CCNP Security Cisco Secure Firewall and Intrusion Prevention System

Official Cert Guide

NAZMUL RAJIB

Cisco Press

CCNP Security Cisco Secure Firewall and Intrusion Prevention System Official Cert Guide

Nazmul Rajib

1 2022

Library of Congress Control Number: 2022933632

ISBN-13: 978-0-13-658970-9

ISBN-10: 0-13-658970-7

Warning and Disclaimer

This book is designed to provide information about the CCNP Security exam concentrating on Cisco Secure Firewall and Intrusion Prevention System (IPS). Every effort has been made to make this book as complete and as accurate as possible, but no warranty or fitness is implied.

The information is provided on an "as is" basis. The author, Cisco Press, and Cisco Systems, Inc. shall have neither liability nor responsibility to any person or entity with respect to any loss or damages arising from the information contained in this book or from the use of the discs or programs that may accompany it.

The opinions expressed in this book belong to the author and are not necessarily those of Cisco Systems, Inc.

Trademark Acknowledgments

All terms mentioned in this book that are known to be trademarks or service marks have been appropriately capitalized. Cisco Press or Cisco Systems, Inc., cannot attest to the accuracy of this information. Use of a term in this book should not be regarded as affecting the validity of any trademark or service mark.

Microsoft and/or its respective suppliers make no representations about the suitability of the information contained in the documents and related graphics published as part of the services for any purpose. All such documents and related graphics are provided "as is" without warranty of any kind. Microsoft and/or its respective suppliers hereby disclaim all warranties and conditions with regard to this information, including all warranties and conditions of merchantability, whether express, implied or statutory, fitness for a particular purpose, title and non-infringement. In no event shall Microsoft and/or its respective suppliers be liable for any special, indirect or consequential damages or any damages whatsoever resulting from loss of use, data or profits, whether in an action of contract, negligence or other tortious action, arising out of or in connection with the use or performance of information available from the services.

Special Sales

For information about buying this title in bulk quantities, or for special sales opportunities (which may include electronic versions; custom cover designs; and content particular to your business, training goals, marketing focus, or branding interests), please contact our corporate sales department at corpsales@pearsoned.com or (800) 382-3419.

For government sales inquiries, please contact governmentsales@pearsoned.com.

For questions about sales outside the U.S., please contact intlcs@pearson.com.

Feedback Information

At Cisco Press, our goal is to create in-depth technical books of the highest quality and value. Each book is crafted with care and precision, undergoing rigorous development that involves the unique expertise of members from the professional technical community.

Readers' feedback is a natural continuation of this process. If you have any comments regarding how we could improve the quality of this book, or otherwise alter it to better suit your needs, you can contact us through email at feedback@ciscopress.com. Please make sure to include the book title and ISBN in your message.

We greatly appreciate your assistance.

Editor-in-Chief: Mark Taub	**Copy Editor:** Chuck Hutchinson
Alliances Manager, Cisco Press: Arezou Gol	**Technical Editors:** Ed Mendez, John Wise
Director, ITP Product Management: Brett Bartow	**Editorial Assistant:** Cindy Teeters
Executive Editor: James Manly	**Cover Designer:** Chuti Prasertsith
Managing Editor: Sandra Schroeder	**Composition:** codeMantra
Development Editor: Ellie Bru	**Indexer:** Timothy Wright
Senior Project Editor: Tonya Simpson	**Proofreader:** Donna Mulder

Pearson's Commitment to Diversity, Equity, and Inclusion

Pearson is dedicated to creating bias-free content that reflects the diversity of all learners. We embrace the many dimensions of diversity, including but not limited to race, ethnicity, gender, socioeconomic status, ability, age, sexual orientation, and religious or political beliefs.

Education is a powerful force for equity and change in our world. It has the potential to deliver opportunities that improve lives and enable economic mobility. As we work with authors to create content for every product and service, we acknowledge our responsibility to demonstrate inclusivity and incorporate diverse scholarship so that everyone can achieve their potential through learning. As the world's leading learning company, we have a duty to help drive change and live up to our purpose to help more people create a better life for themselves and to create a better world.

Our ambition is to purposefully contribute to a world where

- Everyone has an equitable and lifelong opportunity to succeed through learning

- Our educational products and services are inclusive and represent the rich diversity of learners

- Our educational content accurately reflects the histories and experiences of the learners we serve

- Our educational content prompts deeper discussions with learners and motivates them to expand their own learning (and worldview)

While we work hard to present unbiased content, we want to hear from you about any concerns or needs with this Pearson product so that we can investigate and address them.

Please contact us with concerns about any potential bias at https://www.pearson.com/report-bias.html.

About the Author

Nazmul Rajib is a senior product marketing manager of Cisco Systems, Inc. He leads Cisco's global initiatives on cybersecurity enablement, focusing on the firewall and intrusion prevention technologies. As a senior member of the Security Business Group (SBG), Nazmul regularly advises Cisco on security product roadmaps, content strategies, and technical communications. He develops training programs for the Global Security Sales Organization (GSSO) and worldwide channel partners. Nazmul also worked as a technical marketing engineer in the product management organization, where he was responsible for validating security designs, researching best practices, publishing white papers, and presenting new security capabilities.

Prior to joining Cisco's core business group, Nazmul served as a senior information security consultant in the Cisco advanced services organization. With more than a decade of experience, Nazmul assisted many Fortune 500 companies, government agencies, and international organizations. He frequently met Cisco customers to address their critical security concerns and to run workshops.

Previously, Nazmul was a technical lead in the Cisco Customer Experiences (CX) organization, where he consistently assisted the security engineers, and spearheaded the engineering efforts to solve business-critical escalations. He developed several training programs and taught many Cisco engineers worldwide. Nazmul published numerous articles on the Cisco website. In addition to this book, he has authored the best-selling security book *Cisco Firepower Threat Defense* (ISBN: 9781587144806).

Nazmul is a veteran of Sourcefire, Inc., which developed the world's greatest open-source intrusion prevention system. At Sourcefire, Nazmul created and managed the customer knowledge base, new hire onboarding process, and partner certification program. He routinely trained Sourcefire's security engineers and managed security service providers (MSSP) in the United States.

Nazmul has a master of science degree in Internetworking. He also holds many certifications in the areas of cybersecurity, information technology, technical communication, and product marketing. He is a Sourcefire Certified Expert and Sourcefire Certified Security Engineer.

About the Technical Reviewers

Ed Mendez is a senior instructional design and training manager with Cisco Systems, Inc. He has been an education specialist and instructor of many IT security products and technologies for more than 20 years. Ed works with the Cisco certification development team and develops courseware for various Cisco security certification programs. He came to Cisco from the Sourcefire acquisition, where he developed courseware, designed lab infrastructure, and delivered training on many Sourcefire products, including Firepower NGFW, NGIPS, AMP, and Snort. Before joining Sourcefire, he worked at Internet Security Systems (ISS) in the professional services and education departments. Besides holding certifications on many products for which he developed training courses, he also earned CISSP certification in 2002.

John Wise is a senior security instructor and courseware developer with Cisco Systems, Inc., specializing in Cisco Secure Firewall Threat Defense (FTD) and Advanced Malware Protection (AMP). He develops and delivers the Cisco training offerings on next-generation firewall (NGFW) and next-generation intrusion prevention systems (NGIPS). With his decade of teaching and security experiences, John also coaches new instructors at the Cisco Customer Experience (CX) organization. John has been recognized as a Distinguished Speaker at various Cisco Live events held in the United States, Europe, and Latin America.

Dedications

My Lord!

Grant me wisdom, and join me with the righteous.

Bless me with honorable mention among later generations.

Glory be to You!

We have no knowledge except what You have taught us.

You are truly the All-Knowing, All-Wise.

(The Quran)

Acknowledgments

My journey to write this book commenced in early 2020. The plan was to conclude the project within a year. However, 2020 turned out to be an unprecedented year. All praise belongs to God for keeping me safe throughout the pandemic and giving me the ability to complete this book.

It took hundreds of hours to write this book. I would not be able to concentrate on research and writing without my wife's support and sacrifice. I am grateful for her unfailing patience and unwavering devotion.

Sometimes I needed a smile, strength, and stamina to keep going with writing. My marvelous princesses did an amazing job to keep their dad motivated. Their big hugs, kind words, and prayers inspire me to persevere.

I would also like to extend my gratitude to all my colleagues, students, and readers around the world for encouraging me with great feedback on my publications. It is delightful to see the photos of my books on your blog posts.

Many thanks to the technical reviewers for taking the time to review the chapters and providing me invaluable feedback. Their comments, compliments, and commitments have been indispensable to this book.

Finally, I would like to recognize all the editors at Cisco Press for working with me diligently and keeping me on track to get this book published.

Contents at a Glance

Introduction   xxv

Part I   General Deployment

Chapter 1   Introduction to Cisco Secure Firewall and IPS   2

Chapter 2   Deployment of Secure Firewall Virtual   24

Chapter 3   Licensing and Registration   48

Chapter 4   Firewall Deployment in Routed Mode   70

Chapter 5   Firewall Deployment in Transparent Mode   90

Chapter 6   IPS-Only Deployment in Inline Mode   120

Chapter 7   Deployment in Detection-Only Mode   138

Part II   Basic Security Operations

Chapter 8   Capturing Traffic for Advanced Analysis   156

Chapter 9   Network Discovery Policy   172

Chapter 10   Access Control Policy   194

Chapter 11   Prefilter Policy   224

Chapter 12   Security Intelligence   248

Chapter 13   Domain Name System (DNS) Policy   282

Chapter 14   URL Filtering   310

Part III   Advanced Configurations

Chapter 15   Network Analysis and Intrusion Policies   342

Chapter 16   Malware and File Policy   380

Chapter 17   Network Address Translation (NAT)   416

Chapter 18   Traffic Decryption Policy   460

Chapter 19   Virtual Private Network (VPN)   482

Chapter 20   Quality of Service (QoS)   536

Chapter 21   System Logging (Syslog)   556

Part IV   Conclusion

Chapter 22   Final Preparation   582

Part V   Appendixes

Appendix A   Answers to the "Do I Know This Already?" Questions   588

Appendix B   *CCNP Security Cisco Secure Firewall and Intrusion Prevention System Official Cert Guide* Updates   598

Glossary   601

Index   608

Online Elements

Appendix C   Memory Tables

Appendix D   Memory Tables Answer Key

Appendix E   Study Planner

Glossary

Reader Services

Other Features

In addition to the features in each of the core chapters, this book has additional study resources on the companion website, including the following:

■ Practice exams: The companion website contains an exam engine that enables you to review practice exam questions. Use these to prepare with a sample exam and to pinpoint topics where you need more study.

■ Interactive exercises and quizzes: The companion website contains interactive hands-on exercises and interactive quizzes so that you can test your knowledge on the spot.

■ Glossary quizzes: The companion website contains interactive quizzes that enable you to test yourself on every glossary term in the book.

To access this additional content, simply register your product. To start the registration process, go to www.ciscopress.com/register and log in or create an account*. Enter the product ISBN 9780136589709 and click Submit. After the process is complete, you will find any available bonus content under Registered Products.

*Be sure to check the box that you would like to hear from us to receive exclusive discounts on future editions of this product.

Contents

Introduction xxv

Part I   **General Deployment**

Chapter 1   **Introduction to Cisco Secure Firewall and IPS 2**

"Do I Know This Already?" Quiz 3

Foundation Topics 4

Evolution of Next-Generation Firewall 4

Cisco Secure Firewall Solutions 8

Product Evolution and Lifecycle 11

Software and Hardware Architecture 14

Scalability and Resiliency 18

    Clustering 18

    Multi-Instance 19

    High Availability 20

    Resiliency in Connectivity 21

Summary 22

Exam Preparation Tasks 22

Review All Key Topics 22

Complete Tables and Lists from Memory 23

Define Key Terms 23

Chapter 2   **Deployment of Secure Firewall Virtual 24**

"Do I Know This Already?" Quiz 24

Foundation Topics 26

Cisco Secure Firewall on a Virtual Platform 26

    Hosting Environment Settings 27

    Virtual Resource Allocation 28

    Software Package Selection 28

Best Practices 30

Configuration 31

    Virtual Network for Management Traffic 32

    Virtual Network for Data Traffic 33

    Virtual Machine Creation for Secure Firewall 35

System Initialization and Validation 41

Summary 45

Exam Preparation Tasks   46

Review All Key Topics   46

Complete Tables and Lists from Memory   46

Define Key Terms   46

Chapter 3   Licensing and Registration   48

Do I Know This Already?   48

Foundation Topics   50

Cisco Licensing Architecture   50

   Direct Cloud Access   52

   On-Premises Server   52

   Offline Access   53

Cisco Secure Firewall Licenses   54

   Feature License   54

   Export-Controlled License   55

   Evaluation License   56

Validation of Licensing   59

Device Registration   61

   Best Practices for Registration   61

   Configurations on Threat Defense   62

   Configurations on Management Center   63

   Management Communication over the Internet   65

Validation of Registration   67

Summary   68

Exam Preparation Tasks   69

Review All Key Topics   69

Complete Tables and Lists from Memory   69

Define Key Terms   69

Chapter 4   Firewall Deployment in Routed Mode   70

"Do I Know This Already?" Quiz   70

Foundation Topics   72

Routed Mode Essentials   72

Best Practices for Routed Mode Configuration   73

Fulfilling Prerequisites   73

   Enabling the Routed Firewall Mode   75

Configuration of the Routed Interface   75

    Configuring Interfaces with Static IP Addresses   76

    Configuring Interfaces with Automatic IP Addresses   80

Validation of Interface Configuration   82

Summary   88

Exam Preparation Tasks   89

Review All Key Topics   89

Complete Tables and Lists from Memory   89

Define Key Terms   89

Chapter 5   **Firewall Deployment in Transparent Mode   90**

"Do I Know This Already?" Quiz   90

Foundation Topics   92

Transparent Mode Essentials   92

Best Practices for Transparent Mode Configuration   93

Fulfilling Prerequisites   94

    Enabling the Transparent Firewall Mode   95

Configuring Transparent Mode in a Layer 2 Network   96

    Configuring the Physical and Virtual Interfaces   96

    Verifying the Interface Status   103

    Verifying Basic Connectivity and Operations   104

Deploying a Threat Defense Between Layer 3 Networks   108

    Selecting a Default Action   108

    Adding an Access Control Rule for a Routing Protocol   111

    Creating an Access Control Rule for the SSH Protocol   113

    Verifying Access Control Lists   115

Integrated Routing and Bridging (IRB)   118

Summary   118

Exam Preparation Tasks   118

Review All Key Topics   118

Memory Tables and Lists   119

Define Key Terms   119

Chapter 6   **IPS-Only Deployment in Inline Mode   120**

"Do I Know This Already?" Quiz   120

Foundation Topics   122

Inline Mode Essentials   122

Inline Mode Versus Passive Mode   123

Inline Mode Versus Transparent Mode   125

Best Practices for Inline Mode   125

Inline Mode Configuration   126

Fulfilling Prerequisites   126

Interface Setup   127

Inline Set Configuration   129

Verification   132

Event Analysis in IPS-Only Mode   135

Summary   136

Exam Preparation Tasks   136

Review All Key Topics   136

Memory Tables and Lists   137

Define Key Terms   137

Chapter 7   Deployment in Detection-Only Mode   138

"Do I Know This Already?" Quiz   139

Foundation Topics   141

Detection-Only Mode Essentials   141

Passive Monitoring Technology   141

Interface Modes: Inline, Inline Tap, and Passive   142

Best Practices for Detection-Only Deployment   143

Inline Tap Mode   145

Configuration of Inline Tap Mode   145

Verification of Inline Tap Configuration   147

Passive Interface Mode   149

Configuration of Passive Interface Mode   149

Configuring Passive Interface Mode on a Threat Defense   150

Configuring a SPAN Port on a Switch   151

Verification of Passive Interface Configuration   152

Event Analysis in Detection-Only Mode   153

Summary   154

Exam Preparation Tasks   154

Review All Key Topics   155

Complete Tables and Lists from Memory   155

Define Key Terms   155

Part II   **Basic Security Operations**

Chapter 8   **Capturing Traffic for Advanced Analysis   156**

"Do I Know This Already?" Quiz   157

Foundation Topics   158

Packet Capture Essentials   158

Best Practices for Capturing Traffic   160

Capturing of Packets Using Secure Firewall   162

    Configuration   162

    Verification   165

    Packet Capture versus Packet Tracer   169

Summary   170

Exam Preparation Tasks   170

Review All Key Topics   170

Memory Tables and Lists   171

Define Key Terms   171

Chapter 9   **Network Discovery Policy   172**

"Do I Know This Already?" Quiz   172

Foundation Topics   174

Network Discovery Essentials   174

    Application Detectors   175

    Network Discovery Operations   176

Best Practices for Network Discovery   178

Fulfilling Prerequisites   179

Configurations   180

    Reusable Objects   181

    Network Discovery Policy   183

Verification   186

    Analyzing Application Discovery   186

    Analyzing Host Discovery   186

    Undiscovered New Hosts   188

Summary   191

Exam Preparation Tasks   191

Review All Key Topics   191

Complete Tables and Lists from Memory   192

Define Key Terms   192

Chapter 10   Access Control Policy   194

"Do I Know This Already?" Quiz   194

Foundation Topics   196

Access Control Policy Essentials   196

    Policy Editor   196

    Rule Editor   198

Best Practices for Access Control Policy   199

Access Control Policy Configuration   200

    Fulfilling Prerequisites   201

    Creating Rules   202

Verification   208

Summary   222

Exam Preparation Tasks   222

Review All Key Topics   222

Complete Tables and Lists from Memory   222

Define Key Terms   222

Chapter 11   Prefilter Policy   224

"Do I Know This Already?" Quiz   224

Foundation Topics   226

Prefilter Policy Essentials   226

    Prefilter Policy: Rules and Actions   226

    Bypassing Deep Packet Inspection   227

Best Practices for a Prefilter Policy   230

Enabling Bypass Through a Prefilter Policy   230

    Fulfilling Prerequisites   230

    Configuring a Rule in a Prefilter Policy   230

    Invoking a Prefilter Policy into an Access Control Policy   235

Establishing Trust Through an Access Control Policy   237

Verification   240

Managing Encapsulated Traffic Inspection   242

Summary   245

Exam Preparation Tasks   245

Review All Key Topics   245

Complete Tables and Lists from Memory   246

Define Key Terms   246

Chapter 12   Security Intelligence   248

"Do I Know This Already?" Quiz   249

Foundation Topics   251

Security Intelligence Essentials   251

Best Practices for Security Intelligence   256

Fulfilling Prerequisites   257

Automatic Blocking Using Cisco Intelligence Feed   259

Verifying the Action of Cisco Intelligence Feed   262

Overriding the Cisco Intelligence Feed Outcome   265

Instant Blocking Using Context Menu   267

Adding an Address to the Block List   267

Deleting an Address from the Block List   268

Manual Blocking Using Custom List   269

Enabling Security Intelligence in Monitor-Only Mode   272

Threat Intelligence Director   274

Enabling Threat Intelligence Director   276

Adding Sources and Importing Indicators   277

Summary   280

Exam Preparation Tasks   281

Review All Key Topics   281

Complete Tables and Lists from Memory   281

Define Key Terms   281

Chapter 13   Domain Name System (DNS) Policy   282

"Do I Know This Already?" Quiz   282

Foundation Topics   284

DNS Policy Essentials   284

Domain Name System (DNS)   284

Blocking of a DNS Query Using a Secure Firewall   285

DNS Rule Actions   287

Actions That Can Interrupt DNS Queries   288

Actions That Allow DNS Queries   292

Sources of Intelligence   293

Best Practices for Blocking DNS Queries   295

Fulfilling Prerequisites   296

Configuring DNS Policy   297

Add a New Rule to a DNS Policy   298

Invoke the DNS Policy   301

Verification   302

Summary   307

Exam Preparation Tasks   307

Review All Key Topics   308

Complete Tables and Lists from Memory   308

Define Key Terms   308

Chapter 14   URL Filtering   310

"Do I Know This Already?" Quiz   310

Foundation Topics   312

URL Filtering Essentials   312

Category and Reputation   312

URL Database   314

Fulfilling Prerequisites   315

Best Practices for URL Filtering Configuration   317

Enabling URL Filtering   322

Blocking URLs of a Certain Category   323

Verifying the Operation of a URL Filtering Rule   325

Allowing a Specific URL   329

Analyzing the Default Category Override   331

Handling Uncategorized URLs   335

Investigating the Uncategorized URLs   338

Summary   340

Exam Preparation Tasks   341

Review All Key Topics   341

Complete Tables and Lists from Memory   341

Define Key Terms   341

Part III   Advanced Configurations

Chapter 15   Network Analysis and Intrusion Policies   342

"Do I Know This Already?" Quiz   343

Foundation Topics   345

Intrusion Prevention System Essentials   345

Network Analysis Policy   346

Intrusion Policy   346

System-Provided Variable Sets   352

System-Provided Base Policies   353

Best Practices for Intrusion Policy Deployment   356

Configuring a Network Analysis Policy   359

Configuring an Intrusion Policy   364

Creating a Policy with a Default Ruleset   364

Incorporating Intrusion Rule Recommendations   365

Enabling or Disabling an Intrusion Rule   368

Setting Up a Variable Set   369

Policy Deployment   371

Verification   373

Summary   379

Exam Preparation Tasks   379

Review All Key Topics   379

Complete Tables and Lists from Memory   379

Define Key Terms   379

Chapter 16   Malware and File Policy   380

"Do I Know This Already?" Quiz   380

Foundation Topics   382

File Policy Essentials   382

File Type Detection   382

Malware Analysis   382

Best Practices for File Policy Configuration   386

Fulfilling Prerequisites   387

Configuring a File Policy   390

Creating a File Policy   390

Deploying a File Policy   396

Verification   398

Analyzing File Events   399

Analyzing Malware Events   404

*The Management Center Is Unable to Communicate with the
Cloud*   404

The Management Center Performs a Cloud Lookup   408

The Threat Defense Blocks Malware   409

Overriding a Malware Disposition   412

Network Trajectory   413

Summary   414

Exam Preparation Tasks   414

Review All Key Topics   414

Complete Tables and Lists from Memory   415

Define Key Terms   415

Chapter 17   Network Address Translation (NAT)   416

"Do I Know This Already?" Quiz   417

Foundation Topics   418

NAT Essentials   418

NAT Techniques   420

NAT Rule Types   422

Best Practices for NAT Deployment   423

Fulfilling Prerequisites   425

Configuring NAT   427

Masquerading a Source Address (Source NAT for Outbound
Connection)   427

Configuring a Dynamic NAT Rule   427

Verifying the Configuration   433

Verifying the Operation: Inside to Outside   434

Verifying the Operation: Outside to Inside   441

Connecting to a Masqueraded Destination (Destination NAT for Inbound
Connection)   446

Configuring a Static NAT Rule   446

Verifying the Operation: Outside to DMZ   449

Summary   457

Exam Preparation Tasks   457

Review All Key Topics   457

Complete Tables and Lists from Memory   458

Define Key Terms   458

Chapter 18   Traffic Decryption Policy   460

"Do I Know This Already?" Quiz   460

Foundation Topics   462

Traffic Decryption Essentials   462

Overview of SSL and TLS Protocols   462

Decryption Techniques on Secure Firewall   466

Best Practices for Traffic Decryption   467

Configuring a Decryption Policy   468

    PKI Objects   468

    Internal CAs Object   *469*

    Internal Certs Object   *469*

    SSL Policy   470

    File Policy   474

    Access Control Policy   474

Verification   476

Summary   480

Exam Preparation Tasks   480

Review All Key Topics   481

Complete Tables and Lists from Memory   481

Define Key Terms   481

Chapter 19   Virtual Private Network (VPN)   482

"Do I Know This Already?" Quiz   483

Foundation Topics   484

VPN Essentials   484

    Site-to-Site VPN   485

    Remote Access VPN   488

IPsec Essentials   489

    Mode of Operation   490

    Security Association and Key Exchange   492

    IKEv1   *492*

    IKEv2   *494*

    Authentication   495

Site-to-Site VPN Deployment   496

    Prerequisites   496

    Configurations   499

    Access Control Policy   *503*

    NAT Policy   *504*

    Verification   507

Remote Access VPN Deployment   513

    Prerequisites   513

    Configuration   516

    AnyConnect File   *517*

    RADIUS Server Group   *518*

Certificate Enrollment 518

Network and IP Address Pool 521

Remote Access VPN Policy 522

Verification 527

Summary 534

Exam Preparation Tasks 535

Review All Key Topics 535

Complete Tables and Lists from Memory 535

Define Key Terms 535

Chapter 20 Quality of Service (QoS) 536

"Do I Know This Already?" Quiz 536

Foundation Topics 538

Quality of Service Essentials 538

Best Practices for Enabling QoS 541

Fulfilling Prerequisites 541

Configuring QoS Policy 542

Verification 546

Analyzing QoS Events and Statistics 550

Summary 554

Exam Preparation Tasks 554

Review All Key Topics 554

Complete Tables and Lists from Memory 555

Define Key Terms 555

Chapter 21 System Logging (Syslog) 556

"Do I Know This Already?" Quiz 557

Foundation Topics 558

Secure Firewall Logging Essentials 558

Best Practices for Logging 560

Prerequisites 560

Sending Syslog from Threat Defense 564

Add a Syslog Server on Platform Settings 564

Enable Logging on Access Control Policy 568

Verification 568

Sending Syslog from Management Center 569

Create Syslog Alerts 569

Verification   572

Correlate Events to Send Syslog Alerts   574

Troubleshooting Logs   578

Summary   581

Exam Preparation Tasks   581

Review All Key Topics   581

Complete Tables and Lists from Memory   581

Define Key Terms   581

Part IV   Conclusion

Chapter 22   Final Preparation   582

Getting Ready for the Exam   582

Tools for Final Review   582

Exam Day   583

Practice Tests   583

Pearson Cert Practice Test Engine and Questions on the Website   583

Accessing the Pearson Test Prep Software Online   584

Accessing the Pearson Test Prep Software Offline   584

Customizing Your Exams   585

Updating Your Exams   585

Premium Edition   586

Chapter-Ending Review Tools   586

Summary   586

Part V   Appendixes

Appendix A   Answers to the "Do I Know This Already?" Questions   588

Appendix B   CCNP Security Cisco Secure Firewall and Intrusion Prevention System Official Cert Guide Updates   598

Glossary   601

Index   608

Online Elements

Appendix C   Memory Tables

Appendix D   Memory Tables Answer Key

Appendix E   Study Planner

Glossary

Command Syntax Conventions

The conventions used to present command syntax in this book are the same conventions used in the IOS Command Reference. The Command Reference describes these conventions as follows:

- **Boldface** indicates commands and keywords that are entered literally as shown. In actual configuration examples and output (not general command syntax), boldface indicates commands that are manually input by the user (such as a **show** command).

- *Italic* indicates arguments for which you supply actual values.

- Vertical bars (|) separate alternative, mutually exclusive elements.

- Square brackets ([ ]) indicate an optional element.

- Braces ({ }) indicate a required choice.

- Braces within brackets ([{ }]) indicate a required choice within an optional element.

Introduction

Welcome to the world of Cisco career certification. Most importantly, welcome to the world of the Cisco Secure Firewall and Intrusion Prevention System (IPS). If you are reading this Introduction, you have probably decided to obtain Cisco's professional-level security certification—CCNP Security.

Obtaining a Cisco certification ensures that you have a solid understanding of computer networking principles along with Cisco's networking solutions. Cisco has one of the largest market shares of network architectural components, such as routers, switches, firewalls, and intrusion prevention systems, with a global footprint. Cisco's professional-level certifications have been an important part of the computing industry for many years and will continue to be more important. There are many reasons to obtain Cisco certifications, but the most popularly cited reason is their credibility and acceptability. All other factors being equal, a Cisco certified employee, consultant, or job candidate is considered more valuable than one who is not certified.

Primarily, Cisco provides three levels of certifications: Cisco Certified Network Associate (CCNA), Cisco Certified Network Professional (CCNP), and Cisco Certified Internetwork Expert (CCIE). Each certification level has its own technology track. CCNP Security is one of the industry's most respected cybersecurity certifications. Achieving the CCNP Security certification proves your professional-level skills with Cisco's cybersecurity solutions. To earn the CCNP Security certification, you need to pass two exams:

- One core exam that covers the core Cisco security technologies and tests your knowledge of security infrastructure

- One security concentration exam of your choice, so you can customize your certification to your technical area of focus

This book helps you study for the CCNP Security exam, concentrating on the Cisco Secure Firewall and Intrusion Prevention System (formerly known as Cisco Firepower). You may find the use of both brands "Secure Firewall" and "Firepower" on the Cisco websites and in this book, but please note that they refer to the same product. You can find more information about the product rebranding in Chapter 1 of this book. Be sure to visit www.cisco.com to find the latest information on the CCNP Security certification and to keep up-to-date with any concentration exams and certification requirements.

How This Book Is Organized

As of writing this book, the name of the CCNP Security exam concentrating on Cisco Secure Firewall and Intrusion Prevention System is *Securing Networks with Cisco Firepower*. This exam was announced in early 2020 when the Cisco Secure Firewall version 6.x was the latest software train. However, a year later, Cisco introduced many new features in software version 7.x. This version also presents a new product brand and enhances user interface. Because Cisco releases new software versions every few months, it is challenging to update the static contents of a certification book every time a new software version is released. Therefore, to provide you with as up-to-date information as possible, this book has been written based on software version 7.x, which is above the current scope of the exam. Remember, the fundamental knowledge of Cisco Secure Firewall and Intrusion Prevention System is almost identical in most software versions.

It is important to understand that this book is a *static* reference, whereas the exam topics are *dynamic*. To keep the exam outline up to date, Cisco reserves the right to change the exam topics without any notice. Each version of an exam can emphasize different topics and different software releases.

Although this book could be read cover-to-cover, it is designed to be flexible and allow you to easily move between chapters and sections of chapters to cover just the material that you need to more work with. In 22 chapters, this book covers the following topics:

■ **Chapter 1, "Introduction to Cisco Secure Firewall and IPS":** This chapter provides an overview of different types of firewalls and introduces Cisco's next-generation firewall solution—the Cisco Secure Firewall. It also discusses Secure Firewall's architectural and software components and presents various options to enable scalability and resiliency in a Secure Firewall.

■ **Chapter 2, "Deployment of Secure Firewall Virtual":** This chapter describes the requirements for Secure Firewall deployment on a virtual environment. As an example, this chapter demonstrates the steps to build a Secure Firewall lab on VMware ESXi.

■ **Chapter 3, "Licensing and Registration":** This chapter provides a foundational knowledge of different Cisco licensing models and describes their use cases— obtaining and maintaining licenses over the Internet or without any Internet connections. You learn about the capabilities of various feature licenses, purposes of export-controlled licenses, and how to enable evaluation licenses. The last part of this chapter demonstrates the registration processes between a management center and a threat defense.

■ **Chapter 4, "Firewall Deployment in Routed Mode":** This chapter describes the firewall characteristics in routed mode and demonstrates the steps to configure a threat defense in routed firewall mode. Later, it provides tips to verify the interface status and shows connection events.

■ **Chapter 5, "Firewall Deployment in Transparent Mode":** This chapter describes the key components of a transport mode firewall, such as bridge group and Bridge Virtual Interface (BVI). It also details the steps to configure a threat defense in transparent mode and deploy in the Layer 2 and Layer 3 networks. Finally, it describes the integrated routing and bridging (IRB) capability in a threat defense.

- **Chapter 6, "IPS-Only Deployment in Inline Mode":** This chapter describes the deployment of a threat defense as a dedicated intrusion prevention system, also known as IPS-only mode. It delineates the key differences among inline, passive, and transparent modes.

- **Chapter 7, "Deployment in Detection-Only Mode":** This chapter demonstrates the deployment of a threat defense for detection purposes only. It walks you through the steps to configure the threat defense interfaces in inline tap mode and passive mode.

- **Chapter 8, "Capturing Traffic for Advanced Analysis":** This chapter takes a deep dive into the threat defense security engines. This can help you to understand the root cause of a packet drop by the threat defense. To equip you with advanced troubleshooting tools, this chapter demonstrates the process of capturing traffic from a threat defense using the management center GUI.

- **Chapter 9, "Network Discovery Policy":** This chapter describes different types of application detectors and explains the configuration and operation of a network discovery policy. It also demonstrates the setup, usage, and benefits of reusable objects. At the end of the chapter, you learn how to display discovery data using the event viewer and dashboard.

- **Chapter 10, "Access Control Policy":** This chapter introduces you to various options of the access control rule editor and policy editor. It walks you through the configuration of an access control policy with different rule conditions. The "Best Practices for Access Control Policy" section in this chapter enables you to fine-tune the ruleset of an access control policy and experience optimized system performance. Finally, it demonstrates various tools that you can use for troubleshooting purposes.

- **Chapter 11, "Prefilter Policy":** This chapter demonstrates the configuration and deployment of a prefilter policy. A prefilter policy is a great choice to manage encapsulated traffic and to bypass inspection. This chapter also shares an alternative to prefilter rules for bypassing inspection.

- **Chapter 12, "Security Intelligence":** This chapter describes the architectural elements of Cisco Security Intelligence technology. It discusses automatic blocking of harmful IP addresses using the Cisco-provided intelligence category and verification of the Security Intelligence operations using the CLI tools and GUI options. It also shows the methods to override the default behavior of Security Intelligence. The last section explains the Threat Intelligence Director, a feature to import third-party threat intelligence data into Secure Firewall.

- **Chapter 13, "Domain Name System (DNS) Policy":** This chapter describes DNS operation and the configuration of a DNS policy on Secure Firewall. It discusses the best practices for blocking DNS queries and various CLI-based troubleshooting tools to validate DNS policy operations.

- **Chapter 14, "URL Filtering":** This chapter describes the categorization and reputation of URLs using Secure Firewall's URL Filtering feature. It also explains the workflow of URL lookup and URL dataset updates and the configuration of an access control policy with URL Filtering rule constraints. Finally, it demonstrates the operational impact of URL Filtering on live network traffic.

- **Chapter 15, "Network Analysis and Intrusion Policies":** This chapter describes the configuration of the key components of an intrusion prevention system, such as network analysis policy, intrusion policy, variable sets, and base policies. It uses both Snort 2 and Snort 3 versions of the policies in the configuration examples. This chapter also shares the best practices for intrusion policy deployment. Ways to optimize policies with system-generated intrusion rule recommendations and fine-tuned variable sets are also discussed. The final section demonstrates the action of an intrusion policy on live traffic and then exhibits different types of intrusion events using the management center event viewer and dashboard.

- **Chapter 16, "Malware and File Policy":** This chapter describes the Cisco malware defense technologies (formerly advanced malware protection, or AMP, for network), and the configuration of malware and file policies. It delineates both major features: file type detection and malicious file analysis. In the last part of this chapter, you learn how to analyze file and malware events using the GUI and CLI.

- **Chapter 17, "Network Address Translation (NAT)":** This chapter describes the operations and categories of Network Address Translation (NAT) and Port Address Translation (PAT). It demonstrates the implementation of different types of NAT and validation of NAT configurations using the CLI.

- **Chapter 18, "Traffic Decryption Policy":** This chapter describes the encryption protocols, TLS handshakes, and techniques to decrypt traffic using Secure Firewall. It demonstrates the steps to configure an SSL policy to decrypt network traffic and then enable a next-generation security policy to analyze the decrypted traffic further. The chapter uses the event viewer and dashboard to realize the benefits of decrypting traffic.

- **Chapter 19, "Virtual Private Network (VPN)":** This chapter describes various cryptographic protocols and algorithms that are used in different stages of VPN connections and operations. It demonstrates the configurations of site-to-site VPN and remote access VPN, and shows various command-line tools to verify the VPN configurations.

- **Chapter 20, "Quality of Service (QoS)":** This chapter describes various quality of service (QoS) techniques and demonstrates the steps to implement a QoS policy on a threat defense. It also provides useful tips to analyze QoS configurations and operations.

- **Chapter 21, "System Logging (Syslog)":** This chapter describes the syslog implementation over UDP and TCP, and different components of the syslog messages, such as security levels and facilities. It demonstrates how to send syslog from both the management center and threat defense, and shares tips to optimize Secure Firewall performance when syslog is enabled. This chapter also describes the techniques to correlate different types of events and sends alerts to a syslog server only when certain conditions are fulfilled. Finally, this chapter explains the process to generate troubleshooting files that include all the configuration and log files from Secure Firewall.

- **Chapter 22, "Final Preparation":** This chapter describes tools for the final review and instructions to access the practice tests, and it also shares some preparation tips for exam day.

Learning Objectives of the Chapters

The Cisco Learning Network publishes a list of topics to provide you with general guidelines for any Cisco certification exam. Because the general guidelines change at any time without notice, any other topics may also appear on the exam outside of the published guidelines. According to the general guidelines, the CCNP Security exam concentrating on Cisco Secure Firewall and IPS tests your knowledge on policy configurations, integrations, deployments, management, and troubleshooting. Table I-1 provides a list of all the chapters in this book and their objectives.

Table I-1   The Objectives of the Chapters in This Book

Number	Chapter Name	Objectives
1	Introduction to Cisco Secure Firewall and IPS	Evolution of next-generation firewall
		Cisco Secure Firewall components
		Scalable and highly available deployments
2	Deployment of Secure Firewall Virtual	Deployment of Cisco Secure Firewall on a virtual platform
		Building a cost-effective lab environment for the CCNP Security exam preparation
3	Licensing and Registration	Cisco Secure Firewall licensing systems
		Enabling licenses on Secure Firewall
		Registration and initial deployment of Secure Firewall

Number	Chapter Name	Objectives
4	Firewall Deployment in Routed Mode	Deployment of Secure Firewall in routed firewall mode
		Verification of threat defense configurations in routed mode
5	Firewall Deployment in Transparent Mode	Deployment of Secure Firewall in transparent firewall mode
		Verification of threat defense configurations in transparent mode
		Integrated routing and bridging (IRB) mode
6	IPS-Only Deployment in Inline Mode	Deployment of a threat defense as a dedicated intrusion prevention system (IPS)
		Verification of threat defense configurations in inline interface mode
7	Deployment in Detection-Only Mode	Deployment of a threat defense with detection-only capability
		Verification of threat defense configurations in inline tap and passive interface modes
8	Capturing Traffic for Advanced Analysis	Packet capture utility on the management center GUI
		Capturing of live traffic from the threat defense data interfaces
		Differences between the packet capture and packet tracer tools
9	Network Discovery Policy	Network discovery policy operation and configuration
		Application detectors
		Reusable object management
		Dashboard and event viewer
		Discovery data analysis
10	Access Control Policy	Configuration and deployment of access control policy
		Verification of access control policy settings using CLI
		Analysis of access control policy operations for advanced troubleshooting purpose
11	Prefilter Policy	Configuration and deployment of prefilter policy
		Differences between prefilter policy and access control policy
		Different ways to bypass deep packet inspection
		Inspection of encapsulated traffic

Number	Chapter Name	Objectives
12	Security Intelligence	Operation of Security Intelligence technology components
		Implementation of intelligence-based access control policy
		Managing Security Intelligence objects and intelligence feed
		Implementation of the Cisco Threat Intelligence Director (TID)
13	Domain Name System (DNS) Policy	Domain Name System (DNS) operations and rule actions
		Implementation of a DNS policy on Secure Firewall
		Verification of DNS policy configurations using CLI tools
14	URL Filtering	URL Filtering technology and its operational architecture
		Configuration of an access control policy with URL Filtering
		Verification of URL Filtering operations using CLI tools
15	Network Analysis and Intrusion Policies	Implementation of a network analysis policy
		Description and implementation of an intrusion policy
		Snort rule syntax and Snort variable sets
		Intrusion rule recommendations generation
		System-provided base policies
		Verification of intrusion policy operation on a threat defense
16	Malware and File Policy	Architecture of malware defense technology (also known as advanced malware protection or AMP)
		Implementation of malware defense on Secure Firewall
		Configuration of the malware and file policy
		Verification of malware and file policy operation
		Analysis of file events using event viewer and dashboard

Number	Chapter Name	Objectives
17	Network Address Translation (NAT)	Network Address Translation (NAT) and Port Address Translation (PAT) technologies
		Implementation of various NAT techniques on Secure Firewall
		Verification and troubleshooting of address translation operation
		Introduction to platform settings
18	Traffic Decryption Policy	SSL and TLS protocols
		Traffic decryption techniques
		Implementation of an SSL policy on Secure Firewall
		Public key infrastructure (PKI) certificate-based objects
		Verification of traffic decryption operation on a threat defense
19	Virtual Private Network (VPN)	Virtual private network (VPN) technologies and protocols
		Implementation of site-to-site VPN topology
		Implementation of remote access VPN topology
		Verification and troubleshooting of VPN configurations
20	Quality of Service (QoS)	Quality of service (QoS) operation on Secure Firewall
		Implementation of QoS on a threat defense
		Verification of QoS configurations on a threat defense
21	System Logging (Syslog)	Syslog messages, security levels, and facilities
		Configuration of syslog services on Secure Firewall
		Configuration of correlation policy
		Configuration of alerts for security and system events
		Generation and collection of troubleshooting logs using GUI
22	Final Preparation	Tips for exam preparation
		Instructions to access the practice tests

You should be proficient with these topics for the exam as well as for designing and implementing Cisco's firewall technology in the real world. Each version of the exam can have topics that emphasize different functions or features, and some topics can be rather broad and generalized. The goal of this book is to provide the most comprehensive coverage to ensure that you are well prepared for the exam.

Although some chapters might not address specific exam topics, they provide a foundation that is necessary for a clear understanding of important topics. Your short-term goal might be to pass the exam, but your long-term goal should be to become a qualified CCNP security engineer with an understanding of firewall technology.

It is important to understand that this book is a static reference, whereas the exam topics are dynamic. Cisco can and does change the topics covered on certification exams often.

This book should not be your only reference when preparing for the certification exam. You can find a wealth of information at Cisco.com that covers each topic in great detail. If you think you need more detailed information on a specific topic, read the Cisco documentation that focuses on that topic.

Note that as firewall technologies continue to evolve, Cisco reserves the right to change the exam topics without notice. Check cisco.com to verify the actual list of topics to ensure that you are prepared before taking the exam. You can view the current exam topics on any current Cisco certification exam by visiting the cisco.com website, choosing Menu, choosing Training & Events, and selecting from the Certifications list. Note also that, if needed, Cisco Press might post additional preparatory content on the web page associated with this book, at http://www.ciscopress.com/title/9780136589709. It's a good idea to check the website a couple of weeks before taking your exam to be sure you have up-to-date content.

Figure Credits

Figures 1.1, 12.20, 16.30:	Microsoft
Figure 2.1:	American Megatrends, Inc
Figures 2.6 through 2.18:	VMware, Inc
Figures 8.11, 15.35, 16.2:	Wireshark
Figures 20.16:	WinSCP
Figures 21.2, 21.13, 21.18, 21.19:	SolarWinds Worldwide, LLC

Goals and Methods

The focus of this book is to teach how to develop and deliver Cisco firewall solutions. By accomplishing the learning objectives in this book, you will prepare yourself for taking the CCNP Security exam concentrating on Cisco Secure Firewall and Intrusion Prevention System (IPS). The goal of the book is to both help you pass the exam and serve as a go-to resource when you are deploying and managing firewall technology. This book combines technical concepts with real-world experience, including tips and tricks for troubleshooting firewall deployment problems.

Many parts of this book are inspired by our work with customers to deploy firewall technology. One key methodology used in this book is to help you discover the exam topics that you need to review in more depth, to help you fully understand and remember those details, and to help you prove to yourself that you have retained your knowledge of those topics.

Our goal is not to help you pass the CCNP Security exam simply through memorization. The mixture of technology and lab concepts in this book is meant to help you truly learn and understand the firewall topics needed for both the exam and real-world deployments. This book will help you pass the exam by using the following methods:

- Demonstrating the implementation with detailed step-by-step instructions and screenshots

- Providing explanations and information to fill in your knowledge gaps

- Supplying exercises and scenarios that enhance your ability to recall and deduce the answers to test questions

Who Should Read This Book?

This book is ideal for anybody interested in taking the CCNP Security exam concentrating on Cisco Secure Firewall and Intrusion Prevention System. However, anyone else who needs a resource for firewall concepts and Cisco firewall technology will also benefit from this book. We have a handful of objectives for writing this book but the primary focus is to help you pass the exam.

Strategies for Exam Preparation

The strategy you use to study for the CCNP Security exam might be slightly different than strategies used by other readers, depending on the skills, knowledge, and experience you have already obtained. For instance, if you have attended a CCNP Security course in a classroom, you might take a different approach than someone whose knowledge is based on job experience alone.

Regardless of the strategy you use or the background you have, this book is designed to help you get to the point where you can pass the exam in the least amount of time possible. For instance, there is no need for you to practice or read about encryption concepts if you fully understand them already. However, many people like to make sure that they truly know a topic and thus read over material that they already know. Several book features will help you gain the confidence you need to be convinced that you know some material already and to also help you know what topics you need to study more.

The Companion Website for Online Content Review

All the electronic review elements, as well as other electronic components of the book, exist on this book's companion website. To access the companion website, start by establishing a login at www.ciscopress.com and registering your book. To do so, simply go to www. ciscopress.com/register and enter the ISBN of the print book: 9780136589709.

After you have registered your book, go to your account page and click the Registered Products tab. From there, click the Access Bonus Content link to get access to the book's companion website. Note that if you buy the Premium Edition eBook and Practice Test version of this book from Cisco Press, your book will automatically be registered on your account page. Simply go to your account page, click the Registered Products tab, and select Access Bonus Content to access the book's companion website.

How to Access the Pearson Test Prep (PTP) App

You have two options for installing and using the Pearson Test Prep application: a web app and a desktop app. To use the Pearson Test Prep application, start by finding the access code that comes with the book. You can find the code in these ways:

- **Print book:** Look in the cardboard sleeve in the back of the book for a piece of paper with your book's unique access code.

- **Premium Edition:** If you purchase the Premium Edition eBook and Practice Test directly from the Cisco Press website, the code will be populated on your account page after purchase. Just log in at www.ciscopress.com, click Account to see details of your account, and click the Digital Purchases tab.

- **Amazon Kindle:** For those who purchase a Kindle edition from Amazon, the access code will be supplied directly by Amazon.

- **Other bookseller eBooks:** Note that if you purchase an eBook version from any other source, the practice test is not included because other vendors to date have not chosen to vend the required unique access code.

## CHAPTER 1

Introduction to Cisco Secure Firewall and IPS

This chapter provides an overview of the following topics:

Evolution of Next-Generation Firewall: This section provides an introduction to different types of firewalls, such as host-based, network-based, stateless, stateful, and next-generation firewalls.

Cisco Secure Firewall Solutions: This section summarizes a high-level architecture of a typical Cisco Secure Firewall deployment. It also introduces different management platforms and shares a glimpse of their historical evolution.

Product Evolution and Lifecycle: This section discusses the naming convention of the Cisco Secure Firewall and discusses the software lifecycle policy.

Software and Hardware Architecture: This section describes various software components and hardware architecture of a Secure Firewall.

Scalability and Resiliency: This section summarizes various advanced features to enable scalability and ensure resiliency in a Secure Firewall.

The objectives of this chapter are to learn about

- Evolution of next-generation firewall
- Cisco Secure Firewall components
- Scalable and highly available deployments

The heart of the Cisco Secure Firewall is Snort—one of the most popular open-source intrusion detection and prevention systems capable of real-time traffic inspection. In 1998, Martin Roesch developed Snort, and subsequently, in 2001, he founded Sourcefire, Inc., in Columbia, Maryland. Within a short period of time, Sourcefire won the trust of thousands of security professionals around the world, and Snort became the de facto tool for the intrusion detection system (IDS) and intrusion prevention system (IPS). Cisco acquired Sourcefire in 2013. This acquisition enabled Cisco to develop a world-class next-generation security solution—Cisco Secure Firewall. This chapter provides a glimpse into the world of Cisco Secure Firewall: how it has evolved from Sourcefire's core technology, how the security features are integrated into various software components, and what hardware and virtual platforms are available to support the cutting-edge functionalities.

"Do I Know This Already?" Quiz

The "Do I Know This Already?" quiz enables you to assess whether you should read this entire chapter thoroughly or jump to the "Exam Preparation Tasks" section. If you are in doubt about your answers to these questions or your own assessment of your knowledge of the topics, read the entire chapter. Table 1-1 lists the major headings in this chapter and their corresponding "Do I Know This Already?" quiz questions. You can find the answers in Appendix A, "Answers to the 'Do I Know This Already?' Quizzes."

Table 1-1 "Do I Know This Already?" Section-to-Question Mapping

Foundation Topics Section	Questions
Evolution of Next-Generation Firewall	1
Cisco Secure Firewall Solutions	2, 3
Product Evolution and Lifecycle	4
Software and Hardware Architecture	5, 6
Scalability and Resiliency	7, 8

CAUTION The goal of self-assessment is to gauge your mastery of the topics in this chapter. If you do not know the answer to a question or are only partially sure of the answer, you should mark that question as wrong for purposes of the self-assessment. Giving yourself credit for an answer you correctly guess skews your self-assessment results and might provide you with a false sense of security.

1. Which of the following firewalls provides application visibility and control (AVC)?
   a. Stateless firewall
   b. Stateful firewall
   c. Next-generation firewall
   d. Management Center

2. Which of the following platforms can be used to manage threat defense?
   a. Secure Firewall Management Center
   b. Secure Firewall Device Manager
   c. Cisco Defense Orchestrator
   d. All of these answers are correct.

3. Which of the following management platforms can manage only one threat defense?
   a. Secure Firewall Management Center
   b. FireSIGHT Management Center
   c. Secure Firewall Device Manager
   d. Cisco Defense Orchestrator

4. Which release of the Cisco Secure Firewall is chosen for government certification?
   a. STR
   b. LTR

    c. XLTR

    d. All of these answers are correct.

5. Which of the following software components contains intrusion rules?

    a. Operating system

    b. SRU/LSP

    c. VDB

    d. GeoDB

6. Which of the following software components contains the fingerprint of various applications, services, and operating systems?

    a. Operating system

    b. SRU/LSP

    c. VDB

    d. GeoDB

7. Which of the following features enables a Secure Firewall to deliver higher throughput?

    a. Clustering

    b. High availability

    c. Hardware bypass

    d. All of these answers are correct.

8. What does a multi-instance deployment enable you to isolate?

    a. Firewall policy management

    b. Firewall software maintenance

    c. Potential failure of a firewall

    d. All of these answers are correct.

Foundation Topics

Evolution of Next-Generation Firewall

A firewall, generally speaking, is an obstacle deployed between two structures to prevent the spread of fire from one structure to another. In computer networking, a firewall is software or hardware that enables you to filter unwanted traffic and to restrict access from one computer to another, or from one network to another. It plays a vital role in securing a network infrastructure. A firewall can be host-based or network-based.

A *host-based firewall* service is installed locally on a computer system. In this case, the end user's computer system takes the final action—to permit or to deny traffic. It consumes the resources of a local computer to run the firewall services, which can impact the other applications running on that particular computer. Furthermore, in a host-based firewall architecture, traffic traverses all the network components and can consume the underlying network resources until the traffic reaches its target.

Figure 1-1 shows the settings for the Windows Firewall running on a Windows 10 operating system.

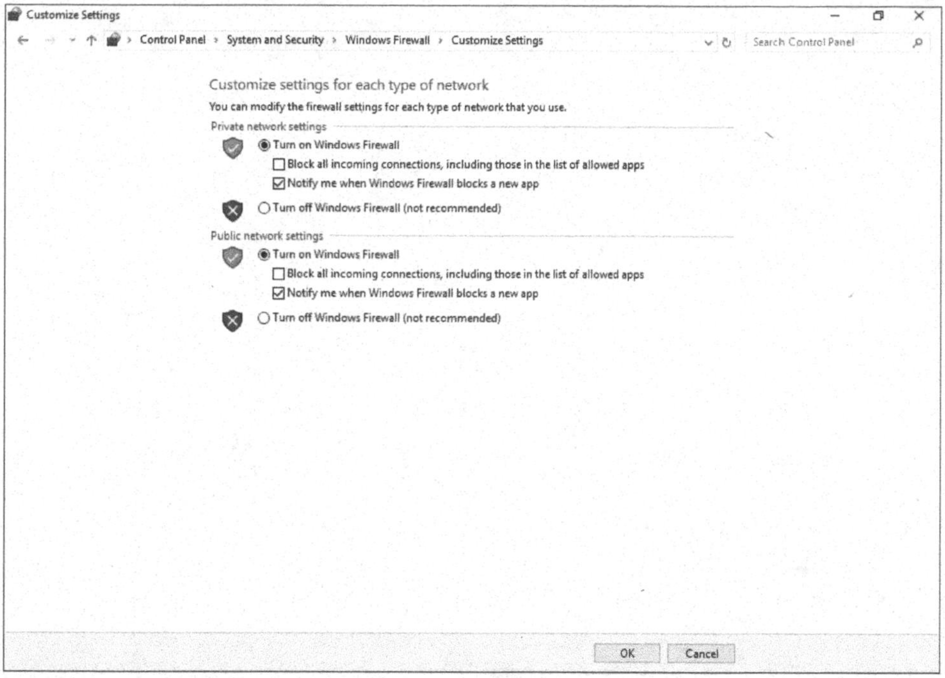

Figure 1-1   *Host-Based Firewall on Microsoft Windows 10*

A *network-based firewall*, on the other hand, can be entirely transparent to an end user. Typically, you deploy it in a perimeter network or at the Internet edge where you want to prevent unwanted traffic from entering your network. The end-user computer system remains unaware of any control of traffic by an intermediate device. In a network-based firewall deployment, you do not need to install any additional software or daemon on the end-user computer systems.

The early generation of firewalls could allow or block packets only based on the static elements in a packet, such as source address, destination address, source port, destination port, and protocol information. These elements are also known as the 5-tuple. When an early generation firewall examined a particular packet, it was unaware of any prior packets that passed through it before, because it was agnostic of the states of the Transmission Control Protocol (TCP). Due to the nature of its operation, this type of firewall is called a *stateless firewall*. A stateless firewall is unable to distinguish the state of a particular packet. For example, it could not determine if a packet is part of an existing connection or trying to establish a legitimate new connection, or whether the packet is a manipulated, rogue packet.

Figure 1-2 indicates the position of the five static elements, known as the 5-tuple, in the Open Systems Interconnection (OSI) model. A stateless firewall utilizes the source address, destination address, source port, destination port, and protocol information of the transport and network layers to filter traffic.

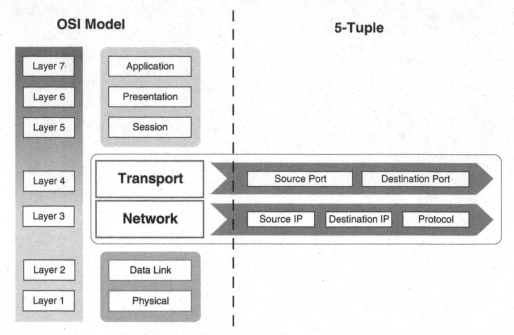

Figure 1-2 *Stateless Firewall Packet Filtering Criteria with Respect to the OSI Layers*

A *stateful firewall* has been developed to overcome the limitations of a stateless firewall. It can hold the connection state in its memory for a certain period, which allows the firewall to track the stages of a TCP handshake, and then take an action based on the state of current and prior packets, rather than based on just a static access control rule constraint.

Figure 1-3 illustrates the states of a TCP connection. During its lifetime, each TCP connection goes through a series of states, which can be used by a stateful firewall to filter traffic. To learn more about TCP operation, read RFC 793.

However, as threats emerge, a traditional firewall—either stateless or stateful—has proven to be ineffective in blocking cyber attacks on present-day applications. You need a firewall that can not only filter traffic at layers 2–4 but also can provide application visibility and control, perform deep packet inspection at layers 3–7, prevent a network from intrusion attempts, decrypt encrypted traffic, detect anomalies in protocols, and correlate security events using various contextual data. The *next-generation firewall (NGFW)* is designed to provide all of these security services from one single box.

Figure 1-4 exhibits the major security features that you can expect on a next-generation firewall (NGFW). Other services are also available on an NGFW but not displayed in this figure, such as routing, geolocation, quality of service (QoS), and Network Address Translation (NAT).

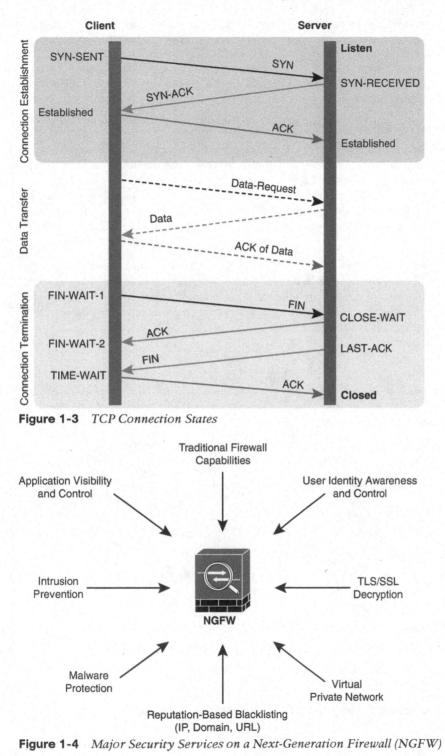

Figure 1-3 *TCP Connection States*

Figure 1-4 *Major Security Services on a Next-Generation Firewall (NGFW)*

The next-generation firewall solution is primarily composed of two components: a manager and a sensor. You use a manager to configure all the security policies and then deploy them to a sensor. Depending on the security policies, a sensor acts on inbound and outbound traffic in real time and generates events. A manager receives those events from its managed sensors, correlates them with various contextual data, and displays them in a graphical user interface (GUI) for an analyst to review.

Cisco Secure Firewall Solutions

The Cisco Secure Firewall is Cisco's next-generation firewall solution. It offers world-class security, visibility, and control through its industry-leading threat intelligence and intrusion prevention capabilities. Its simplified policy management and consistent policy enforcement functionalities enable you to deploy the Secure Firewall solutions in any small-scale to large-scale network environment. In a Secure Firewall deployment, you use a management platform (the manager component) to configure and manage one or more threat defenses (the sensor component).

Figure 1-5 shows the high-level design (HLD) of a typical Cisco Secure Firewall deployment. In the real world, the architecture is larger and can be more complicated, depending on the deployment use cases. For instance, the firewall deployment in an enterprise branch network can be simpler than the deployment in a headquarters or data center network. Likewise, the security requirements of a small and medium-sized business (SMB) network can be different than the requirements of a service provider network.

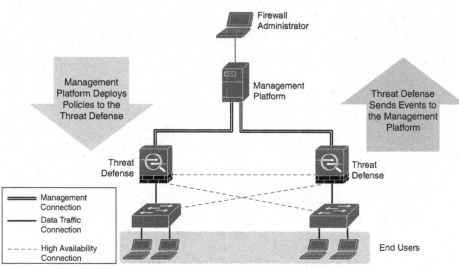

Figure 1-5 *Typical Architecture of Cisco Secure Firewall Deployment*

To meet the need of different types of businesses, Cisco offers manifold solutions to manage the threat defense. You can manage a threat defense locally, remotely, or from the cloud. The current management solutions are

■ **Secure Firewall Device Manager (FDM):** The device manager allows you to manage a single threat defense locally without registering it to any remote management platform. This simple web-based manager application comes with the threat defense

software package by default. This means that when you install the threat defense software, you can enable its built-in device manager application without installing any additional software. Once it is enabled, you can access it simply through a browser.

■ **Secure Firewall Management Center (FMC):** The management center allows you to manage multiple threat defenses from a centralized location. If you need to position hundreds of threat defenses worldwide in various geographical locations, you can use a management center to configure and deploy security policies to all of your threat defenses. The management center enables you to administer hundreds of threat defenses and analyze their security events from a single pane of glass. This book uses the management center in its illustrations and configuration examples.

■ **Cisco Defense Orchestrator (CDO):** Cisco Defense Orchestrator is a cloud-delivered management platform. It enables you to configure and manage policies simultaneously for multiple Cisco security platforms. Because the CDO application is hosted at the Cisco cloud in a Software as a Service (SaaS) model, Cisco regularly takes care of its maintenance tasks and ensures uptime. You do not need to worry about updating its software. You can access its user interface from anywhere, anytime, over the Internet.

The network architecture of each organization can be unique. Different deployment use cases can have significantly different throughput requirements (see Figure 1-6). To fulfill the diverse demands of organizations around the world, Cisco regularly releases a wide variety of new on-premises hardware platforms for Secure Firewall, as well as extends support on many private cloud and public cloud platforms (see Figure 1-7).

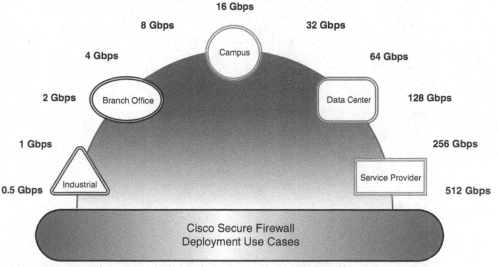

Figure 1-6 *Wide Range of Throughput Requirements in Different Deployment Use Cases*

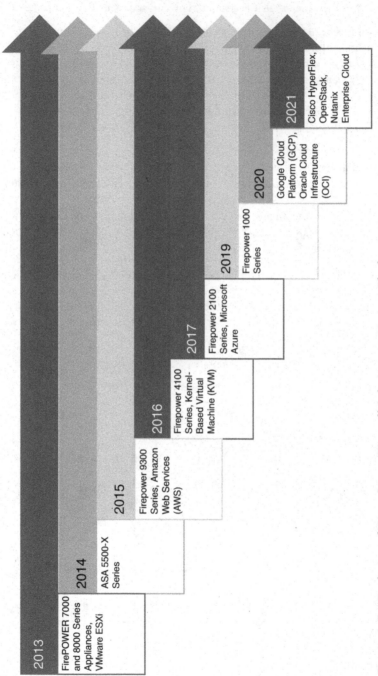

Figure 1-7 *Evolution of Cisco Secure Firewall Solutions on Various Platforms*

Product Evolution and Lifecycle

Sourcefire originally had two different software trains: Version 4.x was primarily intended for intrusion prevention system (IPS) functionality, and Version 5.x was developed with the next-generation firewall (NGFW) features. Depending on the software train, the management platforms had different names. For example, in Version 4.x, it was known as Sourcefire Defense Center, and in Version 5.x, it was known as FireSIGHT Management Center (FMC). Similarly, a sensor was known as 3D Sensor in Version 4.x and a FirePOWER Appliance in Version 5.x. Therefore, it would be correct to say that, in Version 4.x, a Sourcefire Defense Center manages the 3D Sensors, whereas, in Version 5.x, a FireSIGHT Management Center manages the FirePOWER Appliances. Here, note the two different terms—FireSIGHT and FirePOWER.

To make the nomenclature simple as well as to retain the brand reputation, Cisco rebranded them with one simple word: Firepower (note that *power* is written in lowercase). Starting from Version 6.x, Cisco also streamlined the name of the management platform as Firepower Management Center (FMC). Cisco did not retrospectively change the name of the legacy Sourcefire software and hardware from uppercase FirePOWER to lowercase Firepower; for example, the Cisco *FirePOWER* appliances and the Cisco ASA with FirePOWER services. Here, *FirePOWER* (in uppercase format) refers to the developments prior to the Sourcefire acquisition. Only the newly released hardware and software used *Firepower* (in lowercase format) to indicate that this hardware series was introduced after the acquisition.

Table 1-2 shows the branding of management platforms in different software versions.

Table 1-2 Evolution of Cisco Secure Firewall Management Center

Version	Solution Name	Management Platform Name
Version 4.x	3D System	Defense Center
Version 5.x	FireSIGHT System	FireSIGHT Management Center
Version 6.x	Firepower System	Firepower Management Center
Version 7.x	Cisco Secure Firewall	Cisco Secure Firewall Management Center

Figure 1-8 and Figure 1-9 show the login pages of the management platforms in different major software releases.

As with the Sourcefire acquisition, Cisco has been periodically acquiring companies that develop cutting-edge products and technologies. In 2020, Cisco unified all the security product names with the *Cisco Secure* brand. This rebranding simplifies the product names and reflects their use and purpose. For example, the Firepower System is rebranded as Cisco Secure Firewall; the Firepower Management Center is rebranded as Cisco Secure Firewall Management Center, and the Firepower Threat Defense (FTD) is rebranded as Cisco Secure Firewall Threat Defense. Table 1-3 shows some of the new product names according to the Cisco Secure branding architecture.

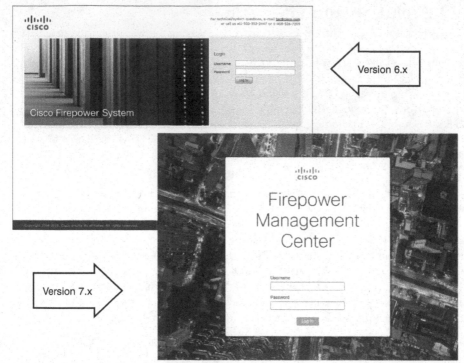

Figure 1-8   *The Login Pages of the Management Platforms in Versions 7.x and 6.x*

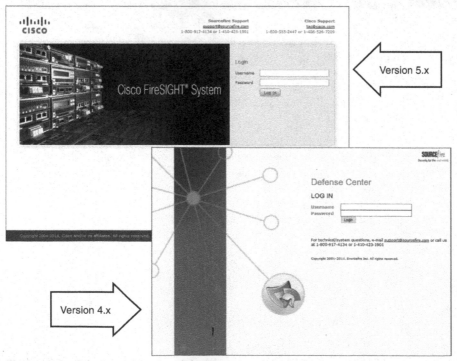

Figure 1-9   *The Login Pages of the Management Platforms in Versions 5.x and 4.x*

Table 1-3 Cisco Secure Branding Architecture

New Name	Previous Name
Cisco Secure Firewall	Firepower Next-Generation Firewall (NGFW)
Cisco Secure Firewall Threat Defense	Firepower Threat Defense
Cisco Secure Firewall Management Center	Firepower Management Center
Cisco Secure IPS	Firepower Threat Defense IPS Mode
Malware Defense	Advanced Malware Protection (AMP) for Networks
Malware Analytics Cloud	Advanced Malware Protection (AMP) Cloud
Cisco Secure Endpoint	Advanced Malware Protection (AMP) for Endpoints
Cisco Secure Client	Cisco AnyConnect Secure Mobility Client
Cisco Secure Malware Analytics	Cisco Threat Grid

Cisco releases two software versions for Secure Firewall, usually about six months apart. The Short-Term Release (STR) has a shorter lifecycle, but it includes the latest feature set. The Long-Term Release (LTR) provides a longer lifecycle. If you are looking for a release that has the latest features and longer support duration, this should be your choice. Every two years, Cisco releases an extended version of LTR, called Extra Long-Term Release (XLTR). This release not only offers the longest lifecycle but also is chosen for government certification. Figure 1-10 displays the longevity of different types of software releases from the first customer shipment (FCS) date.

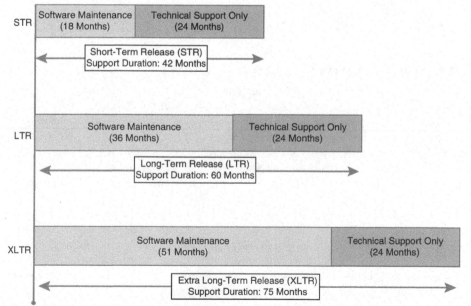

Figure 1-10 *The Software Release Lifecycle of Cisco Secure Firewall*

This book is written based on Cisco Secure Firewall Version 7.0, which is an XLTR. If you are running a different software version, you may find your management center's GUI slightly different. For instance, the banner may show *Firepower Management Center* or *Firewall Management Center*, depending on the version you are using. That's okay for your CCNP Security lab environment because they both refer to the same type of firewall manager. Furthermore, to capture additional contexts in a screenshot, it was often necessary to zoom in/out the browser. Due to dynamic rendering of browser, both *Firepower Management Center* and *FMC* appear in the screenshots. Please don't be confused: they are the same thing (see Figure 1-11). If your management center's GUI looks different from the screenshots provided in this book, you can still use this book to prepare for the CCNP Security exam because the fundamental knowledge of the Cisco Secure Firewall remains the same across all the versions and platforms.

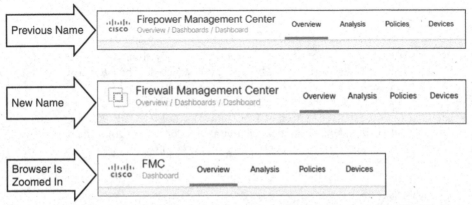

Figure 1-11 *Variation in Banners, Referring to the Same Management Platform*

Software and Hardware Architecture

Right after acquisition, Cisco integrated Sourcefire's next-generation security technologies on Cisco's existing firewall solutions, called the Adaptive Security Appliances (ASA). In that early implementation, Sourcefire technologies were running as a separate service module. Later, Cisco designed new hardware platforms to support Sourcefire technologies natively. They are named *Cisco Firepower*, which was later rebranded as *Cisco Secure Firewall*. In the new implementation, Cisco converges Sourcefire's next-generation security features, open-source Snort, and ASA's firewall functionalities into a single unified software image. This unified software is called the *Firepower Threat Defense (FTD)*. After rebranding, this software is now known as the *Cisco Secure Firewall Threat Defense*, or in short, the threat defense. The unified image of the threat defense software reduces processing overhead and increases overall system performance because all the security services run natively on the operating system, not as a separate service module. The functionalities of software components are elaborated in the later chapters of this book; however, before we dive deep into the features, let's take a quick look at the purpose of each component.

Figure 1-12 illustrates various software components that interact with a Cisco Secure Firewall.

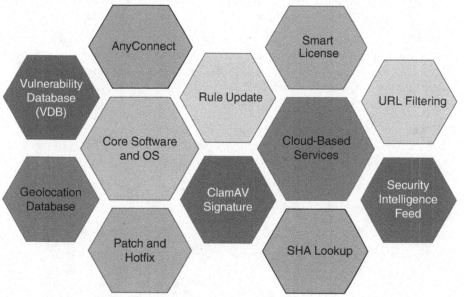

Figure 1-12 *Cisco Secure Firewall Software Components*

- **Core Software and Operating System (OS):** The core part of the software includes the operating system, Snort inspection engine for intrusion detection and prevention, a web server for the graphical user interface, a database to store events, firmware for hardware components, and so on.

- **Maintenance Release and Patch:** Cisco regularly publishes maintenance releases to provide fixes for any defects with the Secure Firewall software and to address any security vulnerabilities that may be found in a public release.

- **Rule Update:** The inspection engine on Secure Firewall uses intrusion rules, based on Snort, to detect and prevent intrusion attempts. The Cisco threat intelligence group, known as Talos, develops the intrusion rules to provide coverage on the latest security threats and vulnerabilities, and package the ruleset separately for different versions of Snort. The rule update package for Snort 2 is known as Cisco **Secure Rule Update (SRU)**. In Snort 3, this rule update package is called the **Lightweight Security Package (LSP)**. In a newly installed Secure Firewall with software version 7.0 or higher, Snort 3 is the default inspection engine.

- **Vulnerability Database (VDB):** This database stores vulnerability information and fingerprints of various applications, services, and operating systems. Secure Firewall uses the information on this database to identify a network host by determining the application, service, or operating system. Furthermore, the VDB allows a Secure Firewall to determine whether a certain file type is eligible for Dynamic File Analysis (an advanced feature of Fire and Malware policy).

- **Geolocation Database (GeoDB):** This database stores the geographical information of an IP address. For instance, when a Secure Firewall displays an intrusion event in the GUI, GeoDB allows you to view the name and flag of the country that originated that intrusion attempt. It helps you to recognize and act on traffic based on the geographical location.

Figure 1-13 shows the default software components that come with a management center running software version 7.0. To find the current versions of your management center, go to the Help menu (the ? icon), which is located at the top-right corner, and select the About page.

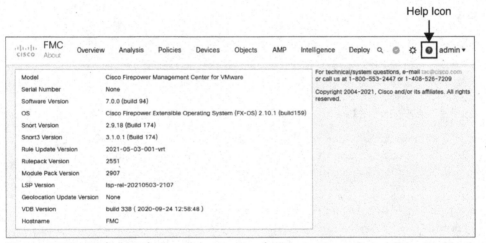

Figure 1-13   *Default Software Components of a Management Center Running Version 7.0*

The architecture of Secure Firewall is modular. A high-end single chassis can be comprised of multiple blade servers, also known as security modules. The threat defense software runs on a supervisor. Both supervisor and security modules are driven by a distinct operating system, called the Firepower eXtensible Operating System (FXOS). Figure 1-14 shows some popular low-end and high-end Secure Firewall hardware models. The top two firewalls are members of the 1000 series family, which is designed for small to medium business networks. The firewall at the bottom is 9000 series hardware, which is capable of handling a large volume of traffic in a data center or a service provider network. Figure 1-15 illustrates the modular architecture of 9000 series hardware in a simple diagram.

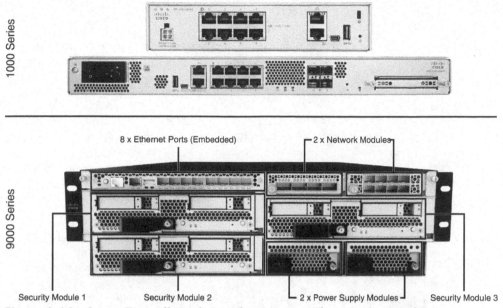

Figure 1-14 *Secure Firewall Hardware That Supports Threat Defense Software*

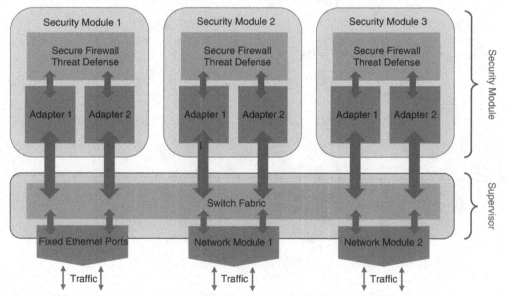

Figure 1-15 *Architecture of the Cisco Secure Firewall 9000 Series Hardware*

Scalability and Resiliency

Secure Firewall is a highly flexible security solution. There are multiple ways to enable scalability and ensure resiliency in a Secure Firewall deployment, such as using **clustering**, **multi-instance**, **high availability**, and more. This section summarizes the key characteristics and advantages of some of these features.

Clustering

As your organization grows, your Secure Firewall deployment can also expand to support its network growth. If you are running a higher Cisco Secure Firewall model, you do not need to replace your existing devices for additional horsepower; you can simply add extra threat defense devices to your existing deployment and group them into a single logical cluster to support additional throughput. A clustered logical device offers higher performance, scalability, and resiliency at the same time.

You can create a cluster between multiple chassis or between multiple security modules of the same chassis. When a cluster is built with multiple independent chassis, it is called *inter-chassis clustering*. When you build a cluster between multiple security modules of the same chassis, it is known as *intra-chassis clustering*. The system automatically designates one of the members of a cluster as the *control unit*. The remaining members are considered the *data units*. In inter-chassis clustering, your configurations on the control unit are automatically replicated to the data units using a cluster control link (CCL). In intra-chassis clustering, the cluster members use backplane for cluster communications.

See Figure 1-16 and Figure 1-17 to understand the differences between inter- and intra-chassis clustering architectures. In Figure 1-16, an intra-chassis cluster is formed between three separate service modules of the same chassis. Figure 1-17 shows an inter-chassis cluster established between two separate chassis. All of the six service modules in two chassis are logically grouped into a cluster. Layer 2 switching is used to establish a cluster control link (CCL) network.

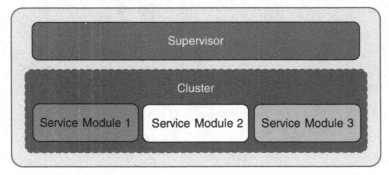

Secure Firewall Hardware Chassis

Figure 1-16 *Logical Diagram of an Intra-Chassis Cluster*

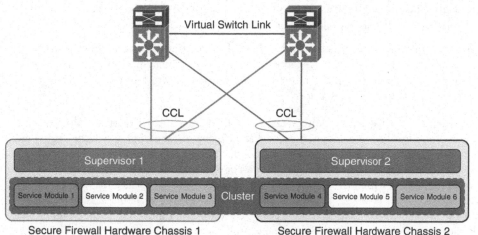

Figure 1-17 *Logical Diagram of an Inter-Chassis Cluster*

Multi-Instance

The higher Secure Firewall models also offer multi-instance capability powered by the Docker container technology. It enables you to create and run multiple application instances using a small subset of the total hardware resources of a chassis. You can manage the threat defense application instances independently, as if they are separate threat defense devices (see Figure 1-18). Multi-instance capability enables you to isolate many critical elements, such as

- Firewall policy management

- Firewall software maintenance

- Any failure and troubleshooting

- Data traffic processing

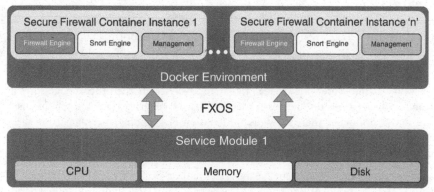

Figure 1-18 *Secure Firewall Implementation in the Docker Container Environment*

In a container-based environment, a threat defense application instance can be deployed in two ways:

- **Native instance:** This utilizes all the hardware resources of a Secure Firewall to build a single threat defense application instance.

- **Container instance:** This shares the physical resources of a Secure Firewall to create multiple logical threat defense application instances. The number of container instances you can create is dependent on the underlying hardware resources, such as CPU, memory, storage, and interface.

Depending on your use case requirements, you can take the advantage of both logical grouping functionalities—container instance and cluster—at the same time. This combined deployment is known as *multi-instance clustering*. This type of clustering offers additional flexibility in your security architecture design. For example, the members of a cluster can be of different models within the same hardware series. A security module can have multiple container instances, as long as sufficient hardware resources are available. It is also not necessary to include all the container instances on a security module into a cluster. Figure 1-19 illustrates this design flexibility in a logical diagram.

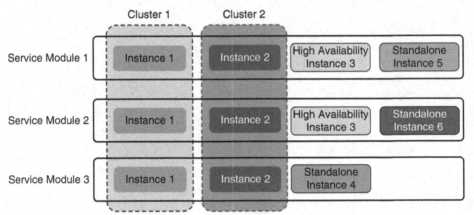

Figure 1-19 *Logical Diagram of a Multi-Instance Cluster Environment*

High Availability

The high availability capability of Secure Firewall enables you to ensure business continuity during an unplanned outage. You can enable high availability on both Secure Firewall components—management center and threat defense. Both participating peers in a high availability pair must be the same model and be running the same software version.

In a high availability architecture, one device operates actively while the other device stays in standby. A standby device does not actively process traffic or security events. If a failure is detected in the active device, or there's any discontinuation of keepalive messages from the active device, the standby device takes over the role of the active device and starts operating actively to maintain continuity in firewall operations.

An active device periodically sends keepalive messages and replicates its configurations to a standby device. The communication channel between the peers of a high-availability pair must be robust, and with much less latency. In terms of connectivity, the management centers of a high-availability pair use their regular management interfaces to communicate with the peers; however, the threat defense devices of a high-availability pair use dedicated links to exchange failover status and data. You can configure an unused data interface to operate as a dedicated failover link. Figures 1-20 and 1-21 illustrate the connections between the active and standby peers of a high-availability pair.

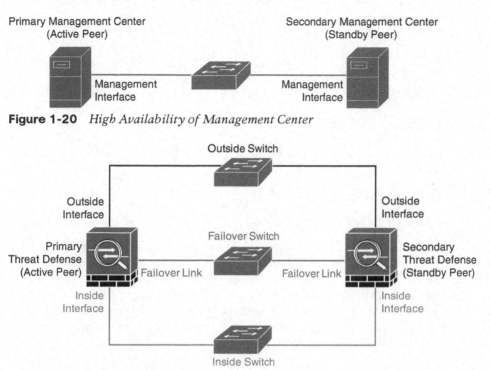

Figure 1-20   *High Availability of Management Center*

Figure 1-21   *High Availability of Threat Defense*

Resiliency in Connectivity

Cisco Secure Firewall supports resiliency in the network port level to ensure business continuity in case of a link failure. The following are the two predominant features to consider, depending on your use cases:

■ **EtherChannel:** EtherChannel is a link aggregation technology (IEEE 802.3ad) that enables you to combine multiple physical ports into a logical group, and then achieve a higher throughput from that aggregated channel group. The other benefit is its fault tolerance for link failure. If one member interface of a channel group goes down, traffic is still transferred and load-balanced through the remaining interfaces of the channel group. Threat defense enables you to configure EtherChannel with its physical interfaces. To establish redundancy, you can consider EtherChannel for any data links as well as for the failover links. The addition, removal, or replacement of links to an EtherChannel is automatically processed by the Link Aggregation Control Protocol (LACP).

Figure 1-22 shows two links bundled into a single channel group. Due to the EtherChannel configurations, the links between the threat defense devices are now more resilient, compared to the topology displayed in Figure 1-21.

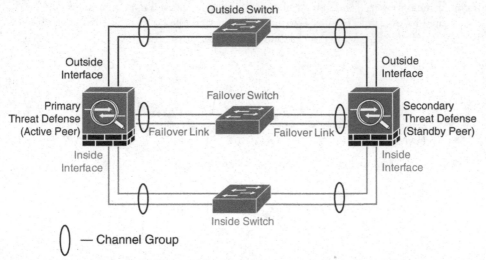

Figure 1-22 *EtherChannel Enabling Fault Tolerance at the Link Level*

- **Hardware Bypass:** This functionally enables traffic to go through a threat defense in case of any hardware failure or power outage. To enable this feature, your threat defense must be equipped with a specially designed network module that is supported only in inline sets (configuration of inline sets is detailed in Chapter 15, "Network Analysis and Intrusion Policies"). The hardware bypass ports are not supported in high availability mode, and they can't participate in an EtherChannel logical group.

Summary

This chapter provides a foundation of the next-generation firewall solutions and reveals a brief history of Cisco Secure Firewall. It also introduces you to the software components and hardware architecture of Secure Firewall. The chapter also describes the advanced features to enable scalability and resiliency in a threat defense. In the next chapter, you will learn about the deployment and initialization of Secure Firewall software.

Exam Preparation Tasks

As mentioned in the section "How to Use This Book" in the Introduction, you have a couple of choices for exam preparation: the exercises here, Chapter 22, "Final Preparation," and the exam simulation questions in the Pearson Test Prep practice test software.

Review All Key Topics

Review the most important topics in this chapter, noted with the Key Topic icon in the outer margin of the page. Table 1-4 lists a reference of these key topics and the page numbers on which each is found.

Key Topic

Table 1-4   Key Topics for Chapter 1

Key Topic Element	Description	Page
Paragraph	Next-generation firewall components	8
List	Secure Firewall management platforms	8
List	Cisco Secure Firewall software components	15
Paragraph	Clustering	18
Paragraph	Multi-instance	19
Paragraph	Multi-instance clustering	20
Paragraph	High availability	20

Complete Tables and Lists from Memory

Print a copy of Appendix C, "Memory Tables" (found on the companion website), or at least the section for this chapter, and complete the tables and lists from memory. Appendix D, "Memory Tables Answer Key," also on the companion website, includes completed tables and lists to check your work.

Define Key Terms

Define the following key terms from this chapter and check your answers in the glossary:

Secure Firewall Device Manager (FDM), Secure Firewall Management Center (FMC), Cisco Defense Orchestrator (CDO), Secure Rule Update (SRU), Lightweight Security Package (LSP), Vulnerability Database (VDB), Geolocation Database (GeoDB), clustering, multi-instance, high availability

## CHAPTER 2

Deployment of Secure Firewall Virtual

This chapter provides an overview of the following topics:

Cisco Secure Firewall on a Virtual Platform: This section discusses the supported platforms and resource allocation requirements for Secure Firewall virtual appliances.

Best Practices: This section provides a list of best practices to deploy Secure Firewall software in a virtual platform.

Configuration: This section describes the VMware ESXi configurations to deploy the Secure Firewall software.

System Initialization and Validation: This section shares ways to verify whether the deployment of Secure Firewall completed successfully.

The objectives of this chapter are to learn about

- Deployment of Cisco Secure Firewall on a virtual platform
- Building a cost-effective lab environment for the CCNP Security exam preparation

The procedure to deploy the Secure Firewall software is different in on-premises hardware, on a virtual environment, or in a public cloud infrastructure. However, after the software is installed and a threat defense is registered with a management center, the steps to configure and deploy various security policies using the graphical user interface (GUI) are identical across all the management center or threat defense models. In other words, if you learn to configure Secure Firewall using a specific model, you can apply the knowledge on any other platforms. To prepare for the CCNP Security exam, you may find a virtual lab is a more cost-effective alternative than building a lab with Cisco proprietary hardware. Keeping that in mind, this chapter demonstrates how to deploy Secure Firewall in a virtual lab environment.

"Do I Know This Already?" Quiz

The "Do I Know This Already?" quiz enables you to assess whether you should read this entire chapter thoroughly or jump to the "Exam Preparation Tasks" section. If you are in doubt about your answers to these questions or your own assessment of your knowledge of the topics, read the entire chapter. Table 2-1 lists the major headings in this chapter and their corresponding "Do I Know This Already?" quiz questions. You can find the answers in Appendix A, "Answers to the 'Do I Know This Already?' Quizzes."

Table 2-1 "Do I Know This Already?" Section-to-Question Mapping

Foundation Topics Section	Questions
Cisco Secure Firewall on a Virtual Platform	1–3
Best Practices	4
Configuration	5, 6
System Initialization and Validation	7, 8

CAUTION The goal of self-assessment is to gauge your mastery of the topics in this chapter. If you do not know the answer to a question or are only partially sure of the answer, you should mark that question as wrong for purposes of the self-assessment. Giving yourself credit for an answer you correctly guess skews your self-assessment results and might provide you with a false sense of security.

1. Which of the following virtual platforms is supported to run Secure Firewall Version 7.0?

   a. VMware Workstation

   b. VMware Player

   c. VMware Fusion

   d. VMware ESXi

2. What is the recommended amount of memory you should allocate to a management center virtual appliance to manage eight threat defense devices?

   a. 16 GB

   b. 28 GB

   c. 32 GB

   d. 64 GB

3. Which of the following is a disk file of a Secure Firewall virtual appliance?

   a. TAR.GZ

   b. VMDK

   c. OVF

   d. MF

4. Which network adapter provides the maximum throughput?

   a. E1000

   b. VMXNET2 (Enhanced)

   c. VMXNET3

   d. VMXNET-X

5. How many total interfaces are required to deploy a threat defense virtual appliance?

   a. One

   b. Two

   c. Three

   d. Four

6. Which of the following statements is true?

   a. You can install an ISO image file to deploy a management center virtual appliance.

   b. A threat defense virtual appliance supports a maximum of four interfaces.

   c. An OVF template for ESXi can also be used to deploy Secure Firewall in the cloud.

   d. Promiscuous mode must be enabled in all the data interfaces of a threat defense virtual appliance.

7. Which of the following statements is false?

   a. Abruptly powering off a virtual appliance can corrupt its system database.

   b. Answering Yes to the question "Manage the Device Locally" enables device manager services.

   c. Secure Firewall software enables you to configure the management IP address both manually and using DHCP.

   d. For security reasons, SSH access to Secure Firewall is disabled by default.

8. Which protocols can be used to connect to Secure Firewall for management purposes?

   a. HTTP and HTTPS.

   b. HTTPS and SSH.

   c. SSH and Telnet.

   d. All of these answers are correct.

Foundation Topics

Cisco Secure Firewall on a Virtual Platform

The Cisco Secure Firewall components—both management center and threat defense—are fully interoperable with any hardware and virtual appliance models. For example, you can deploy a management center in a virtual environment while its threat defense devices may be based on Cisco hardware, or vice versa. Deployment of Secure Firewall in a virtual environment is a multistep process. It requires careful design of a virtual network and allocation of sufficient virtual resources. When you choose a virtual environment, you must understand its compatibilities, limitations, and underlying costs. You might be able to install Secure Firewall software on any virtual platforms; however, Cisco might not support all available platforms. Read the software release notes at cisco.com to determine whether your chosen virtual platform is supported by your desired version of Secure Firewall software. Table 2-2 provides a list of supported virtual/cloud platforms for Secure Firewall Version 7.0.

Table 2-2   Supported Platforms for Secure Firewall Virtual Appliance Running Version 7.0 or Higher

Private Cloud (On-Premises)	Public Cloud
VMware vSphere/ESXi	Amazon Web Services (AWS)
Kernel-Based Virtual Machine (KVM)	Microsoft Azure
OpenStack	Google Cloud Platform (GCP)
Nutanix Enterprise Cloud	Oracle Cloud Infrastructure (OCI)

This chapter demonstrates the steps to deploy a management center and a threat defense in an on-premises virtual environment. During the demonstration, Secure Firewall Version 7.0 is deployed on VMware ESXi 6.5 as an example. If you use a different version or platform, the user interface may appear different; however, you can still use this chapter to understand the core concept of the deployment workflow.

Hosting Environment Settings

Make sure the Virtualization Technology (VT) is enabled on your hosting server where VMware is running. It improves the performance of virtual machines running on VMware. You can enable it using the BIOS setup utility of your system, as shown in Figure 2-1. The latest processors from Intel and AMD support this functionality.

Figure 2-1 shows Virtualization Technology enabled in the BIOS setup utility.

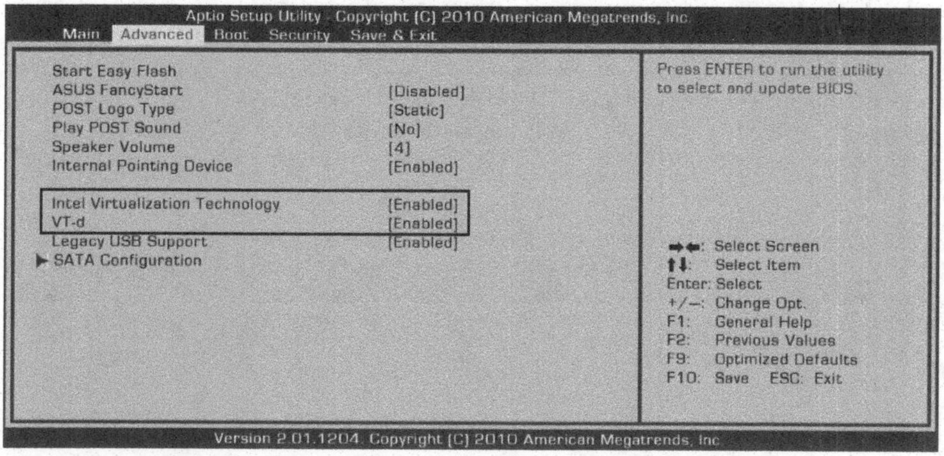

Figure 2-1   *Enabling Virtualization Technology in the BIOS Setup Utility*

Disable hyperthreading on the hosting environment where you will run a threat defense virtual appliance. Hyperthreading technology can make a single *physical* processor core act like two *logical* processors; however, this is not necessary for a threat defense virtual appliance powered by Snort 3. Snort 3 natively supports multiple packet processing threads, which allows a threat defense virtual appliance to perform faster inspection by design. To disable hyperthreading, first disable it in the system's BIOS settings and then turn it off in the vSphere Client.

Virtual Resource Allocation

A virtual appliance obtains its memory, virtual processor, and storage from the resource pools of its host server. The performance of a virtual appliance is subject to the resources you allocate from that resource pool. For optimal performance, you should always consider allocating the Cisco recommended number of resources to your Secure Firewall.

Table 2-3 shows the minimum resource requirements for different management center virtual appliance models. The FMCv25 model can manage up to 25 threat defense devices, whereas an FMCv300 model can manage up to 300 threat defense devices. FMCv300 is designed for larger networks. To build a lab for the CCNP Security exam preparation, you can simply choose FMCv25.

Table 2-3   Secure Firewall Management Center Virtual Appliance Specifications

Component	FMCv25	FMCv300
Processor	4 vCPU–8 vCPU	32 vCPU
Memory	32 GB	64 GB
Storage	250 GB	2.2 TB
Maximum Number of Managed Threat Defense	25	300
Maximum Network Map (Hosts/Users)	50,000/50,000	150,000/150,000
Maximum Intrusion Events	10 million	60 million

Table 2-4 shows the specifications of threat defense virtual appliances in different performance tiers. The more resources you allocate, the better performance a threat defense virtual appliance can offer. However, the smaller the average packet size, the less throughput a threat defense virtual appliance can deliver. The throughput statistics in this table are estimated considering three security features: firewall, application visibility and control (AVC), and intrusion prevention system (IPS). For your CCNP Security exam preparation lab, the FTDv5 model should be sufficient.

Table 2-4   Secure Firewall Threat Defense Virtual Appliance Specifications

Component	FTDv5	FTDv10	FTDv20	FTDv30	FTDv50	FTDv100
Processor	4 vCPU	4 vCPU	4 vCPU	8 vCPU	12 vCPU	16 vCPU
Memory	8 GB	8 GB	8 GB	16 GB	24 GB	32 GB
Storage	48 GB	48 GB	48 GB	48 GB	48 GB	48 GB
Throughput (1024 B)	100 Mbps	1 Gbps	3 Gbps	5.5 Gbps	10 Gbps	15.5 Gbps
Throughput (450 B)	100 Mbps	1 Gbps	1 Gbps	2 Gbps	3 Gbps	7 Gbps
Maximum New Connections per Second	12,500	20,000	20,000	20,000	40,000	130,000
Maximum Concurrent Sessions	100,000	100,000	100,000	250,000	500,000	2,000,000

Software Package Selection

In a Secure Firewall deployment, the management center software version should be equal to or greater than the version running on its managed threat defense devices. For example, if you deploy a threat defense with Version 7.0, its remote manager—the management center—must be running Version 7.0 or greater. You must choose the appropriate software version and package for your hosting environment. For example, if your virtual platform is based on VMware ESXi, use the Open Virtualization Format (.ovf) file, which is provided in a compressed tar.gz file. Similarly, if you run a KVM-based infrastructure, use the QEMU Copy On Write (.qcow2) file. For public cloud platforms, software packages are published separately. For example, for the Microsoft Azure cloud environment, the Virtual Hard Disk (.vhd.bz2) file is available for download. Do not use any ISO image files to create a virtual appliance. They are packaged for Cisco hardware.

Figure 2-2 highlights the installation packages for VMware platform. You can download them from the Cisco Software Download portal.

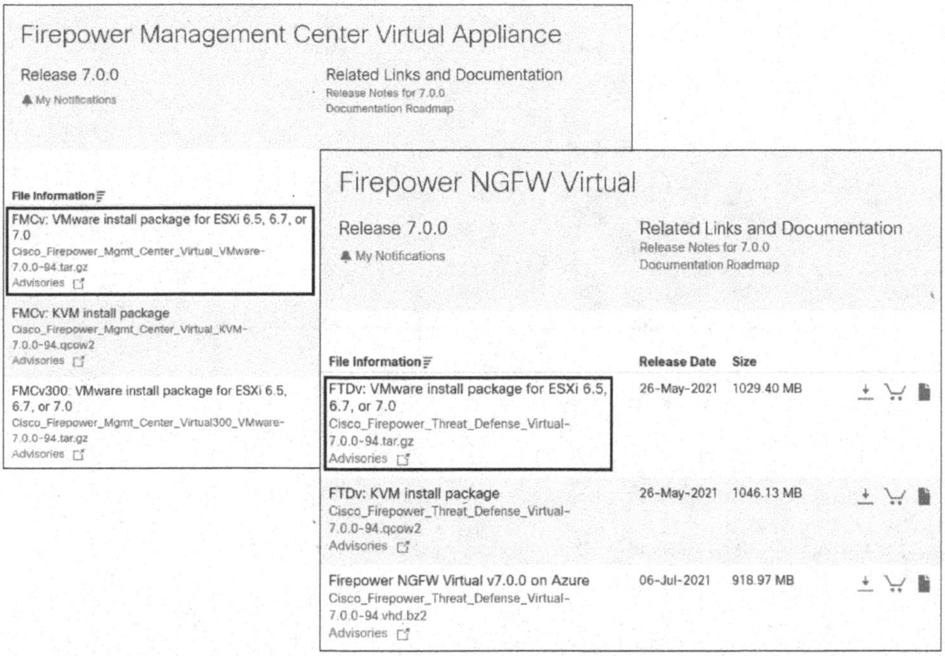

Figure 2-2 *Secure Firewall Virtual Appliance Installation Packages Available at Cisco.com*

A tarball (tar.gz file) for VMware ESXi includes templates for ESXi and the virtual infrastructure (VI). The key difference between them is the initial setup process, which includes network configurations, password setup for the admin account, and other configuration options. In a VI template deployment, you use a deployment wizard to configure the initial system settings before the Secure Firewall software is deployed. In an ESXi template, however, you configure the initial settings from the VMware console after a virtual appliance is deployed. The examples in this chapter use the ESXi template to deploy a Secure Firewall virtual appliance on VMware.

A tarball for a Secure Firewall virtual appliance installation package includes the following types of files:

■ **Open Virtual Format (.ovf) file:** An XML file that stores references to many elements of a Secure Firewall software installation package.

- **Virtual Machine Disk (.vmdk) file:** A compressed virtual disk that stores the Secure Firewall software.

- **Manifest (.mf) file:** A clear-text file that stores the SHA1 digests of the OVF and VMDK files in a package.

Figure 2-3 shows the installation files to create new virtual machines for management center (top image) and threat defense (bottom image). You can obtain these files after you extract the tarballs that you downloaded from the Cisco Software Download portal.

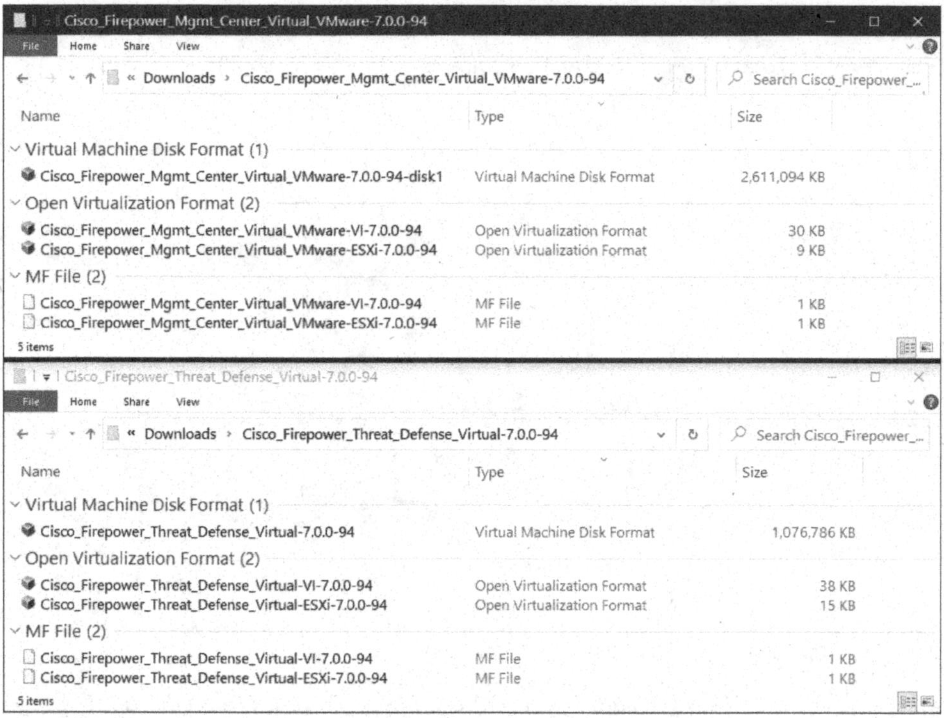

Figure 2-3 *Secure Firewall Virtual Appliance Installation Files*

Best Practices

Best practices for deploying a Secure Firewall virtual appliance on VMware ESXi are as follows:

1. After you download the appropriate file for a Secure Firewall virtual appliance from cisco.com, always verify the checksum of the file you have downloaded to confirm that the file is not corrupt and has not been modified during download. You can find the checksum values in the manifest file (MF files are shown in Figure 2-3), which is included in the tarball package.

2. Read the release notes and getting started guide to determine any version-specific requirements. Plan for additional time to fulfill any prerequisites and to complete the virtual appliance deployment processes. For instance, just to set up a virtual network on the hosting environment, deploy the software from scratch, and complete the

system initialization, you need about an hour (depending on the hardware resource capacity). Additional time is necessary for licensing, registration, and initial setup.

3. If your ESXi server has unused resources, allocate them to your Secure Firewall virtual appliances for enhanced performance. To change virtual resource allocation, you must gracefully power off the virtual machine at first. When you allocate additional resources, you must consider a supported combination of CPU and memory, indicated in Tables 2-3 and 2-4.

4. Never power off a virtual appliance when the deployment or initialization is in progress. It can corrupt the system database. Upon successful initialization of Secure Firewall, a login prompt appears at the VMware console.

5. A Secure Firewall virtual appliance supports the **VMXNET3** network adapter, which is designed to minimize network processing overhead in a virtual environment. If you are running an earlier version of the Secure Firewall software, the network adapter type may be set to E1000 by default. For higher throughput, change the adapter type from E1000 to VMXNET3. The main difference between an E1000 and a VMXNET3 adapter is in the maximum throughput limit. The throughput of a VMXNET3 adapter is 10 Gbps, whereas an E1000 adapter supports up to 1 Gbps. To find more detail on different types of network adapters in the VMware platforms, visit vmware.com.

Configuration

Deployment of a Secure Firewall virtual appliance in VMware is a multistep process. After you build a VMware ESXi host server, you need to design and set up a virtual network in your host environment using the virtual switches and virtual network adapters. This virtual network should be able to segregate the management traffic from the data traffic. Although any VMware-specific configurations, such as setting up a virtual network on VMware, are beyond the scope of this CCNP Security book, this section highlights some of the key steps to help you prepare the lab.

Figure 2-4 shows the key steps to deploy a Secure Firewall virtual appliance on a VMware ESXi host.

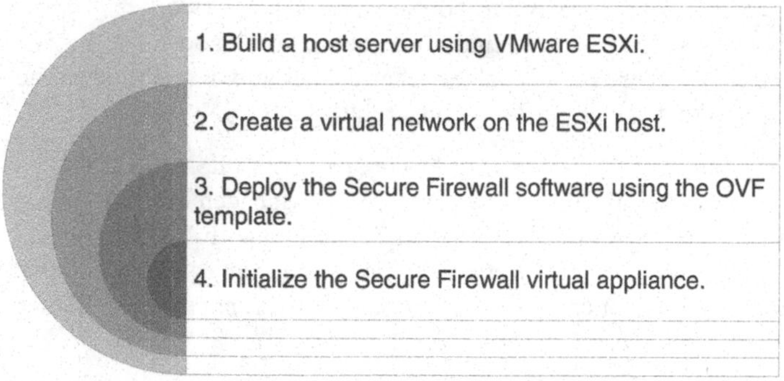

1. Build a host server using VMware ESXi.

2. Create a virtual network on the ESXi host.

3. Deploy the Secure Firewall software using the OVF template.

4. Initialize the Secure Firewall virtual appliance.

Figure 2-4 *Major Steps to Deploy a Secure Firewall Virtual Appliance*

Figure 2-5 exhibits a logical topology where Secure Firewall is deployed in a virtual environment. While the end user's data traverses from the inside network to the Internet through a threat defense virtual appliance over a virtual data network, the management center virtual appliance and threat defense virtual appliance communicate over a separate virtual network for management purposes. All the servers and end users are connected to the virtual network via vmnics.

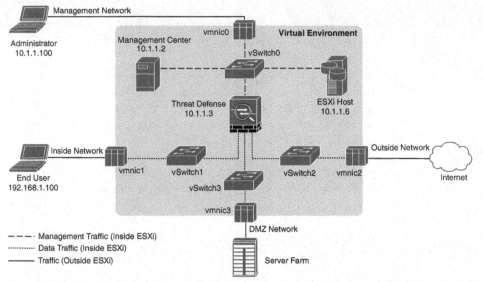

Figure 2-5   *Logical Topology of a Virtual Network on the VMware ESXi Environment*

Virtual Network for Management Traffic

A management center virtual appliance requires only one interface for management communication, whereas a threat defense virtual appliance requires at least four interfaces—one interface for management communication and three interfaces for traffic inspection. The virtual network interfaces are predefined in the ESXi and VI templates. However, before you attempt to deploy an OVF template, you need to configure a virtual network in your VMware ESXi server using virtual switches and virtual ports. Later, you associate them with the predefined virtual network interfaces. The virtual switches are actually mapped with the hardware network interface cards that are physically connected to your ESXi server.

Figure 2-6 shows the default virtual switch vSwitch0 that is created by an ESXi host. A physical adapter vmnic0 is connected to the default virtual port group's Management Network and VM Network. The Management Network is automatically mapped with *VMkernel*—the management interface of an ESXi host. The VM Network is created automatically for guest virtual machines. You can utilize it as the management network for your management center virtual appliance and threat defense virtual appliance.

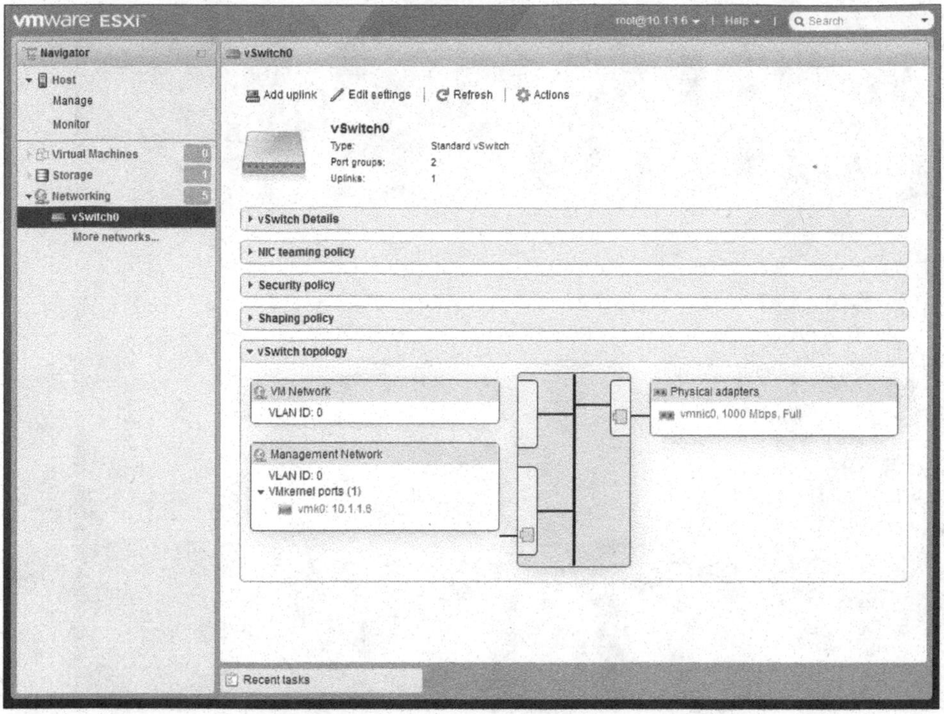

Figure 2-6 *Mapping of Default Virtual Switch with ESXi Management Network*

Virtual Network for Data Traffic

When you deploy Secure Firewall on a virtual platform, there are some special considerations for data interface configurations. For instance, when deploying a threat defense virtual appliance, you must enable **promiscuous mode** on all the connected virtual ports of a virtual switch. It allows a virtual switch to see any frames that traverse through the threat defense virtual appliance.

Figure 2-7 shows how to enable promiscuous mode during the addition of a virtual switch for the inside network. Select Accept for the Promiscuous Mode and other security options in this configuration window.

A threat defense virtual appliance can support up to 10 interfaces in total. Although the default template of a threat defense virtual appliance comes with 10 interfaces, you may not need all of them. To power on a threat defense virtual appliance during its first bootup, at least four interfaces need to be enabled.

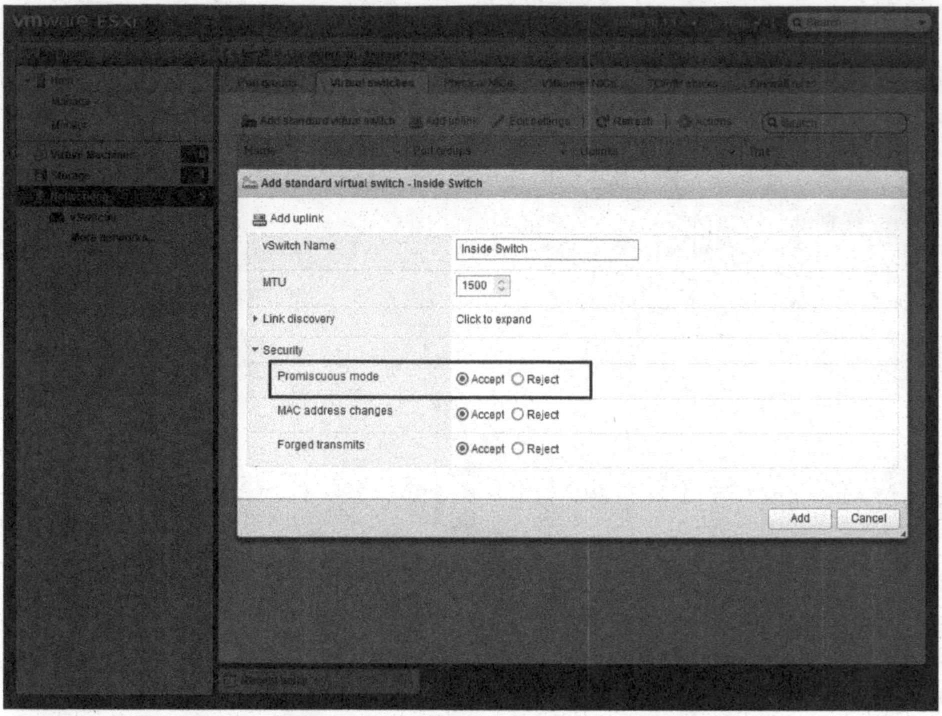

Figure 2-7 *Configuration Window to Add a Standard Virtual Switch*

Table 2-5 shows a typical mapping of the virtual ports with physical network adapters.

Table 2-5 Mapping of Virtual Ports with Physical Adapters

Virtual Port	Physical Adapter	Purpose
VM Network	vmnic0	For management traffic
Inside Network	vmnic1	For internal network
Outside Network	vmnic2	Toward the outside world
DMZ Network	vmnic3	For server farm

Figure 2-8 shows some port groups and their associations with individual virtual switches in VMware ESXi.

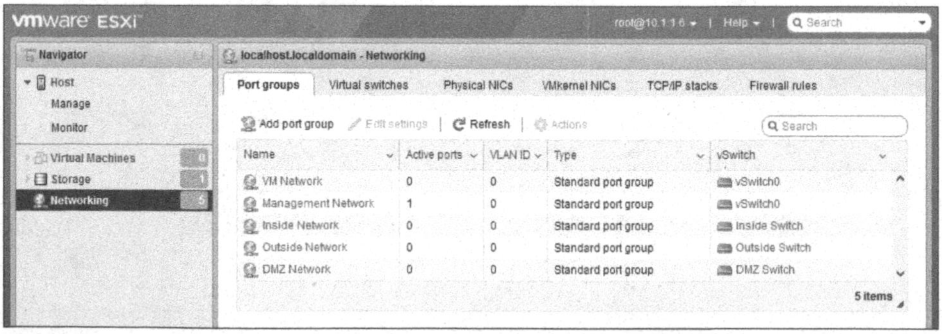

Figure 2-8 *Mapping of Virtual Port Groups with Separate Virtual Switches*

Virtual Machine Creation for Secure Firewall

Once a virtual network is built in the VMware ESXi host, and the desired software package for the Secure Firewall virtual appliance is downloaded and extracted, you are ready to deploy and set up a virtual appliance. Log in to the web client of your ESXi server using a browser, and follow these steps to deploy an OVF template file for the Secure Firewall virtual appliance:

Step 1. Under the Navigator panel, select **Virtual Machines**. The Create/Register VM option appears.

Figure 2-9 shows the option to create a new virtual machine.

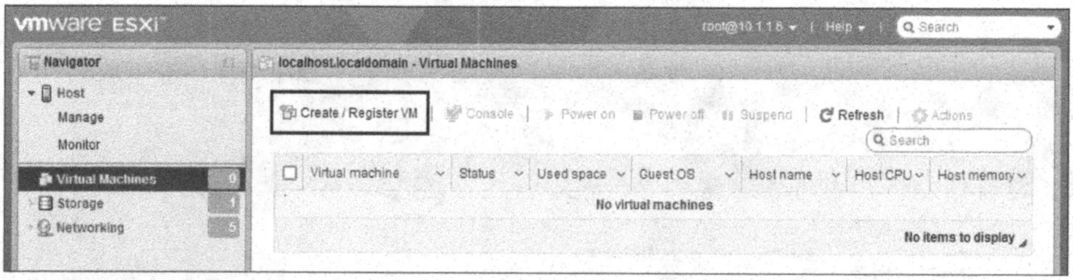

Figure 2-9 *Navigation to the Virtual Machine Creation Option*

Step 2. Click the **Create/Register VM** option. The New Virtual Machine window appears. This wizard walks you through the steps to create a new virtual machine.

Figure 2-10 shows the wizard for creating a new virtual machine.

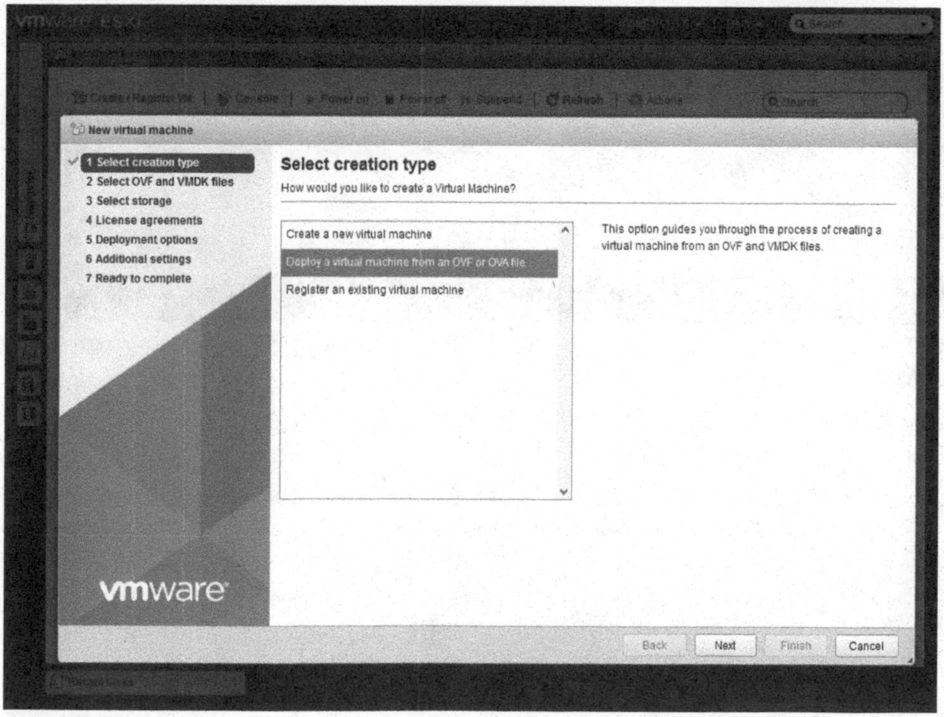

Figure 2-10 *New Virtual Machine Creation Wizard*

Step 3.   Select the **Deploy a Virtual Machine from an OVF or OVA File** option. Click **Next** to continue.

Step 4.   Enter a name for the virtual machine. Select the appropriate OVF and VMDK files that you found in the tarball earlier. Click **Next** to continue.

Figure 2-11 and Figure 2-12 show the selection of .ovf and .vmdk files for the Secure Firewall virtual appliances. To deploy a management center virtual appliance of Version 7.0 on an ESXi host, select the **Cisco_Firepower_Mgmt_Center_Virtual_VMware-ESXi-7.0.0-94.ovf** file, as shown in Figure 2-11. Similarly, to deploy a threat defense virtual appliance of Version 7.0, select the **Cisco_Firepower_Threat_Defense_Virtual-ESXi-7.0.0-94.ovf** file, as shown in Figure 2-12.

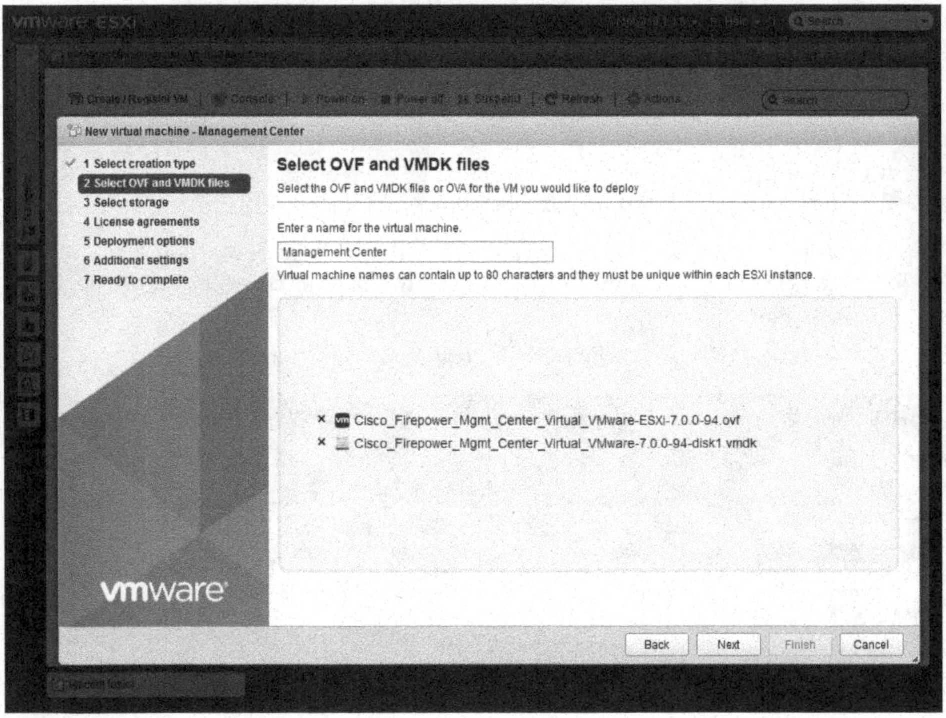

Figure 2-11   *Selection of the OVF and VMDK Files for a Management Center Virtual Appliance*

Step 5.   Select the storage where you want to store the configurations and disk files. Click **Next** to continue.

Figure 2-13 shows the selection for storage, named datastore1, for the new management center virtual appliance.

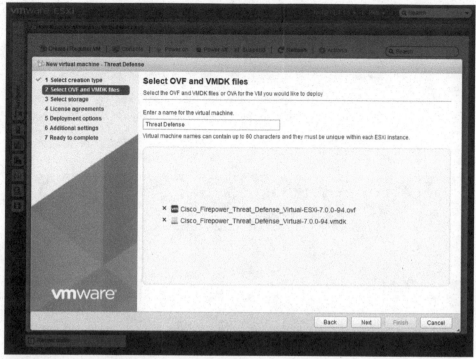

Figure 2-12 *Selection of the OVF and VMDK Files for a Threat Defense Virtual Appliance*

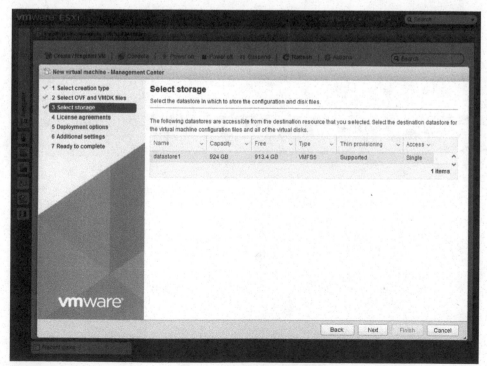

Figure 2-13 *Selection of Storage for the Virtual Machine*

Step 6.   In the Deployment Options stage, first, select the virtual port group that you created for the management network traffic (see the "Virtual Network for Management Traffic" section for details). Next, select one of the following Disk Provisioning options for the virtual disk, and click **Next** to continue.

■ **Thick Provision:** Disk space is allocated at the time of a virtual disk creation.

■ **Thin Provision:** Disk space is allocated on demand. The size of a virtual disk grows whenever there is a need, up to the maximum allocated limit.

Figure 2-14 shows the selection VM Network for the management network and Thick for the Disk Provisioning option for the management center.

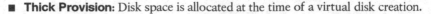

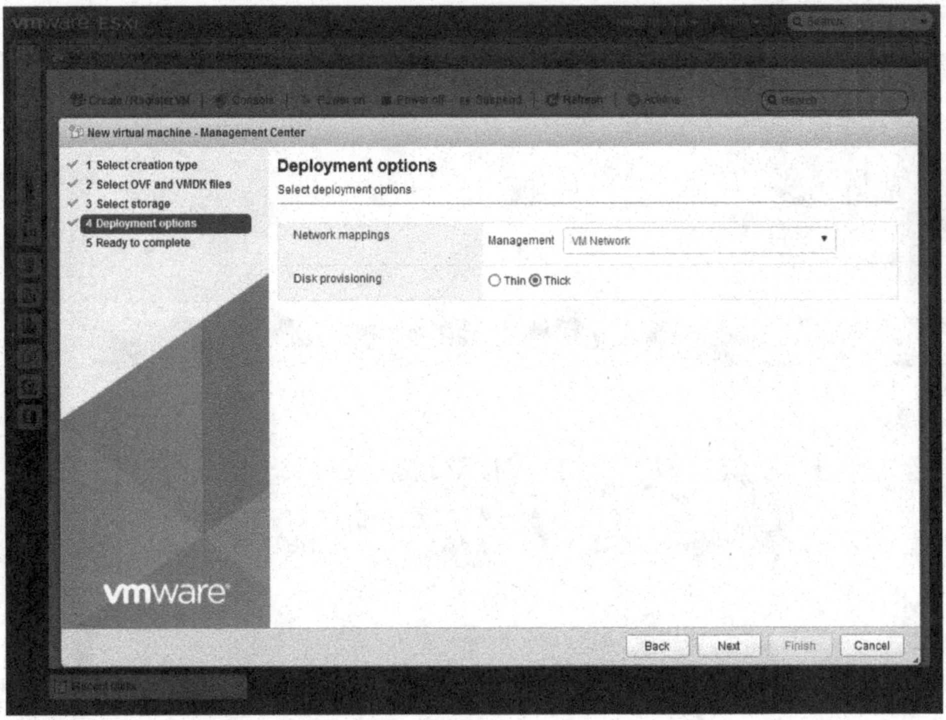

Figure 2-14   *Deployment Options Selection for the Management Center Virtual Appliance*

The number of networks you need to map depends on the type of the virtual appliance you are deploying. For example, a management center virtual appliance needs only one interface for management purposes, whereas a threat defense virtual appliance requires at least four interfaces—one interface for management traffic and three interfaces for data traffic.

Figure 2-15 shows the mapping of virtual port groups with management, diagnostic, and data interfaces of a threat defense virtual appliance.

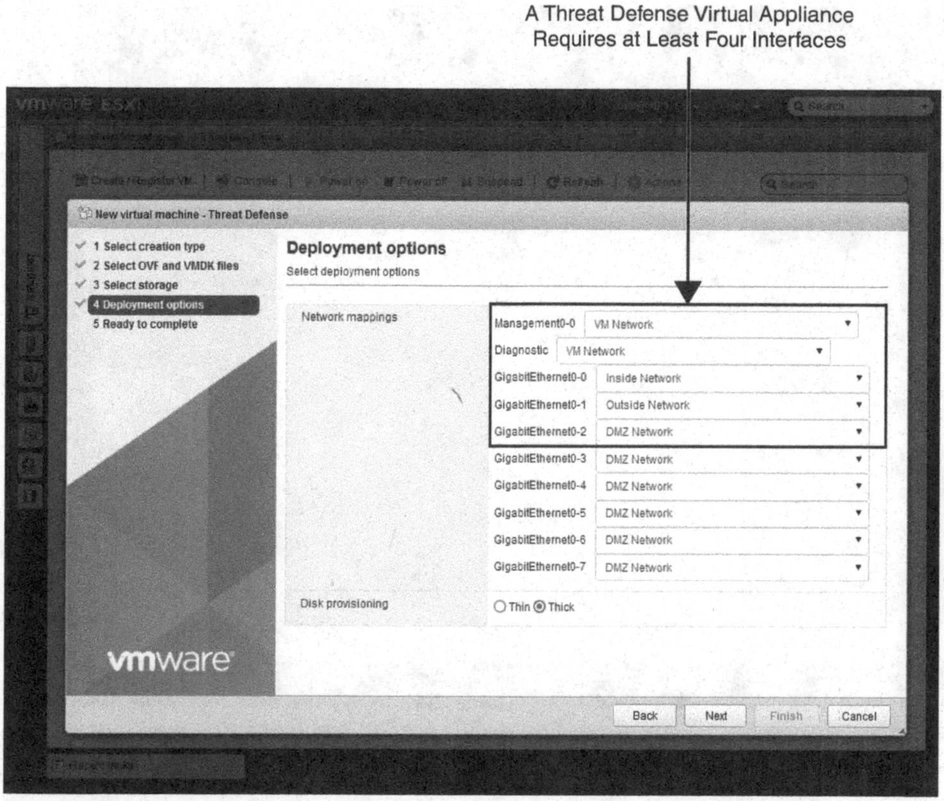

Figure 2-15   *Deployment Options Selection for the Threat Defense Virtual Appliance*

Step 7.   When you are in the final stage named Ready to Complete, review all the selections. If everything looks correct, click the **Finish** button to complete the configuration.

Figure 2-16 shows a summary of the selections for the management center virtual appliance.

Step 8.   As soon as you click the Finish button, the deployment process begins. Uploading a .vmdk file from your local computer to the ESXi server can take several minutes to complete.

Figure 2-17 shows the status of a .vmdk file upload.

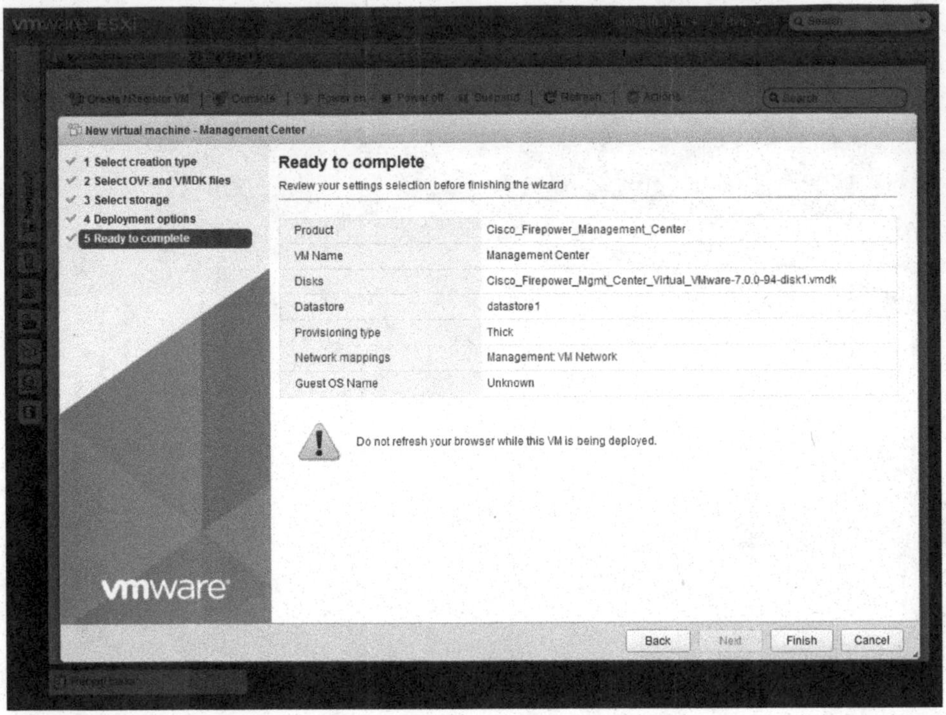

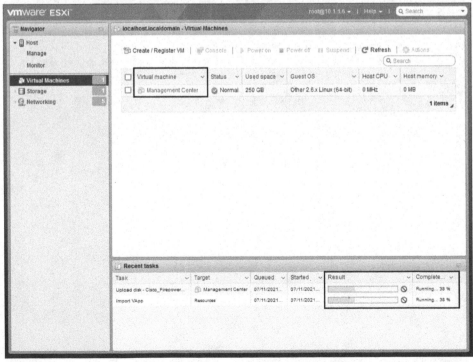

Figure 2-16   *Final Prompt to Confirm the Settings of the Management Center Virtual Appliance*

Figure 2-17   *Upload of the .vmdk File for the Management Center Virtual Appliance*

System Initialization and Validation

After the .ovf and .vmdk files are uploaded, the virtual machine is powered on automatically. If it doesn't power on, you can manually click the Power On button in the virtual machine to begin the initialization process. The initialization process of a management center virtual appliance can take about an hour to complete. For a threat defense virtual appliance, it takes about half an hour. During this time, the system runs many scripts and builds databases. You can view the progress from the virtual machine console. The GUI of the ESXi server allows you to access the console directly from a browser, as shown in Figure 2-18.

CAUTION   Do not power off a virtual machine while the initialization process is in progress. It can render the Secure Firewall database into an unstable state. After the initialization is complete, you can run the **shutdown** command on the Secure Firewall command-line interface (CLI), which is accessible via the VMware console.

Figure 2-18   *Initialization of a Management Center Virtual Appliance After the First Bootup*

In the last part of system initialization, a login prompt appears. Use the default login credentials (username: **admin**, password: **Admin123**) to log in. After your first login, you will be prompted to accept the end-user license agreement (EULA) and to set up basic network settings.

Example 2-1 shows the initialization of a management center virtual appliance followed by the login to its CLI for the first time.

Example 2-1   *Initialization of a Management Center Virtual Appliance After the First Login*

```
Network Management Interface (eth0) Status as of Sun Jul 11 22:32:35 UTC 2021
Management IP: 192.168.45.45. Mask: 255.255.255.0
MAC Address: 00:1A:2B:3C:4D:5E
firepower login: admin
Password: Admin123


Copyright 2004-2021, Cisco and/or its affiliates. All rights reserved.
Cisco is a registered trademark of Cisco Systems, Inc.
All other trademarks are property of their respective owners.


Cisco Firepower Extensible Operating System (FX-OS) v2.10.1 (build 159)
Cisco Firepower Management Center for VMware v7.0.0 (build 94)


You must accept the EULA to continue.
Press <ENTER> to display the EULA:
.


.
! EULA messages are omitted for brevity. Press 'q' to exit the EULA screen.
.

.

Please enter 'YES' or press <ENTER> to AGREE to the EULA: YES
For system security, you must change the admin password before configuring this
device.
Password must meet the following criteria:
- At least 8 characters
- At least 1 lower case letter
- At least 1 upper case letter
- At least 1 digit
- At least 1 special character such as @#*-_+!
- No more than 2 sequentially repeated characters
- Not based on a simple character sequence or a string in password cracking
dictionary
Enter new password:
Confirm new password:
Enter a hostname or fully qualified domain name for this system [firepower]: FMC
Configure IPv4 via DHCP or manually? (dhcp/manual) [manual]: manual
Enter an IPv4 address for the management interface [192.168.45.45]: 10.1.1.2
Enter an IPv4 netmask for the management interface [255.255.255.0]: 255.255.255.0
Enter the IPv4 default gateway for the management interface []: 10.1.1.1
Enter a comma-separated list of DNS servers or 'none' []: 10.1.1.7
Enter a comma-separated list of NTP servers [0.sourcefire.pool.ntp.org,
1.sourcefire.pool.ntp.org]: 10.1.1.8


hostname:                               FMC
IPv4 configured via:                    manual configuration
```

```
Management interface ipv4 address:        10.1.1.2
Management interface ipv4 netmask:        255.255.255.0
Management interface IPv4 gateway:        10.1.1.1
DNS servers:                              10.1.1.7
NTP servers:                              10.1.1.8


Are these settings correct? (y/n) y
If your networking information has changed, you will need to reconnect.


Updated network configuration.
>
```

Example 2-2 shows the initialization of a threat defense virtual appliance. During this process, you will be prompted with a question: Manage the device locally (yes/no). Answering no to this question allows a threat defense to be managed by a remote management center; otherwise, the threat defense device enables its local management application—the Secure Firewall device manager. The > prompt at the end of the example confirms that the system initialization is complete.

Example 2-2 *Initialization of a Threat Defense Virtual Appliance After the First Login*

```
Cisco Firepower Threat Defense for VMware v7.0.0 (build 94)
firepower login: admin
Password: Admin123


Copyright 2004-2021, Cisco and/or its affiliates. All rights reserved.
Cisco is a registered trademark of Cisco Systems, Inc.
All other trademarks are property of their respective owners.


Cisco Firepower Extensible Operating System (FX-OS) v2.10.1 (build 159)
Cisco Firepower Threat Defense for VMware v7.0.0 (build 94)


You must accept the EULA to continue.
Press <ENTER> to display the EULA: YES
.


! EULA messages are omitted for brevity. Press 'q' to exit the EULA screen.
.

.

System initialization in progress. Please stand by.
You must change the password for 'admin' to continue.
Enter new password:
Confirm new password:
You must configure the network to continue.
```

```
You must configure at least one of IPv4 or IPv6.
Do you want to configure IPv4? (y/n) [y]: y
Do you want to configure IPv6? (y/n) [y]: n
Configure IPv4 via DHCP or manually? (dhcp/manual) [manual]: manual
Enter an IPv4 address for the management interface [192.168.45.45]: 10.1.1.3
Enter an IPv4 netmask for the management interface [255.255.255.0]: 255.255.255.0
Enter the IPv4 default gateway for the management interface []: 10.1.1.1
Enter a fully qualified hostname for this system [firepower]: ThreatDefense
Enter a comma-separated list of DNS servers or 'none' [208.67.222.222,
208.67.220.220]: 10.1.1.7
Enter a comma-separated list of search domains or 'none' []: none
If your networking information has changed, you will need to reconnect.
Interface eth0 speed set to '10000baseT/Full'
For HTTP Proxy configuration, run 'configure network http-proxy'

Manage the device locally? (yes/no) [yes]: no
Configure firewall mode? (routed/transparent) [routed]: routed
Configuring firewall mode ...

Update policy deployment information
    - add device configuration
    - add network discovery
    - add system policy

You can register the sensor to a Firepower Management Center and use the Firepower
Management Center to manage it. Note that registering the sensor to a Firepower
Management Center disables on-sensor Firepower Services management capabilities.

When registering the sensor to a Firepower Management Center, a unique alphanumeric
registration key is always required.  In most cases, to register a sensor to a Fire-
power Management Center, you must provide the hostname or the IP address along with
the registration key.
'configure manager add [hostname | ip address ] [registration key ]'

However, if the sensor and the Firepower Management Center are separated by a NAT
device, you must enter a unique NAT ID, along with the unique registration key.
'configure manager add DONTRESOLVE [registration key ] [ NAT ID ]'

Later, using the web interface on the Firepower Management Center, you must use the
same registration key and, if necessary, the same NAT ID when you add this sensor to
the Firepower Management Center.
>
```

When initialization is complete and all the processes of a management center virtual appliance start properly, you should be able to access the landing page of its GUI over the network. To access the GUI, open a browser on your computer and enter the IP address of the management interface in this format: https://*<management_IP_address>*.

Figure 2-19 shows the successful loading of the login page of a management center virtual appliance running Version 7.0.

Alternatively, you can connect to the CLI of the management center virtual appliance and threat defense virtually through the Secure Shell (SSH) protocol. If the network settings that you entered during the system initialization are correct, and the IP addresses of the management interfaces are routable, you should be able to connect to your newly deployed management center virtual appliance and threat defense virtual appliance using the default login credentials.

Figure 2-19 *Login Page of a Secure Firewall Management Center Running Version 7.0*

Summary

This chapter describes how to deploy a Secure Firewall virtual appliance and highlights the best practices for a new deployment. It also demonstrates the system initialization processes of a newly deployed Secure Firewall.

Exam Preparation Tasks

As mentioned in the section "How to Use This Book" in the Introduction, you have a couple of choices for exam preparation: the exercises here, Chapter 22, "Final Preparation," and the exam simulation questions in the Pearson Test Prep practice test software.

Review All Key Topics

Review the most important topics in this chapter, noted with the Key Topic icon in the outer margin of the page. Table 2-6 lists a reference of these key topics and the page numbers on which each is found.

Table 2-6 Key Topics for Chapter 2

Key Topic Element	Description	Page
Table 2-2	Supported Platforms for Secure Firewall Virtual Appliance Running Version 7.0 or Higher	27
Paragraph	VMXNET3 network adapter	31
List	Disk provision	38

Complete Tables and Lists from Memory

Print a copy of Appendix C, "Memory Tables" (found on the companion website), or at least the section for this chapter, and complete the tables and lists from memory. Appendix D, "Memory Tables Answer Key," also on the companion website, includes completed tables and lists to check your work.

Define Key Terms

Define the following key terms from this chapter and check your answers in the Glossary.

thin provision, thick provision, promiscuous mode, Virtual Machine Disk (.vmdk) file, Open Virtual Format (.ovf) file, Manifest (.mf) file, VMXNET3

## CHAPTER 3

Licensing and Registration

This chapter provides an overview of the following topics:

Cisco Licensing Architecture: This section provides a foundational knowledge of different Cisco licensing models and describes their use cases. It helps you understand how Secure Firewall can obtain, maintain, and validate licenses over the Internet or without any Internet connections.

Cisco Secure Firewall Licenses: In this section, you learn about the capabilities of various feature licenses, purposes of export-controlled licenses, and how to enable evaluation licenses.

Validation of Licensing: This section discusses the options to determine the status of smart licenses on a management center.

Device Registration: This section demonstrates the registration processes between a management center and a threat defense.

Validation of Registration: This section shares the techniques to verify the registration status through a management center GUI and threat defense CLI.

The objectives of this chapter are to learn about

- Cisco Secure Firewall licensing systems
- Enablement of licenses on Secure Firewall
- Registration and initial deployment of Secure Firewall

After you deploy the Secure Firewall management center and threat defense on your platform of choice and complete the initial network setup, you are ready to register your threat defense with your management center. However, you cannot complete the registration process until your management center is licensed. A management center accepts two types of licenses: a classic license and a smart license. To manage a Secure Firewall threat defense, you need a smart license. A classic license is used for the earlier implementations of Sourcefire technologies, such as running the FirePOWER software as a separate service module on Adaptive Security Appliances (ASA). Because this book focuses on the latest implementation of Secure Firewall, this chapter discusses various aspects of the smart license.

Do I Know This Already?

The "Do I Know This Already?" quiz enables you to assess whether you should read this entire chapter thoroughly or jump to the "Exam Preparation Tasks" section. If you are in doubt about your answers to these questions or your own assessment of your knowledge of the topics, read the entire chapter. Table 3-1 lists the major headings in this chapter and their corresponding "Do I Know This Already?" quiz questions. You can find the answers in Appendix A, "Answers to the 'Do I Know This Already?' Quizzes."

Table 3-1 "Do I Know This Already?" Section-to-Question Mapping

Foundation Topics Section	Questions
Cisco Licensing Architecture	1
Cisco Secure Firewall Licenses	2, 3
Validation of Licensing	4
Device Registration	5
Validation of Registration	6

CAUTION The goal of self-assessment is to gauge your mastery of the topics in this chapter. If you do not know the answer to a question or are only partially sure of the answer, you should mark that question as wrong for purposes of the self-assessment. Giving yourself credit for an answer you correctly guess skews your self-assessment results and might provide you with a false sense of security.

1. Which method does Secure Firewall use to obtain a license from Cisco?
   a. Direct Internet access.
   b. Through an on-premises SSM server.
   c. A manual process (copy and paste).
   d. All of these answers are correct.

2. Which functionality cannot be enabled without a threat license?
   a. Intrusion prevention.
   b. Malware analysis.
   c. URL filtering.
   d. All of these answers are correct.

3. Which statement is correct about the smart licensing model?
   a. The threat defense connects to the Smart License Server to obtain licenses.
   b. The Cisco SSM application is available only through the Cisco cloud.
   c. You can enable the security features on Secure Firewall completely free for a limited time.
   d. The smart licensing model does not support any air-gap solution.

4. Which option enables you to know about the status of licenses *before* they expire or go out of compliance?
   a. By viewing the license status in the Smart License Status page, available at **System > Smart Licenses**.
   b. By enabling the Smart License Monitor module in the health policy.
   c. By running the **show managers** command in the threat defense CLI.
   d. All of these answers are correct.

5. Which statement is incorrect about registration?

  a. Always begin the registration process from a threat defense.

  b. NAT ID is necessary only when there is an intermediate NAT device between a management center and threat defense.

  c. Before you attempt to register any threat defense, you must enable a license on the management center.

  d. You do not need to select and deploy an access control policy during the device registration process.

6. Which command confirms whether a threat defense is registered with a management center?

  a. > show mgmt status

  b. > show management console

  c. > show managers

  d. > show registration status

Foundation Topics

Cisco Licensing Architecture

The Cisco Secure Firewall supports both smart licensing and classic licensing models. A smart license provides a pool of software licenses that you can apply to any applicable devices throughout your company. Unlike a traditional classic license, a smart license enables you to register a device without its product activation key (PAK). Moreover, it enables you to enable a security feature immediately while its purchase order is still in progress; thus, you can avoid any initial delays due to logistics and approval. Classic license is used to enable security features in the legacy firewall devices.

Table 3-2 describes the key differences between the two licensing models: the classic license and smart license.

Table 3-2 Comparisons Between Classic License and Smart License

	Classic License	Smart License
Supervision	Provides a limited view. You are unable to view all of the licenses that are owned and used by your company.	Provides a complete view. You can view the usages of all of your licenses and devices from a single portal in real time.
Scope	Device-specific licensing. Licenses are specific to only one device.	Company-specific licensing. You can apply licenses across any applicable devices in your company.
Activation	A PAK is required to unlock and register a device.	A PAK is not required to complete registration.

After you purchase the Secure Firewall solution, Cisco assigns your smart licenses and entitlement to a smart account that is created exclusively for your organization. You can manage the smart licenses of your company using the **Cisco Smart Software Manager (SSM)**—a cloud-based web application at cisco.com. With administrative privileges, you can create additional virtual accounts within your company's master account and organize the licenses based on the departments or locations. When necessary, you can also transfer licenses and entitlements between the virtual accounts.

Figure 3-1 shows the web interface of the Cisco SSM cloud application where you can generate a new token for your Cisco Secure Firewall products. By entering this token into your management center, you can connect your management center with the Cisco SSM cloud.

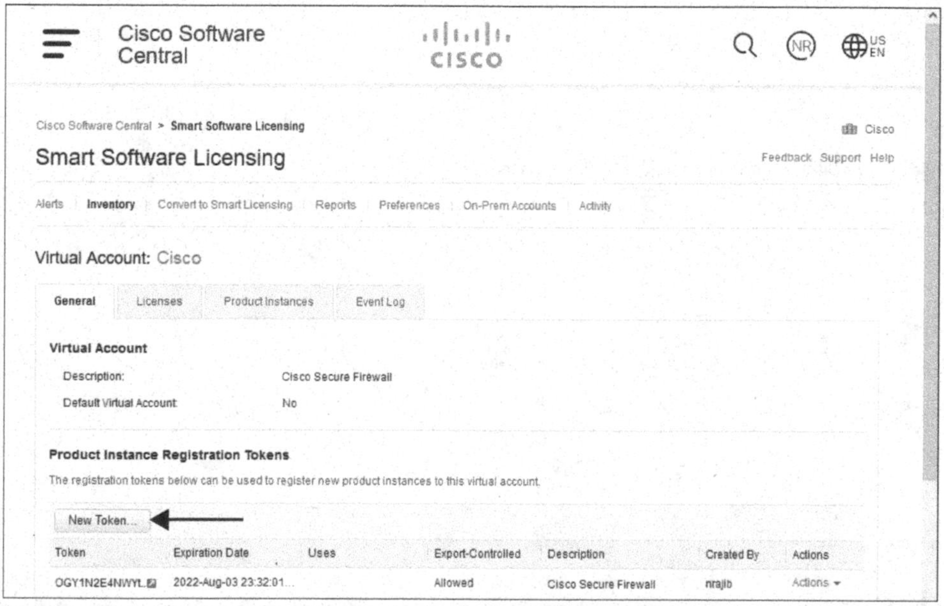

Figure 3-1   *Cisco Smart Software Manager (SSM) at Cisco.com*

Depending on a company's security posture and policy, Cisco offers different architectures to enable smart licenses. They are

- Direct cloud access

- On-premises server

- Offline access

Direct Cloud Access

In the direct cloud access architecture, the Secure Firewall managers—management center and device manager—obtain smart licenses from the Cisco Smart Licensing Cloud. They can connect to the cloud directly over the Internet or via a proxy server. The manager applications use a process called *Smart Agent*, which communicates with the Cisco Smart Licensing Cloud and registers the manager with it. After a successful registration, the Cisco cloud issues an ID certificate. The Smart Agent process uses this certificate to communicate with the Cisco cloud from time to time and to track the status of entitlements.

Figure 3-2 shows the communication between the Smart Agent of a management center and the Cisco Smart Licensing Cloud. When they are connected over the Internet, you can add, remove, and transfer your company's smart licenses using the Cisco SSM cloud application.

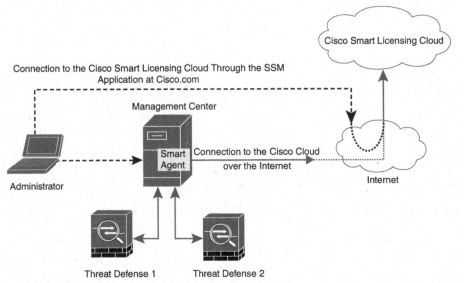

Figure 3-2 *Connections Between a Management Center and the Cisco Smart Licensing Cloud*

On-Premises Server

Because the Cisco Smart Licensing Cloud is hosted at cisco.com, your management center needs to connect to the Internet to obtain a smart license from Cisco. However, some organizations may have a limited Internet access policy, which can prevent a management center from connecting to the Internet directly. In that environment, you can use the Cisco Smart Software Manager on-premises server as an air-gapped solution. In this licensing model, the management center connects to an on-premises version of the Cisco SSM server deployed from an OVA image, which is registered to the Cisco Smart Licensing Cloud through the Internet.

Figure 3-3 illustrates the connection of a management center to the Cisco Smart Licensing Cloud through the Cisco SSM server and Internet.

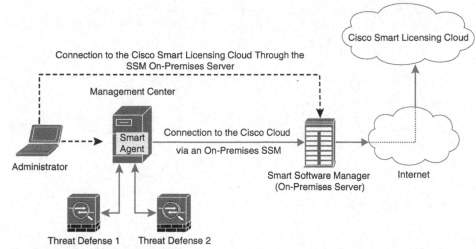

Figure 3-3 *Management Center Connects to the Cisco Smart Licensing Cloud via On-Premises SSM Server*

Figure 3-4 shows the options to connect a management center to the Cisco Smart Licensing system. By default, the Connect Directly to Cisco Smart Software Manager option is selected.

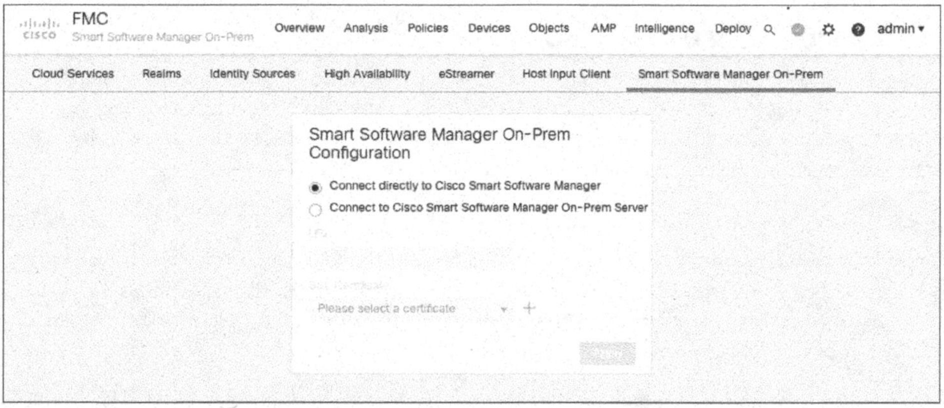

Figure 3-4 *Options to Connect a Management Center to Different Types of Smart Software Manager for Licensing*

Offline Access

Some organizations may want to deploy Secure Firewall in a restricted network where Internet connectivity to the firewall's management network is prohibited. For this type of air-gapped environment, Cisco allows you to reserve licenses from your smart account. This is known as **Permanent License Reservation (PLR)**. In the PLR licensing model, the management center can operate without any connection to the Cisco SSM cloud application. You can manually copy and paste licensing information between the management center and cisco.com to check the licenses in and out.

The PLR model offers two options for license reservation: Specific License Reservation (for a specific term) and Universal Permanent License Reservation (for an unlimited term).

However, to reserve any licenses, you need to obtain approval from your Cisco account representative, because the PLR model allows you to license Secure Firewall without any connection to the Cisco SSM—either a direct connection or via an on-premises server.

Table 3-3 highlights two predominant differences between Specific License Reservation (SLR) and Universal Permanent License Reservation (PLR) models.

Table 3-3 Major Differences Between SLR and PLR Models

Criteria	SLR	PLR
Duration	Licenses are reserved for a specific period.	Licenses are perpetual.
Enforcement	Once it expires, the management center does not allow new registration and deployment.	Enforcement is not a concern because the license never expires.

NOTE The smart licensing managers—Cisco SSM cloud application and the on-premises SSM server—are not limited to Cisco Secure Firewall only. You can register many Cisco products using them. To learn more about various smart licensing models, read the publications at cisco.com. To get access to the Cisco SSM, contact Cisco Support or your Cisco account representative.

Cisco Secure Firewall Licenses

The Cisco Secure Firewall offers many security features to protect your network. Some licenses are permanent, and some are term based. Some features are subject to country-specific laws, and some are available to anyone. The following sections discuss various licenses to enable security functionalities on Secure Firewall.

Feature License

A **base license** is included with your Secure Firewall purchase. However, a base license does not enable all the security features. To enable security functionality, separate **feature licenses** are necessary. Feature licenses are not hardware specific; they entitle you to enable particular security features on your managed threat defense devices.

Table 3-4 describes the functionalities of the Secure Firewall licenses. Keep in mind that a threat license is a prerequisite for Malware and URL Filtering functionalities.

Table 3-4 Secure Firewall License Capabilities

License	It Allows You to
Base	Update the system Control applications and users Perform switching, routing, and NAT
Threat	Detect and prevent intrusion attempts Blacklist traffic based on intelligence Block transfer of certain types of files

License	It Allows You to
Malware	Protect the network from malware, and enable malware defense feature (formerly AMP for networks and AMP Threat Grid)
URL Filtering	Filter URLs based on reputation and category

Table 3-5 describes the subscription codes for the Secure Firewall licenses. The Malware and URL Filtering licenses are available in two formats: as an add-on or in a bundle with a threat license.

Table 3-5   Secure Firewall License Subscription Options

License	Expiry	Which One to Purchase
Base	Permanent	No separate purchase; included automatically during a device purchase
Threat	Term based	**T:** Threat license only
Malware	Term based	**TM:** Threat and malware licenses in a bundle **AMP:** Malware license only; purchased if a threat license is already available
URL Filtering	Term based	**TMC:** Threat, Malware, and URL filtering licenses in a bundle **URL:** URL filtering license only; purchased if a threat license is already available

Export-Controlled License

In addition to the base and feature licenses, Cisco also offers a special kind of license, the **export-controlled license**, for export-controlled functionalities that are subject to the approval of Cisco and permission from the local government. If approved, you can enable this license by selecting the Allow Export-Controlled Functionality on the Products Registered with This Token option in your smart account.

Figure 3-5 shows the option at your smart account that allows export-controlled functionality before generating a registration token for a management platform.

The export-controlled functionalities utilize strong encryption. A popular application of encryption is Remote Access Virtual Private Network (RAVPN). To implement RAVPN on Secure Firewall, you need not only export-controlled functionality enabled on the management center but also an AnyConnect license. The Cisco AnyConnect Secure Mobility client allows you to connect to your organization's network over the Internet and access internal resources from a remote location as if you were connecting from within your organization's local networks.

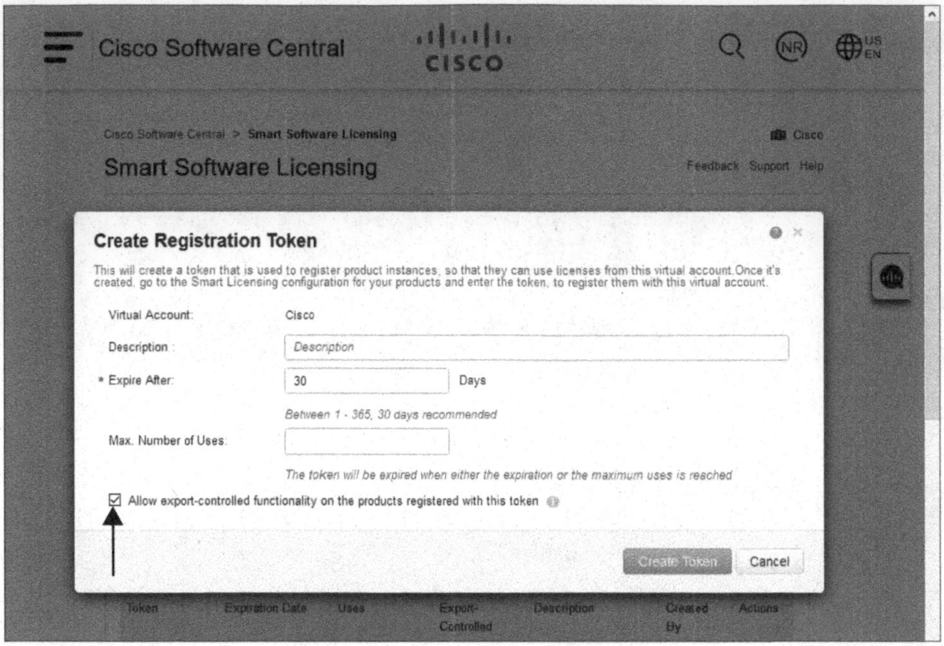

Figure 3-5   *Option That Allows Export-Controlled Functionality*

Table 3-6 lists different types of AnyConnect licenses and their capabilities.

Table 3-6   High-Level Comparison of AnyConnect Licenses

License	Capabilities
AnyConnect Plus	Provides basic VPN services and security features
AnyConnect Apex	Includes all capabilities offered by the AnyConnect Plus license and many more advanced services
AnyConnect VPN Only	Focuses on a high volume of remote users exclusively for RAVPN services

Evaluation License

Enabling security feature licenses on Secure Firewall is not a straightforward process. Especially after you purchase a brand-new firewall, you have to perform several steps to obtain smart licenses and to apply them on your Secure Firewall. Figure 3-6 shows a general workflow to procure smart licenses using Cisco SSM and then enable them on Secure Firewall.

As a CCNP Security exam candidate, however, you can always take advantage of Evaluation Mode. It enables you to use the next-generation security features on Secure Firewall for 90 days. Evaluation Mode is easy to enable. After your first login to the management center GUI, you are prompted to configure a smart license. If you have all the information available to register your management center with Cisco SSM, you can enter it now. Alternatively, you can choose to start the 90-day evaluation period without registration, as shown in Figure 3-7.

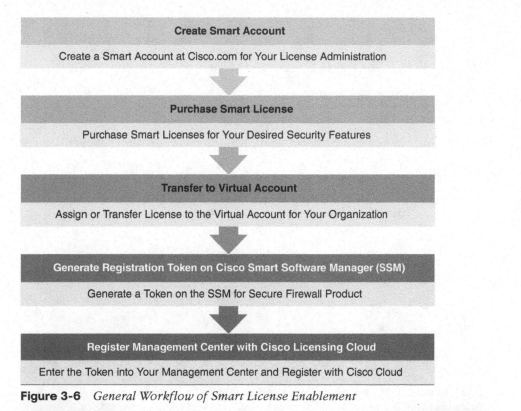

Figure 3-6   *General Workflow of Smart License Enablement*

Figure 3-7   *Smart License Configuration Wizard*

NOTE   Export-controlled features that are subject to national security review and that are based on advanced encryption are unavailable in Evaluation Mode. For example, Virtual Private Network (VPN) is not available.

If you skipped the smart licensing configuration during your first login, you can still enable Evaluation Mode by following these steps:

Step 1.   Click the **System** icon and select the **Smart Licenses** option. The Smart License Status page appears.

Figure 3-8 shows the available options for licensing under the System menu.

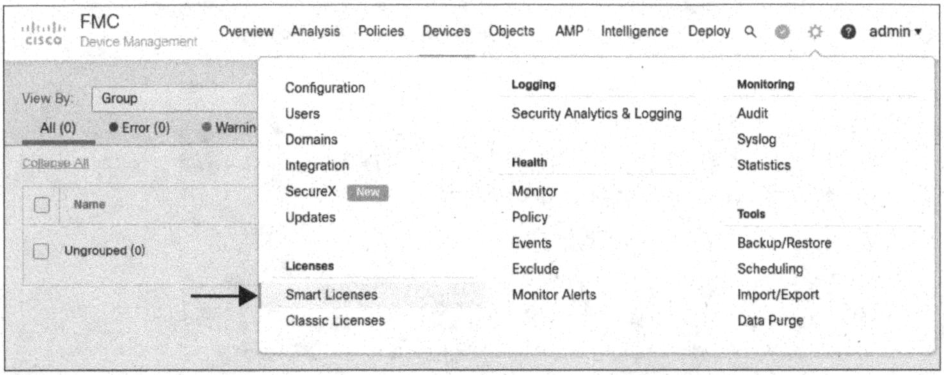

Figure 3-8   *Navigation to the Smart Licenses Page Using the System Menu*

Step 2.   On the Smart Licenses page, you will find two buttons: Register and Evaluation Mode. Select **Evaluation Mode**.

TIP   The Evaluation Mode button does not appear if it was already used for the 90-day evaluation period. However, every time you deploy a brand-new management center (either a fresh install or reimage), you can enable Evaluation Mode for another 90-day period. This is a great tool for a CCNP Security exam candidate to perform hands-on testing of the system.

Step 3.   The Evaluation Mode pop-up window appears to remind you that the evaluation mode is a one-time option, and available for 90 days from the day of its enablement. Select **Yes** to begin the 90-day period.

Figure 3-9 displays a pop-up window that prompts to confirm the enablement of Evaluation Mode for 90 days.

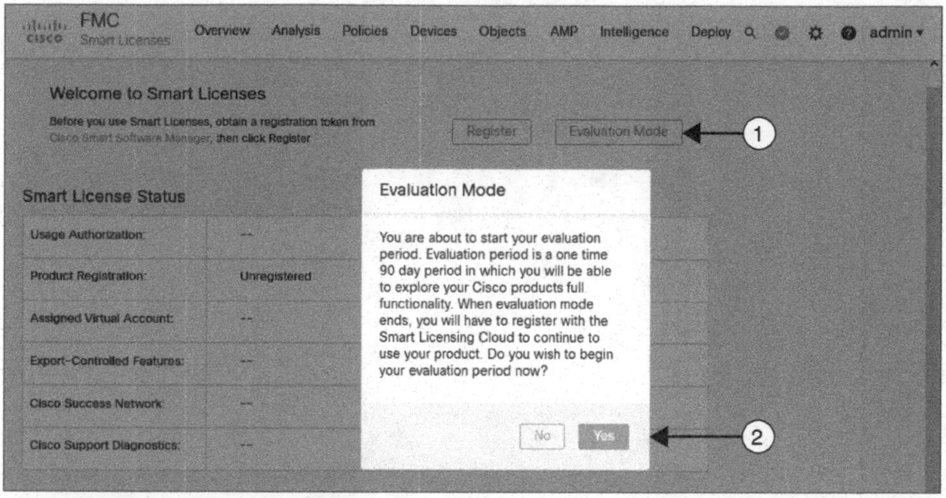

Figure 3-9 *Enablement of Evaluation Mode*

CAUTION   If you enable Evaluation Mode in a production environment, make sure to purchase and apply valid smart licenses before the evaluation period expires. Otherwise, you can experience an interruption in traffic inspection and miss any critical security events.

Validation of Licensing

Using the management center GUI, you can verify the entitlement status of your smart licenses and the registration status of management center with the Cisco Smart Licensing Cloud. Navigate to **System > Smart Licenses** to view the status in the Smart License Status page.

If the management center is successfully registered with the Cisco Smart Licensing Cloud, you will find the smart license status Authorized.

Figure 3-10 confirms the enablement of a smart license for a 90-day evaluation period.

Figure 3-11 shows a successful registration of the management center with the Cisco Smart Licensing Cloud. Note the Edit Performance Tier and Edit Licenses options in this page. You can use them to modify the selections of performance tiers and feature licenses for any particular threat defense.

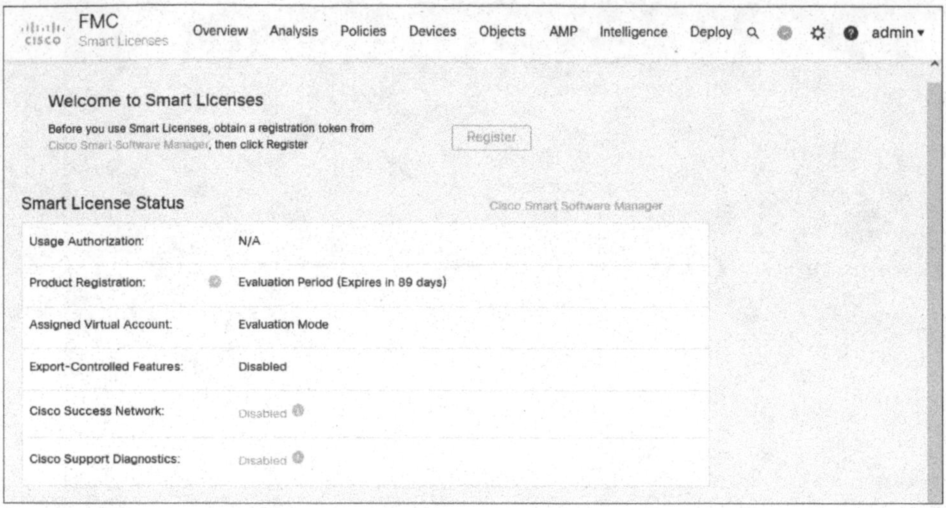

Figure 3-10 *Evaluation Mode Is Enabled*

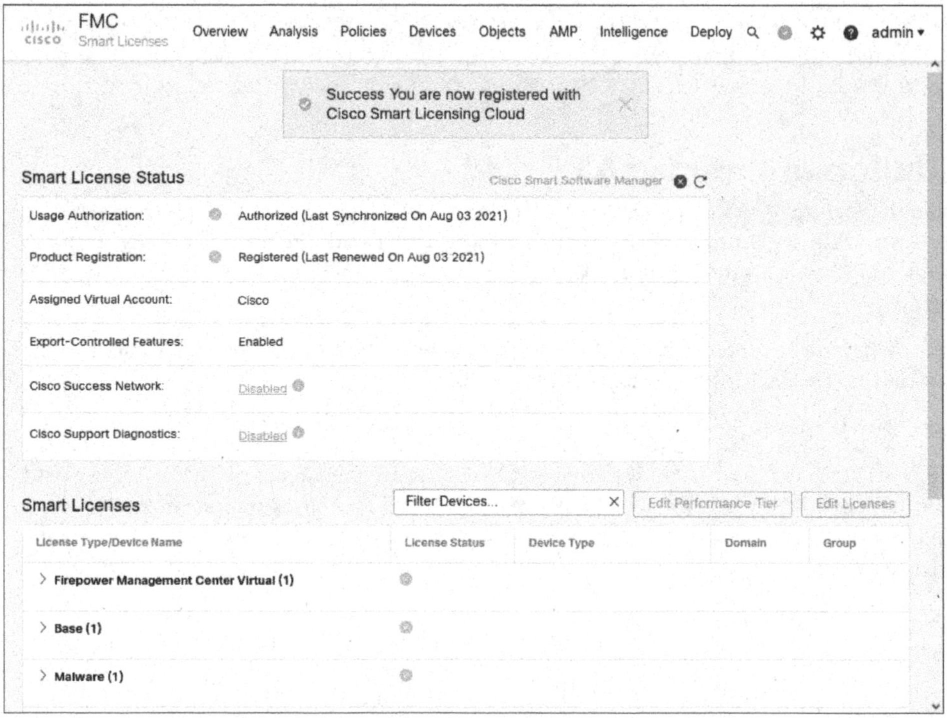

Figure 3-11 *Management Center Is Registered with the Cisco Smart Licensing Cloud*

If the license expires or the management center is unable to validate the license with the Cisco Smart Licensing Cloud, you will find an out-of-compliance status. By enabling the Smart License Monitor module in the health policy, you can receive health alerts if there is any communication issue between your management center and the Cisco Smart Licensing Cloud, or if the license is expired or out of compliance.

Figure 3-12 shows the enablement of the Smart License Monitor module in a health policy. After you enable the module, you must save the policy and deploy it to Secure Firewall.

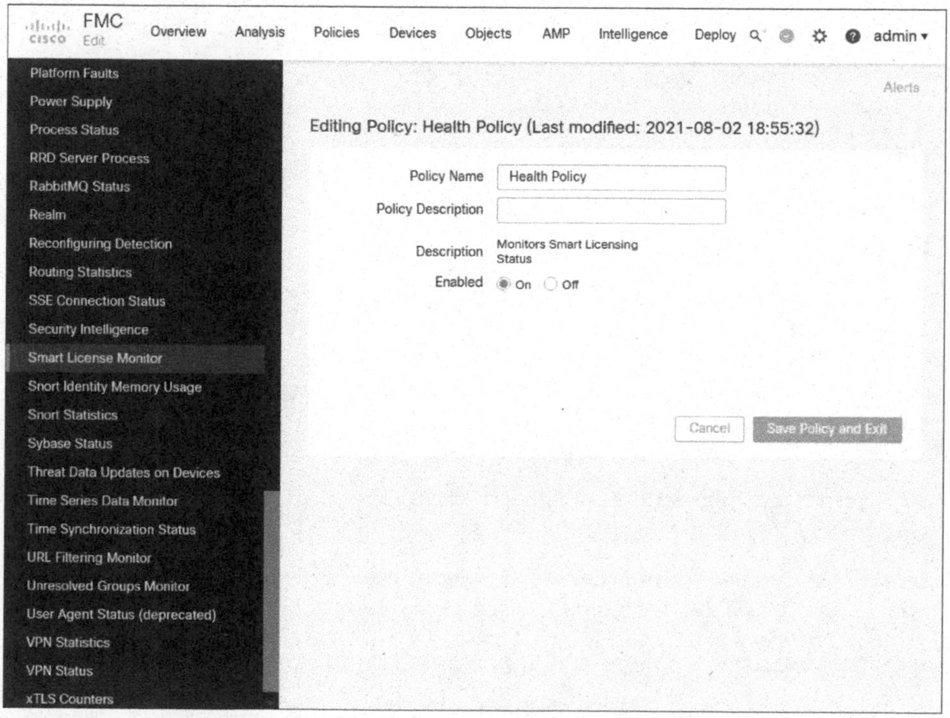

Figure 3-12   *Health Module for Smart License Monitoring*

Device Registration

After your management center is registered with the Cisco smart licensing system or enabled with Evaluation Mode, you are ready to register your threat defense devices with the management center. To complete registration, you need to have access to the CLI of the threat defense and to the GUI of the management center.

Best Practices for Registration

When you register a threat defense with a management center, there are a few points to keep in mind:

1. You must begin the registration process from your threat defense. At first, you enter the management center information on the threat defense CLI, and then you provide the threat defense detail in the management center GUI.

2. Instead of using the hostname or fully qualified domain name (FQDN), use the IP address directly. It assures that a failure of the registration process is not due to a DNS failure.

3. If an intermediate device translates the management IP addresses of your management center and threat defense, use a unique NAT ID during their registration process.

Configurations on Threat Defense

After system initialization is complete and the management network is set up, you should be able to connect to the threat defense CLI through the Secure Shell (SSH) or console terminal. Upon a successful login to the threat defense CLI, you will see the default CLI prompt: >.

Example 3-1 confirms that the threat defense is currently not registered with a remote management center or enabled with the local device manager service.

Example 3-1   *Output of the* **show managers** *Command*

```
> show managers
No managers configured.
>
```

To add a management center to a threat defense, run the **configure manager add** command along with the management IP address of the management center. You also have to provide a one-time registration key that is used only during the registration process. A unique NAT ID is necessary if an intermediate networking device translates the IP addresses of the management interfaces. The command syntax is as follows:

```
> configure manager add IP_Address_of_management_center
Registration_Key NAT_ID
```

Example 3-2 demonstrates the successful addition of a management center using its management IP address 10.1.1.2. The configuration uses RegKey as the one-time temporary registration key and NatId as a NAT ID. Although the use of a NAT ID is optional, you should use it if you are unsure about any possible translation of IP addresses by an intermediate device.

Example 3-2   *Adding a Management Center to a Threat Defense*

```
> configure manager add 10.1.1.2 RegKey NatId
Manager successfully configured.
Please make note of reg_key as this will be required while adding Device in FMC.
>
```

After you complete the configuration on the threat defense, the next step is to add the threat defense on the management center. Before going to the next step, though, check the current status of the registration.

Example 3-3 shows the pending registration status after you add the management center to threat defense. The registration status changes to *completed* after you perform the next step successfully.

Example 3-3   *Pending Registration Status Appears After Entering the Management Center Detail in Threat Defense*

```
> show managers
Host                    : 10.1.1.2
Registration Key        : ****
Registration            : pending
RPC Status              :
>
```

Configurations on Management Center

The second step of the registration process is to enter the details of the threat defense in the web interface of the management center. When you provide the details, you must use the same registration key (and the same NAT ID, if used) that you configured on the threat defense previously. Here are the steps you have to follow:

Step 1. Log in to the web interface of your management center. Select **Devices > Device Management.** The Device Management page appears.

Figure 3-13 shows navigation to the Device Management page.

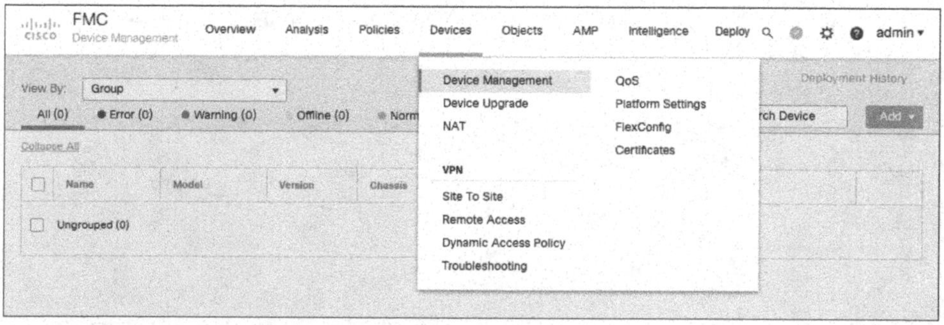

Figure 3-13 *Selections Under the Devices Menu*

Step 2. Select **Device** from the Add drop-down. The Add Device window appears. Here, you enter the details of the threat defense.

Figure 3-14 shows navigation to the Add Device window.

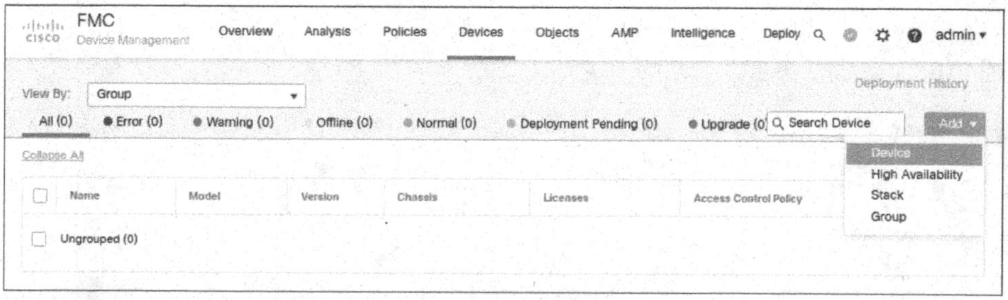

Figure 3-14 *Navigation to the Add Device Window*

Step 3. In the Host field, enter the IP address of the threat defense management interface.

Step 4. In the Display Name field, provide a name that will be displayed in the management center web interface to represent this particular threat defense.

Step 5. In the Registration Key field, enter the same registration key that you used earlier in the threat defense CLI.

Step 6. Select an Access Control Policy that you want to apply to your threat defense initially. If this is a new deployment, the management center may not have an access control policy preconfigured. You can, however, create a policy on the fly by choosing **Create New Policy** from the drop-down.

Figure 3-15 shows that the Add Device window is populated with the detail of the threat defense. Note that the same registration key (RegKey) and NAT ID (NatId) are used on management center and threat defense. A new access control policy called AC Policy is created on the fly. The New Policy window appears when you select Create New Policy from the drop-down. The image shows a basic setup that is sufficient to complete registration. You can edit and enhance this policy later.

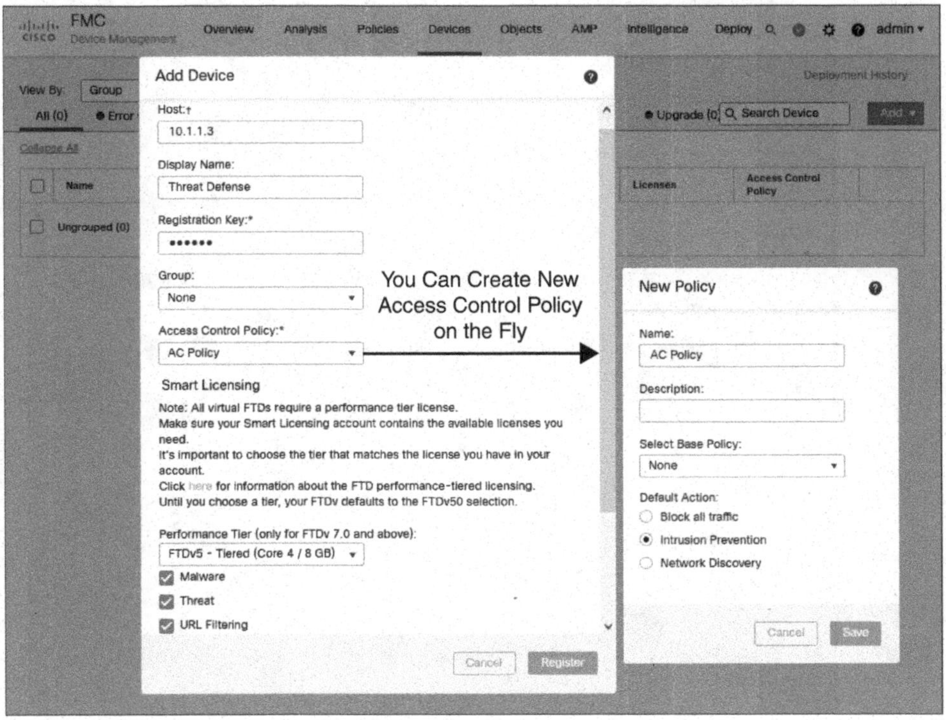

Figure 3-15 *Filling in the Fields in the Add Device Window*

Step 7. In the Smart Licensing section of the Add Device window, select a Performance Tier if you are registering a threat defense virtual. Here, the tier selection is dependent on the firewall you purchased from Cisco. For the CCNP Security exam preparation, a lower tier would suffice the need for any hands-on exercises.

Step 8.   Make sure to select all the security features that you want to configure on the threat defense, such as Malware, Threat, URL Filtering, and so on.

Step 9.   Under the Advanced section, provide a unique NAT ID if there is an intermediate device that translates the IP addresses of the Secure Firewall management interfaces.

Step 10.   The Transfer Packets option enables a threat defense to send the associated packets to the management center when any security events are generated. This option is enabled, by default.

Step 11.   Click the **Register** button to begin the registration process. All the communications between the management center and threat defense happen through an encrypted tunnel, known as *sftunnel*.

Figure 3-16 illustrates the registration process in the management center GUI. During the registration process, the system goes through a device discovery phase. When the discovery is complete, the system automatically applies the policies to threat defense. The spinning wheel next to the threat defense name and the real-time notifications confirm that the process is going on.

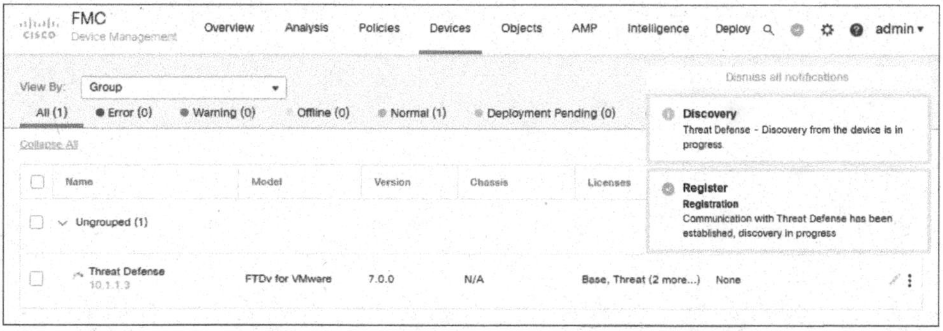

Figure 3-16   *Management Center GUI Shows the Status of Ongoing Registration Process*

Management Communication over the Internet

This section may be optional for your lab environment, but it describes a real-world deployment use case. Some organizations require you to position Secure Firewall in various geographical locations and ensure their registration and management communications over the Internet. For example, threat defense devices are deployed in remote branch offices, and they need to be managed using a management center located in a remote data center. In that case, Internet connectivity is necessary for any management communications between them. There are two ways to connect a threat defense with a management center over the Internet. If the threat defense management interface is connected to a private network or you want the management traffic to be inspected, you can use the inside interface as the gateway to the management center (as shown in Figure 3-17). If the threat defense is deployed as an edge device in your network, you can enable the management functionalities on its outside data interface and use that outside interface to communicate directly with a remote management center over the Internet (as shown in Figure 3-18). This feature is called FMC access. If you want to enable FMC access on a threat defense prior to its registration, you can use the threat defense CLI (this option is available under the **configure network** command). Alternatively, to manage this functionality after registration, you can use the threat defense interface configuration page on the management center GUI (as shown in Figure 3-19). The FMC access feature is supported on the routed interface. The next chapter describes routed firewall mode in detail.

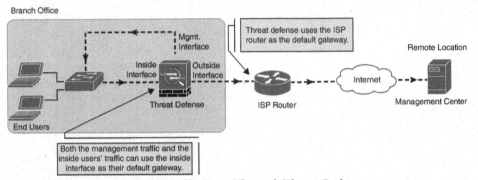

Figure 3-17   *Management Traffic Goes Through Threat Defense*

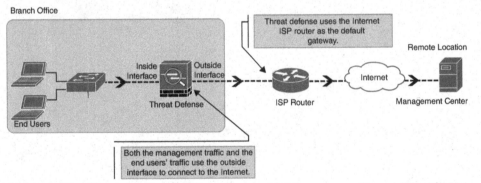

Figure 3-18   *Threat Defense Communicates with Management Center Directly Using Its Data Interface (FMC Access)*

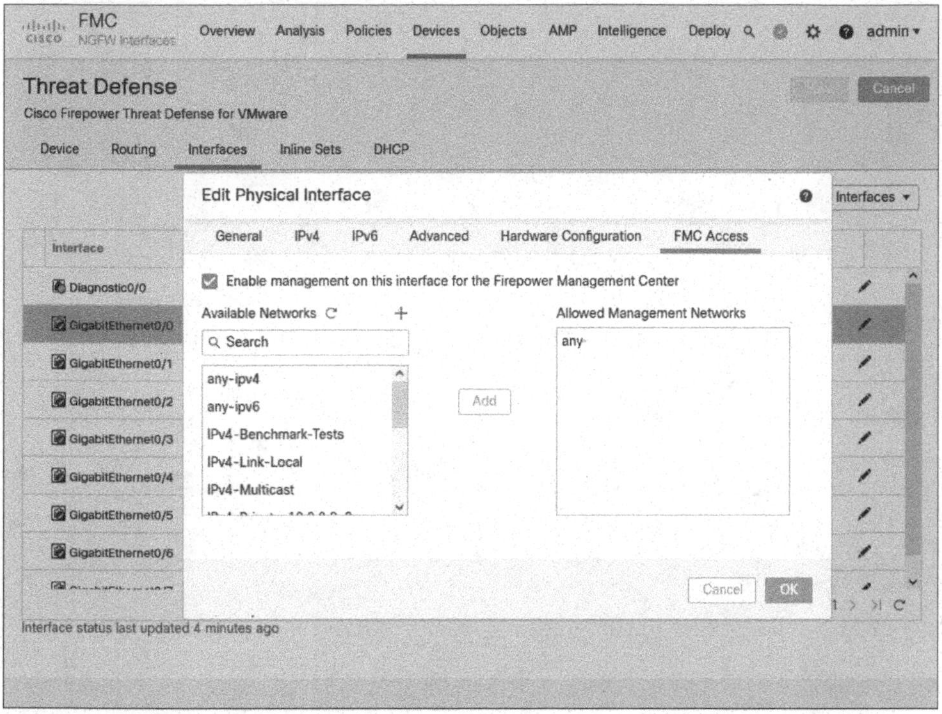

Figure 3-19   *FMC Access Options Is Enabled in the Threat Defense Data Interface*

Validation of Registration

If the registration process is successful, the health status of the threat defense appears as healthy (check mark) in the device management page. Likewise, the tasks window displays successful completion of various registration-related activities. Additionally, you can run the **show managers** command in the threat defense CLI to confirm the status.

Figure 3-20 confirms a successful registration. The check mark next to the threat defense device name indicates this status. Similarly, the task status window shows successful completion of various automatic post-registration activities.

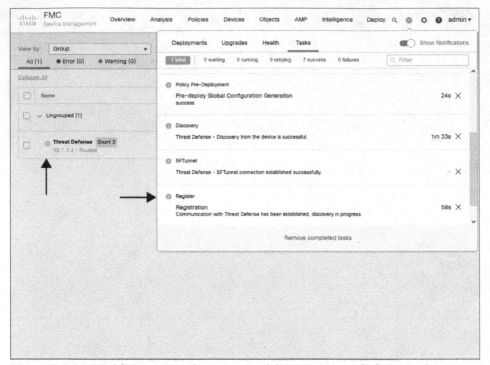

Figure 3-20   *Health Status Confirms Successful Registration of Threat Defense*

Example 3-4 shows the completed registration status after the threat defense is added to a management center successfully.

Example 3-4   *Status Confirms That the Registration Is Complete*

```
> show managers
Type                   : Manager
Host                   : 10.1.1.2
Registration           : Completed
>
```

Summary

This chapter describes licensing and registration—two important initial tasks of Secure Firewall deployment. The first part of this chapter explains the capabilities of different licensing architecture and the steps to enable licenses on Secure Firewall. Later, the chapter demonstrates the registration of a threat defense with a management center and shares some tips to validate registration status.

Exam Preparation Tasks

As mentioned in the section "How to Use This Book" in the Introduction, you have a couple of choices for exam preparation: the exercises here, Chapter 22, "Final Preparation," and the exam simulation questions in the Pearson Test Prep practice test software.

Review All Key Topics

Review the most important topics in this chapter, noted with the Key Topic icon in the outer margin of the page. Table 3-7 lists a reference of these key topics and the page numbers on which each is found.

Table 3-7 Key Topics for Chapter 3

Key Topic Element	Description	Page
Paragraph	Feature license	54
Paragraph	Evaluation Mode	56
List	Best practices for registration	61

Complete Tables and Lists from Memory

Print a copy of Appendix C, "Memory Tables" (found on the companion website), or at least the section for this chapter, and complete the tables and lists from memory. Appendix D, "Memory Tables Answer Key," also on the companion website, includes completed tables and lists to check your work.

Define Key Terms

Define the following key terms from this chapter, and check your answers in the Glossary:

Cisco Smart Software Manager (SSM), feature license, export-controlled license, base license, Permanent License Reservation (PLR)

## CHAPTER 4

Firewall Deployment in Routed Mode

This chapter provides an overview of the following topics:

Routed Mode Essentials: This section describes the characteristics of a firewall in routed mode.

Best Practices for Routed Mode Configuration: This section discusses some of the best practices that you should consider before you place your threat defense into routed firewall mode.

Fulfilling Prerequisites: In this section, you learn the commands to enable routed firewall mode on a threat defense.

Configuration of the Routed Interface: This section demonstrates the steps to configure routed interfaces with static and dynamic IP addresses.

Validation of Interface Configuration: The last section of this chapter provides useful tips to verify the status of routed interfaces and view the connection events.

The objectives of this chapter are to learn about

- Deployment of Secure Firewall in routed firewall mode
- Verification of threat defense configurations in routed mode

You can deploy a Secure Firewall threat defense as a default gateway for your network so that the end users can use the threat defense to communicate with a different subnet or to connect to the Internet. You can also deploy a threat defense transparently so that it stays invisible to your network hosts. In short, you can deploy a threat defense in two ways: routed mode and transparent mode. This chapter describes the processes to deploy a threat defense in routed mode. Chapter 5, "Firewall Deployment in Transparent Mode," discusses the transparent mode.

"Do I Know This Already?" Quiz

The "Do I Know This Already?" quiz enables you to assess whether you should read this entire chapter thoroughly or jump to the "Exam Preparation Tasks" section. If you are in doubt about your answers to these questions or your own assessment of your knowledge of the topics, read the entire chapter. Table 4-1 lists the major headings in this chapter and their corresponding "Do I Know This Already?" quiz questions. You can find the answers in Appendix A, "Answers to the 'Do I Know This Already?' Quizzes."

Table 4-1 "Do I Know This Already?" Section-to-Question Mapping

Foundation Topics Section	Questions
Routed Mode Essentials	1
Best Practices for Routed Mode Configuration	2
Fulfilling Prerequisites	3
Configuration of the Routed Interface	4
Validation of Interface Configuration	5, 6

> **CAUTION**   The goal of self-assessment is to gauge your mastery of the topics in this chapter. If you do not know the answer to a question or are only partially sure of the answer, you should mark that question as wrong for purposes of the self-assessment. Giving yourself credit for an answer you correctly guess skews your self-assessment results and might provide you with a false sense of security.

1. Which of the following statements is true?

    a. Threat defense in transparent mode cannot be configured by a management center.

    b. You can change the firewall deployment mode by using the management center.

    c. You cannot change the firewall mode until you unregister the threat defense from the management center.

    d. When you change the firewall mode, the threat defense saves the running configurations.

2. Which of the following statements is false?

    a. When configured in Layer 3 mode, each data interface on a threat defense is required to be on a different network.

    b. Backing up a security policy configuration on a threat defense is not necessary because the security policies are defined and stored on the management center.

    c. Changing the firewall mode does not affect the existing configurations on a threat defense.

    d. None of these answers are correct.

3. Which of the following commands is used to configure a threat defense from transparent mode to routed mode?

    a. configure routed

    b. configure firewall routed

    c. configure interface routed

    d. configure transparent disable

4. Which of the following statements is false for IP address configuration?

    a. A threat defense data interface must be configured with a static IP address.

    b. A threat defense can function as a DHCP client as well as a DHCP server.

c. When you create an address pool for the DHCP server, it must be within the same subnet as the connected interface.

d. None of these answers are correct.

5. Which of the following commands is used to debug and analyze ping requests?

a. **debug icmp**

b. **debug ip icmp**

c. **debug icmp trace**

d. **debug icmp reply**

6. Which of the following commands can be run to determine any interface-related issues?

a. **show interface ip brief**

b. **show interface** *interface_ID*

c. **show running-config interface**

d. All of these answers are correct.

Foundation Topics

Routed Mode Essentials

Key Topic

In **routed mode**, a threat defense acts like a Layer 3 hop. Each interface on a threat defense can be connected to a different subnet, and the threat defense can act as the default gateway for that subnet. The threat defense can also route traffic between different subnets, like a Layer 3 router.

Figure 4-1 shows how a host interacts with a threat defense as its next Layer 3 hop. In routed mode, each threat defense interface connects to a unique subnet.

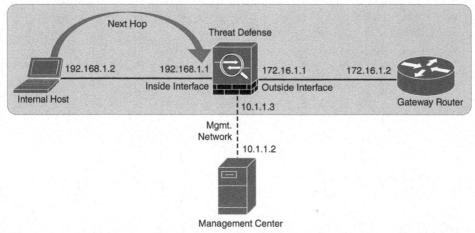

Figure 4-1 *Communication of a Host with a Threat Defense in Routed Mode*

Best Practices for Routed Mode Configuration

If you want to deploy a threat defense in routed mode, consider the following suggestions:

- Do not configure the diagnostic interface with an IP address. This simplifies the network design and reduces configuration overhead. When a diagnostic interface is configured with an IP address, a threat defense treats it like a data interface. When configured in Layer 3 mode, each data interface on a threat defense is required to be on a different network. Therefore, the diagnostic interface (which must be on the same subnet as the logical management interface, br1) and the inside interface must be on two different subnets. To transfer traffic between two different subnetworks, the routing service is required.

- Changing the firewall mode wipes out any existing configurations on a threat defense. Therefore, before you change the firewall mode from transparent to routed or vice versa, take note of your threat defense settings for future reference, in case you want to revert the threat defense to the prior state. To view the current threat defense configuration, run the **show running-config** command in the CLI.

- If you just want to change the firewall mode of a threat defense, backing up your security policy configuration is not necessary because the next-generation security policies are defined and stored on the management center. After you configure the security policies, the management center allows you to deploy the same policies to one or more threat defense devices.

Fulfilling Prerequisites

Do you remember the last part of the threat defense installation and initialization process? During the initialization, the threat defense prompts to confirm the firewall mode, and you can select between routed mode and transparent mode (see Example 4-1). If you selected routed mode during the system initialization, you can skip this section and read the section "Configuration of the Routed Interface."

Example 4-1   *Configuring the Firewall Mode During the Initialization*

```
<Output Omitted>
.
.
.
Manage the device locally? (yes/no) [yes]: no
Configure firewall mode? (routed/transparent) [routed]:
Configuring firewall mode ...
Update policy deployment information
   - add device configuration
   - add network discovery
   - add system policy
.
.
.
<Output Omitted>
```

If you selected transparent mode during the system initialization and now you want to reconfigure your threat defense to routed mode, you must unregister the threat defense from the management center. You cannot change the firewall mode when a manager is configured. To verify whether a threat defense is currently registered with the management center, run the **show managers** command at the threat defense CLI.

Example 4-2 shows that the threat defense is currently registered with a management center with IP address 10.1.1.2.

Example 4-2 *Threat Defense Is Currently Registered with a Management Center*

```
> show managers
Type          : Manager
Host          : 10.1.1.2
Registration : Completed
>
```

If your threat defense is currently in transparent mode and registered with a management center, you can unregister it by using the management center web interface. To delete registration, go to **Devices > Device Management**, click the three dots next to threat defense name, and select Delete (see Figure 4-2).

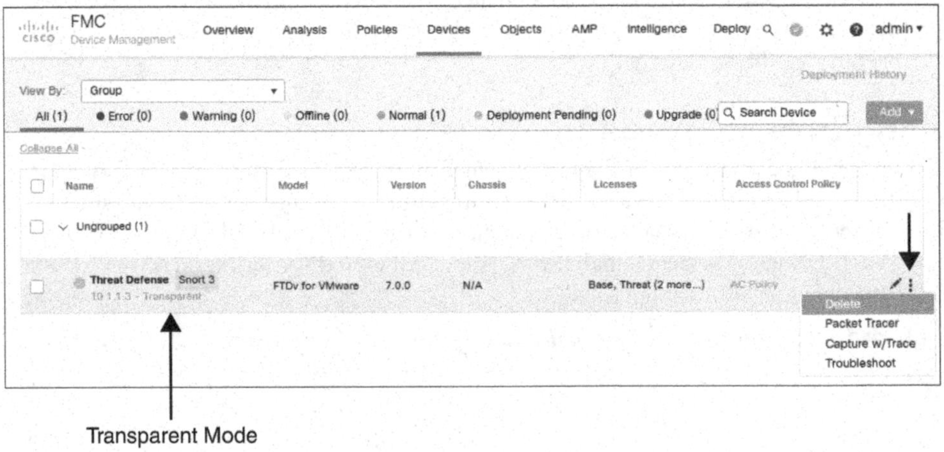

Transparent Mode

Figure 4-2 *Deleting the Registration of a Threat Defense in Transparent Mode*

Example 4-3 shows confirmation that the threat defense is neither registered with the management center nor enabled with its local device manager service.

Example 4-3 *Threat Defense Is Not Managed by a Management Center or Built-in Local Manager*

```
> show managers
No managers configured.
>
```

Enabling the Routed Firewall Mode

You can change the firewall mode of a threat defense if it is currently not registered with a management center. To configure a threat defense with routed mode, log in to the threat defense CLI and run the **configure firewall routed** command (see Example 4-4).

Example 4-4 *Configuring the Routed Mode*

```
> configure firewall routed

This will destroy the current interface configurations, are you sure that you want
to proceed? [y/N] y
The firewall mode was changed successfully.
```

After configuring the threat defense to the desired mode, you can determine the status from the CLI. Example 4-5 confirms that the threat defense is in routed mode.

Example 4-5 *Verifying the Firewall Deployment Mode*

```
> show firewall
Firewall mode: Router
>
```

Alternatively, upon a successful registration, the management center GUI also displays the current firewall deployment mode. You can view it by navigating to **Devices > Device Management**. Figure 4-3 indicates that the threat defense is configured in routed mode.

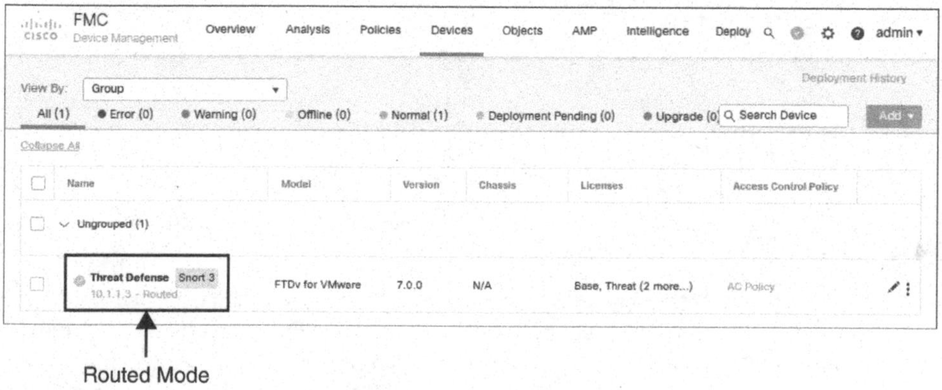

Figure 4-3 *Threat Defense Is Deployed in Routed Mode*

Configuration of the Routed Interface

In threat defense, you can configure a data interface with a static IP address. A threat defense can also operate as a DHCP client and obtain an IP address from a DHCP server. Furthermore, you can enable the **DHCP service** on a threat defense and configure it to assign IP addresses dynamically to its hosts.

Configuring Interfaces with Static IP Addresses

To configure a routed interface with a static IP address, follow these steps:

Step 1. Navigate to **Devices > Device Management**. A list of the managed devices appears.

Step 2. Click the pencil icon that is next to the threat defense name you want to configure. The device management editor page appears, showing all the interfaces of threat defense on the Interfaces tab (see Figure 4-4).

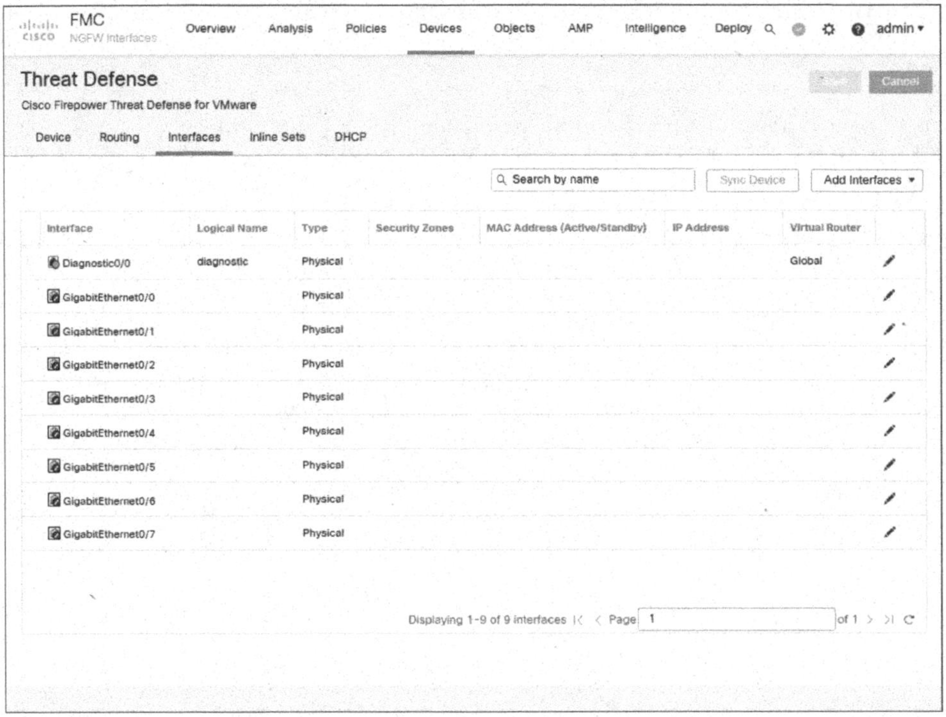

Figure 4-4 *Interfaces Tab of the Virtual Threat Device*

Depending on the threat defense platform you run, you may come across different types of interfaces and model-specific options. For example, threat defense model 1010 comes with an Ethernet type interface with built-in switch ports, as shown in Figure 4-5. To configure this model in routed mode, you need to disable access mode **switch ports**.

Step 3. On the Interfaces tab, click the pencil icons next to GigabitEthernet0/0 and GigabitEthernet0/1 to configure these interfaces for the inside and outside networks, respectively. Use the settings shown in Table 4-2 to configure these two interfaces.

To enable an interface, you must give it a name; this is a requirement. However, configuring a security zone is an optional step. Here, in the Edit Physical Interface window, you can create a security zone and associate it with an interface on the fly. In future, you could use the **Objects > Object Management > Interface** page to manage the security zones.

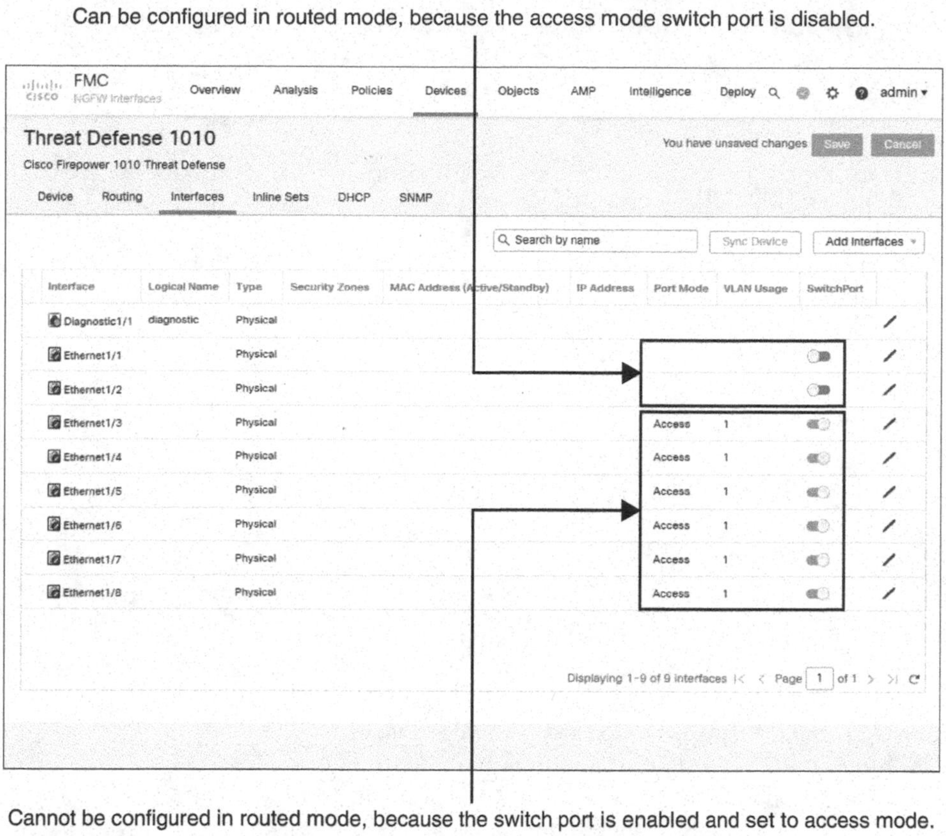

Can be configured in routed mode, because the access mode switch port is disabled.

Cannot be configured in routed mode, because the switch port is enabled and set to access mode.

Figure 4-5 *Interfaces Tab of Threat Defense Model 1010 Shows Switch Port Modes*

Table 4-2 Settings for Ingress and Egress Interfaces

	GigabitEthernet0/0	GigabitEthernet0/1
Interface name	INSIDE_INTERFACE	OUTSIDE_INTERFACE
Security zone (optional)	INSIDE_ZONE	OUTSIDE_ZONE
IP address	192.168.1.1/24	172.16.1.1/24

Figure 4-6 shows the general settings for GigabitEthernet0/0; for example, it is named INSIDE_INTERFACE. Make sure to enable an interface using the **Enabled** check box.

Figure 4-7 shows the manual assignment of a static IP address to the GigabitEthernet0/0 interface.

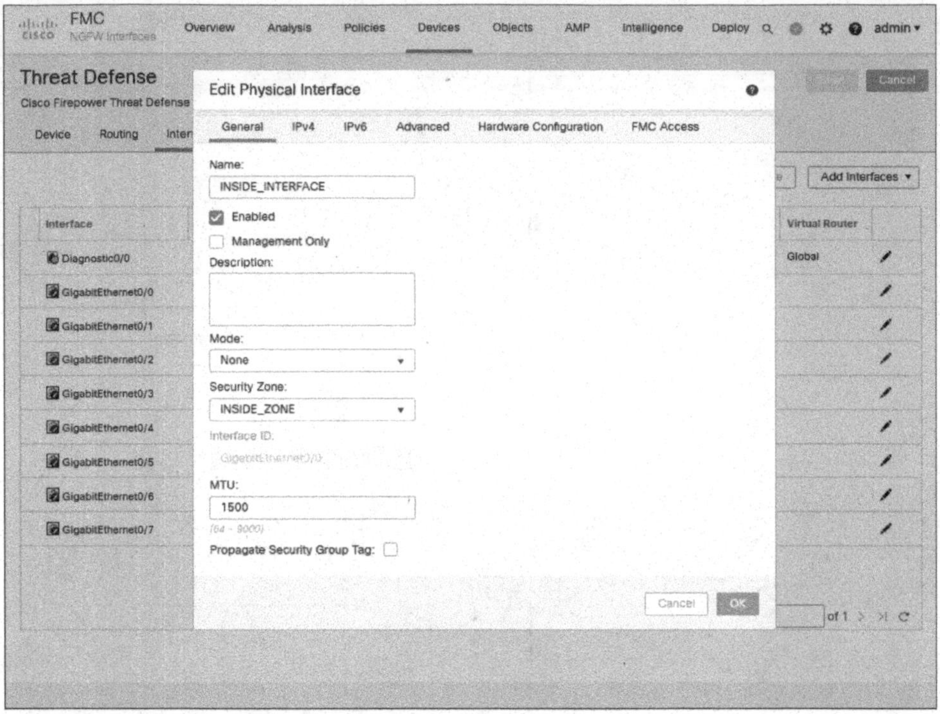

Figure 4-6   *General Configurations of the Inside Interface*

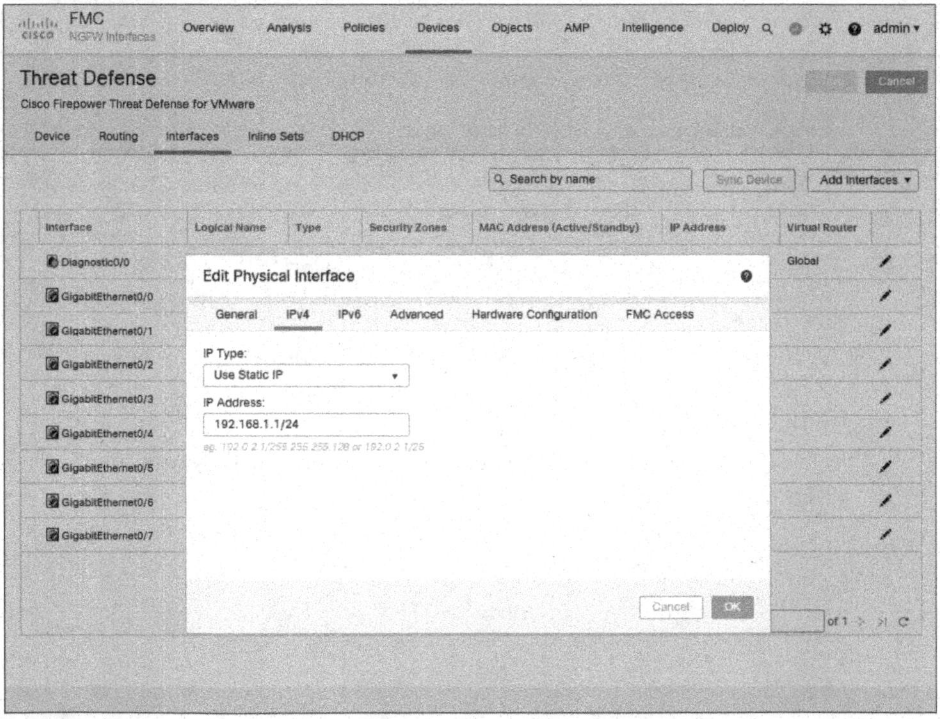

Figure 4-7   *Static IP Address on the Inside Interface GigabitEthernet0/0*

Step 4. Repeat the preceding steps for GigabitEthernet0/1 to enable it for the outside network. When you're finished, click the **Save** button to save the changes.

Figure 4-8 shows the configurations of ingress and egress routed interfaces.

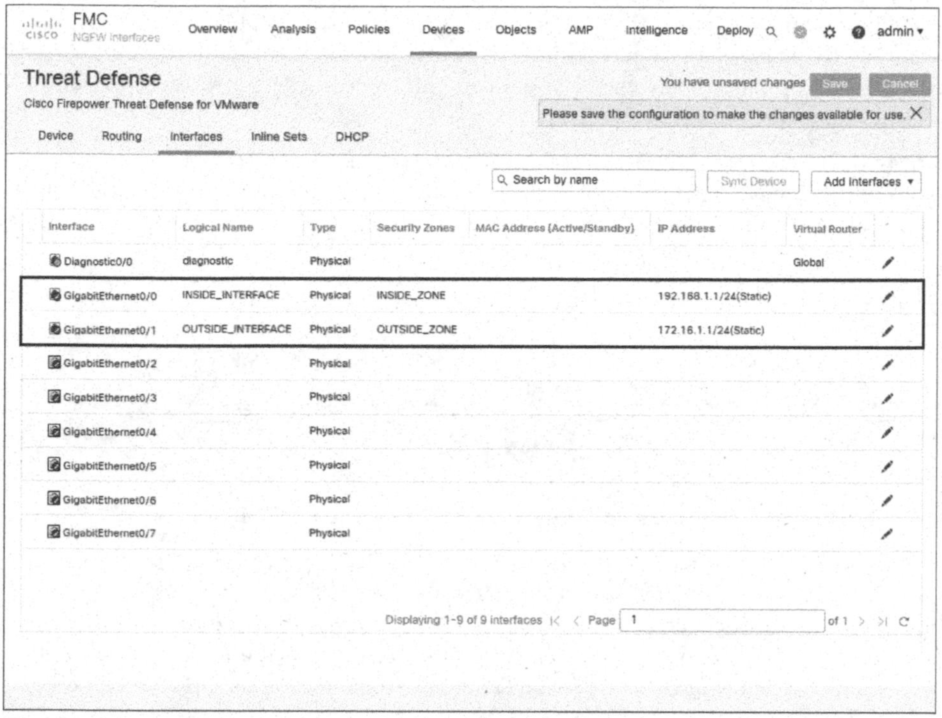

Figure 4-8 *Inside and Outside Interface Configurations*

Step 5. After the configuration is saved, navigate to **Deploy > Deployment**. Select the threat defense where you want to apply the changes and click the **Deploy** button to apply the configurations (see Figure 4-9).

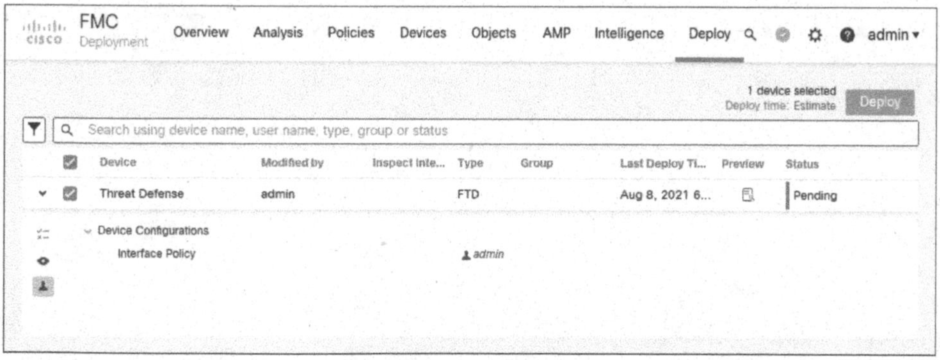

Figure 4-9 *Threat Defense Configuration Deployment*

Configuring Interfaces with Automatic IP Addresses

A threat defense can function as a DHCP client as well as a DHCP server. For example, if you deploy a threat defense between the outside interface and an Internet service provider (ISP), the device can obtain an IP address dynamically for its outside interface from the ISP router. Simultaneously, a threat defense can act as a DHCP server and provide IPv4 addresses dynamically to the hosts it inspects through its inside interface. Configuring a threat defense as a DHCP server is an optional choice; it does not influence the deep packet inspection capability.

Figure 4-10 illustrates two scenarios: The inside network obtains an IP address from the DHCP service running on a threat defense, while the outside interface of the threat defense gets an IP address from a service provider.

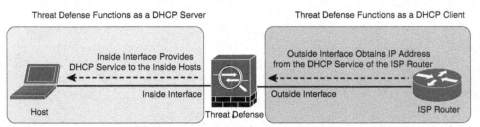

Figure 4-10   *A Threat Defense as a DHCP Server and a DHCP Client*

Enabling an interface to obtain an IP address from a DHCP server is a straightforward process. For example, during the outside interface configuration, when you assign a static IP address to the interface, you simply select Use DHCP from the drop-down instead of selecting the Use Static IP option. That's it. When this interface configuration is deployed, the outside interface attempts to obtain the IP address from an external DHCP server or the ISP router. See Figure 4-11 to find the Use DHCP option.

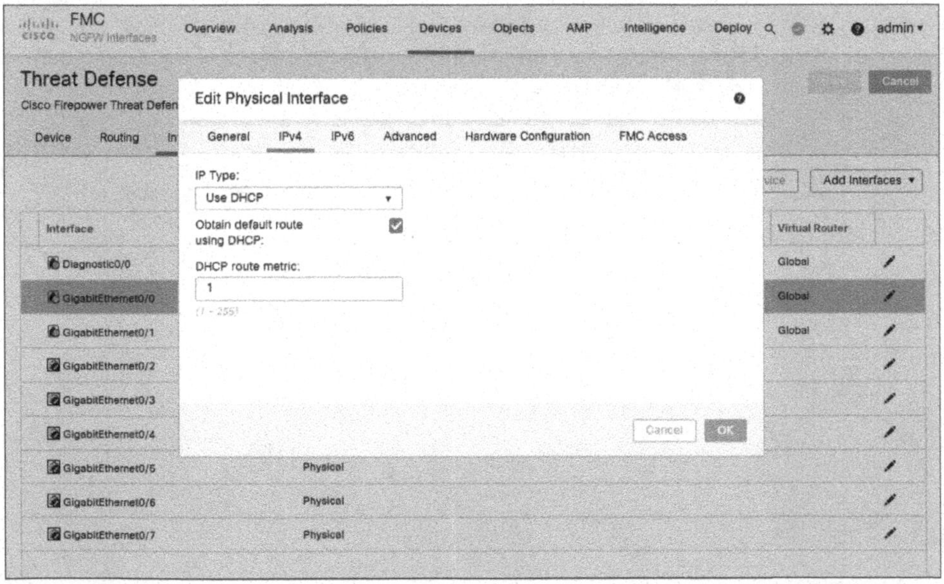

Figure 4-11   *Interface Configuration to Run a Threat Defense as a DHCP Client*

However, if you want the threat defense to provide IP addresses dynamically to its connected hosts, you need to enable DHCP services on it. The following steps describe how to configure a threat defense with DHCP services and allow its inside interface to provide IP addresses to its connected host computers:

Step 1. Go to **Devices > Device Management** and click the pencil icon to edit the threat defense configuration.

Step 2. Assign the static IP address **192.168.1.1** on GigabitEthernet0/0—the inside interface of the threat defense. Your end users (DHCP clients) will be using this IP address as their default gateway. (Figure 4-10 illustrates the purpose of the inside interface.)

Step 3. On the device editor page, go to the DHCP tab. By default, the DHCP Server page appears.

Step 4. Click the **Add** button on the Server tab (located near the bottom part of the DHCP Server page). The Add Server window appears.

Step 5. In the Add Server window, select the inside interface from the drop-down list because it will be offering IP addresses to the inside network.

Step 6. Create an address pool for the DHCP server. Remember that the addresses in the pool must be within the same subnet as the connected interface. For example, if you assign 192.168.1.1/24 to the inside interface, the DHCP address pool should be between 192.168.1.2 and 192.168.1.254.

Figure 4-12 shows that a DHCP server is enabled on the threat defense's inside interface with the address pool 192.168.1.2 to 192.168.1.10.

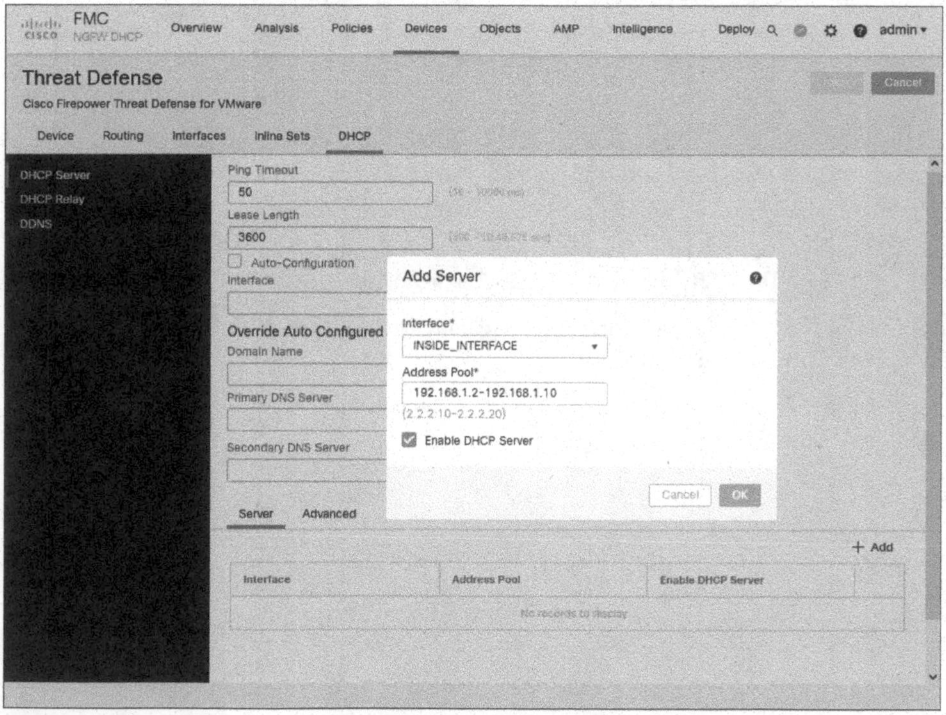

Figure 4-12 *DHCP Server Configurations on a Threat Defense*

Step 7.   Select the **Enable DHCP Server** check box to enable the service and click **OK**. You return to the device editor page.

Step 8.   Optionally, through the DHCP service, a threat defense can transfer any DNS-related information to your DHCP clients. The DHCP Server page allows you to enter domain names and DNS addresses manually. Alternatively, you can select the **Auto-Configuration** check box to let the threat defense obtain any DNS information automatically from a DHCP client connected to a predefined interface.

Step 9.   Click the **Save** button to save the configurations. To deploy the configurations to your threat defense, go to **Deploy > Deployment**, select the threat defense you wish to configure, and click the **Deploy** button (shown previously in Figure 4-9).

Validation of Interface Configuration

After the configurations are deployed to the threat defense, the hosts between the inside network and outside network should be able to communicate successfully. To test connectivity, you can simply run an ICMP ping test between the inside and outside hosts. If the hosts are running any services (such as web or Secure Shell), you can also use them to verify connectivity.

In a brand-new deployment, the management center does not display **connection events**. If you would like to use your management center to validate any connection attempts through your threat defense, you need to enable logging in the access control policy. By default, a new access control policy does not come with any customizable access control rule. Because we describe the operation of an access control rule in later chapters, for now, you can add a simple access control rule to allow the traffic and enable logging within that rule (see Figure 4-13). Alternatively, in an access control policy without any rule, you can simply enable logging in the default action (see Figure 4-14), which can also trigger connection events.

If you deployed the access control policy with logging functionality enabled, you can now view events for any associated connections by navigating to **Analysis > Connections > Events** of your management center.

Figure 4-15 exhibits connection attempts from an inside host (IP: 192.168.1.2) to an outside host (IP: 172.168.1.2) over ICMP, SSH, and HTTPS protocols.

While you run ICMP traffic, you can view the details of how the system is processing the ICMP packets by using the **debug** command.

Example 4-6 shows ICMP requests and replies exchanged between two computers located in the inside and outside networks.

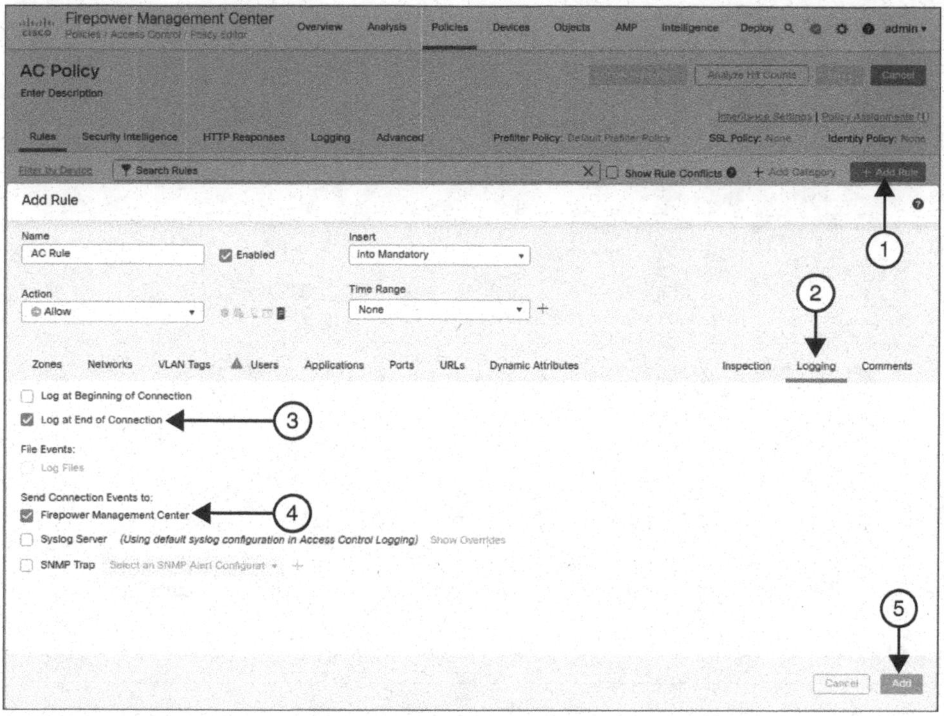

Figure 4-13   *Enabling Logging Within an Access Control Rule*

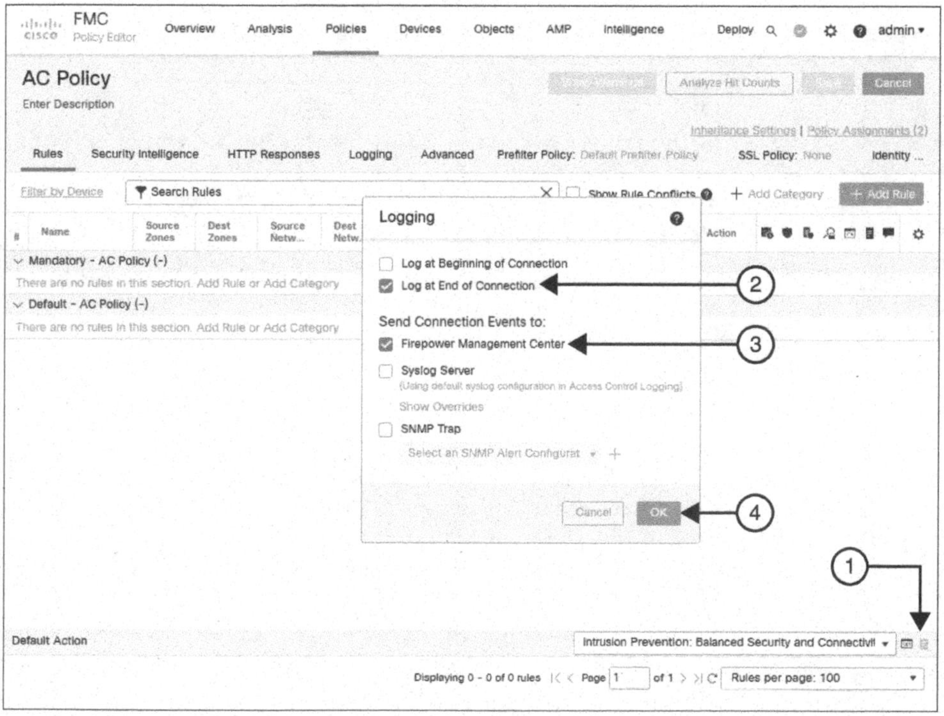

Figure 4-14   *Enabling Logging in an Access Control Policy as a Default Action*

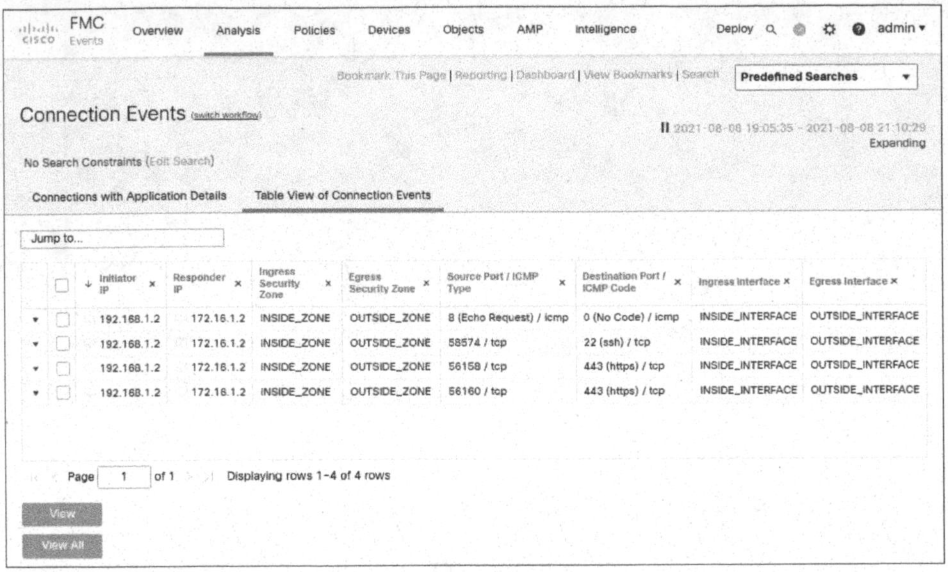

Figure 4-15   *Table View of Connection Events Between Inside and Outside Hosts*

Example 4-6   *Debugging ICMP Traffic in a Threat Defense*

```
> debug icmp trace
debug icmp trace enabled at level 1
>
ICMP echo request from INSIDE_INTERFACE:192.168.1.2 to OUTSIDE_INTERFACE:172.16.1.100
ID=4101 seq=1 len=56
ICMP echo reply from OUTSIDE_INTERFACE:172.16.1.100 to INSIDE_INTERFACE:192.168.1.2
ID=4101 seq=1 len=56
ICMP echo request from INSIDE_INTERFACE:192.168.1.2 to OUTSIDE_INTERFACE:172.16.1.100
ID=4101 seq=2 len=56
ICMP echo reply from OUTSIDE_INTERFACE:172.16.1.100 to INSIDE_INTERFACE:192.168.1.2
ID=4101 seq=2 len=56
.

.

<Output Omitted>

> undebug all
>
```

If the ping test fails, you need to determine the status of the interfaces. You can run the following commands on the threat defense to determine the interface status and to verify the configurations you applied from the management center to the threat defense. Command outputs are slightly different depending on the configuration method (static versus dynamic).

- **show ip**
- **show interface ip brief**

- show interface *interface_ID*

- show running-config interface

Example 4-7 shows output of the **show ip** command. You can view the mapping between the interface, logical name, and IP address in this output. You cannot, however, view the current status in the output.

Example 4-7   *Output of the* **show ip** *Command*

```
> show ip
System IP Addresses:
Interface            Name              IP address      Subnet mask      Method
GigabitEthernet0/0   INSIDE_INTERFACE  192.168.1.1     255.255.255.0    CONFIG
GigabitEthernet0/1   OUTSIDE_INTERFACE 172.16.1.1      255.255.255.0    CONFIG
Current IP Addresses:
Interface            Name              IP address      Subnet mask      Method
GigabitEthernet0/0   INSIDE_INTERFACE  192.168.1.1     255.255.255.0    CONFIG
GigabitEthernet0/1   OUTSIDE_INTERFACE 172.16.1.1      255.255.255.0    CONFIG
>
```

Example 4-8 confirms that both the GigabitEthernet0/0 and GigabitEthernet0/1 interfaces are up and configured manually (using static IP addresses). The **show interface ip brief** command provides an overview, including the current status, of each of the interfaces.

Example 4-8   *Overview of the Interface Status*

```
> show interface ip brief
Interface           IP-Address      OK? Method Status               Protocol
GigabitEthernet0/0  192.168.1.1     YES CONFIG up                   up
GigabitEthernet0/1  172.16.1.1      YES CONFIG up                   up
GigabitEthernet0/2  unassigned      YES unset  administratively down up
GigabitEthernet0/3  unassigned      YES unset  administratively down up
GigabitEthernet0/4  unassigned      YES unset  administratively down up
GigabitEthernet0/5  unassigned      YES unset  administratively down up
GigabitEthernet0/6  unassigned      YES unset  administratively down up
GigabitEthernet0/7  unassigned      YES unset  administratively down up
Internal-Control0/0 127.0.1.1       YES unset  up                   up
Internal-Control0/1 unassigned      YES unset  up                   up
Internal-Data0/0    unassigned      YES unset  down                 up
Internal-Data0/0    unassigned      YES unset  up                   up
Internal-Data0/1    169.254.1.1     YES unset  up                   up
Internal-Data0/2    unassigned      YES unset  up                   up
Management0/0       unassigned      YES unset  up                   up
>
```

Example 4-9 shows detailed statistics of the GigabitEthernet0/0 interface. By using the **show interface** *interface_ID* command, you can determine any errors and drops that may have occurred on an interface.

Example 4-9 *Detailed Statistics of Packets in the Interface Level*

```
> show interface GigabitEthernet 0/0
Interface GigabitEthernet0/0 "INSIDE_INTERFACE", is up, line protocol is up
  Hardware is net_vmxnet3, BW 10000 Mbps, DLY 10 usec
        Auto-Duplex(Full-duplex), Auto-Speed(10000 Mbps)
        Input flow control is unsupported, output flow control is unsupported
        MAC address 000a.000b.abcd, MTU 1500
        IP address 192.168.1.1, subnet mask 255.255.255.0
        277 packets input, 60997 bytes, 0 no buffer
        Received 0 broadcasts, 0 runts, 0 giants
        0 input errors, 0 CRC, 0 frame, 0 overrun, 0 ignored, 0 abort
        0 pause input, 0 resume input
        0 L2 decode drops
        215 packets output, 77346 bytes, 0 underruns
        0 pause output, 0 resume output
        0 output errors, 0 collisions, 0 interface resets
        0 late collisions, 0 deferred
        0 input reset drops, 0 output reset drops
        input queue (blocks free curr/low): hardware (0/0)
        output queue (blocks free curr/low): hardware (0/0)
  Traffic Statistics for "INSIDE_INTERFACE":
        277 packets input, 57079 bytes
        215 packets output, 74336 bytes
        7 packets dropped
      1 minute input rate 0 pkts/sec,  0 bytes/sec
      1 minute output rate 0 pkts/sec,  0 bytes/sec
      1 minute drop rate, 0 pkts/sec
      5 minute input rate 0 pkts/sec,  0 bytes/sec
      5 minute output rate 0 pkts/sec,  0 bytes/sec
      5 minute drop rate, 0 pkts/sec
>
```

Example 4-10 displays the interface configurations from the CLI. You can find all the settings you configured on the management center and applied to the threat defense.

Example 4-10 *Running Configurations of GigabitEthernet0/0 and GigabitEthernet0/1*

```
> show running-config interface
!
interface GigabitEthernet0/0
 nameif INSIDE_INTERFACE
 cts manual
  propagate sgt preserve-untag
  policy static sgt disabled trusted
 security-level 0
```

```
 ip address 192.168.1.1 255.255.255.0
!
interface GigabitEthernet0/1
 nameif OUTSIDE_INTERFACE
 cts manual
  propagate sgt preserve-untag
  policy static sgt disabled trusted
 security-level 0
 ip address 172.16.1.1 255.255.255.0
!
interface GigabitEthernet0/2
 shutdown
 no nameif
 no security-level
 no ip address
 .

 .
<Output Omitted for Brevity>
 .

 .
>
```

If the threat defense does not offer an IP address to its DHCP clients, or if the threat defense cannot obtain an IP address from any external DHCP server, you can debug any DHCP transactions to and from the DHCP server.

Example 4-11 proves that the threat defense has dynamically assigned the IP address 192.168.1.2 to a host with the MAC address C4:2C:03:3C:98:A8. This IP address is the first address from the DHCP address pool 192.168.1.2 to 192.168.1.10.

Example 4-11   *Verifying the IP Address Assignment from a DHCP Address Pool*

```
> show dhcpd binding

IP address     Client Identifier   Lease expiration    Type
 192.168.1.2    c42c.033c.98a8       3580 seconds  Automatic
>
```

If you do not see any DHCP binding, you can debug the DHCP packets on the threat defense.

Example 4-12 demonstrates the process of a DHCP server assigning an IP address. In the debug output, you can analyze the four major stages of the DHCP protocol: Discovery, Offer, Request, and Acknowledgment (DORA).

Example 4-12 *Exchange of DHCP Packets Between a Threat Defense and a DHCP Server*

```
> debug dhcpd packet
debug dhcpd packet enabled at level 1
>


DHCPD/RA: Server msg received, fip=ANY, fport=0 on INSIDE_INTERFACE interface
DHCPD: DHCPDISCOVER received from client c42c.033c.98a8 on interface
INSIDE_INTERFACE.
DHCPD: send ping pkt to 192.168.1.2
DHCPD: ping got no response for ip: 192.168.1.2
DHCPD: Add binding 192.168.1.2 to radix tree
DHCPD/RA: Binding successfully added to hash table
DHCPD: Sending DHCPOFFER to client c42c.033c.98a8 (192.168.1.2).

DHCPD: Total # of raw options copied to outgoing DHCP message is 0.
DHCPD/RA: creating ARP entry (192.168.1.2, c42c.033c.98a8).
DHCPD: unicasting BOOTREPLY to client c42c.033c.98a8(192.168.1.2).
DHCPD/RA: Server msg received, fip=ANY, fport=0 on INSIDE_INTERFACE interface
DHCPD: DHCPREQUEST received from client c42c.033c.98a8.
DHCPD: Extracting client address from the message
DHCPD: State = DHCPS_REBOOTING
DHCPD: State = DHCPS_REQUESTING
DHCPD: Client c42c.033c.98a8 specified it's address 192.168.1.2
DHCPD: Client is on the correct network
DHCPD: Client accepted our offer
DHCPD: Client and server agree on address 192.168.1.2
DHCPD: Renewing client c42c.033c.98a8 lease
DHCPD: Client lease can be renewed
DHCPD: Sending DHCPACK to client c42c.033c.98a8 (192.168.1.2).
DHCPD: Total # of raw options copied to outgoing DHCP message is 0.
DHCPD/RA: creating ARP entry (192.168.1.2, c42c.033c.98a8).
DHCPD: unicasting BOOTREPLY to client c42c.033c.98a8(192.168.1.2).

>
```

Summary

This chapter explains how to configure a threat defense in routed mode. It describes the steps to configure the routed interfaces of a threat defense with static IP addresses as well as dynamic IP addresses. In addition, this chapter discusses various command-line tools you can use to determine any potential interface-related issues.

Exam Preparation Tasks

As mentioned in the section "How to Use This Book" in the Introduction, you have a couple of choices for exam preparation: the exercises here, Chapter 22, "Final Preparation," and the exam simulation questions in the Pearson Test Prep practice test software.

Review All Key Topics

Review the most important topics in this chapter, noted with the Key Topic icon in the outer margin of the page. Table 4-3 lists a reference of these key topics and the page numbers on which each is found.

Table 4-3   Key Topics for Chapter 4

Key Topic Element	Description	Page
Paragraph	Routed firewall mode	72
Paragraph	DHCP client vs. DHCP server	80

Complete Tables and Lists from Memory

There are no Memory Tables or Lists in this chapter.

Define Key Terms

Define the following key terms from this chapter, and check your answers in the Glossary:

routed mode, switch port, DHCP service, connection event

## CHAPTER 5

Firewall Deployment in Transparent Mode

This chapter provides an overview of the following topics:

Transparent Mode Essentials: This section describes the characteristics of a firewall in transparent mode. It also introduces the bridge group and Bridge Virtual Interface (BVI).

Best Practices for Transparent Mode Configuration: This section discusses some of the best practices that you should consider when you configure your threat defense with the transparent firewall mode.

Fulfilling Prerequisites: In this section, you learn the commands to enable transparent firewall mode on a threat defense.

Configuring Transparent Mode in a Layer 2 Network: This section provides the steps to enable the transparent interface and bridge group interface. You also learn the commands that you can run on a threat defense CLI and verify the operation of transparent mode.

Deploying a Threat Defense Between Layer 3 Networks: This section demonstrates the techniques to deploy a threat defense between two routers.

Integrated Routing and Bridging (IRB): This section defines the integrated routing and bridging (IRB) capability of a threat defense.

The objectives of this chapter are to learn about

- Deployment of Secure Firewall in transparent firewall mode

- Verification of threat defense configurations in transparent mode

- Integrated Routing and Bridging (IRB) mode

The threat defense's transparent mode allows you to control your network traffic like a firewall, while the threat defense device stays invisible to the hosts in your network. This chapter discusses the configuration of a threat defense in transparent mode.

"Do I Know This Already?" Quiz

The "Do I Know This Already?" quiz enables you to assess whether you should read this entire chapter thoroughly or jump to the "Exam Preparation Tasks" section. If you are in doubt about your answers to these questions or your own assessment of your knowledge of the topics, read the entire chapter. Table 5-1 lists the major headings in this chapter and their corresponding "Do I Know This Already?" quiz questions. You can find the answers in Appendix A, "Answers to the 'Do I Know This Already?' Quizzes."

Table 5-1 "Do I Know This Already?" Section-to-Question Mapping

Foundation Topics Section	Questions
Transparent Mode Essentials	1
Best Practices for Transparent Mode Configuration	2
Fulfilling Prerequisites	3
Configuring Transparent Mode in a Layer 2 Network	4
Deploying a Threat Defense Between Layer 3 Networks	5, 6
Integrated Routing and Bridging (IRB)	7

CAUTION The goal of self-assessment is to gauge your mastery of the topics in this chapter. If you do not know the answer to a question or are only partially sure of the answer, you should mark that question as wrong for purposes of the self-assessment. Giving yourself credit for an answer you correctly guess skews your self-assessment results and might provide you with a false sense of security.

1. Which of the following statements is true about a bridge group?

    a. It represents a unique Layer 2 network.

    b. A threat defense supports multiple bridge groups at the same time.

    c. Hosts from different bridge groups cannot communicate with each other without a router.

    d. All of these answers are correct.

2. Which of the following statements is true about deployment?

    a. Transparent mode allows you to configure the connected interfaces as the default gateway for end users.

    b. Switching between transparent mode and routed mode requires a restart.

    c. You can use the management center to configure a threat defense from routed mode to transparent mode.

    d. Changing a firewall from routed to transparent mode erases any existing configuration.

3. What is the supported way to enable transparent firewall mode on a threat defense?

    a. Using the **Devices > Device Management** page of the management center GUI

    b. Reimaging the threat defense software with the **transparent** parameter enabled

    c. Issuing the **configure firewall transparent** command in the threat defense CLI

    d. Running the **configure transparent firewall** command on the threat defense CLI, followed by a system reboot

4. Which of the following statements is true about an IP address?

  a. You should use the IP address of a BVI as the default gateway for the hosts in a bridged network.

  b. The IP address of a BVI should be on a different subnet than any hosts in the bridge group.

  c. The BVI's IP address is used as the source IP address for packets that originate from a threat defense.

  d. All physical interfaces on a threat defense require an IP address.

5. Which of the following statements is true when you select the Access Control: Block All Traffic policy as the default action?

  a. It overrides any "allow" access control rules deployed on a threat defense.

  b. It blocks the traffic when the threat defense detects an intrusion attempt.

  c. This policy is equivalent to the **deny tcp any any** access control rule.

  d. It blocks the traffic as soon as malware is found in the network.

6. Which of the following commands displays the access control rule entries?

  a. **show access-list**

  b. **show access-control-rule**

  c. **show access-control**

  d. **show access-list-config**

7. Which of the following functionalities is supported in integrated routing and bridging (IRB)?

  a. Switching between interfaces and subinterfaces.

  b. Routing between bridge groups.

  c. Routing between a bridge group and a routed interface.

  d. All of these answers are correct.

Foundation Topics

Transparent Mode Essentials

In **transparent mode**, a threat defense bridges the inside and outside interfaces into a single Layer 2 network and remains transparent to the hosts. When a threat defense is in transparent mode, the management center does not allow you to assign an IPv4 address to a directly connected interface. As a result, the hosts are unable to communicate with any connected interfaces on the threat defense. Unlike with routed mode, you cannot configure the connected interfaces as the default gateway for the hosts.

You can, however, assign an IP address to the Bridge Virtual Interface (BVI) that comes with each **bridge group**. A bridge group represents a unique Layer 2 network. You can create multiple bridge groups on a single threat defense, but the hosts within different bridge groups cannot communicate with each other without a router. Within a bridge group, both the BVI and the hosts must have IP addresses from the same subnet. A threat defense uses the IP address of the BVI when it communicates with its hosts.

Figure 5-1 shows how a host finds its next hop when you configure a threat defense in transparent mode.

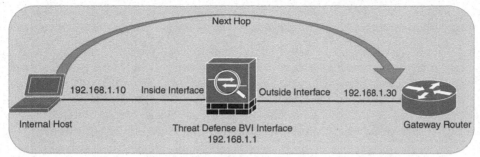

Figure 5-1 *Host Communication Through a Threat Defense in Transparent Mode*

Figure 5-2 shows a real-world deployment of a threat defense in transparent mode. The management interfaces of the management center and threat defense are connected to the end users through the 192.168.1.0/24 subnet. The default gateway for the 192.168.1.0/24 subnet is the gateway router IP address 192.168.1.30/24.

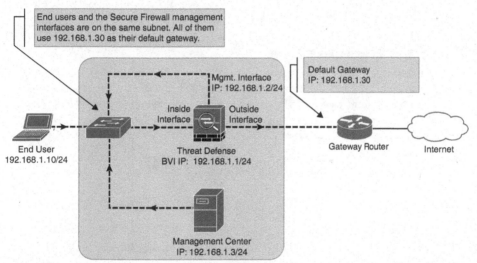

Figure 5-2 *A Threat Defense in Transparent Mode Is Deployed in a Typical Network*

Best Practices for Transparent Mode Configuration

Consider the following when you plan to deploy a threat defense in transparent mode:

- Changing the firewall mode wipes out any existing threat defense configurations. Therefore, before you change the firewall mode from routed to transparent or vice versa, take note of your threat defense configuration settings for future reference, in case you want to revert the threat defense to the initial state. To view the current threat defense configuration, run the **show running-config** command in the CLI.

- If you just want to change the firewall mode on a threat defense, performing a backup of your security policy configuration is not necessary because the next-generation security policies are defined and stored on the management center. Once registered, you can deploy the same policies to one or more threat defense devices from the management center.

- Do not use the BVI IP address as the default gateway for the connected hosts. Instead, use any connected router as the default gateway for the hosts in the bridged network.

- Do not forget to add access control rules to allow any necessary network management traffic. By default, threat defense in transparent mode blocks the DHCP traffic, multicast traffic, and Dynamic Routing Protocol traffic (such as RIP, OSPF, EIGRP, BGP, and so on). If you select Access Control: Block All Traffic as the default action, make sure you have added access control rules explicitly to allow any essential traffic. If you are not sure, you can use Intrusion Prevention: Balanced Security and Connectivity as the default action; it allows any unmatched traffic, as long as no malicious activities are found.

- If your ultimate goal is to perform transparent inspection, you can also choose the dedicated IPS-only deployment in inline mode instead of the transparent firewall mode. While both modes allow you to deploy the threat defense as a bump in the wire, a dedicated IPS-only deployment has less configuration overhead than transparent mode. In addition, a dedicated IP address for each BVI is not necessary. To learn more, read Chapter 6, "IPS-Only Deployment in Inline Mode."

Fulfilling Prerequisites

During system initialization, a threat defense provides an option to choose between routed mode and transparent mode (see Example 5-1). To set up a threat defense with transparent mode, just type **transparent** when the system prompts and press Enter. If you selected transparent mode during the system initialization, you could skip this section and read the section "Configuring Transparent Mode in a Layer 2 Network." If you selected routed mode, read on.

Example 5-1 *Configuring Transparent Firewall Mode During Initialization*

```
<Output Omitted>
.
.
.
Manage the device locally? (yes/no) [yes]: no
Configure firewall mode? (routed/transparent) [routed]: transparent
Configuring firewall mode ...
.
.
<Output Omitted>
```

You cannot change the firewall mode if the threat defense is currently registered with the management center. If you initially configured the threat defense to routed mode and now you want to reconfigure it to transparent mode, you must unregister the threat defense from the management center. To verify the registration status, run the **show managers** command at the threat defense CLI.

Example 5-2 shows that the threat defense is currently registered with a management center with IP address 10.1.1.2.

Example 5-2   *Verifying the Registration Status—Threat Defense Is Currently Registered*

```
> show managers
Type         : Manager
Host         : 10.1.1.2
Registration : Completed
>
```

If you find that a threat defense is currently registered with a management center, unregister it by using the management center web interface. To delete the registration, go to **Devices > Device Management**, click the three dots next to the threat defense name, and select the Delete option, as shown in Figure 5-3.

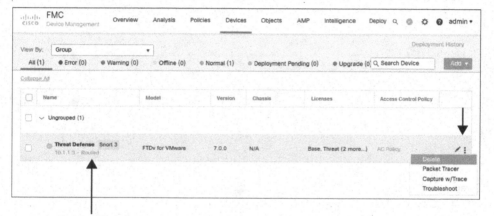

Routed Mode

Figure 5-3   *Unregistering a Threat Defense from the Management Center*

Example 5-3 confirms that the threat defense is currently not registered with a management center.

Example 5-3   *Verifying the Registration Status—Threat Defense Is Not Registered*

```
> show managers
No managers configured.
>
```

Enabling the Transparent Firewall Mode

If a threat defense is currently not registered with a manager, you can change the firewall deployment mode. To configure a threat defense with transparent mode, log in to the threat defense CLI and run the **configure firewall transparent** command (see Example 5-4).

Example 5-4   *Configuring Transparent Mode*

```
> configure firewall transparent

This will destroy the current interface configurations, are you sure that you want
to proceed? [y/N] y
The firewall mode was changed successfully.
```

After configuring the threat defense with the desired mode, you can determine the status from the CLI, as shown in Example 5-5.

Example 5-5   *Verifying Firewall Deployment Mode*

```
> show firewall
Firewall mode: Transparent
>
```

Alternatively, upon a successful registration, the web interface of the management center also displays the current firewall deployment mode. You can view it by navigating to **Devices > Device Management** (see Figure 5-4).

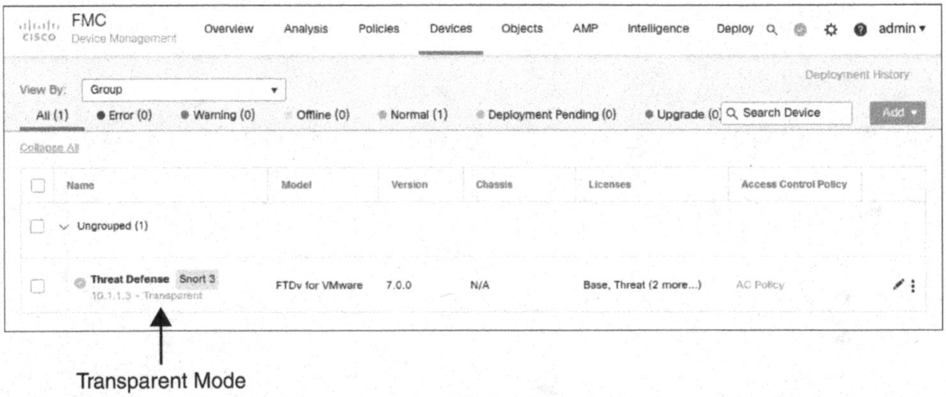

Transparent Mode

Figure 5-4   *Confirmation of Registration of a Threat Defense in Transparent Mode*

Configuring Transparent Mode in a Layer 2 Network

A threat defense in transparent mode can control traffic as a firewall and inspect traffic as an intrusion prevention system while it stays transparent in the network, like a Layer 2 switch. It supports the following deployment scenarios:

■ You can deploy it in a single Layer 2 network, where all the hosts reside in the same subnet and can communicate without a dynamic routing protocol. This type of deployment works when you configure the physical and virtual interfaces in a bridge group.

■ You can also deploy a threat defense between the Layer 3 networks, where hosts from different subnets communicate using a routing protocol. By default, when you configure a threat defense in transparent mode, it blocks any underlying dynamic routing protocol traffic. Therefore, to allow this traffic, you need to add access control rules explicitly.

Configuring the Physical and Virtual Interfaces

To configure the interfaces when a threat defense is in transparent mode, follow these steps:

Step 1.   Navigate to **Devices > Device Management**. A list of the managed threat defense devices appears.

Step 2.   Click the pencil icon that is next to the threat defense you want to configure. The device management editor page appears, showing all the interfaces of a threat defense on the Interfaces tab (see Figure 5-5).

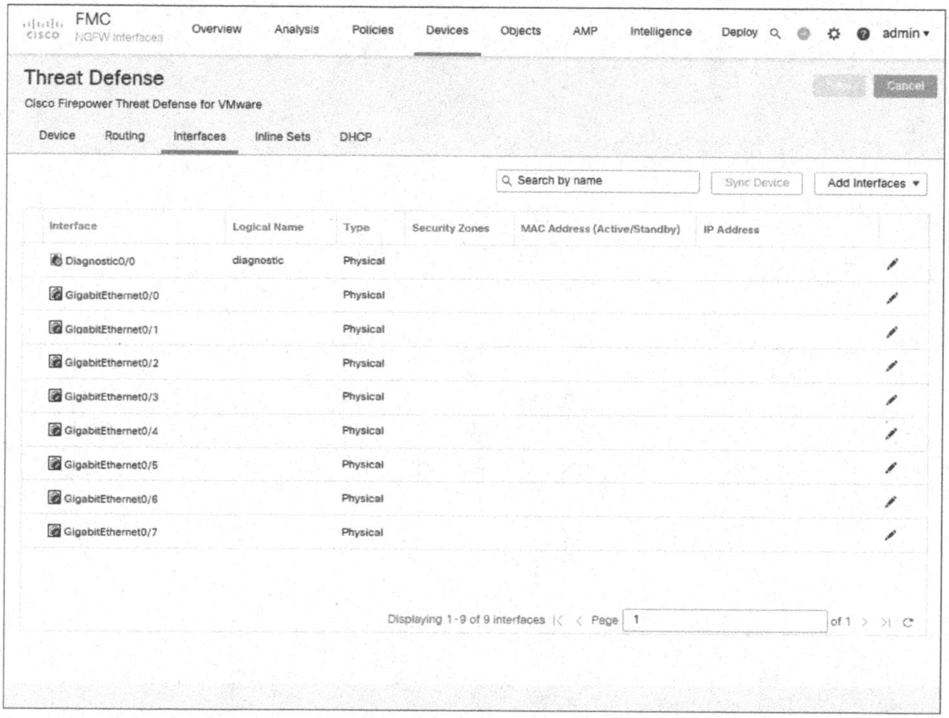

Figure 5-5   *The Interfaces Tab Shows All the Interfaces of a Threat Defense Virtual*

Depending on the threat defense platform you run, you may come across different types of interfaces and model-specific options. For example, threat defense model 1010 comes with Ethernet type interfaces with built-in switch ports. However, you cannot enable transparent mode on an interface if it is set to switch port access mode. To configure the interfaces of threat defense model 1010 in transparent mode, you need to disable the switch port by clicking the slider icon next to the desired interface, as shown in Figure 5-6.

Step 3.   On the Interfaces tab, click the pencil icons next to GigabitEthernet0/0 and GigabitEthernet0/1 to configure these interfaces for the inside and outside networks. Use the settings shown in Table 5-2 to configure these two interfaces.

To enable an interface, you must give it a name; this is a requirement. However, configuring a security zone is an optional step. Here, in the interface configuration window, you can create a security zone and associate it with an interface on the fly. Alternatively, you can navigate to **Objects > Object Management > Interface** to add, remove, or modify the assignment of security zones.

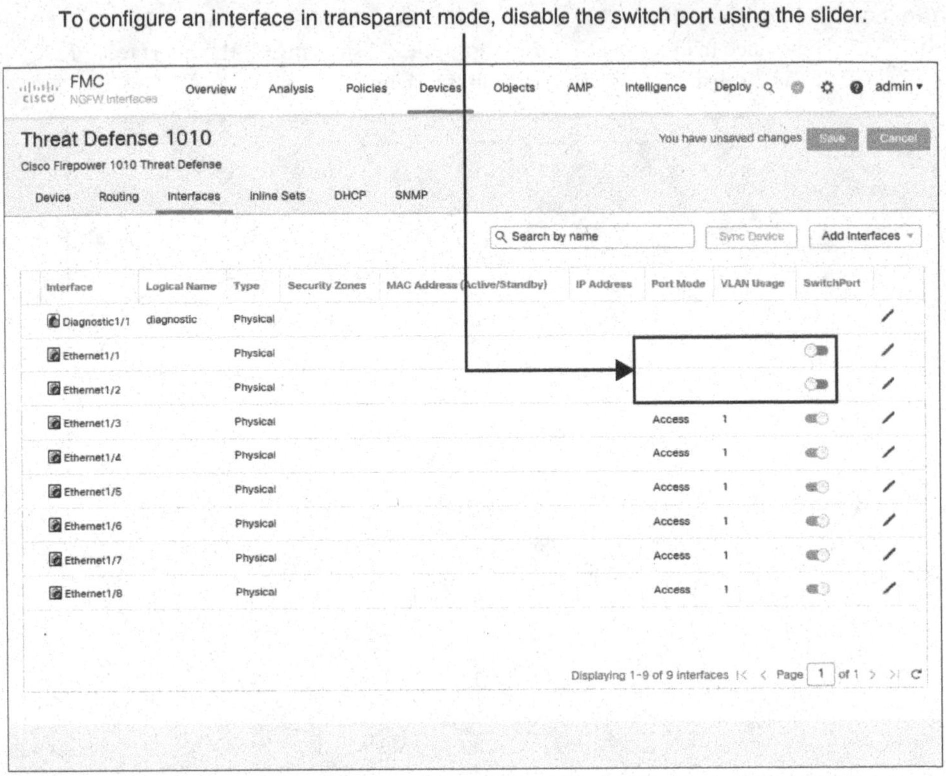

To configure an interface in transparent mode, disable the switch port using the slider.

Figure 5-6 *Threat Defense Hardware Appliance Shows Hardware-Specific Options (Switch Port)*

Table 5-2 Configuration Settings for GigabitEthernet0/0 and GigabitEthernet0/1

	GigabitEthernet0/0	GigabitEthernet0/1
Interface name	INSIDE_INTERFACE	OUTSIDE_INTERFACE
Security zone (optional)	INSIDE_ZONE	OUTSIDE_ZONE
IP address	In transparent mode, an IP address is not required on a data interface. Instead, assign an IP address to the BVI.	

Figure 5-7 shows the general settings of GigabitEthernet0/0; for example, it is named INSIDE_INTERFACE. Make sure to enable the interface using the Enabled check box. Note that there is no option to configure an IPv4 address.

Step 4. Repeat the preceding steps for GigabitEthernet0/1 to enable it for the outside network.

Step 5. After you configure both interfaces, click the **Save** button to save the changes you have made so far (see Figure 5-8). The interface settings are now saved on the management center.

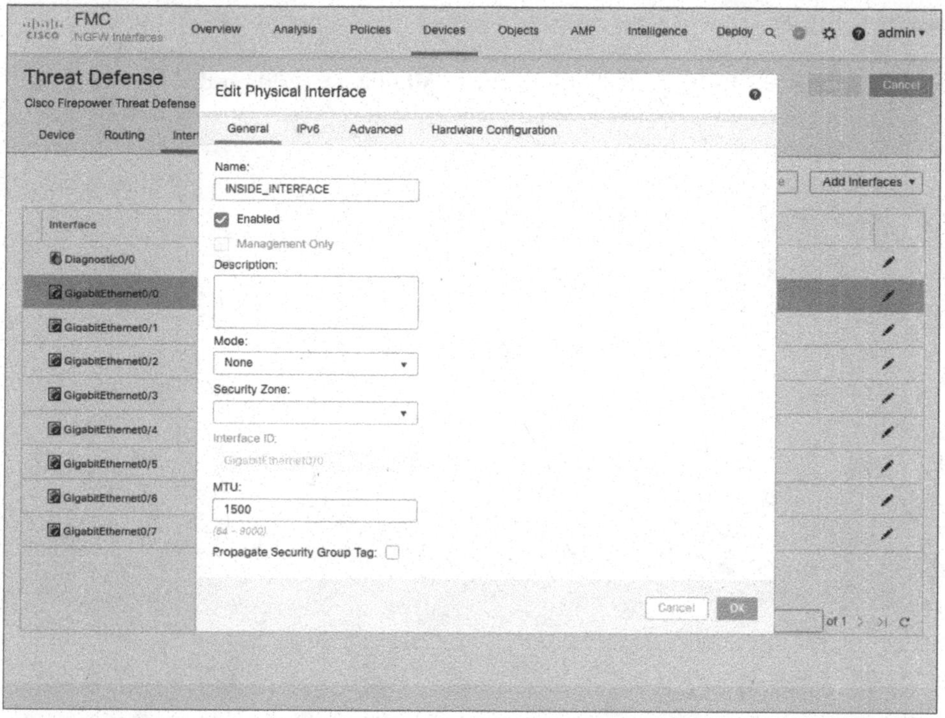

Figure 5-7   *Physical Interface Configuration Window*

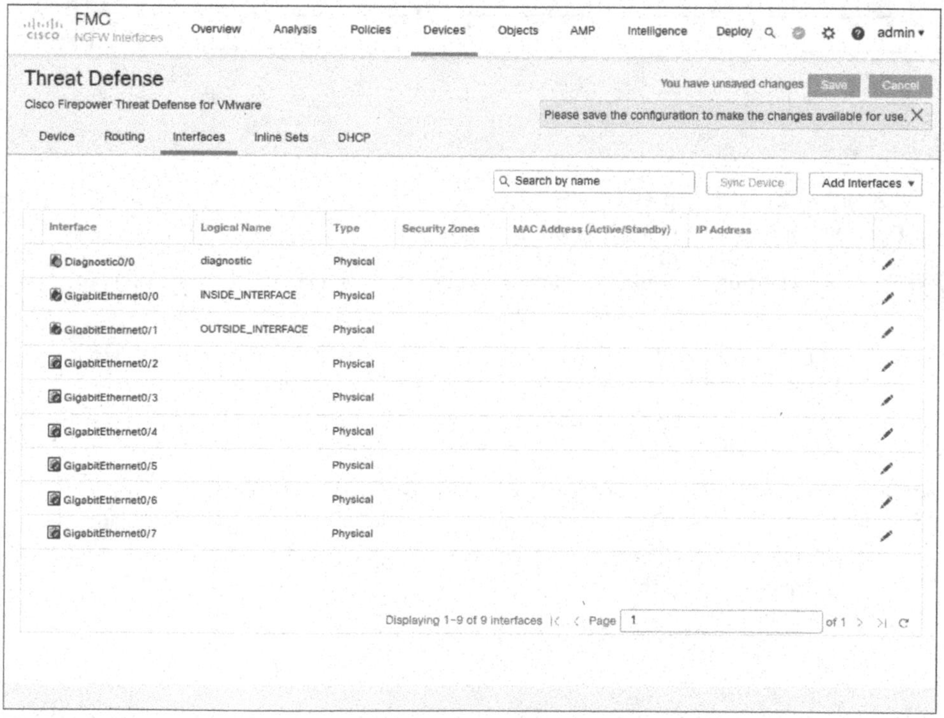

Figure 5-8   *Transparent Interfaces for the Inside and Outside Networks*

Step 6.   Before you deploy the configuration to the threat defense, there is still one more component to set up in a transparent mode firewall: the Bridge Virtual Interface (BVI). To add a BVI, click the **Add Interfaces** drop-down located at the right side of this Interfaces tab. A list of different types of interfaces appears (see Figure 5-9).

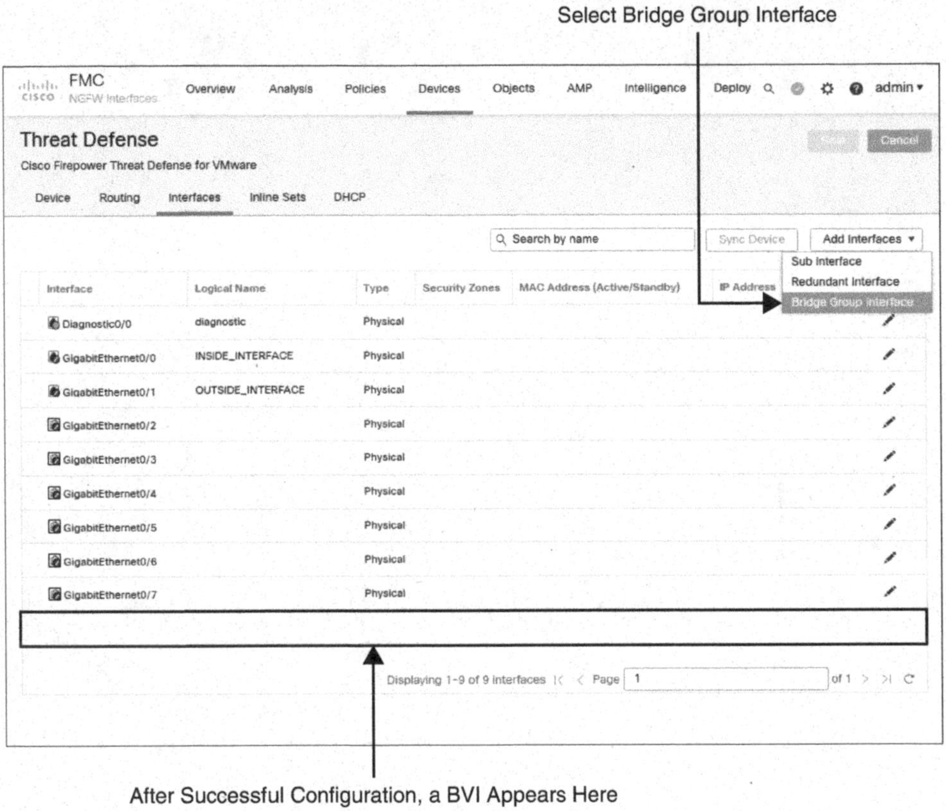

Figure 5-9   *Option to Add a Bridge Group Interface*

Step 7.   Select **Bridge Group Interface** from the list of interfaces. The Add Bridge Group Interface window appears.

Step 8.   On the Add Bridge Group Interface window, provide a bridge group ID between 1 and 250 and select the interfaces that are part of the bridged network—in this case, GigabitEthernet0/0 and GigabitEthernet0/1, as shown in Figure 5-10.

Step 9.   On the IPv4 subtab, configure the address 192.168.1.1 for the BVI (see Figure 5-11). The IP address must be on the same subnet as the hosts and default gateway router, and in this case, it is within the same /24 subnet as its hosts.

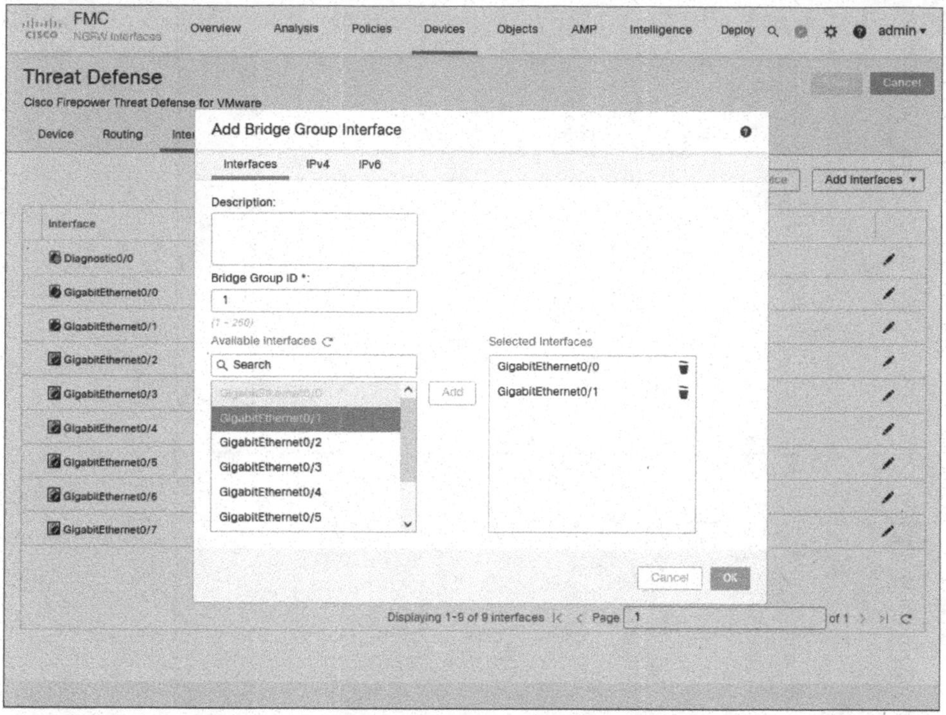

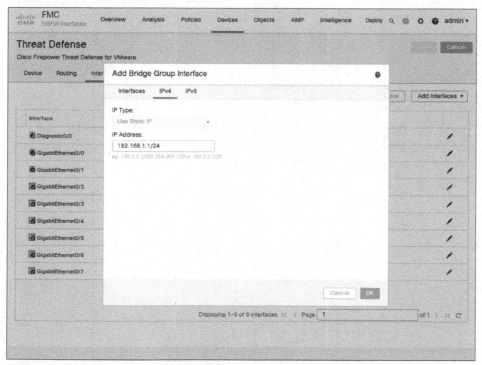

Figure 5-10 *Selection of Interfaces for the Bridge Group*

Figure 5-11 *IP Address of the Bridge Group Interface*

Step 10. Click **OK** to exit the Add Bridge Group Interface window. Figure 5-12 confirms the setup of a bridge group BVI1. Make sure to click the **Save** button to save the changes.

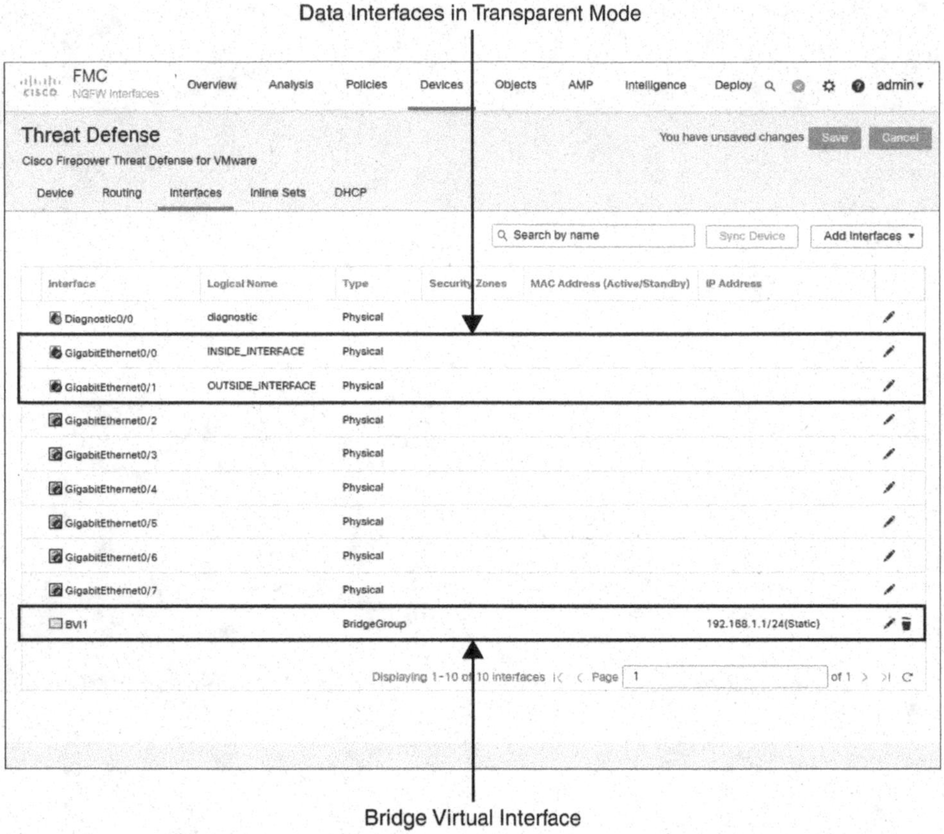

Figure 5-12 *Configuration of Interfaces on a Threat Defense in Transparent Mode*

Step 11. To deploy the configurations to your threat defense, navigate to **Deploy > Deployment**, select the threat defense, and click the **Deploy** button, as shown in Figure 5-13.

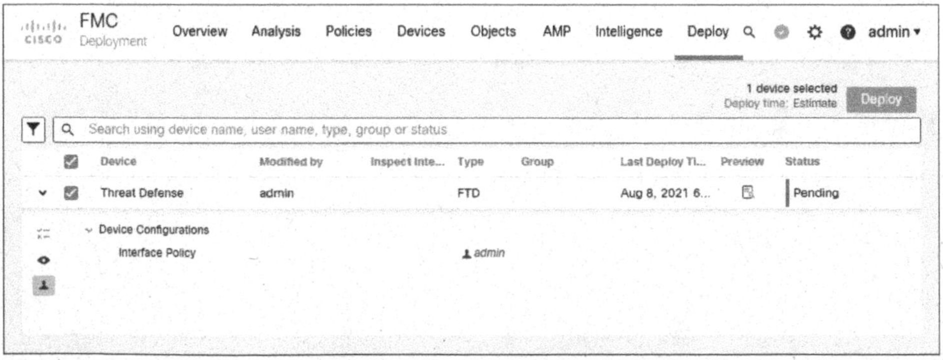

Figure 5-13 *Deployment of Policy on a Threat Defense*

Verifying the Interface Status

After deploying a threat defense by using the management center web interface, you can verify any configuration settings from the threat defense CLI.

Example 5-6 shows the interface configuration of a threat defense in transparent mode. Both member interfaces are in bridge group 1 and have no IP addresses. Only BVI1 has an IP address (192.168.1.1/24).

Example 5-6 *Interface Configurations on a Threat Defense in Transparent Mode*

```
> show running-config interface
!
interface GigabitEthernet0/0
 bridge-group 1
 nameif INSIDE_INTERFACE
 cts manual
  propagate sgt preserve-untag
  policy static sgt disabled trusted
 security-level 0
!
interface GigabitEthernet0/1
 bridge-group 1
 nameif OUTSIDE_INTERFACE
 cts manual
  propagate sgt preserve-untag
  policy static sgt disabled trusted
 security-level 0
!
interface GigabitEthernet0/2
 shutdown
 no nameif
 no security-level
 .
 .
<Output Omitted for Brevity>
 .
 .
interface BVI1
 ip address 192.168.1.1 255.255.255.0
>
```

Example 5-7 highlights the status of the interfaces on a threat defense in transparent mode. Although you do not configure IP addresses for the member interfaces of a bridge group, they use the same IP address as the BVI when you communicate with any connected hosts.

Example 5-7 *Interface Status of a Threat Defense in Transparent Mode*

```
> show interface ip brief
Interface             IP-Address      OK? Method Status                Protocol
GigabitEthernet0/0    192.168.1.1     YES unset  up                    up
GigabitEthernet0/1    192.168.1.1     YES unset  up                    up
GigabitEthernet0/2    unassigned      YES unset  administratively down up
GigabitEthernet0/3    unassigned      YES unset  administratively down up
GigabitEthernet0/4    unassigned      YES unset  administratively down up
GigabitEthernet0/5    unassigned      YES unset  administratively down up
GigabitEthernet0/6    unassigned      YES unset  administratively down up
GigabitEthernet0/7    unassigned      YES unset  administratively down up
Internal-Control0/0   127.0.1.1       YES unset  up                    up
Internal-Control0/1   unassigned      YES unset  up                    up
Internal-Data0/0      unassigned      YES unset  down                  up
Internal-Data0/0      unassigned      YES unset  up                    up
Internal-Data0/1      169.254.1.1     YES unset  up                    up
Internal-Data0/2      unassigned      YES unset  up                    up
Management0/0         unassigned      YES unset  up                    up
BVI1                  192.168.1.1     YES manual up                    up
>
```

Verifying Basic Connectivity and Operations

After configuring a threat defense in transparent mode, you might want to verify whether the transparent mode is operating as expected. Is the threat defense really invisible to the network hosts? You can prove this by using Address Resolution Protocol (ARP). When a host computer communicates through a threat defense, the host cannot see the threat defense. Instead, it sees the devices deployed on the other side of the threat defense.

Before testing the functionality, you can determine the MAC and IP addresses of all the participating interfaces. Figure 5-14 shows the Layer 1, Layer 2, and Layer 3 addresses of the network devices in the OSPF area 1 network. Instead of seeing the threat defense inside interface, the inside router sees the outside router as its next hop.

Example 5-8 shows the commands that allow you to find the MAC and IP addresses of the interfaces on the threat defense and router.

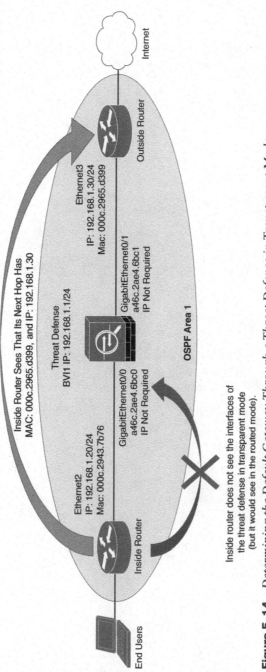

Inside Router Sees That Its Next Hop Has
MAC: 000c.2965.d399, and IP: 192.168.1.30

Threat Defense
BVI1 IP: 192.168.1.1/24

Ethernet3
IP: 192.168.1.30/24
Mac: 000c.2965.d399

GigabitEthernet0/1
a46c.2ae4.6bc1
IP Not Required

Ethernet2
IP: 192.168.1.20/24
Mac: 000c.2943.7b76

GigabitEthernet0/0
a46c.2ae4.6bc0
IP Not Required

OSPF Area 1

Internet

Outside Router

Inside Router

End Users

Inside router does not see the interfaces of
the threat defense in transparent mode
(but it would see in the routed mode).

Figure 5-14 *Determining the Default Gateway Through a Threat Defense in Transparent Mode*

5

Example 5-8 *Determining the MAC and IP Addresses*

```
! On Threat Defense:

> show interface GigabitEthernet 0/0 | include address
        MAC address a46c.2ae4.6bc0, MTU 1500
        IP address 192.168.1.1, subnet mask 255.255.255.0

> show interface GigabitEthernet 0/1 | include address
        MAC address a46c.2ae4.6bc1, MTU 1500
        IP address 192.168.1.1, subnet mask 255.255.255.0


! On Router:

Inside-Router# show interfaces Ethernet2 | include address
 Hardware is CSR vNIC, address is 000c.2943.7b76 (bia 000c.2943.7b76)
 Internet address is 192.168.1.20/24

Outside-Router## show interfaces Ethernet3 | include address
 Hardware is CSR vNIC, address is 000c.2965.d399 (bia 000c.2965.d399)
 Internet address is 192.168.1.30/24
```

If you configured the interfaces according to the instructions in the previous section, you should be able to successfully ping from the inside router to the outside router.

Example 5-9 shows a successful ping test from the inside router to the outside router through the threat defense. The dropping of the first packet is an expected behavior. It happens because the ARP table is empty at the beginning.

Example 5-9 *Sending a Successful Ping Request from Inside to Outside*

```
Inside-Router# ping 192.168.1.30
Type escape sequence to abort.
Sending 5, 100-byte ICMP Echos to 192.168.1.30, timeout is 2 seconds:
.!!!!
Success rate is 80 percent (4/5), round-trip min/avg/max = 5/5/6 ms
Inside-Router#
```

The ping test by the inside router (shown in Example 5-9) does not prove whether the ping replies come from the outside router or from the BVI of the threat defense. You can determine this by enabling debugging on the threat defense for ICMP traffic, like this:

```
> debug icmp trace

debug icmp trace enabled at level 1

>
```

Once again, you can send the ping requests to the outside router (IP: 192.168.1.30) from the inside router (IP: 192.168.1.20). The requests go through the threat defense as in the previous example. However, this time, the threat defense shows a log for the through traffic. There are two lines for each ping request—one for sending a request and one for receiving a reply:

```
ICMP echo request from INSIDE_INTERFACE:192.168.1.20 to
OUTSIDE_INTERFACE:192.168.1.30 ID=8 seq=1 len=72
```

```
ICMP echo reply from OUTSIDE_INTERFACE:192.168.1.30 to
INSIDE_INTERFACE:192.168.1.20 ID=8 seq=1 len=72
```

Now check the ARP table on the inside router to view the mapping of IP addresses with the inside interface. Compare the entries in the table with the MAC addresses that you found in the command output shown in Example 5-8.

Example 5-10 displays the mapping of the MAC addresses with the IP addresses. Besides the MAC address of its own interface (000c.2943.7b76), the ARP table of the inside router shows the MAC address of its next hop—the outside router (000c.2965.d399), not the threat defense (a46c.2ae4.6bc0), which is transparent in the network.

Example 5-10   *Inside Router ARP Table—After Pinging from the Inside Router to the Outside Router*

```
Inside-Router# show arp
Protocol Address      Age (min) Hardware Addr Type Interface
Internet 192.168.1.20      -   000c.2943.7b76 ARPA Ethernet2
Internet 192.168.1.30      2   000c.2965.d399 ARPA Ethernet2
Inside-Router#
```

If you send a ping request directly from the threat defense, the threat defense uses its BVI IP address to send that request. In that case, the ARP table on the router shows the MAC address of the threat defense interface that communicates with the router.

Example 5-11 demonstrates that when you ping from the threat defense to the inside router, it uses the BVI address 192.168.1.1 as its IP address. Remember that in transparent mode, you do not configure any IPv4 address on the threat defense physical interface.

Example 5-11   *BVI IP Address Used When Traffic Originates from the Threat Defense Itself*

```
> debug icmp trace
debug icmp trace enabled at level 1


> ping 192.168.1.20
ICMP echo request from 192.168.1.1 to 192.168.1.20 ID=52779 seq=30330 len=72
ICMP echo reply from 192.168.1.20 to 192.168.1.1 ID=52779 seq=30330 len=72


<Output Omitted for Brevity>


! To disable the debug of ICMP traffic:
> no debug icmp trace
debug icmp trace disabled.
>


! Alternatively, to disable all the running debug processes:
> undebug all
>
```

Example 5-12 shows a new entry in the ARP table after you send the ping requests to the inside router from the threat defense. It now displays the MAC address of the GigabitEthernet0/0 interface (a46c.2ae4.6bc0) in the threat defense.

Example 5-12 *Inside Router ARP Table—After Pinging from the Threat Defense to the Inside Router*

```
Inside-Router# show arp
Protocol Address      Age (min) Hardware Addr Type Interface
Internet 192.168.1.1      1     a46c.2ae4.6bc0 ARPA Ethernet2
Internet 192.168.1.20     -     000c.2943.7b76 ARPA Ethernet2
Internet 192.168.1.30     5     000c.2965.d399 ARPA Ethernet2
Inside-Router#
```

Deploying a Threat Defense Between Layer 3 Networks

After configuring the physical and virtual interfaces, you can communicate with any hosts, through a threat defense, within the same subnet. However, if you want to communicate with hosts that are in different subnets, a routing protocol is necessary.

When you configure a dynamic routing protocol across the network, the threat defense blocks the underlying routing traffic until you allow it in an access control policy. You can choose one of following options:

- Select a nonblocking policy as the default action (fewer steps to set up).

- Add an access control rule to allow desired traffic (more steps to set up).

Figure 5-15 shows a threat defense deployed between an inside router and an outside router. Both routers use loopback interfaces to simulate a host and the Internet. The loopback and routing interfaces are on different subnets, and all of them are included in OSPF area 1.

Selecting a Default Action

The default action in an access control policy determines how a threat defense handles traffic when no matching access control rule is available in the current ruleset. To define the default action, first you need to go to **Policies > Access Control**. Here, you can choose to create a new policy or edit an existing one, as shown in Figure 5-16.

When you are on the policy editor page, use the Default Action drop-down to select one of the system-provided policies that can allow the hosts in your lab. From a security standpoint, you can consider selecting a policy that allows traffic upon inspection. If you are unsure about choosing an appropriate policy, select the Intrusion Prevention: Balanced Security and Connectivity policy, as shown in Figure 5-17. It allows the unmatched traffic to go through the threat defense only if the traffic passes a deep packet inspection.

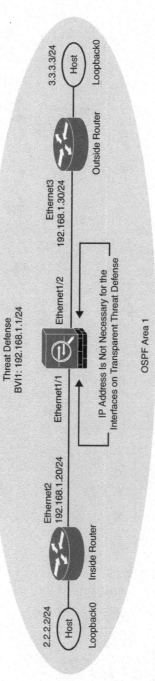

Figure 5-15 *Deployment of a Threat Defense (in Transparent Mode) Between Two Routers*

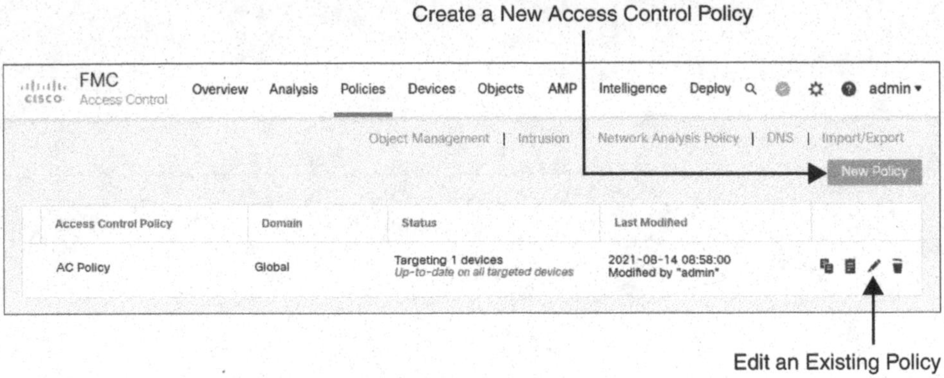

Create a New Access Control Policy

Figure 5-16 *Options to Create and Modify an Access Control Policy*

List of System-Provided Policies for Default Action

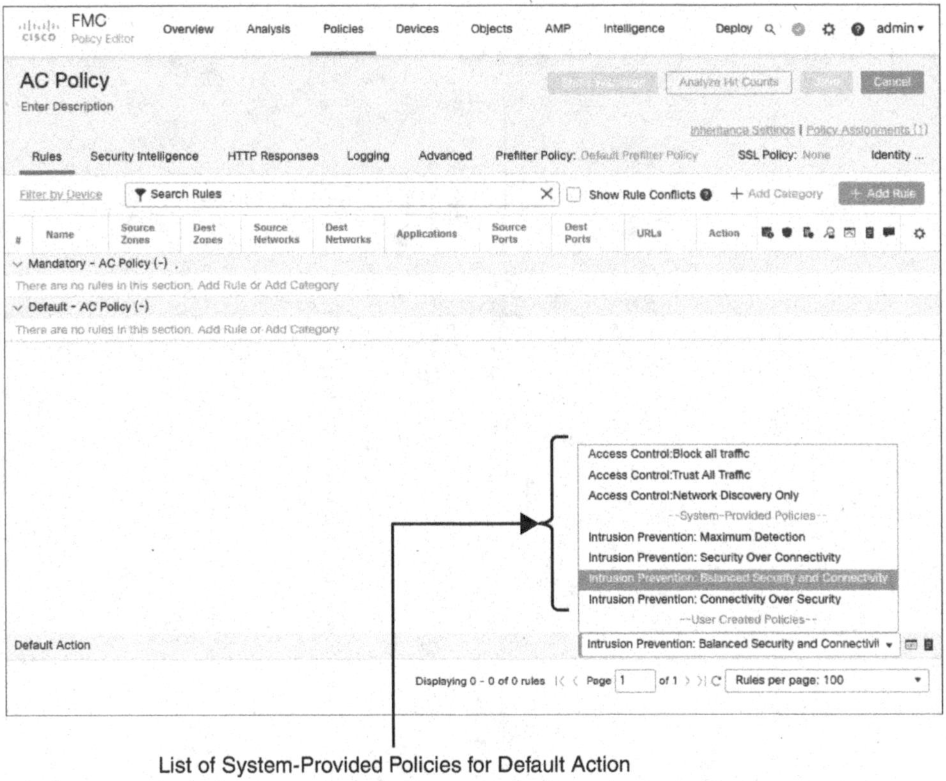

Figure 5-17 *Selecting a System-Provided Policy as the Default Action*

A new access control policy does not come with any access control rule, by default. When there is no access control in the policy, your selections in the Default Action section can impact all traffic that goes through a threat defense. For example, in an empty access control policy, if you enable logging in the default action, following the steps shown in Figure 5-18, it enables a threat defense to trigger events for any connection attempts. The management center displays those connection events at **Policies > Connections > Events**. Remember, to activate any new settings on an access control policy, you must save the policy and then deploy it to the threat defense by navigating to **Deploy > Deployment** and making selections there.

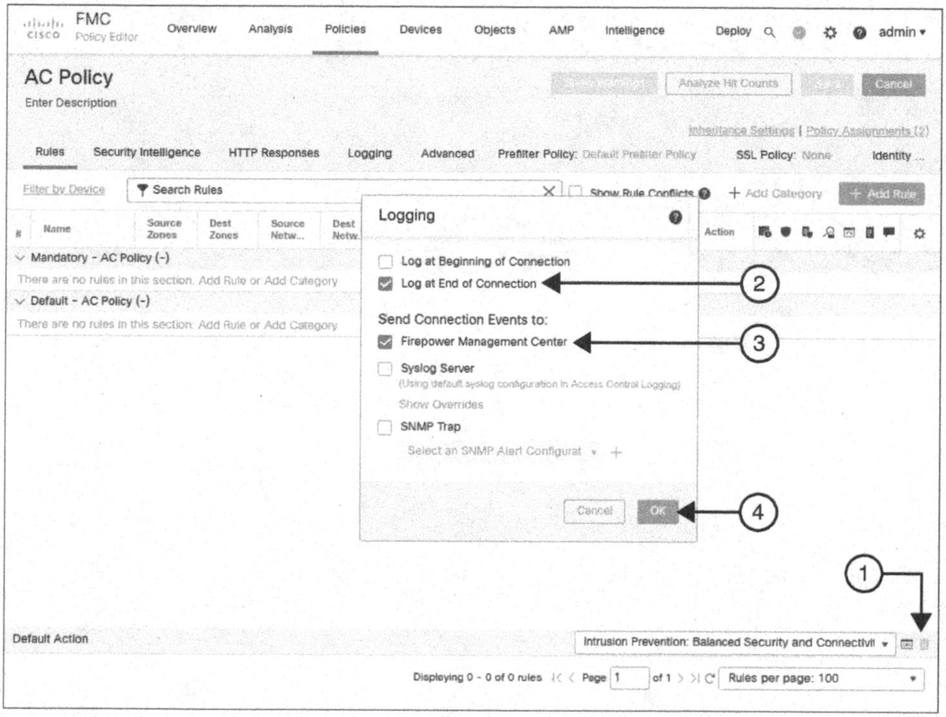

Figure 5-18   *Enabling Logging for Traffic Matching Default Action*

Adding an Access Control Rule for a Routing Protocol

If you select the Access Control: Block All Traffic policy as the default action, traffic is blocked when it does not match with any custom access control rules. Only the traffic that exclusively matches a rule is allowed through the threat defense.

If you create an access control rule to allow a particular routing protocol, such as OSPF, and select the Access Control: Block All Traffic policy as the default action, the threat defense allows only OSPF management traffic. Any other data traffic, however, is dropped due to the default blocking action. In this scenario, two routers can build an OSPF neighbor relationship through a threat defense, but you are unable to ping the inside router from the outside router and vice versa. Similarly, you cannot use Secure Shell (SSH) to access a router from the other router even though the neighbor relation is established. To permit additional traffic, you can add their associated protocols to an access control rule and select the Allow action.

The following configuration example shows how to create two access control rules—one for the routing traffic (OSPF) and one for the data traffic (SSH).

To create an access control rule for OSPF traffic, follow these steps:

Step 1.   Go to **Policies > Access Control**. Click the **New Policy** button to create a new policy or click the pencil icon to edit an existing policy. The policy editor page appears.

Step 2.   To create a new access control rule, on the policy editor page, click the **Add Rule** button (see Figure 5-19). The Add Rule window appears.

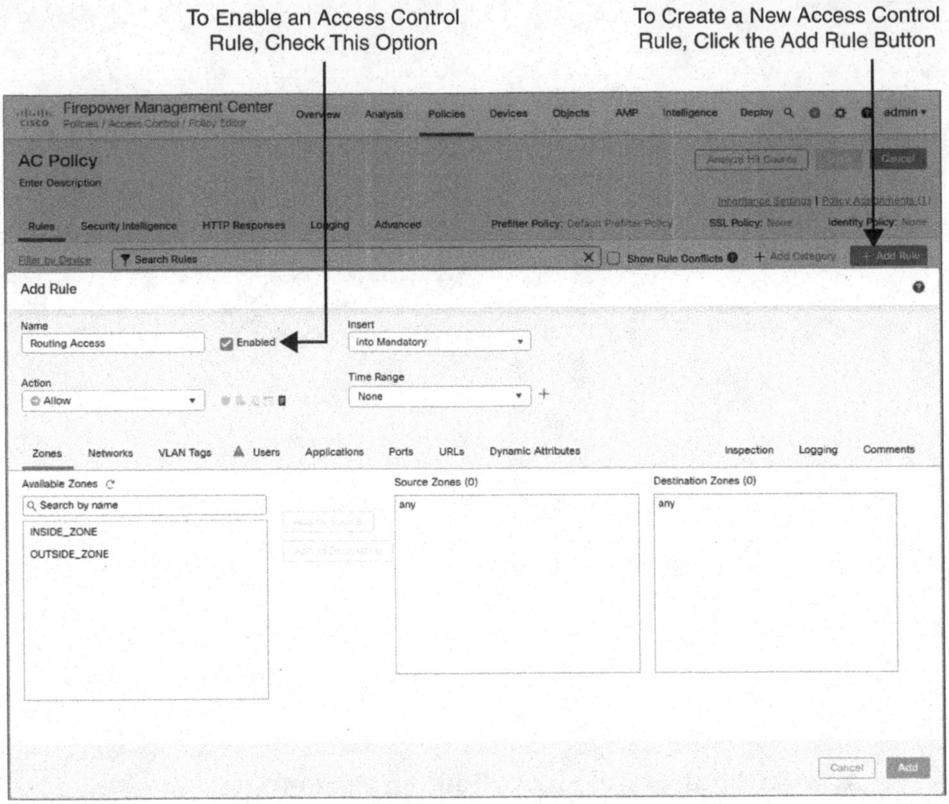

To Enable an Access Control
Rule, Check This Option

To Create a New Access Control
Rule, Click the Add Rule Button

Figure 5-19   *Adding and Enabling an Access Control Rule*

Step 3.   Give a name to this particular access control rule, select the **Enabled** check box, and set the action to **Allow**. Figure 5-19 shows how to enable a new access control rule called Routing Access with the rule action set to Allow.

CAUTION   Routers exchange keepalives to determine the states of the neighbors. If a threat defense deployed between two routers inspects a very high volume of traffic, it may delay keepalive packets from traversing the device even if you add an access control rule to allow them. As a result, a router may take a longer time to call its neighbor, which makes any reachability issues worse.

TIP   Cisco Secure Firewall offers two unique rule actions—Trust and Fastpath—that can expedite management traffic traversing the device. In an access control rule, you can set the action to Trust to let the OSPF traffic go through the threat defense without any further inspection. However, the more optimal method for bypassing an inspection is to add a prefilter rule for the OSPF protocol and set the action for it to Fastpath. Chapter 11 describes the Prefilter policy in detail.

Step 4.   Go to the Ports tab and click the **Protocol** drop-down that is under the Selected Destination Ports field.

Step 5.   Select the OSPF/OSPFIGP protocol and click the **Add** button next to the protocol drop-down. The selected protocol should be listed under the Selected Destination Ports box. Figure 5-20 shows the sequence for adding an access control rule called Routing Access to allow the OSPF protocol.

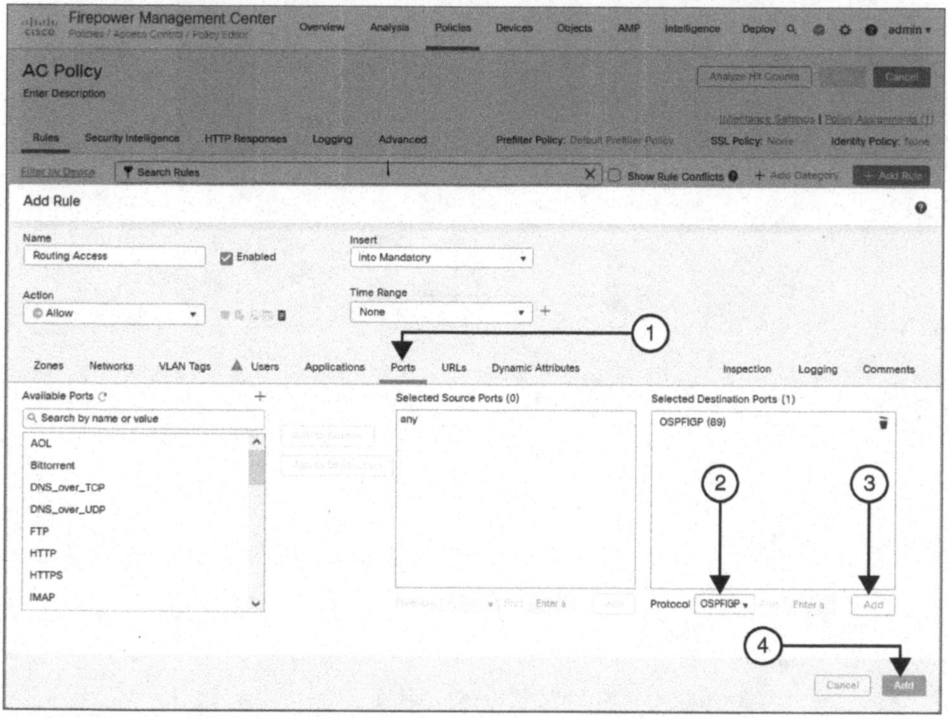

Figure 5-20   *Adding a Rule Condition to Match Traffic for OSPF Protocol*

Step 6.   Click the **Add** button to return to the policy editor page, where you can see the rule you just created.

Creating an Access Control Rule for the SSH Protocol

You can create a rule to allow data traffic through the SSH protocol. The following steps show how to allow destination port 22—the default port for SSH:

Step 1.   Click the **Add Rule** button once again. In the Add Rule window, provide a name for the rule, select the **Enabled** check box, and set the **Allow** action.

Step 2.   In the Available Ports section, select **SSH** and click the **Add to Destination** button. The SSH protocol appears under the Selected Destination Ports box. Figure 5-21 shows the steps to create an access control rule named Shell Access to allow the SSH traffic via port 22.

NOTE Step 2 allows SSH traffic that is destined for port 22, which is also the default port for the SSH protocol. If you want to allow any SSH application traffic, regardless of its destination port, you can create a rule by using the Applications tab.

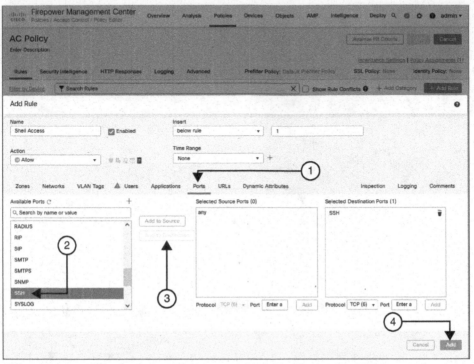

Figure 5-21 *Adding a Rule Condition to Match Traffic for the SSH Protocol*

Step 3. Optionally, go to the Logging tab to enable logging for this access control rule (see Figure 5-22). It allows you to see connection events when the rule matches the SSH traffic.

Step 4. Click the **Add** button to return to the policy editor page and select the **Access Control: Block All Traffic** policy as the Default Action. Figure 5-23 shows that two rules—Routing Access and Shell Access—are added. As the default action, Access Control: Block All Traffic is chosen.

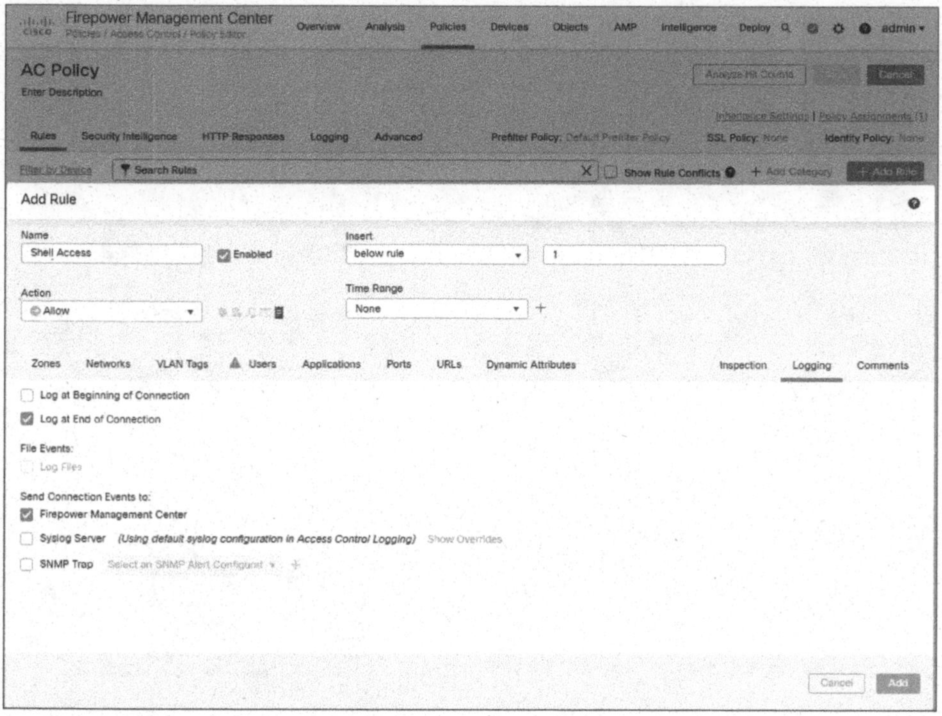

Figure 5-22 *Enabling Logging for an Access Control Rule*

Step 5. Add more access control rules as necessary. For now, in this configuration example, just create the preceding two access control rules. After the desired rules are added, save the policy using the **Save** button, and then go to **Deploy > Deployment** to deploy the new configurations on your threat defense.

Verifying Access Control Lists

When traffic is not blocked or allowed according to the configurations on the management center, you can use the threat defense CLI to verify whether the desired access control rules are applied. You can run the **show access-list** command to view the custom access control rules you created, as well as any implicit or system-generated rules that are applied to the threat defense.

Example 5-13 shows the system-generated access control rules when an access control policy with no custom rule is applied. The last rule on line 10, **permit ip any any**, is applied implicitly when you select a nonblocking default action. The following example uses the Balanced Security and Connectivity policy as the default action.

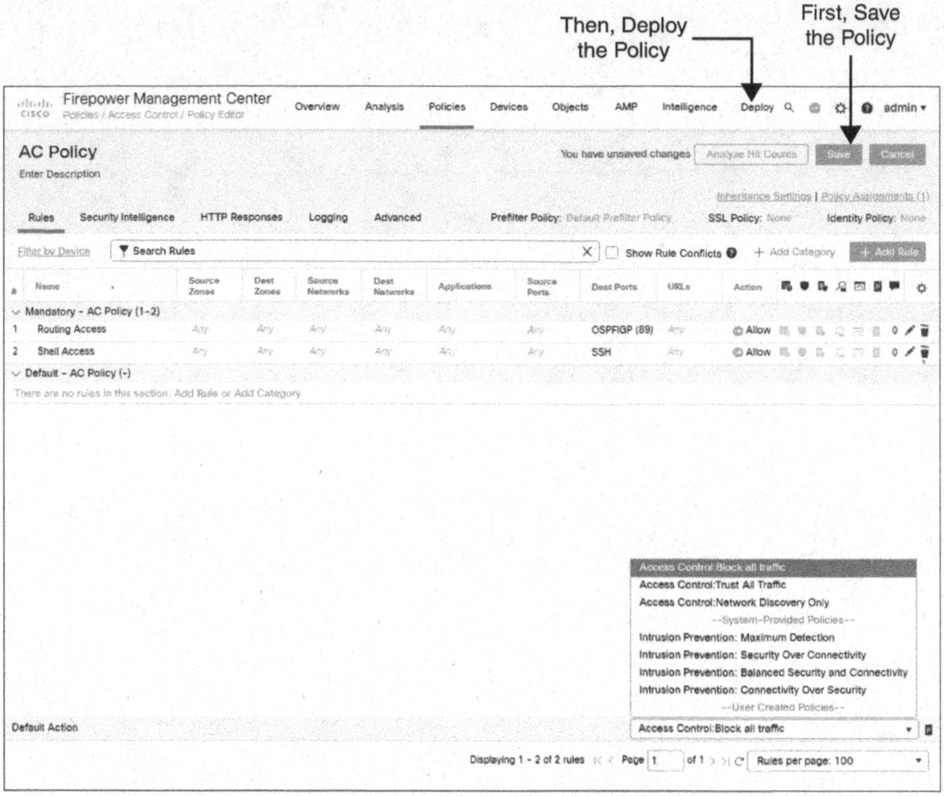

Then, Deploy
the Policy

First, Save
the Policy

Figure 5-23 *The Access Control Policy Is Set to Transfer Traffic in Transparent Mode*

Example 5-13 *No Custom Rule with the Balanced Security and Connectivity Default Policy*

```
> show access-list
access-list cached ACL log flows: total 0, denied 0 (deny-flow-max 4096)
            alert-interval 300
access-list CSM_FW_ACL_; 6 elements; name hash: 0x4a69e3f3
access-list CSM_FW_ACL_ line 1 remark rule-id 9998: PREFILTER POLICY: Default Tunnel
and Priority Policy
access-list CSM_FW_ACL_ line 2 remark rule-id 9998: RULE: DEFAULT TUNNEL ACTION RULE
access-list CSM_FW_ACL_ line 3 advanced permit ipinip any any rule-id 9998 (hitcnt=0)
0xf5b597d6
access-list CSM_FW_ACL_ line 4 advanced permit 41 any any rule-id 9998 (hitcnt=0)
0x06095aba
access-list CSM_FW_ACL_ line 5 advanced permit gre any any rule-id 9998 (hitcnt=0)
0x52c7a066
access-list CSM_FW_ACL_ line 6 advanced permit udp any eq 3544 any range 1025 65535
rule-id 9998 (hitcnt=0) 0x46d7839e
access-list CSM_FW_ACL_ line 7 advanced permit udp any range 1025 65535 any eq 3544
rule-id 9998 (hitcnt=0) 0xaf1d5aa5
```

```
access-list CSM_FW_ACL_ line 8 remark rule-id 268434432: ACCESS POLICY: AC
Policy - Default/1
access-list CSM_FW_ACL_ line 9 remark rule-id 268434432: L4 RULE: DEFAULT ACTION
RULE
access-list CSM_FW_ACL_ line 10 advanced permit ip any any rule-id 268434432
(hitcnt=3281) 0xa1d3780e
>
```

Example 5-14 shows two custom access control rules on lines 10 and 13, along with other
system-generated rules, that are created on the management center and applied to the threat
defense. These rules allow the threat defense to permit OSPF and SSH traffic. The last rule
on line 16, **deny ip any any**, is applied implicitly when you select Access Control: Block All
Traffic as the default action.

Example 5-14 *Two Custom Rules with Block All Traffic as the Default Policy*

```
> show access-list
access-list cached ACL log flows: total 0, denied 0 (deny-flow-max 4096)
            alert-interval 300
access-list CSM_FW_ACL_; 8 elements; name hash: 0x4a69e3f3
access-list CSM_FW_ACL_ line 1 remark rule-id 9998: PREFILTER POLICY: Default Tunnel
and Priority Policy
access-list CSM_FW_ACL_ line 2 remark rule-id 9998: RULE: DEFAULT TUNNEL ACTION RULE
access-list CSM_FW_ACL_ line 3 advanced permit ipinip any any rule-id 9998 (hitcnt=0)
0xf5b597d6
access-list CSM_FW_ACL_ line 4 advanced permit 41 any any rule-id 9998 (hitcnt=0)
0x06095aba
access-list CSM_FW_ACL_ line 5 advanced permit gre any any rule-id 9998 (hitcnt=0)
0x52c7a066
access-list CSM_FW_ACL_ line 6 advanced permit udp any eq 3544 any range 1025 65535
rule-id 9998 (hitcnt=0) 0x46d7839e
access-list CSM_FW_ACL_ line 7 advanced permit udp any range 1025 65535 any eq 3544
rule-id 9998 (hitcnt=0) 0xaf1d5aa5
access-list CSM_FW_ACL_ line 8 remark rule-id 268437504: ACCESS POLICY: AC
Policy - Mandatory/1
access-list CSM_FW_ACL_ line 9 remark rule-id 268437504: L7 RULE: Routing Access
access-list CSM_FW_ACL_ line 10 advanced permit ospf any any rule-id 268437504
(hitcnt=4) 0x385cc1f6
access-list CSM_FW_ACL_ line 11 remark rule-id 268437505: ACCESS POLICY: AC
Policy - Mandatory/2
access-list CSM_FW_ACL_ line 12 remark rule-id 268437505: L7 RULE: Shell Access
access-list CSM_FW_ACL_ line 13 advanced permit tcp any any object-group SSH rule-id
268437505 (hitcnt=8) 0x030eea01
 access-list CSM_FW_ACL_ line 13 advanced permit tcp any any eq ssh rule-id 268437505
(hitcnt=8) 0xf8ca4a86
access-list CSM_FW_ACL_ line 14 remark rule-id 268434432: ACCESS POLICY: AC
Policy - Default/1
access-list CSM_FW_ACL_ line 15 remark rule-id 268434432: L4 RULE: DEFAULT ACTION
RULE
access-list CSM_FW_ACL_ line 16 advanced deny ip any any rule-id 268434432 event-log
flow-start (hitcnt=826) 0x97aa021a
>
```

If you set the default action to block all traffic and do not permit the OSPF traffic through an access list, the neighbor relationship breaks. When a neighbor goes down, the threat defense triggers an alert on the CLI similar to the following:

```
Aug 14 04:00:51.434: %OSPF-5-ADJCHG: Process 1, Nbr 3.3.3.3 on
Ethernet2 from FULL to DOWN, Neighbor Down: Dead timer expired
```

Integrated Routing and Bridging (IRB)

You have just learned how to create a Layer 2 bridge group on a threat defense in transport mode. Also, the preceding chapter described how to configure Layer 3 interfaces in routed mode. On a traditional firewall, when you enable a firewall mode, all the interfaces on that firewall solely support that particular mode. Because each routed interface or Bridge Virtual Interface (BVI) represents a separate subnet, a router is essential to route traffic between the different subnets. However, in your deployment use case, if you need to configure some interfaces in routed mode, while the other interfaces will run in bridge groups, you can configure your threat defense to do so. A single threat defense can route traffic between any regular routed interfaces and Bridge Virtual Interfaces natively and simultaneously. This functionality is known as **integrated routing and bridging (IRB)**. IRB enables you to deploy a threat defense in diverse design scenarios, as it integrates the capabilities of separate Layer 2 and Layer 3 devices into a single device.

Summary

This chapter discusses the transparent firewall mode and how to configure the physical and virtual interfaces. It discusses integrated routing and bridging (IRB). Furthermore, it describes various command-line tools that enable you to investigate any potential configuration issues.

Exam Preparation Tasks

As mentioned in the section "How to Use This Book" in the Introduction, you have a couple of choices for exam preparation: the exercises here, Chapter 22, "Final Preparation," and the exam simulation questions in the Pearson Test Prep practice test software.

Review All Key Topics

Review the most important topics in this chapter, noted with the Key Topic icon in the outer margin of the page. Table 5-3 lists a reference of these key topics and the page numbers on which each is found.

Table 5-3 Key Topics for Chapter 5

Key Topic Element	Description	Page
Paragraph	Transparent mode	92
Bullet list	Bridge Virtual Interface (BVI)	94
Bullet list	Special handling of traffic	94
Paragraph	Integrated routing and bridging (IRB)	118

Memory Tables and Lists

There are no Memory Tables or Lists for this chapter.

Define Key Terms

Define the following key terms from this chapter, and check your answers in the Glossary:

transparent mode, bridge group, integrated routing and bridging (IRB)

5

## CHAPTER 6

IPS-Only Deployment in Inline Mode

This chapter provides an overview of the following topics:

Inline Mode Essentials: This section describes the characteristics of IPS-only deployment mode. It delineates the key differences among inline, passive, and transparent modes.

Best Practices for Inline Mode: In this section, you learn some of the best practices to ensure uninterrupted traffic flow through a threat defense in inline deployment mode.

Inline Mode Configuration: This section walks you through the steps to configure a threat defense in inline mode.

Verification: In the last section of this chapter, you learn some useful commands that you can run on the CLI to investigate and troubleshoot an issue.

The objectives of this chapter are to learn about

- Deployment of threat defense as a dedicated intrusion prevention system (IPS)
- Verification of threat defense configurations in inline interface mode

A threat defense in inline interface mode can block unintended traffic while it remains invisible to the network hosts. However, in the preceding chapter, you learned about transparent mode, which also blocks traffic and keeps itself transparent in the network. So, why would someone choose inline mode? This chapter explores the advantages of inline mode and demonstrates its functionality and configuration.

"Do I Know This Already?" Quiz

The "Do I Know This Already?" quiz enables you to assess whether you should read this entire chapter thoroughly or jump to the "Exam Preparation Tasks" section. If you are in doubt about your answers to these questions or your own assessment of your knowledge of the topics, read the entire chapter. Table 6-1 lists the major headings in this chapter and their corresponding "Do I Know This Already?" quiz questions. You can find the answers in Appendix A, "Answers to the 'Do I Know This Already?' Quizzes."

Table 6-1 "Do I Know This Already?" Section-to-Question Mapping

Foundation Topics Section	Questions
Inline Mode Essentials	1
Best Practices for Inline Mode	2
Inline Mode Configuration	3, 4
Verification	5

CAUTION   The goal of self-assessment is to gauge your mastery of the topics in this chapter. If you do not know the answer to a question or are only partially sure of the answer, you should mark that question as wrong for purposes of the self-assessment. Giving yourself credit for an answer you correctly guess skews your self-assessment results and might provide you with a false sense of security.

1. Which of the following statements is false?

   a. A threat defense supports NAT in the inline mode.

   b. An inline set is a logical group of one or more interface pairs.

   c. A threat defense does not support blocking with reset or interactive blocking.

   d. Both inline mode and transparent mode work like bump in the wire.

2. Which of the following options offer better handling of traffic in an IPS-only deployment?

   a. Enabling portfast on the switch ports that are connected to the inline interface pair.

   b. Enabling the fail open features for the inline interface set.

   c. Allowing the inline set to propagate its link state.

   d. All of these answers are correct.

3. Which of the following statements is true?

   a. The steps to configure inline mode and transparent mode are identical.

   b. An inline pair uses loopback IP addresses to transfer traffic.

   c. The Snort fail open feature is enabled on an inline set by default.

   d. The Propagate Link State feature is not enabled by default on an inline set.

4. Which of the following statements is true?

   a. You should include both interface pairs in the same inline set to ensure the recognition of asynchronous traffic.

   b. The fail open feature allows a threat defense device to continue its traffic flow through the device by bypassing the detection.

   c. Propagate Link State reduces the routing convergence time when one of the interfaces in an inline set goes down.

   d. All of these answers are correct.

5. Which command displays the advanced settings of an inline interface set?

   a. show interface ip brief

   b. show inline-set

   c. show interface detail

   d. show interface inline detail

Foundation Topics

Inline Mode Essentials

A threat defense supports a wide variety of block actions, such as simple blocking, blocking with reset, interactive blocking, and interactive blocking with reset. However, a block action cannot drop any suspicious packet if the interfaces are misconfigured or set up with an improper mode.

Figure 6-1 shows a list of the actions that you can apply to an access control rule. Note the different types of block actions a threat defense supports.

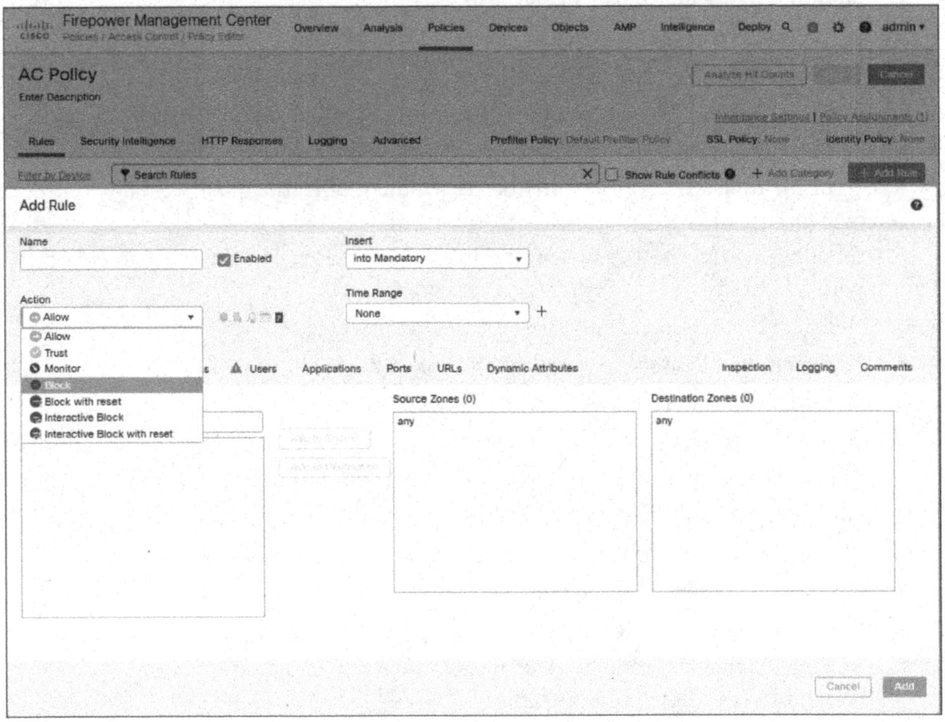

Figure 6-1 *Available Actions for an Access Control Rule*

A threat defense enables you to choose any interface mode, regardless of the underlying deployment mode—routed or transparent. However, ultimately, the capability of an interface mode defines whether a threat defense is able to block any suspicious traffic it sees.

Table 6-2 lists various threat defense modes and describes their capabilities to block traffic. The deployment mode in this table defines how a threat defense functions as a firewall.

The interface mode defines how a threat defense acts on the traffic in case of any suspicious activities.

Table 6-2 Capability to Block Traffic in Various Modes

Deployment Mode	Interface Mode	Able to Block Traffic?
Routed		Yes
Transparent		Yes
	Inline	Yes
	Inline-tap	No
	Passive	No
	Passive (ERSPAN)	No

Inline Mode Versus Passive Mode

An intrusion detection and prevention system can detect suspicious activities and prevent network attacks. You can deploy a threat defense either as an intrusion detection system (IDS) or as an intrusion prevention system (IPS). To prevent any potential intrusion attempt in real time, you must deploy a threat defense in inline mode. In **inline mode**, the ingress and egress interfaces are bundled into an interface pair. Each pair must be associated with an **inline set**, which is a logical group of one or more interface pairs.

Figure 6-2 illustrates how two interfaces (GigabitEthernet0/0 with GigabitEthernet0/1 and GigabitEthernet0/2 with GigabitEthernet0/3) can build the inline pairs. Note that both of the inline pairs are included in Inline Set 1 in this illustration.

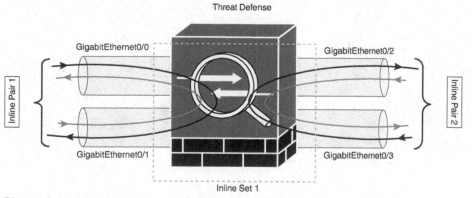

Figure 6-2 *Understanding an Inline Interface, Interface Pair, and Inline Set*

A threat defense in passive mode, in contrast, detects intrusion attempts but is unable to block them. A switch or tap mirrors all the packets it receives and sends a copy of each packet to the threat defense using port mirroring. Because the original traffic does not go through a threat defense, the threat defense is unable to take any action on a packet. In other words, a threat defense in passive mode cannot stop an intrusion attempt; it can only detect an attempt based on the traffic it sees.

Figure 6-3 provides an example of a typical threat defense deployment. The topology shows two threat defense devices deployed in two different modes—inline (IPS) and passive (IDS).

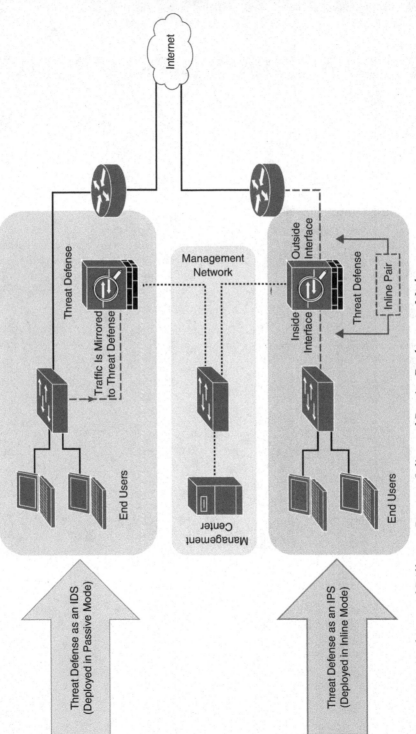

Figure 6-3 *Architectural Difference Between Inline and Passive Deployment Modes*

Inline Mode Versus Transparent Mode

Both inline mode and transparent mode work like *bump in the wire*, which means they are invisible to the connected devices. However, they are two different techniques.

In inline mode, the interfaces on an interface pair are network agnostic. They can send and receive any traffic, as long as the policies permit. In addition, you do not need to configure IP addresses on any of the member interfaces of an inline pair.

In contrast, a threat defense in transparent mode places the inside and outside networks into a virtual bridge group and creates a Layer 2 bridging network. Traffic that originates from a threat defense uses a Bridged Virtual Interface (BVI) as its source interface. The BVI, inside network, and outside network must all be configured with the IP addresses from a single subnet.

You can enable Network Address Translation (NAT) in transparent mode; however, a threat defense does not support NAT in the inline mode.

Best Practices for Inline Mode

When you create an inline set, consider the following:

- If your network uses asynchronous routing, and the inbound and outbound traffic go through two different interface pairs, you should include both interface pairs in the same interface set. Doing so ensures that the threat defense does not see just half of the traffic; it can see the flows from both directions and recognize them when they are part of a single connection.

- If the interfaces of an inline pair are connected to switches that run Spanning Tree Protocol (STP), you should enable portfast on the associated switch ports. It allows those switch ports to transition to the forwarding state immediately and reduces hardware bypass time.

- You should enable the fail open features for the inline interface set. In case of an inspection failure, this feature allows a threat defense to continue moving traffic through the device without interruption.

- Likewise, you should allow the inline set to propagate its link state. Doing so reduces the routing convergence time when one of the interfaces in an inline set goes down.

Figure 6-4 shows the options to enable fail open and link state propagation functionalities on an inline set. The detailed configuration workflow is described in the following configuration section.

6

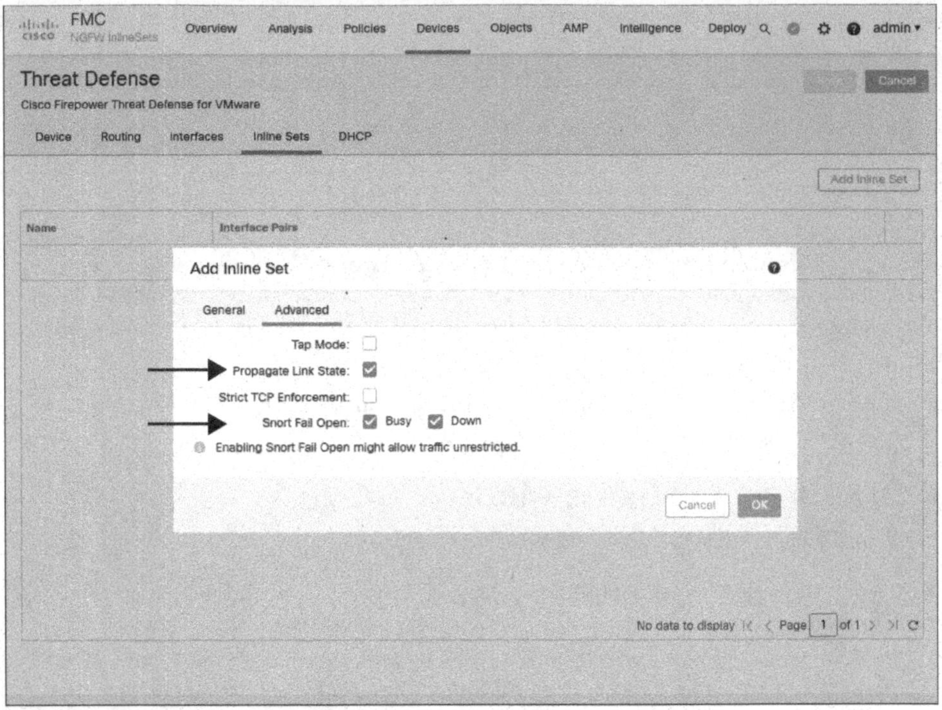

Figure 6-4   *Advanced Options to Provide Uninterrupted Traffic Flow*

Inline Mode Configuration

In the following sections, you configure an inline set and then deploy the interface settings to a threat defense. The configuration example also includes the fault-tolerance features that can help you avoid downtime in case of a failure.

Figure 6-5 provides an overview of the lab topology that is used in this chapter. The configuration examples and the command outputs in this chapter are based on this topology.

Fulfilling Prerequisites

This chapter assumes that you completed the exercises in the previous chapters and are familiar with the following items at this point:

■ In the access control policy, enable logging on the access control rule and on the default action (illustrated in Figure 4-13 and Figure 4-14). It allows you to see events for any connections that go through the threat defense in IPS-only mode.

■ This book primarily uses a virtual threat defense to demonstrate configuration steps. However, depending on the threat defense platform you run, you may come across different types of interfaces and model-specific options. For example, if you are running threat defense model 1010, you will find an Ethernet type interface with built-in switch ports (as opposed to the GigabitEthernet type interface on the virtual threat defense). For the interfaces that will participate in an inline set, disable the access mode switch ports (illustrated in Figure 4-5).

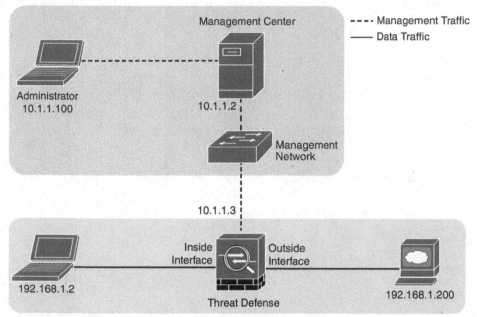

Figure 6-5 *Lab Topology Used in the Configuration Examples in This Chapter*

- On the virtual environment, enable promiscuous mode on all the connected virtual ports of the virtual switch (illustrated in Figure 2-7). It allows a virtual switch to see any frames that traverse through the threat defense virtual appliance.

Key Topic

- Finally, if you plan to enable the hardware bypass feature, read the official hardware installation guide to determine whether your threat defense model and its network module support this feature. The **hardware bypass** functionality of Secure Firewall ensures continuity of traffic flow between an inline interface pair in case of any unplanned failure. You will find the feature very helpful if your threat defense experiences any software reboot, hardware crash, or even a power outage.

Interface Setup

An inline set is a logical group of one or more interface pairs. Before you add an inline set, you must create an inline interface pair and associate the pair with the inline set you want to add. To create an inline set, follow these steps:

Step 1. Navigate to **Devices > Device Management**. A list of all the devices that are registered with management center appears (see Figure 6-6).

Step 2. Click the pencil icon that is next to the threat defense you want to configure. The device editor page appears, showing all the physical interfaces of a threat defense on the Interfaces tab.

Step 3. Select the pencil icon next to each interface that will be part of an inline pair—in this case, the GigabitEthernet0/0 and GigabitEthernet0/1 interfaces (see Figure 6-7).

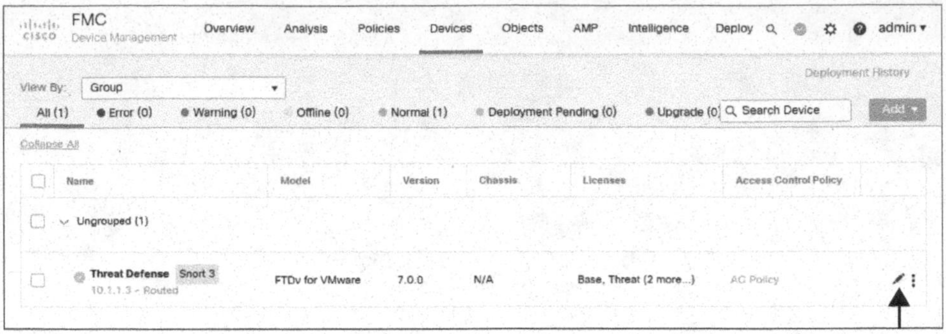

Figure 6-6 *The Device Management Page Displays a List of Managed Devices*

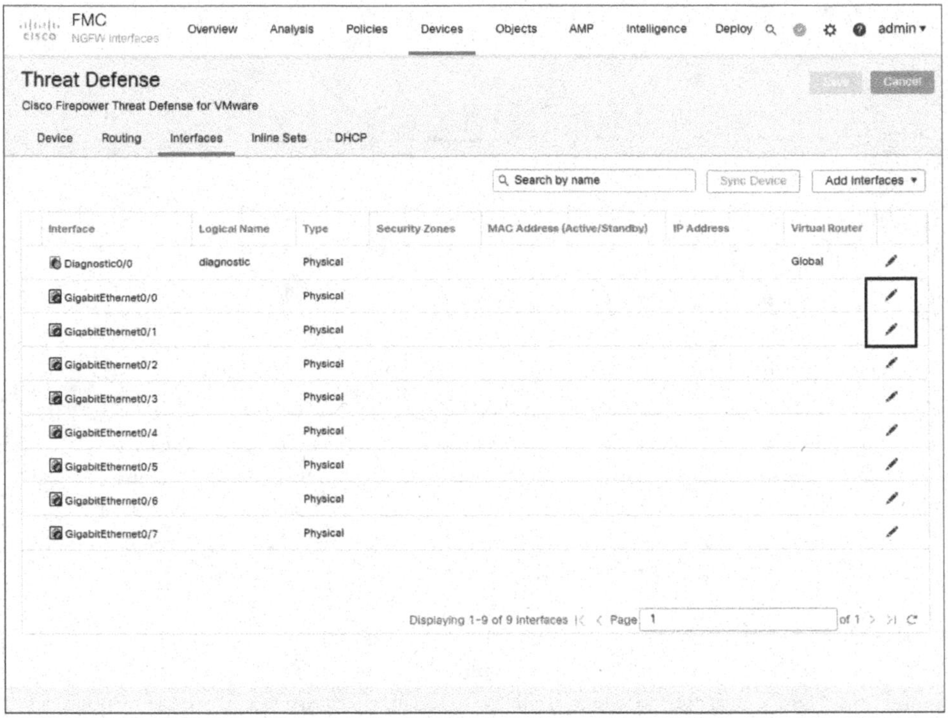

Figure 6-7 *The Interfaces Tab Shows the List of Interfaces on a Threat Defense*

Step 4. In the Edit Physical Interface window, the default value of the Mode drop-down is None. Keep it unchanged, because this setting represents inline mode. Then assign a name to the interface and click the **Enabled** check box to enable it. Assigning an IP address is not necessary for an inline interface. Click **OK** to return to the Interfaces tab.

Figure 6-8 shows the settings on the GigabitEthernet0/0 interface. This example uses the name INSIDE_INTERFACE for the GigabitEthernet0/0 interfaces.

Step 5. Repeat step 4 for the other interface in the inline pair. For example, you can enable the GigabitEthernet0/1 interface with the name OUTSIDE_INTERFACE.

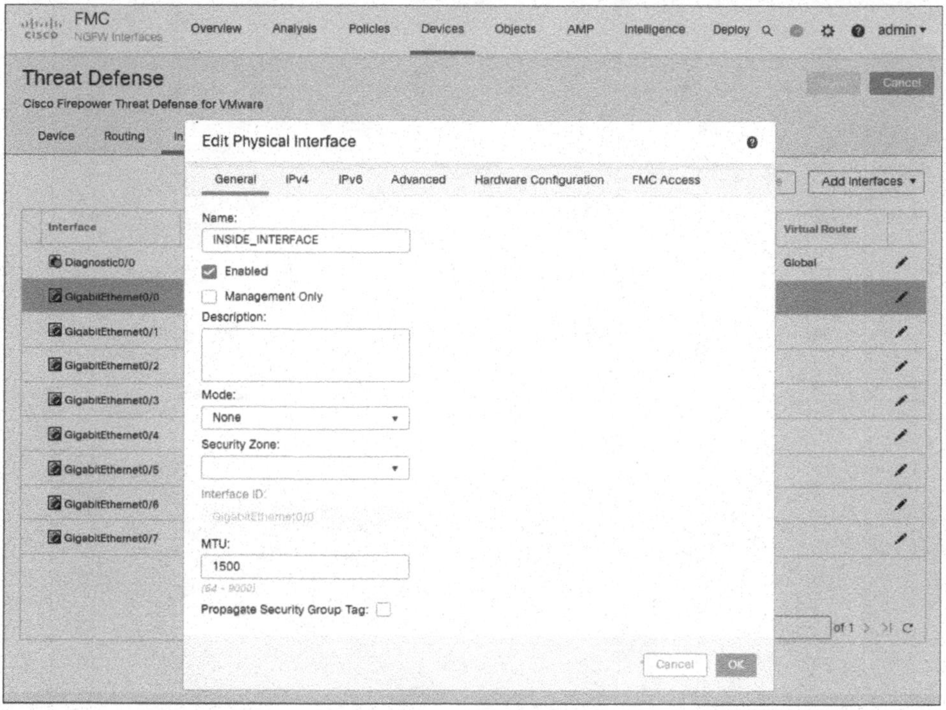

Figure 6-8 *The Edit Physical Interface Window*

Step 6.   After both interfaces are named and enabled, click the **Save** button to save the changes.

Figure 6-9 shows an overview of each interface configuration. Note that the IP address or security zone is not configured. Only the logical interface is necessary for an inline interface.

Inline Set Configuration

Now, begin the second part of the configuration—adding the interface pair to an inline set—by following these steps:

Step 1.   On the Device Management page of your selected threat defense, go to the Inline Sets tab and click the **Add Inline Set** button. The Add Inline Set window appears.

Step 2.   Under the General tab, give a name to the inline set, select an interface pair, and add it to the inline set (see Figure 6-10).

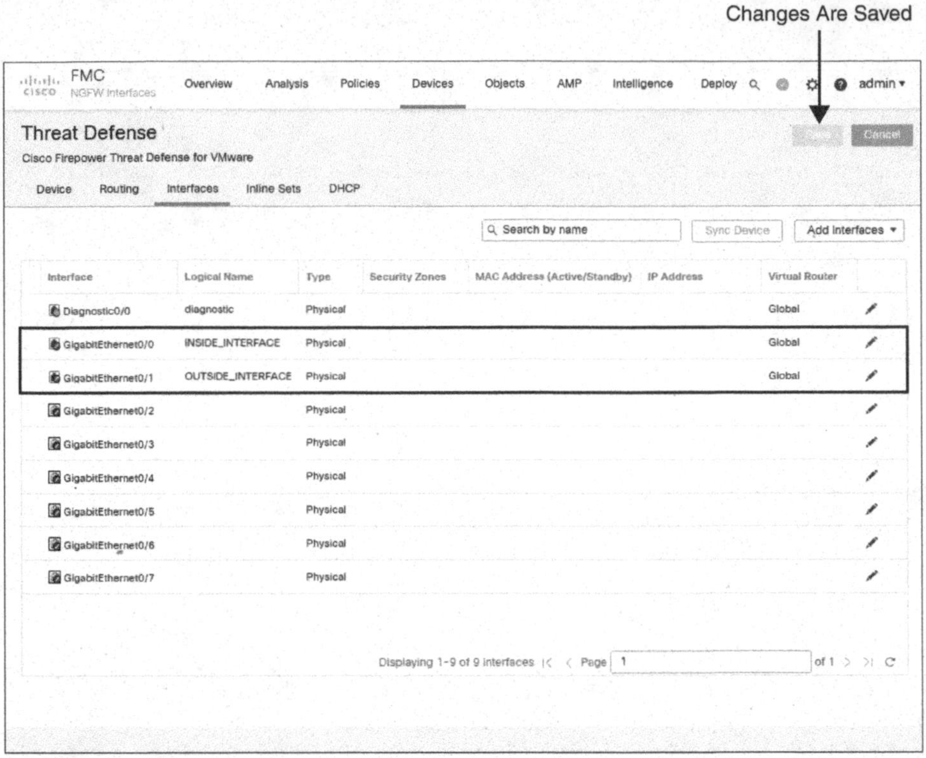

Figure 6-9 *Overview of the Interface Configuration*

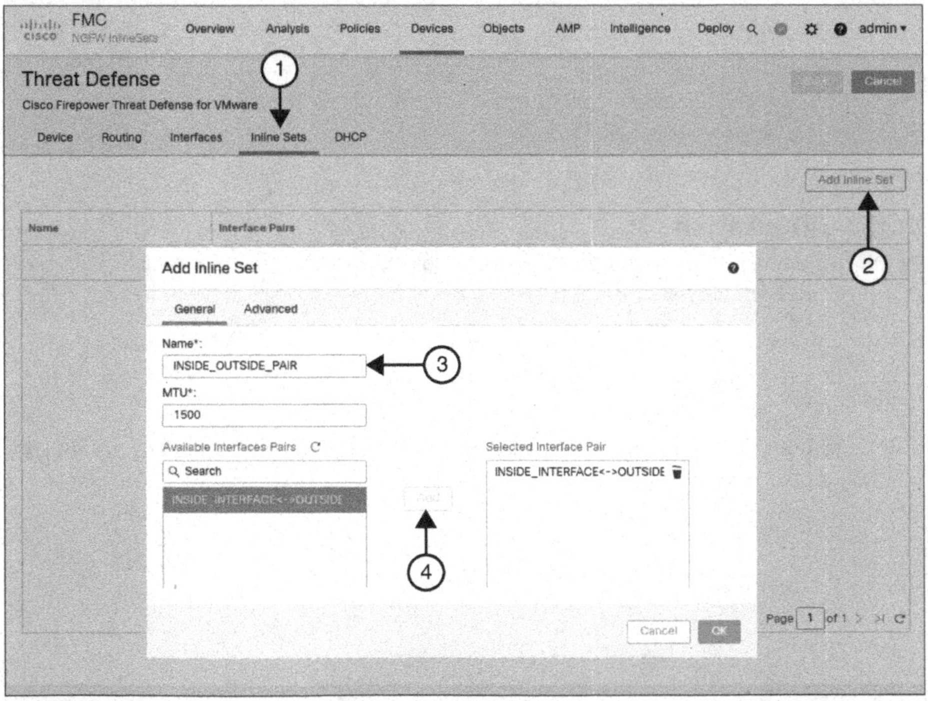

Figure 6-10 *Inline Set Configuration Window*

Step 3. Optionally, under the Advanced tab, enable the **Propagate Link State** and **Snort Fail Open** features (both **Busy** and **Down**), as shown in Figure 6-11. These features allow a threat defense to continue its traffic flow in case of an operational failure, thus avoiding a network outage. Following are some failure scenarios:

- **Propagate Link State:** If one of the links of an inline pair goes down, the second link can stay up and able to receive traffic. However, the threat defense cannot transfer traffic through an interface that has no link. The Propagate Link State feature automatically brings the remaining interface down if one of the interfaces in an inline pair goes down. This feature improves routing convergence time by not sending traffic through a failed link.

- **Snort Fail Open (Busy):** When the interface buffer is full and drops traffic, this option allows a threat defense to pass traffic without inspection.

- **Snort Fail Open (Down):** When Snort—the inspection engine of threat defense—goes down due to a restart, this fail open feature allows a threat defense to continue its traffic flow through the device without inspection.

Step 4. Click **OK**. A warning message appears, warning about the removal of existing settings from the interfaces (see Figure 6-11).

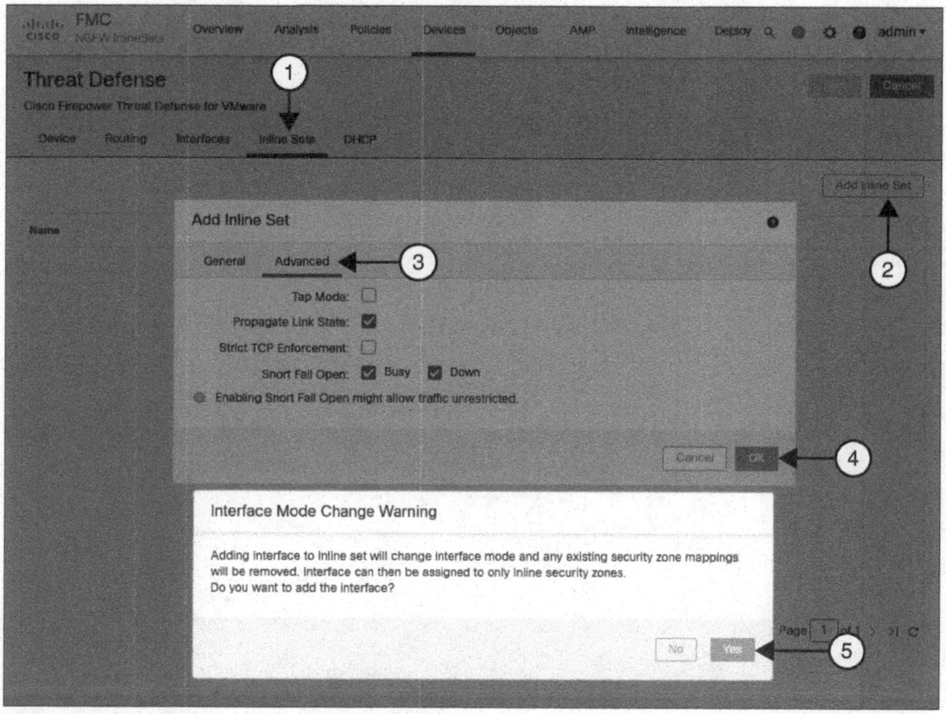

Figure 6-11 *Advanced Settings of Inline Set*

Step 5. Select **Yes** to accept the configuration changes. You return to the Inline Sets page. Click **Save** to save the configurations (see Figure 6-12).

Step 6. Finally, go to **Deploy > Deployment**, select your threat defense, and deploy the configurations to the threat defense.

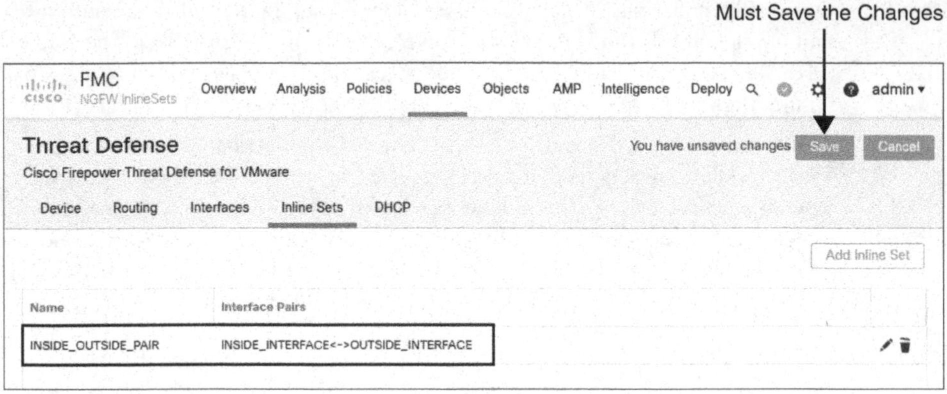

Figure 6-12 *An Inline Set Showing the Selection of Interface Pairs*

Verification

Upon a successful deployment, your inside host should be able to communicate with the outside host, and vice versa. If any connection attempt fails, you can verify the configurations on the GUI and check the status in the CLI.

Figure 6-13 shows the table view of connection events. The events confirm that hosts 192.168.1.2 and 192.168.1.200 are able to communicate through the threat defense.

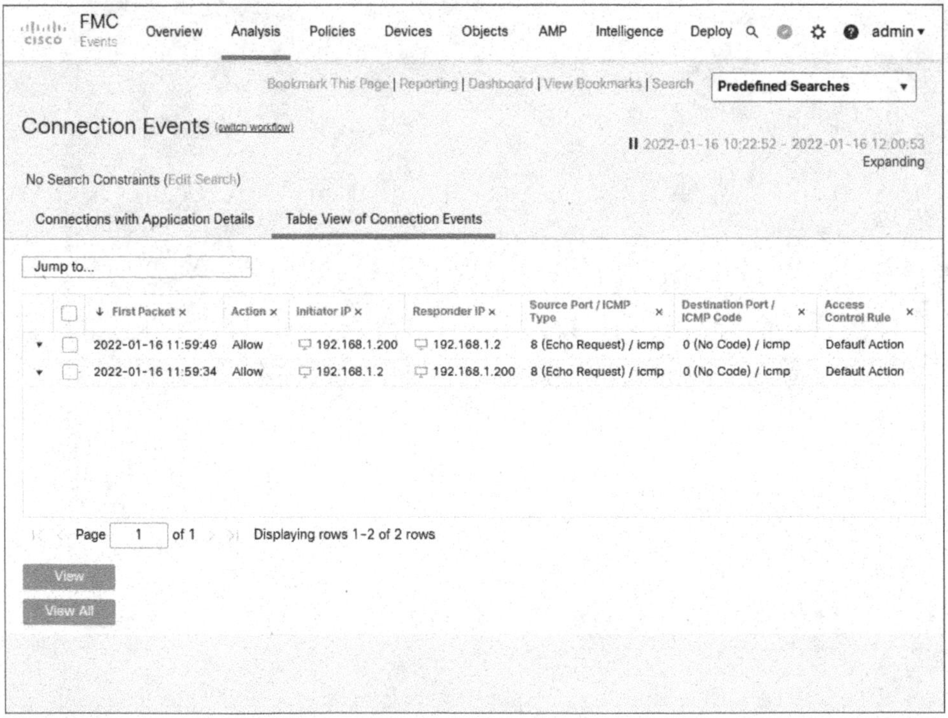

Figure 6-13 *Connection Events for the ICMP Traffic*

Example 6-1 shows the overall status of the available interfaces on a threat defense. It confirms that the GigabitEthernet0/0 and GigabitEthernet0/1 interfaces are up and configured with no IP address. However, it does not confirm whether they are part of an inline pair.

Example 6-1 *Summary of the Threat Defense Interface Status*

```
> show interface ip brief

Interface               IP-Address      OK? Method Status                Protocol
GigabitEthernet0/0      unassigned      YES unset  up                        up
GigabitEthernet0/1      unassigned      YES unset  up                        up
GigabitEthernet0/2      unassigned      YES unset  administratively down up
GigabitEthernet0/3      unassigned      YES unset  administratively down up
GigabitEthernet0/4      unassigned      YES unset  administratively down up
GigabitEthernet0/5      unassigned      YES unset  administratively down up
GigabitEthernet0/6      unassigned      YES unset  administratively down up
GigabitEthernet0/7      unassigned      YES unset  administratively down up
Internal-Control0/0     127.0.1.1       YES unset  up                        up
Internal-Control0/1     unassigned      YES unset  up                        up
Internal-Data0/0        unassigned      YES unset  down                      up
Internal-Data0/0        unassigned      YES unset  up                        up
Internal-Data0/1        169.254.1.1     YES unset  up                        up
Internal-Data0/2        unassigned      YES unset  up                        up
Management0/0           unassigned      YES unset  up                        up
>
```

Example 6-2 confirms that the GigabitEthernet0/0 interface is in inline mode, and it is included in an inline pair called INSIDE_OUTSIDE_PAIR. It also provides detailed statistics about the traffic.

Example 6-2 *Detailed Statistics About the GigabitEthernet0/0 Interface*

```
> show interface GigabitEthernet 0/0

Interface GigabitEthernet0/0 "INSIDE_INTERFACE", is up, line protocol is up
  Hardware is net_vmxnet3, BW 10000 Mbps, DLY 10 usec
        Auto-Duplex(Full-duplex), Auto-Speed(10000 Mbps)
        Input flow control is unsupported, output flow contrBX1_CODE_MIDol is
        unsupported
        MAC address 000c.2916.38a3, MTU 1500
        IPS Interface-Mode: inline, Inline-Set: INSIDE_OUTSIDE_PAIR
        IP address unassigned
        295 packets input, 37845 bytes, 0 no buffer
        Received 0 broadcasts, 0 runts, 0 giants
        0 input errors, 0 CRC, 0 frame, 0 overrun, 0 ignored, 0 abort
        0 pause input, 0 resume input
        0 L2 decode drops
        349 packets output, 63902 bytes, 0 underruns
```

```
        0 pause output, 0 resume output
        0 output errors, 0 collisions, 0 interface resets
        0 late collisions, 0 deferred
        0 input reset drops, 0 output reset drops
        input queue (blocks free curr/low): hardware (0/0)
        output queue (blocks free curr/low): hardware (0/0)
Traffic Statistics for "INSIDE_INTERFACE":
        293 packets input, 33555 bytes
        348 packets output, 59576 bytes
        8 packets dropped
    1 minute input rate 1 pkts/sec,   122 bytes/sec
    1 minute output rate 1 pkts/sec,   250 bytes/sec
    1 minute drop rate, 0 pkts/sec
    5 minute input rate 0 pkts/sec,   0 bytes/sec
    5 minute output rate 0 pkts/sec,   0 bytes/sec
    5 minute drop rate, 0 pkts/sec
>
```

Example 6-3 shows the output of the **show inline-set** command on the threat defense CLI. This command provides various components of an inline set configuration, such as member interfaces of an inline pair, the status of each interface, and advanced settings.

Example 6-3 *Status of the INSIDE_OUTSIDE_PAIR Inline Set*

```
> show inline-set

Inline-set INSIDE_OUTSIDE_PAIR
  Mtu is 1500 bytes
  Fail-open for snort down is on
  Fail-open for snort busy is on
  Tap mode is off
  Propagate-link-state option is on
  hardware-bypass mode is disabled
  Interface-Pair[1]:
    Interface: GigabitEthernet0/0 "INSIDE_INTERFACE"
      Current-Status: UP
    Interface: GigabitEthernet0/1 "OUTSIDE_INTERFACE"
      Current-Status: UP
    Bridge Group ID: 501
>
```

Event Analysis in IPS-Only Mode

If a threat defense is deployed in the dedicated IPS-only mode with an inline interface pair, and a packet matches against an intrusion rule with block action, the management center marks the connection event with Intrusion Block. Let's see how it works on live traffic.

Figure 6-14 shows two different connection events triggered by the same source and destination hosts. In both cases, the intrusion rule 1:718 is enabled to block an incorrect login attempt to a Telnet server. In this example, when the login attempt is successful, the management center simply displays an Allow connection event; however, the next time an incorrect login credential is entered, threat defense blocks that connection attempt, and the management center displays a Block connection event with the marking of Intrusion Block.

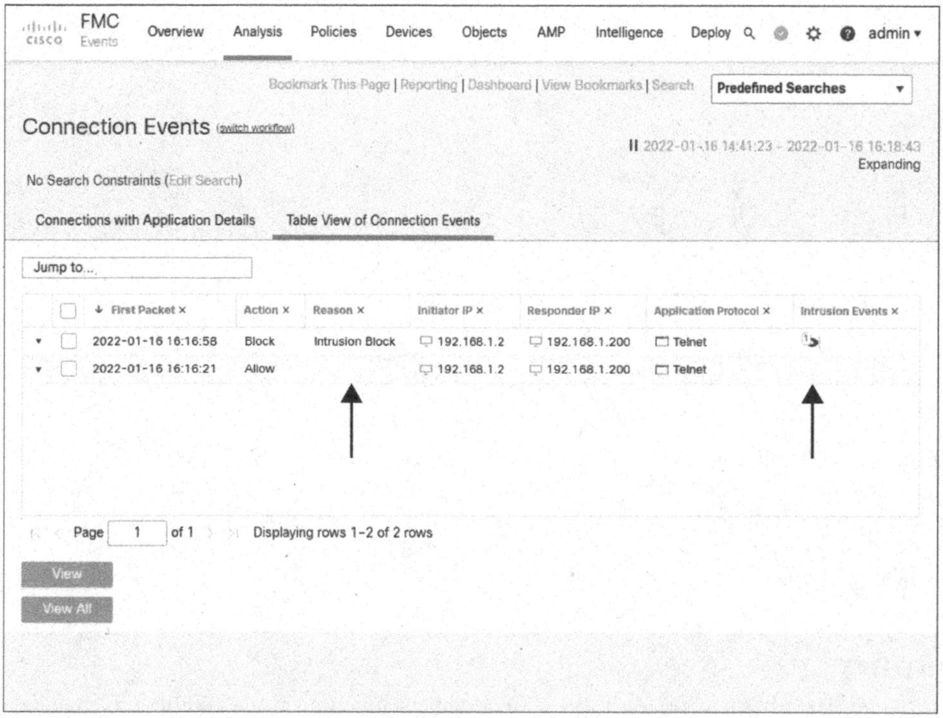

Figure 6-14 *Connection Events in IPS-Only Mode (Customized Table View of Events)*

Figure 6-15 shows the corresponding intrusion event for both Telnet connections, as shown in Figure 6-14. The management center is showing only one intrusion event for two login attempts. This is because the first login attempt is successful, so the threat defense does not find packets that can match the syntax of intrusion rule 1:718. However, the next time the threat defense detects an incorrect login attempt, the connection is blocked and the intrusion rule 1:718 is triggered.

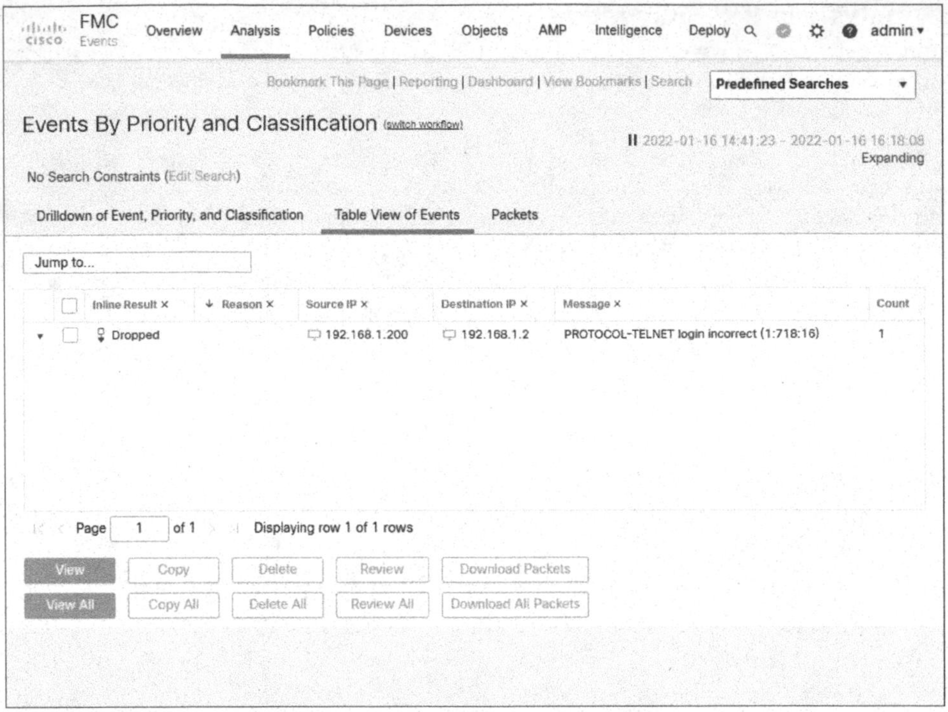

Figure 6-15 *Intrusion Event in IPS-Only Mode (Customized Table View of Events)*

> **NOTE**   Because this chapter focuses on understanding the dedicated IPS-only mode, the primary objective is to demonstrate the behavior of a threat defense when an access control and an intrusion policy are deployed in inline interface mode. The intrusion policy configuration and the intrusion rule 1:718 are described in detail in Chapter 15, "Network Analysis and Intrusion Policies."

Summary

This chapter describes how to configure a threat defense in inline mode and how to enable fault-tolerance features on an inline set. The chapter also describes various command-line tools that you can use to verify the status of an interface, an inline pair, and an inline set.

Exam Preparation Tasks

As mentioned in the section "How to Use This Book" in the Introduction, you have a couple of choices for exam preparation: the exercises here, Chapter 22, "Final Preparation," and the exam simulation questions in the Pearson Test Prep practice test software.

Review All Key Topics

Review the most important topics in this chapter, noted with the Key Topic icon in the outer margin of the page. Table 6-3 lists a reference of these key topics and the page numbers on which each is found.

Key Topic

Table 6-3 Key Topics for Chapter 6

Key Topic Element	Description	Page
Paragraph	Inline mode	123
Paragraph	Passive mode	123
Bullet list	Hardware bypass	127
Bullet list	Propagate Link State	131
Bullet list	Snort Fail Open	131

Memory Tables and Lists

Print a copy of Appendix B, "Memory Tables" (found on the companion website), or at least the section for this chapter, and complete the tables and lists from memory. Appendix C, "Memory Tables Answer Key," also on the companion website, includes completed tables and lists to check your work.

Define Key Terms

Define the following key terms from this chapter, and check your answers in the Glossary:

inline mode, inline set, Propagate Link State, hardware bypass

6

CHAPTER 7

Deployment in Detection-Only Mode

This chapter provides an overview of the following topics:

Detection-Only Mode Essentials: This section describes the key network elements of a detection-only deployment. It delineates the differences between various detection-only modes that are supported by a threat defense.

Best Practices for Detection-Only Deployment: This section provides guidelines for architecting a detection-only mode in different scenarios.

Inline Tap Mode: This section demonstrates how to configure a threat defense in inline tap mode using a management center. Later, it provides some command-line tools that you can use to validate configurations.

Passive Interface Mode: This section demonstrates how to configure a threat defense in passive mode using a management center. It also shares some commands that you can run on the CLI to verify a deployment.

Event Analysis in Detection-Only Mode: This section exhibits the operations of a threat defense in various detection-only modes. You can view the actions of detection-only modes through the connection events displayed on a management center.

The objectives of this chapter are to learn about

- Deployment of threat defense with detection-only capability

- Verification of threat defense configurations in inline tap and passive interface modes

A threat defense can block packets when you deploy it in inline interface mode. However, in some scenarios you might not want to block packets right away but instead want to watch the traffic pattern, determine the effectiveness of your access control rules or intrusion rules on live traffic, and then tune the overall access control policy accordingly. Sometimes, you want to allow and analyze any suspicious activities on your honeypot and identify any potential attackers. Occasionally, an organization's security compliance and business continuity policy demand a passive detection capability rather than inline protection. In this chapter, you learn how to deploy a threat defense to inspect traffic and detect any suspicious activities without dropping the traffic in real time.

"Do I Know This Already?" Quiz

The "Do I Know This Already?" quiz enables you to assess whether you should read this entire chapter thoroughly or jump to the "Exam Preparation Tasks" section. If you are in doubt about your answers to these questions or your own assessment of your knowledge of the topics, read the entire chapter. Table 7-1 lists the major headings in this chapter and their corresponding "Do I Know This Already?" quiz questions. You can find the answers in Appendix A, "Answers to the 'Do I Know This Already?' Quizzes."

Table 7-1 "Do I Know This Already?" Section-to-Question Mapping

Foundation Topics Section	Questions
Detection-Only Mode Essentials	1–4
Best Practices for Detection-Only Deployment	5
Inline Tap Mode	6
Passive Interface Mode	7
Event Analysis in Detection-Only Mode	8

CAUTION The goal of self-assessment is to gauge your mastery of the topics in this chapter. If you do not know the answer to a question or are only partially sure of the answer, you should mark that question as wrong for purposes of the self-assessment. Giving yourself credit for an answer you correctly guess skews your self-assessment results and might provide you with a false sense of security.

1. Which of the following interface modes does not block packets?

   a. Transparent mode

   b. Routed mode

   c. Inline tap mode

   d. All of these answers are correct.

2. Which of the following actions ensures the analysis of maximum traffic when it goes through a threat defense?

   a. Using a SPAN port on a switch.

   b. Deploying a TAP to replicate traffic.

   c. Deploying passive mode instead of inline mode.

   d. Any threat defense model is capable of handling all the traffic and ensures 100 percent detection.

3. Which of the following statements is true?

   a. Passive mode can work with just one interface, whereas an inline set requires at least two interfaces.

   b. An inline interface does not require that port mirroring features, such as a TAP or SPAN port, be available.

    c. Transition between detection-only mode and prevention mode is faster and easier in inline tap mode.

    d. All of these answers are correct.

4. What is the advantage of considering inline tap mode over passive mode?

    a. A threat defense in inline tap mode can handle more traffic than any other modes.

    b. Passive mode cannot block any intrusion attempt.

    c. You can easily transition to the inline mode without touching any physical cables.

    d. Both inline tap and passive modes are the same; there are no administrative differences.

5. An administrator wants to position a threat defense permanently in detection-only mode. What is the best option to consider?

    a. Transparent mode

    b. Inline tap mode

    c. Passive mode

    d. All of these answers are correct.

6. Which of the following commands shows whether an interface is set to inline tap mode?

    a. **show inline-tap**

    b. **show inline-set**

    c. **show interface ip brief**

    d. **show interface inline-tap**

7. If a threat defense interface is configured with passive mode, which of the following commands can help you to determine the passive deployment mode?

    a. **show nameif**

    b. **show interface** *<interface_name>*

    c. **show passive-interface**

    d. **show monitor session**

8. Which of the following settings enable a threat defense to run in detection-only mode?

    a. Interface Mode: **Inline Tap**

        Inspection Mode: **Prevention**

    b. Interface Mode: **Passive**

        Inspection Mode: **Prevention**

    c. Interface Mode: **Inline**

        Inspection Mode: **Detection**

    d. All of the above

Foundation Topics

Detection-Only Mode Essentials

When you consider deploying a threat defense for detection-only purposes, you mainly have two choices: passive mode and inline tap mode. The following sections emphasize the differences between various interface modes and monitoring technologies.

Passive Monitoring Technology

To understand the architecture of a passive deployment, you must be familiar with the underlying technologies, including the following:

- **Promiscuous mode:** Promiscuous mode allows an interface to see any packet in a network segment—even packets that are not aimed at that interface. On a threat defense, when you configure an interface in passive mode, you set the interface into promiscuous mode. This capability enables a threat defense to monitor the network activities without being an active part of a network.

  Figure 7-1 introduces promiscuous mode and SPAN port, which are the technologies used in a threat defense deployed in passive mode.

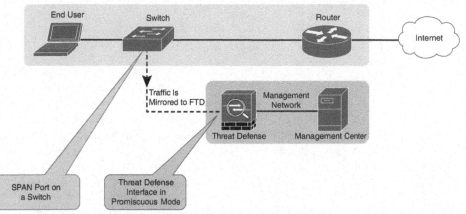

Figure 7-1 *Basic Architecture of a Passive Deployment*

- **SPAN port:** Some switch models can replicate traffic from multiple switch ports and send the copies to a specific switch port. Using that switch port, the switch sends all the replicated traffic to its connected threat defense to monitor the network traffic without being an active part of the traffic flow; this functionality of the switch is known as *port mirroring*. A switch port enabled with the port mirroring feature is known as the **Switched Port Analyzer (SPAN)** port.

  A SPAN port can receive mirrored traffic from the same Layer 2 switch. However, if you want to send the replicated traffic to multiple switches, you can use the **Encapsulated Remote Switched Port Analyzer (ERSPAN)** technology. ERSPAN transports mirrored traffic over a Layer 3 network by encapsulating it using the Generic Routing Encapsulation (GRE) tunneling protocol.

A threat defense supports inspection of both SPAN and ERSPAN traffic. However, the configuration examples in this chapter use only the SPAN port.

Figure 7-2 illustrates the differences between two types of passive deployments using SPAN and ERSPAN ports.

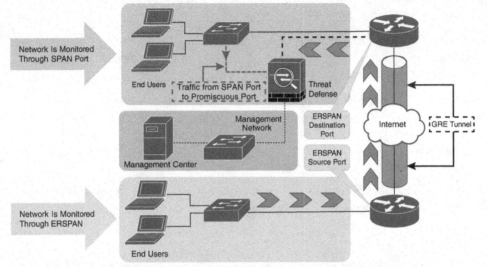

Figure 7-2   *Difference Between a SPAN Port and an ERSPAN Port*

- **TAP:** A TAP is a network device that copies and transfers traffic to another system. Unlike a SPAN port on a switch, which is configured at the software level, a network TAP is dedicated hardware that is designed to replicate and transfer traffic. For an additional cost, a TAP offers numerous advantages over a SPAN port. One of the most important benefits is that a TAP is able to capture and copy all the traffic (including any errors) from a highly utilized network and transfer it to a monitoring device, such as a threat defense, without any packets dropping.

  A SPAN port, in contrast, drops packets if the utilization of a SPAN link exceeds its capacity. In a highly utilized network, if a SPAN port fails to transfer all the traffic from all the switch ports, a threat defense loses the complete visibility of a network and may miss detecting any suspicious activities.

Figure 7-3 shows two types of cabling that a threat defense supports. Both deployments are operational in detection-only mode.

Interface Modes: Inline, Inline Tap, and Passive

In Chapter 6, "IPS-Only Deployment in Inline Mode," you learned about the deployment of a threat defense in inline mode. Inline mode allows a threat defense to block traffic based on the access control and intrusion rules you enable. In contrast, in inline tap mode and in passive mode, if you apply an access control rule or intrusion rule with block action, the threat defense does not actually block the original traffic. It only generates an event and lets the original traffic go through the threat defense.

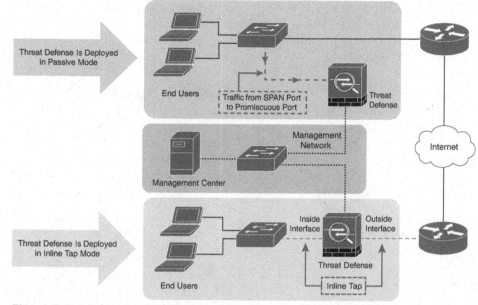

Figure 7-3 *Cabling of Interfaces in Passive Mode and Inline Tap Mode*

From a user standpoint, a block action in both modes—passive and inline tap—has the same effect. For example, if a packet matches an access control rule with block action, it triggers a connection event displaying the block action, while the original packet goes through. Likewise, if a packet matches an intrusion rule with block action, the threat defense lets the traffic go through it, while the management center displays an intrusion event with the Would Have Dropped inline result (demonstrated later in this chapter).

Although the outcomes are the same, the big advantage of inline tap mode over passive mode is the ease of transition to the inline mode, when necessary. The physical cabling of inline mode and inline tap mode is exactly the same. If your threat defense is currently deployed in inline tap mode, and you decide to switch to inline mode to block traffic in real time, you can do so simply by changing a setting in the GUI.

Best Practices for Detection-Only Deployment

Consider the following best practices before you deploy a threat defense in passive mode:

- If your plan is to deploy a threat defense in a detection-only mode so that you could gauge the impact of current security policies without disrupting the traffic flow, you may choose inline tap mode over the traditional passive mode. This allows you to switch to inline mode faster without touching any physical cables.

- If your ultimate plan is to deploy a threat defense in detection-only mode permanently, choose passive mode over inline tap mode to eliminate any chance of traffic interruption due to an accidental outage of the threat defense. Furthermore, depending on the traffic, the inline tap mode configurations can impact the threat defense performance more than the passive mode configurations.

■ If your threat defense is already deployed in inline mode, and you want to test the efficacy of a new intrusion policy, you can simply choose the Detection inspection mode option in that intrusion policy (in older Secure Firewall software, this option is known as Drop When Inline). It enables you to identify and tune any intrusion rules that may generate false positive alerts without changing the interface configurations.

Figure 7-4 displays various ways to enable detection-only modes on a Secure Firewall. Depending on your deployment use case, you can choose any one of them. Describing the images clockwise, image A shows the selection of passive mode in the interface configuration window. Image B shows the selection of inline tap mode for an inline pair. Image C shows the selection of Detection mode during the creation of a new intrusion policy. Image D shows the selection of Detection mode within an already created intrusion policy.

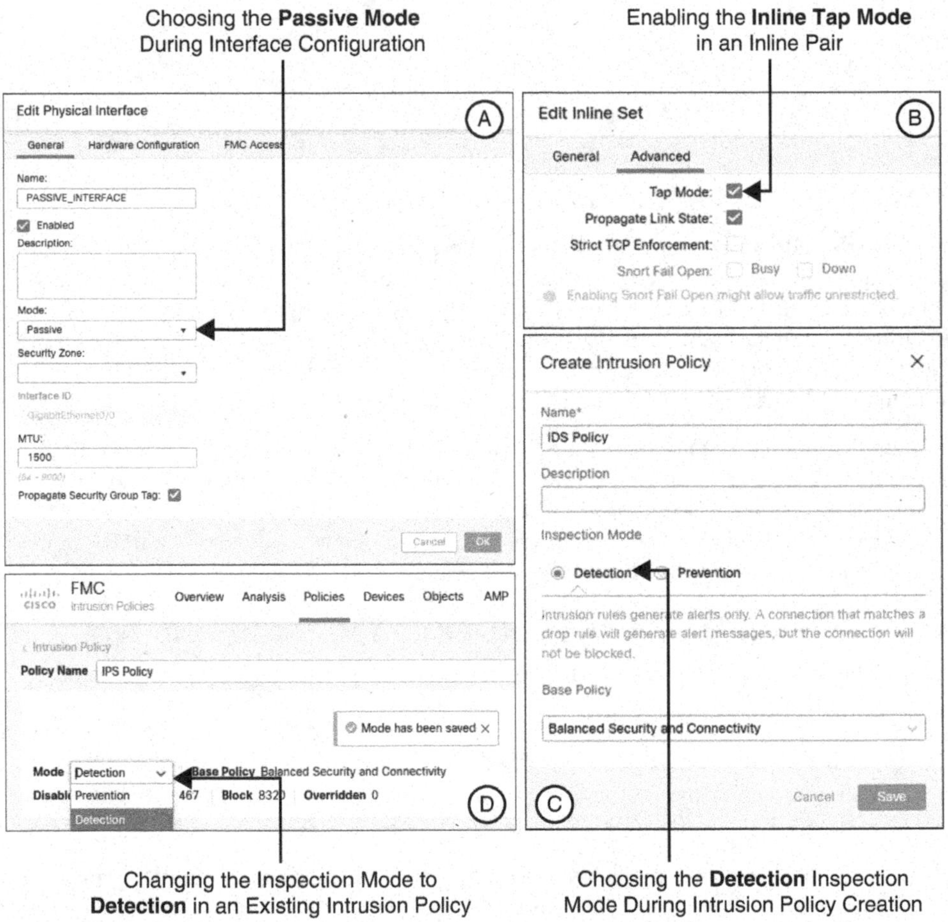

Figure 7-4 *Various Ways to Enable Detection-Only Mode on a Secure Firewall*

■ If the utilization of a network is medium to high, use a TAP instead of a SPAN port to mirror traffic.

■ Although a threat defense in passive mode cannot block traffic, you should still select a threat defense model after carefully reviewing the hardware specifications and your throughput requirements. This ensures that the threat defense can analyze all the traffic without any packet drop.

Inline Tap Mode

Inline tap mode configurations are similar to the regular inline mode setup, which are detailed in the previous chapter. Broadly speaking, you will need to perform the following tasks to configure the threat defense interfaces in inline tap mode:

1. Configure general settings of interfaces.
2. Build an inline pair (General setting).
3. Enable inline tap (Advanced setting).
4. Save the configuration changes.
5. Deploy the configurations to threat defense.

Configuration of Inline Tap Mode

Inline tap mode comes as an add-on feature to an existing inline set. This section assumes your threat defense is currently running in inline interface mode, and discusses only the additional steps to change its interface mode from inline to inline tap mode.

To enable inline tap mode, follow these steps:

Step 1. Log in to the management center GUI.

Step 2. Navigate to **Devices > Device Management**. A list of managed threat defense devices appears (see Figure 7-5).

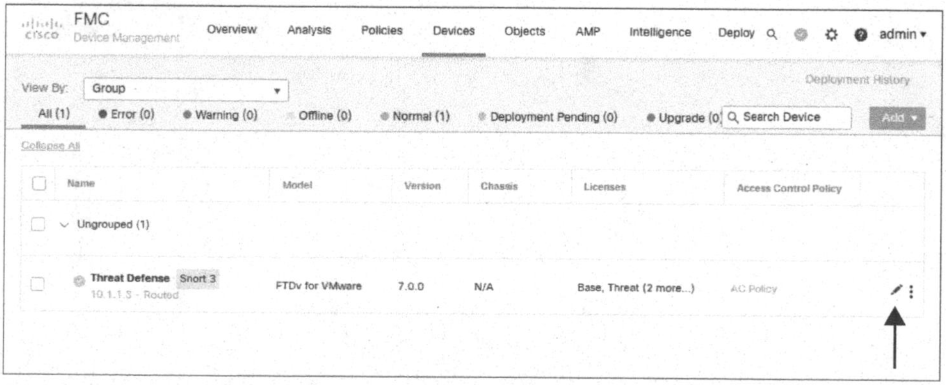

Figure 7-5 *List of Threat Defense Devices Managed by This Management Center*

Step 3. Click the pencil icon next to the threat defense where you want to enable inline tap mode. The device editor page appears.

Step 4. Select the **Inline Sets** tab. If you configured an inline interface pair in Chapter 6, it should appear here (see Figure 7-6).

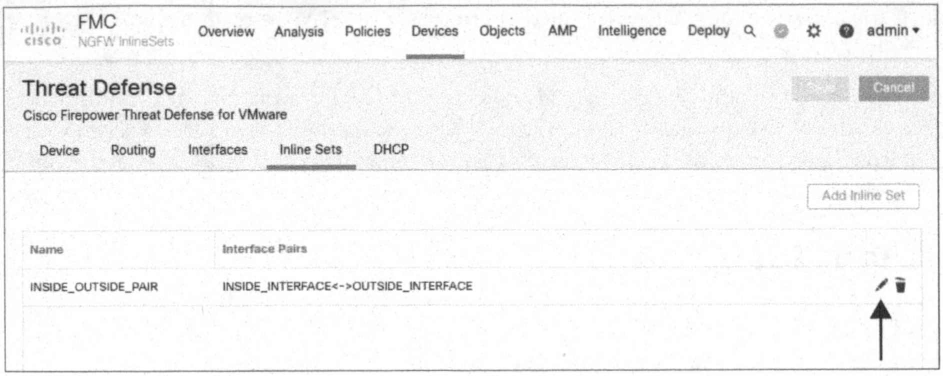

Figure 7-6 *List of Interface Pairs Shown on the Inline Sets Tab*

Step 5. Click the pencil icon next to the inline interface pair to modify the existing settings. The Edit Inline Set window appears.

Step 6. Select the **Advanced** tab.

Step 7. Enable the **Tap Mode** check box (see Figure 7-7).

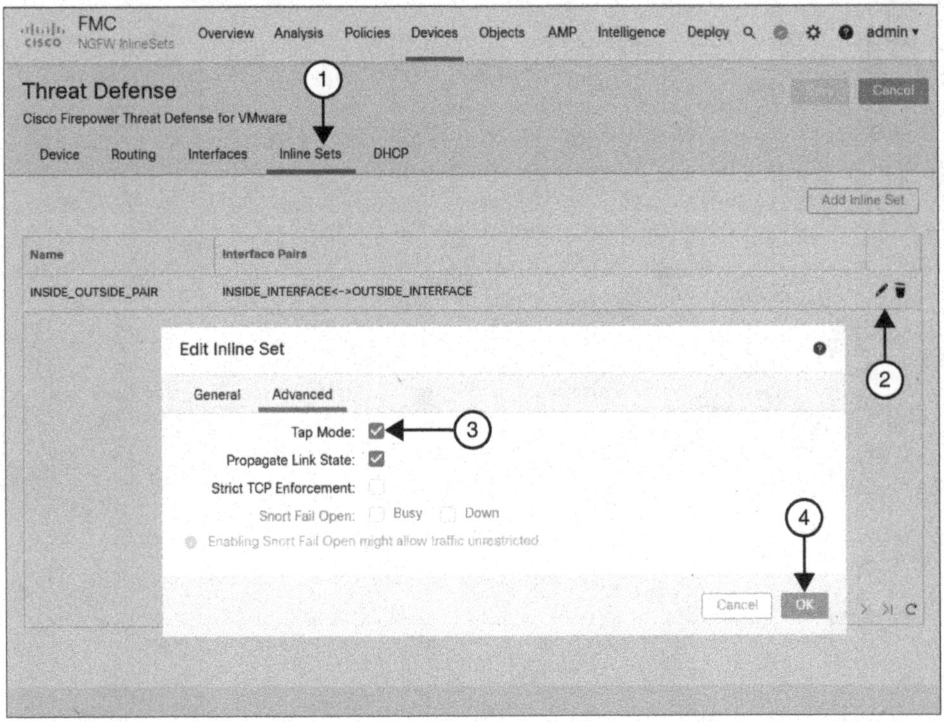

Figure 7-7 *Advanced Settings for an Inline Set Configuration*

Step 8. Click **OK** to return to the Inline Sets tab. A warning message appears (see Figure 7-8) to warn about the removal of existing settings from the interfaces.

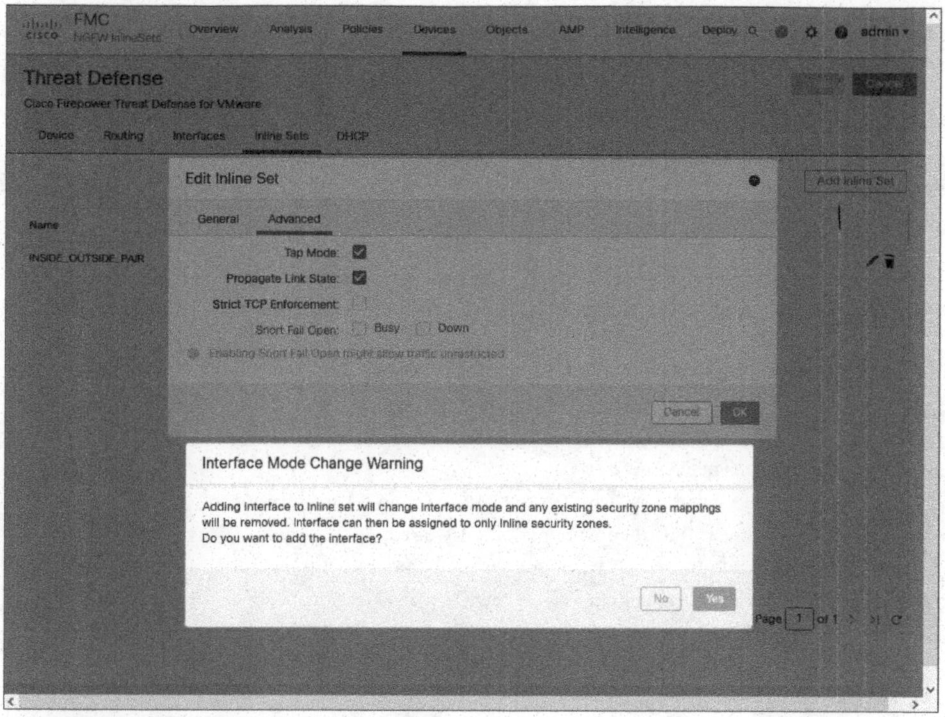

Figure 7-8 *Interface Mode Change Warning*

Step 9.   Click **Save** to save the settings.

Step 10. Navigate to **Deploy > Deployment** to deploy the configurations to the threat defense.

Verification of Inline Tap Configuration

You can use the command-line interface to verify the inline tap configuration and interface status. The CLI commands are helpful to investigate the root cause of any connectivity issues.

Example 7-1 confirms that inline tap mode is enabled on the interface set. The command output also shows the detailed configuration settings of an inline set, such as member interfaces of an inline pair, their status, and advanced settings.

Example 7-1 *Tap Mode Is Enabled on the INSIDE_OUTSIDE_PAIR Inline Set*

```
> show inline-set

Inline-set INSIDE_OUTSIDE_PAIR
  Mtu is 1500 bytes
  Fail-open for snort down is off
  Fail-open for snort busy is off
  Tap mode is on
  Propagate-link-state option is on
```

```
hardware-bypass mode is disabled
Interface-Pair[1]:
  Interface: GigabitEthernet0/0 "INSIDE_INTERFACE"
    Current-Status: UP
  Interface: GigabitEthernet0/1 "OUTSIDE_INTERFACE"
    Current-Status: UP
  Bridge Group ID: 507
>
```

Example 7-2 demonstrates that the GigabitEthernet 0/0 and GigabitEthernet 0/1 interfaces are in inline tap mode. Both interfaces are part of the inline pair called INSIDE_OUTSIDE_PAIR. The command output also provides detailed statistics about the packet drops.

Example 7-2 *Status of Each Interface of an Inline Pair*

```
> show interface GigabitEthernet 0/0
Interface GigabitEthernet0/0 "INSIDE_INTERFACE", is up, line protocol is up
  Hardware is net_vmxnet3, BW 10000 Mbps, DLY 10 usec
        Auto-Duplex(Full-duplex), Auto-Speed(10000 Mbps)
        Input flow control is unsupported, output flow control is unsupported
        MAC address 000c.2916.38a3, MTU 1500
        IPS Interface-Mode: inline-tap, Inline-Set: INSIDE_OUTSIDE_PAIR
        IP address unassigned
        368 packets input, 50414 bytes, 0 no buffer
        Received 0 broadcasts, 0 runts, 0 giants
        0 input errors, 0 CRC, 0 frame, 0 overrun, 0 ignored, 0 abort
        0 pause input, 0 resume input
        0 L2 decode drops
        50 packets output, 6123 bytes, 0 underruns
        0 pause output, 0 resume output
        0 output errors, 0 collisions, 0 interface resets
        0 late collisions, 0 deferred
        0 input reset drops, 0 output reset drops
        input queue (blocks free curr/low): hardware (0/0)
        output queue (blocks free curr/low): hardware (0/0)
  Traffic Statistics for "INSIDE_INTERFACE":
        185 packets input, 20589 bytes
        0 packets output, 0 bytes
        35 packets dropped
      1 minute input rate 0 pkts/sec,  2 bytes/sec
      1 minute output rate 0 pkts/sec,  0 bytes/sec
      1 minute drop rate, 0 pkts/sec
      5 minute input rate 0 pkts/sec,  41 bytes/sec
      5 minute output rate 0 pkts/sec,  0 bytes/sec
      5 minute drop rate, 0 pkts/sec
>
```

```
> show interface GigabitEthernet 0/1
Interface GigabitEthernet0/1 "OUTSIDE_INTERFACE", is up, line protocol is up
  Hardware is net_vmxnet3, BW 10000 Mbps, DLY 10 usec
        Auto-Duplex(Full-duplex), Auto-Speed(10000 Mbps)
        Input flow control is unsupported, output flow control is unsupported
        MAC address 000c.2916.38ad, MTU 1500
        IPS Interface-Mode: inline-tap, Inline-Set: INSIDE_OUTSIDE_PAIR
        IP address unassigned
        50 packets input, 6143 bytes, 0 no buffer
        Received 0 broadcasts, 0 runts, 0 giants
        0 input errors, 0 CRC, 0 frame, 0 overrun, 0 ignored, 0 abort
        0 pause input, 0 resume input
        0 L2 decode drops
        346 packets output, 48092 bytes, 0 underruns
        0 pause output, 0 resume output
        0 output errors, 0 collisions, 0 interface resets
        0 late collisions, 0 deferred
        0 input reset drops, 0 outputreset drops
        input queue (blocks free curr/low): hardware (0/0)
        output queue (blocks free curr/low): hardware (0/0)
  Traffic Statistics for "OUTSIDE_INTERFACE":
        48 packets input, 5331 bytes
        0 packets output, 0 bytes
        27 packets dropped
      1 minute input rate 0 pkts/sec,  0 bytes/sec
      1 minute output rate 0 pkts/sec,  0 bytes/sec
      1 minute drop rate, 0 pkts/sec
      5 minute input rate 0 pkts/sec,  17 bytes/sec
      5 minute output rate 0 pkts/sec,  0 bytes/sec
      5 minute drop rate, 0 pkts/sec
  >
```

Passive Interface Mode

Configuration of a passive interface is much simpler than the configuration of an inline set. You can use just one interface to receive traffic from a mirror port. An egress interface is not necessary because a threat defense does not forward traffic in passive mode.

Configuration of Passive Interface Mode

A threat defense supports both SPAN and ERSPAN ports, but the ports on a switch or router require additional configurations. You can also deploy a plug-and-play TAP that can mirror traffic without any additional software configuration.

The following section details the steps to connect a threat defense passive interface with a SPAN port on a switch—one of the most common port mirroring options.

Configuring Passive Interface Mode on a Threat Defense

To configure a passive interface on a threat defense, follow these steps:

Step 1. Log in to the management center GUI.

Step 2. Navigate to **Devices > Device Management**. A list of managed devices appears.

Step 3. Click the pencil icon next to the device name where you want to enable the passive interface mode. The device editor page appears.

> **NOTE** For passive interface configuration, if you want to use the same interfaces that you used in the previous exercises to configure inline mode or inline tap mode, you can do so by removing the existing inline set from the Inline Sets tab.

Step 4. On the Interfaces tab, select an interface that will function in promiscuous mode. The interface connects to a SPAN port on a switch. The Edit Physical Interface window appears. Figure 7-9 shows the configuration of Gigabit Ethernet 0/0 interface as a passive interface.

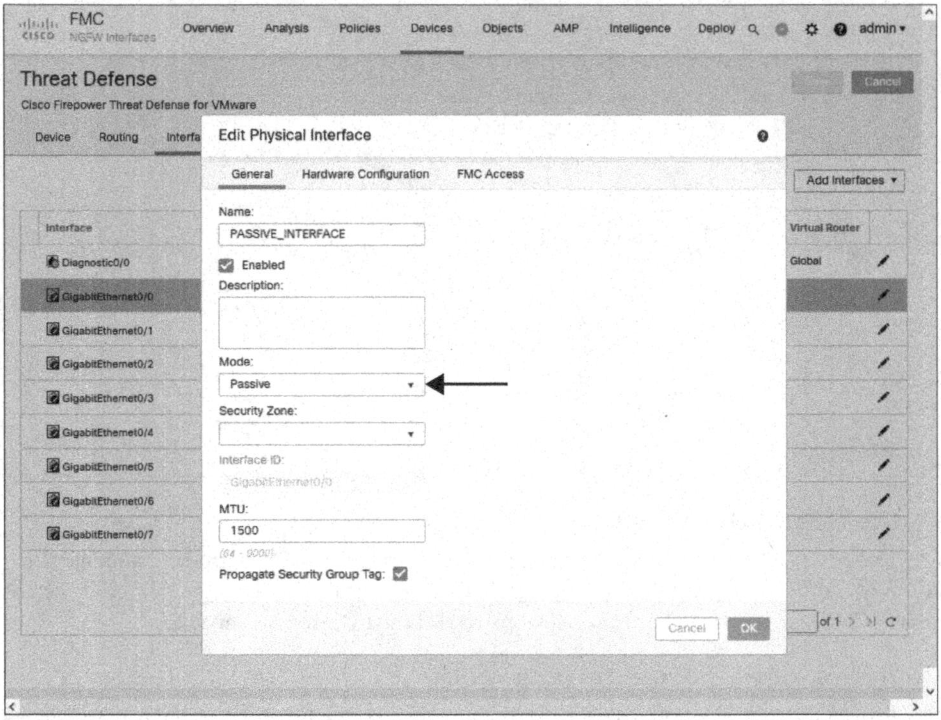

Figure 7-9 *Configuration of a Passive Interface*

Step 5. Give the interface a name and select the **Enabled** check box.

Step 6. From the Mode drop-down, select **Passive**.

Step 7. Click **OK** to return to the device editor page.

Step 8. Click **Save** to save the configuration.

Figure 7-10 shows an overview of the threat defense interfaces. Note that GigabitEthernet 0/0 is configured in passive mode. No IP address or security zone is associated with it because they are not required for a passive interface. The inline settings on GigabitEthernet 0/1 are also removed.

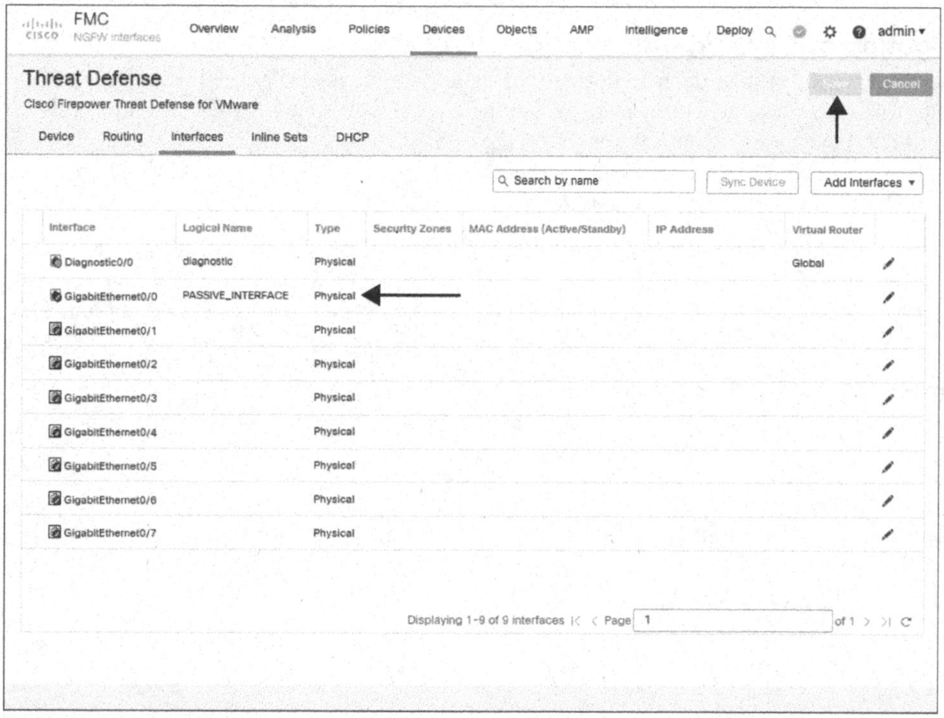

Figure 7-10 *Overview of Threat Defense Interface Configurations*

Step 9. Navigate to **Deploy > Deployment** to deploy the configurations to the threat defense.

Configuring a SPAN Port on a Switch

If you are using a Cisco switch to transmit mirrored traffic to a threat defense, you have to define the source ports (the ports from which the traffic is copied) and a destination port (the port that sends duplicated traffic to a threat defense).

Example 7-3 shows the setup of a SPAN port on a Cisco switch. According to the following configuration, this switch receives traffic on the GigabitEthernet0/1 and GigabitEthernet0/2 interfaces, duplicates them, and retransmits the duplicated traffic through the GigabitEthernet0/8 interface.

Example 7-3 *Essential Commands to Configure a SPAN Port*

```
Switch(config)# monitor session 1 source interface gigabitEthernet 0/1
Switch(config)# monitor session 1 source interface gigabitEthernet 0/2

Switch(config)# monitor session 1 destination interface g0/8
```

Verification of Passive Interface Configuration

In passive mode, a threat defense does not block any traffic regardless of the action you assign to a rule; it just generates events when there are matches against rule conditions. If you find a passive deployment is not triggering desired events, you need to check both devices—the threat defense and switch. The following examples demonstrate some commands that you run during investigation.

Example 7-4 offers two useful commands that you can run on a threat defense. First, enter the **show nameif** command to determine the active interfaces. Then you can run the **show interface** command with the interface to identify the interface status, mode, traffic statistics, and so on.

Example 7-4 *Verifying a Passive Interface*

```
> show nameif
Interface                   Name                        Security
GigabitEthernet0/0          PASSIVE_INTERFACE           0
Management0/0               diagnostic                  0
>
> show interface GigabitEthernet 0/0
Interface GigabitEthernet0/0 "PASSIVE_INTERFACE", is up, line protocol is up
  Hardware is net_vmxnet3, BW 10000 Mbps, DLY 10 usec
        Auto-Duplex(Full-duplex), Auto-Speed(10000 Mbps)
        Input flow control is unsupported, output flow control is unsupported
        MAC address 000c.2916.38a3, MTU 1500
        IPS Interface-Mode: passive
        IP address unassigned
        379 packets input, 51238 bytes, 0 no buffer
        Received 0 broadcasts, 0 runts, 0 giants
        0 input errors, 0 CRC, 0 frame, 0 overrun, 0 ignored, 0 abort
        0 pause input, 0 resume input
        0 L2 decode drops
        55 packets output, 6689 bytes, 0 underruns
        0 pause output, 0 resume output
        0 output errors, 0 collisions, 0 interface resets
        0 late collisions, 0 deferred
        0 input reset drops, 0 output reset drops
        input queue (blocks free curr/low): hardware (0/0)
        output queue (blocks free curr/low): hardware (0/0)
```

```
Traffic Statistics for "PASSIVE_INTERFACE":
      9 packets input, 504 bytes
      0 packets output, 0 bytes
      2 packets dropped
   1 minute input rate 0 pkts/sec,  0 bytes/sec
   1 minute output rate 0 pkts/sec,  0 bytes/sec
   1 minute drop rate, 0 pkts/sec
   5 minute input rate 0 pkts/sec,  0 bytes/sec
   5 minute output rate 0 pkts/sec,  0 bytes/sec
   5 minute drop rate, 0 pkts/sec
>
```

Example 7-5 provides two useful commands to confirm the SPAN port status on a switch.

Example 7-5 *Configuring and Verifying a SPAN Port*

```
Switch# show running-config | include monitor
monitor session 1 source interface Gi0/1 - 2
monitor session 1 destination interface Gi0/8
Switch#



Switch# show monitor session 1
Session 1
---------
Type                 : Local Session
Source Ports         :
   Both              : Gi0/1-2
Destination Ports    : Gi0/8
   Encapsulation     : Native
        Ingress      : Disabled

Switch#
```

Event Analysis in Detection-Only Mode

In Chapter 6, you saw how a blocked intrusion attempt is recorded in the management center when its threat defense is deployed in inline interface mode: an intrusion event appeared with a Dropped inline result, and the associated connection event displayed its reason as Intrusion Block. (See the "Event Analysis in IPS-Only Mode" section in Chapter 6.)

Now, in a detection-only mode, the threat defense can operate differently for the same intrusion policy: any matching packet is allowed to go through the threat defense because of its deployment mode. However, the management center marks the intrusion event with the Would Have Dropped inline result, and indicates the reason as Interface in Passive or Tap Mode (see Figure 7-11.) A management center with an older software version may display black and gray arrows to indicate IPS-only and detection-only modes, respectively.

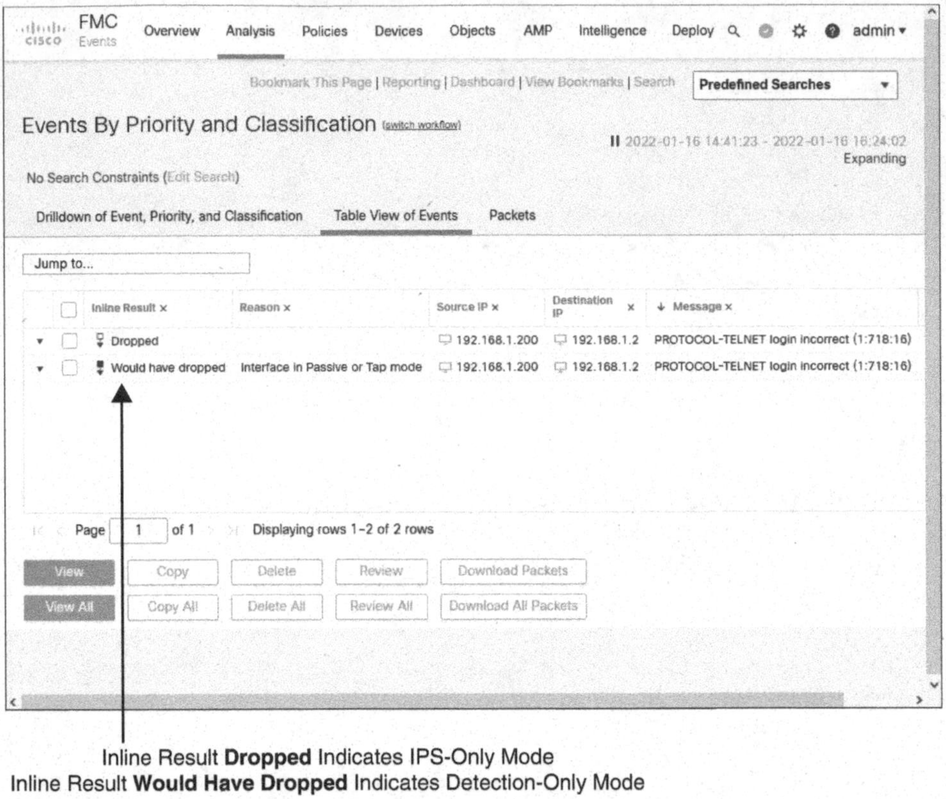

Inline Result **Dropped** Indicates IPS-Only Mode
Inline Result **Would Have Dropped** Indicates Detection-Only Mode

Figure 7-11 *Intrusion Events in IPS-Only and Detection-Only Modes (Customized Table View of Events)*

A threat defense can operate in a detection-only mode when its interfaces are set to inline tap or passive mode (regardless of the inspection mode of the intrusion policy). A threat defense with inline interface mode can also operate in detection-only mode if its intrusion policy is configured with Detection inspection mode. In older Secure Firewall software, this option is known as Drop When Inline. This option enables you to test and tune an intrusion policy without modifying the interface mode configurations. The intrusion policy configuration is described in detail in Chapter 15, "Network Analysis and Intrusion Policies."

Summary

This chapter explains the configuration of different detection-only modes of a threat defense, such as passive mode and inline tap mode. It also shows various commands that you can use to determine the status of interfaces and traffic.

Exam Preparation Tasks

As mentioned in the section "How to Use This Book" in the Introduction, you have a couple of choices for exam preparation: the exercises here, Chapter 22, "Final Preparation," and the exam simulation questions in the Pearson Test Prep practice test software.

Review All Key Topics

Review the most important topics in this chapter, noted with the Key Topic icon in the outer margin of the page. Table 7-2 lists a reference of these key topics and the page numbers on which each is found.

Key Topic

Table 7-2   Key Topics for Chapter 7

Key Topic Element	Description	Page
List	Underlying technologies of passive deployment	141
Paragraph	Inline versus inline tap	142
Paragraph	Inline tap versus passive mode	143

Complete Tables and Lists from Memory

There are no Memory Tables or Lists in this chapter.

Define Key Terms

Define the following key terms from this chapter, and check your answers in the Glossary:

promiscuous mode, Switched Port Analyzer (SPAN), Encapsulated Remote Switched Port Analyzer (ERSPAN), TAP

7

## CHAPTER 8

Capturing Traffic for Advanced Analysis

This chapter provides an overview of the following topics:

Packet Capture Essentials: This section illustrates the threat defense security engines and their components. The illustrations help you understand the root cause of a packet drop by the threat defense.

Best Practices for Capturing Traffic: In this section, you learn some of the best practices for keeping system performance at the optimal level while capturing traffic.

Capturing of Packets Using Secure Firewall: This section demonstrates the process of capturing traffic from the data interfaces of a threat defense using the management center GUI.

The objectives of this chapter are to learn about

- The packet capture utility on the management center GUI

- Capturing live traffic from the threat defense data interfaces

- The differences between the packet capture and packet tracer tools

After configuring a threat defense in the desired deployment mode, you start creating various security policies. When the policies are deployed, you expect that only the desired traffic will go through the threat defense. However, if your deployment exhibits any connectivity issues, you should first verify your configurations. When you are unable to find any issues with the configurations, you might want to capture live traffic and analyze it. Capturing traffic is an advanced but critical step in investigating any connectivity issues in a network. This chapter discusses the processes to capture live traffic from the data interfaces of a threat defense.

"Do I Know This Already?" Quiz

The "Do I Know This Already?" quiz enables you to assess whether you should read this entire chapter thoroughly or jump to the "Exam Preparation Tasks" section. If you are in doubt about your answers to these questions or your own assessment of your knowledge of the topics, read the entire chapter. Table 8-1 lists the major headings in this chapter and their corresponding "Do I Know This Already?" quiz questions. You can find the answers in Appendix A, "Answers to the 'Do I Know This Already?' Quizzes."

Table 8-1   "Do I Know This Already?" Section-to-Question Mapping

Foundation Topics Section	Questions
Packet Capture Essentials	1
Best Practices for Capturing Traffic	2
Capturing of Packets Using Secure Firewall	3, 4

CAUTION   The goal of self-assessment is to gauge your mastery of the topics in this chapter. If you do not know the answer to a question or are only partially sure of the answer, you should mark that question as wrong for purposes of the self-assessment. Giving yourself credit for an answer you correctly guess skews your self-assessment results and might provide you with a false sense of security.

1. Which engine is responsible for analyzing traffic in a threat defense?

   a. ASA engine.

   b. Snort engine.

   c. Lina engine.

   d. All of these answers are correct.

2. Which of the following statements is true?

   a. Capturing traffic can increase the CPU utilization of a threat defense.

   b. A threat defense is designed to capture traffic only for troubleshooting purposes.

   c. You can use the management center GUI to capture traffic from the threat defense interfaces.

   d. All of these answers are correct.

3. What does the Stop When Full option do?

   a. It stops a threat defense from further packet inspection.

   b. It stops a threat defense from capturing traffic when the database is full.

   c. It stops a threat defense from capturing traffic when the buffer is full.

   d. It stops a threat defense from filling up the buffer when excessive traffic is in interfaces.

4. Which of the following statements is true about captured packets?

   a. You can store captured packets into a file directly using the management center.

   b. You can store the traces of captured packets in a cleartext format.

   c. Packets that are seen live by the threat defense interfaces can be viewed offline.

   d. All of these answers are correct.

Foundation Topics

Packet Capture Essentials

Threat defense software is a unified image that converges the features of a traditional Cisco ASA firewall, Snort-based IDS/IPS, and next-generation security features, including various advanced security technologies, such as network discovery, security intelligence, application control, file control, and an intrusion detection and prevention system. When a threat defense blocks the traversal of a packet from the ingress to the egress interface, it could happen due to any of these security components. Therefore, if two hosts experience any connectivity issues while sending traffic through a threat defense, it is essential to analyze packets to determine the root cause of the issue.

Figure 8-1 illustrates the various reasons for a packet drop by a threat defense.

After receiving packets on the ingress interface, a threat defense analyzes them based on all the enabled security policies. After the packets pass the security checks, the threat defense sends them to its egress interface. Primarily, two types of security engines analyze the packets throughout this process. They are the Snort engine and the firewall engine (see Figure 8-2 and Figure 8-3). So, when a packet is dropped by the threat defense, how could you determine the engine or the component that is responsible for that drop? The packet analysis can be a great troubleshooting step in this case.

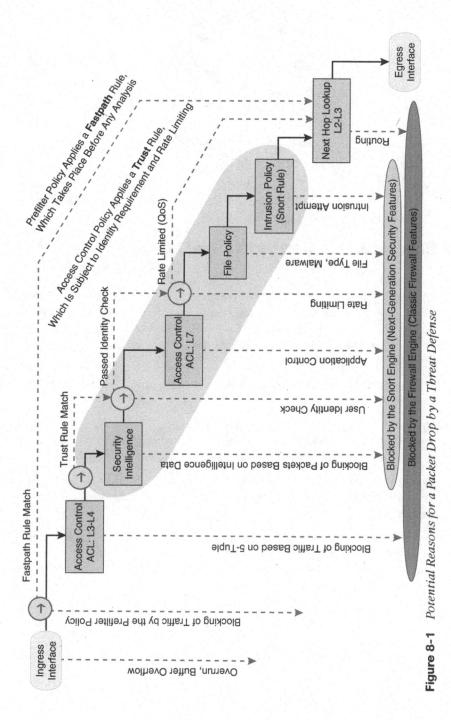

Figure 8-1   *Potential Reasons for a Packet Drop by a Threat Defense*

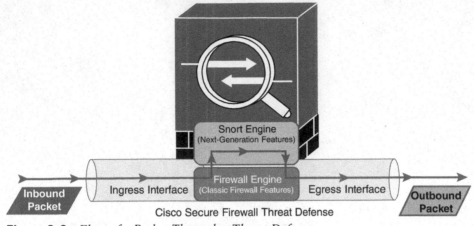

Figure 8-2   *Flow of a Packet Through a Threat Defense*

Best Practices for Capturing Traffic

Before you consider capturing traffic, make sure you understand the following:

- The primary objective of a threat defense is not to capture live traffic all the time. Besides controlling and inspecting traffic, a threat defense supports capturing live traffic only for troubleshooting purposes. If you need to capture traffic for a long period, you should find a dedicated system designed for this purpose.

- Capturing live traffic on a production system can increase the CPU utilization; hence, it can degrade system performance. When necessary, capture traffic during a maintenance window.

- Use specific packet filtering criteria to capture traffic. For example, define the source host and destination host precisely instead of including a broader subnet. Similarly, specify your desired protocol name instead of capturing traffic of all protocols.

- Do not turn on the capture process to capture packets continuously because it can fill the buffer quickly. Use the Stop When Full feature to limit the number of packets to capture.

- Use the management center GUI to capture traffic. Although the threat defense CLI allows you to capture traffic, the GUI offers a robust and easy-to-use web-based tool to capture traffic from any data interfaces of a threat defense. You can use the management center GUI to define packet filtering criteria, to capture traffic, to manage the capture process, and to save the captured packets into a **PCAP file**.

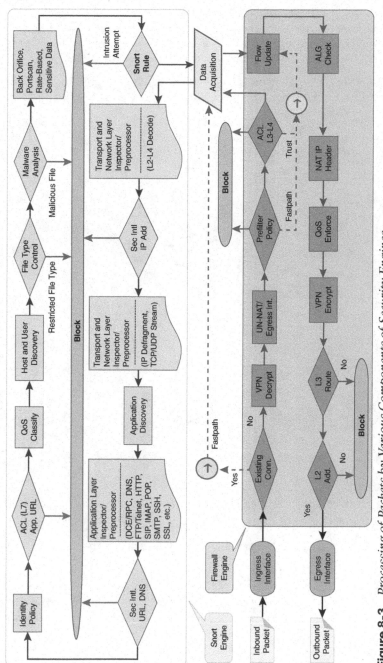

Figure 8-3 *Processing of Packets by Various Components of Security Engines*

Capturing of Packets Using Secure Firewall

You can use the management center to capture traffic from any of its managed threat defense devices. The management center allows you to probe on any data interfaces that are configured and enabled on a threat defense. In the following sections, you learn how to capture packets from the ingress and egress interfaces of a threat defense, save them into a file (in PCAP file format), and then view them in **packet analyzer** software.

Figure 8-4 shows the lab topology that is used in this chapter to capture traffic. To generate live traffic, the outside host 192.168.1.200 will access the web server 192.168.1.2, located in the inside network.

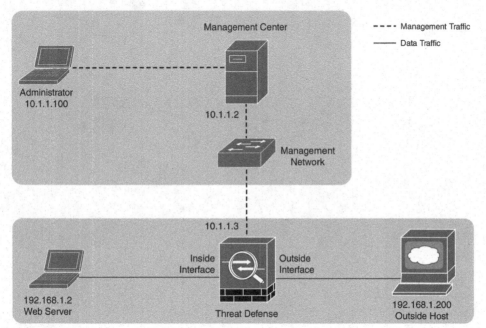

Figure 8-4   *Lab Topology—Used in Chapter to Capture Packets*

Configuration

To capture traffic from an interface of a managed device, follow these steps:

Step 1.   Log in to the management center using a browser.

Step 2.   Navigate to **Devices > Device Management**. The list of managed devices appears.

Step 3.   Next to the threat defense name is an icon with three dots. Click the three dots. The device menu for that threat defense appears (see Figure 8-5).

Step 4.   Select the **Capture w/Trace** option. The Advanced Troubleshooting page appears.

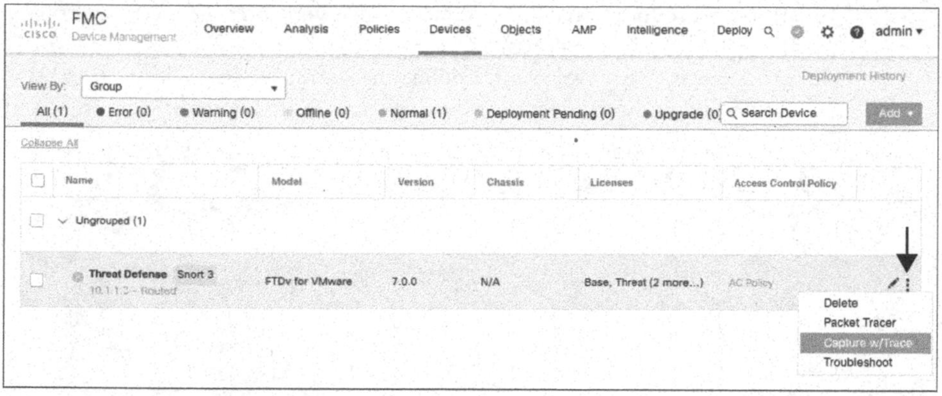

Figure 8-5 *Navigation to the Packet Capture Tool*

Step 5.   On the Advanced Troubleshooting page, go to the Capture w/Trace tab. There, you can find a web interface for the packet capturing tool (see Figure 8-6).

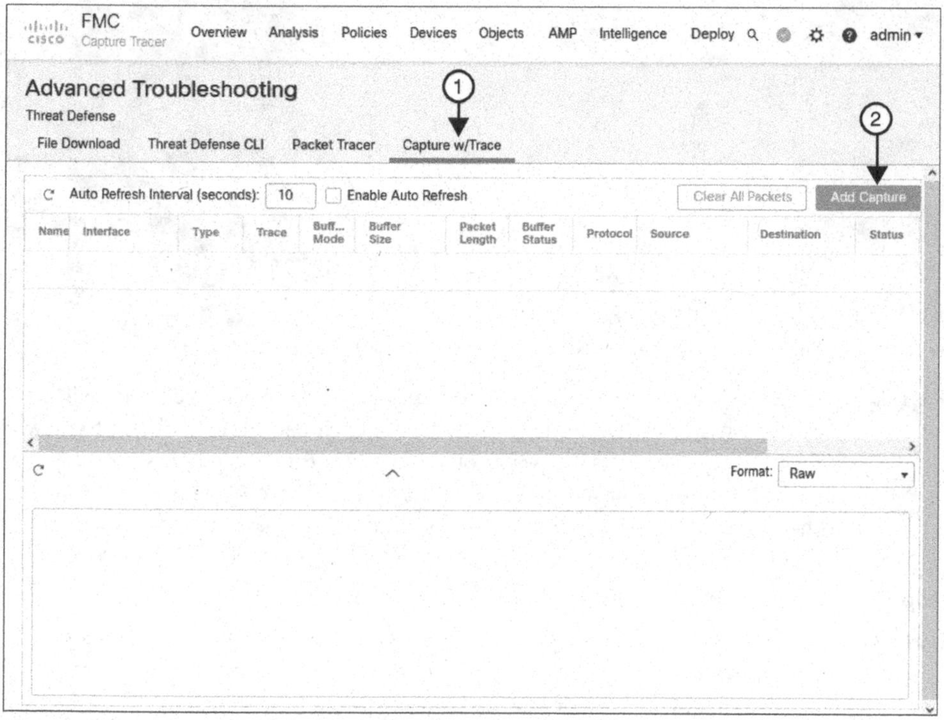

Figure 8-6 *User Interface for the Packet Capture Tool*

Step 6.   Click the **Add Capture** button. The Add Capture window appears.

Step 7. Create a capture for the outside interface. When you enter the matching criteria, try to be as specific as possible. For example, select the protocol that you want to analyze. Most importantly, define the source host and destination host precisely instead of including their broader subnet (see Figure 8-7).

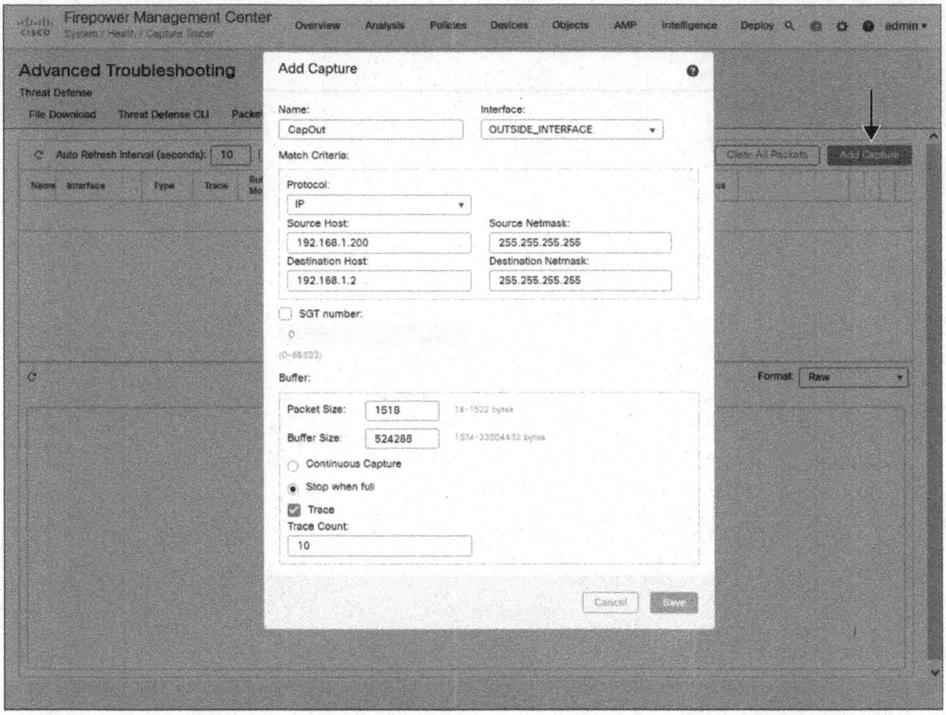

Figure 8-7 *Adding a Capture for the Outside Interface with Specific Filters*

Step 8. You should select the **Stop When Full** option to ensure that the buffer will not be inundated by continuous packets. For each packet, if you want to view the actions and verdicts by every component of a threat defense, select the **Trace** check box. You should limit the number of packets you want to trace; otherwise, the buffer can fill up quickly. Figure 8-8 illustrates a scenario where packets are dropped due to overrun and no buffer.

Step 9. Save the capture. The capture process should begin automatically.

Step 10. Optionally, you can add a separate capture for the inside interface if you want to compare the packets received on both inside and outside interfaces. It can help to investigate the root cause of any connectivity issues.

Figure 8-9 shows two captures that are running on the inside and outside interfaces. You can use this page to stop, pause, modify, and save a capture.

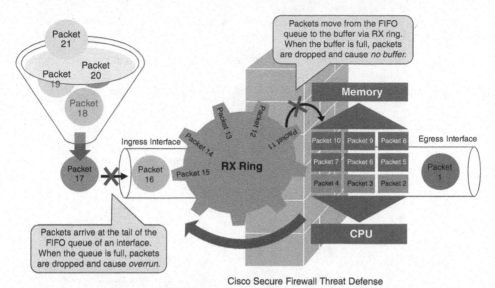

Figure 8-8 *Impact on Packets When the Buffer Is Full*

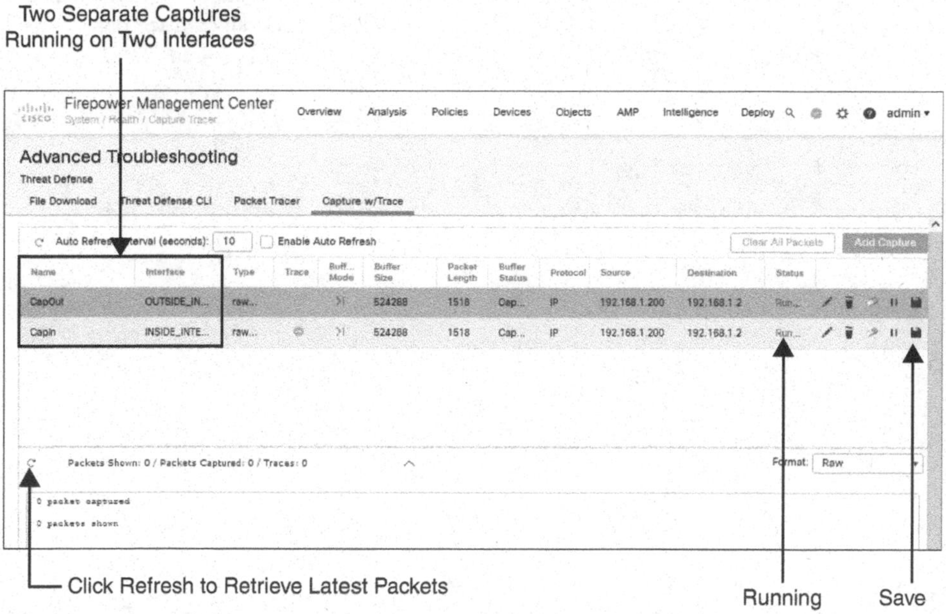

Two Separate Captures
Running on Two Interfaces

Figure 8-9 *Two Independent Capture Processes Are Running*

Verification

After the packets are captured, you will start seeing them in the bottom frame of the Capture w/Trace page. If this is a lab environment (as shown in Figure 8-4), you can use the outside host to access the internal web server. It will generate traffic. If you do not see them being captured, make sure the process is running and click the circular refresh icon to retrieve the latest packets, as shown in Figure 8-9.

Figure 8-10 shows the detail of captured packets in the frame. The detail data appears when you enable the Trace option. You can scroll down to see the complete trace. Alternatively, you can copy and paste the text and save it in a text editor for future reference.

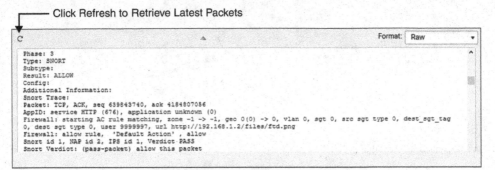

Click Refresh to Retrieve Latest Packets

```
Phase: 3
Type: SNORT
Subtype:
Result: ALLOW
Config:
Additional Information:
Snort Trace:
Packet: TCP, ACK, seq 639843740, ack 4184807056
AppID: service HTTP (676), application unknown (0)
Firewall: starting AC rule matching, zone -1 -> -1, geo 0(0) -> 0, vlan 0, sgt 0, src sgt type 0, dest_sgt_tag
0, dest sgt type 0, user 9999997, url http://192.168.1.2/files/ftd.png
Firewall: allow rule, 'Default Action' , allow
Snort id 1, NAP id 2, IPS id 1, Verdict PASS
Snort Verdict: (pass-packet) allow this packet
```

Figure 8-10 *Trace of a Captured Packet (Partial View on the GUI)*

Example 8-1 provides the trace data of two packets (packets 1 and 4) that are generated during the connection attempt of an outside host to a web server. The detail of trace data demonstrates how a packet is analyzed and allowed by each component of a threat defense.

Example 8-1 *Detail Trace of Captured Packets (Copied from GUI)*

```
1: 00:40:58.699258      192.168.1.200.52280 > 192.168.1.2.80: S
639843739:639843739(0) win 29200 <mss 1460,sackOK,timestamp 13333800 0,nop,wscale 7>
Phase: 1
Type: NGIPS-MODE
Subtype: ngips-mode
Result: ALLOW
Config:
Additional Information:
The flow ingressed an interface configured for NGIPS mode and NGIPS services will be
applied

Phase: 2
Type: ACCESS-LIST
Subtype: log
Result: ALLOW
Config:
access-group CSM_FW_ACL_ global
access-list CSM_FW_ACL_ advanced permit ip any any rule-id 268439552
access-list CSM_FW_ACL_ remark rule-id 268439552: ACCESS POLICY: AC Policy - Mandatory
```

```
access-list CSM_FW_ACL_ remark rule-id 268439552: L7 RULE: Ping Test
Additional Information:
 This packet will be sent to snort for additional processing where a verdict will be
reached


Phase: 3
Type: NGIPS-EGRESS-INTERFACE-LOOKUP
Subtype: Resolve Egress Interface
Result: ALLOW
Config:
Additional Information:
Ingress interface OUTSIDE_INTERFACE is in NGIPS inline mode.
Egress interface INSIDE_INTERFACE is determined by inline-set configuration


Phase: 4
Type: FLOW-CREATION
Subtype:
Result: ALLOW
Config:
Additional Information:
New flow created with id 195, packet dispatched to next module


Phase: 5
Type: EXTERNAL-INSPECT
Subtype:
Result: ALLOW
Config:
Additional Information:
Application: 'SNORT Inspect'


Phase: 6
Type: SNORT
Subtype:
Result: ALLOW
Config:
Additional Information:
Snort Trace:
Packet: TCP, SYN, seq 639843739
Session: new snort session
AppID: service unknown (0), application unknown (0)
Firewall: starting AC rule matching, zone -1 -> -1, geo 0 -> 0, vlan 0, sgt 0, src
sgt type 0, dest_sgt_tag 0, dest sgt type 0, user 9999997, icmpType 0, icmpCode 0
Firewall: allow rule,  'Default Action' , allow
Snort id 1, NAP id 2, IPS id 1, Verdict PASS
Snort Verdict: (pass-packet) allow this packet
```

8

```
Result:
input-interface: OUTSIDE_INTERFACE(vrfid:0)
input-status: up
input-line-status: up
Action: allow
.

.

<Traces of packet 2 and 3 are truncated for brevity>

.

.

4: 00:40:58.700342        192.168.1.200.52280 > 192.168.1.2.80: P 639843740:
639844072(332) ack 4184807056 win 229 <nop,nop,timestamp 13333801 2375771791>
Phase: 1
Type: FLOW-LOOKUP
Subtype:
Result: ALLOW
Config:
Additional Information:
Found flow with id 195, using existing flow


Phase: 2
Type: EXTERNAL-INSPECT
Subtype:
Result: ALLOW
Config:
Additional Information:
Application: 'SNORT Inspect'


Phase: 3
Type: SNORT
Subtype:
Result: ALLOW
Config:
Additional Information:
Snort Trace:
Packet: TCP, ACK, seq 639843740, ack 4184807056
AppID: service HTTP (676), application unknown (0)
Firewall: starting AC rule matching, zone -1 -> -1, geo 0(0) -> 0, vlan 0, sgt 0,
src sgt type 0, dest_sgt_tag 0, dest sgt type 0, user 9999997, url
http://192.168.1.2/files/ftd.png
Firewall: allow rule, 'Default Action' , allow
Snort id 1, NAP id 2, IPS id 1, Verdict PASS
Snort Verdict: (pass-packet) allow this packet
```

```
Result:
input-interface: OUTSIDE_INTERFACE(vrfid:0)
input-status: up
input-line-status: up
Action: allow
```

In addition to the detail trace data (displayed in Example 8-1), you can also save the original packets in the PCAP file format for future reference. Later, for further analysis, you can open the PCAP file in a packet analyzer tool like Wireshark (see Figure 8-11). Additionally, you can replay the captured packets in a PCAP file to emulate the connections in a lab environment. PCAP files are critical to an incident response team for forensic analysis.

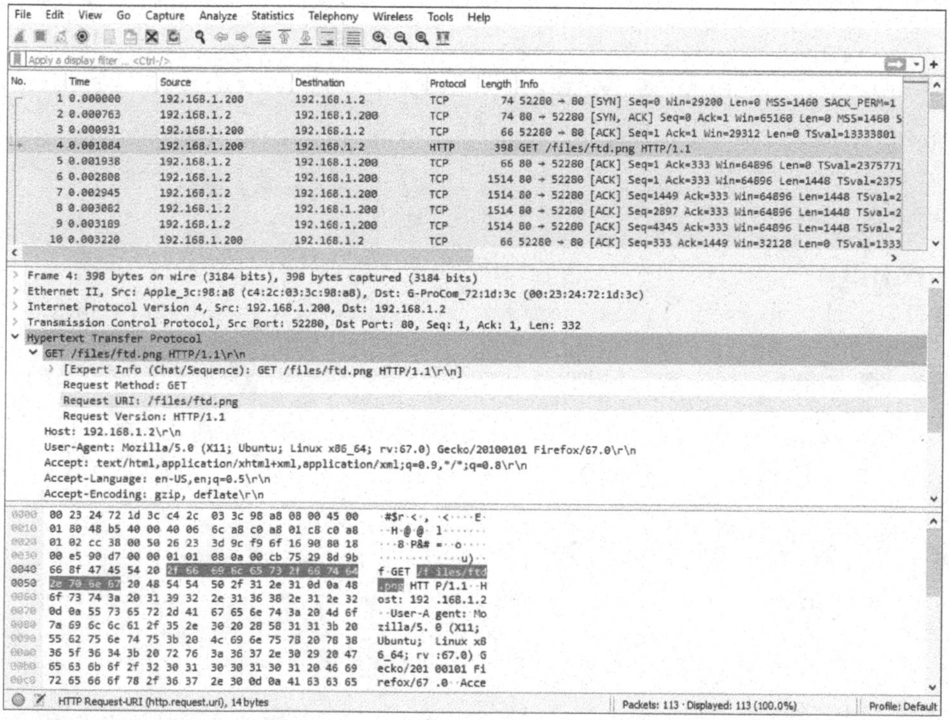

Figure 8-11 *Captured Packets Are Saved and Viewed in a Packet Analyzer*

Packet Capture versus Packet Tracer

The previous sections demonstrate the use of the packet capture tool. The example shows how to capture live traffic and how the trace option provides additional packet flow data. Because capturing live packets can be a CPU-intensive process, running the tool in a production environment requires careful planning. For a quick packet flow analysis, the packet tracer tool can be an easy alternative.

The packet tracer tool enables you to simulate the flow of a packet based on the security policies you deployed on a threat defense. The process is simple: you select an interface and packet type and provide the host detail, as shown in Figure 8-12. The tool uses that information to create a virtual packet. After you start the simulation, the virtual packet is evaluated against the security policies deployed on a threat defense. The verdict on a virtual packet can enable you to predict the potential impact of the security policies on live traffic. You can leverage this tool to investigate any connectivity issues in your real-world network.

Figure 8-12 *User Interface for the Packet Tracer Tool*

Summary

This chapter demonstrates the generation of live traffic between a web server and a client, provides detailed steps for capturing traffic between them using the management center, and then describes how to use a packet analyzer tool for further analysis. The chapter also illustrates the possible reasons for a packet drop and delineates the packet flow through different components of a threat defense. It empowers you to prepare for the next chapters because they will describe various security policies.

Exam Preparation Tasks

As mentioned in the section "How to Use This Book" in the Introduction, you have a couple of choices for exam preparation: the exercises here, Chapter 22, "Final Preparation," and the exam simulation questions in the Pearson Test Prep practice test software.

Review All Key Topics

Review the most important topics in this chapter, noted with the Key Topic icon in the outer margin of the page. Table 8-2 lists a reference of these key topics and the page numbers on which each is found.

Key Topic

Table 8-2   Key Topics for Chapter 8

Key Topic Element	Description	Page
Paragraph	Benefit of the packet capture tool	158
List	Optimal performance during packet capture	160
Paragraph	Packet tracer	169

Memory Tables and Lists

There are no Memory Tables or Lists for this chapter.

Define Key Terms

Define the following key terms from this chapter, and check your answers in the Glossary:

PCAP file, packet analyzer

8

## CHAPTER 9

Network Discovery Policy

This chapter provides an overview of the following topics:

Network Discovery Essentials: This section describes different types of application detectors and explains the operation of network discovery components on a threat defense.

Best Practices for Network Discovery: In this section, you learn important best practices to improve the effectiveness of network discovery.

Fulfilling Prerequisites: This section discusses the settings that you should not overlook before configuring a network discovery policy.

Configurations: This section describes the reusable objects on Secure Firewall and then uses objects to configure discovery rule conditions.

Verification: In this section, you find different ways to view network discovery data on a management center GUI.

The objectives of this chapter are to learn about

- Network discovery policy operation and configuration

- Application detectors

- Reusable object management

- Dashboard and event viewer

- Discovery data analysis

Secure Firewall can automatically discover the applications and services running in a network. It can dynamically identify the hosts and users who are running an application. It also can discover applications with or without the help of any active scanner. Secure Firewall allows you to monitor or block traffic solely based on the type of application a user might be running. This chapter describes how to enable application visibility and control (AVC) on Secure Firewall using the network discovery policy.

"Do I Know This Already?" Quiz

The "Do I Know This Already?" quiz enables you to assess whether you should read this entire chapter thoroughly or jump to the "Exam Preparation Tasks" section. If you are in doubt about your answers to these questions or your own assessment of your knowledge of the topics, read the entire chapter. Table 9-1 lists the major headings in this chapter and their corresponding "Do I Know This Already?" quiz questions. You can find the answers in Appendix A, "Answers to the 'Do I Know This Already?' Quizzes."

Table 9-1 "Do I Know This Already?" Section-to-Question Mapping

Foundation Topics Section	Questions
Network Discovery Essentials	1–2
Best Practices for Network Discovery	3–5
Fulfilling Prerequisites	6
Configurations	7
Verification	8

CAUTION The goal of self-assessment is to gauge your mastery of the topics in this chapter. If you do not know the answer to a question or are only partially sure of the answer, you should mark that question as wrong for purposes of the self-assessment. Giving yourself credit for an answer you correctly guess skews your self-assessment results and might provide you with a false sense of security.

1. Which of the following statements about application detectors is true?

   a. Internal detectors are always on; they are built in the software.

   b. The management center leverages OpenAppID to create custom detectors.

   c. Secure Firewall software comes with a set of application detectors, by default.

   d. All of these answers are correct.

2. Which of the following databases contain the fingerprint information?

   a. Snort rule database

   b. URL filtering database

   c. Vulnerability Database

   d. Discovery event database

3. What does a network discovery policy allow Secure Firewall to discover?

   a. Hosts

   b. Users

   c. Applications

   d. All of these answers are correct.

4. For accurate discovery of the latest applications, which of the following should you consider?

   a. Ensure that the network discovery policy is set to monitor the load-balancer devices.

   b. Use the network addresses instead of network objects.

   c. Generate Rule Recommendations in an intrusion policy.

   d. Keep the Vulnerability Database (VDB) version up to date.

5. Which of the following is considered a best practice when deploying network discovery policy?

   a. Deploy the threat defense as close as possible to the gateway.

   b. Add the addresses 0.0.0.0/0 and ::/0 in the rule for an accurate host profile.

   c. Exclude the IP addresses of any NAT and load-balancing devices from the list of monitored networks.

   d. For precise detection of the latest application, create a rule to discover private IP addresses.

6. Which of the following statements is not true?

   a. To discover applications, hosts, or users from certain subnets, you can trust the traffic from that subnet to expedite the discovery process.

   b. Secure Firewall uses the Adaptive Profiles option to perform application control.

   c. The Adaptive Profiles option should be always enabled to ensure superior detection.

   d. Trusted connections are not subject to deep inspection or discovery.

7. Which of the following statements is false?

   a. If you forgot to create an object using the Object Management page, you can still create one on the fly directly from the Add Rule window.

   b. Creating objects for the network resources and reusing them in the discovery rules are optional; however, it helps with rule management in the long term.

   c. You can create objects only for three elements: network addresses, port numbers, and interfaces.

   d. You can group multiple objects into a single configuration.

8. What is the reason that some operating systems appear as pending?

   a. The network discovery policy deployment is not complete.

   b. The threat defense is currently waiting on further packets to conclude analysis.

   c. The management center has reached its license limit.

   d. The operating system is currently being updated by the host.

Foundation Topics

Network Discovery Essentials

When you access a website, you interact with at least three types of applications: a browser on a client computer that originates the web communication, an underlying protocol that establishes the communication channel to the web, and the web contents from a server with which you are communicating. When a threat defense is deployed between the client and server, it can discover all three of these applications in a network. Moreover, it can categorize applications based on risk level, business relevance, content category, and so on.

Application Detectors

Secure Firewall uses application detectors to identify the network applications running on a monitored network. The detection capability can vary, depending on the source of the detectors. There are mainly two sources for detectors:

■ **System-provided detectors:** Secure Firewall software comes with detectors for various applications and operating systems. The default set of detectors is different in different software versions. Cisco provides the latest detectors in a separate software package, called the **Vulnerability Database (VDB)**. The VDB contains the fingerprints of various applications, operating systems, and client software. It also keeps a record of the known vulnerabilities. When Secure Firewall discovers an application, it can correlate the application with any known vulnerabilities to determine its impact within a network.

■ **User-created detectors:** You can create your own detectors based on patterns you notice on custom applications. The management center provides full administrative control over your custom detectors so that you can modify or disable them as necessary. Behind the scenes, it leverages **OpenAppID**—an open-source application detection module.

> **NOTE** When a host from a monitored network connects to a server in a nonmonitored network, the management center infers the application protocol (on the nonmonitored network) by using the information on the client software (of the monitored network).

Table 9-2 shows the types of application detectors supported by Secure Firewall. Except for the built-in internal detectors, you can activate or deactivate any type of detector, as necessary.

Table 9-2 Types of Application Detector

Type of Detector	Functions
Internal detector	Detects protocol, client, and web applications. Internal detectors are always turned on; they are built in the software.
Client detector	Detects client traffic. It also helps to infer an application protocol on a nonmonitored network.
Web application detector	Detects traffic based on the contents in a payload of HTTP traffic.
Port-based application protocol detector	Detects traffic based on well-known ports.
Fingerprint-based application protocol detector	Detects traffic based on application fingerprints.
Custom application detector	Detects traffic based on user-defined patterns.

Figure 9-1 shows the application detector page on the management center. To find this page, go to **Policies > Application Detectors**. You can search for any desired application to determine its coverage. For example, Figure 9-1 shows retrieval of 40 detectors that are related to

Facebook. The total number of detectors can vary, depending on the VDB version running on the management center.

Search for Detectors That Are Related to Facebook Application

40 Detectors Found for *Facebook*

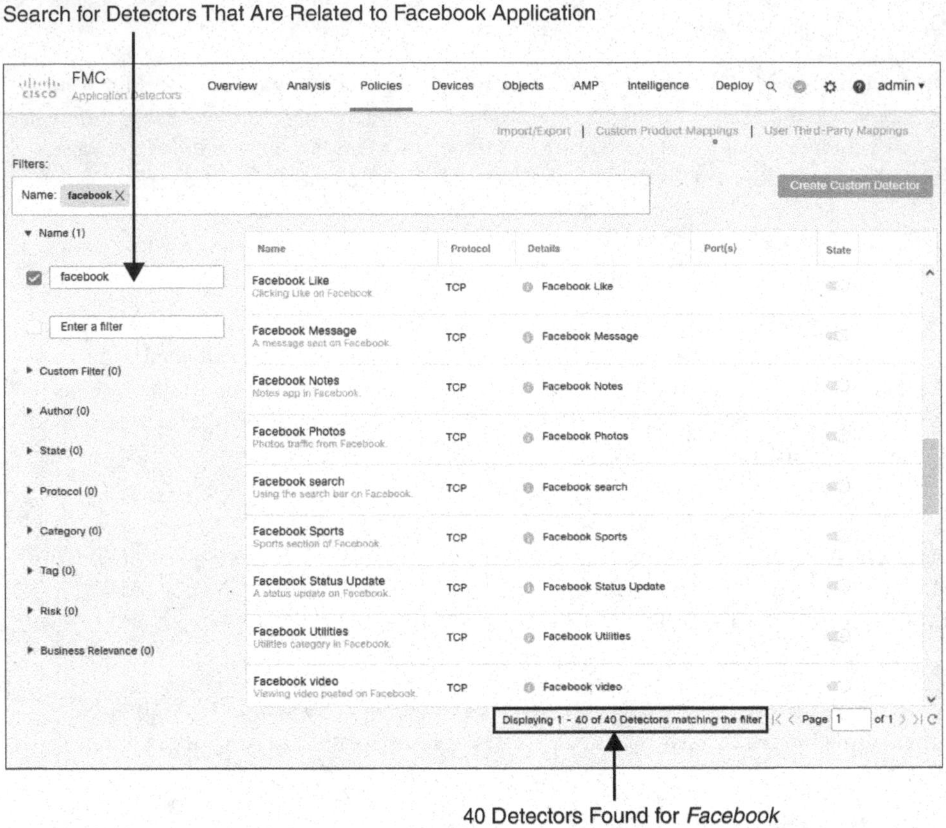

Figure 9-1   *The Application Detector Page on the Management Center*

Network Discovery Operations

A threat defense can control an application when a monitored connection is established between a client and server, and the application in a session is identified. To identify an application, the threat defense has to analyze the first few packets in a session. Until the identification is complete, the threat defense cannot apply an application rule. To ensure protection during the analysis period, the threat defense inspects those early packets by using the default intrusion policy of an active access control policy. Upon successful identification, the threat defense is able to act on the rest of the session traffic based on the access control rule created using an application filtering condition. If a prefilter policy or an access control policy is configured to block any particular traffic, the threat defense does not evaluate the traffic further against a network discovery policy.

Figure 9-2 illustrates the operational workflow of a threat defense. Note the two separate stages of the application visibility and control (AVC)—application discovery, and host and user discovery. A connection is subject to application discovery only if it passes the inspection by the IP-based security intelligence component. The URL- and DNS-based security intelligence component can act on a connection after its underlying application is discovered.

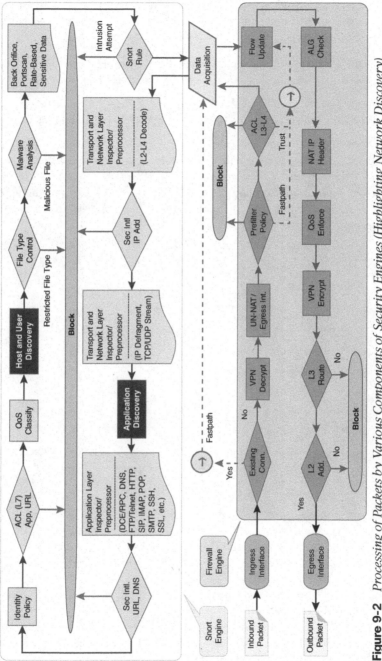

Figure 9-2 *Processing of Packets by Various Components of Security Engines (Highlighting Network Discovery)*

Best Practices for Network Discovery

A network discovery policy enables Secure Firewall to discover applications, hosts, and users in a network. A threat defense discovers a network passively; it does not directly affect the traffic flow. However, to ensure optimal performance, you should consider the following best practices when you enable network discovery:

- Keep the VDB version up to date. Installing the latest version ensures the detection of the latest software and application with more precise version information.

   Figure 9-3 shows the current VDB version on the Help > About page. This page also confirms the versions of all the software components running on the management center.

- By default, the management center comes with an application discovery rule, which uses 0.0.0.0/0 and ::/0 as the network address. This address enables Secure Firewall to discover applications from any observed networks. Snort leverages this application discovery data for intrusion detection and prevention by detecting the service metadata of a packet.

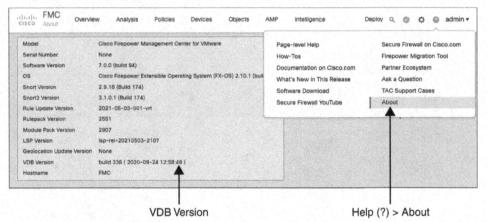

VDB Version   Help (?) > About

Figure 9-3 *Current VDB Version on a Management Center*

- When you add a custom rule for host and user discovery, include only the network addresses you own, such as the private IP addresses of your organization (see RFC 1918). Do not add the network address 0.0.0.0/0 and ::/0 to a host and user discovery rule because it encompasses all the subnets in the Internet. Attempting to discover host and user data from the entire Internet traffic can deplete the host and user licenses quickly. Likewise, excessive user discovery and host profile data can fill the management center database rapidly. As the threat defense continues to discover new hosts from the Internet, the management center continues to accommodate this new data by dropping the older discovery events and respective host profiles from the database. This continuous process can eventually impact management center database performance. Therefore, always limit the scope of your discovery policy within your internal network.

Key Topic

- Exclude the IP addresses of any NAT and load-balancing devices from the list of monitored networks. These types of devices can hide computers running behind them, which leads a threat defense to generate excessive discovery events depending on the operating system and applications running on the hosts behind the device. Exclusion of NAT and load-balancing IP addresses can improve threat defense performance.

  Figure 9-4 shows the positions of two types of intermediate devices—a router and a load balancer—that can each represent multiple network hosts.

- You can also exclude any ports from being monitored if you are sure about the service a port might be running. Doing so reduces the number of discovery events for known ports and services.

- Avoid creating overlapping rules that include the same hosts multiple times to prevent performance degradation.

- Deploy the threat defense as close as possible to the hosts. The lower the hop count between a threat defense and a host, the faster the threat defense detects the host and with a higher confidence value.

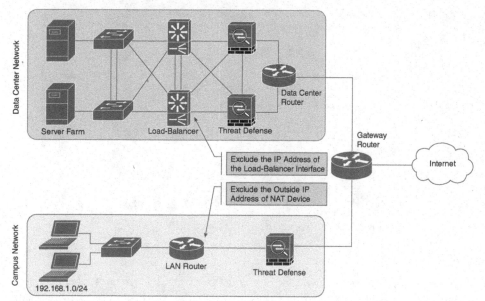

Figure 9-4 *NAT Device (Router) and Load-Balancer Interface Representing Multiple Hosts*

Fulfilling Prerequisites

Before you begin configuring a network discovery rule, consider the following issues:

- If you want to discover certain subnets or ports, do not use an access control rule or a prefilter rule to trust connections from those subnets or ports because the trusted connections are not subject to deep inspection or discovery; hence, they do not contain detailed information during discovery.

■ Secure Firewall uses the Adaptive Profiles option to perform application control. This option enhances detection capabilities of a threat defense. The Adaptive Profile Updates option leverages the service metadata and helps a threat defense to determine whether a particular intrusion rule is pertinent to an application running on a particular host and whether the rule should be enabled. To ensure superior detection, this option should be always enabled. You can verify the configuration status in the Advanced tab of an access control policy, under Detection Enhancement Settings (see Figure 9-5).

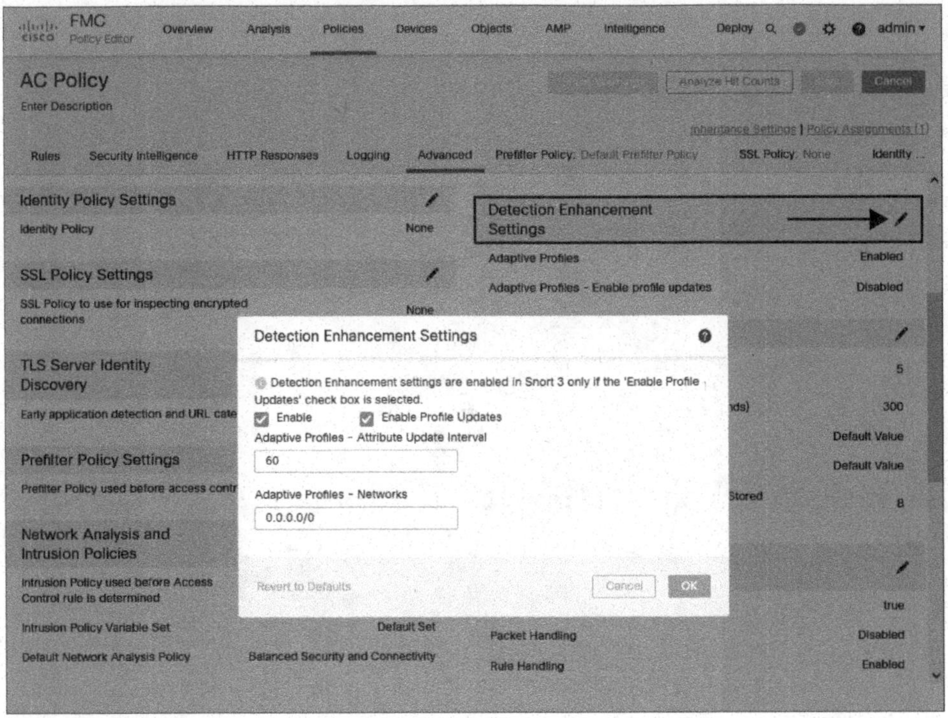

Figure 9-5 *Adaptive Profiles Setting for an Access Control Policy*

Configurations

In the following section, you first learn the options to create reusable objects for network resources. Then you learn the steps to configure a network discovery policy using predefined objects. To demonstrate the impact of an intermediate networking device representing multiple internal hosts, a router has been placed between the threat defense and the LAN switch in the topology.

Figure 9-6 shows the topology that is used in the lab exercise of this chapter to demonstrate the configuration of a network discovery policy. Here, a router performs the Network Address Translation (NAT) operation. It translates all the end-user traffic from the 192.168.1.0/24 subnet to the IP address 172.16.100.110. The following lab exercise shows how to exclude this translated address in a network discovery policy from being monitored.

Reusable Objects

Managing the rules using IP addresses could be cumbersome when you have an access control policy with thousands of rules. However, if you use objects in a rule, you don't need to remove the old rule and add a new one to reflect the new IP addresses; rather, you simply edit and update the value of the related named object. After you redeploy the policy, the new values of the objects are applied automatically in the ruleset.

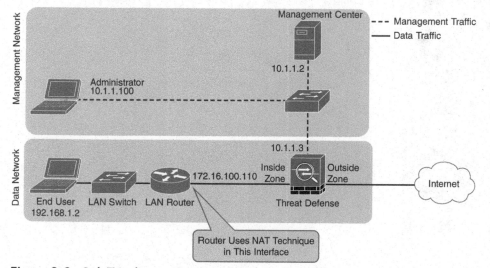

Figure 9-6 *Lab Topology to Demonstrate the Operation of a Network Discovery Policy*

Creating named objects for the network resources and reusing them in access control or discovery rules are optional; however, it helps you to manage configurations in the long term. For example, in your network discovery policy, you can exclude all the load balancers from being monitored by Secure Firewall. To do that, you can add them in a discovery rule one by one. Next time, if any IP addresses are changed, you need to remove the rule and add the new ones to reflect the changes.

Secure Firewall allows you to create named objects for network addresses, port numbers, interfaces, VLAN tags, URLs, time ranges, access lists, and many more variable components in a policy. You can also group multiple objects into a single configuration, which is called an object group. Furthermore, you can invoke an object group into another object group. This type of object is called a nested object.

You can add, delete, and modify an object by navigating to **Objects > Object Management** on the GUI. On the left panel of the Object Management page is a list of components that you can group into objects. A management center comes with predefined objects that are based on well-known addresses or port numbers. You can use them in a policy but cannot modify their values.

Figure 9-7 shows a list of network objects as an example. If an object is modifiable, it provides an option (a pencil icon) to edit.

To add an object of a particular type, select the object type from the left panel. For example, Figure 9-8 and Figure 9-9 show the configuration windows of a network object and port object, respectively. You can also create an object on the fly directly from the rule editor window, which is shown in Figure 9-11, later in the chapter.

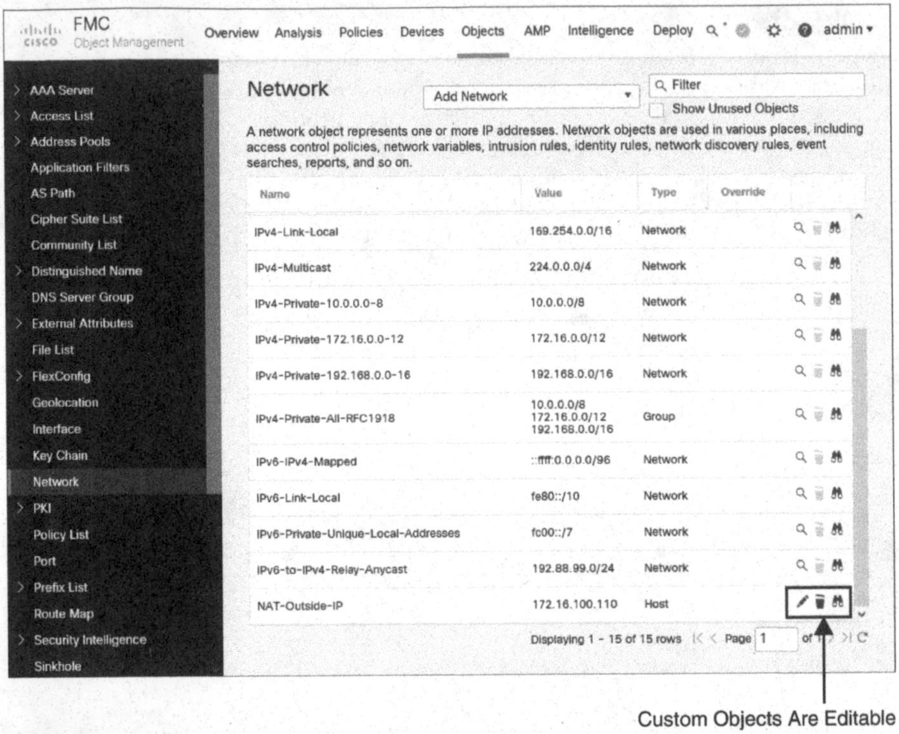

Custom Objects Are Editable

Figure 9-7 *Network Objects*

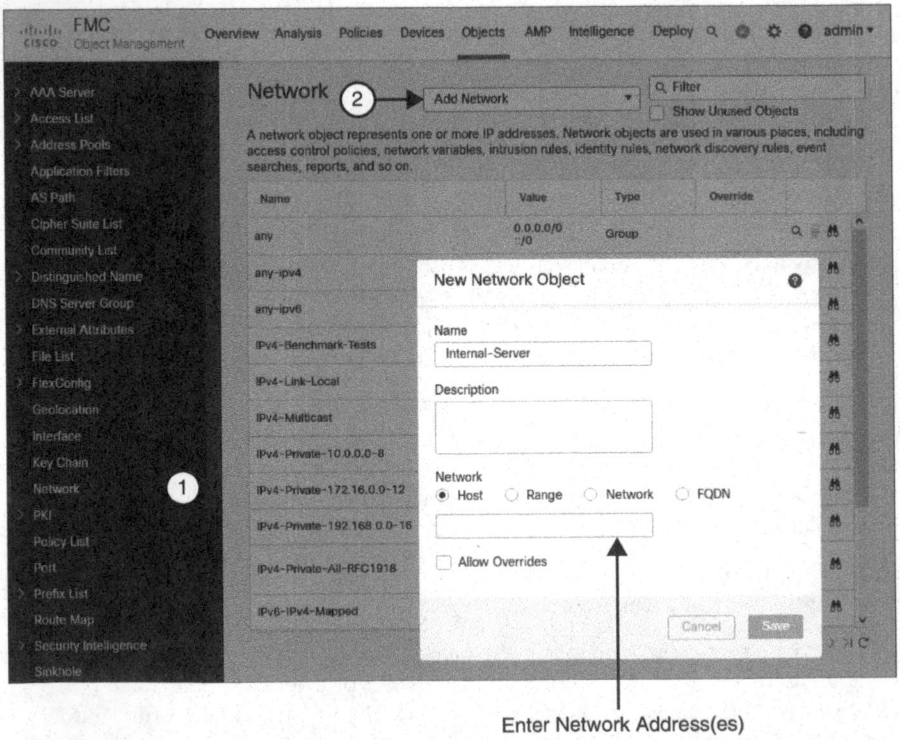

Enter Network Address(es)

Figure 9-8 *Network Object Configuration Window*

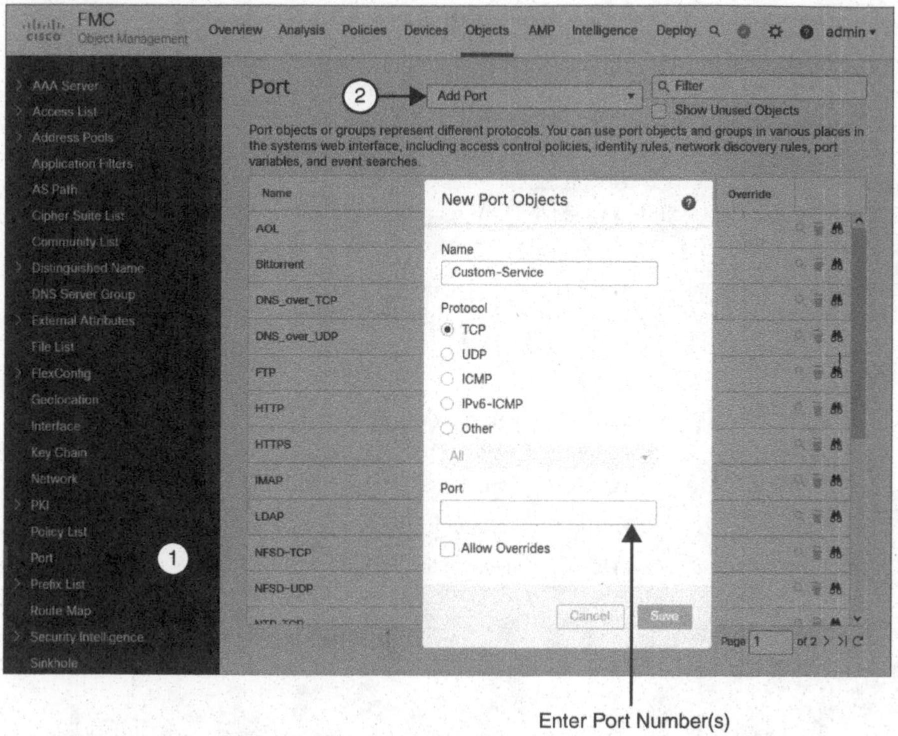

Figure 9-9 *Port Object Configuration Window*

Network Discovery Policy

To configure a network discovery policy, follow these steps:

Step 1.   In the management center, navigate to **Policies > Network Discovery.** The default rule for application discovery appears (see Figure 9-10). The 0.0.0.0/0 and ::/0 networks in default rule enable a Secure Firewall to discover applications from any observed networks. Keep this rule as is, because Snort leverages this application discovery data for intrusion detection.

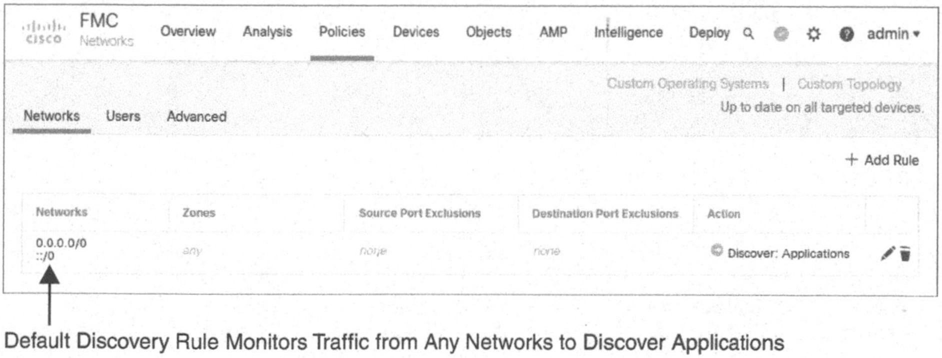

Default Discovery Rule Monitors Traffic from Any Networks to Discover Applications

Figure 9-10 *Default Rule for a Network Discovery Policy*

Step 2.   Click the **Add Rule** button. The Add Rule window appears.

Step 3.   First, add a rule to exclude the IP address of any intermediate NAT and load-balancing devices. To do that, select the **Exclude** action from the drop-down, and then select a network object that represents your desired IP address. The Exclude action excludes the hosts from being discovered; hence, no discovery events are recorded for the excluded hosts. However, any connection attempts between the excluded hosts are still recorded in the connection events database.

> **TIP**   If you did not create a network object previously, you can do it now on the fly using the plus icon. Alternatively, you can add a network address directly on the rule editor window.

Figure 9-11 shows a discovery rule that excludes a network object, NAT-Outside-IP. The object maps the IP address of the router's outside interface. The figure also highlights the available options to add an object or address on the fly.

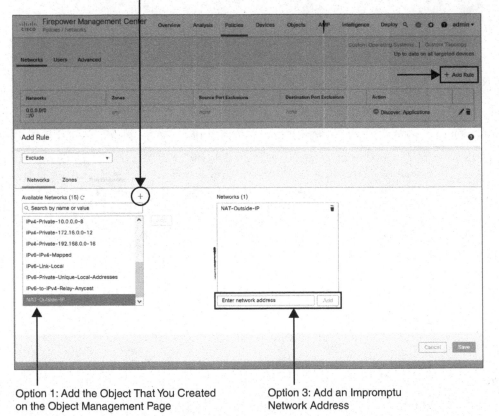

Figure 9-11   *Adding a Rule to Exclude a Network Object*

Step 4.   Click the **Save** button to return to the network discovery policy page.

Step 5.   To include the network you want to monitor, click the **Add Rule** button again. The Add Rule window appears.

Step 6.   Select the **Discover** action from the drop-down. Make sure the options are checked for Hosts, Users, and Applications.

Step 7.   Select a network object that represents your desired IP network and add it to the rule.

Figure 9-12 shows a network discovery rule that can discover hosts, users, and applications running on a network with private IP addresses (RFC 1918).

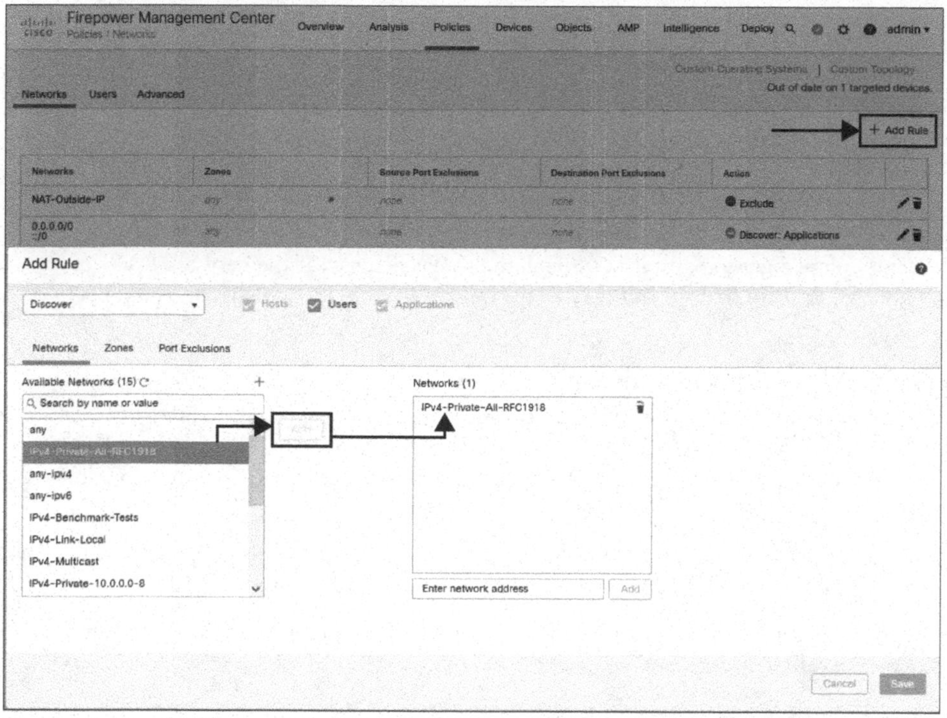

Figure 9-12   *Adding a Rule to Discover Hosts, Users, and Applications*

Step 8.   Click the **Save** button to return to the network discovery policy page.

Step 9.   Go to the **Deploy** page to deploy the network discovery policy on your threat defense.

Figure 9-13 shows the two network discovery rules you just created.

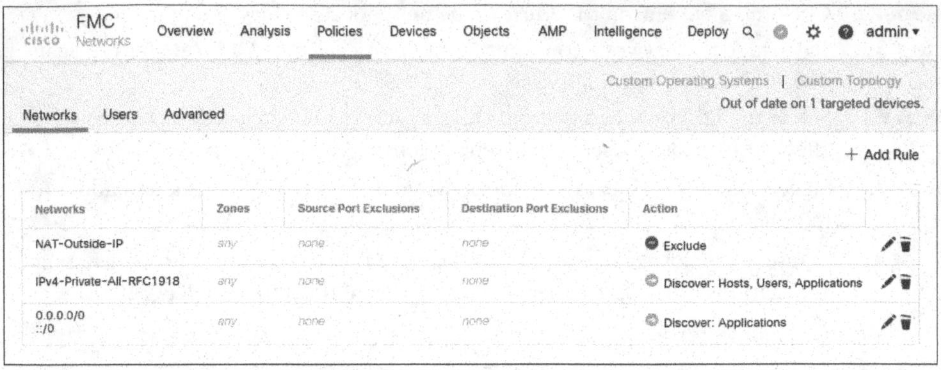

Figure 9-13   *An Exclusion Rule, a Custom Discovery Rule, and the Default Rule to Discover Applications*

Verification

Now you can verify the functionality of network discovery by passing network traffic through a threat defense. First, from your client computers, go to various websites on the Internet. Doing so generates traffic through the threat defense. If the network discovery policy is properly configured and deployed, you will be able to view discovery events in the management center GUI.

Analyzing Application Discovery

You can view a summary of the application data by using the Application Statistics dashboard, located at **Overview > Dashboards > Application Statistics**. The dashboard shows several data points in different widgets. The management center allows you to add, remove, or modify any widgets, as desired.

Figure 9-14 shows four widgets in the Application Statistics dashboard. Each widget displays a unique statistic of the application running in a monitored network.

Figure 9-15 shows different types of discovery events. They are generated when a new port, protocol, operating system, and host are discovered.

Analyzing Host Discovery

You can view the operating systems running on a monitored network by navigating to **Analysis > Hosts > Hosts**. Secure Firewall can identify most of the operating systems, along with their version detail. Click the Summary of the OS Versions tab to view the version information.

If some operating systems appear as *pending*, it's because the threat defense is currently analyzing the collected data or waiting on further information to come to an accurate conclusion. The *unknown* state indicates that the pattern of packets does not match an application detector. Updating the VDB to the latest version can reduce the number of unknown discovery events.

Figure 9-16 shows the name and version of operating systems running on a monitored network. It also shows examples of *unknown* and *pending* operating systems.

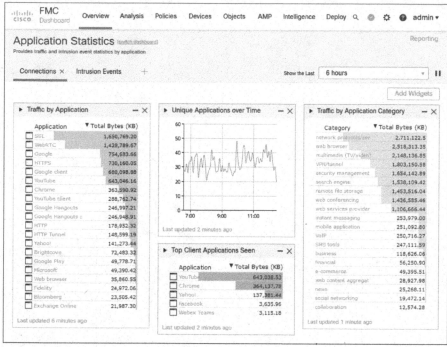

Figure 9-14 *Application Statistics Dashboard*

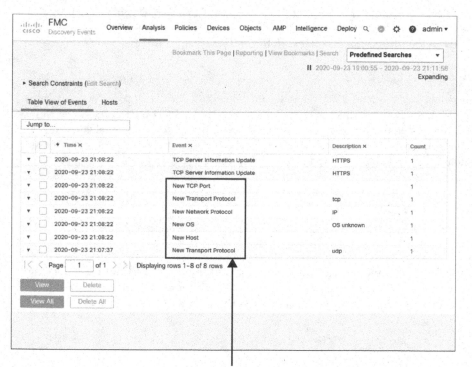

Discovery of Port, Protocol, New Operating System, Host

Figure 9-15 *Network Discovery Events*

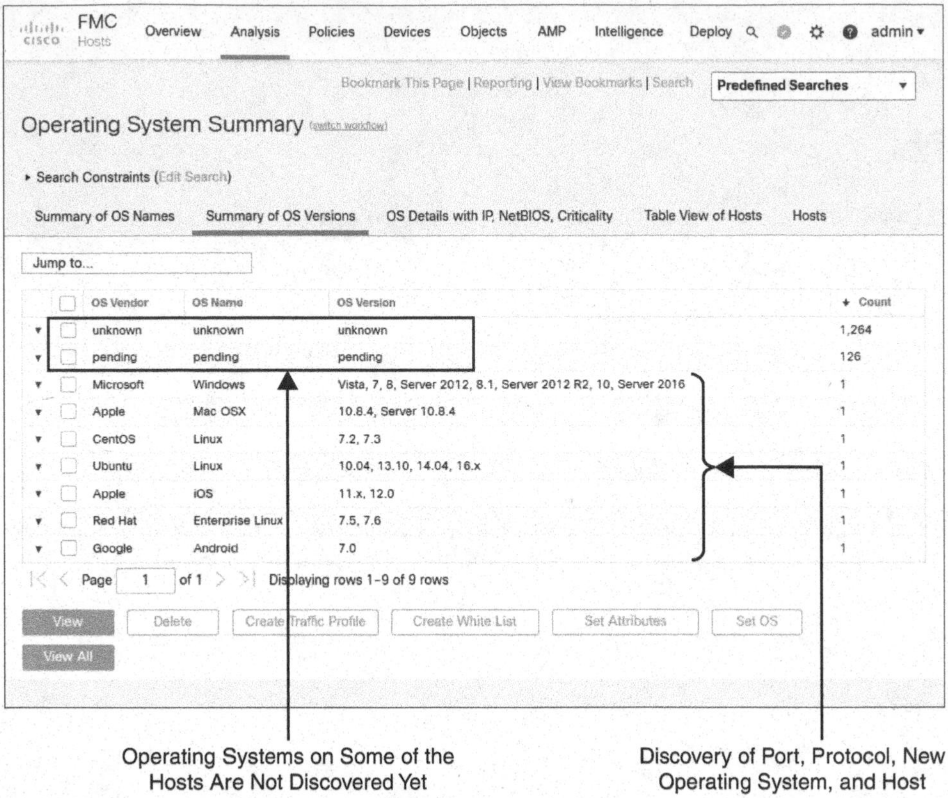

Operating Systems on Some of the   Discovery of Port, Protocol, New
Hosts Are Not Discovered Yet   Operating System, and Host

Figure 9-16   *Operating Systems on the Monitored Hosts*

> **TIP**   Remember this best practice: The lower the hop count between a threat defense and a host, the faster the threat defense detects the host and with a higher confidence value. Moreover, additional intermediate devices between a threat defense and hosts can alter or truncate important packet data. Therefore, consider deploying your threat defense as close as possible to the monitored hosts.

Undiscovered New Hosts

If you identify a host that has not been detected by the threat defense, there are some items you can check to help you determine the cause:

- Check whether the management center generates any health alerts for exceeding the host limits. To receive an alert due to the oversubscription of host discovery, the health monitor module for Host Limit must be enabled.

Figure 9-17 shows the option to enable a health module that can trigger an alert when the management center exceeds its host limit. To find this page, go to **System > Health > Policy** and edit a health policy you want to apply.

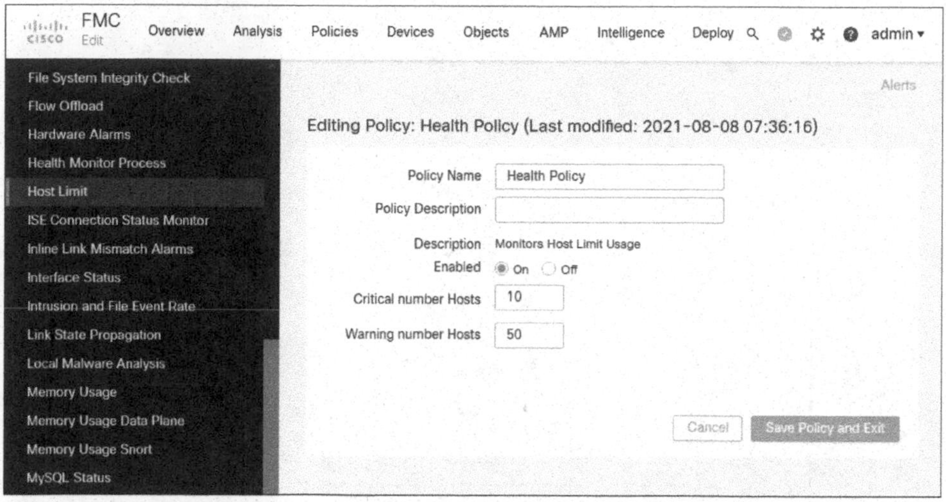

Figure 9-17   *Health Module to Monitor Host Limit Usage*

■ By analyzing the network map on the management center, you can determine the number of unique hosts identified by Secure Firewall and compare the number with the host limit for a management center model. You can also recognize any hosts that might be representing multiple hosts, such as a router with the NAT feature enabled or a load balancer. These are hosts you should consider excluding with a network discovery policy exclusion rule.

Table 9-3 shows the maximum number of hosts a management center can discover at any time. While this table shows the host limits of the virtual models, you can find the limits of the latest hardware models in the management center data sheet, available at the Cisco website.

Table 9-3   Host Discovery Limitation on Management Center Virtual Models

Management Center Model	Host Limit
FMCv25	50,000
FMCv300	150,000

Figure 9-18 demonstrates the discovery of hundreds of external hosts within a few minutes. If it continues, this can deplete discover licenses from Secure Firewall quickly and can impact system resource utilization. To find this page, go to **Analysis > Hosts > Network Map.**

The Threat Defense Can Discover Hundreds of Hosts from the Internet in Few Minutes

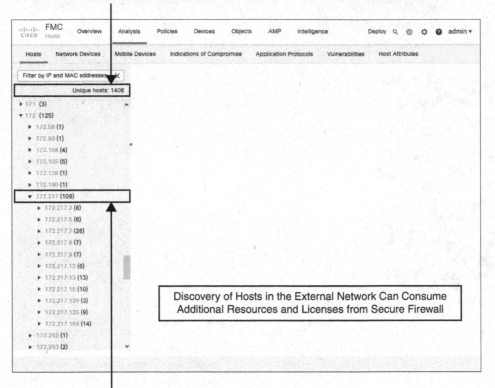

The Subnets Can Be Expanded to Find Details of the Discovered Hosts

Figure 9-18   *The Network Map Shows All the Discovered Hosts*

■ Check how the network discovery policy is configured to handle a host when the management center reaches the threshold for the host limit. You can configure a policy to stop discovering any new hosts or to drop the earliest discoveries when the management center reaches its limit.

Figure 9-19 shows the navigation to a drop-down where you can choose between dropping an old host and locking down any new entries.

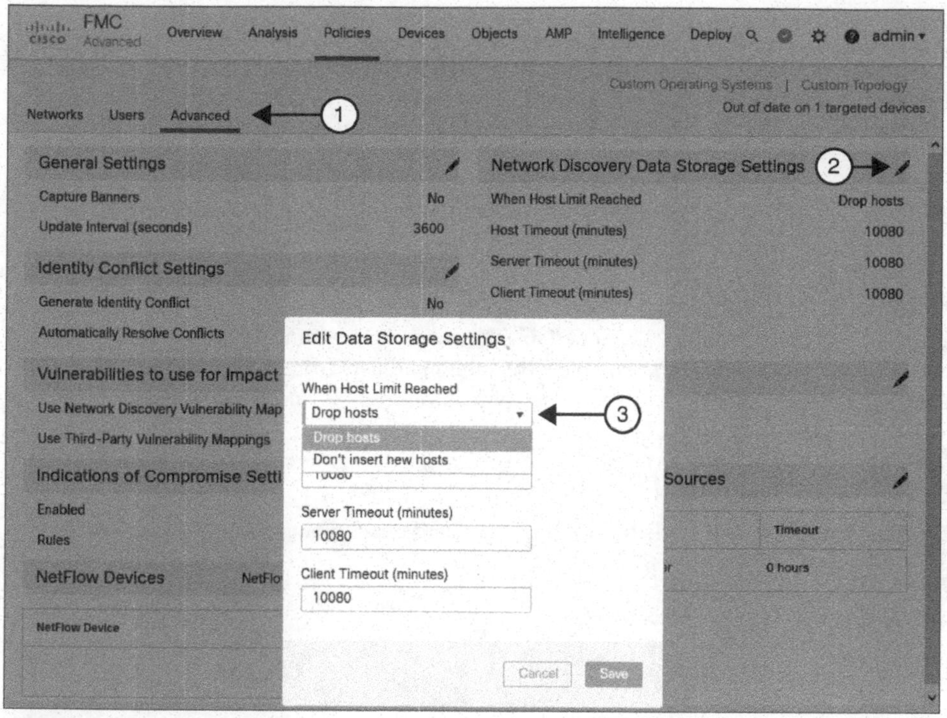

Figure 9-19 *Advanced Network Discovery Settings*

Summary

This chapter describes how to configure Secure Firewall to discover hosts, users, and applications running on a network. It shows the usage of reusable objects in the network discovery policy. It also presents the discovered data on the management center's dashboard widget and event viewer.

Exam Preparation Tasks

As mentioned in the section "How to Use This Book" in the Introduction, you have a couple of choices for exam preparation: the exercises here, Chapter 22, "Final Preparation," and the exam simulation questions in the Pearson Test Prep practice test software.

Review All Key Topics

Review the most important topics in this chapter, noted with the Key Topic icon in the outer margin of the page. Table 9-4 lists a reference of these key topics and the page numbers on which each is found.

Key Topic

Table 9-4   Key Topics for Chapter 9

Key Topic Element	Description	Page
Bullet list	Vulnerability Database (VDB)	175
Paragraph	Application visibility and control operation	176
Bullet list	Impact of broader discovery rule	178
Bullet list	Discovery rule exclusion	179

Complete Tables and Lists from Memory

Print a copy of Appendix C, "Memory Tables" (found on the companion website), or at least the section for this chapter, and complete the tables and lists from memory. Appendix D, "Memory Tables Answer Key," also on the companion website, includes completed tables and lists to check your work.

Define Key Terms

Define the following key terms from this chapter, and check your answers in the Glossary:

OpenAppID, Vulnerability Database (VDB)

## CHAPTER 10

Access Control Policy

This chapter provides an overview of the following topics:

Access Control Policy Essentials: This section introduces you to various options of the access control rule editor and policy editor.

Best Practices for Access Control Policy: This section provides useful tips to fine-tune the ruleset of an access control policy. Following the best practices can help you to optimize system performance.

Access Control Policy Configuration: This section discusses the prerequisites for configuring an access control policy, followed by the detailed steps to configure a policy with different rule conditions.

Verification: In this section, you learn how to use various commands and tools that you can run on the CLI and GUI. They are instrumental to verify the configuration of an access control policy and to troubleshoot any connectivity and performance issues.

The objectives of this chapter are to learn about

■ Configuration and deployment of access control policy

■ Verification of access control policy settings using CLI

■ Analysis of access control policy operations for advanced troubleshooting purposes

As the name suggests, an access control policy allows you to create access control rules to match traffic and apply an action on matching traffic per business requirements. You use access control rules to associate next-generation security policies, such as file policies and intrusion policies, with the matching traffic. An access control policy is the central place for invoking all the security policies that you create on Secure Firewall. Before we dive into various next-generation security policies, let's look at various components of an access control policy and how to configure one.

"Do I Know This Already?" Quiz

The "Do I Know This Already?" quiz enables you to assess whether you should read this entire chapter thoroughly or jump to the "Exam Preparation Tasks" section. If you are in doubt about your answers to these questions or your own assessment of your knowledge of the topics, read the entire chapter. Table 10-1 lists the major headings in this chapter and their corresponding "Do I Know This Already?" quiz questions. You can find the answers in Appendix A, "Answers to the 'Do I Know This Already?' Quizzes."

Table 10-1 "Do I Know This Already?" Section-to-Question Mapping

Foundation Topics Section	Questions
Access Control Policy Essentials	1
Best Practices for Access Control Policy	2, 3
Access Control Policy Configuration	4
Verification	5

CAUTION The goal of self-assessment is to gauge your mastery of the topics in this chapter. If you do not know the answer to a question or are only partially sure of the answer, you should mark that question as wrong for purposes of the self-assessment. Giving yourself credit for an answer you correctly guess skews your self-assessment results and might provide you with a false sense of security.

1. Which of the following pages provide the option to select an action for unmatched traffic?

    a. Policy editor

    b Rule editor

    c. Inspection tab of the Add Rule window

    d. Advanced tab of the policy editor page

2. Which of the following choices could improve system performance?

    a. Place the precisely defined rules before a broader rule.

    b. Do not use access control rules to filter traffic based on 5-tuple.

    c. Place the block rules at the top of the access control ruleset.

    d. All of these answers are correct.

3. Which option or command allows you to identify the shadowed rule?

    a. Firewall Engine Debug

    b. Analyze Hit Counts

    c. Show Rule Conflict

    d. show access-list

4. Which of the following options is false?

    a. A default action can act on unmatched traffic only.

    b. An interactive block with a reset action sends a response message before sending a reset packet to the requestor.

    c. Do not enable logging simultaneously for both phases—beginning and end of connections—to avoid any performance issues.

    d. Secure Firewall allows you to select a default action for every rule with a monitor action.

5. Which of the following commands can you use to debug the operations of a threat defense security engine?

a. **system support app-id-debug**

b. **system support firewall-debug**

c. **system support firewall-engine-debug**

d. **system support application-identification-debug**

Foundation Topics

Access Control Policy Essentials

To create a simple access control policy, you basically work on two types of editors: the access control policy editor and the access control rule editor. The other security policies, such as intrusion policies and file policies, have their own policy editors. After you configure the other policies using their respective policy editors, you need to invoke them into an access control policy that will be deployed to a threat defense. The following sections briefly introduce both editors.

Policy Editor

To navigate to the access control policy editor page, go to **Policies > Access Control** on your management center. When the list of existing access control policies appears, click the pencil icon next to a policy name to open it in the policy editor (see Figure 10-1). If no access control policy has been created yet, you can create a new one anytime by clicking the New Policy button.

cisco FMC Access Control	Overview	Analysis	Policies	Devices	Objects	AMP	Intelligence	Deploy Q ◎ ✿ ❷ admin ▼

Object Management | Intrusion | Network Analysis Policy | DNS | Import/Export

New Policy

Access Control Policy	Domain	Status	Last Modified	
AC Policy	Global	Targeting 1 devices *Up-to-date on all targeted devices*	2021-09-19 07:58:26 Modified by "admin"	🗎 🖹 ✏ 🗑

Click the Pencil Icon to Edit the Policy

Figure 10-1 *Navigating to the Access Control Policy Editor*

When you open an access control policy in a policy editor, you will find many options to enhance the security policy. Here is a summary of some of the options:

■ **Policy Assignment:** To select a target threat defense where an access control policy is deployed. While you can create and save many access control policies on your management center, you can deploy only one access control policy to your threat defense at any time.

■ **Rules:** To view the access control rules with their rule conditions. Traffic is evaluated against access control rules in top-down order.

■ **Security Intelligence:** To block connections based on reputation and intelligence data.

- **HTTP Responses:** To display a response page when a threat defense detects an attempt to access a website.

- **Logging:** To set up destinations for syslog messages that will be generated by all the components of the access control policy.

- **Advanced:** To configure advanced options that can influence the performance of a threat defense. In most cases, the default settings do not require any changes.

- **Default Action:** To define how the traffic that does not match any existing access control rule conditions is handled by a threat defense. You can choose to apply one of the following actions to the remaining unmatched traffic:

  - Block all the remaining unmatched traffic.

  - Trust all the remaining unmatched traffic.

  - Discover only the host, user, and application details.

  - Inspect traffic against an intrusion policy.

Figure 10-2 shows an overview of the access control policy editor page.

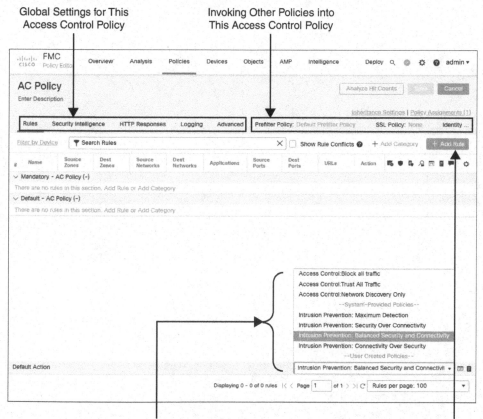

Figure 10-2 *Access Control Policy Editor Page*

Rule Editor

You can create or modify access control rules using the rule editor. To open the rule editor window, click the Add Rule button on the policy editor. Similarly, to open an existing access control rule on the rule editor, click the pencil icon next to a rule.

Figure 10-3 shows the navigation to the access control rule editor window. The Add Rule window (shown in the foreground) appears when you click the Add Rule button on the policy editor page (shown in the background).

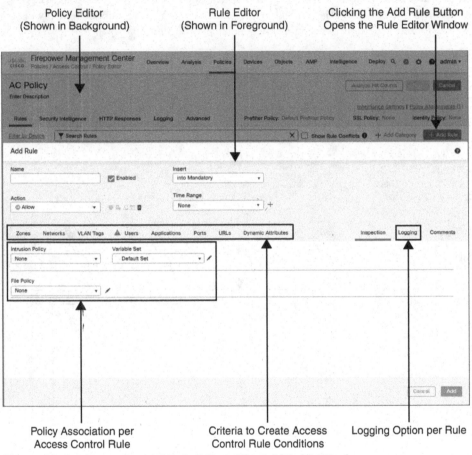

Figure 10-3 *Access Control Rule Editor (The Add Rule) Window*

An access control rule can have single or multiple matching conditions. You can use various networking criteria as conditions, such as interface zones, network addresses, ports, users, applications, and URLs. You can also specify any days and times when a rule will become active. When a packet matches a rule condition, the threat defense handles the traffic based on the action you select in the access control rule. The available options are to allow, trust, monitor, or block a connection.

As you know, an access control policy is the central place to invoke all the other security policies. You can associate a preconfigured file policy and intrusion policy with each rule individually. The other security policies, such as prefilter policies, SSL policies, and identity policies, are invoked globally in the access control policy editor page. Figure 10-3 highlights the association of different policies in the access control rule editor and policy editor pages.

Best Practices for Access Control Policy

Placement of access control rules in an access control policy can impact the CPU and memory utilization of a threat defense. The access control rules are evaluated sequentially from top to bottom. Therefore, consider the following best practices when you configure an access control policy:

- First, place the rules with block actions at the top of the access control policy. It enables a threat defense to deny traffic faster. During the rule evaluation process, when a packet matches the rule constraints and finds a rule with block action, it stops evaluating the packet further against the remaining rules in the policy.

- Next, place the precisely defined rules before a broader rule. When traffic matches a broader rule first, it will not be evaluated further against any rules with more specific conditions.

- Rules that are not associated with an intrusion policy or file policy should be placed before the rules that are associated with them.

- If you want to allow or block traffic solely based on 5-tuple (such as source IP address, destination IP address, source port number, destination port number, and protocol), consider using a prefilter rule for them. It improves system performance. The configuration of a prefilter policy is described in the next chapter.

- After adding all the access control rules, use the **Show Rule Conflict** check box to determine if there are any duplicate or overlapping rules (also known as **shadowed rules**). Shadowed rules can degrade system performance.

- Once an access control policy is deployed and running for some time, use the **Analyze Hit Counts** option to determine if there are any rules that never matched any traffic. Based on the statistics, you can fine-tune the rules to improve efficacy.

Figure 10-4 shows two built-in optimization tools—Show Rule Conflict and Analyze Hit Counts—that enable you to fine-tune an access control policy.

Figure 10-5 shows the options to view access control rule hit counts. To identify the rules that never matched any traffic, select your threat defense and then choose the Never Hit Rules option from the drop-down.

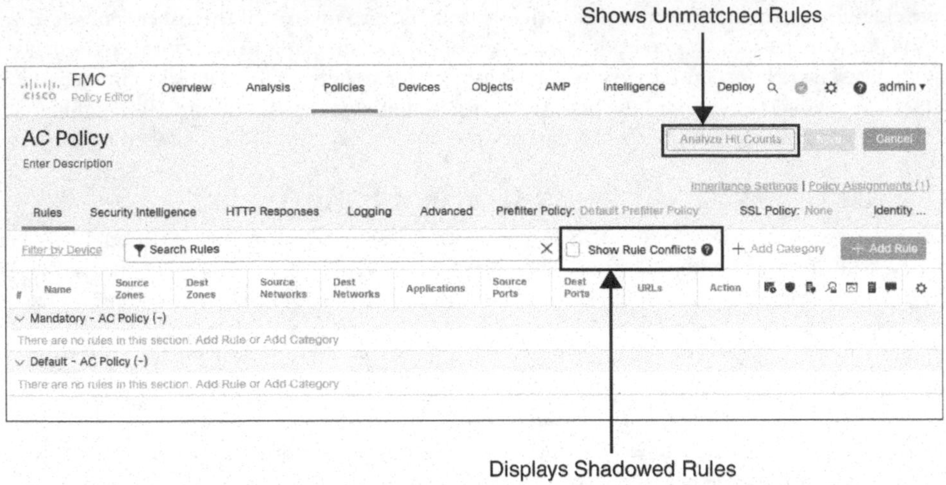

Shows Unmatched Rules

Displays Shadowed Rules

Figure 10-4 *Show Rule Conflict and Analyze Hit Counts Options*

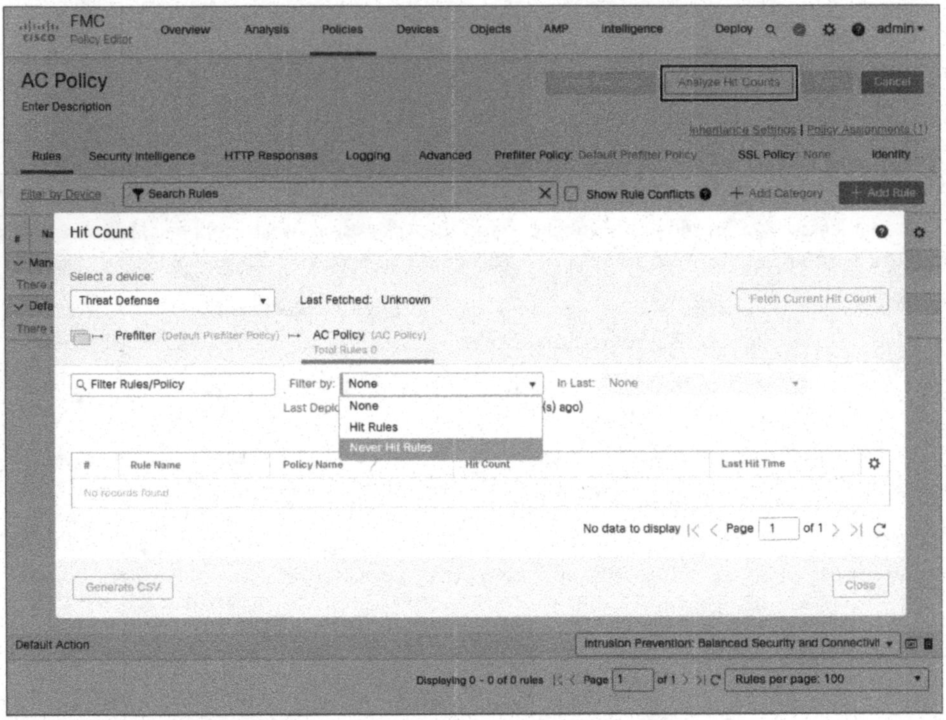

Figure 10-5 *Window for Hit Count Analysis*

Access Control Policy Configuration

In the following sections, you learn how to configure a simple access control policy and deploy it to a threat defense. As you learned earlier in the "Rule Editor" section, an access control rule can be created with wide variety of rule conditions. This chapter primarily focuses on the concept of rule creation rather than creating many rules with every possible combination. To demonstrate the impact of different rule conditions, in these exercises, you configure two access control rules with two different actions: Telnet traffic will be blocked, and Secure Shell (SSH) traffic will be allowed. Any other traffic will be subject to intrusion inspection by default. You also learn how to associate intrusion and file policies with individual access control rules.

Figure 10-6 shows the topology that is used in the lab exercises for this chapter to demonstrate the operation of an access control policy.

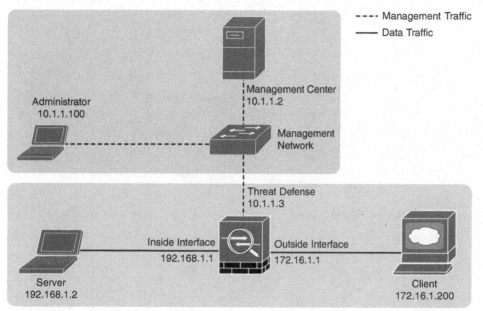

Figure 10-6 *Topology to Demonstrate the Operation of an Access Control Policy*

Fulfilling Prerequisites

This chapter assumes that the following prerequisites are fulfilled:

- Your Secure Firewall is licensed with the features that you want to include in the access control rule condition. Without applying an appropriate feature license, you might be able to configure the feature in an access control policy; however, the management center will not allow you to deploy the policy to a threat defense.

- During device registration, you have the option to create a new access control policy or select an existing policy. You must do one or the other because implementation of an access control policy is a requirement for the registration process to complete successfully.

- Threat defense data interfaces can be configured per the design requirements of your organization. Previous chapters described various interface deployment modes.

10

Creating Rules

To create an access control rule, follow these steps:

Step 1. Navigate to **Policies > Access Control > Access Control**. A list of available access control policies appears (refer to Figure 10-1).

Step 2. Use the pencil icon next to the policy name to open the policy editor. The access control policy editor page appears. If you want to use a new policy, click the **New Policy** button to create a new one.

Step 3. In the policy editor, click the **Add Rule** button. The Add Rule window opens (refer to Figure 10-3).

Step 4. Now you add two access control rules. First, create a rule to block Telnet traffic. In the Add Rule window, do the following:

a. Give a name to the rule.

b. Use the Action drop-down to select a block action. There are four types of block actions (see Figure 10-7). All of them deny the matching traffic without any further inspection but have different approaches:

- Select **Block** to simply deny the traffic.

- Select **Block with Reset** to deny the traffic as well as to send a reset packet to the requestor.

- Select **Interactive Block** to send an interactive response message to the requestor.

- Select **Interactive Block with Reset** to send a response message *before* sending a reset packet to the requestor.

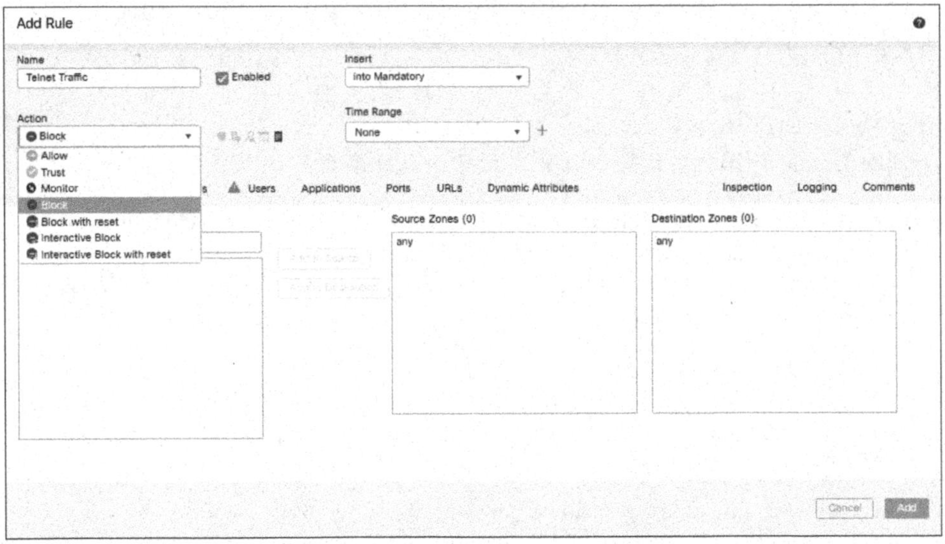

Figure 10-7 *Available Actions for an Access Control Rule*

c. Go to the Ports tab to find the ports that you want to block. To select a well-known port, you can simply search for its associated protocol name. For example, if you want to block TCP port 23, you can select **TELNET**, and click **Add to Destination**, as shown in Figure 10-8.

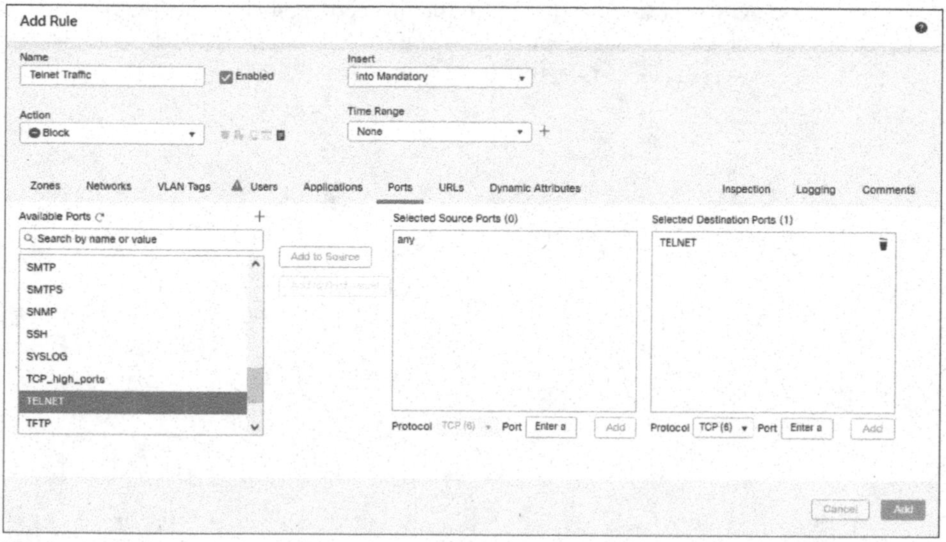

Figure 10-8 *The Port Used for Telnet Service Is Selected as the Destination Port*

d. On the Logging tab, enable **Log at Beginning of Connection** to log the denied connections (see Figure 10-9). This could be helpful for troubleshooting connectivity issues. You cannot enable Log at End of Connection because blocked traffic is denied instantaneously without further inspection at the beginning of connections.

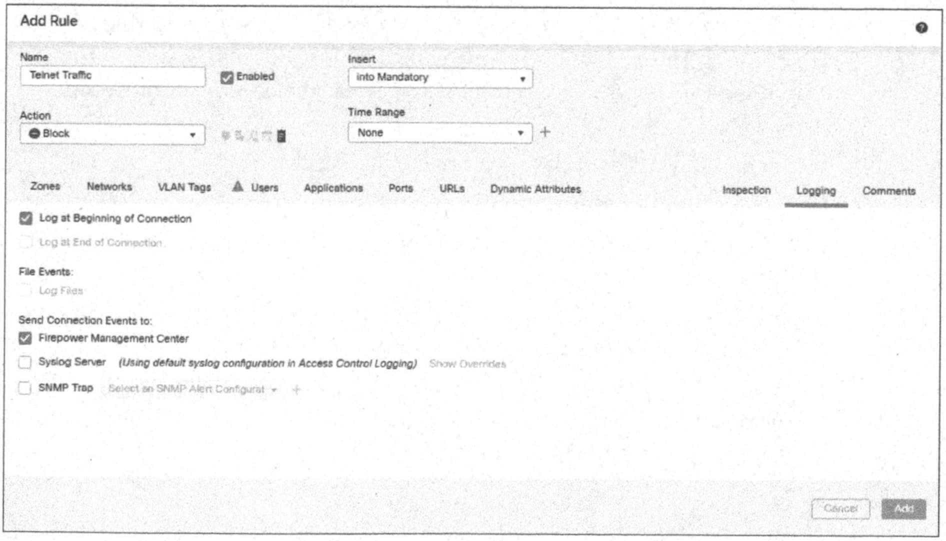

Figure 10-9 *Logging Settings for a Rule with the Block Action*

e. Additionally, you could use objects from the remaining tabs in the rule con-figuration interface to add more specific or complex rule conditions. In this example, we are keeping the rule simple because the primary objective of this exercise is to introduce you to the rule creation process in general.

■ As you create this rule, go to the Inspection tab and note that you cannot associate an intrusion or file policy when the Block action is selected (see Figure 10-10).

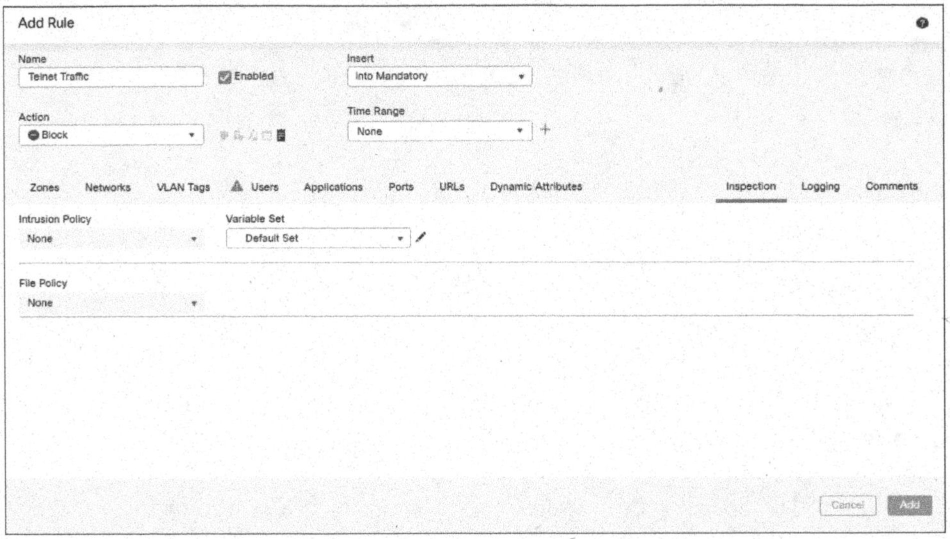

Figure 10-10 *Rules with the Block Action Are Not Inspected Further*

f. Click the **Add** button to complete the creation. You then return to the policy editor page. The new rule should be listed there.

Step 5. Click the **Add Rule** button again to add the second access control rule of this exercise. The Add Rule window reappears. This rule allows web traffic (HTTP and HTTPS) and also is subject to advanced next-generation security inspection.

a. On the Add Rule window, give a name to the rule.

b. Select **Allow** from the Action drop-down.

c. On the Ports tab, select **HTTP** and **HTTPS** from the list of available ports and add them as destination ports (see Figure 10-11).

d. On the Inspection tab, use the Intrusion Policy and File Policy drop-downs to select your desired next-generation security policies.

Figure 10-12 shows the selection of a custom intrusion policy and a custom file policy. Chapter 15, "Intrusion Policy," and Chapter 16, "Malware and File Policy," describe these policies in detail.

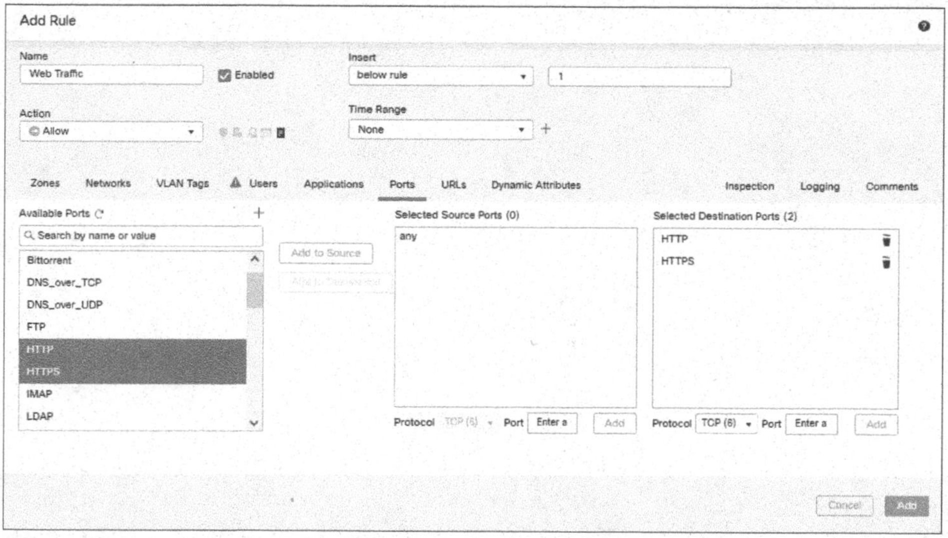

Add Rule

Name
| Web Traffic | ☑ Enabled |

Insert
| below rule ▼ | 1 |

Action
| ☉ Allow ▼ | ● ▲ ☐ ⊟ ▣ |

Time Range
| None ▼ | + |

Zones   Networks   VLAN Tags ⚠ Users   Applications   **Ports**   URLs   Dynamic Attributes   Inspection   Logging   Comments

| Available Ports ⟳ | + | | Selected Source Ports (0) | Selected Destination Ports (2) |

🔍 Search by name or value

Bittorrent			any	HTTP	🗑
DNS_over_TCP		**Add to Source**		HTTPS	🗑
DNS_over_UDP		Add to Destination			
FTP					
HTTP					
HTTPS					
IMAP					
LDAP			Protocol TCP (6) ▼ Port Enter a Add	Protocol TCP (6) ▼ Port Enter a Add

Cancel   Add

Figure 10-11 *Selection of Web Services (TCP Ports 80 and 443)*

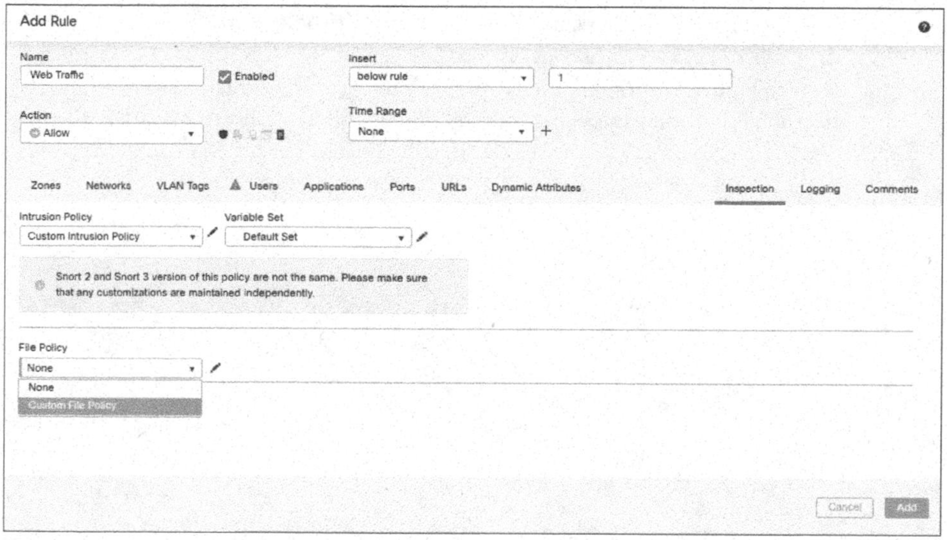

Add Rule

Name
| Web Traffic | ☑ Enabled |

Insert
| below rule ▼ | 1 |

Action
| ☉ Allow ▼ | ● ▲ ☐ ⊟ ▣ |

Time Range
| None ▼ | + |

Zones   Networks   VLAN Tags ⚠ Users   Applications   Ports   URLs   Dynamic Attributes   **Inspection**   Logging   Comments

Intrusion Policy   Variable Set
| Custom Intrusion Policy ▼ | ✎ | | Default Set ▼ | ✎ |

ⓘ Snort 2 and Snort 3 version of this policy are not the same. Please make sure
   that any customizations are maintained independently.

File Policy
| None ▼ | ✎ |
| None |
| Custom File Policy |

Cancel   Add

Figure 10-12 *Association of Advanced Security Policies with an Access Control Rule*

e. On the Logging tab, select **Log at End of Connection** to enable logging
for any matching connections (see Figure 10-13). This is an optional step,
but it allows you to view a connection event when a threat defense allows
web traffic. Do not enable logging simultaneously for both phases—the
beginning and end of connections—to avoid any performance issues.

f. Click the **Add** button to add the rule into the policy. You then return to the
policy editor page.

10

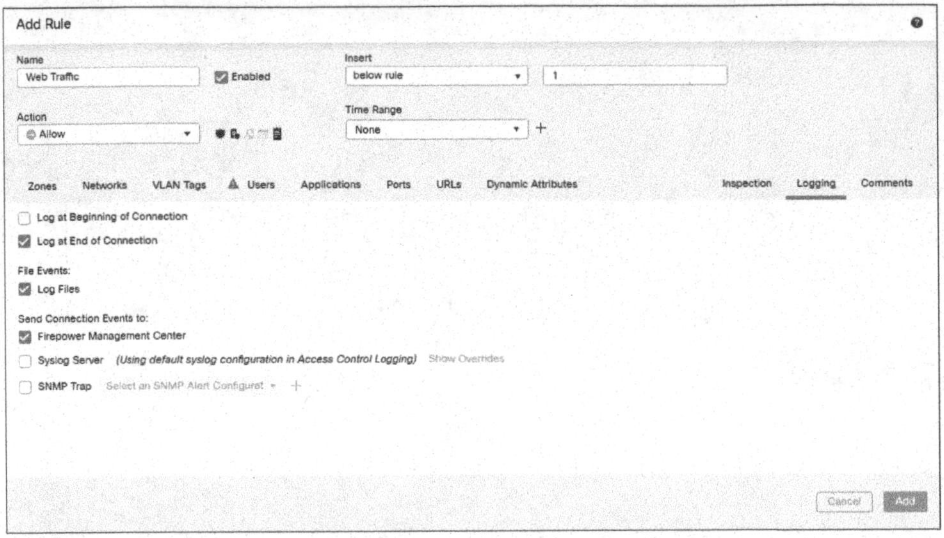

Figure 10-13 *Logging Settings for a Rule with the Allow Action*

Step 6. Select an action for the traffic that will not match any of the access control rules you have added so far. At the bottom of the policy editor page, click the drop-down next to **Default Action** to choose an action for the unmatched traffic (see Figure 10-14). Optionally, to generate logs for connections matching the default action, enable logging for the default action, as shown in Figure 10-15.

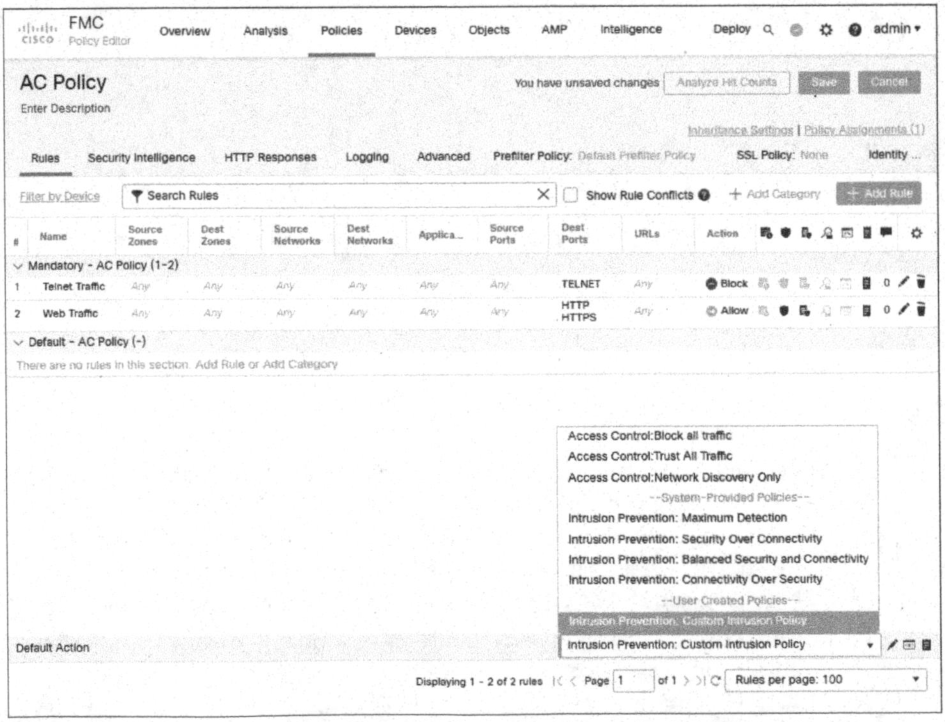

Figure 10-14 *Selecting a Default Action for the Unmatched Traffic*

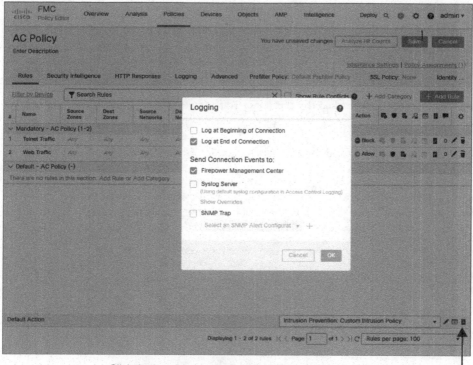

Click the Logging Icon to Enable Logging
for Connections Matching Default Action

Figure 10-15 *Enabling Logging for Connections Matching the Default Action*

Step 7.   Click the **Save** button to save the changes in this policy.

Step 8.   Go to **Deploy > Deployment** to deploy the access control policy to your desired threat defense, as shown in Figure 10-16.

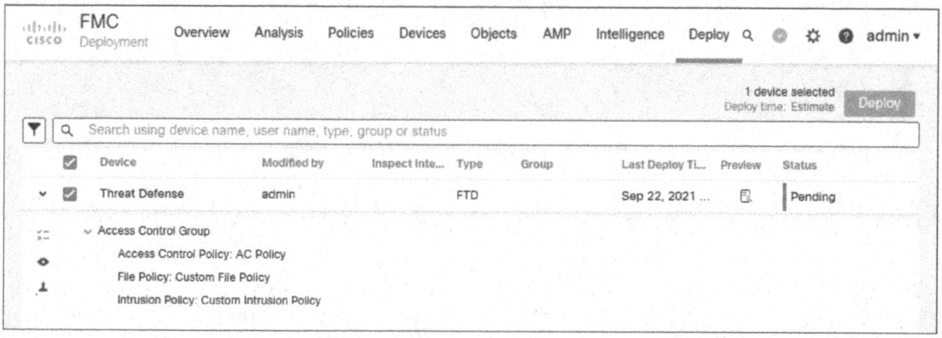

Figure 10-16 *Deployment of an Access Control Policy to a Threat Defense*

Verification

After you deploy the policy, it is time to verify whether the policy works as expected in the lab environment (refer to Figure 10-6). From the client computer (IP address: 172.16.1.200), try to connect to the server (IP address: 192.168.1.2) through the threat defense. Here are the test scenarios and their results that you can expect per the access control policy:

- Telnet connection: Blocked (by the Telnet Traffic rule)

- Web access: Allowed (by the Web Traffic rule)

- SSH connection: Allowed (by the Default Action of the policy)

Figure 10-17 shows three types of connections from the client to the server. Per the access control policy, the Telnet traffic is blocked, and the web traffic is allowed by the custom access control rules. However, when a connection does not match any custom rules, it hits the default action. In this case, the SSH traffic was allowed by the default action.

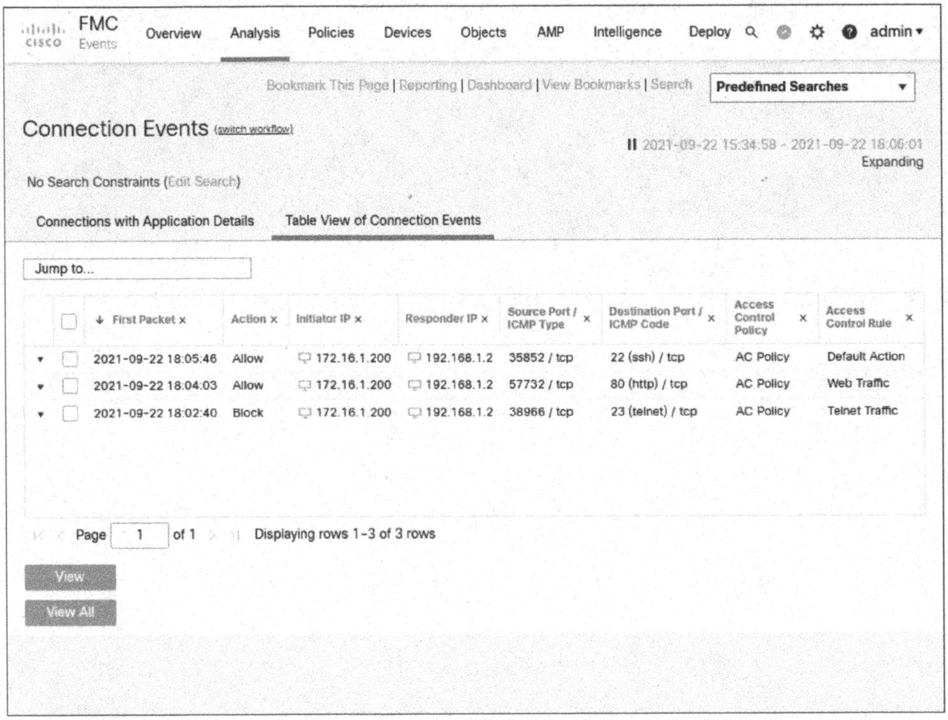

Figure 10-17 *Connection Events Confirm the Actions by the Access Control Policy*

You can use the management center's GUI to view the rule hit counts. On the policy editor page, select the Analyze Hit Counts button. It opens the Hit Count window. Click the Refresh button to load the latest statistics in this window.

Figure 10-18 shows hit counts for the access control rules.

Alternatively, you can view all the access control rules and their respective hit counts by using the command-line interface of the threat defense.

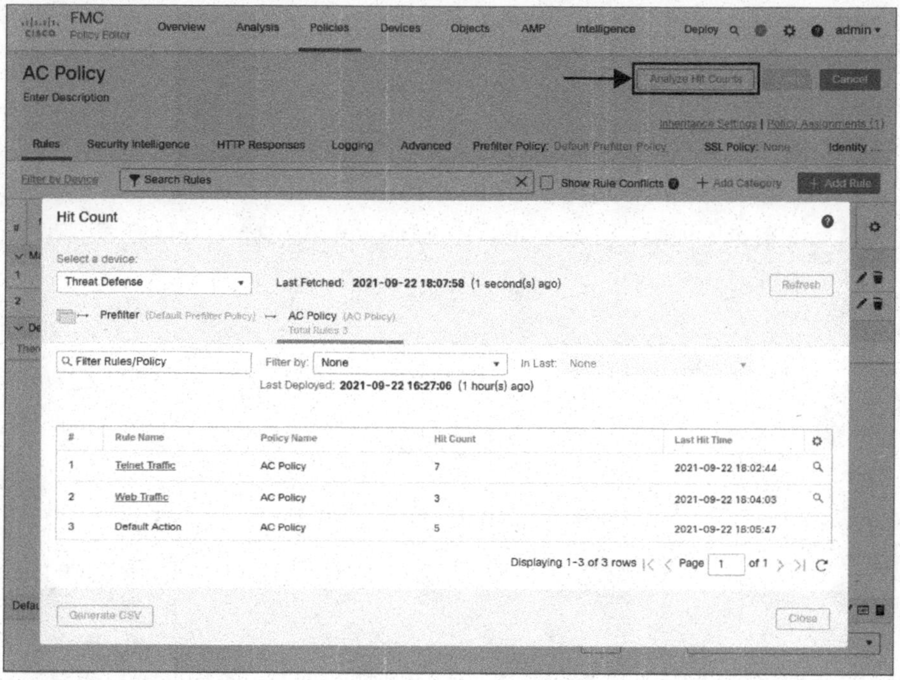

Figure 10-18 *Hit Counts of the Access Control Policy*

Example 10-1 uses the CLI to show the currently deployed access control rules on a threat defense. Both custom rules—Telnet Traffic and Web Traffic—and their hit counts are highlighted in the output. Also, the rules for the default action are available at the end of the output.

Example 10-1 *Currently Deployed Access Control Rules and Their Hit Counts*

```
> show access-list
access-list cached ACL log flows: total 0, denied 0 (deny-flow-max 4096)
          alert-interval 300
access-list CSM_FW_ACL_; 9 elements; name hash: 0x4a69e3f3
access-list CSM_FW_ACL_ line 1 remark rule-id 9998: PREFILTER POLICY: Default Tunnel
and Priority Policy
access-list CSM_FW_ACL_ line 2 remark rule-id 9998: RULE: DEFAULT TUNNEL ACTION RULE
access-list CSM_FW_ACL_ line 3 advanced permit ipinip any any rule-id 9998
(hitcnt=0) 0xf5b597d6
access-list CSM_FW_ACL_ line 4 advanced permit udp any eq 3544 any range 1025 65535
rule-id 9998 (hitcnt=0) 0x46d7839e
access-list CSM_FW_ACL_ line 5 advanced permit udp any range 1025 65535 any eq 3544
rule-id 9998 (hitcnt=0) 0xaf1d5aa5
access-list CSM_FW_ACL_ line 6 advanced permit 41 any any rule-id 9998 (hitcnt=0)
0x06095aba
access-list CSM_FW_ACL_ line 7 advanced permit gre any any rule-id 9998 (hitcnt=0)
0x52c7a066
access-list CSM_FW_ACL_ line 8 remark rule-id 268443648: ACCESS POLICY:
AC Policy - Mandatory
access-list CSM_FW_ACL_ line 9 remark rule-id 268443648: L4 RULE: Telnet Traffic
access-list CSM_FW_ACL_ line 10 advanced deny tcp any any object-group TELNET
rule-id 268443648 event-log flow-start (hitcnt=7) 0xae7f8544
```

10

```
    access-list CSM_FW_ACL_ line 10 advanced deny tcp any any eq telnet rule-id
268443648 event-log flow-start (hitcnt=7) 0x2bcbaf06
access-list CSM_FW_ACL_ line 11 remark rule-id 268443649: ACCESS POLICY: AC
Policy - Mandatory
access-list CSM_FW_ACL_ line 12 remark rule-id 268443649: L7 RULE: Web Traffic
access-list CSM_FW_ACL_ line 13 advanced permit tcp any any object-group HTTP
rule-id 268443649 (hitcnt=8) 0x5f6af719
    access-list CSM_FW_ACL_ line 13 advanced permit tcp any any eq www rule-id
268443649 (hitcnt=8) 0x548e4473
access-list CSM_FW_ACL_ line 14 advanced permit tcp any any object-group HTTPS
rule-id 268443649 (hitcnt=0) 0x0eb6ef10
    access-list CSM_FW_ACL_ line 14 advanced permit tcp any any eq https rule-id
268443649 (hitcnt=0) 0x355e77bc
access-list CSM_FW_ACL_ line 15 remark rule-id 268434432: ACCESS POLICY: AC
Policy - Default
access-list CSM_FW_ACL_ line 16 remark rule-id 268434432: L4 RULE: DEFAULT ACTION
RULE
access-list CSM_FW_ACL_ line 17 advanced permit ip any any rule-id 268434432
(hitcnt=26) 0xa1d3780e
>
```

A threat defense enables you to debug the operation of the threat defense security engines. By running the **system support firewall-engine-debug** command on the CLI, you can see the details behind the processing of traffic flowing through the threat defense (see Example 10-2). When you run this command, specify as many filters as possible to limit the scope of what gets reported from this command in the CLI console.

Example 10-2 *Debug Messages Generated by the Threat Defense Engines*

```
> system support firewall-engine-debug

Please specify an IP protocol: tcp
Please specify a client IP address:
Please specify a client port:
Please specify a server IP address:
Please specify a server port:
Monitoring firewall engine debug messages
.
.

! Client attempts to connect to the server using Telnet service
.
172.16.1.200-41090 > 192.168.1.2-23 6 AS 1-1 I 1 Got start of flow event from
hardware with flags 00020001
17
2.16.1.200-41090 > 192.168.1.2-23 6 AS 1-1 I 1 Logging SOF for event from hardware
with rule_id = 268443648 ruleAction = 4 ruleReason = 0
.
.
```

```
! Client uses a browser to access the web server

.

.

172.16.1.200-33498 > 192.168.1.2-80 6 AS 1-1 I 0 new firewall session
172.16.1.200-33498 > 192.168.1.2-80 6 AS 1-1 I 0 using HW or preset rule order 3,
'Web Traffic', action Allow and prefilter rule 0
172.16.1.200-33498 > 192.168.1.2-80 6 AS 1-1 I 0 HitCount data sent for rule
id: 268443649,
172.16.1.200-33498 > 192.168.1.2-80 6 AS 1-1 I 0 allow action
172.16.1.200-33498 > 192.168.1.2-80 6 AS 1-1 I 0 File policy verdict is None
172.16.1.200-33498 > 192.168.1.2-80 6 AS 1-1 I 0 deleting firewall session
flags = 0x14001, fwFlags = 0x1100
172.16.1.200-33498 > 192.168.1.2-80 6 AS 1-1 I 0 Logging EOF as part of session
delete with rule_id = 268443649 ruleAction = 2 ruleReason = 0

.

.

! Client connects to the server using Secure Shell (SSH) protocol

.

.

172.16.1.200-59178 > 192.168.1.2-22 6 AS 1-1 I 0 new firewall session
172.16.1.200-59178 > 192.168.1.2-22 6 AS 1-1 I 0 using HW or preset rule order 4,
'Default Action', action Allow and prefilter rule 0
172.16.1.200-59178 > 192.168.1.2-22 6 AS 1-1 I 0 HitCount data sent for rule
id: 268434432,
172.16.1.200-59178 > 192.168.1.2-22 6 AS 1-1 I 0 allow action
172.16.1.200-59178 > 192.168.1.2-22 6 AS 1-1 I 0 deleting firewall session
flags = 0x28003, fwFlags = 0x1100

^C
Caught interrupt signal
Exiting.
>
```

When you confirm that traffic is dropped by the threat defense, but you are unable to
determine the root cause of that drop, you can analyze the trace data of the packet capture.
The trace command feedback can point you to the threat defense component that causes a
packet drop. Figure 10-19 illustrates various reasons for a packet drop by a threat defense,
and Figure 10-20 details the processing of a packet through different elements of a threat
defense. Note that both images highlight the positions of the access control components.

The following three examples exhibit the trace data of three connection attempts that
are analyzed by the current access control policy. Example 10-3 shows the denied Telnet
attempt, Example 10-4 displays access to the web server, and Example 10-5 shows a successful SSH connection. The process to capture packets using the management center's GUI is
described in Chapter 8, "Capturing Traffic for Advanced Analysis." Assuming you know the
process by now, the following examples only display the output from the packet capturing
tool.

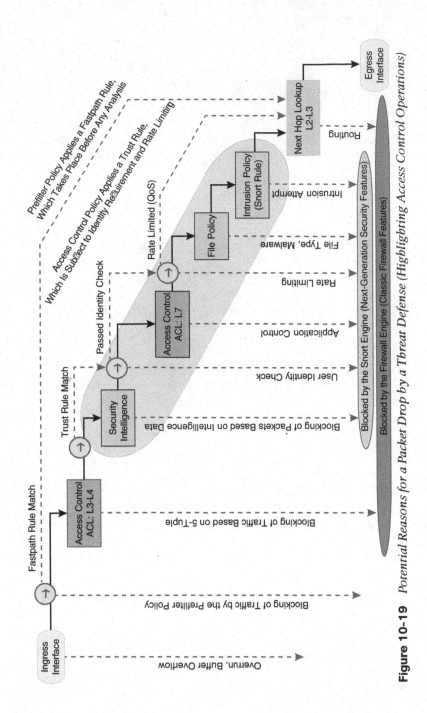

Figure 10-19 *Potential Reasons for a Packet Drop by a Threat Defense (Highlighting Access Control Operations)*

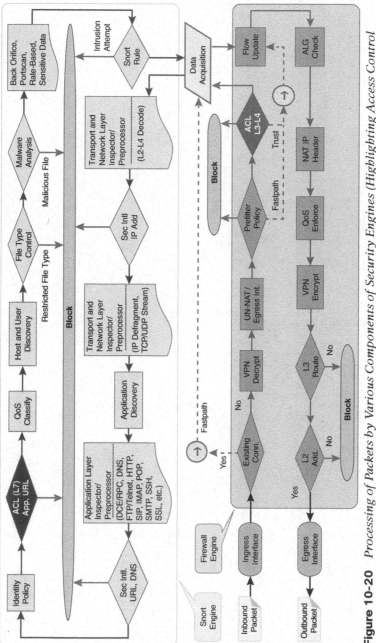

Figure 10-20 *Processing of Packets by Various Components of Security Engines (Highlighting Access Control Operations)*

10

Example 10-3   *Trace of Live Telnet Traffic, Blocked by an Access Control Rule*

```
1: 12:29:41.654369        172.16.1.200.41090 > 192.168.1.2.23: S 1576044869:
1576044869(0) win 29200 <mss 1460,sackOK,timestamp 1299709 0,nop,wscale 7>
Phase: 1
Type: CAPTURE
Subtype:
Result: ALLOW
Config:
Additional Information:
MAC Access list

Phase: 2
Type: ACCESS-LIST
Subtype:
Result: ALLOW
Config:
Implicit Rule
Additional Information:
MAC Access list

Phase: 3
Type: ROUTE-LOOKUP
Subtype: No ECMP load balancing
Result: ALLOW
Config:
Additional Information:
Destination is locally connected. No ECMP load balancing.
Found next-hop 192.168.1.2 using egress ifc  INSIDE_INTERFACE(vrfid:0)

Phase: 4
Type: ACCESS-LIST
Subtype: log
Result: DROP
Config:
access-group CSM_FW_ACL_ global
access-list CSM_FW_ACL_ advanced deny tcp any any object-group TELNET rule-id
268443648 event-log flow-start
access-list CSM_FW_ACL_ remark rule-id 268443648: ACCESS POLICY: AC
Policy - Mandatory
access-list CSM_FW_ACL_ remark rule-id 268443648: L4 RULE: Telnet Traffic
object-group service TELNET tcp
 port-object eq telnet
Additional Information:
```

```
Result:
input-interface: OUTSIDE_INTERFACE(vrfid:0)
input-status: up
input-line-status: up
Action: drop
Drop-reason: (acl-drop) Flow is denied by configured rule, Drop-location: frame
0x00005651a4470720 flow (NA)/NA
```

Example 10-4   *Trace of Live Web Traffic, Allowed by an Access Control Rule*

```
1: 12:30:49.669307        172.16.1.200.33498 > 192.168.1.2.80: S
797583708:797583708(0) win 29200 <mss 1460,sackOK,timestamp 1316712 0,nop,wscale 7>
Phase: 1
Type: CAPTURE
Subtype:
Result: ALLOW
Config:
Additional Information:
MAC Access list


Phase: 2
Type: ACCESS-LIST
Subtype:
Result: ALLOW
Config:
Implicit Rule
Additional Information:
MAC Access list


Phase: 3
Type: ROUTE-LOOKUP
Subtype: No ECMP load balancing
Result: ALLOW
Config:
Additional Information:
Destination is locally connected. No ECMP load balancing.
Found next-hop 192.168.1.2 using egress ifc  INSIDE_INTERFACE(vrfid:0)


Phase: 4
Type: ACCESS-LIST
Subtype: log
Result: ALLOW
Config:
```

10

```
access-group CSM_FW_ACL_ global
access-list CSM_FW_ACL_ advanced permit tcp any any object-group HTTP rule-id
268443649
access-list CSM_FW_ACL_ remark rule-id 268443649: ACCESS POLICY: AC
Policy - Mandatory
access-list CSM_FW_ACL_ remark rule-id 268443649: L7 RULE: Web Traffic
object-group service HTTP tcp
 port-object eq www
Additional Information:
 This packet will be sent to snort for additional processing where a verdict will be
reached

Phase: 5
Type: CONN-SETTINGS
Subtype:
Result: ALLOW
Config:
class-map class-default
 match any
policy-map global_policy
 class class-default
  set connection advanced-options UM_STATIC_TCP_MAP
service-policy global_policy global
Additional Information:

Phase: 6
Type: NAT
Subtype: per-session
Result: ALLOW
Config:
Additional Information:

Phase: 7
Type: IP-OPTIONS
Subtype:
Result: ALLOW
Config:
Additional Information:

Phase: 8
Type: CAPTURE
Subtype:
Result: ALLOW
Config:
Additional Information:
```

```
Phase: 9
Type: NAT
Subtype: per-session
Result: ALLOW
Config:
Additional Information:

Phase: 10
Type: IP-OPTIONS
Subtype:
Result: ALLOW
Config:
Additional Information:

Phase: 11
Type: CAPTURE
Subtype:
Result: ALLOW
Config:
Additional Information:

Phase: 12
Type: FLOW-CREATION
Subtype:
Result: ALLOW
Config:
Additional Information:
New flow created with id 37, packet dispatched to next module

Phase: 13
Type: EXTERNAL-INSPECT
Subtype:
Result: ALLOW
Config:
Additional Information:
Application: 'SNORT Inspect'

Phase: 14
Type: SNORT
Subtype:
Result: ALLOW
Config:
Additional Information:
Snort Trace:
```

10

```
Packet: TCP, SYN, seq 797583708
Session: new snort session
AppID: service unknown (0), application unknown (0)
Firewall: allow rule,  'Web Traffic' , allow
Snort id 0, NAP id 2, IPS id 1, Verdict PASS
Snort Verdict: (pass-packet) allow this packet


Phase: 15
Type: INPUT-ROUTE-LOOKUP-FROM-OUTPUT-ROUTE-LOOKUP
Subtype: Resolve Preferred Egress interface
Result: ALLOW
Config:
Additional Information:
Found next-hop 192.168.1.2 using egress ifc  INSIDE_INTERFACE(vrfid:0)


Phase: 16
Type: ADJACENCY-LOOKUP
Subtype: Resolve Nexthop IP address to MAC
Result: ALLOW
Config:
Additional Information:
Found adjacency entry for Next-hop 192.168.1.2 on interface  INSIDE_INTERFACE
Adjacency :Active
MAC address 0023.2472.1d3c hits 105 reference 1


Result:
input-interface: OUTSIDE_INTERFACE(vrfid:0)
input-status: up
input-line-status: up
output-interface: INSIDE_INTERFACE(vrfid:0)
output-status: up
output-line-status: up
Action: allow
```

Example 10-5 *Trace of Live SSH Traffic, Allowed by Default Action*

```
1: 12:31:53.714104      172.16.1.200.59178 > 192.168.1.2.22: S 2673341661:
2673341661(0) win 29200 <mss 1460,sackOK,timestamp 1332724 0,nop,wscale 7>
Phase: 1
Type: CAPTURE
Subtype:
Result: ALLOW
Config:
Additional Information:
MAC Access list
```

```
Phase: 2
Type: ACCESS-LIST
Subtype:
Result: ALLOW
Config:
Implicit Rule
Additional Information:
MAC Access list


Phase: 3
Type: ROUTE-LOOKUP
Subtype: No ECMP load balancing
Result: ALLOW
Config:
Additional Information:
Destination is locally connected. No ECMP load balancing.
Found next-hop 192.168.1.2 using egress ifc  INSIDE_INTERFACE(vrfid:0)


Phase: 4
Type: ACCESS-LIST
Subtype: log
Result: ALLOW
Config:
access-group CSM_FW_ACL_ global
access-list CSM_FW_ACL_ advanced permit ip any any rule-id 268434432
access-list CSM_FW_ACL_ remark rule-id 268434432: ACCESS POLICY: AC Policy - Default
access-list CSM_FW_ACL_ remark rule-id 268434432: L4 RULE: DEFAULT ACTION RULE
Additional Information:
 This packet will be sent to snort for additional processing where a verdict will be
reached


Phase: 5
Type: CONN-SETTINGS
Subtype:
Result: ALLOW
Config:
class-map class-default
 match any
policy-map global_policy
 class class-default
  set connection advanced-options UM_STATIC_TCP_MAP
service-policy global_policy global
Additional Information:
```

10

```
Phase: 6
Type: NAT
Subtype: per-session
Result: ALLOW
Config:
Additional Information:

Phase: 7
Type: IP-OPTIONS
Subtype:
Result: ALLOW
Config:
Additional Information:

Phase: 8
Type: CAPTURE
Subtype:
Result: ALLOW
Config:
Additional Information:

Phase: 9
Type: NAT
Subtype: per-session
Result: ALLOW
Config:
Additional Information:

Phase: 10
Type: IP-OPTIONS
Subtype:
Result: ALLOW
Config:
Additional Information:

Phase: 11
Type: CAPTURE
Subtype:
Result: ALLOW
Config:
Additional Information:

Phase: 12
Type: FLOW-CREATION
```

```
Subtype:
Result: ALLOW
Config:
Additional Information:
New flow created with id 38, packet dispatched to next module


Phase: 13
Type: EXTERNAL-INSPECT
Subtype:
Result: ALLOW
Config:
Additional Information:
Application: 'SNORT Inspect'


Phase: 14
Type: SNORT
Subtype:
Result: ALLOW
Config:
Additional Information:
Snort Trace:
Packet: TCP, SYN, seq 2673341661
Session: new snort session
AppID: service unknown (0), application unknown (0)
Firewall: allow rule, 'Default Action' , allow
Snort id 0, NAP id 2, IPS id 1, Verdict PASS
Snort Verdict: (pass-packet) allow this packet


Phase: 15
Type: INPUT-ROUTE-LOOKUP-FROM-OUTPUT-ROUTE-LOOKUP
Subtype: Resolve Preferred Egress interface
Result: ALLOW
Config:
Additional Information:
Found next-hop 192.168.1.2 using egress ifc  INSIDE_INTERFACE(vrfid:0)


Phase: 16
Type: ADJACENCY-LOOKUP
Subtype: Resolve Nexthop IP address to MAC
Result: ALLOW
Config:
Additional Information:
Found adjacency entry for Next-hop 192.168.1.2 on interface  INSIDE_INTERFACE
Adjacency :Active
MAC address 0023.2472.1d3c hits 112 reference 1
```

10

```
Result:
input-interface: OUTSIDE_INTERFACE(vrfid:0)
input-status: up
input-line-status: up
output-interface: INSIDE_INTERFACE(vrfid:0)
output-status: up
output-line-status: up
Action: allow
```

Summary

This chapter describes various components of an access control policy. To demonstrate the configuration workflow, this chapter provides step-by-step instructions on how to add access control rules with different actions and associate a rule for advanced security inspection. Later, various tools are used to verify the successful deployment of an access control policy and to explain the detailed operations of access control rules.

Exam Preparation Tasks

As mentioned in the section "How to Use This Book" in the Introduction, you have a couple of choices for exam preparation: the exercises here, Chapter 22, "Final Preparation," and the exam simulation questions in the Pearson Test Prep practice test software.

Review All Key Topics

Review the most important topics in this chapter, noted with the Key Topic icon in the outer margin of the page. Table 10-2 lists a reference of these key topics and the page numbers on which each is found.

Table 10-2   Key Topics for Chapter 10

Key Topic Element	Description	Page
Bullet list	Understanding the access control policy editor	196
Bullet list	Placement of access control rules	199
Bullet list	Finding shadowed and unused rules	199
Bullet list	Different ways to block traffic	202
Step list	Best practices for logging enablement	205

Complete Tables and Lists from Memory

There are no Memory Tables or Lists in this chapter.

Define Key Terms

Define the following key terms from this chapter, and check your answers in the Glossary:

shadowed rules, Show Rule Conflict, Analyze Hit Counts, default action

## CHAPTER 11

Prefilter Policy

This chapter provides an overview of the following topics:

Prefilter Policy Essentials: This section describes the functions of a prefilter policy and the actions you can take on traffic using a prefilter rule.

Best Practices for a Prefilter Policy: This section provides guidelines for considering a prefilter policy to handle traffic.

Enabling Bypass Through a Prefilter Policy: This section demonstrates the configuration and deployment of a prefilter policy on Secure Firewall.

Establishing Trust Through an Access Control Policy: This section shows an alternative to prefilter rules when you want to bypass inspection.

Verification: In this section, you learn the command to find the prefilter rules using the threat defense CLI. You also learn how to use the management center's GUI to determine whether a connection is handled by an access control policy or a prefilter policy.

Managing Encapsulated Traffic Inspection: This section discusses the options in a prefilter policy that you can use to manage encapsulated traffic through a threat defense.

The objectives of this chapter are to learn about

- Configuration and deployment of prefilter policy
- Differences between prefilter policy and access control policy
- Different ways to bypass deep packet inspection
- Inspection of encapsulated traffic

A prefilter policy is the first line of defense among all the security components of Secure Firewall. Both security policies—the prefilter policy and access control policy—allow a threat defense to block traffic or bypass deep packet inspection. A prefilter policy, however, acts on traffic earlier and faster than traffic passed to the access control policy. This chapter describes the prefilter policy and demonstrates its operational advantages over an access control policy by using a bypass operation as an example.

"Do I Know This Already?" Quiz

The "Do I Know This Already?" quiz enables you to assess whether you should read this entire chapter thoroughly or jump to the "Exam Preparation Tasks" section. If you are in doubt about your answers to these questions or your own assessment of your knowledge of the topics, read the entire chapter. Table 11-1 lists the major headings in this chapter and their corresponding "Do I Know This Already?" quiz questions. You can find the answers in Appendix A, "Answers to the 'Do I Know This Already?' Quizzes."

Table 11-1 "Do I Know This Already?" Section-to-Question Mapping

Foundation Topics Section	Questions
Prefilter Policy Essentials	1, 2
Best Practices for a Prefilter Policy	3
Enabling Bypass Through a Prefilter Policy	4
Establishing Trust Through an Access Control Policy	5
Verification	6
Managing Encapsulated Traffic Inspection	7

CAUTION The goal of self-assessment is to gauge your mastery of the topics in this chapter. If you do not know the answer to a question or are only partially sure of the answer, you should mark that question as wrong for purposes of the self-assessment. Giving yourself credit for an answer you correctly guess skews your self-assessment results and might provide you with a false sense of security.

1. Which of the following rules can bypass security inspection?

   a. Prefilter rule

   b. Tunnel rule

   c. Access control rule

   d. All of these answers are correct.

2. What is the difference between a prefilter rule and an access control rule?

   a. A prefilter rule matches for traffic prior to an access control rule.

   b. A prefilter rule analyzes traffic based on the outermost header of a packet, whereas an access control rule analyzes the innermost header.

   c. A prefilter rule supports limited constraints to create a rule, whereas an access control rule offers many granular options.

   d. All of these answers are correct.

3. Which of the following is a best practice for rule creation?

   a. To block traffic based on network address or port number, a prefilter rule is a better choice than an access control rule.

   b. To bypass inspection, consider a prefilter rule over an access control rule.

   c. Bypassing deep packet inspection on management traffic can improve network performance.

   d. All of these answers are correct.

4. Which of the following items is not mandatory when deploying a prefilter policy?

   a. Invoking a prefilter policy into an access control policy.

   b. Enabling logging in a prefilter rule.

   c. Choosing a default action for tunnel traffic.

   d. All of these items are mandatory.

5. Which of the following rules can be used to bypass traffic that is destined to a specific URL?

   a. Tunnel rule.

   b. Prefilter rule with Fastpath action.

   c. Access control rule with Trust action.

   d. All of these answers are correct.

6. Which of the following commands displays the rules that are configured in a prefilter policy?

   a. **show access-list**

   b. **show acl all**

   c. **show prefilter-policy**

   d. **show prefilter-list**

7. With which encapsulation protocols can Secure Firewall analyze traffic?

   a. GRE

   b. IP-in-IP

   c. IPv6-in-IP

   d. All of these answers are correct.

Foundation Topics

Prefilter Policy Essentials

If you trust certain hosts in your network and do not want their traffic to be inspected, you can instruct a threat defense to bypass any traffic to and from those hosts with a prefilter policy. The threat defense can bypass inspection of particular traffic while the rest of the network traffic can be subject to deep packet inspection. Because bypassing inspection reduces processing overhead, it can eventually improve network latency and overall user experiences.

Prefilter Policy: Rules and Actions

In a prefilter policy, there are three ways to assign an action to the traffic: the tunnel rule, prefilter rule, and default action (see Figure 11-1).

- **Tunnel rule:** A tunnel rule, as the name suggests, filters tunnel traffic that is encapsulated by an additional IP header—for example, GRE, IP-in-IP, and IPv6-in-IP. A tunnel rule can rezone the inner sessions of tunnels for further analysis by next-generation security policies.

- **Prefilter rule:** A prefilter rule allows you to filter traffic based on basic networking constraints, such as IP address, port number, VLAN tag, and interface. However, it does not support rezoning.

- **Default action:** The default action is applicable only for tunnel traffic. The default action offers two actions on tunnel traffic: analyze and block. However, you cannot rezone tunnels. When a tunnel does not match any rules in the prefilter policy, the default action can block the tunnel or forward the encapsulated/tunneled traffic to the access control policy for further analysis.

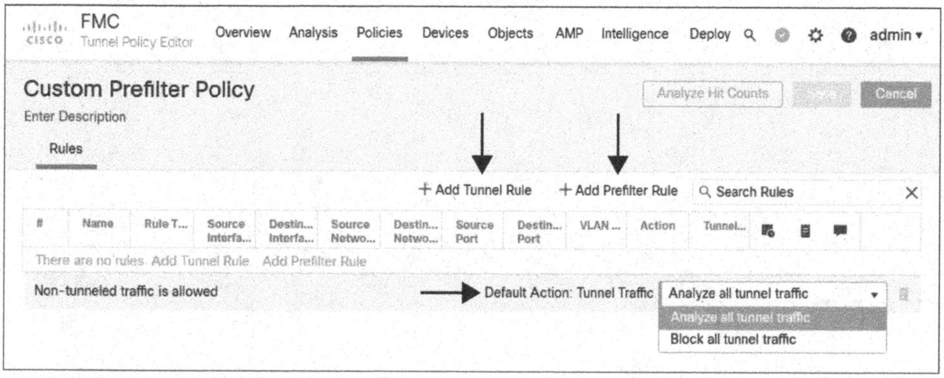

Figure 11-1 *Prefilter Policy Editor*

A rule's action determines how a threat defense handles the matching traffic. Both a tunnel rule and prefilter rule offer three types of actions:

- **Analyze:** This action allows a threat defense to perform further analysis on matching traffic. The traffic will continue to be inspected and controlled by the rules on next-generation security policies, such as access control policies, intrusion policies, and malware and file policies.

- **Block:** This action blocks matching traffic immediately. No further inspection is performed by any policy components of Secure Firewall.

- **Fastpath:** This action bypasses any further security analysis by a threat defense. Moreover, the matching traffic is no longer subject to rate limit and identity requirements.

Bypassing Deep Packet Inspection

Secure Firewall offers two types of rule actions to bypass deep packet inspection. While the end result appears to be identical, the implementation and operation of each action are different. For example,

- **Fastpath action:** This action is enabled through a prefilter policy. A prefilter rule with the Fastpath action can enable a threat defense to bypass traffic before a packet even reaches the firewall engine and Snort engine. This functionality is known as Fastpath. You can apply the Fastpath action on both the tunnel rule and prefilter rule. A prefilter rule with the Fastpath action is also known as a **fastpath rule**.

11

■ **Trust action:** This action is invoked by way of an access control policy rule rather than a prefilter policy rule. An access control rule with the Trust action allows a threat defense to bypass deep packet inspection. Trusted traffic checks for identity and quality of service (QoS) requirements as configured in their respective policies. An access control rule with the Trust action is known as a **trust rule**.

Access control policy rules offer more granular filtering capability. For example, you can match and trust traffic based on applications, URLs, users, and so on. Unlike a prefilter rule, an access control rule uses the innermost header of a packet to filter traffic. Figure 11-2 exhibits the differences between the prefilter rule editor and access control rule editor.

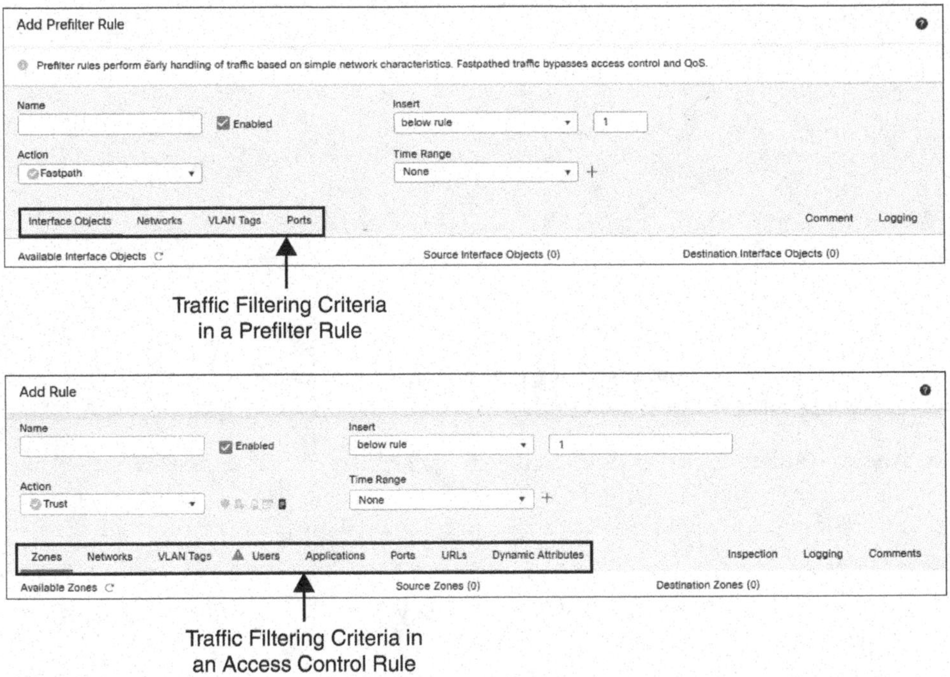

Traffic Filtering Criteria
in a Prefilter Rule

Traffic Filtering Criteria in
an Access Control Rule

Figure 11-2 *A Prefilter Rule Can Filter Traffic Based on Interface, Network, VLAN, and Port*

Figure 11-3 shows the workflow of a trust rule and a fastpath rule on Secure Firewall. When a packet matches a trust rule or a fastpath rule, it bypasses various inspection components.

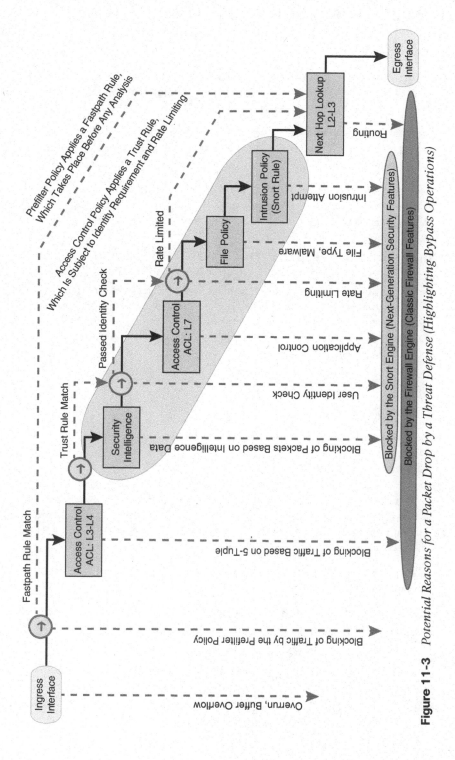

Figure 11-3 *Potential Reasons for a Packet Drop by a Threat Defense (Highlighting Bypass Operations)*

Best Practices for a Prefilter Policy

If you are debating between a prefilter rule and an access control rule, the following guidelines could help:

- When you want to block traffic or bypass inspection based on simple conditions, such as network address, port number, VLAN tags, and interface objects, you should use a prefilter rule instead of an access control rule.

- Network management traffic is time sensitive. Enabling advanced deep packet inspection on management traffic can introduce latency in the network. If you trust the management traffic, consider bypassing inspection using a prefilter policy.

- Likewise, in the High Frequency Trading (HFT) and High-Performance Computing (HPC) environments, where higher speed and higher performance are extremely critical, you can deploy a prefilter policy for latency-sensitive traffic.

Enabling Bypass Through a Prefilter Policy

The default prefilter policy that comes with Secure Firewall out of the box provides limited configurable options. However, to take advantage of all the features and filtering conditions of a prefilter rule, you need to create your own prefilter policy. As an example, the following sections demonstrate how to create a custom prefilter policy and add a prefilter rule to it to bypass trusted traffic over port 22—the default port for the SSH protocol. Mainly, there are two phases in this configuration process:

- **In prefilter policy:** Create a custom prefilter policy and add a prefilter rule with a Fastpath action to match SSH traffic.

- **In access control policy:** Invoke the custom prefilter policy into the access control policy that will be deployed on the threat defense.

Fulfilling Prerequisites

This chapter uses a lab environment where a threat defense is registered with a management center and is deployed between an inside host and an outside host in routed firewall mode. The hosts use the Secure Shell (SSH) and web (HTTP, HTTPS) services for communication. The configuration examples in this chapter use SSH, HTTP, and HTTPS protocols to demonstrate the actions of the fastpath and trust rules.

Figure 11-4 shows the simple lab topology that is used in this chapter to demonstrate bypassing inspection.

Configuring a Rule in a Prefilter Policy

To create a custom prefilter policy and add a prefilter rule to it, follow these steps:

Step 1.   Navigate to **Policies > Access Control > Prefilter**. The Prefilter Policy page appears. It shows a list of currently available prefilter policies. By default, the management center comes with the default prefilter policy.

Step 2.   Click the **New Policy** button to create a new prefilter policy. The New Policy configuration window appears (see Figure 11-5).

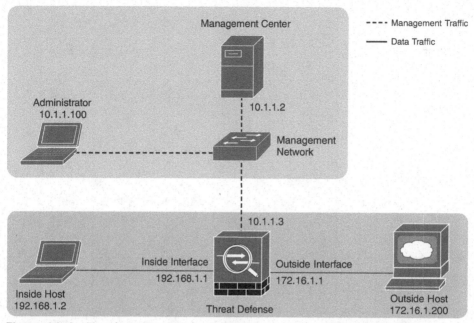

Figure 11-4   *Topology Used in the Configuration Examples of This Chapter*

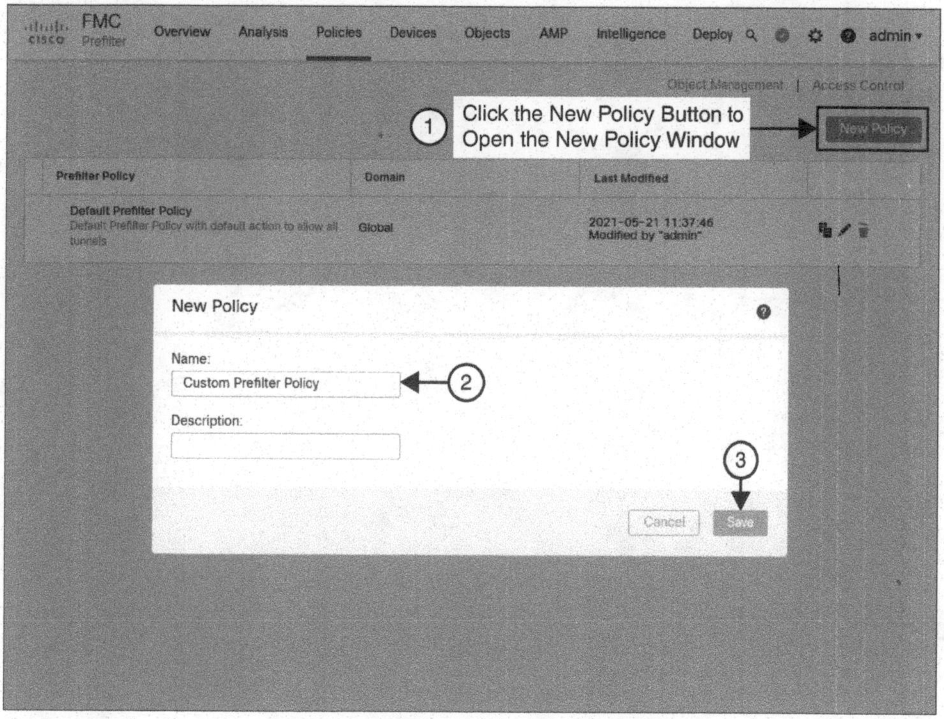

Figure 11-5   *The Window to Create a New Prefilter Policy*

Step 3.   Give a name to the new policy. Click the **Save** button to create the new prefilter policy. It opens the new policy in the policy editor (see Figure 11-6).

11

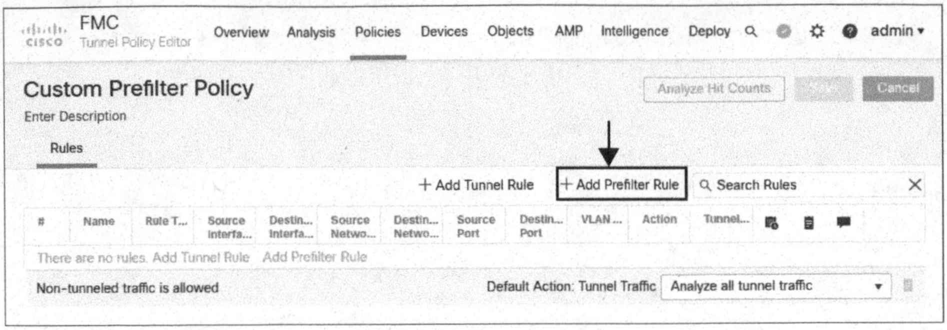

Figure 11-6 *The Prefilter Policy Editor Page*

Step 4. In the prefilter policy editor page, click the **Add Prefilter Rule** button. The Add Prefilter Rule window appears. This window enables you to create and modify a prefilter rule.

Step 5. On the Add Prefilter Rule window, give a name to the rule and set the Action to **Fastpath.**

Step 6. Click the **Port** tab and select **SSH** from the Available Ports list.

Step 7. Click the **Add to Destination** button to select SSH (TCP port 22) as the destination port. It will match traffic that is destined to port 22. Figure 11-7 shows the creation of a custom prefilter rule, named Shell Prefilter. The rule uses the Fastpath action and selects the default port for the SSH protocol (TCP port 22) as the destination port.

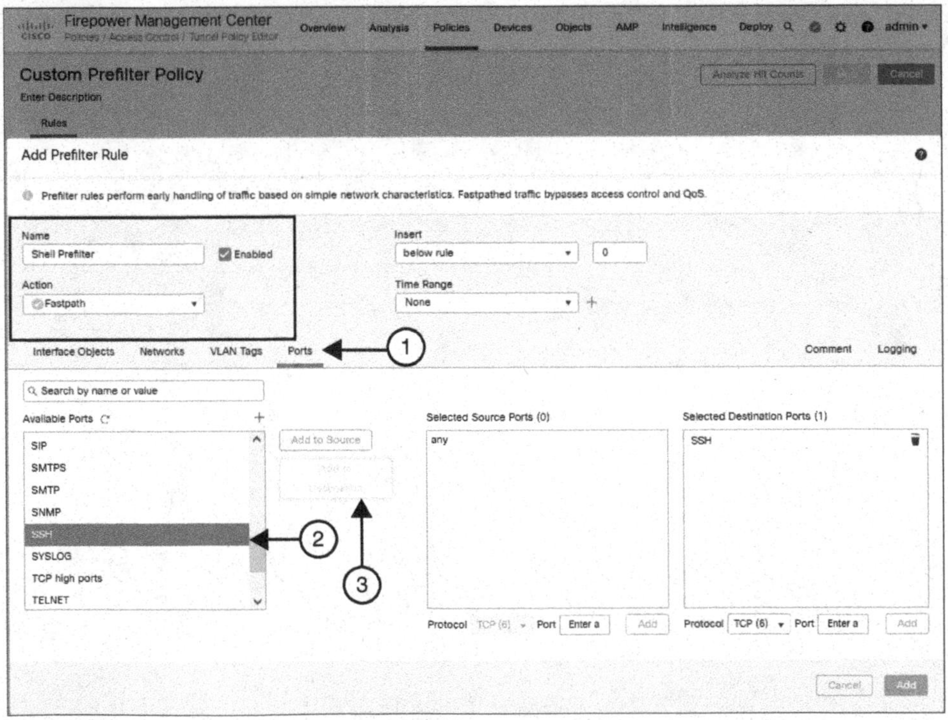

Figure 11-7 *Configuration of a Prefilter Rule to Match the Destination Port*

NOTE   You could save the rule right here (after Step 7). It would match and fastpath any traffic that is transferred over port 22. However, if you want to bypass inspection for traffic that originated from a particular subnet, complete Steps 8 and 9.

Step 8.   Select the **Networks** tab. By default, the management center comes with pre-configured objects for some well-known network addresses, such as private IP addresses and multicast addresses. If they match with your network-addressing scheme, you can select them here. Alternatively, you can create a network object on the fly, or just add an IP address directly as a source or destination. Figure 11-8 illustrates the available options to match the source and destination networks for a prefilter rule.

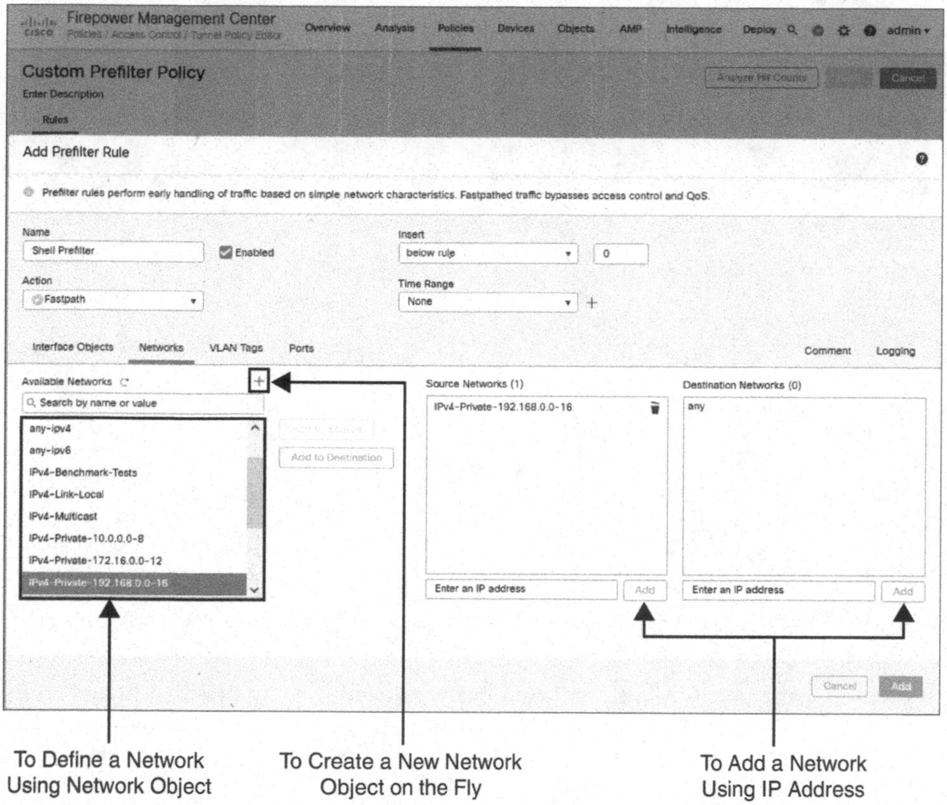

To Define a Network Using Network Object   To Create a New Network Object on the Fly   To Add a Network Using IP Address

Figure 11-8   *Options to Add Networks*

Step 9.   After you select your desired network object, click the **Add to Source** button. This makes the prefilter rule to match traffic coming from your desired subnet. Figure 11-8 shows the selection of private IP addresses 192.168.0.0/16 as the source network.

11

Step 10.   Optionally, enable logging for this prefilter rule so that every time traffic matches the conditions in this rule, the threat defense generates a log and sends it to the management center. This helps you to determine whether a policy is operational and any desired traffic is bypassing inspection. To do this, go to the Logging tab and select either **Log at Beginning of Connection** or **Log at End of Connection** (see Figure 11-9). Do not select both because doing so can affect the system performance.

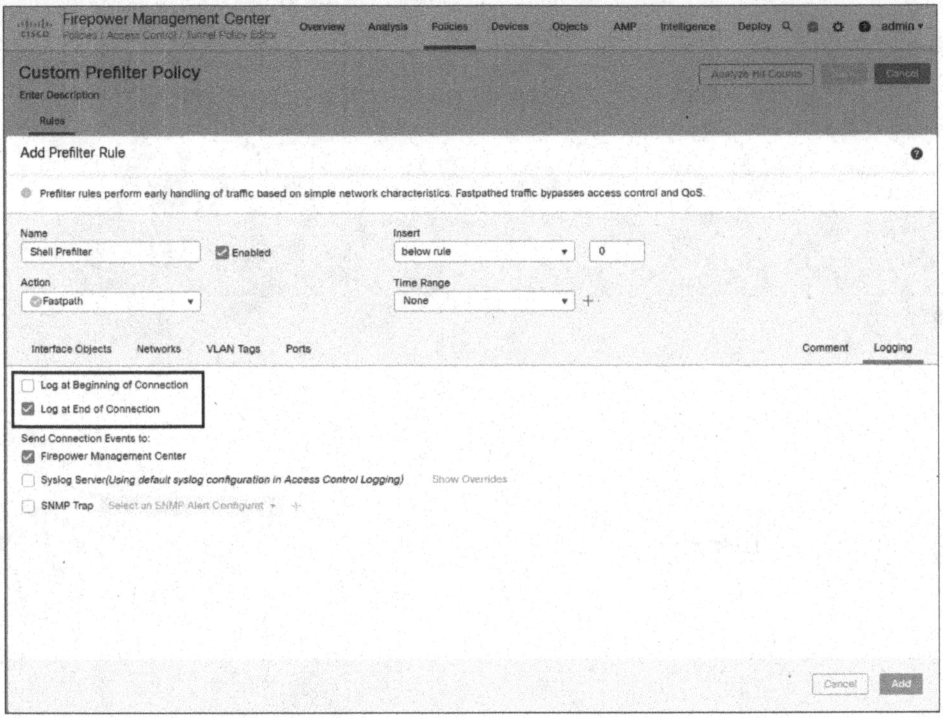

Figure 11-9   *Options to Log Connections*

Step 11.   Click the **Add** button to complete the rule configuration, and you return to the policy editor page.

Step 12.   On the policy editor page, keep the default action as **Analyze All Tunnel Traffic.** Click the **Save** button to save all the changes you have made in this custom prefilter policy (see Figure 11-10).

NOTE   Do not deploy a new prefilter policy at this stage. You need to make sure that your desired prefilter policy is invoked by way of the access control policy you intend to deploy to the threat defense. The next section, "Invoking a Prefilter Policy in an Access Control Policy," describes how to do that. For now, just click the Save button to store the changes.

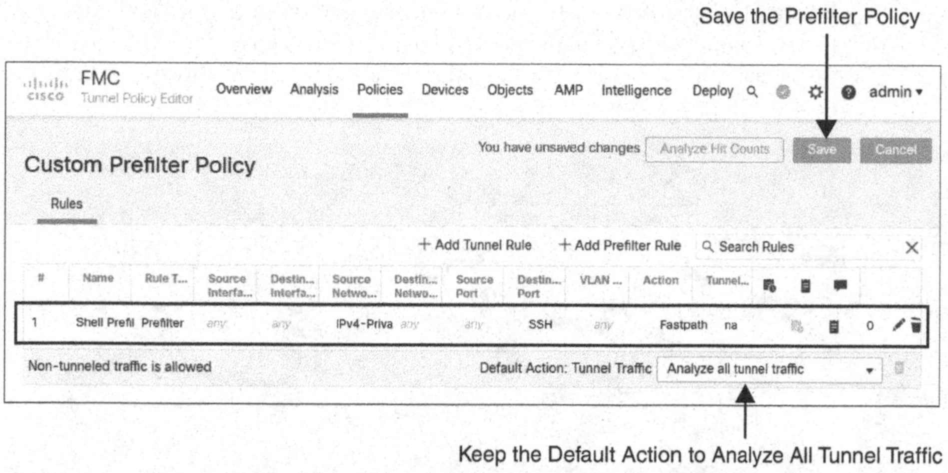

Save the Prefilter Policy

Figure 11-10 *Overview of the Prefilter Policy Setup*

Invoking a Prefilter Policy into an Access Control Policy

To invoke a custom prefilter policy in your desired access control policy, follow these steps:

Step 1.   Navigate to **Policies > Access Control > Access Control**. The Access Control Policy page appears.

Step 2.   To modify the policy that you want to deploy to your threat defense, click the pencil icon next to the policy name. The access control policy opens into the policy editor page (see Figure 11-11).

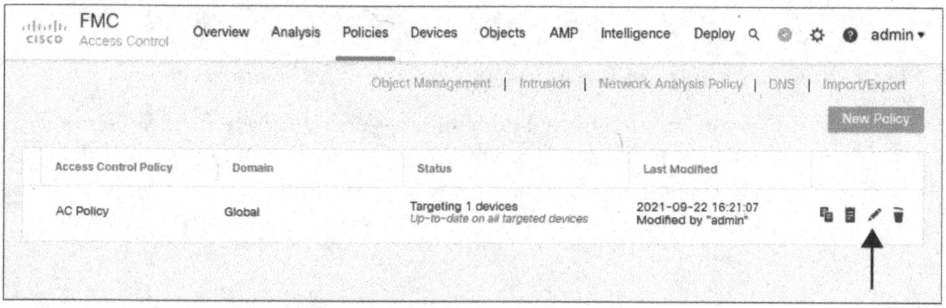

Figure 11-11 *Option to Edit an Access Control Policy*

Step 3.   Look at the upper side of the policy editor page. You will find the currently selected prefilter policy. By default, an access control policy uses the default prefilter policy. Click the current prefilter policy name. The Prefilter Policy pop-up window appears.

Step 4.   The Prefilter Policy window presents the available prefilter policies in a drop-down. Select **Custom Prefilter Policy** and click **OK**.

Figure 11-12 shows the selection of a custom prefilter policy in the Prefilter Policy pop-up window. In the background, you can see the current selection—the default prefilter policy. Clicking the current policy name opens the Prefilter Policy selection window.

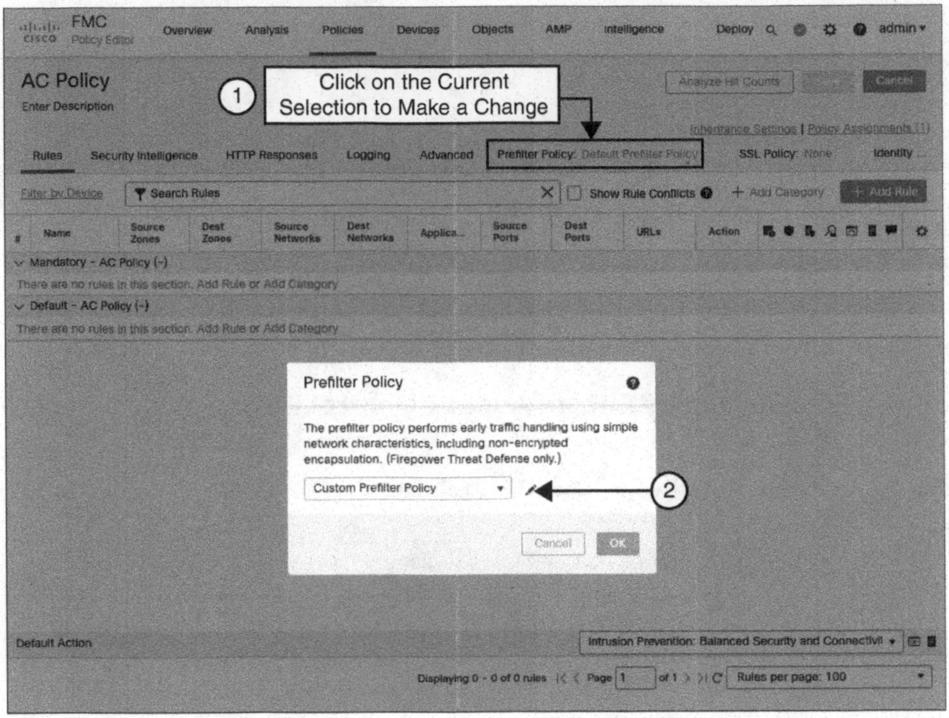

Figure 11-12 *Invoking a Custom Prefilter Policy into an Access Control Policy*

Step 5. Now that you have completed both phases—configuring a new prefilter policy and invoking it into an access control policy—you are ready to deploy the policies. Go to **Deploy > Deployment**, select the threat defense where you want to deploy the policy, and click the **Deploy** button to begin deployment (see Figure 11-13).

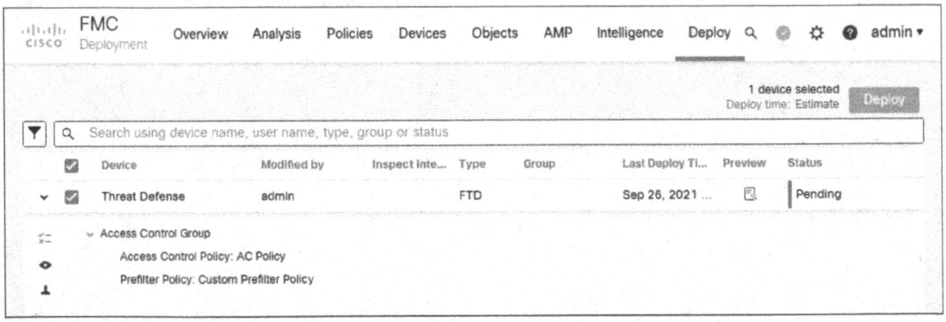

Figure 11-13 *Deployment of a Prefilter and Access Control Policy*

Establishing Trust Through an Access Control Policy

NOTE   Completing the steps in this section is not necessary for a prefilter policy configuration. The objective of this section is to demonstrate the configuration of a trust rule—another way to bypass deep packet inspection. Later, we analyze the operational differences between a fastpath rule and a trust rule.

CAUTION   This chapter uses a web service to demonstrate the flow of a TCP packet. However, you should not trust any connection unless you have a complete understanding of the particular traffic and its source and destination.

A trust rule bypasses traffic without performing any deep packet inspection and network discovery. It supports granular filters based on Security Intelligence data, application fingerprints, URL filtering, user identities, and so on. This section describes how to trust traffic using an access control policy. As an example, the default ports of the web services (HTTP and HTTPS protocols) will be trusted. Here are the steps:

Step 1.   Navigate to **Policies > Access Control > Access Control**. The access control policy page appears (refer to Figure 11-11).

Step 2.   To edit the policy that you want to deploy to your threat defense, click the pencil icon next to your desired policy name. It opens the access control policy editor page (see Figure 11-14).

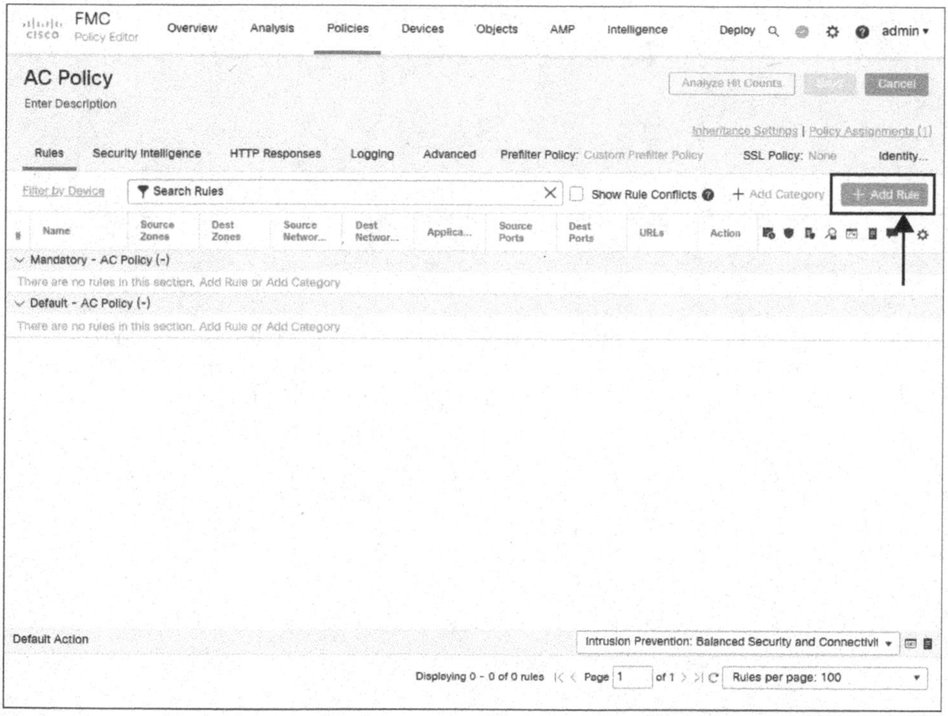

Figure 11-14   *Access Control Policy Editor Showing the Add Rule Button*

Step 3. On the policy editor, click the **Add Rule** button to create a new access control rule. The Add Rule window appears.

Step 4. Give a name to the access control rule and select the **Trust** action.

Step 5. Define a rule condition to match web traffic that is originated only from the inside network. Go to the Ports tab and select **HTTP** and **HTTPS** as the destination ports. Similarly, on the Networks tab, select the inside subnet 192.168.0.0/16 as the source network. Figure 11-15 and Figure 11-16 show the configurations of the Web Access rule to trust web traffic coming from the inside network subnet 192.168.0.0/16.

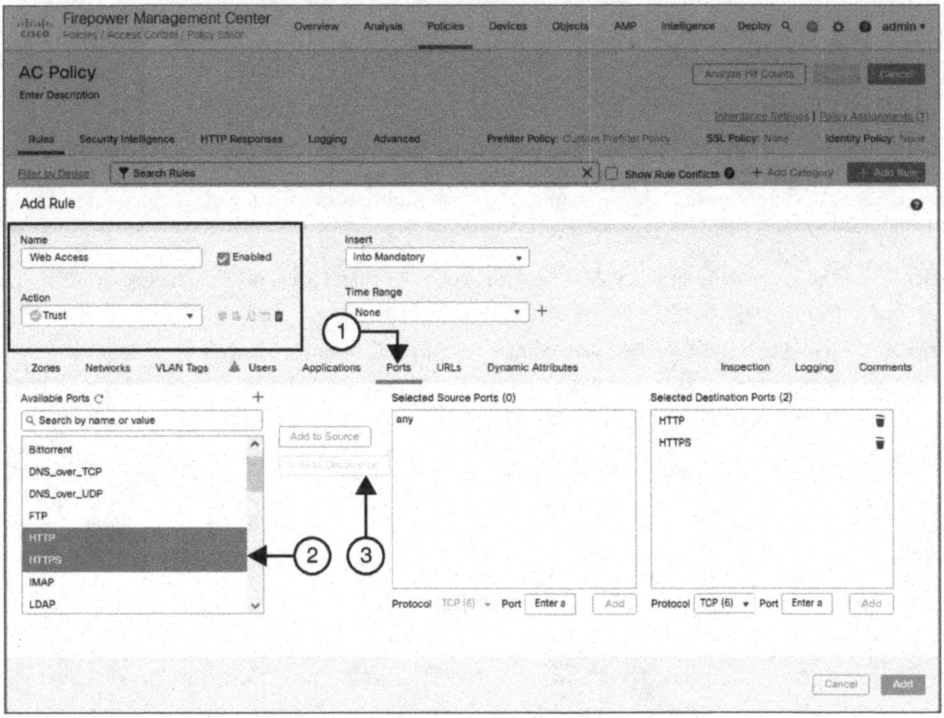

Figure 11-15 *Rule Condition to Trust Web Traffic Using Destination Ports*

Step 6. Optionally, go to the Logging tab to enable logging so that you can determine when the threat defense trusts a connection. Select either **Log at Beginning of Connection** or **Log at End of Connection**. Do not select both options because doing so can affect the system performance (see Figure 11-17).

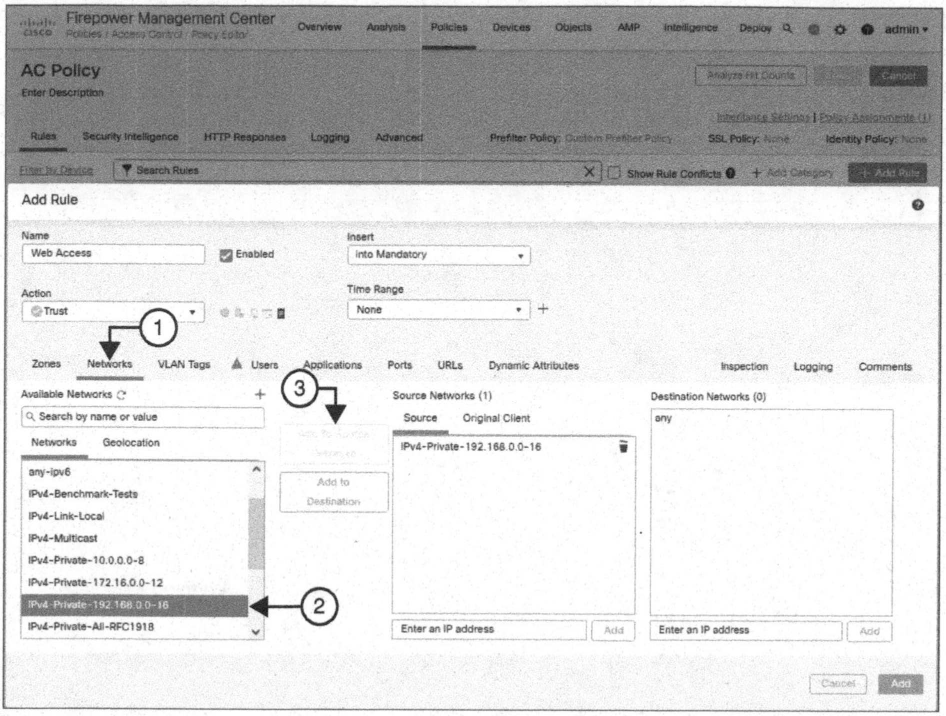

Figure 11-16 *Rule Condition to Trust Traffic from a Specific Source Network*

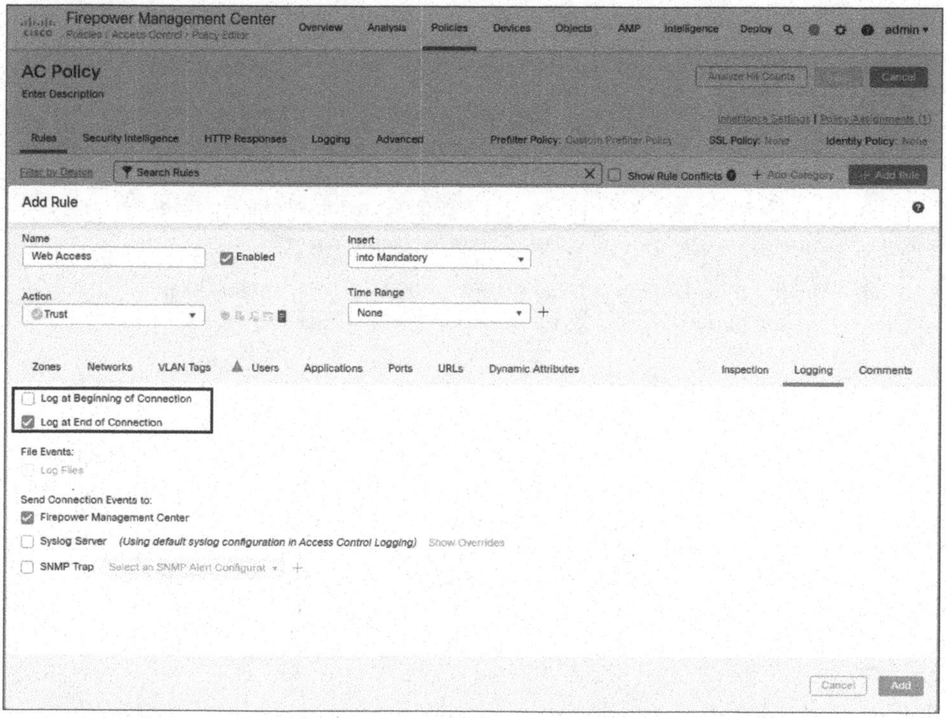

Figure 11-17 *Enabling Logging at the End of Trusted Connection*

Step 7. Click the **Add** button to complete the trust rule configuration. You return to the policy editor page.

Step 8. Select a default action using the drop-down. Choosing an intrusion prevention policy confirms the deep packet inspection of unmatched traffic.

Step 9. Click the **Save** button to save the changes (see Figure 11-18).

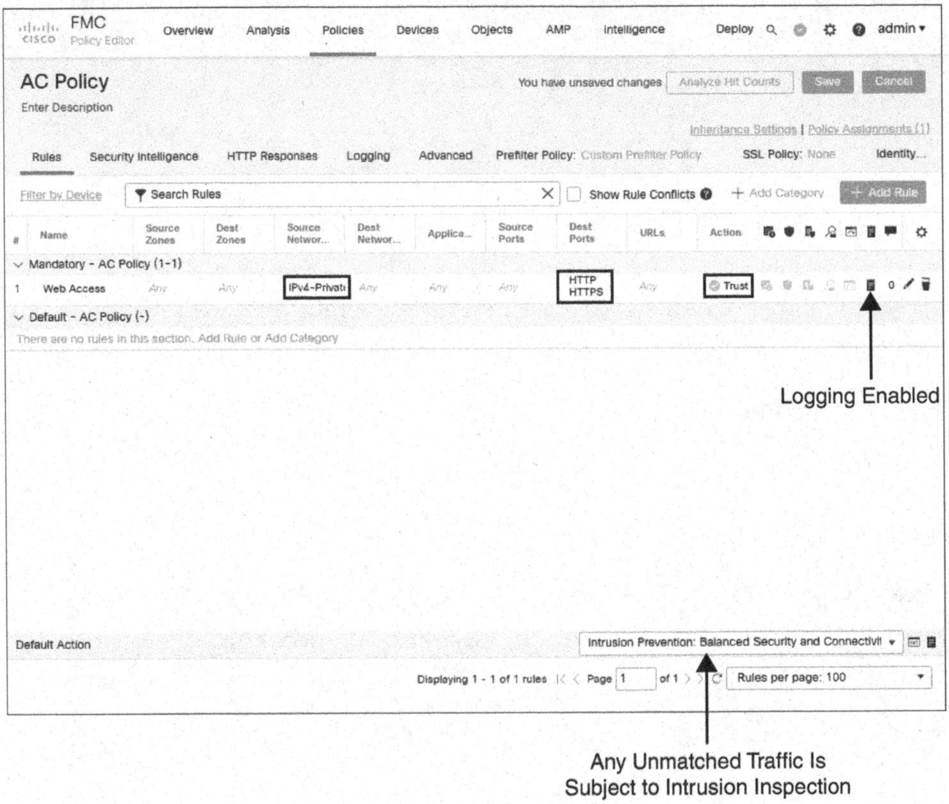

Figure 11-18 *Save Any Changes on a Policy Before Deployment*

Step 10. Finally, go to **Deploy > Deployment** and select your threat defense. Click the **Deploy** button to activate the rule on the threat defense.

Verification

When the policy deployment is complete, you can use the CLI to verify whether the new prefilter and access control rules are deployed on the threat defense. For example, you can use the **show access-list** command to view the list of prefilter rules and access control rules that are active on a threat defense. Example 11-1 shows that the custom prefilter rule Shell Prefilter is positioned on top of any other access control rules because a prefilter policy acts on traffic prior to any security policies.

Example 11-1 *Position of a Prefilter Rule on the Active Ruleset*

```
> show access-list
access-list cached ACL log flows: total 0, denied 0 (deny-flow-max 4096)
          alert-interval 300
access-list CSM_FW_ACL_; 9 elements; name hash: 0x4a69e3f3
access-list CSM_FW_ACL_ line 1 remark rule-id 268446721: PREFILTER POLICY: Custom
Prefilter Policy
access-list CSM_FW_ACL_ line 2 remark rule-id 268446721: RULE: Shell Prefilter
access-list CSM_FW_ACL_ line 3 advanced trust tcp object IPv4-Private-192.168.0.0-16
any object-group SSH rule-id 268446721 event-log flow-end (hitcnt=3) 0xca6c38d1
  access-list CSM_FW_ACL_ line 3 advanced trust tcp 192.168.0.0 255.255.0.0 any eq
ssh rule-id 268446721 event-log flow-end (hitcnt=3) 0xeb962600
access-list CSM_FW_ACL_ line 4 remark rule-id 268445696: PREFILTER POLICY: Custom
Prefilter Policy
access-list CSM_FW_ACL_ line 5 remark rule-id 268445696: RULE: DEFAULT TUNNEL ACTION
RULE
access-list CSM_FW_ACL_ line 6 advanced permit ipinip any any rule-id 268445696
(hitcnt=0) 0xf5b597d6
access-list CSM_FW_ACL_ line 7 advanced permit udp any eq 3544 any range 1025 65535
rule-id 268445696 (hitcnt=0) 0x46d7839e
access-list CSM_FW_ACL_ line 8 advanced permit udp any range 1025 65535 any eq 3544
rule-id 268445696 (hitcnt=0) 0xaf1d5aa5
access-list CSM_FW_ACL_ line 9 advanced permit 41 any any rule-id 268445696
(hitcnt=0) 0x06095aba
access-list CSM_FW_ACL_ line 10 advanced permit gre any any rule-id 268445696
(hitcnt=0) 0x52c7a066
access-list CSM_FW_ACL_ line 11 remark rule-id 268447745: ACCESS POLICY: AC
Policy - Mandatory
access-list CSM_FW_ACL_ line 12 remark rule-id 268447745: L7 RULE: Web Access
access-list CSM_FW_ACL_ line 13 advanced permit tcp object IPv4-Private-
192.168.0.0-16 any object-group HTTP rule-id 268447745 (hitcnt=0) 0x8beb8bbd
  access-list CSM_FW_ACL_ line 13 advanced permit tcp 192.168.0.0 255.255.0.0 any eq
www rule-id 268447745 (hitcnt=0) 0x8f3560b5
access-list CSM_FW_ACL_ line 14 advanced permit tcp object IPv4-Private-
192.168.0.0-16 any object-group HTTPS rule-id 268447745 (hitcnt=0) 0x5cff7517
  access-list CSM_FW_ACL_ line 14 advanced permit tcp 192.168.0.0 255.255.0.0 any eq
https rule-id 268447745 (hitcnt=0) 0x32aaadf6
access-list CSM_FW_ACL_ line 15 remark rule-id 268434432: ACCESS POLICY: AC
Policy - Default
access-list CSM_FW_ACL_ line 16 remark rule-id 268434432: L4 RULE: DEFAULT ACTION
RULE
access-list CSM_FW_ACL_ line 17 advanced permit ip any any rule-id 268434432
(hitcnt=3) 0xa1d3780e
>
```

Now is the time to verify the actions of prefilter and access control rules on live traffic in a lab environment (refer to Figure 11-4). To perform a test, use inside host 192.168.1.2 to connect to outside host 172.16.1.200. You can use the SSH client to connect over the SSH protocol and a web browser to connect over HTTP/HTTPS. Both connection attempts should be successful, and the inside user should not notice any difference.

11

You can use the management center to view the respective connection events. In the management center, go to **Analysis > Connections > Events**. There, you should see two connection events with two different types of actions. Figure 11-19 demonstrates that when the Shell Prefilter rule is triggered, a Fastpath action bypasses the SSH connection. Similarly, when the Web Access rule finds matching HTTP/HTTPS traffic, the Trust action bypasses that connection.

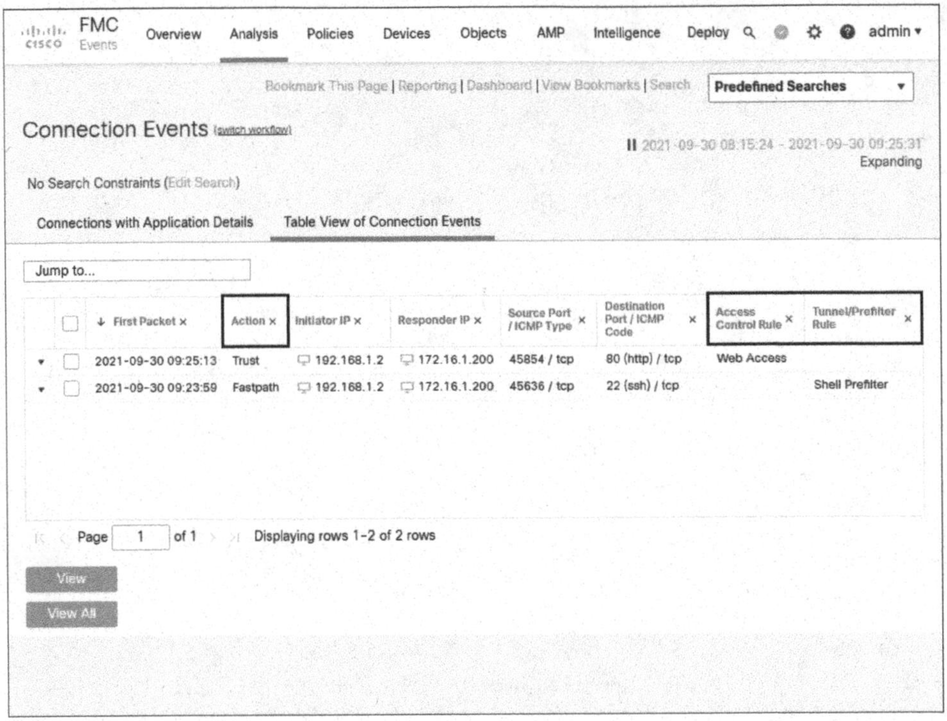

	↓ First Packet ×	Action ×	Initiator IP ×	Responder IP ×	Source Port / ICMP Type ×	Destination Port / ICMP Code ×	Access Control Rule ×	Tunnel/Prefilter Rule ×
▼	2021-09-30 09:25:13	Trust	192.168.1.2	172.16.1.200	45854 / tcp	80 (http) / tcp	Web Access	
▼	2021-09-30 09:23:59	Fastpath	192.168.1.2	172.16.1.200	45636 / tcp	22 (ssh) / tcp		Shell Prefilter

Figure 11-19 *Connection Events Triggered by Prefilter and Access Control Rules*

Managing Encapsulated Traffic Inspection

An encapsulation protocol, also known as a tunneling protocol, is used to mask the original IP header of a packet and encapsulate the packet with a completely different IP header. Routers can leverage this protocol to transport certain types of traffic that may not be allowed via the underlying network. Some of that traffic includes (but is not limited to) multicast traffic, nonroutable IP traffic, and non-IP traffic. Through encapsulation technology, a user is able to access a network or service that may be denied in the original network.

Figure 11-20 shows how a GRE header and an IP header (outer) encapsulate a TCP header and its original IP header (inner). When a GRE tunnel is implemented between two sites, one tunnel endpoint encapsulates data packets with an additional header and forwards them to another tunnel endpoint for decapsulation. In that case, each perimeter router acts as a GRE tunnel endpoint (see Figure 11-21).

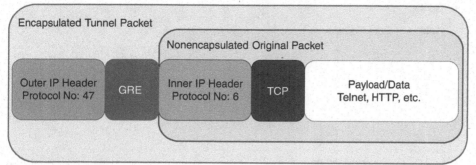

Figure 11-20 *GRE Encapsulated Packet*

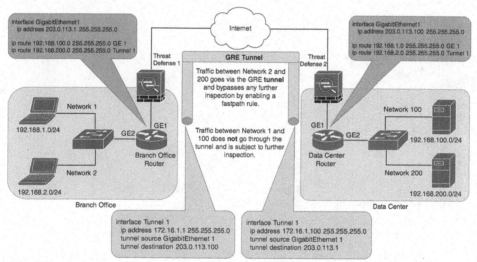

Figure 11-21 *Two Sites Communicate over the Internet via the GRE Tunnel*

You can deploy a prefilter policy to a threat defense to analyze, block, or fastpath encapsulated packets based on their outermost protocol headers. Secure Firewall supports various encapsulation protocols, such as Generic Routing Encapsulation (GRE), IP-in-IP, IPv6-in-IP, and Teredo encapsulation protocols. Figure 11-22 shows a list of supported encapsulation protocols and the actions you can apply on a tunnel.

Secure Firewall comes with a default prefilter policy, which you cannot delete or fine-tune. The only configurable option is the default action against the encapsulated traffic. There are two choices: Analyze All Tunnel Traffic and Block All Tunnel Traffic. The Analyze All Tunnel Traffic option in the default prefilter policy forwards all encapsulated packets to the access control policy for the next level of inspection (see Figure 11-23). The Block All Tunnel Traffic option denies the encapsulated traffic right away.

11

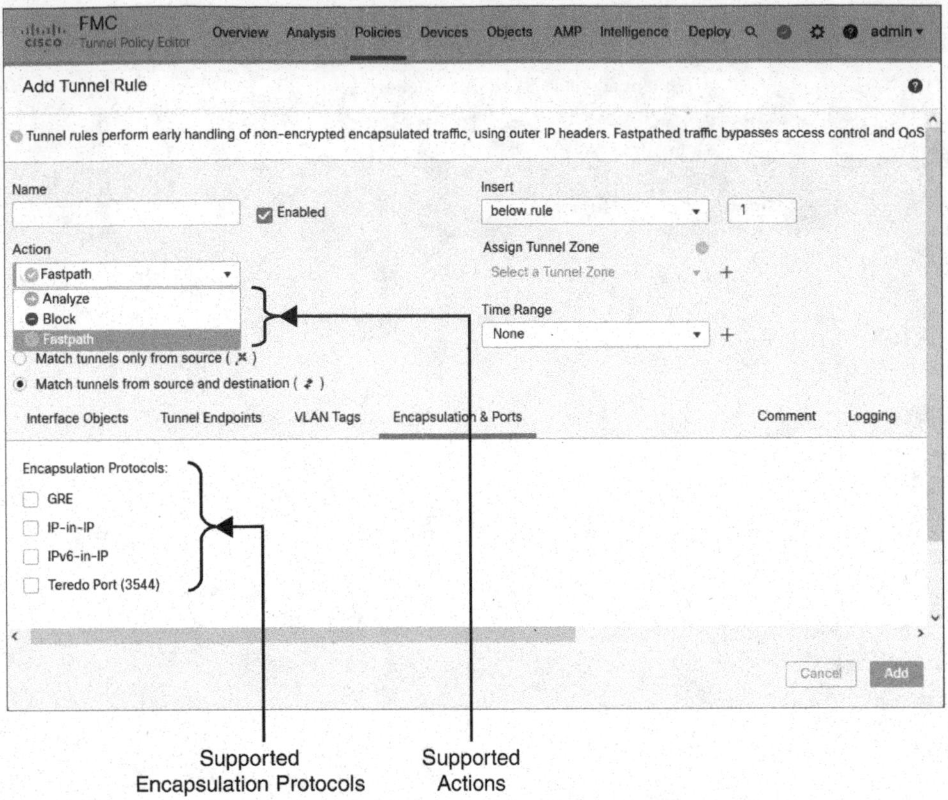

Figure 11-22 *Encapsulation Protocol Support on Secure Firewall*

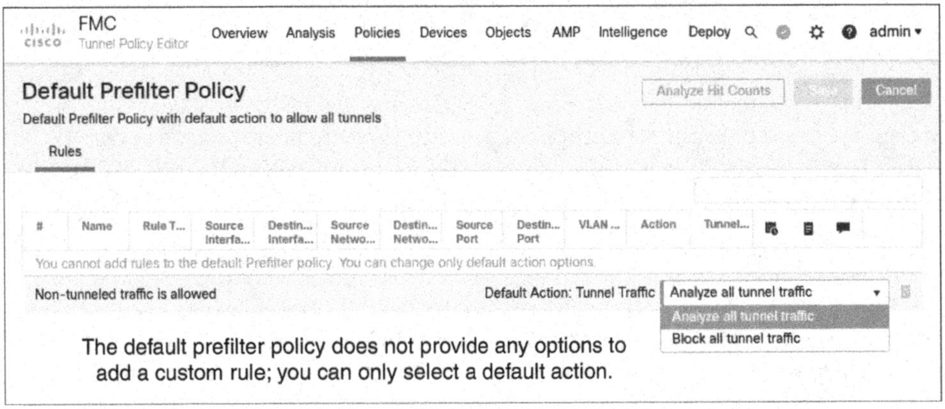

Figure 11-23 *Available Default Actions for Encapsulated Traffic*

A custom prefilter policy, on the other hand, allows you to add a tunnel rule, which offers granular control over different types of tunnel traffic. By using a custom tunnel rule, you can instruct a threat defense to bypass certain types of encapsulated passthrough traffic from any further inspection, while the remaining tunneled traffic is denied or forwarded to the next level of inspection. For example, Figure 11-24 shows a tunnel rule, GRE Traffic, that is configured to fastpath only the GRE encapsulation traffic, while any other tunnel traffic is blocked by the default action.

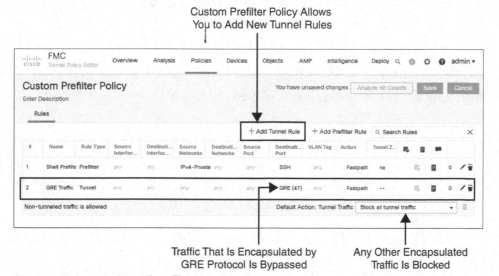

Figure 11-24 *Policy That Blocks All Encapsulated Traffic Except the GRE Protocol*

Because the steps to add a tunnel rule are similar to the steps to add a prefilter rule, this section just highlights their key differences.

Summary

This chapter discusses the prefilter policy and techniques for bypassing deep packet inspection. It provides the steps to configure different methods. The chapter also shows how to verify the deployment and view the connection events for bypassed traffic.

Exam Preparation Tasks

As mentioned in the section "How to Use This Book" in the Introduction, you have a couple of choices for exam preparation: the exercises here, Chapter 22, "Final Preparation," and the exam simulation questions in the Pearson Test Prep practice test software.

Review All Key Topics

Review the most important topics in this chapter, noted with the Key Topic icon in the outer margin of the page. Table 11-2 lists a reference of these key topics and the page numbers on which each is found.

11

Key Topic

Table 11-2   Key Topics for Chapter 11

Key Topic Element	Description	Page
Bullet list	Prefilter rule actions	227
Bullet list	Prefilter rule versus access control rule	227
Paragraph	Encapsulation protocol	242

Complete Tables and Lists from Memory

There are no Memory Tables or Lists for this chapter.

Define Key Terms

Define the following key terms from this chapter, and check your answers in the Glossary:

tunnel rule, prefilter rule, default action, fastpath rule, trust rule

CHAPTER 12

Security Intelligence

This chapter provides an overview of the following topics:

Security Intelligence Essentials: This section illustrates the operation of Security Intelligence in Secure Firewall. It also describes different mechanisms for inputting IP addresses.

Best Practices for Security Intelligence: This section provides some best practices for engaging Security Intelligence techniques in a packet filtering process.

Fulfilling Prerequisites: This section discusses the prerequisites for enabling Security Intelligence. You must read and fulfill them before you begin the configurations.

Automatic Blocking Using Cisco Intelligence Feed: In this section, you learn the steps to configure Security Intelligence in an access control policy and to block harmful IP addresses using the Cisco-provided intelligence-based category. It also demonstrates how to use CLI commands to verify the Security Intelligence categorization and the GUI option to override a default behavior.

Instant Blocking Using Context Menu: This section shares a useful option to block or unblock traffic on the fly without modifying an access control policy.

Manual Blocking Using Custom List: This section demonstrates how to input custom IP addresses manually to block them in bulk. It also shows the steps to change the default behavior of Security Intelligence from Block to Monitor-only.

Threat Intelligence Director: In the last section, you learn about an advanced feature that allows you to import third-party threat intelligence data into Secure Firewall.

The objectives of this chapter are to learn about

- Operation of Security Intelligence technology components

- Implementation of intelligence-based access control policy

- Managing Security Intelligence objects and intelligence feed

- Implementation of the Cisco Threat Intelligence Director (TID)

To compromise a network, an attacker uses various techniques, such as spam, command-and-control (CNC) servers, phishing, malware, and so on. The number, types, and sources of new threats are increasing every day. As a security engineer, you might find it challenging to keep the access control list of a firewall up to date with all the new suspicious addresses. To make your job easier, Secure Firewall offers a unique threat defense mechanism called Security Intelligence. This chapter describes the processes of configuring Security Intelligence technology using the Cisco intelligence feed and third-party sources.

"Do I Know This Already?" Quiz

The "Do I Know This Already?" quiz enables you to assess whether you should read this entire chapter thoroughly or jump to the "Exam Preparation Tasks" section. If you are in doubt about your answers to these questions or your own assessment of your knowledge of the topics, read the entire chapter. Table 12-1 lists the major headings in this chapter and their corresponding "Do I Know This Already?" quiz questions. You can find the answers in Appendix A, "Answers to the 'Do I Know This Already?' Quizzes."

Table 12-1 "Do I Know This Already?" Section-to-Question Mapping

Foundation Topics Section	Questions
Security Intelligence Essentials	1, 2, 3
Best Practices for Security Intelligence	4
Fulfilling Prerequisites	5
Automatic Blocking Using Cisco Intelligence Feed	6
Instant Blocking Using Context Menu	7
Manual Blocking Using Custom List	8
Threat Intelligence Director	9

CAUTION The goal of self-assessment is to gauge your mastery of the topics in this chapter. If you do not know the answer to a question or are only partially sure of the answer, you should mark that question as wrong for purposes of the self-assessment. Giving yourself credit for an answer you correctly guess skews your self-assessment results and might provide you with a false sense of security.

1. The Security Intelligence mechanism is implemented on which of the following threat defense components?
   a. Firewall engine
   b. Snort engine
   c. Management center
   d. All of these answers are correct.

2. Which of the following statements is true?

   a. When you add an IP address to the Do-Not-Block List, a threat defense allows that address to bypass any further inspection.

   b. A threat defense updates the Cisco intelligence feed once a month.

   c. Adding an IP to the Block List enables you to block an address without redeploying an access control policy.

   d. Monitor-only mode of Security Intelligence works only when the threat defense is deployed in passive mode.

3. Which of the following options can you use to block an IP address using Security Intelligence?

   a. Cisco Security Intelligence feed

   b. Custom List

   c. Context menu for a connection event

   d. All of these answers are correct.

4. To block traffic based on source IP address or destination IP address, which of the following methods would be most optimal for system performance?

   a. Prefilter policy

   b. Access control policy

   c. DNS policy

   d. Security Intelligence

5. You have just installed a new management center, but you have noticed that no intelligence-based objects are available for selection. What could be the root cause of the issue?

   a. The database is corrupt.

   b. The management center is disconnected from the Internet.

   c. The management center is running an older software version.

   d. The management center is not registered with a threat defense.

6. Which of the following commands displays an exact IP address and confirms that the address is included in the current Block List file?

   a. cat *filename.blf*

   b. head *ip_address filename.blf*

   c. egrep *ip_address *.blf*

   d. tail *ip_address filename.blf*

7. You blocked an address by selecting the Add IP to Block List option. But now, you need to allow the address. Which option would be the best to allow that address again?

   a. Adding a prefilter rule for that IP address to fastpath the new connections.

   b. Adding an access control rule for that IP address to trust the new connections.

    c.   Removing that IP address from the Global Block List.

    d.   All of these answers are correct.

  8. When it comes to blocking custom IP addresses using Security Intelligence, which of the following statements is true?

    a.   Security Intelligence can block traffic intelligently only using a Cisco-provided feed, but any custom addresses are not supported.

    b.   You need to input one custom IP address at a time and then choose an action for the address.

    c.   You can create a text file to include custom IP addresses in bulk and input the file directly into a management center.

    d.   When a connection to or from a custom address is blocked, the connection is marked as the "non-default" category in the Connection Events page.

  9. When you enable the Threat Intelligence Director (TID), a threat defense acts as the following:

    a.   Element

    b.   Observable

    c.   Indicator

    d.   Director

Foundation Topics

Security Intelligence Essentials

Security Intelligence enables you to block a suspicious address dynamically without any manual modification to the access control policy. As an early line of defense, it can block a packet before the packet goes through a deeper inspection process in the threat defense. Thus, it helps a threat defense to optimize its CPU and memory utilization, which can improve overall system performance. Figure 12-1 illustrates that traffic that is not blocked or fastpathed by a prefilter policy can be subject to the Security Intelligence evaluation.

Several enhancements have been made to the Security Intelligence technology since Secure Firewall introduced this feature originally. Besides blocking malicious IP addresses, which is one of the most common uses of Security Intelligence data, Secure Firewall can also leverage the intelligence data to block malicious URLs and domain names. To demonstrate the operations of Security Intelligence, this chapter primarily focuses on blocking IP addresses. The next chapter discusses how to block malicious domain names.

Figure 12-2 details the architecture of a threat defense. It helps you to understand how a packet is processed by the Security Intelligence component before it goes through any deep packet inspection.

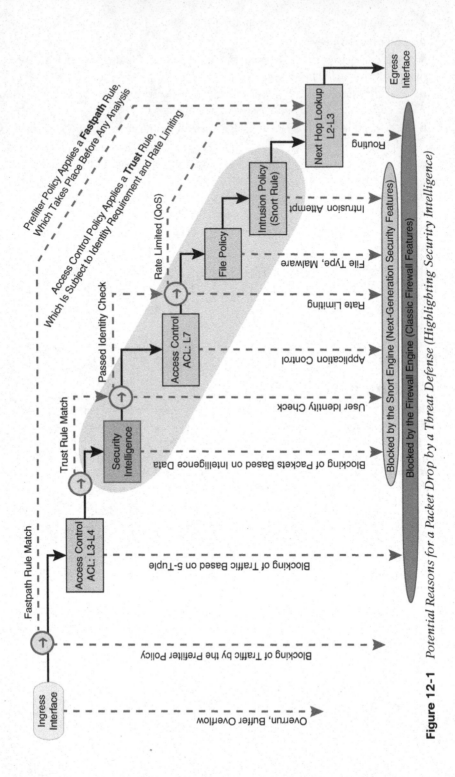

Figure 12-1 *Potential Reasons for a Packet Drop by a Threat Defense (Highlighting Security Intelligence)*

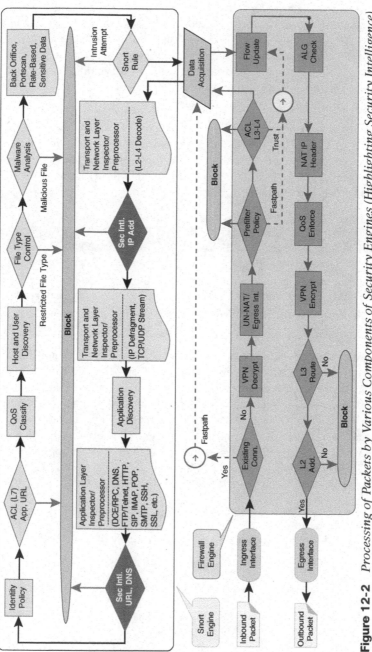

Figure 12-2 *Processing of Packets by Various Components of Security Engines (Highlighting Security Intelligence)*

You can input a potential suspicious address in Secure Firewall in three ways:

- **Feed:** Cisco has a dedicated threat intelligence and research team, known as Talos. The team analyzes the behavior of Internet traffic, performs in-depth analysis on any suspicious activities, categorizes the potential addresses based on their characteristics, and lists these addresses in a file called the Cisco intelligence feed. One of the processes, called the cloud agent, runs on a management center. It periodically communicates with the Cisco cloud to download the latest feed. When the management center downloads a feed, it sends the feed to its managed devices automatically; redeployment of the access control policy is not necessary.

- **List:** The management center also supports input of custom addresses in bulk to the block. You can list the addresses in a text file (.txt format) and upload the file manually to the management center through a web browser. The file requires you to enter one address per line. Table 12-2 shows the key differences between the feed and list types of Security Intelligence input.

Table 12-2   Security Intelligence Feed Versus Security Intelligence List

	Feed	List
Provider	Created by the Cisco threat intelligence team	Created by you
Maintenance	The management center can automatically update an existing feed.	You can manually update an old list on demand.
File transfer	The update file is provided by Cisco over the Internet via a web service.	You can upload an update file using a local web browser.

- **Context Menu:** Secure Firewall enables you to block or allow an IP address instantly—without adding a new access control rule for it. In case of an immediate need, you can use the context menu on the Connection Event page to block or allow any IP addresses. This menu provides options to act on certain IP addresses on the fly without a full-scale maintenance window for policy modification and deployment. Any addresses that you block using the context menu become part of the *Global Block List*. Similarly, any addresses that are allowed using this option become part of the *Global Do-Not-Block List*. The Block List and Do-Not-Block List are also known as the blacklist and whitelist in software versions 5.x and 6.x.

In summary, there are three ways to block an address using the Security Intelligence feature:

- Automatic blocking of an address using the Cisco intelligence feed

- Instant blocking of an address using the context menu of the connection event page

- Manual blocking of addresses in bulk using a custom intelligence list

Figure 12-3 illustrates the key operational steps of the Security Intelligence feature on the management center, threat defense, and Cisco cloud.

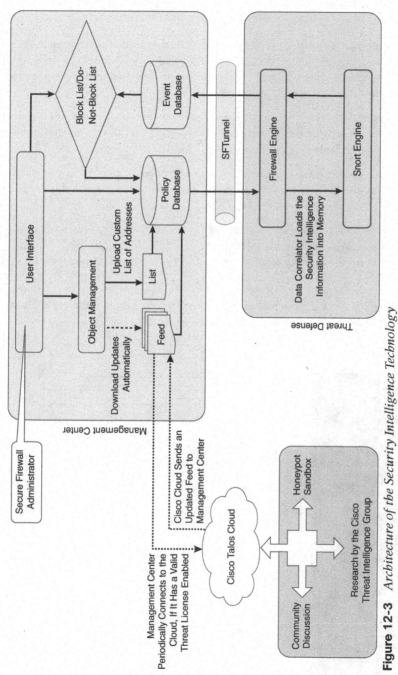

Figure 12-3   *Architecture of the Security Intelligence Technology*

Best Practices for Security Intelligence

Security Intelligence is an effective tool for controlling suspicious activities automatically. Before you enable this tool, consider the following best practices:

- If your goal is to block traffic based on 5-Tuple—source port, destination port, source IP, destination IP, and protocol—you should consider deploying a prefilter rule instead of engaging Security Intelligence as the primary method for blocking traffic. This rule ensures optimal system performance.

- If you want to test a new feed or understand its potential impact on real-world traffic (especially in your production environment), you can set the action of Security Intelligence from Block to Monitor-only mode.

- You can leverage the Security Intelligence technology to block any suspicious addresses that you obtain from third-party security advisories. Later in this chapter, you learn how to input custom addresses in bulk in Secure Firewall.

- You can enable the health module for the Security Intelligence on the health policy. This module allows the management center to generate alerts if the system fails to download the Security Intelligence data or to load the data into system memory.

Figure 12-4 shows the option to enable the health module for Security Intelligence. To find this page, go to **System > Health > Policy**, edit a health policy, and select Security Intelligence from the left panel.

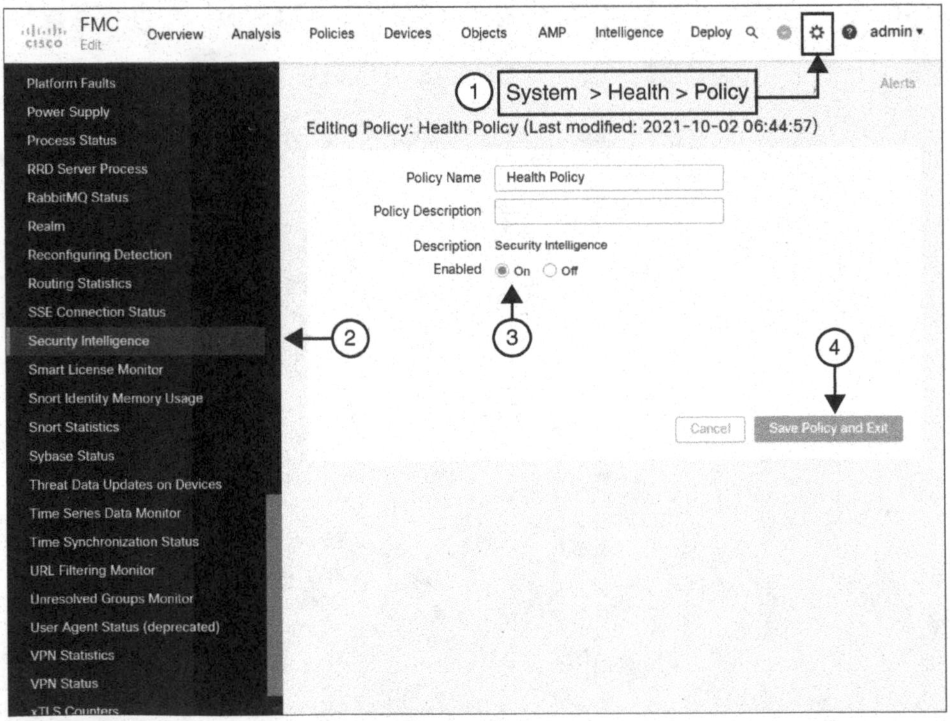

Figure 12-4 *Security Intelligence Health Module*

Fulfilling Prerequisites

To enable the Security Intelligence functionality, the following prerequisites must be fulfilled:

- Security Intelligence requires a *threat* license. Check whether the management center has a valid threat license and that the license is applied on the desired threat defense. If the threat license is disabled or expired, the management center stops obtaining the latest Cisco intelligence feed from the Cisco cloud.

Figure 12-5 shows a simple topology that is used in this chapter to demonstrate the configurations of Security Intelligence.

Figure 12-6 shows the device management page where you can enable and disable a threat license for a managed device.

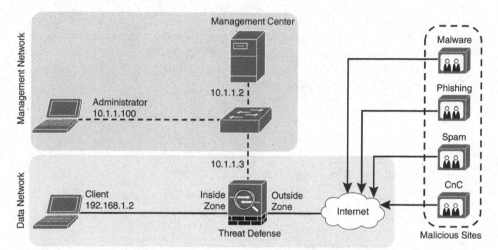

Figure 12-5 *Topology Used in the Configuration Examples of This Chapter*

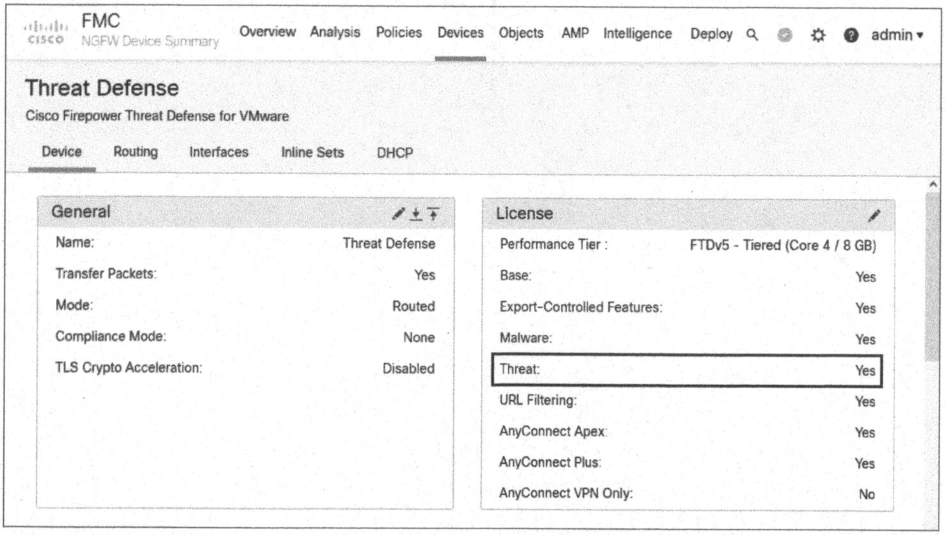

Figure 12-6 *The Device Management Page Shows the Status of Current Licenses*

TIP While you are in the process of purchasing a license, you can enable Evaluation Mode on your management center. It allows you to configure and deploy an access control policy with the Security Intelligence feature. Chapter 3, "Licensing and Registration," describes Evaluation Mode in detail.

Key Topic

- If you are working on a newly installed management center, the list of intelligence-based objects may not be available for selection (see Figure 12-7). To populate the Available Objects field with intelligence-based object categories, you need to update the Cisco intelligence feed from the Cisco cloud. Go to **Objects > Object Management > Security Intelligence > Network Lists and Feeds** and click the Update Feeds button. Doing so updates the management center with the latest intelligence feed over the Internet. If you do not populate the intelligence-based objects, you will not be able to select and use them as rule constraints. Figure 12-8 shows the update of two types of feeds. The Cisco intelligence feed is used by the Security Intelligence feature that you configure in the next section. The other type of feed—the Cisco TID Feed—is used by the Threat Intelligence Director (TID). TID configuration is described in the last part of this chapter.

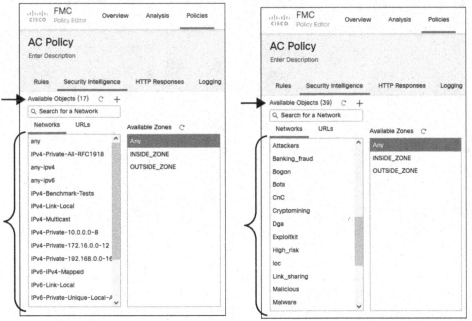

Default Network Objects (Out of the Box)

Intelligence-Based Network Objects (After the Feed Update)

Figure 12-7 *Additional Network Objects Appear After a Cloud Update*

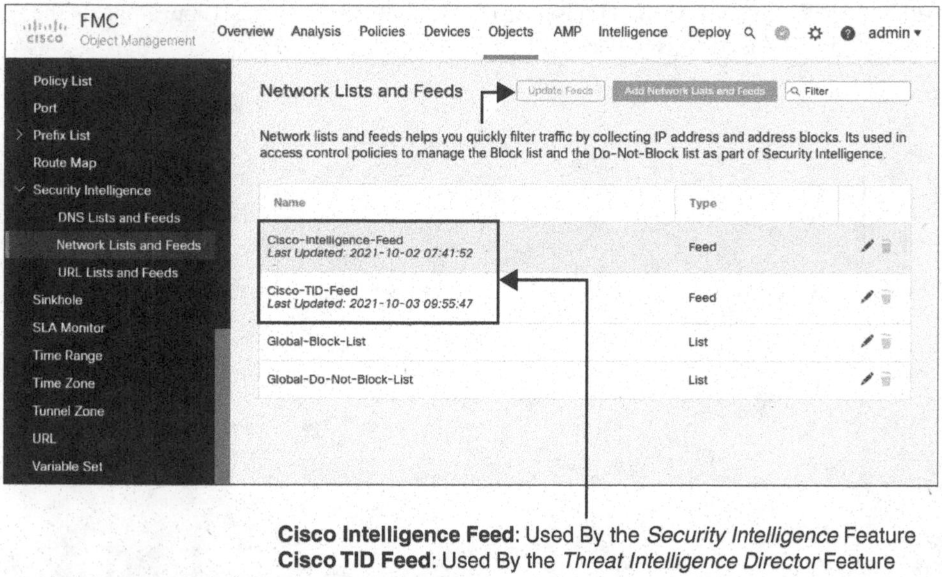

Cisco Intelligence Feed: Used By the *Security Intelligence* Feature
Cisco TID Feed: Used By the *Threat Intelligence Director* Feature

Figure 12-8   *Navigation to the Page That Enables You to Update Feeds*

Automatic Blocking Using Cisco Intelligence Feed

Although Security Intelligence is enabled through an access control policy, it does not require you to add any separate access control rule. To block suspicious traffic by using the Cisco intelligence feed, perform the following steps:

Step 1.   Navigate to **Policies > Access Control > Access Control**. A list of available access control policies appears (see Figure 12-9).

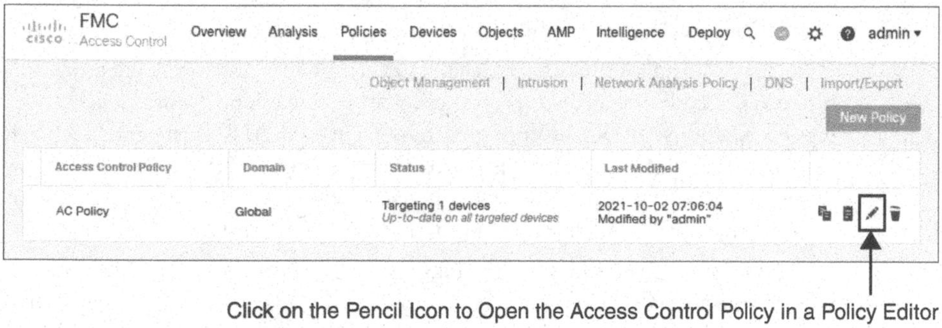

Click on the Pencil Icon to Open the Access Control Policy in a Policy Editor

Figure 12-9   *List of Available Access Control Policies*

Step 2.   Click the pencil icon next to an access control policy that you want to deploy to your threat defense. It opens the policy in the policy editor.

Step 3.   On the access control policy editor page, select the **Security Intelligence** tab. A list of available objects appears.

Step 4.   On the Networks subtab, select the categories that you want to block. Optionally, you can also specify zones for inspection. By default, a threat defense inspects traffic from Any zone.

Step 5.   Click the **Add to Block List** button. The selected categories appear inside the Block List field (see Figure 12-10).

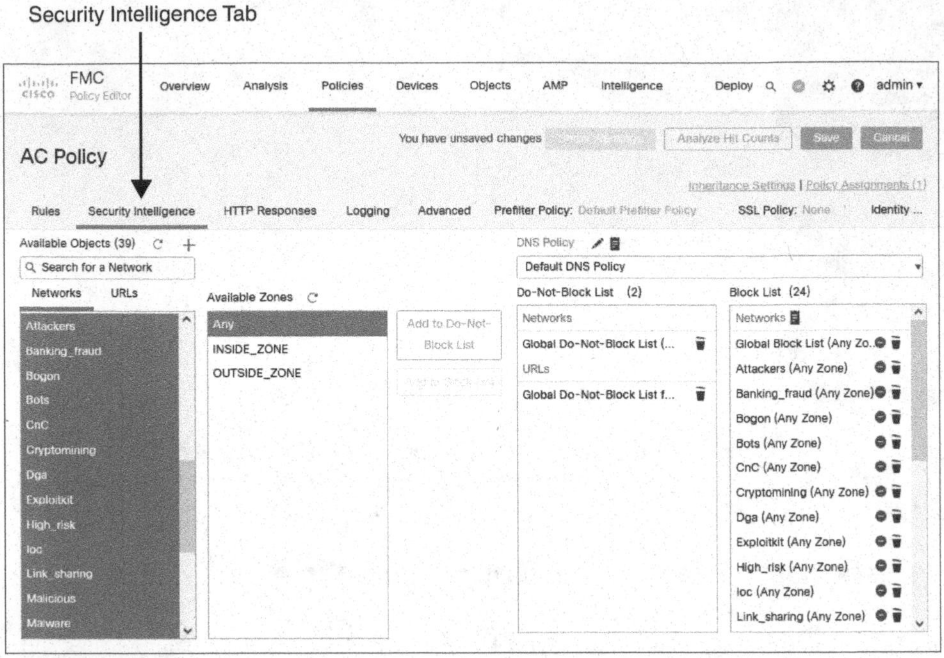

Security Intelligence Tab

Figure 12-10   *Blocking Suspicious Networks Using Security Intelligence*

Figure 12-10 shows the selection of intelligence-based network objects (available under the Networks subtab). If the intelligence-based categories are not available for selection, you need to update the Cisco intelligence feed from the cloud (described in the "Fulfilling Prerequisites" section).

This chapter primarily focuses on enabling the Security Intelligence feature based on IP addresses. However, you can also enable Security Intelligence to block suspicious URLs. The configuration of URL-based Security Intelligence is similar to the configuration of IP address-based Security Intelligence. The only difference is that instead of selecting the Network type intelligence object, you select the URL type intelligence object, as shown in Figure 12-11.

Step 6.   Under the Block List field, click the logging icon to ensure that the Log Connections option is checked for Security Intelligence events, and the events will be sent to the management center (see Figure 12-12). Click **OK** to return to the Security Intelligence tab.

Step 7.   When the configuration is complete, click **Save** on the access control policy editor to save the changes.

URLs Subtab

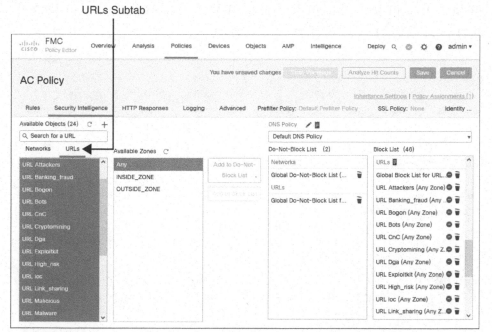

Figure 12-11 *Blocking Suspicious URLs Using Security Intelligence*

Logging Setting for Block List

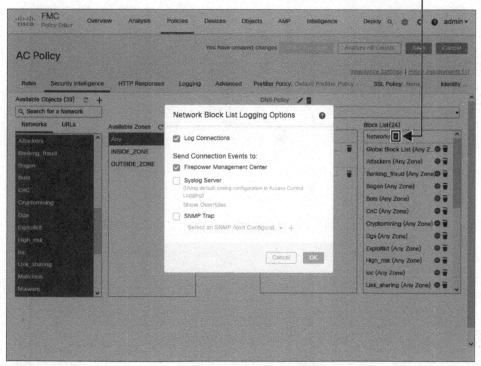

Figure 12-12 *Logging Options for the Security Intelligence Events*

Step 8. Finally, navigate to **Deploy > Deployment** to deploy this new access control policy to your desired threat defense.

> **NOTE** In a real-world network, you must consider intelligence-based protection *comprehensively* to secure your environment from malicious IP, URL, and DNS. The techniques to block access to harmful URLs and prevent queries for malicious domains are described in the next two chapters.

Verifying the Action of Cisco Intelligence Feed

When you deploy an access control policy with the Security Intelligence feature, you can verify the deployment using the management center GUI as well as the threat defense CLI. You can use the management center GUI to view the intelligence-based object categories, but it does not reveal all the malicious addresses within each category. If the policy deployment is successful, you can find the addresses by directly accessing the Cisco intelligence feed data files on a threat defense.

Example 12-1 shows the Security Intelligence Block List files (.blf) on the threat defense CLI. For each intelligence-based object category, a .blf file is available. If the command output does not show any files, it indicates a new deployment, or the Security Intelligence feature is not enabled in the access control policy.

Example 12-1 *Files Containing Intelligence-Based IP Addresses*

```
> expert
admin@ThreatDefense:/$ egrep -i "Cisco intelligence feed" /var/sf/iprep_download/
  *.blf

/var/sf/iprep_download/02213098-6d94-4680-8ce8-2d0816389f56.blf:#Cisco intelligence
feed: High_risk
/var/sf/iprep_download/032ba433-c295-11e4-a919-d4ae5275a468.blf:#Cisco intelligence
feed: Response
/var/sf/iprep_download/03709ed4-faab-47af-bade-4435f8daee27.blf:#Cisco intelligence
feed: Spyware
/var/sf/iprep_download/1b117672-7453-478c-be31-b72e89ca1acb.blf:#Cisco intelligence
feed: Open_proxy
/var/sf/iprep_download/23f2a124-8278-4c03-8c9d-d28fe08b5e98.blf:#Cisco intelligence
feed: Malware
/var/sf/iprep_download/2b15cb6f-a3fc-4e0e-a342-ccc5e5803263.blf:#Cisco intelligence
feed: Tor_exit_node
/var/sf/iprep_download/2ccda18e-ddff-4f5c-af9a-f009852183f4.blf:#Cisco intelligence
feed: Suspicious
/var/sf/iprep_download/30f9e69c-d64c-479c-821d-0e4edab8217a.blf:#Cisco intelligence
feed: Open_relay
/var/sf/iprep_download/3e2af68e-5fc8-4b1c-b5bc-b4e7cab598ba.blf:#Cisco intelligence
feed: Spam
/var/sf/iprep_download/5a0b6d6b-e2c3-436f-b4a1-48248b330a26.blf:#Cisco intelligence
feed: Attackers
/var/sf/iprep_download/5f8148f1-e5e4-427a-aa3b-ee1c2745c350.blf:#Cisco intelligence
feed: Bogon
/var/sf/iprep_download/60f4e2ab-d96c-44a0-bd38-830252b63f46.blf:#Cisco intelligence
feed: CnC
```

```
/var/sf/iprep_download/6ba968f4-7a25-4793-a2c8-7cc77f1ff437.blf:#Cisco intelligence
feed: Bots
/var/sf/iprep_download/8af156ca-8020-4608-9278-01b87458ea46.blf:#Cisco intelligence
feed: Newly_seen
/var/sf/iprep_download/8c3e31be-ca41-43c8-87cb-82a35b0f20e2.blf:#Cisco intelligence
feed: Malicious
/var/sf/iprep_download/937cf5e8-76d1-4ba2-a83c-475dc80c3845.blf:#Cisco intelligence
feed: Ioc
/var/sf/iprep_download/a27c6aae-8e52-4174-a81a-47c59fecc092.blf:#Cisco intelligence
feed: Exploitkit
/var/sf/iprep_download/abdc925f-4f85-4504-90a7-c891979ac517.blf:#Cisco intelligence
feed: Cryptomining
/var/sf/iprep_download/b1df3aa8-2841-4c88-8e64-bfaacec7fedd.blf:#Cisco intelligence
feed: Dga
/var/sf/iprep_download/bde824fd-36dd-4a7c-9cc1-80e40ac7aa35.blf:#Cisco intelligence
feed: Banking_fraud
/var/sf/iprep_download/d3899830-d481-4773-b4e2-7daa7acf5e44.blf:#Cisco intelligence
feed: Link_sharing
/var/sf/iprep_download/d7d996a6-6b92-4a56-8f10-e8506e431ca5.blf:#Cisco intelligence
feed: Phishing
admin@ThreatDefense:/$
```

Now, as an example, select one of the filenames to view the contents in the file. Each .blf file contains a list of malicious IP addresses for the category that you selected in the access control policy. For instance, Example 12-2 shows the IP addresses from the phishing category.

Example 12-2 *Security Intelligence Feed Containing the IP Addresses Susceptible to Phishing Activities*

```
admin@ThreatDefense:/$ cat /var/sf/iprep_download/d7d996a6-6b92-4a56-8f10-
e8506e431ca5.blf
#Cisco intelligence feed: Phishing
158.58.184.213
103.127.31.155
37.220.6.126
100.42.65.207
23.94.7.9
23.254.130.108
.
Output is truncated for brevity
.
admin@ThreatDefense:/$
```

NOTE   If you have enabled Security Intelligence based on URL, you can find the files in the /var/sf/siurl_download directory.

Alternatively, you can follow an opposite workflow to determine if any particular IP address is included in the Cisco intelligence feed. This workflow is helpful when you learn about a harmful IP address in an advisory, but you are unsure if the address is already included in the Cisco intelligence feed, or manual blocking may be necessary for now. To determine the inclusion of a specific IP address, use the following steps:

Step 1.   On the threat defense CLI, go to the expert mode and search for a specific IP address within the Block List files:

```
admin@ThreatDefense:/$ egrep 23.94.7.9 /var/sf/
iprep_download/*.blf
/var/sf/iprep_download/d7d996a6-6b92-4a56-8f10-
e8506e431ca5.blf:23.94.7.9

admin@ThreatDefense:/$
```

This command uses the IP address 23.94.7.9 as an example; you can replace it as needed.

Step 2.   The output from Step 1 shows the list file where the IP address is listed, but it does not display the category. To determine the category type, run the following command to view the first line of the file:

```
admin@ThreatDefense:/$ head -n1 /var/sf/iprep_download/
d7d996a6-6b92-4a56-8f10-e8506e431ca5.blf
#Cisco intelligence feed: Phishing
admin@ThreatDefense:/$
```

Now that you have learned about the investigation techniques using the CLI, it is time to see the action of Security Intelligence on live traffic. From your internal host, try to access one of the IP addresses included in the Cisco Intelligence Feed phishing category (see Example 12-2). The threat defense should block the connection, and the management center should display a Security Intelligence event for this attempt. You can view the event by navigating to **Analysis > Connections > Security Intelligence Events** (see Figure 12-13). The management center also logs an associated connection event for this connection attempt. You can view it in the Connection Events page by navigating to **Analysis > Connections > Events.** Figure 12-14 shows two connection events from the same source and destination addresses. The first connection was allowed because the Security Intelligence was not enabled at that time. After the Security Intelligence was enabled, the threat defense blocked the connection because the IP address was identified as the Phishing category, per the Cisco intelligence feed.

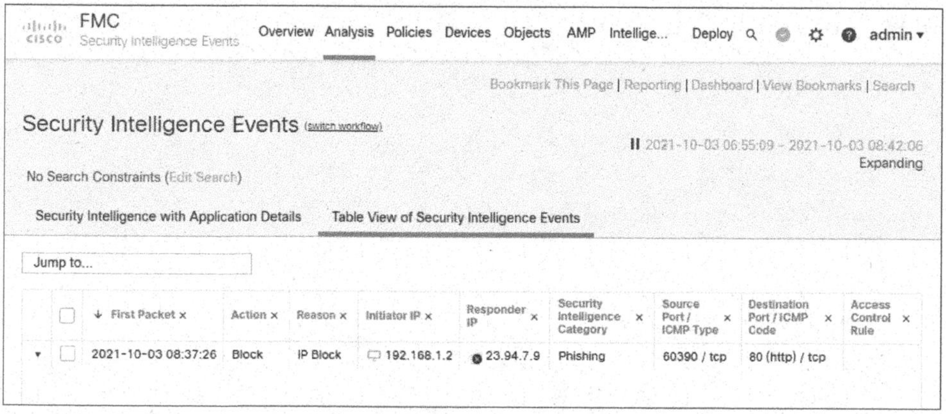

Figure 12-13 *The Security Intelligence Events Page Shows Only the Intelligence-Based Events*

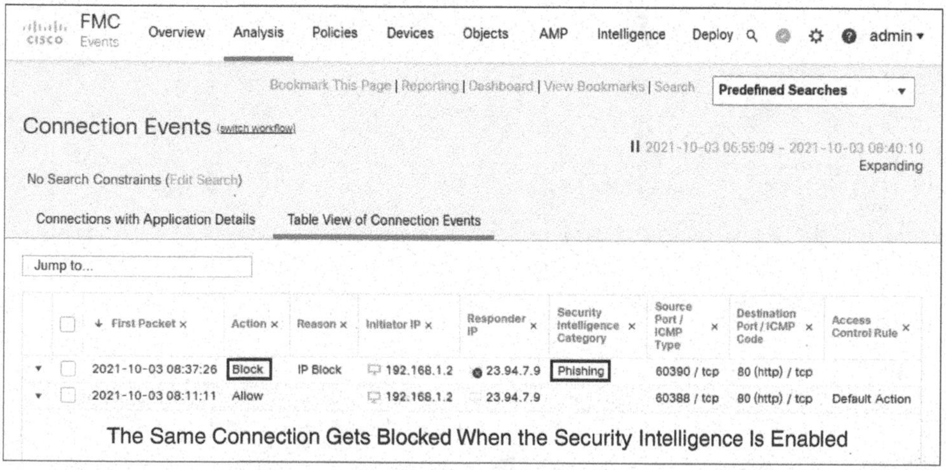

Figure 12-14 *The Connection Events Page Shows a Record for the Security Intelligence Event*

Overriding the Cisco Intelligence Feed Outcome

Key Topic

Cisco regularly updates the intelligence feed with new addresses as soon as they are known for suspicious activities. Therefore, when the Security Intelligence feature is enabled, your threat defense may block a new address without giving you prior notice. However, if you find that an address is blocked by the Cisco intelligence feed, and you disagree with the verdict, you can report it to Cisco. If you want to access the resources at this address anyway while Cisco reinvestigates, you can override the verdict by adding that particular address to the Do-Not-Block List. Although this override enables the traffic to bypass the Security Intelligence check, traffic to and from that address is still subject to any subsequent inspection. If other components of a threat defense find any anomaly with the traffic, the threat defense can still block the connection.

The process of adding an IP address to the Do-Not-Block List is identical to the process of adding an address to the Block List. On the Connection Events page, find your desired IP address that you want to unblock and right-click it. When the context menu appears, select the Add IP to Do-Not-Block List option from the menu, as shown in Figure 12-15.

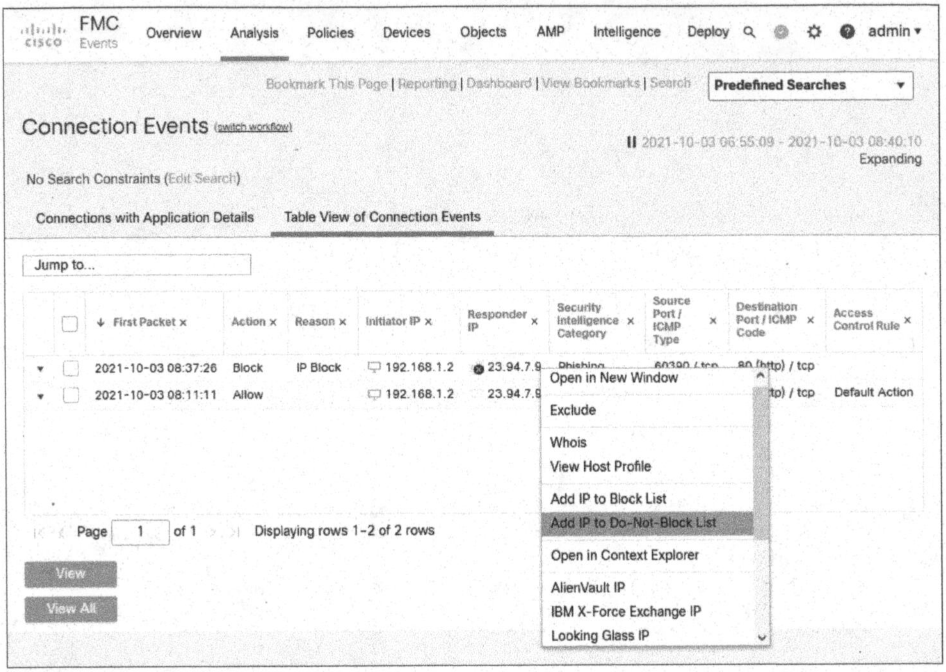

Figure 12-15 *The Add IP to Do-Not-Block List Option (Appears After a Right-Click)*

After an IP address is added to the Do-Not-Block List, the connection is allowed as usual, and the management center logs the incident as a regular connection. You can find the event for that allowed connection in the Connection Events page (see Figure 12-16).

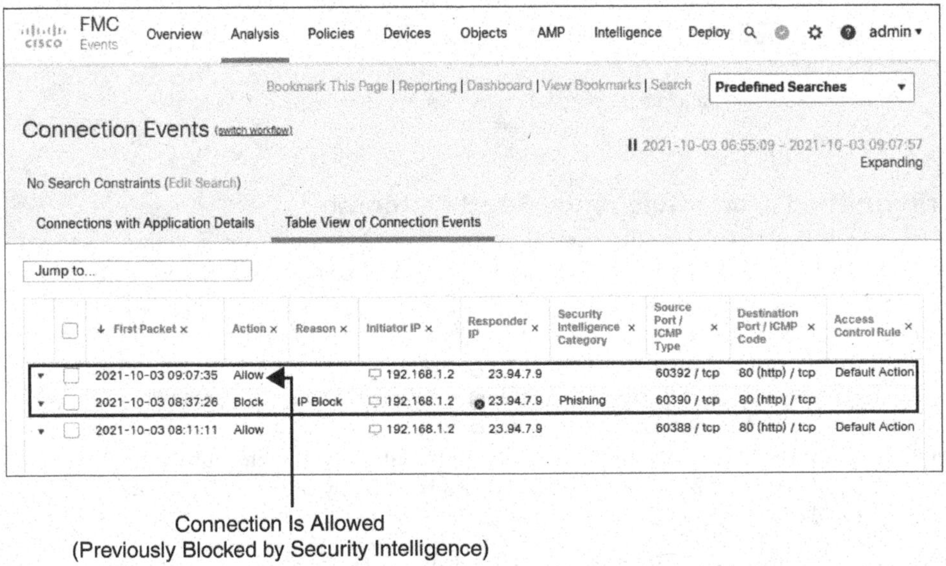

Connection Is Allowed
(Previously Blocked by Security Intelligence)

Figure 12-16 *A Connection Bypasses the Security Intelligence Check*

When you add an address to the Do-Not-Block List, the address is automatically included in the Global Do-Not-Block List object. If you want to reinstate the address to the Security Intelligence check, you can delete the address from the Global Do-Not-Block List object, as shown in Figure 12-17.

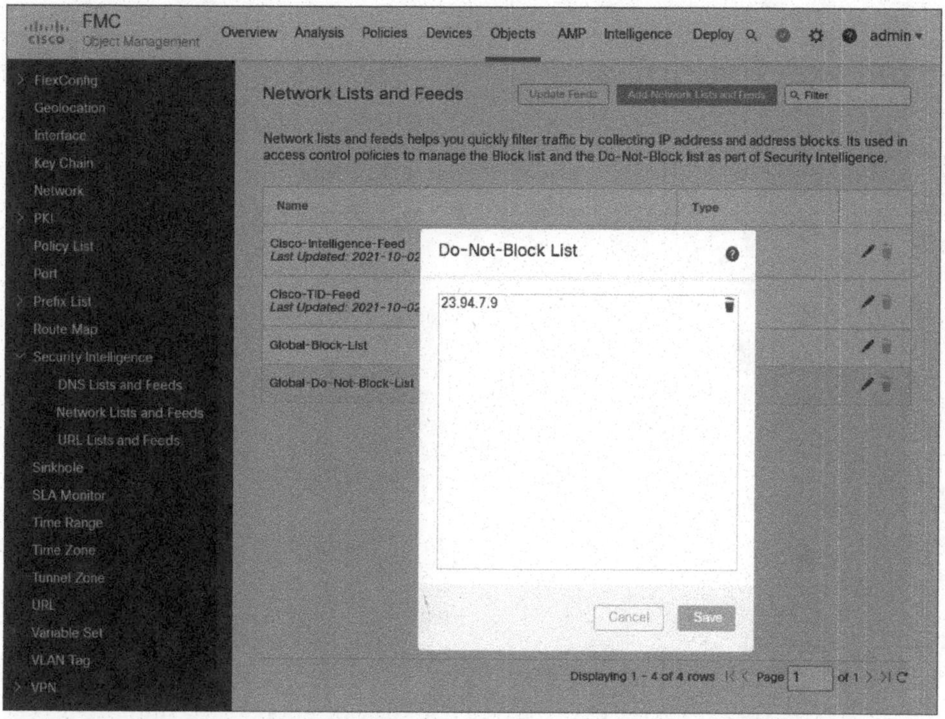

Figure 12-17 *Deleting an Address from the Global Do-Not-Block List Object*

CAUTION On the Security Intelligence configuration page, if you remove the Global Do-Not-Block List object from the Do-Not-Block List field, the access control policy stops enforcing the instantaneous allowance of IP addresses.

Instant Blocking Using Context Menu

Secure Firewall enables you to block an address instantaneously. On the Connection Events page, you right-click an IP address to open a context menu for it. Using the menu, you can add the IP address to the Block List. This feature is useful when you notice a connection event for a suspicious address, but you are not allowed to modify and redeploy the access control policy without a formal change management approval process or without scheduling a maintenance window after business hours.

Adding an Address to the Block List

Let's say you have noticed suspicious activity from an IP address (for example, 172.16.1.200). After doing some research, you learn that this address could be malicious. If you want to block that address immediately, use the following steps:

Step 1. Navigate to **Analysis > Connections > Events.**

Step 2. Right-click the address that you want to block. For example, if you want to block 172.16.1.200, right-click the address (displayed under the Responder IP column). A context menu appears, as shown in Figure 12-18.

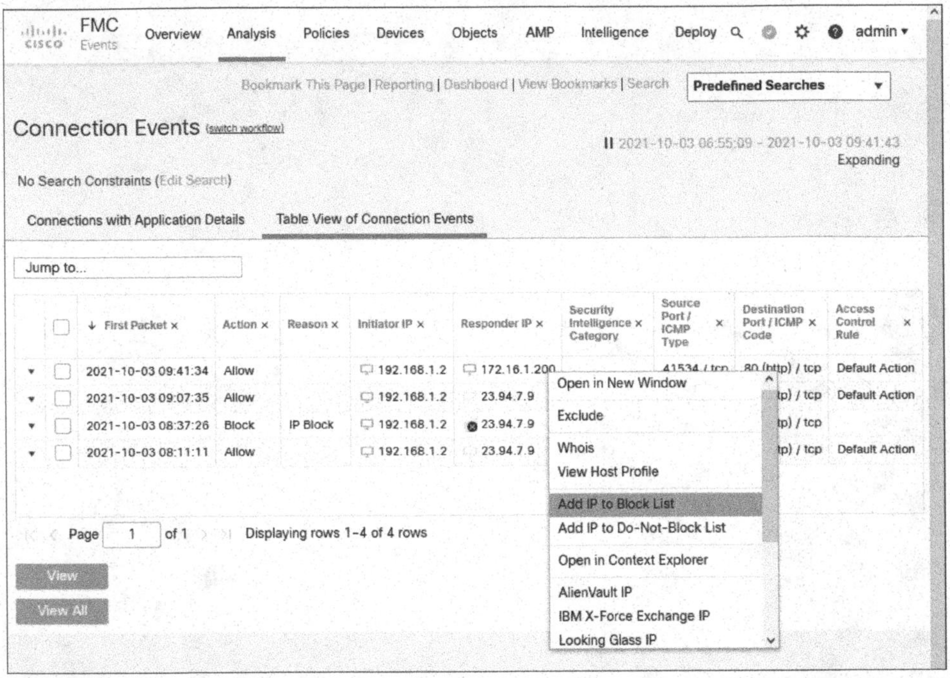

Figure 12-18 *Context Menu Displays the Option to Add IP to the Block List*

Step 3. In the context menu, select the **Add IP to Block List** option. Confirm your selection when the confirmation window appears. That's all. No additional configuration is necessary after this step. Now, if you attempt to connect to that IP address, the threat defense will block it.

Deleting an Address from the Block List

Any address that you block by using the Add IP to Block List option is included in the Global Block List category. If you want to allow the address again, you can go to **Object Management > Security Intelligence**, edit Global Block List to remove the address, and redeploy the access control policy to the threat defense.

TIP In case of unexpected system behavior, such as any desired addresses are not blocked or unblocked by Security Intelligence, you can begin your troubleshooting with a policy redeployment. When you redeploy the access control policy, Secure Firewall can allocate additional memory to Security Intelligence.

> **CAUTION**   On the Security Intelligence configuration page, if you delete the Global Block List object from the Block List field, the access control policy stops enforcing the instantaneous blocking of IP addresses.

Figure 12-19 shows the IP address that you blocked earlier using the Add IP to Block List option. To allow this IP address once again, remove the address from the list and save the changes.

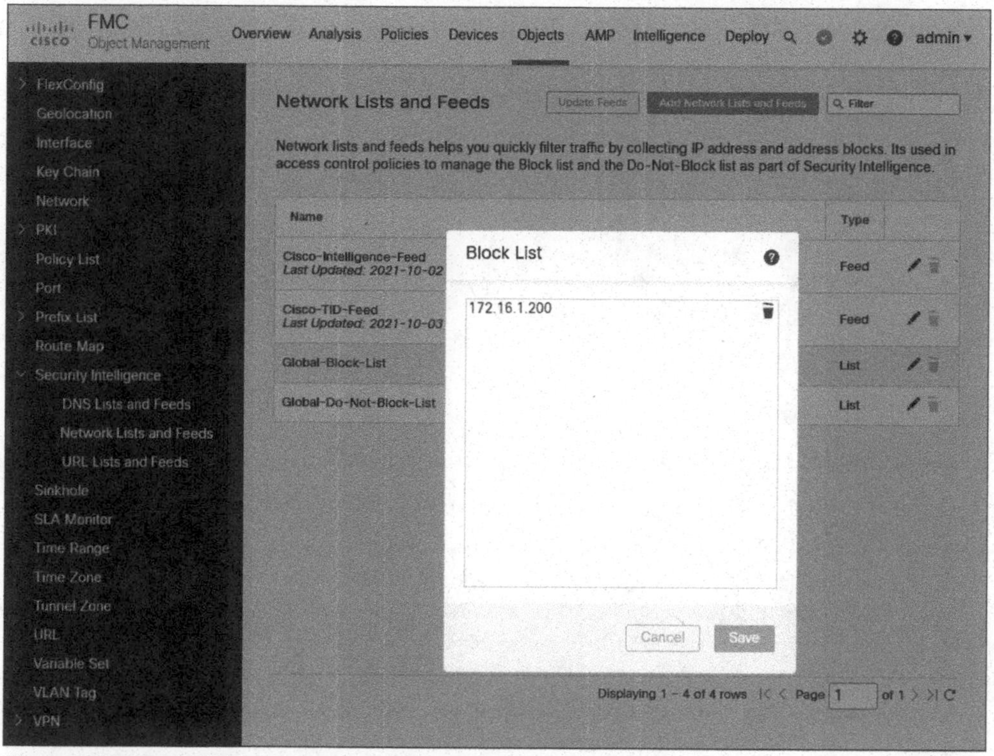

Figure 12-19   *Unblocking a Previously Blocked IP Address*

Manual Blocking Using Custom List

As a security engineer, you always read the latest security advisories to make sure that your network is protected from any zero-day threats. Let's say that you have found a new security advisory in a security-related community forum or website. While Cisco investigates the new information, you just want to block the potential malicious addresses on your own without any delay. Using a text editor, you can create a file to list any potential IP addresses in bulk. Secure Firewall allows you to use this file as input and to block all the custom IP addresses included in the file.

To block a custom list of IP addresses, follow these steps:

Step 1. Write or copy the potential malicious addresses into a text editor and save the file in .txt format. When you create a list, enter one record per line. Optionally, if you want to insert a comment for future reference, use a hash sign (#) at the beginning of the line.

Figure 12-20 shows the creation of a .txt file using Notepad. The file contains a custom list of IP addresses. These addresses are listed for demonstration purposes only and should not be considered as a definitive guideline. Conduct your own research before you decide to block an address; otherwise, a legitimate site might get blocked.

```
Malicious IP List - Notepad                              – σ  ×
File  Edit  Format  View  Help
# This is a comment. The following addresses are
randomly selected for demonstration purposes only.


112.246.46.78
182.254.166.203
152.89.239.115
192.236.147.148
206.126.81.137
```

Figure 12-20 *A .txt File with Custom List of Potential Malicious IP Addresses*

Step 2. In the management center, navigate to **Object > Object Management**.

Step 3. In the left panel, select an appropriate option under Security Intelligence. For example, if you want to add a custom list of IP addresses, select the **Network Lists and Feeds** option. Then click the **Add Network Lists and Feeds** button to upload your text file to the management center. Figure 12-21 shows the window to upload a custom Security Intelligence list. After you select **List** from the Type drop-down, you can browse your text file containing the malicious IP addresses. Upon a successful upload, the management center shows the number of addresses you uploaded.

Step 4. After the file is uploaded, navigate to **Policies > Access Control > Access Control** and edit the access control policy that you want to deploy to a threat defense.

Step 5. When the policy editor page appears, select the **Security Intelligence** tab. A list of available objects and zones appears.

Step 6. In the Network subtab, select the custom object you want to block. Optionally, you can select a specific zone on which you want to enforce the list. By default, the threat defense inspects traffic from Any zone.

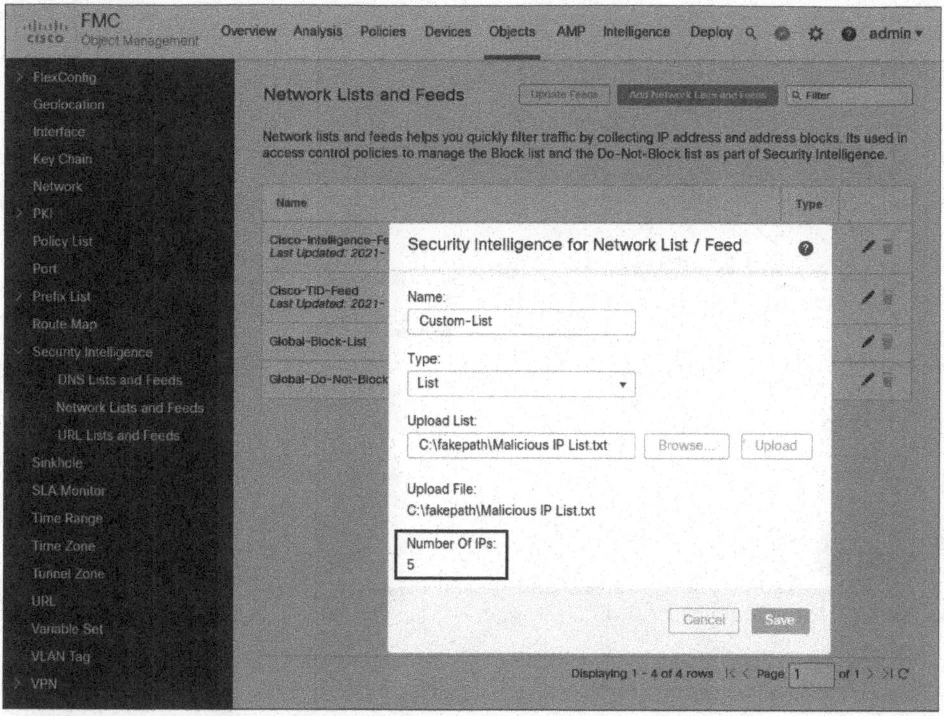

Figure 12-21   *Uploading a Security Intelligence List File*

> **NOTE**   This chapter enables the Security Intelligence feature based on network and IP addresses. If you want to enable this feature based on URL conditions, select the URL subtab. The remaining configuration steps are identical.

Step 7.   Click the **Add to Block List** button. The custom object appears in the Block List field.

Step 8.   Next to the Block List field, click the logging icon to verify whether Log Connections is checked for Security Intelligence events. Click **OK** to return to the Security Intelligence tab. Figure 12-22 illustrates the addition of a custom Security Intelligence list to the Block List.

Step 9.   When the configuration is complete, click **Save** to save the changes. Finally, deploy the new access control policy to your threat defense from the Deploy > Deployment page.

Now if you attempt to access one of the addresses that you included in the text file, the threat defense will block the connection.

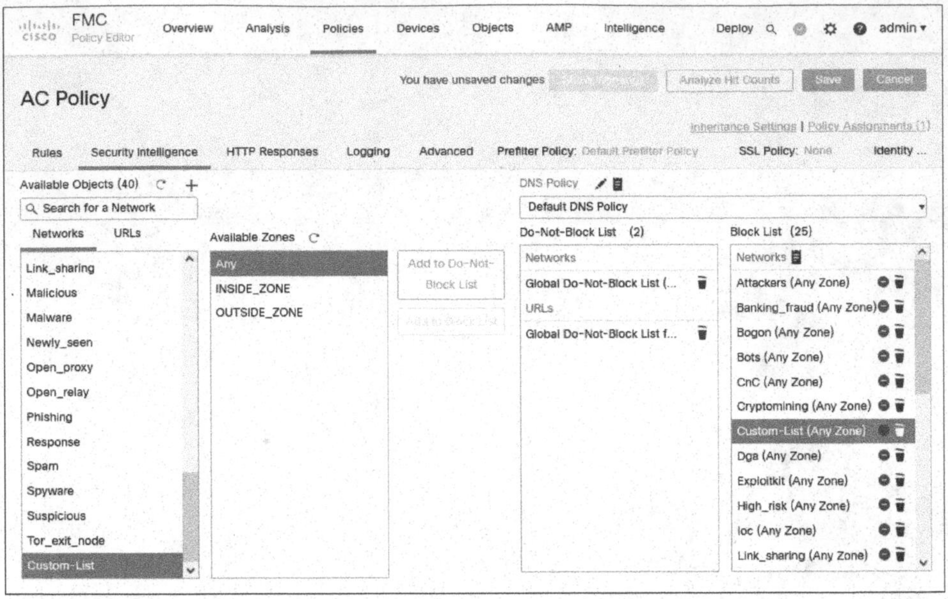

Figure 12-22 *Addition of a Custom Intelligence Object to the Block List*

Figure 12-23 shows how Security Intelligence blocks connections. The Custom-List under Security Intelligence Category confirms the reasons for blocking.

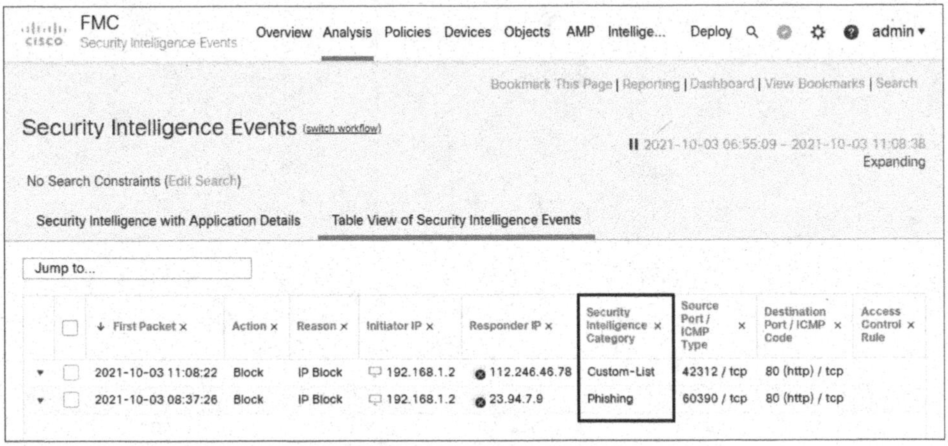

Figure 12-23 *Blocking an IP Address Using Custom List*

Enabling Security Intelligence in Monitor-Only Mode

Occasionally, you might want to monitor the activities of certain hosts in a network instead of blocking them completely. Doing so allows you to analyze the behavior of suspicious traffic and helps you build an appropriate defense. Follow these steps to enable monitoring functionality using Security Intelligence:

> **NOTE**   The following steps assume that you have already blocked certain IP addresses by completing the instructions in the previous sections. This time, you modify the previous configurations and change the action from Block to Monitor-only.

Step 1.   In the access control policy editor page, go to the **Security Intelligence** tab.

Step 2.   From the Block List field, right-click a category that you want to monitor. A context menu appears.

> **NOTE**   The threat defense does not support the Monitor-only mode for the Global Block List category.

Step 3.   From the context menu, select the **Monitor-only (Do Not Block)** option for your desired category. The red icon turns into a down arrow.

Figure 12-24 shows the selection of Monitor-only mode for a specific Security Intelligence category, the Custom-List, while leaving all other categories in Block mode.

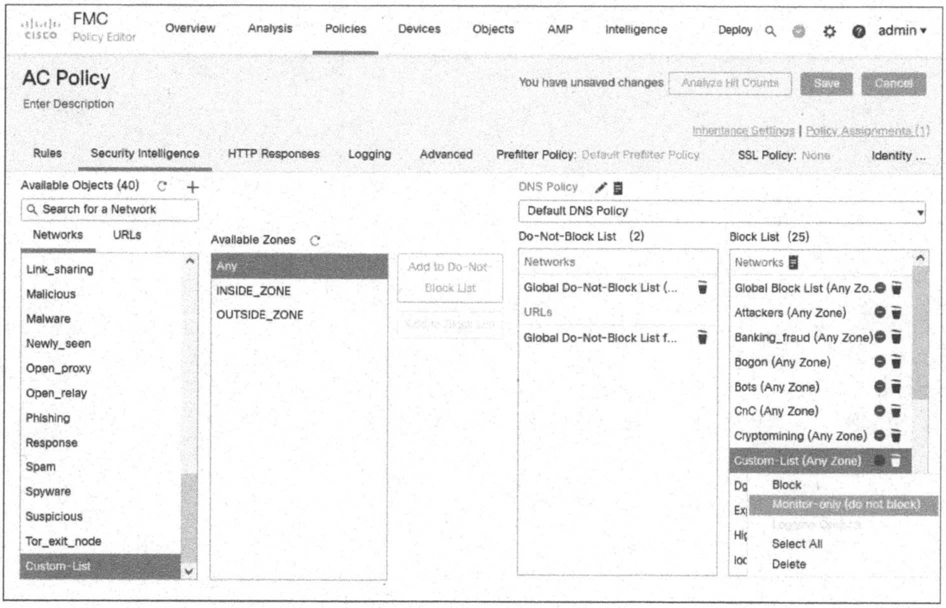

Figure 12-24   *Configuration of Monitor-Only Mode*

Step 4.   When the configuration is complete, click the **Save** button to save the changes and navigate to **Deploy > Deployment** to redeploy the access control policy to the threat defense.

This configuration changes the action from Block to Monitor-only for any addresses in the Custom-List that you created and uploaded earlier. To test the operation of Monitor-only mode, attempt to access one of the addresses from the custom list. This time, the threat defense allows that connection and generates a monitor event.

Figure 12-25 shows the difference between the Block and Monitor-only actions. The first connection attempt from host 192.168.1.2 to 112.246.46.78 was blocked; however, the second attempt was allowed, and the connection was monitored.

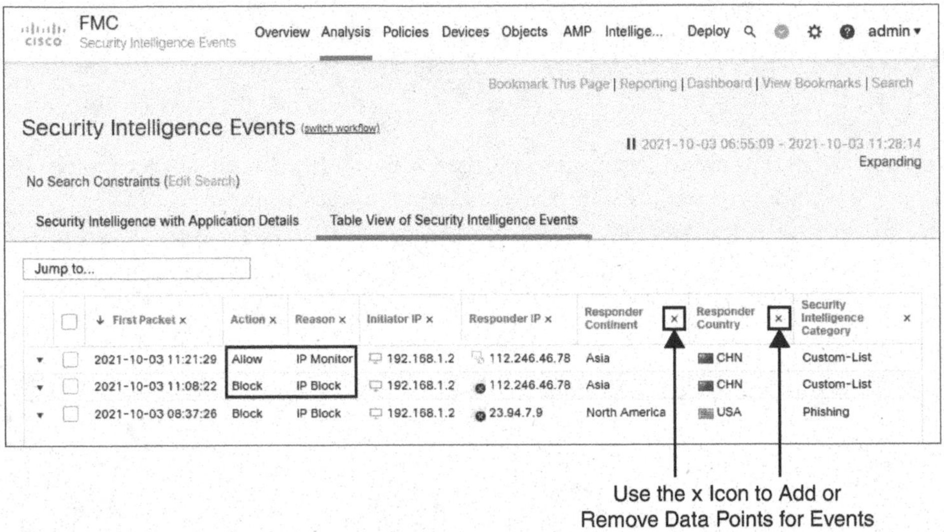

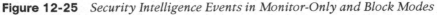

Figure 12-25   *Security Intelligence Events in Monitor-Only and Block Modes*

> **NOTE**   Although both screenshots for Figure 12-23 and Figure 12-25 are captured from the Analysis > Connections > Security Intelligence Events page, they provide different sets of information. For instance, Figure 12-25 shows geographical information in the view. Similarly, you can add and remove additional information by switching to the table view of events.

Threat Intelligence Director

Secure Firewall can also analyze and block connections based on the threat intelligence data published by various community-based cybersecurity sources. You can enable the Threat Intelligence Director (TID) on a management center to obtain and aggregate intelligence data from third-party sources and publish them to all the threat defense devices it manages. Figure 12-26 illustrates the operational workflow of TID. It shows that, after obtaining the *indicators* from *sources*, the management center publishes the *observables* to its threat defense, also known as an *element* in a TID architecture. As the threat defense inspects traffic, it reports the *observations* back to the management center. Upon evaluation of observations, the management center triggers *incidents*.

12

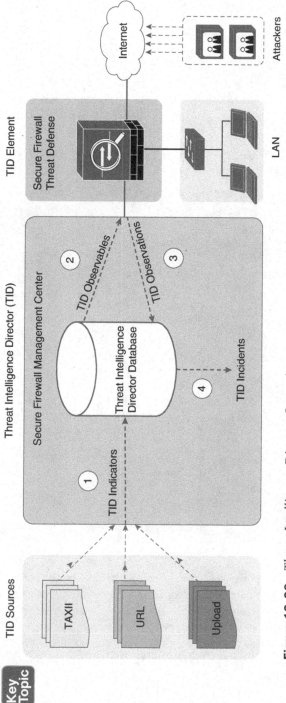

Figure 12-26 *Threat Intelligence Director Operations*

Enabling Threat Intelligence Director

You can enable TID on a threat defense through the access control policy by following these steps:

Step 1. Navigate to **Policies > Access Control > Access Control**. A list of available access control policies appears.

Step 2. Use the pencil icon next to the policy name to open the policy in the policy editor. The access control policy editor page appears.

Step 3. Go to the **Advanced** tab. Click the pencil icon next to the General Settings section.

Step 4. Select the **Enable Threat Intelligence Director** check box, as shown in Figure 12-27. Click **OK** to return to the policy editor page.

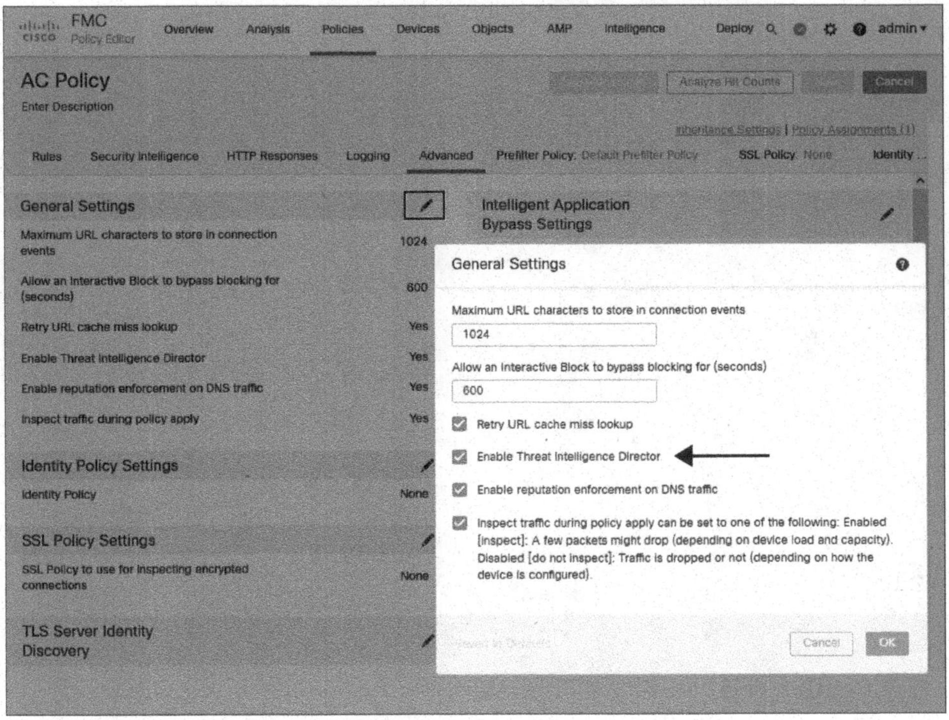

Figure 12-27 *Enabling the Threat Intelligence Director on an Access Control Policy*

Step 5. Add access control rules for the traffic that will be subject to TID inspection. When adding rules, you can optionally associate any other policies with the access control rule, as needed. For example, attach a file policy for malware analysis and an intrusion policy for deep packet inspection. Configuration of these policies is described in detail in separate chapters of this book.

Step 6. Save the changes. Go to **Deploy > Deployment** to deploy the policy to the threat defense.

After the policy deployment is successful, navigate to **Intelligence > Elements**. Your threat defense should be listed on this page. You might need to wait a few seconds for the green status icon to appear (see Figure 12-28).

CISCO FMC Elements	Overview	Analysis	Policies	Devices	Objects	AMP	Intelligence	Deploy	admin ▾

			1 Element
Name	**Element Type**	**Registered On**	**Access Control Policy**
⊘ Threat Defense	Cisco Firepower Threat Defense for VMware	Aug 28, 2021 1:46 PM EDT	AC Policy

Figure 12-28   *The Threat Intelligence Director Is Enabled on a Threat Defense*

Adding Sources and Importing Indicators

After the TID is successfully enabled, you are ready to add the TID sources. A management center supports two types of files to ingest sources:

- **STIX (Structured Threat Information Expression):** STIX is a standard used by cyber-security communities to describe and share threat intelligence information. A STIX file supports complex indicators.

- **Flat file:** Flat files are ASCII text files. They support simple indicators.

A management center can obtain a STIX or a flat file in three ways:

- **TAXII (Trusted Automated eXchange of Indicator Information):** The TAXII service is used to transport the intelligence data represented in a STIX file. To download a large STIX file, use the TAXII service. When an update is available, TAXII adds only the incremental data instead of replacing the existing data.

- **URL:** Using a URL, a management center can reach out to a remote server to fetch files from it.

- **Upload:** If the file is available on your local computer, you can use the browser to upload the file directly from your computer to the management center.

Now, let's add a source using the simplest method—uploading a flat file. For demonstration purposes, the following exercise reuses the same file that was used in the earlier example (refer to Figure 12-20). The later part of this exercise shows how to add a third-party source using the TAXII service.

Step 1.   Navigate to **Intelligence > Sources** in your management center. On the Sources tab, select the plus (**+**) icon. The Add Source window appears.

Step 2.   Choose the **Upload** delivery methods. Select **Flat File** from the Type drop-down. From the Content drop-down, choose **IPv4** because the file in this exercise includes IPv4 addresses only. A file can contain different types of indi-cators as well, as shown in Figure 12-29.

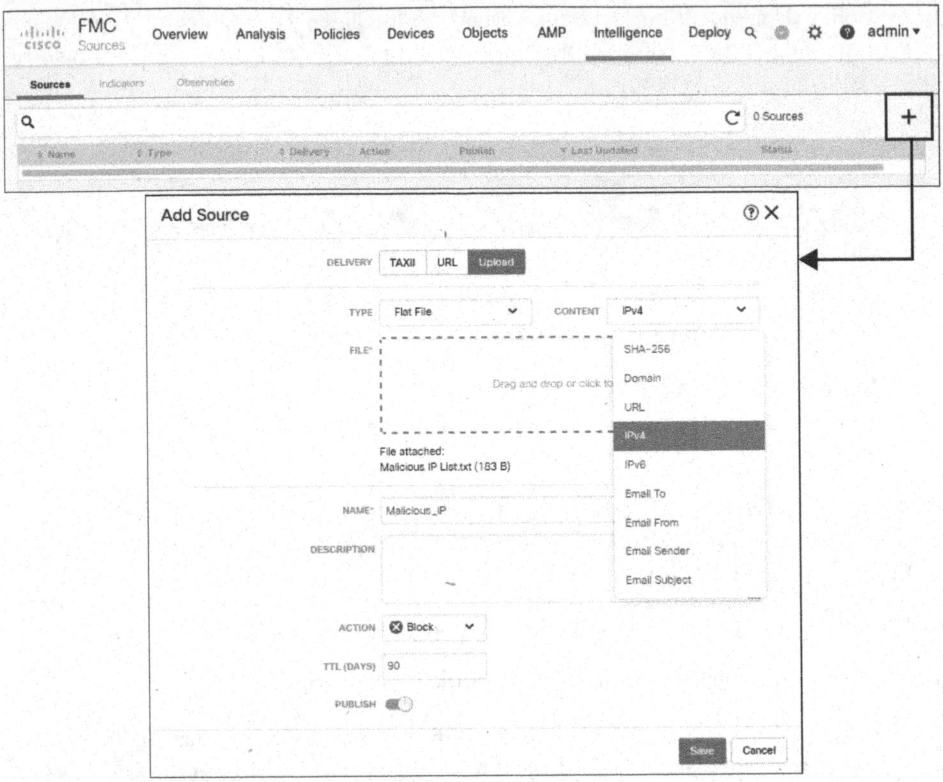

Figure 12-29 *Option to Add Sources to the Threat Intelligence Director*

Step 3.   Upload the file and assign a name to this source. Choose your desired action for the indicators that are obtained from this file.

Step 4.   Click **Save** to save the source.

That's all; the import is complete. Now, if you go to the Indicators tab, you will notice all the IP addresses that are included in the uploaded file are imported as TID indicators (see Figure 12-30).

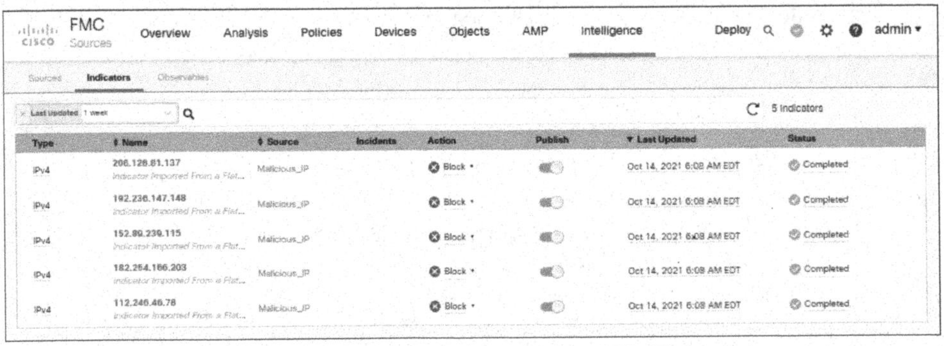

Figure 12-30 *Import of TID Indicators Using a Flat File Upload*

In the previous example, you used a flat file to import a few custom indicators. Next, you are going to import thousands of indicators in bulk from a third-party source using the TAXII service.

Step 1. Assuming you are still on the Intelligence > Sources page, navigate to the Sources tab and select the plus (+) icon. The Add Source window appears.

Step 2. Choose the **TAXII** delivery methods. Enter the URL and credential of the TAXII server. When the management center reaches out to the server, you can select the desired feeds using the Feeds drop-down.

Figure 12-31 shows the addition of a source using the TAXII service. It uses a URL from Hail a TAXII—a repository of open-source cyberthreat intelligence feeds in STIX format. As of the writing of this book, their intelligence data is publicly accessible through http://hailataxii.com/taxii-discovery-service (Username: guest, Password: guest).

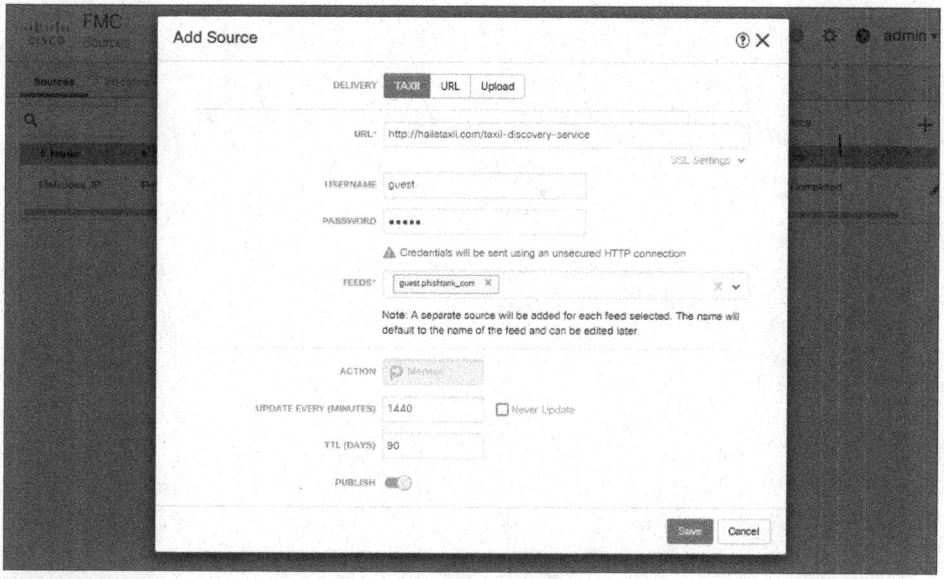

Figure 12-31 *Adding a Source Using the TAXII Service*

Step 3. Click **Save** to save the policy. The management center begins downloading the STIX file from the source immediately, as shown in Figure 12-32. After it is downloaded, data is parsed and observables are published automatically, without any redeployment of the access control policy.

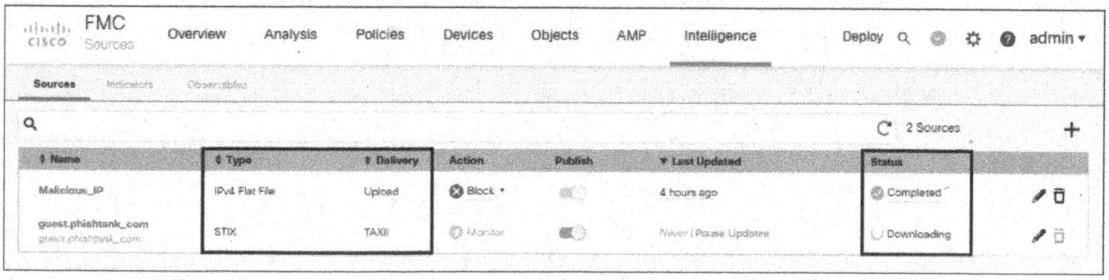

Figure 12-32 *Downloading a STIX File Using the TAXII Service*

If you now go to the Indicators tab again, you will find thousands of indicators that are being populated from the third-party source. By default, indicators that are downloaded using TAXII services are set to monitor traffic. However, if you want to block traffic based on certain indicators or observables, you can always do so by changing the action from Monitor to Block, as shown in Figure 12-33. When traffic is blocked by TID, you can find the events on the Intelligence > Incidents page.

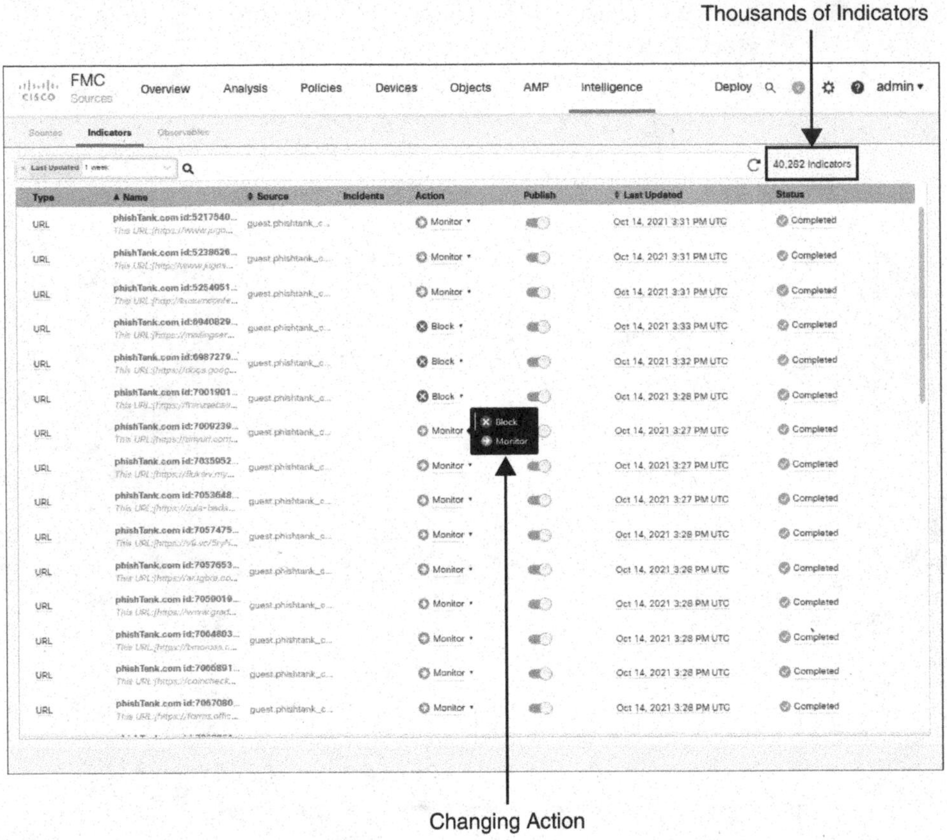

Figure 12-33 *Indicators Obtained from a Third-Party Source Using the TAXII Service*

Summary

This chapter describes how a threat defense can dynamically detect, block, or monitor suspicious addresses by using the Security Intelligence feature. It demonstrates how to enable both a Cisco intelligence feed as well as third-party sources. This chapter also walks you through the CLI configuration files, which can be useful to investigate issues with Security Intelligence.

Exam Preparation Tasks

As mentioned in the section "How to Use This Book" in the Introduction, you have a couple of choices for exam preparation: the exercises here, Chapter 22, "Final Preparation," and the exam simulation questions in the Pearson Test Prep practice test software.

Review All Key Topics

Review the most important topics in this chapter, noted with the Key Topic icon in the outer margin of the page. Table 12-3 lists a reference of these key topics and the page numbers on which each is found.

Key Topic

Table 12-3 Key Topics for Chapter 12

Key Topic Element	Description	Page
Bullet list	Security Intelligence blocking options	254
Bullet list	Updating Security Intelligence feed	258
Paragraph	Possible reasons for override	265
Figure 12-26	TID operation overview	275
Bullet list	STIX	277
Bullet list	TAXII	277

Complete Tables and Lists from Memory

Print a copy of Appendix C, "Memory Tables" (found on the companion website), or at least the section for this chapter, and complete the tables and lists from memory. Appendix D, "Memory Tables Answer Key," also on the companion website, includes completed tables and lists to check your work.

Define Key Terms

Define the following key terms from this chapter, and check your answers in the Glossary:

Security Intelligence, feed, list, context menu

## CHAPTER 13

Domain Name System (DNS) Policy

This chapter provides an overview of the following topics:

DNS Policy Essentials: This section describes the Domain Name System (DNS) and the operation of a DNS policy on Secure Firewall.

Best Practices for Blocking DNS Queries: This section provides tips to deploy and enforce a DNS policy in a real-world network.

Fulfilling Prerequisites: This section discusses the licensing and objects that are necessary for a DNS policy implementation.

Configuring DNS Policy: In this section, you learn how to configure and deploy a DNS policy on Secure Firewall.

Verification: The last section of this chapter introduces you to various command-line tools that you can use to investigate and troubleshoot any issues with a DNS policy.

The objectives of this chapter are to learn about

- Domain Name System (DNS) operations and rule actions

- Implementation of a DNS policy on Secure Firewall

- Verification of DNS policy configurations using CLI tools

Attackers often send phishing emails with links to malicious websites. A user in your network may be deceived by the misleading content and click an obfuscated link by mistake. A threat defense can intelligently prevent a user from accessing a malicious website by blocking its DNS query—one of the first things a client computer performs to access a website. This chapter describes the implementation of a DNS policy on Secure Firewall.

"Do I Know This Already?" Quiz

The "Do I Know This Already?" quiz enables you to assess whether you should read this entire chapter thoroughly or jump to the "Exam Preparation Tasks" section. If you are in doubt about your answers to these questions or your own assessment of your knowledge of the topics, read the entire chapter. Table 13-1 lists the major headings in this chapter and their corresponding "Do I Know This Already?" quiz questions. You can find the answers in Appendix A, "Answers to the 'Do I Know This Already?' Quizzes."

Table 13-1 "Do I Know This Already?" Section-to-Question Mapping

Foundation Topics Section	Questions
DNS Policy Essentials	1, 2, 3
Best Practices for Blocking DNS Queries	4
Fulfilling Prerequisites	5
Configuring DNS Policy	6
Verification	7

CAUTION The goal of self-assessment is to gauge your mastery of the topics in this chapter. If you do not know the answer to a question or are only partially sure of the answer, you should mark that question as wrong for purposes of the self-assessment. Giving yourself credit for an answer you correctly guess skews your self-assessment results and might provide you with a false sense of security.

1. Which of the following actions can detect a harmful domain without interrupting traffic flow?
    a. Domain Not Found
    b. Do-Not-Block List
    c. Block List
    d. Monitor

2. Which of the following actions sends an address of a spoofed DNS server?
    a. Domain Not Found
    b. Sinkhole
    c. Monitor
    d. Drop

3. Which of the following statements is incorrect?
    a. Sinkhole configuration requires a unique type of sinkhole object.
    b. A DNS policy requires a threat license.
    c. A threat defense downloads the latest Cisco intelligence feed directly from the Cisco cloud.
    d. The management center supports the blocking of custom domain lists.

4. Which of the following options can expedite the enforcement of a new DNS policy?
    a. Clearing the DNS cache of the client and server manually.
    b. Disabling the DNS caching on the local workstations by the system administrator.
    c. Positioning a threat defense between the local-area network (LAN) and the DNS server.
    d. All of these answers are correct.

5. Which license is necessary to configure and deploy a DNS policy on Secure Firewall?

   a. Threat license

   b. Malware license

   c. DNS license

   d. No additional license is necessary. This is a basic firewall functionality; you can enable a DNS policy out of the box.

6. Which of the following statements is true about a DNS policy?

   a. A new DNS policy comes with two built-in rules: Global Do-Not-Block List for DNS and Global Block List for DNS.

   b. The default DNS policy is modifiable but not removable.

   c. A DNS policy needs to be invoked within an access control policy to activate it on a threat defense.

   d. All of these answers are correct.

7. Which of the following directories stores the files related to a DNS policy?

   a. /var/sf/sidns_intelligence

   b. /var/sf/sidns_download

   c. /var/log/sidns_policy

   d. /var/log/sidns_list

Foundation Topics

DNS Policy Essentials

Before diving into DNS policy configuration, let's look at how a host computer learns the IP address of a website through a DNS query and how Secure Firewall can prevent a user from making a DNS query for a malicious domain.

Domain Name System (DNS)

When you want to call one of your friends, what do you usually do? You pick up your phone, go to the Contacts app, find your friend in the app, and select that person's name. You do not need to memorize or type the phone number to call a person. The phone originates a call for you, using the number stored in the Contacts app. If you do not find the number you need in your Contacts app, you ask someone who knows your friend for the phone number. This whole process is an analogy of how a DNS server works.

When you want to visit a website, you open a browser and enter the URL. However, before your browser learns the IP address of a website, the following tasks happen behind the scenes:

Key Topic

Step 1.   The browser sends a query to the local DNS server in your network.

Step 2.   If the local network has no internal DNS server or the DNS server has no information about the site you want to visit, a query is sent to the recursive DNS server of your Internet service provider (ISP). If the recursive server has information about the IP address in its cache, your browser receives that information. No additional queries are performed.

Step 3.   However, if the recursive server does not know the IP address, the recursive server sends the query to one of the 13 sets of root name servers located worldwide. A root server knows the DNS information about a top-level domain (TLD).

Step 4.   The DNS server of a TLD sends information about the second-level domain and its authoritative name server. An authoritative name server knows all the addressing information for a particular domain.

Step 5.   The authoritative name server responds to a query by returning the address record (A record) to your ISP. The ISP's recursive server stores the record on its cache for a specific amount of time and sends the IP address to your browser.

Figure 13-1 shows various levels of DNS queries for a domain. Depending on the records on the intermediate server cache, the number of queries can be higher or lower. The process can happen within less than a second.

Blocking of a DNS Query Using a Secure Firewall

You can add an access control rule to your access control policy to block DNS traffic; however, a traditional access control rule is unable to identify any harmful domain based on the characteristics of its web contents.

Figure 13-2 shows an access control rule that blocks DNS traffic solely based on DNS service ports. This static rule is unable to determine the risk level of a domain, and therefore, it cannot block an unsafe domain dynamically.

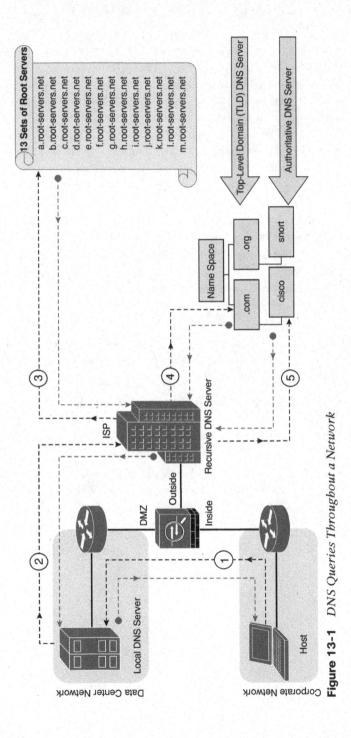

Figure 13-1   *DNS Queries Throughout a Network*

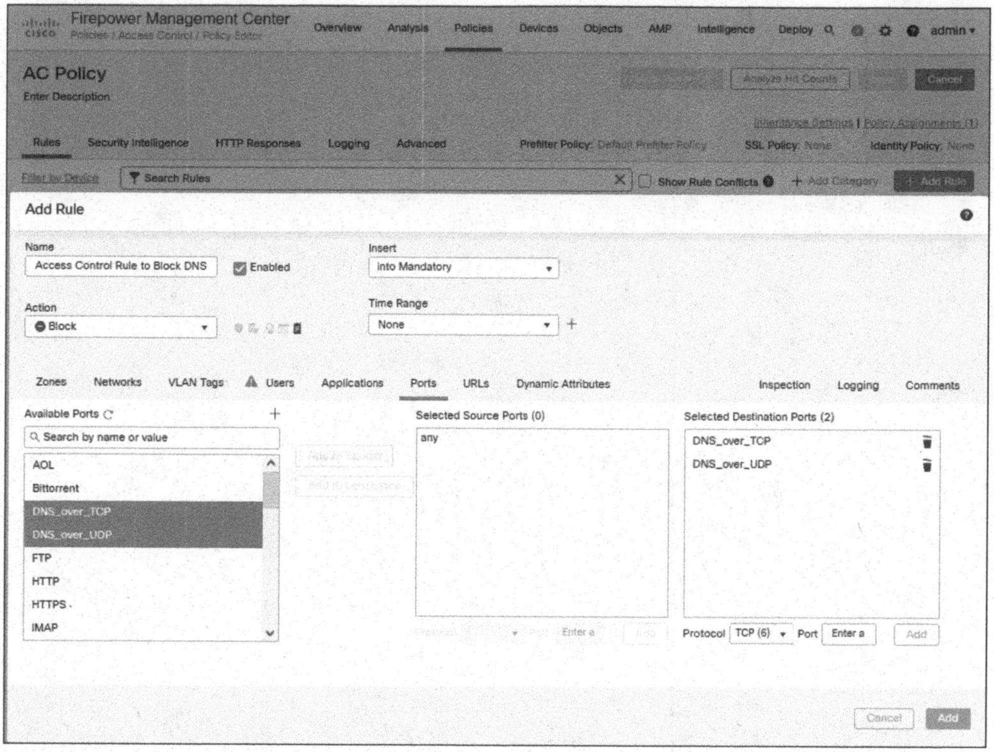

Figure 13-2 *Identifying and Blocking DNS Traffic Based on Service Ports*

The DNS-based Security Intelligence feature of Secure Firewall allows you to identify a susceptible DNS query and block the resolution of an unsafe domain name, while any queries to legitimate websites are allowed. It leads to a browser not being able to obtain the IP address of a malicious website. A threat defense blocks the request for a website before a potential HTTP connection is even established. Consequently, the threat defense does not need to engage its resources for further HTTP inspection.

Figure 13-3 shows the workflow of a DNS query. It also shows where a threat defense functions.

Figure 13-4 shows the low-level architecture of a threat defense. It helps you to understand how a packet is processed by the intelligence-based **DNS Policy** component before it goes through any deep packet inspection.

DNS Rule Actions

Depending on the security policies of your organization, you can add a DNS rule to a Block List or a Do-Not-Block List, or you can monitor a DNS query.

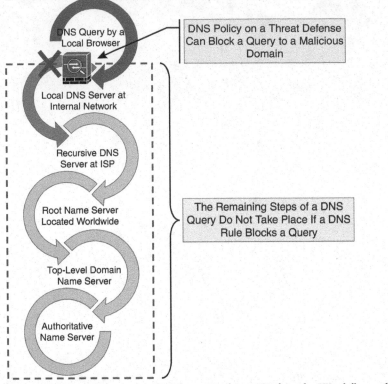

Figure 13-3   *Placement of a Threat Defense Within the Workflow of a DNS Query*

Actions That Can Interrupt DNS Queries

Secure Firewall offers various options for detecting and controlling a DNS query. Figure 13-5 shows the list of actions in the DNS rule configuration window. When you complete the lab exercises in this chapter, you can notice the impact of these actions on real-world traffic. (See Figure 13-20 for a quick comparison now.)

■ **Drop:** With this option, the threat defense simply drops the DNS query for a particular domain. Dropped packets are not subject to any further inspections.

CAUTION   A user may still access a website if the client computer caches the DNS records, and the existing records are not expired.

13

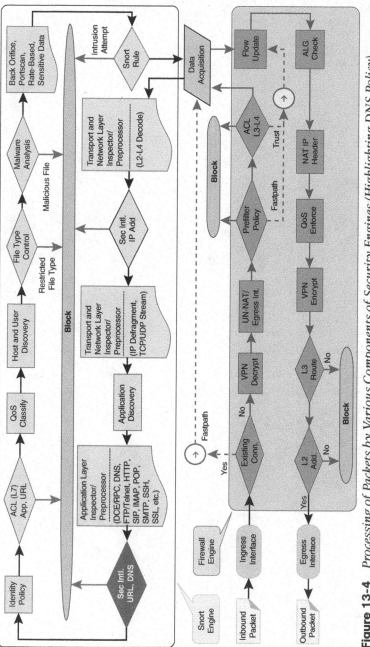

Figure 13-4 *Processing of Packets by Various Components of Security Engines (Highlighting DNS Policy)*

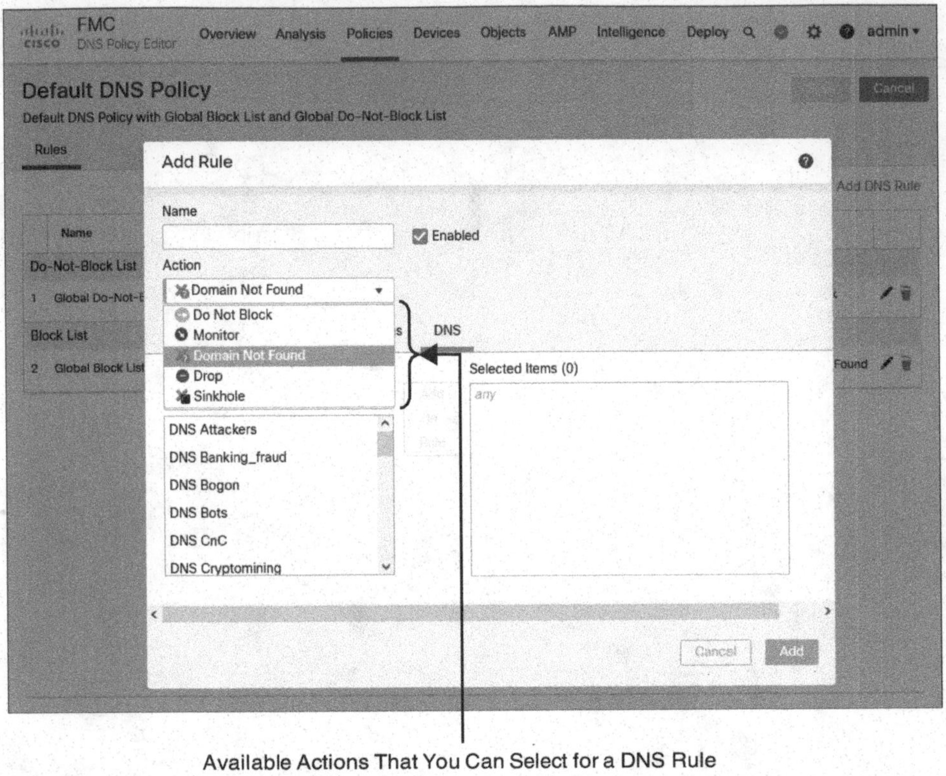

Figure 13-5   *DNS Rule Actions*

Figure 13-6 illustrates the drop action on a threat defense. The device simply drops the DNS query, and no response is provided to the client.

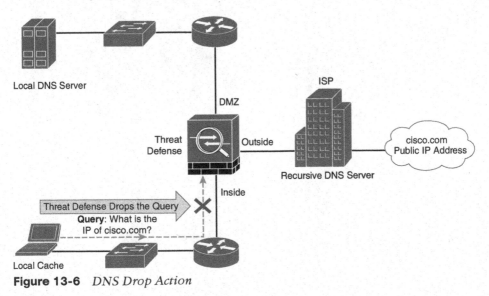

Figure 13-6   *DNS Drop Action*

■ **Domain Not Found:** With this option, as a response to a DNS query, a user receives an **NXDOMAIN (nonexistent domain name)** message (see Figure 13-7). The NXDOMAIN message indicates that the requested domain name does not exist. The browser cannot resolve the IP address for a domain. Consequently, the user fails to access the website.

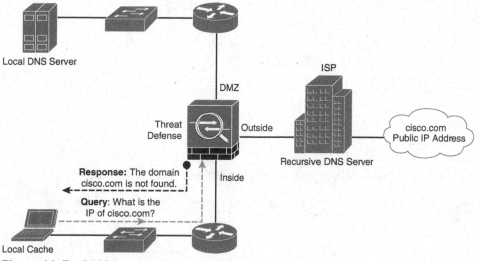

Figure 13-7 *DNS Domain Not Found Action*

■ **Sinkhole:** With this option, the threat defense responds to a DNS query with a false IP address. A browser does not realize that an intermediate security device—the threat defense in this example—acts as a spoofed DNS server, and it responds to its query with a false IP address. The IP address may or may not be assigned to an existing DNS server. Using Sinkhole functionality, you can redirect malicious traffic to an alternate location for further security analysis. The alternate DNS server location must be configured in a sinkhole object. The steps to create a sinkhole object are described in the "Fulfilling Prerequisites" section of this chapter.

Figure 13-8 shows a spoofed DNS server. The threat defense uses the IP address of this spoofed DNS server as a response to a DNS query only when the domain is categorized as harmful.

Figure 13-9 shows the implementation of a sinkhole without a physical spoofed server. You can assign any false IP address within a sinkhole object. Then the threat defense uses this false address to respond to any query to a harmful domain.

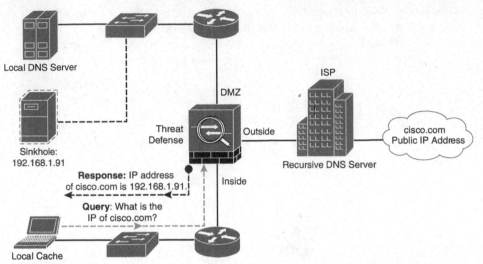

Figure 13-8 *DNS Sinkhole Action (Fake Address Represents a Spoofed DNS Server)*

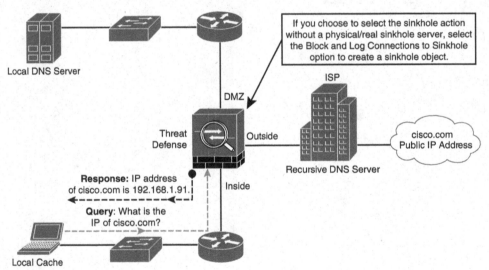

Figure 13-9 *DNS Sinkhole Action (Fake Address Does Not Represent an Actual DNS Server)*

Actions That Allow DNS Queries

Let's say the Cisco intelligence feed blocks a query to your trusted domain. You have asked Cisco to reinvestigate the domain. While you're waiting on Cisco, you can use one of the following actions to allow a desired DNS query:

- **Do Not Block:** This action allows the traffic to bypass an intelligence-based check; however, the traffic is still subject to other security inspections.

- **Monitor:** This action allows a threat defense to generate alerts when there is any match, but the threat defense does not interrupt traffic flow.

Sources of Intelligence

To learn about the new suspicious domains, Secure Firewall updates its intelligence database from the following sources:

- **Feed:** Cisco has a dedicated threat intelligence and research team, known as Talos, that analyzes the behavior of Internet traffic, performs in-depth analysis on any suspicious activities, categorizes the potential domains based on their characteristics, and lists the domains in a file.

  One of the processes running on the management center, known as a cloud agent, periodically communicates with the Cisco cloud to download the latest feed. The frequency for updating the feed is configurable. When the management center downloads a feed, it sends the feed to its managed threat defense devices automatically. Redeployment of the access control policy is not necessary.

  Figure 13-10 shows the selection of an update frequency for the Cisco intelligence feed. To access this configuration window, go to the **Object > Object Management.** Under Security Intelligence, select **DNS Lists and Feeds,** and click the pencil icon next to Cisco-DNS-and-URL-Intelligence-Feed.

  Table 13-2 shows the key differences between the feed and list types of Security Intelligence input.

- **List:** The management center supports the ability to block or allow custom lists of domains. You can list the domains in a text file (.txt format) and upload the file manually to the management center. Upon a successful upload, a custom DNS object appears along with the system-provided DNS objects. The process to add a DNS rule is described later in this chapter, in the section "Configuring DNS Policy."

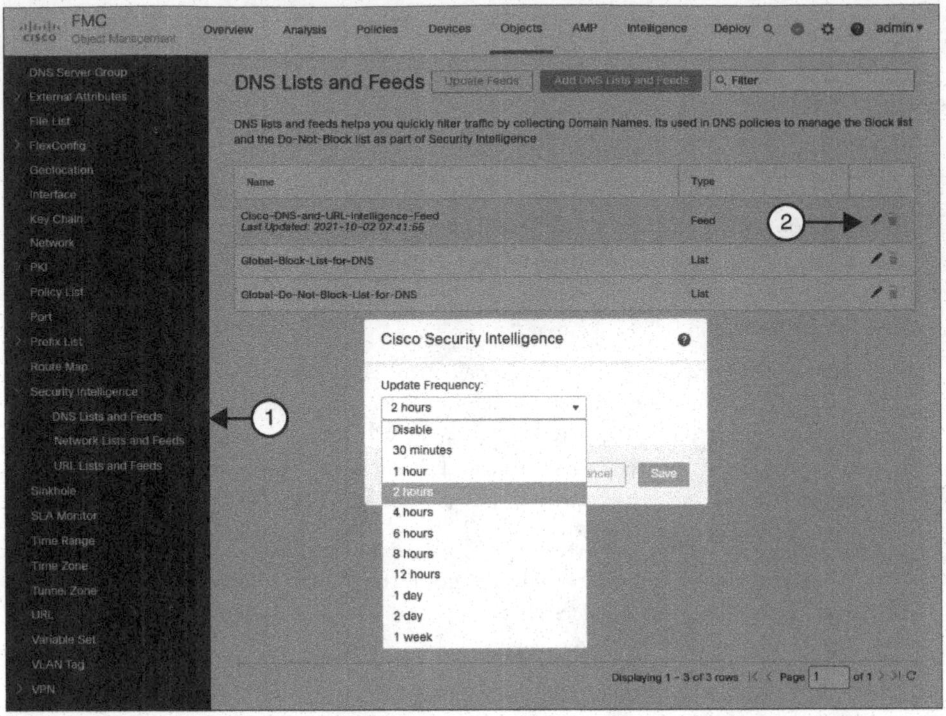

Figure 13-10 *Frequency of Cisco DNS and URL Intelligence Feed Update*

Table 13-2   Intelligence Feed Versus Intelligence List

	Feed	List
Provider	The Cisco threat intelligence team creates and manages the feed. The management center also supports the input of custom domains through an internal feed URL.	You created the feed based on your own research and selection.
Update	The management center can download the latest feed periodically.	You can manually update an old list on demand.

TIP   When you create your own list of domains for the Block List, enter one domain name per line. You can add a comment for future reference. Use the hash sign (#) at the beginning of a line to enter a comment.

Figure 13-11 shows the DNS List/Feed configuration window. To find this option, go to Object Management in the main menu and select the **DNS Lists and Feeds** option under Security Intelligence. Then click the **Add DNS Lists and Feeds** button. The DNS List/Feed configuration window then appears when you select List from the Type drop-down.

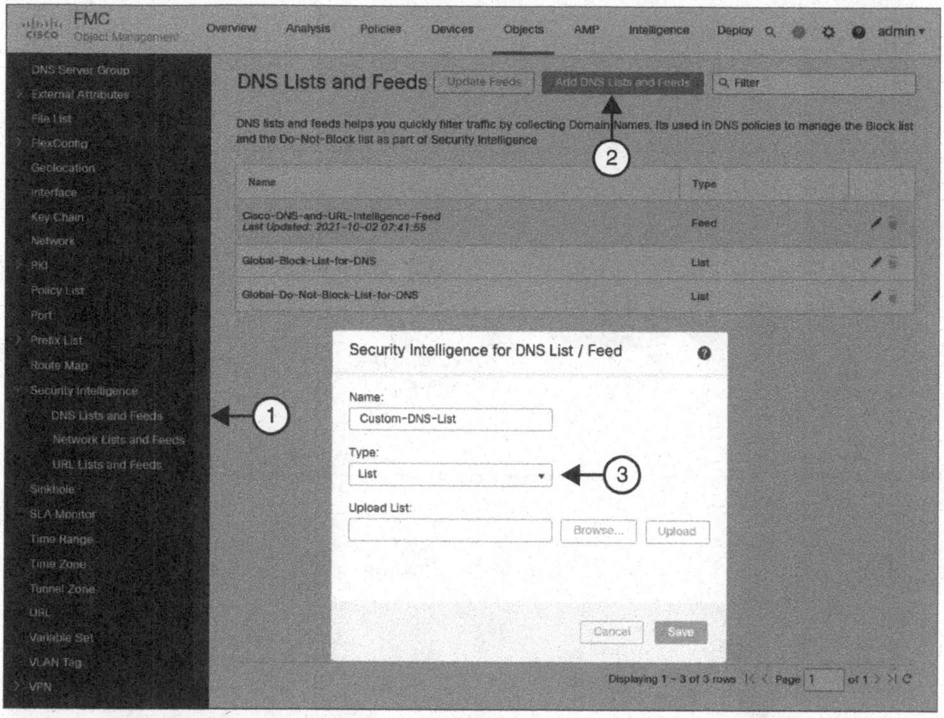

Figure 13-11 *Option to Upload a DNS List File*

Best Practices for Blocking DNS Queries

Depending on the placement of a threat defense in a network, you may have to wait some time before you notice a new DNS policy take effect. For example, if your one and only threat defense is placed at the perimeter edge—between your company network and ISP network—your network hosts may continue resolving an undesired website until the local DNS cache expires. The hosts can notice the effect of a new DNS policy after the DNS cache of the client computer and local DNS server expires.

You can clear the DNS cache of the client and server manually. However, it may not be feasible to clear the cache of *all* of the network hosts manually in real time. To expedite the enforcement of a new DNS policy on Secure Firewall, you can consider the following best practices:

- Enable IP address–based Security Intelligence as well.

- Disable DNS caching on the local workstations. Your organization's system administrator can confirm this setting.

- Position your threat defense between the local-area network (LAN) and the DNS server so that any egress traffic from the LAN is subject to DNS policy inspection. Placing a threat defense at the network edge enables the LAN hosts to resolve addresses directly using the cache of the internal DNS server.

Figure 13-12 shows two different ways to place a threat defense. In Network A, the threat defense allows queries to an internal DNS server and blocks the queries to an external DNS server. However, the threat defense in Network B blocks queries to any DNS servers, local or external.

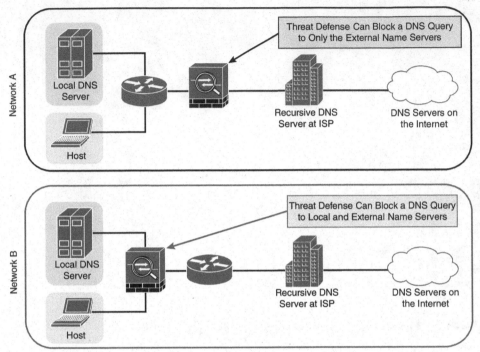

Figure 13-12   *Effectiveness of a DNS Rule in Different Threat Defense Deployments*

Fulfilling Prerequisites

Before you configure a DNS policy, make sure the following prerequisites are fulfilled:

■ A DNS policy requires a threat license. If you are in the process of purchasing a threat license, you can enable Evaluation Mode to avoid any logistic and administrative delays. The 90-day evaluation period allows you to configure and enable security features as if you have already installed a paid license.

■ If you want to redirect a DNS query to a sinkhole, you must configure a sinkhole object (with a real or fake IP address) before you select the Sinkhole action for a DNS rule. You can create multiple sinkhole objects using different IP addresses and use them for different purposes (for example, one object for malware, one object for phishing, and so on).

Figure 13-13 shows the configuration of a sinkhole object. To find this configuration window, navigate to **Objects > Object Management > Sinkhole** and click the **Add Sinkhole** button.

NOTE If you want to set up the sinkhole functionality without a physical DNS server, select the Block and Log Connections to Sinkhole option shown in Figure 13-13.

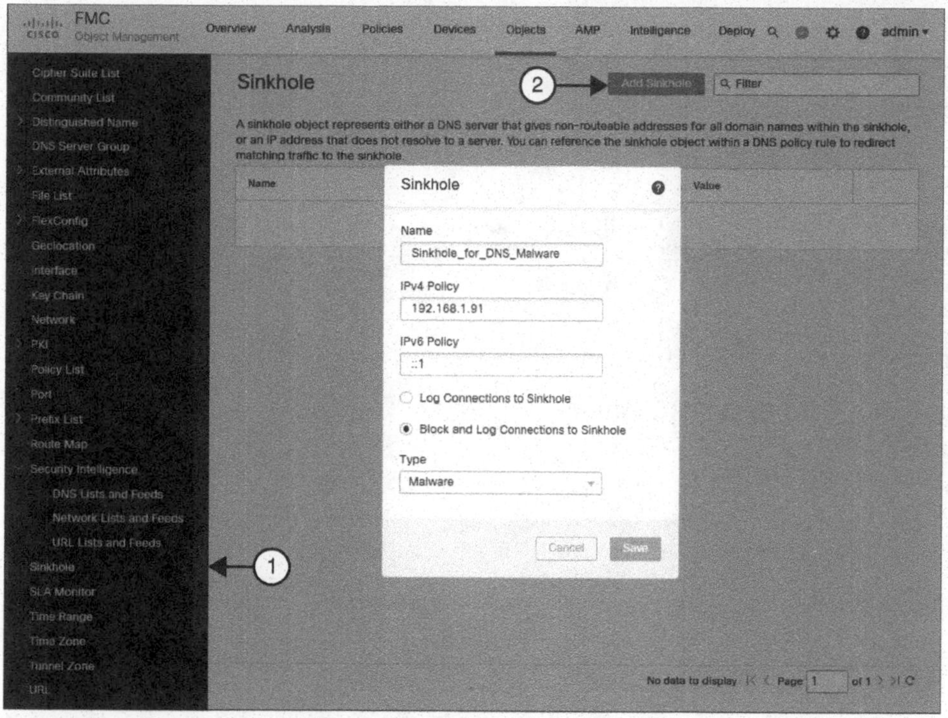

Figure 13-13 *Sinkhole Object Configuration*

Configuring DNS Policy

To block a query to a malicious domain using Secure Firewall, you must perform the following two tasks on your management center:

- Create a new DNS policy or edit an existing one by adding the necessary DNS rule conditions.

- Invoke the desired DNS policy within an access control policy and deploy the policies on a threat defense.

The following sections describe the process of enabling DNS policies successfully on a threat defense. Figure 13-14 shows the lab topology that is used in this chapter to configure DNS-based Security Intelligence (a DNS policy).

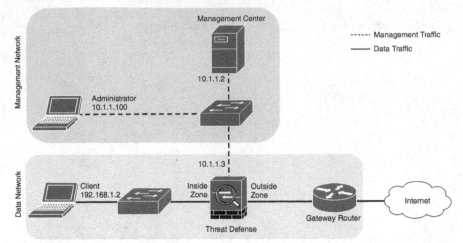

Figure 13-14 *Topology Used in the Configuration Examples of This Chapter*

Add a New Rule to a DNS Policy

To add a new DNS rule, follow these steps:

Step 1. Navigate to **Policies > Access Control > DNS**. The system-provided Default DNS Policy appears. The default policy is modifiable but not removable. You can also create a brand-new DNS policy and customize it. Do that by using the **Add DNS Policy** button. The system prompts you to name your new DNS policy (see Figure 13-15).

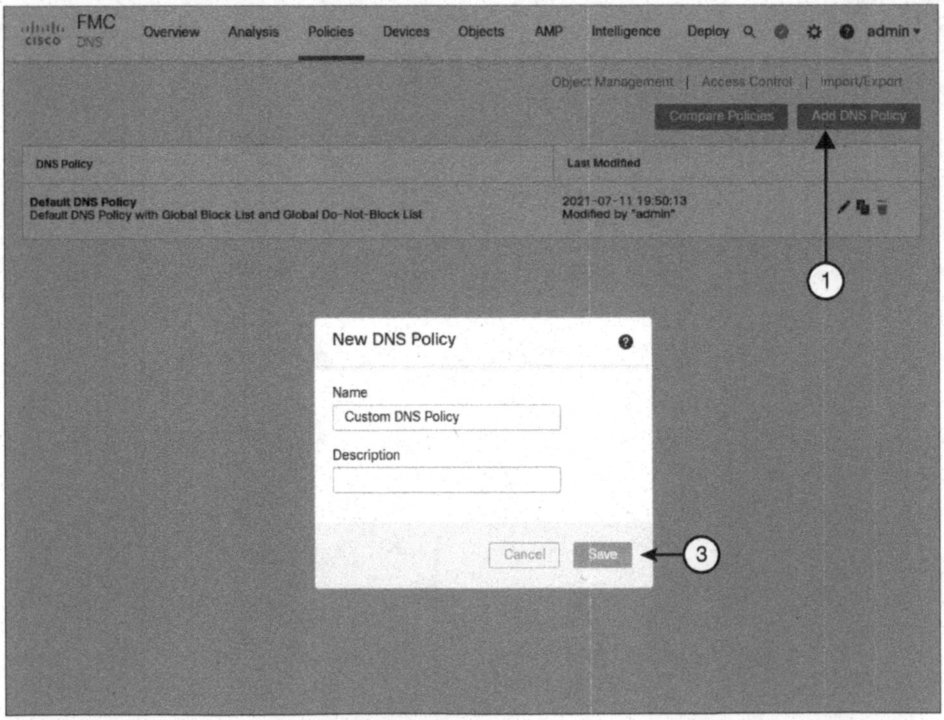

Figure 13-15 *Creation of a New DNS Policy*

Step 2. After you open a DNS policy in the policy editor, click the **Add DNS Rule** button. The Add Rule window appears.

Figure 13-16 shows the DNS policy editor page. Each DNS policy, by default, comes with two rules—Global Do-Not-Block List for DNS and Global Block List for DNS—that have higher precedence than a custom DNS rule.

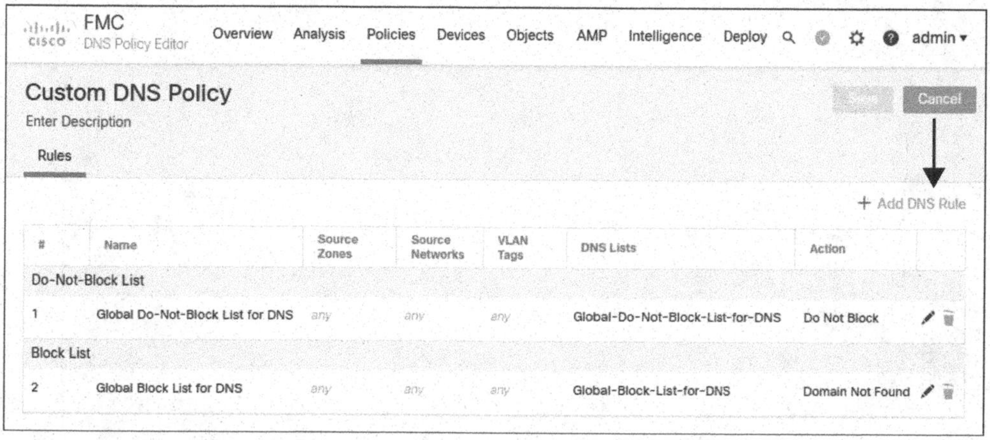

Figure 13-16 *DNS Policy Editor Page*

Step 3. Give a name to your DNS rule and select a desired action from the Action drop-down. The "DNS Rule Actions" section, earlier in this chapter, describes the functions of each action.

Step 4. Select the **DNS** tab, which shows the intelligence-based categories for unsafe DNS traffic. Add the desired categories to your rule.

Figure 13-17 shows the DNS rule editor window, where four different Security Intelligence categories are added to the rule.

Step 5. Optionally, select the **Zones**, **Networks**, and **VLAN** tabs and define the source and destination traffic, as appropriate.

Step 6. When the rule configuration is complete, click the **Add** button to save the rule and exit the DNS rule editor window. For each type of rule action, you need to create a separate DNS rule. So, repeat the previous steps as needed (see Figure 13-18 as an example of multiple DNS rules).

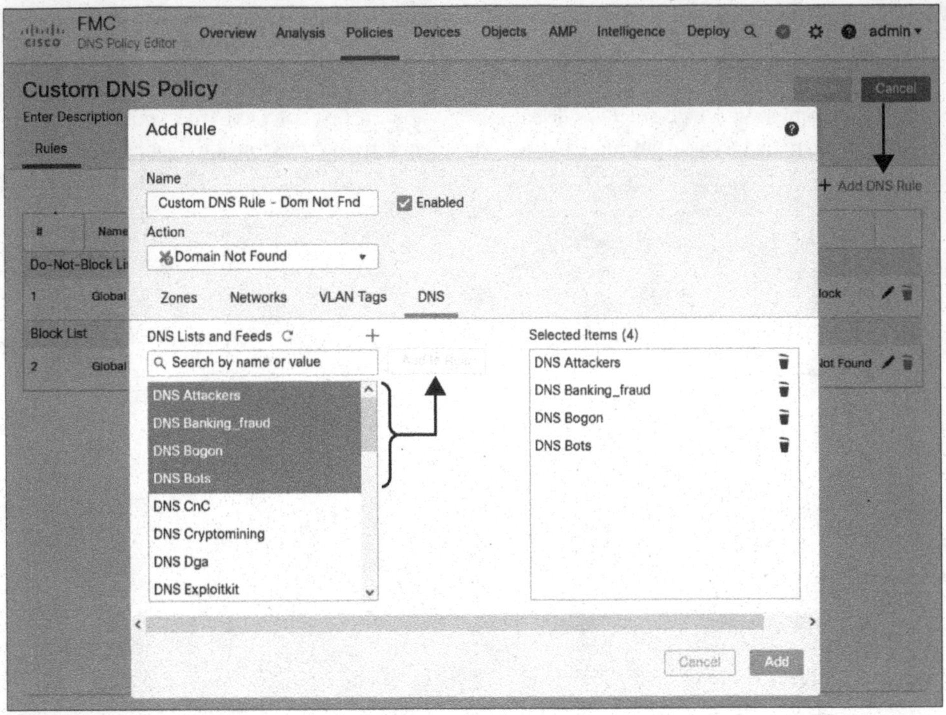

Figure 13-17 *DNS Rule Editor Window*

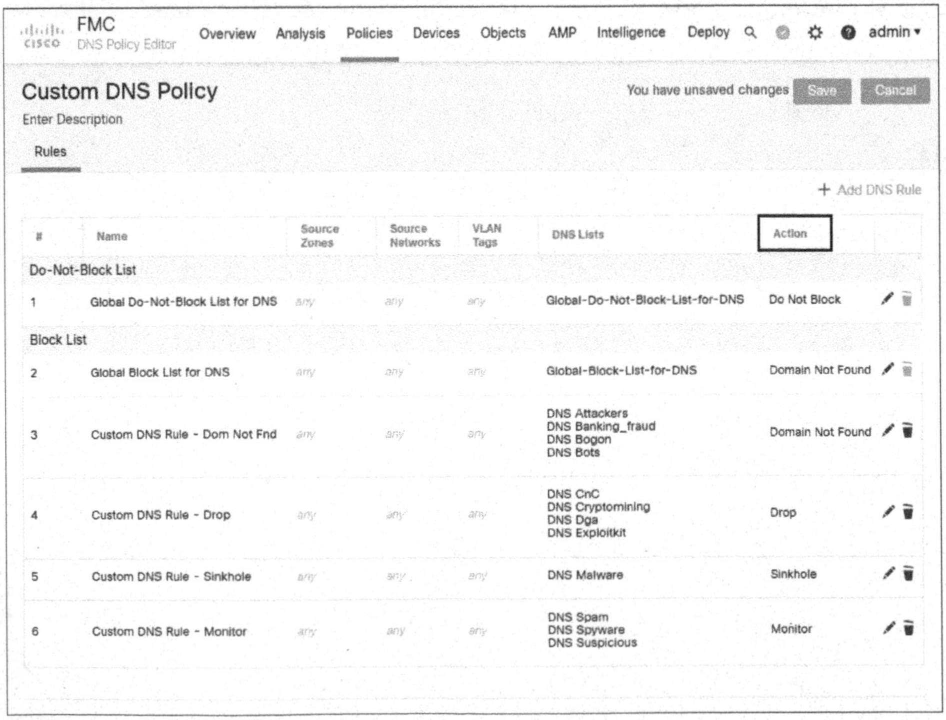

Figure 13-18 *Multiple DNS Rules with Various Rule Actions*

Step 7.   On the DNS policy editor, click the **Save** button to save the changes on your DNS policy.

> **NOTE**   Do not attempt to deploy a new DNS policy at this stage. To enable a DNS policy, you must complete the steps provided in the next section, "Invoke the DNS Policy."

Invoke the DNS Policy

To deploy a DNS policy on a threat defense, you need to invoke it manually within an access control policy. The following steps show how to deploy a newly created DNS policy:

> **NOTE**   If you do not perform the following steps, by default, an access control policy invokes the system-provided default DNS policy.

Step 1.   Navigate to **Policies > Access Control > Access Control**. Edit the access control policy that will be applied on a threat defense.

Step 2.   On the access control policy editor page that appears, select the **Security Intelligence** tab.

Step 3.   On the Security Intelligence tab, from the DNS Policy drop-down, select the desired DNS policy (see Figure 13-19).

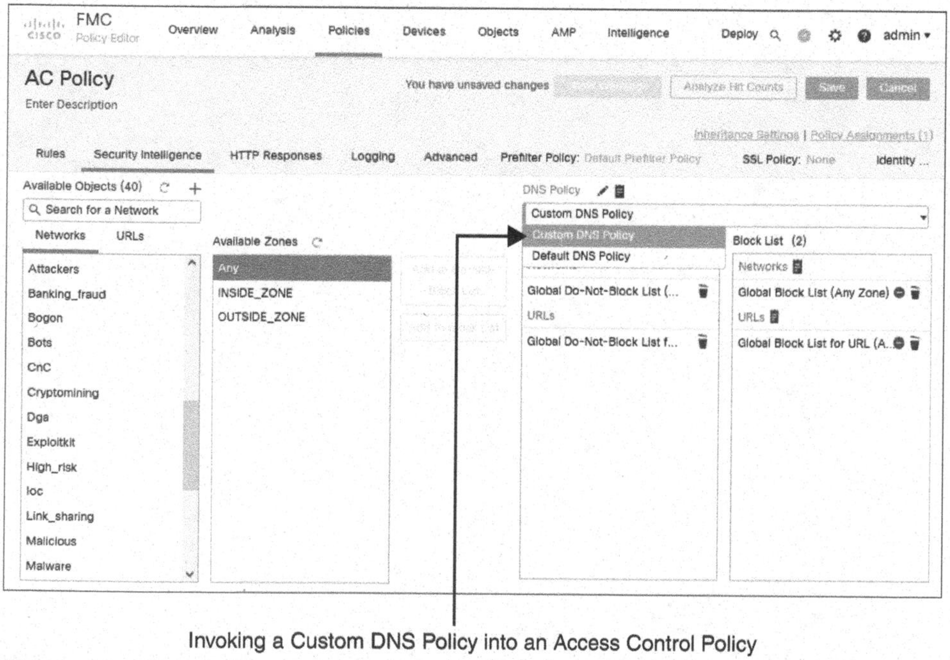

Invoking a Custom DNS Policy into an Access Control Policy

Figure 13-19   *Invoking a Custom DNS Policy into an Access Control Policy*

Step 4.   Click **Save** to save the configuration and deploy the policy to your threat defense.

Verification

You can use the threat defense CLI in expert mode to review the DNS policy configuration and investigate issues related to configuration, deployment, and inspection. Upon a successful deployment, the DNS Security Intelligence rules are stored in the /var/sf/sidns_download directory, in list file (.lf) format. The DNS policy configuration file, dns.rules, is also located in this directory. The threat defense creates all these files at the time when you deploy a DNS policy. Therefore, matching the timestamps of the files, which use the UTC time zone, is an important indicator of whether the latest policy is deployed.

Example 13-1 shows the dns.rules file and the list files (.lf) that are created upon a successful DNS policy deployment. The list files contain the DNS addresses that are assigned with Block and Do-Not-Block actions.

Example 13-1 *Files Containing the DNS Addresses and Policy Configurations*

```
> expert
admin@ThreatDefense:/$ ls -halp /var/sf/sidns_download/
total 50M
drwxrwxr-x  5 www  detection 4.0K Nov 27 00:57 ./
drwxr-xr-x 72 root root      4.0K Nov 27 00:55 ../
-rw-r--r--  1 root root        61 Nov 27 00:56 03709ed4-faab-47af-bade-
4435f8da1013.lf
-rw-r--r--  1 root root       1.3M Nov 27 00:56 23f2a124-8278-4c03-8c9d-
d28fe08b71ab.lf
-rw-r--r--  1 root root       7.7K Nov 27 00:56 2ccda18e-ddff-4f5c-af9a-
f00985219707.lf
-rw-r--r--  1 root root        96 Nov 27 00:56 3e2af68e-5fc8-4b1c-b5bc-
b4e7cab5abcd.lf
-rw-r--r--  1 root root       133 Nov 27 00:56 5a0b6d6b-e2c3-436f-b4a1-
48248b331d39.lf
-rw-r--r--  1 root root        48 Nov 27 00:56 5f8148f1-e5e4-427a-aa3b-
ee1c2745d663.lf
-rw-r--r--  1 root root       8.1M Nov 27 00:56 60f4e2ab-d96c-44a0-bd38-
830252b65259.lf
-rw-r--r--  1 root root        74 Nov 27 00:55 663da2e4-32f4-44d2-ad1f-
8d6182720d32.lf
-rw-r--r--  1 root root        47 Nov 27 00:56 6ba968f4-7a25-4793-a2c8-
7cc77f1f1074.lf
-rw-r--r--  1 root root        17 Nov 27 00:56 IPRVersion.dat
-rw-r--r--  1 root root        53 Nov 27 00:56 a27c6aae-8e52-4174-a81a-
47c59fecd3a5.lf
-rw-r--r--  1 root root       1.7M Nov 27 00:56 abdc925f-4f85-4504-90a7-
c891979ad82a.lf
-rw-r--r--  1 root root       20M Nov 27 00:56 b1df3aa8-2841-4c88-8e64-
bfaacec7111f.lf
-rw-r--r--  1 root root        56 Nov 27 00:56 bde824fd-36dd-4a7c-9cc1-
80e40ac7bd48.lf
-rw-r--r--  1 root root        74 Nov 27 00:55 ded9848d-3580-4ca1-9d3c-
04113549f129.lf
```

```
-rw-rw-r--  1 root root     19M Nov 27 00:57 dm_dns0.acl
-rw-r--r--  1 root root    1.9K Nov 27 00:55 dns.rules
drwxr-xr-x  2 www  www        6 Jul 30 18:16 health/
drwxr-xr-x  2 www  www       22 Jul 30 18:16 peers/
drwxr-xr-x  2 www  www       92 Jul 30 18:16 tmp/
admin@ThreatDefense:/$
```

After you configure a DNS policy using the GUI and deploy it on a threat defense, the threat defense writes the configurations into the dns.rules file. A dns.rules file saves the DNS rule conditions and associates the actions with the related Block List and Do-Not-Block List files. The file also records the time when the latest DNS policy is deployed. Example 13-2 exhibits the contents of the dns.rules file.

Example 13-2   *DNS Policy Configurations—View from the CLI*

```
admin@ThreatDefense:/$ cat /var/sf/sidns_download/dns.rules
#### dns.rules
####################################################################
#
# AC Name        : Custom DNS Policy
# Policy Exported : Fri Nov 27 00:54:09 2020 (UTC)
# File Written    : Fri Nov 27 00:55:25 2020 (UTC)
#
# DC Version      : 6.6.0-90  OS: 37
# SRU             : 2020-01-16-001-vrt
# VDB             : 328
#
####################################################################
#
policy 6d3a2cd0-3020-11eb-9269-908e9e1aaac3
revision c81daa72-3049-11eb-b248-8a9bd317e923


interface 1 9d23ae0a-0639-11eb-8ed7-75e4028dc079
interface 2 8cf056aa-1caa-11eb-b1d4-d466abfe9e0b
dnslist 1048624 03709ed4-faab-47af-bade-4435f8da1013.1f
dnslist 1048622 23f2a124-8278-4c03-8c9d-d28fe08b71ab.1f
dnslist 1048625 2ccda18e-ddff-4f5c-af9a-f00985219707.1f
dnslist 1048623 3e2af68e-5fc8-4b1c-b5bc-b4e7cab5abcd.1f
dnslist 1048614 5a0b6d6b-e2c3-436f-b4a1-48248b331d39.1f
dnslist 1048616 5f8148f1-e5e4-427a-aa3b-ee1c2745d663.1f
dnslist 1048618 60f4e2ab-d96c-44a0-bd38-830252b65259.1f
dnslist 1048575 663da2e4-32f4-44d2-ad1f-8d6182720d32.1f
dnslist 1048617 6ba968f4-7a25-4793-a2c8-7cc77f1f1074.1f
dnslist 1048621 a27c6aae-8e52-4174-a81a-47c59fecd3a5.1f
dnslist 1048619 abdc925f-4f85-4504-90a7-c891979ad82a.1f
dnslist 1048620 b1df3aa8-2841-4c88-8e64-bfaacec7111f.1f
```

```
dnslist 1048615 bde824fd-36dd-4a7c-9cc1-80e40ac7bd48.lf
dnslist 1048576 ded9848d-3580-4ca1-9d3c-04113549f129.lf
sinkhole 1 22e626b6-3020-11eb-b5b7-a08f3b06f9a7 192.168.1.91 ::1


1 allow any   any any 1048575
3 nxdomain any   any any 1048576
5 nxdomain any   any any 1048614
5 nxdomain any   any any 1048615
5 nxdomain any   any any 1048616
5 nxdomain any   any any 1048617
6 block any   any any 1048618
6 block any   any any 1048619
6 block any   any any 1048620
6 block any   any any 1048621
7 sinkhole any   any any 1048622 (sinkhole: 1)
8 monitor any   any any 1048623
8 monitor any   any any 1048624
8 monitor any   any any 1048625
admin@ThreatDefense:/$
```

Example 13-2 also highlights the sinkhole configurations in the dns.rules file. The sinkhole rule (rule ID 7) matches the domain names on the 23f2a124-8278-4c03-8c9d-d28fe08b71ab. lf list file (list ID 1048622). When there is a match with the rule, the threat defense responds to a DNS query with the sinkhole IP address 192.168.1.91.

To find the domains that are listed in a list file (.lf file), you can read the file using simple Linux commands, such as **cat** or **less**. To identify the category of the domains, just view the first line of the file using the **head** command. Example 13-3 confirms that the file 23f2a124-8278-4c03-8c9d-d28fe08b71ab.lf (DNS list ID 1048622) lists all the domains that are susceptible for malware.

Example 13-3 *Viewing the List of Domains Included in a Category*

```
! To display the first ten lines of a file:


admin@ThreatDefense:/$ head /var/sf/sidns_download/23f2a124-8278-4c03-8c9d-
d28fe08b71ab.lf
#Cisco DNS and URL intelligence feed: DNS Malware
www.ukrembtr.com
timnhanhanh12h.com
mavericktannery.com
www.studiocoloccini.it
content.bateriku.com
tecmachine.com.br
nnlamn.kvalitne.cz
security.hsbc.request-authorisation.com
```

```
berharaphiduplebihbaik.com
admin@ThreatDefense:/$


! To display only the first line of a file:
admin@ThreatDefense:/$ head -n1 /var/sf/sidns_download/23f2a124-8278-4c03-
8c9d-d28fe08b71ab.1f
#Cisco DNS and URL intelligence feed: DNS Malware
admin@ThreatDefense:/$
```

The categorization or inclusion of a domain may vary in different versions of the Security Intelligence feed. If you want to determine the inclusion of any particular domain in the current Cisco intelligence feed, you can run the following command to search for that particular domain within all the list files:

```
admin@ThreatDefense:~$ egrep [domain_name] /var/sf/sidns_
download/*.1f
```

Example 13-4 shows how this command is used.

Example 13-4 *Identifying the DNS Intelligence Category for Certain Domains*

```
admin@ThreatDefense:~$ egrep wowize.xyz /var/sf/sidns_download/*.1f
/var/sf/sidns_download/23f2a124-8278-4c03-8c9d-d28fe08b71ab.1f:wowize.xyz
admin@ThreatDefense:~$ head -n1 /var/sf/sidns_download/23f2a124-8278-4c03-
8c9d- d28fe08b71ab.1f
#Cisco DNS and URL intelligence feed: DNS Malware
admin@ThreatDefense:~$


admin@ThreatDefense:~$ egrep dcapib.com /var/sf/sidns_download/*.1f
/var/sf/sidns_download/60f4e2ab-d96c-44a0-bd38-830252b65259.1f:dcapib.com
admin@ThreatDefense:~$ head -n1 /var/sf/sidns_download/60f4e2ab-d96c-44a0-
bd38-830252b65259.1f
#Cisco DNS and URL intelligence feed: DNS CnC
admin@ThreatDefense:~$
```

To verify the operation of a DNS policy and inspection of a DNS query, you need to access some of the domains that are included in the current DNS policy. You can use a browser to connect, but keep in mind that those domains are potentially harmful. You should not attempt to access the contents on those websites until any security device or tool is actively protecting your network. Alternatively, you can also use the **nslookup** command on a client computer and attempt to resolve a domain name. It allows you to view the IP address of a domain without accessing the contents of a malicious website. The tool is available on both Windows and Linux operating systems.

Example 13-5 shows the resolutions of the same domain names used in the previous examples from a network host. The client uses the **nslookup** command-line tool and receives different results for querying different domains from different intelligence-based categories.

Example 13-5 *Resolving Domain Names by Using the* nslookup *Command*

```
! The following answer demonstrates the "Sinkhole" action. It responds with IP
address 192.168.1.91, which is a non-authoritative spoof DNS server.

Users@Linux:~$ nslookup wowize.xyz
Server:        127.0.1.1
Address:       127.0.1.1#53

Non-authoritative answer:
Name: wowize.xyz
Address: 192.168.1.91
Name: wowize.xyz
Address: ::1
Users@Linux:~$



! The following answer reflects the "Domain Not Found" action. The DNS query fails
with NXDOMAIN message, which means the domain appears to be non-existent.

Users@Linux:~$ nslookup iro.bckl.ir
Server:        127.0.1.1
Address:       127.0.1.1#53

** server can't find iro.bckl.ir: NXDOMAIN
Users@Linux:~$



! The following answer reflects the "Monitor" action. The DNS query is able to
resolve the domain name. It shows the public IP address for the domain.

Users@Linux:~$ nslookup news06.biz
Server: 127.0.1.1
Address: 127.0.1.1#53

Non-authoritative answer:
Name: news06.biz
Address: 134.209.136.68
Users@Linux:~$
```

Figure 13-20 demonstrates various rule actions on different domains. The threat defense triggered these events when a client attempted to access any matching websites. Events triggered by the DNS policy are displayed on the **Analysis > Connections > Security Intelligence Events** page.

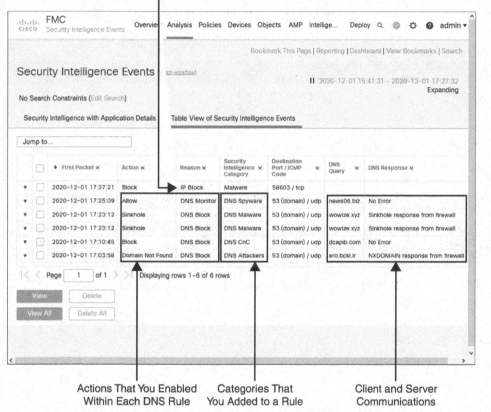

Figure 13-20 *Security Intelligence Event Page Showing Events Triggered by DNS Rules*

Summary

This chapter describes various techniques for administering DNS queries using Secure Firewall. Besides using a traditional access control rule, a threat defense can incorporate the Cisco intelligence feed and dynamically block suspicious domains. This chapter describes various ways to configure and deploy a DNS policy. The chapter also demonstrates several command-line tools you can run to verify, analyze, and troubleshoot issues with DNS policy.

Exam Preparation Tasks

As mentioned in the section "How to Use This Book" in the Introduction, you have a couple of choices for exam preparation: the exercises here, Chapter 22, "Final Preparation," and the exam simulation questions in the Pearson Test Prep practice test software.

Review All Key Topics

Review the most important topics in this chapter, noted with the Key Topic icon in the outer margin of the page. Table 13-3 lists a reference of these key topics and the page numbers on which each is found.

Table 13-3　Key Topics for Chapter 13

Key Topic Element	Description	Page
Step list	DNS server operation	285
Bullet list	Sinkhole	291

Complete Tables and Lists from Memory

Print a copy of Appendix C, "Memory Tables" (found on the companion website), or at least the section for this chapter, and complete the tables and lists from memory. Appendix D, "Memory Tables Answer Key," also on the companion website, includes completed tables and lists to check your work.

Define Key Terms

Define the following key terms from this chapter, and check your answers in the Glossary:

DNS Policy, feed, NXDOMAIN (nonexistent domain name), sinkhole

## CHAPTER 14

URL Filtering

This chapter provides an overview of the following topics:

URL Filtering Essentials: This section explains how the categorization and reputation of URLs can enable Secure Firewall to filter URLs intelligently. It also describes the workflow of URL lookup and URL dataset updates on Secure Firewall.

Fulfilling Prerequisites: This section discusses the licensing requirements for enabling URL Filtering functionality on Secure Firewall.

Best Practices for URL Filtering Configuration: In this section, you learn about the best practices for configuring and managing the URL Filtering feature.

Enabling URL Filtering: This section walks you through the steps to configure an access control policy with a URL Filtering rule constraint and then verify its impact on network traffic.

The objectives of this chapter are to learn about

- URL Filtering technology and its operational architecture

- Configuration of an access control policy with URL Filtering

- Verification of URL Filtering operations using CLI tools

New websites are coming out every day. As a security analyst, you will strive to determine the relevance of a new website for business operations and its risk level for security reasons. However, it is challenging to catch up with the number of new websites growing exponentially every day. In this chapter, you learn how Secure Firewall can empower you with automatic classification of millions of websites using its web reputation technology.

"Do I Know This Already?" Quiz

The "Do I Know This Already?" quiz enables you to assess whether you should read this entire chapter thoroughly or jump to the "Exam Preparation Tasks" section. If you are in doubt about your answers to these questions or your own assessment of your knowledge of the topics, read the entire chapter. Table 14-1 lists the major headings in this chapter and their corresponding "Do I Know This Already?" quiz questions. You can find the answers in Appendix A, "Answers to the 'Do I Know This Already?' Quizzes."

Table 14-1 "Do I Know This Already?" Section-to-Question Mapping

Foundation Topics Section	Questions
URL Filtering Essentials	1, 2
Fulfilling Prerequisites	3
Best Practices for URL Filtering Configuration	4
Enabling URL Filtering	5

> **CAUTION** The goal of self-assessment is to gauge your mastery of the topics in this chapter. If you do not know the answer to a question or are only partially sure of the answer, you should mark that question as wrong for purposes of the self-assessment. Giving yourself credit for an answer you correctly guess skews your self-assessment results and might provide you with a false sense of security.

1. Which of the following statements is true about the URL lookup?

   a. A threat defense, by itself, can resolve the category of all URLs on the Internet.

   b. The management center, by itself, can resolve the category of all URLs on the Internet.

   c. Both the management center and threat defense can collectively resolve URLs on the Internet.

   d. Neither the management center nor the threat defense can resolve URLs independently; they send all the URLs to the Internet to determine the latest categorizations.

2. Which of the following statements about URL database updates is true?

   a. Secure Firewall can download the new URLs directly from the Cisco cloud.

   b. The URL Filtering database can be different in different Secure Firewall models, depending on their available resources.

   c. The management center communicates with Cisco Cloud Services automatically every 30 minutes to check for new updates.

   d. All of these answers are correct.

3. Which of the following licenses is necessary to block a URL based on its category and reputation?

   a. Threat

   b. URL

   c. Malware

   d. Both Threat and URL

4. When enabling URL Filtering on Secure Firewall, which of the following could be one of the best practices to follow?

   a. Enable a health module for URL Filtering.

   b. Enable URL Filtering and automatic updates for Cisco Cloud Services.

   c. Avoid a smaller cache for URLs.

   d. All of these answers are correct.

5. Which of the following is true about uncategorized URLs?

   a. A threat defense can hold uncategorized traffic in the buffer if the URL lookup is pending.

   b. Cloud lookup of uncategorized URLs can lead to performance degradation if the management center is not configured properly.

   c. Uncategorized URLs may be categorized if the management center is able to communicate with Cisco Cloud Services.

   d. All of these answers are correct.

Foundation Topics

URL Filtering Essentials

The URL Filtering feature of Secure Firewall can categorize millions of URLs and domains. You can enable this feature to prevent your network hosts from accessing a specific type of URL. This feature empowers you to enforce your organization's IT security and legal policies dynamically—without continually making manual changes to the access control rule conditions.

Category and Reputation

You can use the management center GUI to download the URL database directly from the Cisco cloud. The cloud contains the analysis of millions of URLs, which are categorized into approximately a hundred different classes. The analysis engine in the cloud can categorize more than 2500 URLs per second. The URL database maintains the Web Reputation Index (WRI), which is calculated dynamically based on data points from various sources, such as age and history of the site, reputation and location of the hosting IP address, and subject and context of the content. Depending on the Secure Firewall software version you run, you will find different names for the reputation levels. Table 14-2 describes the reputation levels on different Secure Firewall software versions.

Table 14-2 Web Reputation Levels and Their Descriptions

Reputation Level	Version 6.5 and Higher	Version 6.4 and Lower	Descriptions
1	Untrusted	High risk	Sites pose a high risk; they are known to have exposed malicious data or malicious software to clients.
2	Questionable	Suspicious	Sites are suspicious. The threat level is higher than average.

Reputation Level	Version 6.5 and Higher	Version 6.4 and Lower	Descriptions
3	Neutral	Benign Sites with Security Risks	These are generally benign sites, but they can expose clients to risk due to the unsafe characteristics of the sites.
4	Favorable	Benign Sites	Benign sites may occasionally expose clients to risk. However, exposures are rare.
5	Trusted	Trustworthy	Well-known trustworthy sites have very strong security features.

Figure 14-1 shows the implementation of URL categories and reputations in the management center web interface.

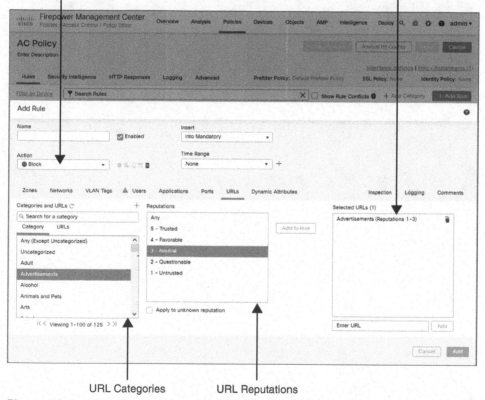

Block Action

When you select the **Block** action, the system automatically selects all the reputation levels that are less trustworthy than your selected level.

URL Categories   URL Reputations

Figure 14-1   *URL Categories and Reputations in the Access Control Rule Editor*

Based on the action—Allow or Block—configured for a rule, the management center automatically adds extra **URL reputation** levels along with your original selection. For example, when you select the Allow action for a certain reputation level, the management center allows all the URLs of that level as well as the URLs that are more benign than your selected level. Likewise, if you select the Block action for a particular reputation level, the management center blocks all the URLs of that level along with any URLs that are riskier than the level you selected.

Figure 14-2 shows different behaviors between the Allow and Block actions. Compare this image with Figure 14-1. Note that both show the same reputation level (3–Neutral) is selected, but the ultimate reputation selections are different due to the rule action—Allow versus Block.

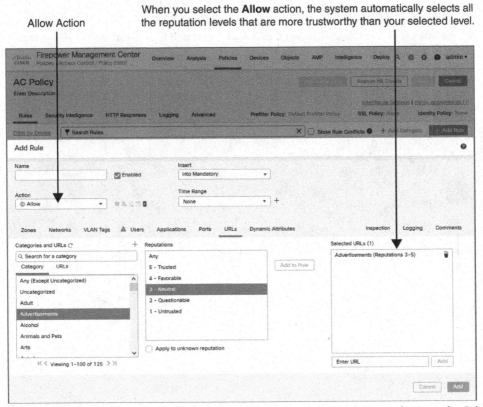

Figure 14-2 *Additional URL Reputation Levels Are Selected—Depending on the Selected Rule Action*

URL Database

Secure Firewall loads the URL dataset into its memory for a faster lookup. Depending on the size of available memory on the management center and threat defense, the Cisco cloud publishes two types of datasets in a **URL database:** 20 million URLs or 1 million URLs. After the initial download of a database, the management center receives updates from the cloud periodically, as long as the automatic update option is enabled. The periodic updates are incremental and smaller. However, the total download time depends on the last URL database installed on the management center and, of course, the download speed.

Table 14-3 shows the relationship between the number of URLs loaded and available memory.

Table 14-3   Available Memory Versus the Number of URLs in a Dataset

Available Memory	Number of URLs in the Dataset
More than 3.4 GB	20 million URLs
Less than or equal to 3.4 GB	1 million URLs

During traffic inspection, a threat defense can resolve most of the URLs the first time it sees them. However, depending on other factors, a threat defense might have to go through multiple steps to resolve a URL by category and reputation. Following are the key steps, in general:

Step 1.   The Snort engine on a threat defense performs an immediate lookup on the local URL dataset. A threat defense can determine the URL category in most cases. If the URL is not found in the threat defense, the query is forwarded to the management center.

Step 2.   If the management center can retrieve the URL category from its local database, it sends the query result to the threat defense so that the threat defense can act on traffic according to the access control policy.

Step 3.   If the management center is unable to resolve the URL category from its local database, it checks the Cisco Cloud Services database in the cloud:

■ If the query to Cloud Services is disabled, the management center places the unknown URL into the Uncategorized group.

■ If the query to Cloud Services is enabled, the management center sends a query to the cloud for the unknown URL.

Figure 14-3 shows the steps to resolve an unknown new URL into its category and reputation.

Fulfilling Prerequisites

Before you begin configuring an access control rule with URL Filtering conditions, your Secure Firewall must meet the following licensing requirements:

■ A URL Filtering license is necessary to use the Cisco-provided URL classifications and reputations. Furthermore, as a prerequisite, the management center also requires you to enable the threat license before you enable URL Filtering.

Figure 14-4 shows the page where you can enable or disable any license for a threat defense. To find this page, navigate to **Devices > Device Management**. Edit the device where you want to enable the URL Filtering license and then select the **Devices** tab.

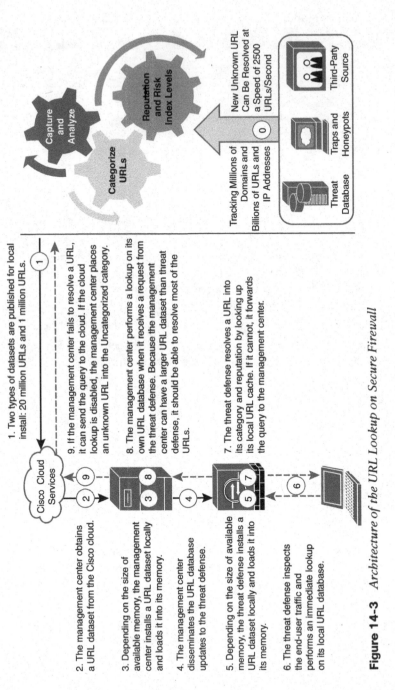

Figure 14-3 *Architecture of the URL Lookup on Secure Firewall*

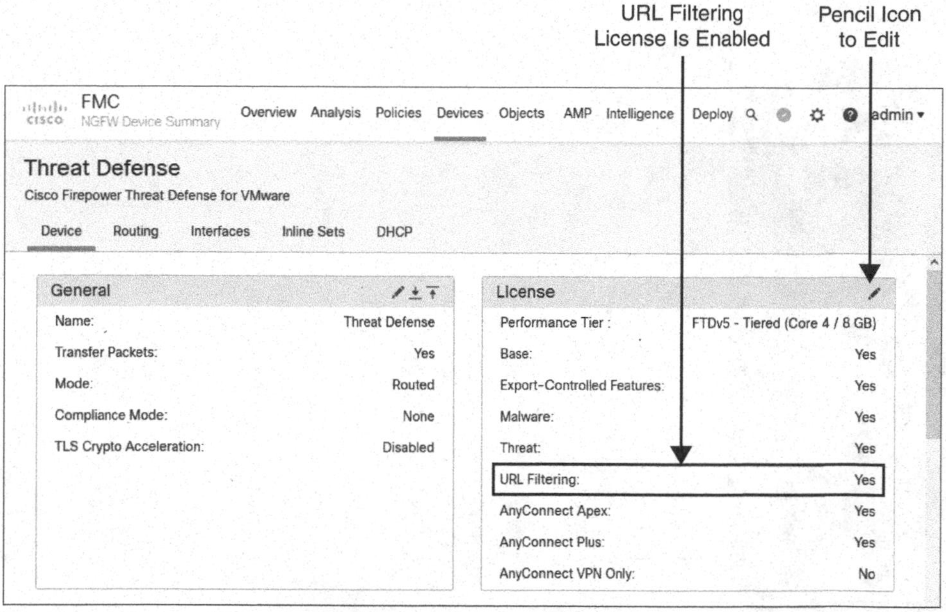

URL Filtering
License Is Enabled

Pencil Icon
to Edit

Figure 14-4 *Enabling the URL Filtering License on a Threat Defense*

■ Without a URL Filtering license, you can create an access control rule based on any URL conditions; however, you cannot deploy the access control policy with URL classifications until you enable a URL Filtering license on the threat defense. Similarly, if the URL license expires after you deploy an access control policy with URL filtering, the threat defense stops matching the rules with URL conditions, and the management center stops updating the URL database.

TIP If you are in the process of purchasing a license, you can enable Evaluation Mode to avoid any administrative delays. Evaluation Mode allows you to configure and deploy any features as if you have already enabled a paid license.

Best Practices for URL Filtering Configuration

Consider the following best practices when enabling the URL Filtering feature in Secure Firewall:

■ Check whether the URL Filtering Monitor health module is enabled in the current health policy. If this module is enabled, the management center generates alerts if it fails to deploy a URL dataset to a threat defense or fails to download the latest URL database from Cisco Cloud Services.

Figure 14-5 shows the option to enable the health module for URL Filtering. To find this page, go to **System > Health > Policy**, edit a health policy, and select **URL Filtering Monitor** from the left panel. You must redeploy a health policy after you change any settings.

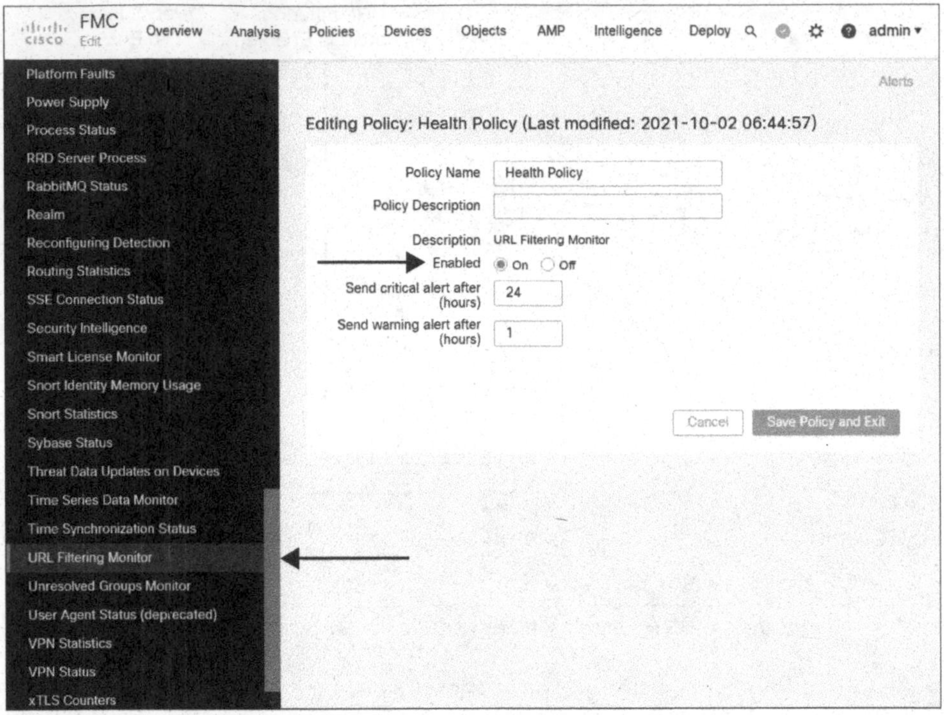

Figure 14-5 *Health Module for URL Filtering Monitor*

- Make sure Cisco Cloud Services is enabled for URL Filtering. It ensures the most up-to-date classification of URLs based on Cisco's latest research. Figure 14-6 confirms the enablement of URL Filtering automatic updates.

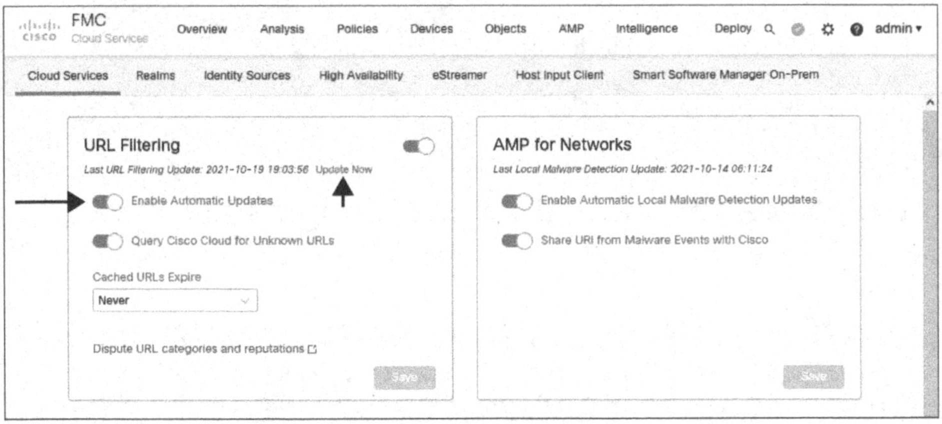

Figure 14-6 *Enabling URL Filtering and Automatic Updating*

- Caching of URL category and reputation data can improve a user's web browsing experiences. It is set for no expiry by default (see Figure 14-6), but be mindful of its consequences: an unexpired cache can lead to stale URL data, while a smaller cache can keep a system busier with more frequent queries to the Cisco cloud.

Key Topic

■ Ensure that the management center is updating its URL database periodically with the latest URL reputation data. You can find the timestamp for the Last URL Filtering Update on the Cloud Services page (see Figure 14-6). The management center communicates with Cisco Cloud Services every 30 minutes to determine whether a new update for the URL Filtering database is available. Therefore, if the automatic update option is enabled, you should not create a separate scheduled task for URL database updates. However, a recurring scheduled task for URL database updates is useful if you want to manage the URL database update manually.

Figure 14-7 shows the options to create a scheduled task for URL database updates. In this configuration, the management center updates the URL Filtering database daily at 11:00 p.m., as opposed to the system default of every 30 minutes.

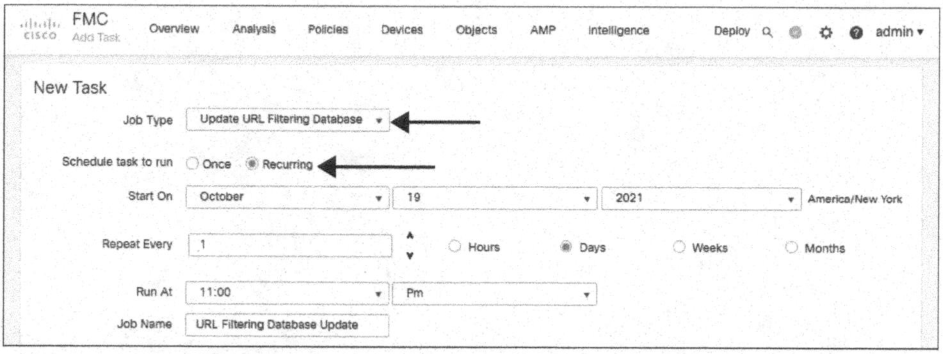

14

Figure 14-7 *Scheduling a Recurring Task to Update the URL Filtering Database*

■ To prevent access to any suspicious websites, you can consider blocking the DNS queries to those domain names. If a threat defense can block a connection during DNS resolution, a URL lookup for that connection will no longer be necessary. Hence, it can improve system performance.

Figure 14-8 highlights the workflow of the various security components on a threat defense. The URL-based Security Intelligence system blocks a packet *before* it is categorized and blocked by a URL-based access control rule.

■ If you want to filter any specific websites using Cisco Talos–defined classifications, but you are unsure about the exact categories and reputations of those websites, you can check them directly using the management center GUI. It can help you to define the rule conditions more confidently.

Figure 14-9 shows the categorizations and reputations of different websites. Running this query on a management center allows you to predetermine that the search engines google.com and monster.com belong to two separate categories. To access this page, navigate to **Analysis > Advanced > URL** on your management center.

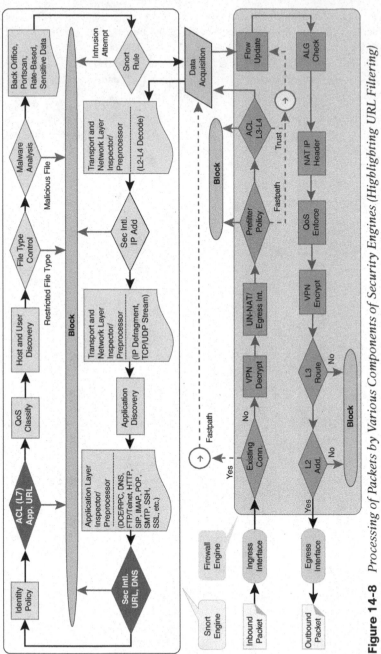

Figure 14-8   *Processing of Packets by Various Components of Security Engines (Highlighting URL Filtering)*

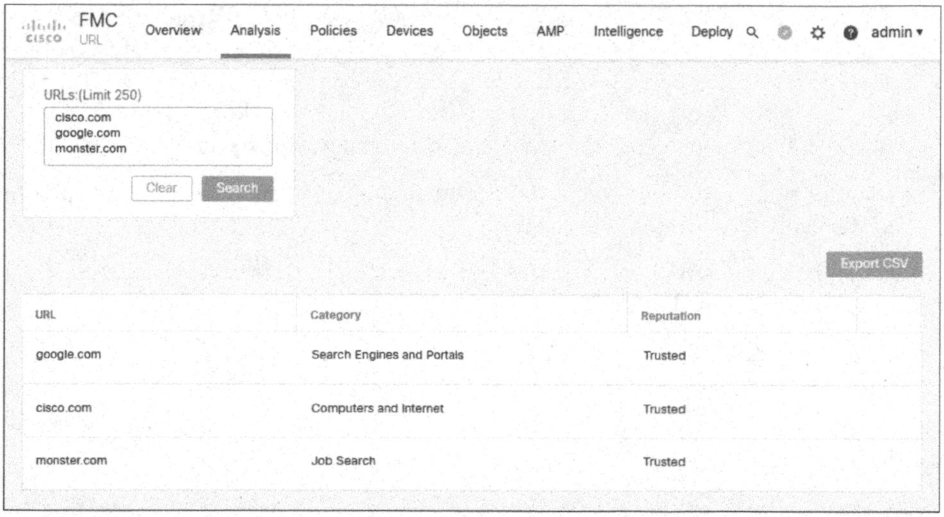

Figure 14-9 *Identifying the Category and Reputation of Specific URLs Using the Management Center*

■ When the web traffic is encrypted with the TLS/SSL protocol (HTTPS sessions), Secure Firewall can utilize their certificate information to determine the URL involved in an encrypted session. In the public key cryptography, certificates are exchanged during the TLS/SSL handshake process. The Subject field of a certificate includes Common Name (CN). The value of CN can be used to determine the URL. Figure 14-10 shows the certificate from the official Cisco website. The CN value indicates that the certificate originated from www.cisco.com.

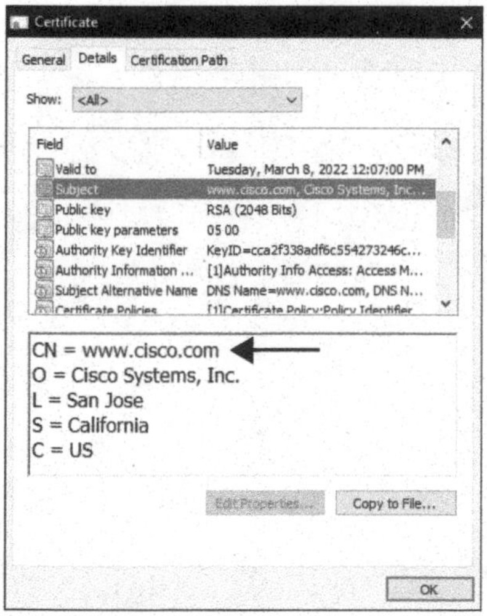

Figure 14-10 *Finding the URL Information from a Certificate*

In TLS 1.3, certificates are encrypted. Secure Firewall can simply extract the TLS certificate information without decrypting the entire packet. To extract a TLS certificate for URL filtering purposes, you do not need to configure a complete SSL/TLS policy (described in detail in Chapter 18). Just make sure the following two options are enabled on the Advanced tab of the access control policy, as shown in Figure 14-11.

- Under the TLS Server Identity Discovery section, the Early Application Detection and URL Categorization option is enabled.

- Under the General Settings section, the Enable Reputation Enforcement on DNS Traffic option is turned on.

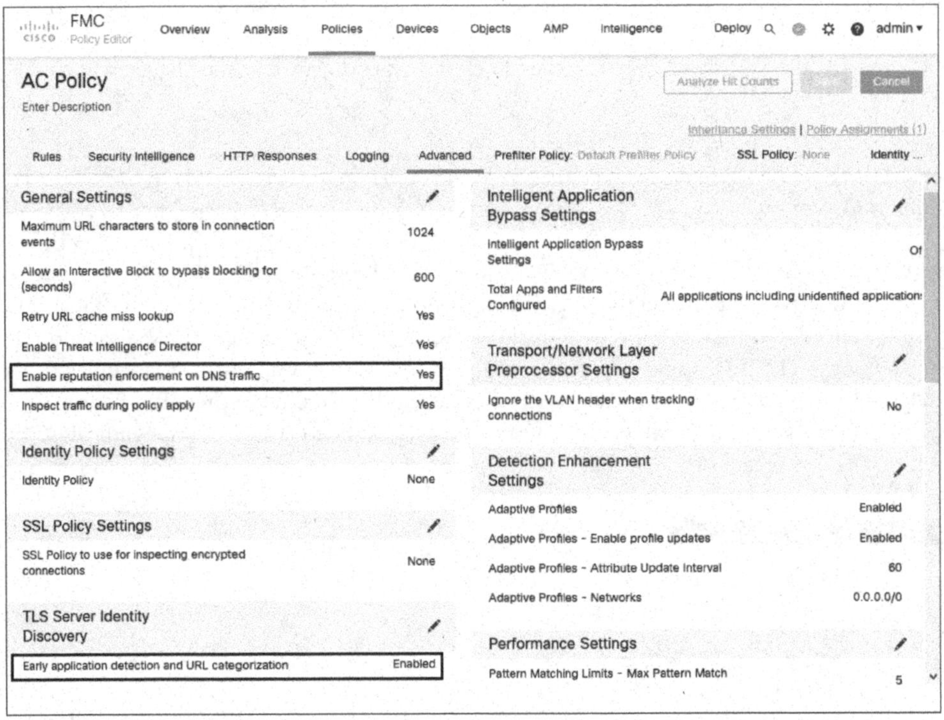

Figure 14-11 *Advanced Settings to Enhance URL Filtering Capability for Encrypted Traffic*

Enabling URL Filtering

Now is the time to learn the configuration of URL Filtering on a Secure Firewall. The next sections demonstrate the following three configurations:

- Blocking URLs of a certain category

- Allowing a specific URL

- Handling **uncategorized URLs**

Blocking URLs of a Certain Category

You can block undesired URLs based on their categories and reputations. You can accomplish this by adding an access control rule with URL Filtering conditions. The following steps describe how to add an access control rule to block certain URL categories:

Step 1.   Navigate to **Policies > Access Control > Access Control** and select an existing access control policy to edit or create a new one.

Step 2.   On the access control policy editor page, click the **Add Rule** button. The Add Rule window appears.

Step 3.   Provide a name to the rule and select an action for it.

Step 4.   Click the **URLs** tab. A list of URL categories and reputations appears. Select the categories and reputations you want to block and add them to the rule. Optionally, you can apply this rule to any URLs with an unknown reputation under the same category.

Figure 14-12 shows the creation of an access control rule with the URL Filtering condition. The rule blocks all the URLs that are related to the Job Search category. It also applies to the URLs with unknown reputation.

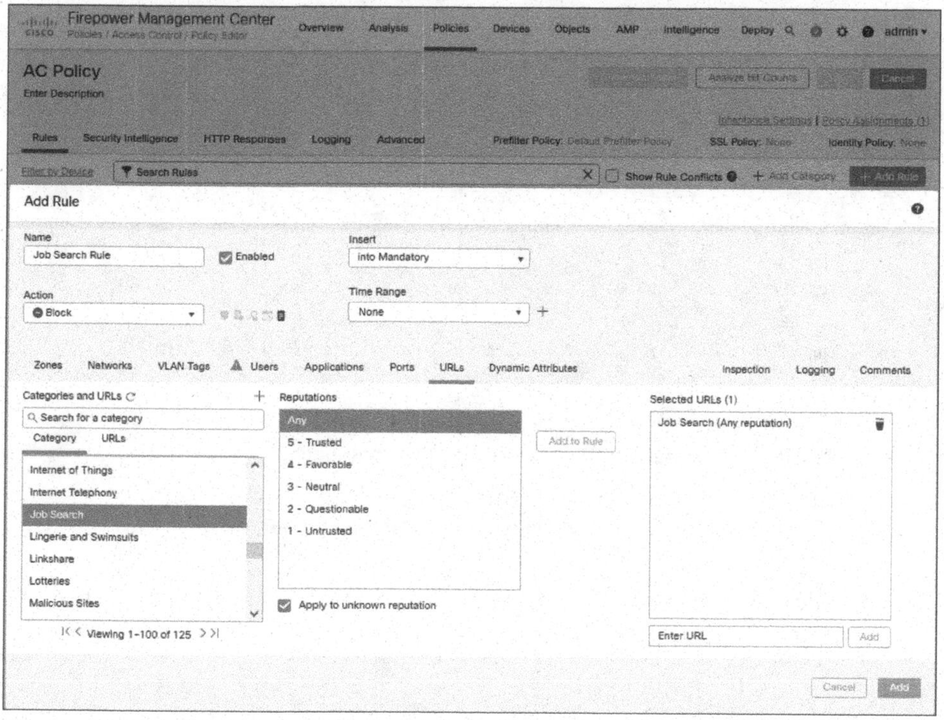

Figure 14-12 *Selecting a URL Category for Any Reputation Levels*

Step 5.   On the Logging tab, enable **Log at Beginning of Connection.** This step is optional, but it allows you to view events when a threat defense blocks a connection due to a URL Filtering condition.

Figure 14-13 shows how to enable logging at the beginning of a connection. When this setting is enabled, the threat defense generates a connection event whenever it blocks a URL in the Job Search category.

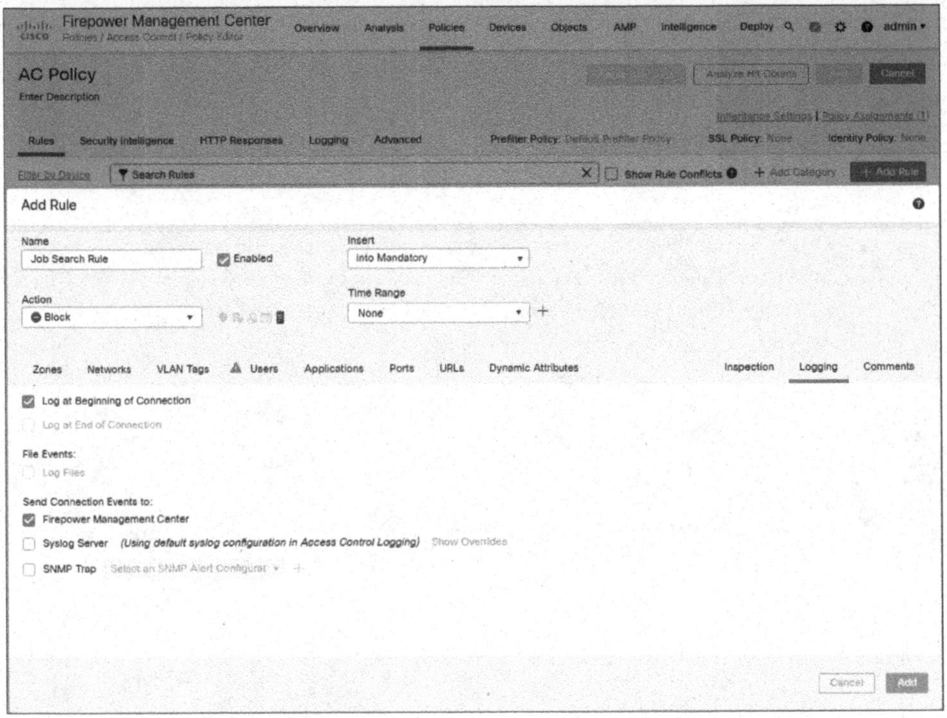

Figure 14-13   *Enabling Logging for an Access Control Rule with a URL Filtering Condition*

Step 6.   Click the **Add** button to create the access control rule.

Figure 14-14 shows the creation of a simple access control rule called the Job Search Rule. This rule blocks any URLs that are within the Job Search category.

Step 7.   Click **Save** to save the changes on the access control policy. Finally, go to **Deploy > Deployment** to deploy the policy on your desired threat defense.

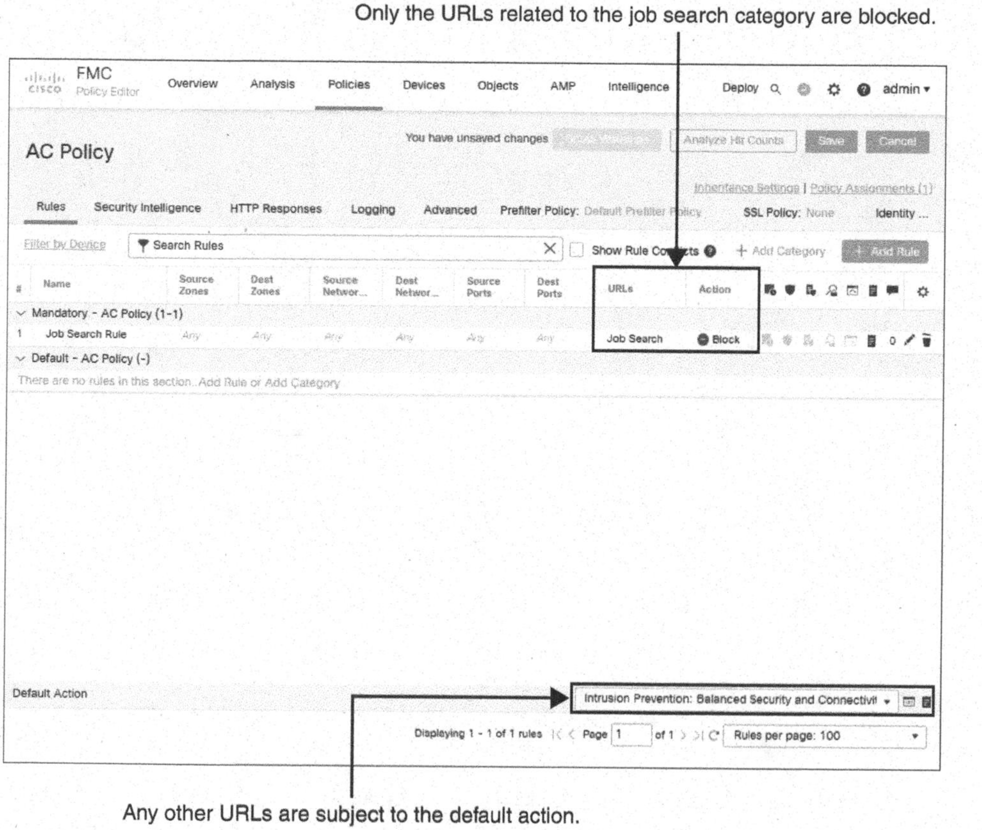

Only the URLs related to the job search category are blocked.

Any other URLs are subject to the default action.

Figure 14-14 *Viewing a Simple URL Filtering Rule on the Access Control Policy Editor*

Verifying the Operation of a URL Filtering Rule

To verify the actions of the access control rule that you created in the preceding section, select two URLs—one URL from the matching category, such as Job Search, and the other URL from any nonmatching category. If an access control rule with a URL condition is operational, it only blocks the Job Search–related URLs, while the default action of the access control policy allows any other URL categories.

Attempt to visit the following websites and notice the result in each case:

- google.com (a general search engine)

- dice.com (a job search engine)

- monster.com (a job search engine)

Figure 14-15 shows the blocking of both job search engines—dice.com and monster.com. However, because of the policy for default action, the threat defense does not block the general search engine google.com.

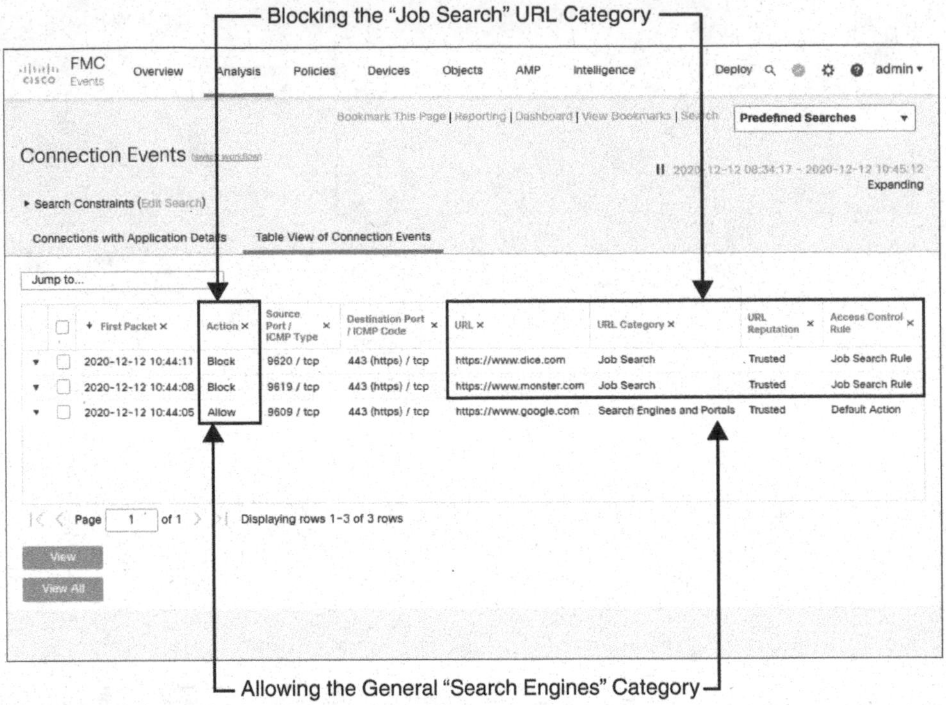

Blocking the "Job Search" URL Category

Figure 14-15 *Access Control Rule with URL Filtering Conditions Blocking Desired Connections*

You can also debug the actions in the threat defense and analyze the **firewall-engine-debug** messages for troubleshooting purposes.

Example 14-1 shows the **firewall-engine-debug** messages when a threat defense allows you access to a general search engine, such as google.com. The debug message shows that the threat defense can perform a URL lookup successfully, but the URL itself does not match with any URL Filtering rules. The default action allows the URL.

Example 14-1 *Debug Messages by an Access Control Rule with a URL Condition (Action: Allow)*

```
> system support firewall-engine-debug

Please specify an IP protocol: tcp
Please specify a client IP address: S.S.S.S
Please specify a client port:
Please specify a server IP address: D.D.D.D
Please specify a server port: 443
Monitoring firewall engine debug messages


# At this point, connect to google.com using a browser. The following debug output
shows the messages related to URL lookup and filtering processes. The initial commu-
nications between client and server are truncated for brevity.
.
.
```

```
S.S.S.S-9609 > D.D.D.D-443 6 AS 4-4 I 0 TLS host name retrieved is  www.google.com
S.S.S.S-9609 > D.D.D.D-443 6 AS 4-4 I 0 URL SI: ShmDBLookupURL("www.google.com")
returned 0
S.S.S.S-9609 > D.D.D.D-443 6 AS 4-4 I 0 Starting AC with minimum 3, 'Job Search
Rule', and SrcZone first with zones -1 -> -1, geo 0(0) -> 0, vlan 0, source sgt
type: 0, sgt tag: 0, ISE sgt id: 0, dest sgt type: 0, ISE dest_sgt_tag: 0, svc 1122,
payload 184, client 1296, misc 0, user 9999997, min url-cat-list 0-0-0, url
www.google.com, xff
S.S.S.S-9609 > D.D.D.D-443 6 AS 4-4 I 0: returned from url lookup, url_info is 90
2020 0 0 0 0 0 0 0
S.S.S.S-9609 > D.D.D.D-443 6 AS 4-4 I 0: DataMessaging_GetURLData: Returning URL_
BCTYPE for www.google.com
S.S.S.S-9609 > D.D.D.D-443 6 AS 4-4 I 0 rule order 3, 'Job Search Rule', URL Lookup
Success: www.google.com waited: 0ms
S.S.S.S-9609 > D.D.D.D-443 6 AS 4-4 I 0 no match rule order 3, 'Job Search Rule',
url=(www.google.com) c=2020 r=90
S.S.S.S-9609 > D.D.D.D-443 6 AS 4-4 I 0 match rule order 4, 'Default Action', action
Allow
S.S.S.S-9609 > D.D.D.D-443 6 AS 4-4 I 0 Logging SOF with rule_id = 268434432
ruleAction = 2 ruleReason = 0
S.S.S.S-9609 > D.D.D.D-443 6 AS 4-4 I 0 MidRecovery data sent for rule id:
268434432,rule_action:2, rev id:767611487, rule_match flag:0x0
S.S.S.S-9609 > D.D.D.D-443 6 AS 4-4 I 0 HitCount data sent for rule id: 268434432,
S.S.S.S-9609 > D.D.D.D-443 6 AS 4-4 I 0 allow action
.
.
```

Example 14-2 shows the **firewall-engine-debug** messages when the threat defense denies you access to both job search engines—monster.com and dice.com. The debug message confirms that the threat defense is able to perform a URL lookup successfully, but the URL itself is blocked due to a matching condition in the Job Search Rule access control rule.

Example 14-2 *Debug Messages, Triggered by an Access Control Rule with URL Condition (Action: Block)*

```
> system support firewall-engine-debug

Please specify an IP protocol: tcp
Please specify a client IP address: S.S.S.S
Please specify a client port:
Please specify a server IP address: D.D.D.D
Please specify a server port: 443
Monitoring firewall engine debug messages


# At this point, connect to monster.com using a browser. The following debug output
shows the messages related to URL lookup and filtering processes. The initial commu-
nications between client and server are truncated for brevity.
.
```

```
S.S.S.S-9619 > D.D.D.D-443 6 AS 4-4 I 1 TLS host name retrieved is  www.monster.com

S.S.S.S-9619 > D.D.D.D-443 6 AS 4-4 I 1 URL SI: ShmDBLookupURL("www.monster.com")
returned 0

S.S.S.S-9619 > D.D.D.D-443 6 AS 4-4 I 1 Starting AC with minimum 3, 'Job Search
Rule', and SrcZone first with zones -1 -> -1, geo 0(0) -> 0, vlan 0, source sgt
type: 0, sgt tag: 0, ISE sgt id: 0, dest sgt type: 0, ISE dest_sgt_tag: 0, svc 1122,
payload 0, client 1296, misc 0, user 9999997, min url-cat-list 0-0-0, url
www.monster.com, xff

S.S.S.S-9619 > D.D.D.D-443 6 AS 4-4 I 1: returned from url lookup, url_info is 90
2004 0 0 0 0 0 0 0 0

S.S.S.S-9619 > D.D.D.D-443 6 AS 4-4 I 1: DataMessaging_GetURLData: Returning
URL_BCTYPE for www.monster.com

S.S.S.S-9619 > D.D.D.D-443 6 AS 4-4 I 1 rule order 3, 'Job Search Rule', URL Lookup
Success: www.monster.com waited: 0ms

S.S.S.S-9619 > D.D.D.D-443 6 AS 4-4 I 1 rule order 3, 'Job Search Rule', URL
www.monster.com Matched Category: 2004:90 waited: 0ms

S.S.S.S-9619 > D.D.D.D-443 6 AS 4-4 I 1 match rule order 3, 'Job Search Rule',
action Block

S.S.S.S-9619 > D.D.D.D-443 6 AS 4-4 I 1 Logging SOF with rule_id = 268452864
ruleAction = 4 ruleReason = 0

S.S.S.S-9619 > D.D.D.D-443 6 AS 4-4 I 1 MidRecovery data sent for rule id:
268452864,rule_action:4, rev id:767611487, rule_match flag:0x0

S.S.S.S-9619 > D.D.D.D-443 6 AS 4-4 I 1 HitCount data sent for rule id: 268452864,

S.S.S.S-9619 > D.D.D.D-443 6 AS 4-4 I 1 deny action

.

.

# At this point, connect to dice.com using a browser. The following debug output
shows the messages related to URL lookup and filtering processes. The initial commu-
nications between client and server are truncated for brevity.

.

S.S.S.S-9620 > D.D.D.D-443 6 AS 4-4 I 0 TLS host name retrieved is  www.dice.com

S.S.S.S-9620 > D.D.D.D-443 6 AS 4-4 I 0 URL SI: ShmDBLookupURL("www.dice.com")
returned 0

S.S.S.S-9620 > D.D.D.D-443 6 AS 4-4 I 0 Starting AC with minimum 3, 'Job Search
Rule', and SrcZone first with zones -1 -> -1, geo 0(0) -> 0, vlan 0, source sgt
type: 0, sgt tag: 0, ISE sgt id: 0, dest sgt type: 0, ISE dest_sgt_tag: 0, svc 1122,
payload 0, client 1296, misc 0, user 9999997, min url-cat-list 0-0-0, url www.dice.
com, xff

S.S.S.S-9620 > D.D.D.D-443 6 AS 4-4 I 0: returned from url lookup, url_info is 90
2004 0 0 0 0 0 0 0 0

S.S.S.S-9620 > D.D.D.D-443 6 AS 4-4 I 0: DataMessaging_GetURLData: Returning
URL_BCTYPE for www.dice.com

S.S.S.S-9620 > D.D.D.D-443 6 AS 4-4 I 0 rule order 3, 'Job Search Rule', URL Lookup
Success: www.dice.com waited: 0ms

S.S.S.S-9620 > D.D.D.D-443 6 AS 4-4 I 0 rule order 3, 'Job Search Rule', URL
www.dice.com Matched Category: 2004:90 waited: 0ms

S.S.S.S-9620 > D.D.D.D-443 6 AS 4-4 I 0 match rule order 3, 'Job Search Rule',
action Block
```

```
S.S.S.S-9620 > D.D.D.D-443 6 AS 4-4 I 0 Logging SOF with rule_id = 268452864
ruleAction = 4 ruleReason = 0
S.S.S.S-9620 > D.D.D.D-443 6 AS 4-4 I 0 MidRecovery data sent for rule id:
268452864,rule_action:4, rev id:767611487, rule_match flag:0x0
S.S.S.S-9620 > D.D.D.D-443 6 AS 4-4 I 0 HitCount data sent for rule id: 268452864,
S.S.S.S-9620 > D.D.D.D-443 6 AS 4-4 I 0 deny action
.
.
```

Allowing a Specific URL

If you do not want a threat defense to block a particular URL along with the other URLs that are in the same category, you can override the default reputation score of that URL. To accomplish this, you just need to add a separate access control rule with the Allow action. The following steps describe how to create an access control rule to allow a certain URL:

Step 1.   Go to **Objects > Object Management**. On the left panel, select **URL** to create an object of type URL. Figure 14-16 shows the workflow to create a new URL object. In this example, the URL-Object-for-Dice.com custom object represents the dice.com site.

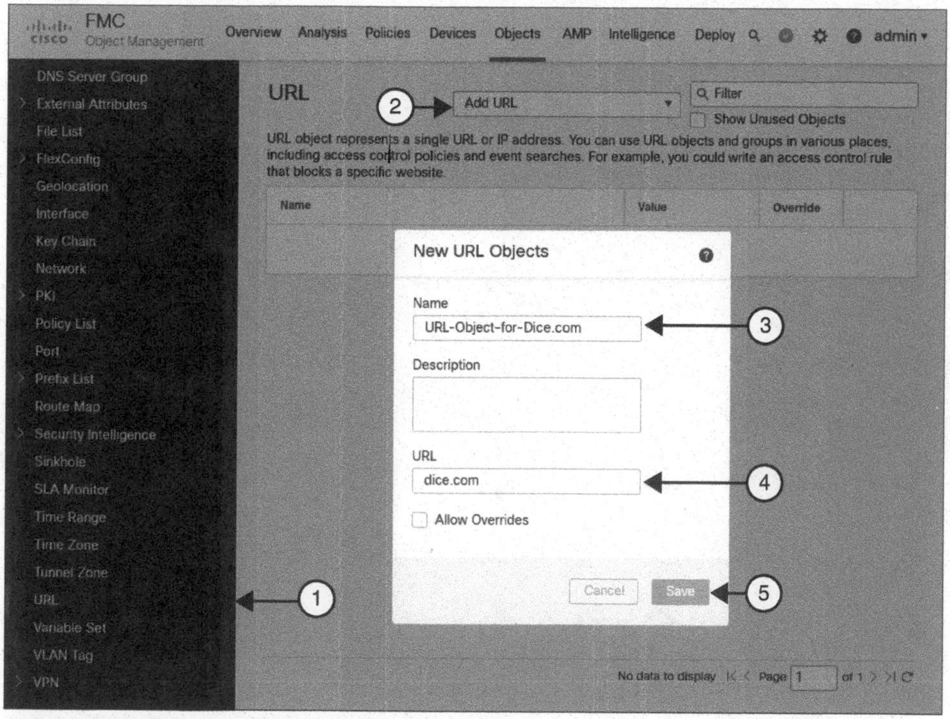

Figure 14-16   *Configuring a New URL Object*

Step 2.   After a URL object is created, create a new access control rule to allow traffic to and from this URL object.

A threat defense analyzes access control rules from top to bottom. Therefore, when you need to allow a specific URL that is part of a blocked URL category, position a specifically defined rule above the broader rule. You can define the position as you add the rule. Alternatively, after adding a rule, you can go to the access control policy editor page to drag and move a rule to a desired position.

Figure 14-17 shows an access control rule that allows the URL-Object-for-Dice. com object. You can find your custom URL object located under the URLs subtab. Note that the Rule Exception rule is placed *above* the existing rule #1, so that it is evaluated before the broader rule.

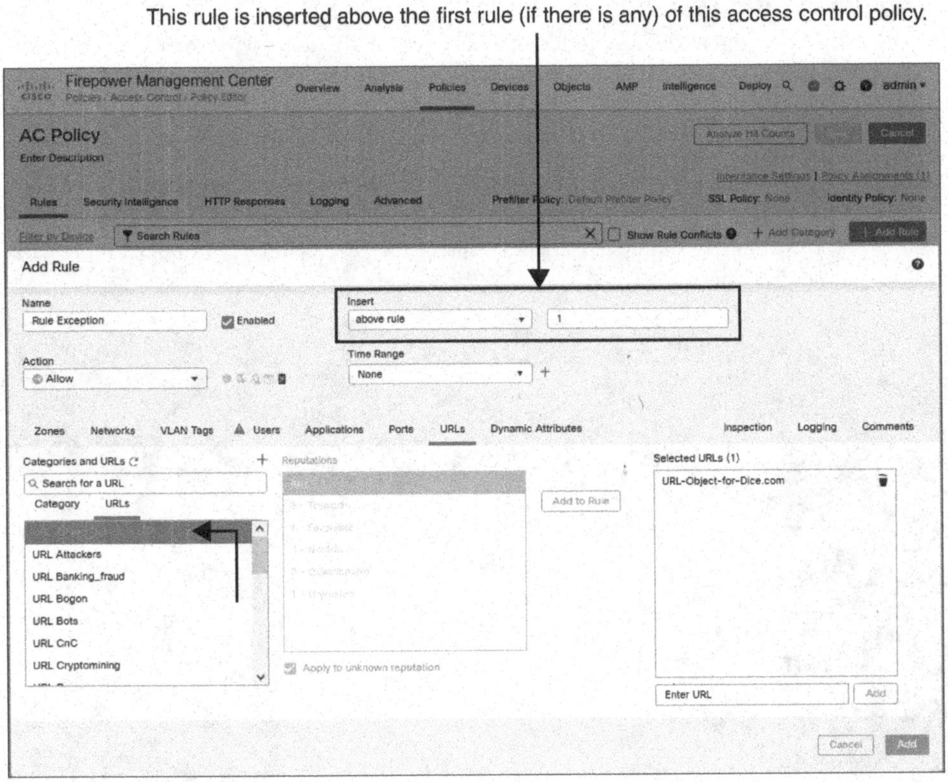

This rule is inserted above the first rule (if there is any) of this access control policy.

Figure 14-17 *Allowing a Desired URL Using a Custom Object*

Step 3. Optionally, go to the Logging tab and enable **Log at End of Connection**. This optional step allows a threat defense to generate events due to any matching URL Filtering conditions. Do not enable both logging options at the same time. Doing so can negatively impact performance.

Figure 14-18 shows the selection of logging at the end of the allowed connection. When this particular rule triggers, this rule causes the related events to log in to the management center GUI.

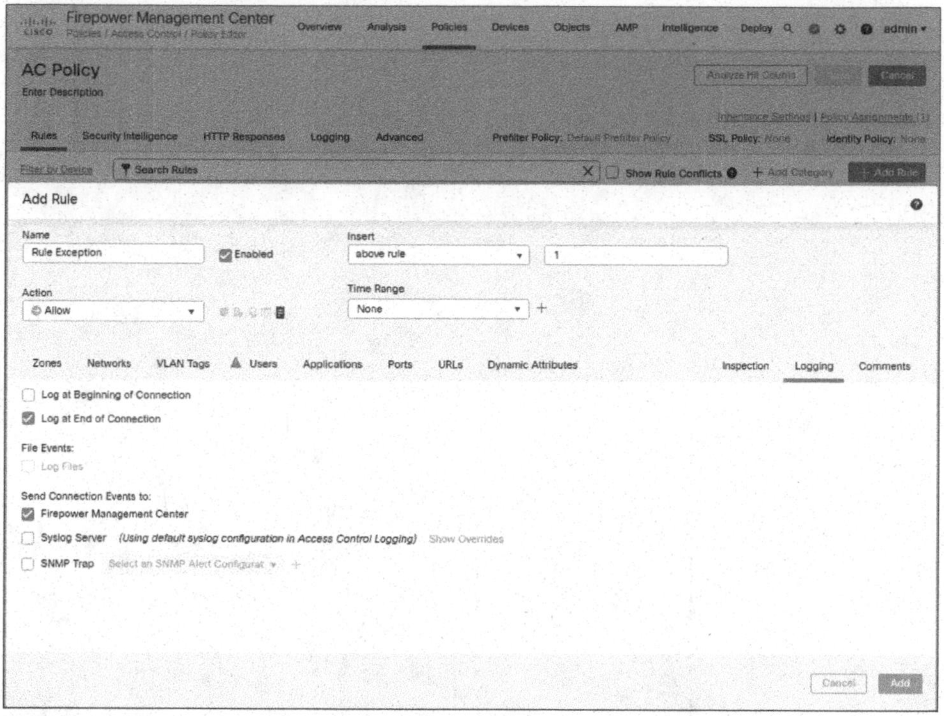

Figure 14-18 *Logging Configuration of an Access Control Rule*

Step 4.   Click the **Add** button to complete the creation of the access control rule. The browser returns to the access control policy editor page.

Figure 14-19 shows all the access control rules in the policy editor page. As you can see, the rule to allow dice.com is positioned above the broader rule that can block the entire Job Search category. Here, you can drag and move the rules to sort them in a different order.

Step 5.   Click **Save** to save the changes in the access control policy, and navigate to **Deploy > Deployment** to deploy the policy to your desired threat defense.

Analyzing the Default Category Override

To verify the operation of the Allow action, perform the same test that you did in the previous section: attempt to visit the same three search engines once again and notice the differences. This time, the threat defense should allow your access to dice.com, although this is a job search engine. However, the threat defense should continue blocking access to other job search engines, such as monster.com. Any URL categories except Job Search are allowed.

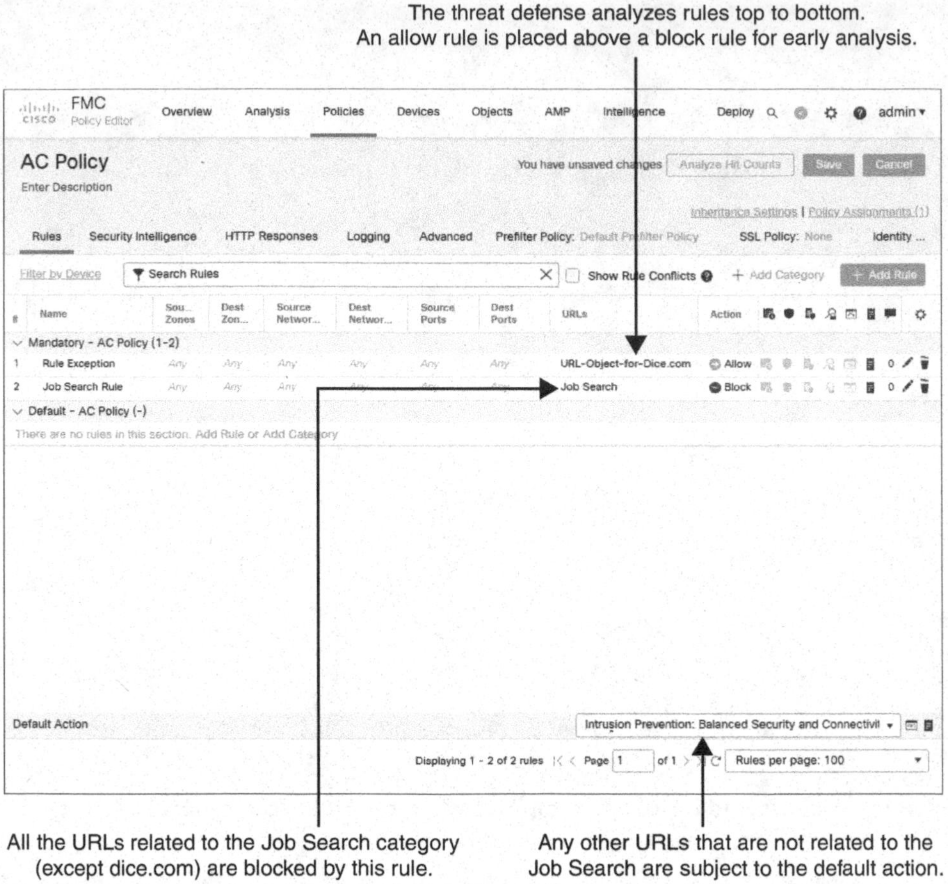

The threat defense analyzes rules top to bottom.
An allow rule is placed above a block rule for early analysis.

All the URLs related to the Job Search category
(except dice.com) are blocked by this rule.

Any other URLs that are not related to the
Job Search are subject to the default action.

Figure 14-19 *Access Control Policy Editor Page Showing an Overview of All the Access Control Rules*

Figure 14-20 shows that dice.com is now allowed, whereas the monster.com site remains blocked. Because of the default action on the access control policy, the threat defense continues to allow the general search engine website google.com.

You can use the **firewall-engine-debug** tool to debug the rule action on traffic. The debug messages are helpful for troubleshooting purposes.

Example 14-3 shows the **firewall-engine-debug** messages when the threat defense allows you to access dice.com, as an exception to the broader URL category, Job Search.

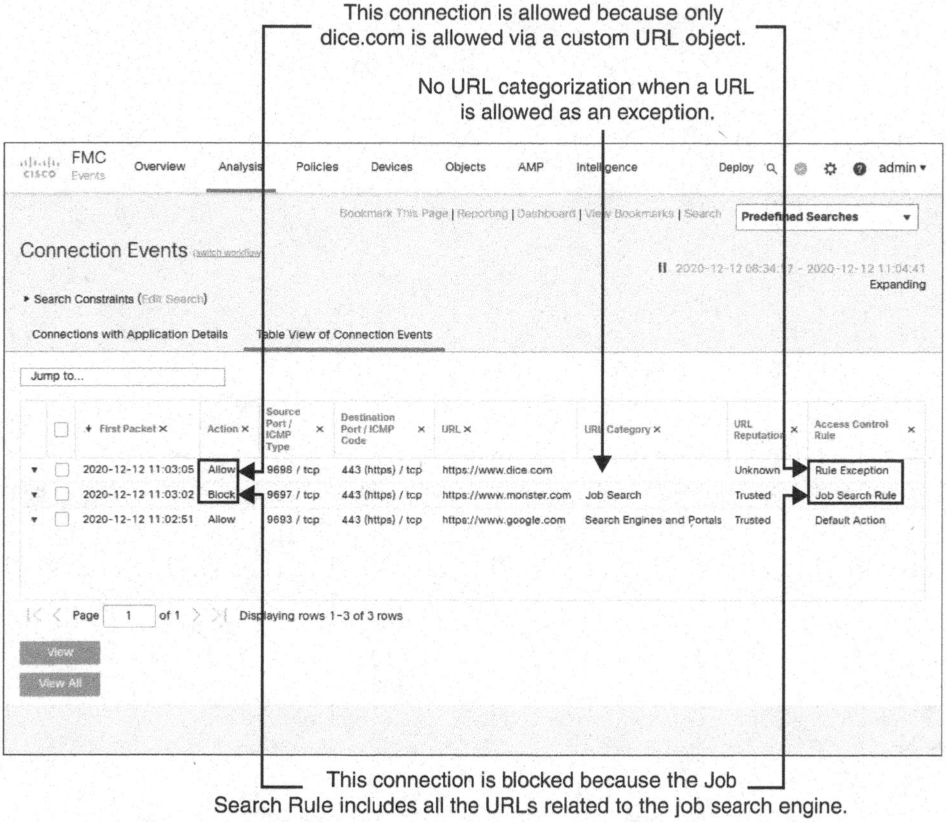

This connection is allowed because only
dice.com is allowed via a custom URL object.

No URL categorization when a URL
is allowed as an exception.

Figure 14-20 *Allowing a Specific URL from a Broader Blocked Category*

This connection is blocked because the Job
Search Rule includes all the URLs related to the job search engine.

Example 14-3 *Debugging Messages When Access to Dice.com Is Allowed*

```
> system support firewall-engine-debug

Please specify an IP protocol: tcp
Please specify a client IP address: S.S.S.S
Please specify a client port:
Please specify a server IP address: D.D.D.D
Please specify a server port: 443
Monitoring firewall engine debug messages


# At this point, connect to dice.com using a browser. The following debug output
shows the messages related to URL lookup and filtering processes. The initial commu-
nications between client and server are truncated for brevity.
.
.
.
```

```
S.S.S.S-9698 > D.D.D.D-443 6 AS 4-4 I 1 TLS host name retrieved is  www.dice.com
S.S.S.S-9698 > D.D.D.D-443 6 AS 4-4 I 1 URL SI: ShmDBLookupURL("www.dice.com")
returned 0
S.S.S.S-9698 > D.D.D.D-443 6 AS 4-4 I 1 Starting AC with minimum 3, 'Rule
Exception', and SrcZone first with zones -1 -> -1, geo 0(0) -> 0, vlan 0, source sgt
type: 0, sgt tag: 0, ISE sgt id: 0, dest sgt type: 0, ISE dest_sgt_tag: 0, svc 1122,
payload 0, client 1296, misc 0, user 9999997, min url-cat-list 0-0-0, url www.dice.
com, xff
S.S.S.S-9698 > D.D.D.D-443 6 AS 4-4 I 1 custom host matcher using: www.dice.com
S.S.S.S-9698 > D.D.D.D-443 6 AS 4-4 I 1 custom host matcher url without slash passed
S.S.S.S-9698 > D.D.D.D-443 6 AS 4-4 I 1 match rule order 3, 'Rule Exception', action
Allow
S.S.S.S-9698 > D.D.D.D-443 6 AS 4-4 I 1 MidRecovery data sent for rule id:
268453888,rule_action:2, rev id:4226208863, rule_match flag:0x2
S.S.S.S-9698 > D.D.D.D-443 6 AS 4-4 I 1 HitCount data sent for rule id: 268453888,
S.S.S.S-9698 > D.D.D.D-443 6 AS 4-4 I 1 allow action
S.S.S.S-9698 > D.D.D.D-443 6 AS 4-4 I 1 Setting flow ID to 268453888
.
.
```

Example 14-4 shows the **firewall-engine-debug** messages when the threat defense denies
your access to the job search engine monster.com. The debugging messages confirm that the
threat defense is able to perform a URL lookup successfully, but the URL itself is blocked
due to a matching condition in the Job Search Rule access control rule.

Example 14-4 *Debugging Messages When Access to monster.com Is Blocked*

```
> system support firewall-engine-debug

Please specify an IP protocol: tcp
Please specify a client IP address: S.S.S.S
Please specify a client port:
Please specify a server IP address: D.D.D.D
Please specify a server port: 443
Monitoring firewall engine debug messages

# At this point, connect to dice.com using a browser. The following debug output
shows the messages related to URL lookup and filtering processes. The initial commu-
nications between client and server are truncated for brevity.
.
```

```
S.S.S.S-9697 > D.D.D.D-443 6 AS 4-4 I 0 TLS host name retrieved is  www.monster.com
S.S.S.S-9697 > D.D.D.D-443 6 AS 4-4 I 0 URL SI: ShmDBLookupURL("www.monster.com")
returned 0
S.S.S.S-9697 > D.D.D.D-443 6 AS 4-4 I 0 Starting AC with minimum 3, 'Rule Excep-
tion', and SrcZone first with zones -1 -> -1, geo 0(0) -> 0, vlan 0, source sgt
type: 0, sgt tag: 0, ISE sgt id: 0, dest sgt type: 0, ISE dest_sgt_tag: 0, svc 1122,
payload 0, client 1296, misc 0, user 9999997, min url-cat-list 0-0-0, url www.
monster.com, xff
S.S.S.S-9697 > D.D.D.D-443 6 AS 4-4 I 0 custom host matcher using: www.monster.com
S.S.S.S-9697 > D.D.D.D-443 6 AS 4-4 I 0 custom host matcher url without slash failed
S.S.S.S-9697 > D.D.D.D-443 6 AS 4-4 I 0 no match rule order 3, 'Rule Exception',
url=(www.monster.com) c=0 r=0
S.S.S.S-9697 > D.D.D.D-443 6 AS 4-4 I 0: returned from url lookup, url_info is 90
2004 0 0 0 0 0 0 0 0
S.S.S.S-9697 > D.D.D.D-443 6 AS 4-4 I 0: DataMessaging_GetURLData: Returning URL_
BCTYPE for www.monster.com
S.S.S.S-9697 > D.D.D.D-443 6 AS 4-4 I 0 rule order 4, 'Job Search Rule', URL Lookup
Success: www.monster.com waited: 0ms
S.S.S.S-9697 > D.D.D.D-443 6 AS 4-4 I 0 rule order 4, 'Job Search Rule', URL
www.monster.com Matched Category: 2004:90 waited: 0ms
S.S.S.S-9697 > D.D.D.D-443 6 AS 4-4 I 0 match rule order 4, 'Job Search Rule',
action Block
S.S.S.S-9697 > D.D.D.D-443 6 AS 4-4 I 0 Logging SOF with rule_id = 268452864
ruleAction = 4 ruleReason = 0
S.S.S.S-9697 > D.D.D.D-443 6 AS 4-4 I 0 MidRecovery data sent for rule id:
268452864,rule_action:4, rev id:4226208863, rule_match flag:0x0
S.S.S.S-9697 > D.D.D.D-443 6 AS 4-4 I 0 HitCount data sent for rule id: 268452864,
S.S.S.S-9697 > D.D.D.D-443 6 AS 4-4 I 0 deny action
.
.
.
```

Handling Uncategorized URLs

Key Topic

In most cases, a threat defense resolves a URL into its category and reputation when it sees a web request for the first time. If the threat defense is unable to resolve a URL, it forwards the query to the management center. The management center performs a lookup on its own URL database. Because the management center typically has a larger URL dataset than the threat defense, it should be able to resolve most of the URLs.

If you enter a new and uncommon URL, the management center may be unable to resolve the category by looking up its local database. In this case, you can enable the management center to send a query to the Cisco Cloud Services cloud. If the cloud lookup times out, or if the query to the Cisco Cloud Services cloud is disabled due to privacy concerns, the management center places the unknown URL into the Uncategorized group. Figure 14-21 illustrates a scenario where a URL is unknown to the management center. As the cloud lookup is disabled (or failed due to Internet connectivity issues), the management center marks that URL as Uncategorized.

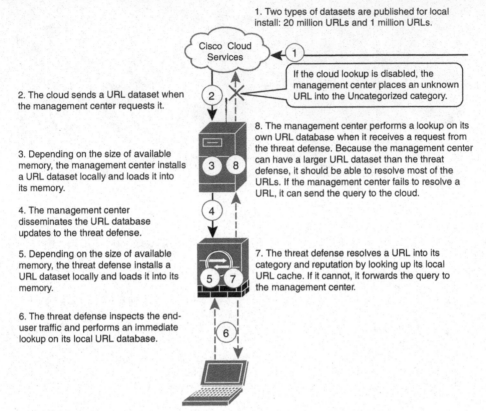

1. Two types of datasets are published for local install: 20 million URLs and 1 million URLs.

If the cloud lookup is disabled, the management center places an unknown URL into the Uncategorized category.

2. The cloud sends a URL dataset when the management center requests it.

3. Depending on the size of available memory, the management center installs a URL dataset locally and loads it into its memory.

4. The management center disseminates the URL database updates to the threat defense.

5. Depending on the size of available memory, the threat defense installs a URL dataset locally and loads it into its memory.

6. The threat defense inspects the end-user traffic and performs an immediate lookup on its local URL database.

8. The management center performs a lookup on its own URL database when it receives a request from the threat defense. Because the management center can have a larger URL dataset than the threat defense, it should be able to resolve most of the URLs. If the management center fails to resolve a URL, it can send the query to the cloud.

7. The threat defense resolves a URL into its category and reputation by looking up its local URL cache. If it cannot, it forwards the query to the management center.

Figure 14-21 *Workflow for Triggering an Uncategorized URL Event*

To allow the management center to perform a cloud lookup for unknown URLs, follow these steps:

Step 1. Go to **System > Integration > Cloud Services.**

Step 2. Enable **URL Filtering** and make sure the **Query Cisco Cloud for Unknown URLs** option is enabled as well.

Step 3. Optionally, click the **Update Now** option to update the URL database immediately with the latest URL data.

Step 4. Save the changes.

Figure 14-22 shows the configuration page to enable cloud lookup for unknown URLs.

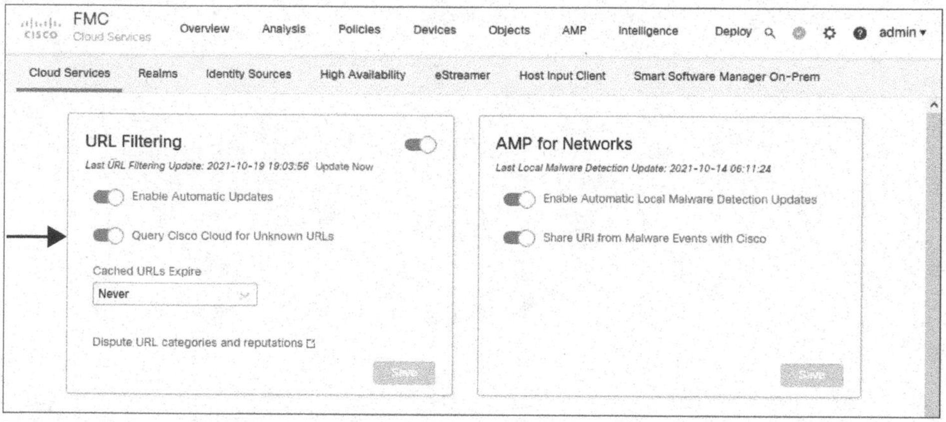

Figure 14-22 *Enabling Cloud Lookup for Unknown URLs*

While resolving a URL category, the threat defense does not let the uncategorized traffic pass until the URL lookup is complete or the lookup process times out, whichever comes first. If the volume of uncategorized traffic grows, the threat defense keeps holding the traffic in memory. The threat defense considers a URL uncategorized until an appropriate category is determined during a cloud lookup. The threat defense allows the initial flows, but for subsequent connections, it continues to look up that URL with the hope of resolving and caching it.

This behavior, however, can lead to performance degradation. To avoid this situation, you can let a threat defense pass traffic immediately whenever a URL appears uncached and the URL category cannot be determined locally. The following steps show how to disable a retry when a local cache fails the first lookup:

Step 1. Go to **Policies > Access Control > Access Control** and edit the access control policy that is deployed on your threat defense.

Step 2. In the access control policy editor page that appears, select the **Advanced** tab.

Step 3. Select the pencil icon next to General Settings. The General Settings configuration window appears.

Step 4. Disable the **Retry URL Cache Miss Lookup** option and click **OK** to return to the access control policy editor page.

Step 5. Click **Save** to save the changes. Navigate to **Deploy > Deployment** to redeploy the policy to your threat defense.

Figure 14-23 shows an advanced setting in an access control policy that allows a threat defense to pass uncategorized traffic immediately, without holding it for continuous cloud lookups.

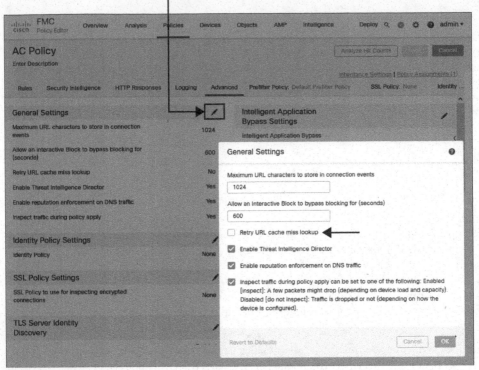

Figure 14-23 *Disabling Retry Attempts When a Local Cache Misses URLs*

Investigating the Uncategorized URLs

To demonstrate the action of threat defense on uncategorized URLs, this chapter uses nazmulrajib.com. Figure 14-24 shows a connection event for accessing nazmulrajib.com. As an end user attempts to access this website, the management center marks the URL as Uncategorized.

Example 14-5 displays the debug messages that result from connecting to the unknown URL nazmulrajib.com. First, the threat defense performs a lookup on its local shared memory (see the keyword **ShmDBLookupURL** in the example). Then it attempts to query the cloud. If the communication to the cloud is unavailable (as shown in this example), the URL lookup eventually fails.

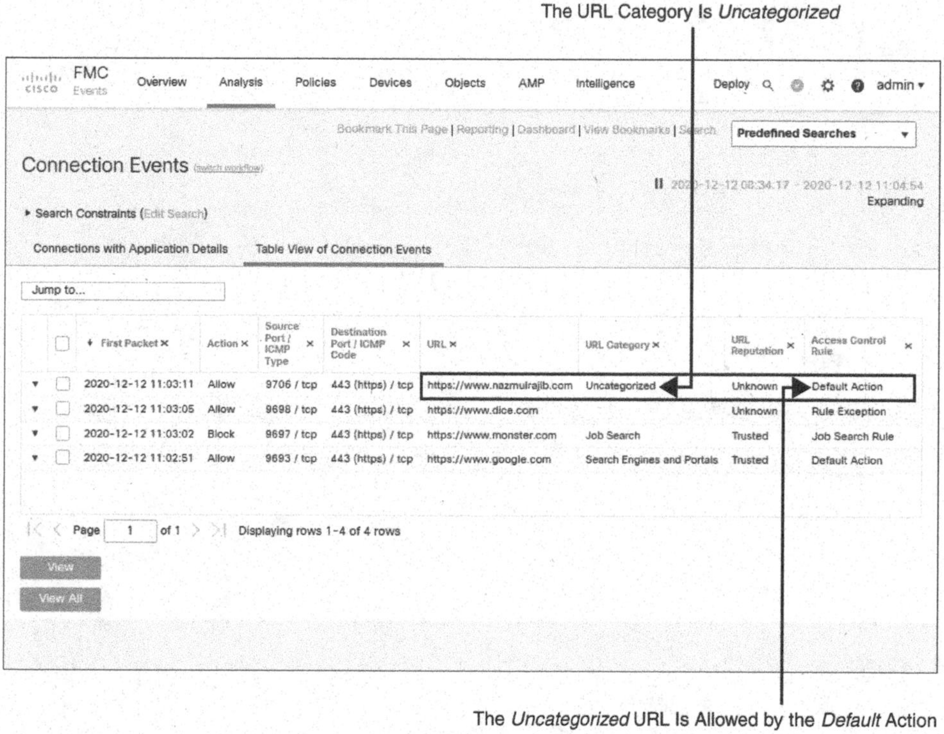

The URL Category Is *Uncategorized*

The *Uncategorized* URL Is Allowed by the *Default* Action

Figure 14-24 *An Uncategorized URL Event*

Example 14-5 *Debugging a Connection to an Uncategorized URL*

```
> system support firewall-engine-debug

Please specify an IP protocol: tcp
Please specify a client IP address: S.S.S.S
Please specify a client port:
Please specify a server IP address: D.D.D.D
Please specify a server port: 443
Monitoring firewall engine debug messages

# At this point, connect to nazmulrajib.com using a browser. The following debug
output shows the messages related to URL lookup and filtering processes. The initial
communications between client and server are truncated for brevity.

.

.

S.S.S.S-9706 > D.D.D.D-443 6 AS 4-4 I 0 TLS host name retrieved is  www.nazmulrajib.
com

S.S.S.S-9706 > D.D.D.D-443 6 AS 4-4 I 0 URL SI: ShmDBLookupURL("www.nazmulrajib.
com") returned 0
```

```
S.S.S.S-9706 > D.D.D.D-443 6 AS 4-4 I 0 Starting AC with minimum 3, 'Rule Excep-
tion', and SrcZone first with zones -1 -> -1, geo 0(0) -> 0, vlan 0, source sgt
type: 0, sgt tag: 0, ISE sgt id: 0, dest sgt type: 0, ISE dest_sgt_tag: 0, svc 1122,
payload 0, client 1296, misc 0, user 9999997, min url-cat-list 0-0-0, url
www.nazmulrajib.com, xff

S.S.S.S-9706 > D.D.D.D-443 6 AS 4-4 I 0 custom host matcher using: www.nazmulrajib.
com

S.S.S.S-9706 > D.D.D.D-443 6 AS 4-4 I 0 custom host matcher url without slash failed

S.S.S.S-9706 > D.D.D.D-443 6 AS 4-4 I 0 no match rule order 3, 'Rule Exception',
url=(www.nazmulrajib.com) c=0 r=0

S.S.S.S-9706 > D.D.D.D-443 6 AS 4-4 I 0: returned from url lookup, url_info is NULL

S.S.S.S-9706 > D.D.D.D-443 6 AS 4-4 I 0: DataMessaging_GetURLData: www.nazmulrajib.
com found in cache, index: 103, rval: 0

S.S.S.S-9706 > D.D.D.D-443 6 AS 4-4 I 0: DataMessaging_GetURLData: REQUEST_FAILED
www.nazmulrajib.com. Return URL_PENDINGTYPE, retry cloud. request_age=731

S.S.S.S-9706 > D.D.D.D-443 6 AS 4-4 I 0: DataMessaging_GetURLData: Adding url
www.nazmulrajib.com to queue

S.S.S.S-9706 > D.D.D.D-443 6 AS 4-4 I 0: DataMessaging_GetURLData: Successfully
added to queue

S.S.S.S-9706 > D.D.D.D-443 6 AS 4-4 I 0 rule order 4, 'Job Search Rule', URL Match
Pending: www.nazmulrajib.com waited: 0ms



# At this point, the Secure Firewall makes another attempt to determine the URL
category. Since the retry attempt also fails, the Secure Firewall marks the URL as
uncategorized and allows it per the Default Action.


S.S.S.S-9706 > D.D.D.D-443 6 AS 4-4 I 0: DataMessaging_GetURLData: REQUEST_FAILED,
returning URL_FAILEDTYPE for www.nazmulrajib.com

S.S.S.S-9706 > D.D.D.D-443 6 AS 4-4 I 0 rule order 4, 'Job Search Rule', URL Lookup
Failed: www.nazmulrajib.com waited: 200ms

S.S.S.S-9706 > D.D.D.D-443 6 AS 4-4 I 0 no match rule order 4, 'Job Search Rule',
url=(www.nazmulrajib.com) c=65534 r=0

S.S.S.S-9706 > D.D.D.D-443 6 AS 4-4 I 0 match rule order 5, 'Default Action', action
Allow

S.S.S.S-9706 > D.D.D.D-443 6 AS 4-4 I 0 Logging SOF with rule_id = 268434432
ruleAction = 2 ruleReason = 0

S.S.S.S-9706 > D.D.D.D-443 6 AS 4-4 I 0 MidRecovery data sent for rule id:
268434432,rule_action:2, rev id:4226208863, rule_match flag:0x0

S.S.S.S-9706 > D.D.D.D-443 6 AS 4-4 I 0 HitCount data sent for rule id: 268434432,

S.S.S.S-9706 > D.D.D.D-443 6 AS 4-4 I 0 allow action
```

Summary

This chapter describes techniques to filter traffic based on the category and reputation of a URL. It illustrates how Secure Firewall performs a URL lookup and how a threat defense takes an action based on the query result. This chapter also explains the connection to a URL through debugging messages, which is critical for troubleshooting.

Exam Preparation Tasks

As mentioned in the section "How to Use This Book" in the Introduction, you have a couple of choices for exam preparation: the exercises here, Chapter 22, "Final Preparation," and the exam simulation questions in the Pearson Test Prep practice test software.

Review All Key Topics

Review the most important topics in this chapter, noted with the Key Topic icon in the outer margin of the page. Table 14-4 lists a reference of these key topics and the page numbers on which each is found.

Table 14-4 Key Topics for Chapter 14

Key Topic Element	Description	Page
Paragraph	URL Filtering operation	314
Bullet list	URL Filtering automatic update	319
Bullet list	URL Filtering of encrypted traffic	322
Paragraph	Uncategorized URL	335

Complete Tables and Lists from Memory

Print a copy of Appendix C, "Memory Tables" (found on the companion website), or at least the section for this chapter, and complete the tables and lists from memory. Appendix D, "Memory Tables Answer Key," also on the companion website, includes completed tables and lists to check your work.

Define Key Terms

Define the following key terms from this chapter, and check your answers in the Glossary:

URL reputation, URL database, uncategorized URLs

CHAPTER 15

Network Analysis and Intrusion Policies

This chapter provides an overview of the following topics:

Intrusion Prevention System Essentials: This section describes the key components of the intrusion prevention system configuration, such as the network analysis policy, intrusion policy, variable sets, and base policies.

Best Practices for Intrusion Policy Deployment: This section provides tips to deploy Secure Firewall optimally for intrusion prevention purposes.

Configuring a Network Analysis Policy: This section describes the steps to configure a network analysis policy based on both Snort 2 and Snort 3 versions.

Configuring an Intrusion Policy: This section explains the steps to create an intrusion policy and to incorporate system-generated intrusion rule recommendations. It also discusses the importance of customizing a variable set.

Policy Deployment: In this section, you learn how to deploy the network analysis and intrusion policies using an access control policy.

Verification: Finally, this section demonstrates the action of an intrusion policy on live traffic and then exhibits different types of intrusion events using the management center event viewer and dashboard.

The objectives of this chapter are to learn about

- Implementation of a network analysis policy

- Describing and implementing an intrusion policy

- Snort rule syntax and Snort variable sets

- Intrusion rule recommendations generation

- System-provided base policies

- Verification of intrusion prevention operation on threat defense

One of the most popular features of Cisco Secure Firewall is that it can function as an intrusion detection system (IDS) as well as an intrusion prevention system (IPS). The IDS/IPS functionality on a threat defense is powered by Snort, one of the leading open-source IPS technologies in the world. You can write Snort rules to sniff network packets, detect malicious activities, generate alerts for users, or even block any harmful packets from entering a network. In Secure Firewall, a Snort rule is also known as an intrusion rule. The operation of intrusion rules is governed by two policies: an intrusion policy and a network analysis policy. This chapter describes both of these policies and demonstrates their configurations on Secure Firewall.

"Do I Know This Already?" Quiz

The "Do I Know This Already?" quiz enables you to assess whether you should read this entire chapter thoroughly or jump to the "Exam Preparation Tasks" section. If you are in doubt about your answers to these questions or your own assessment of your knowledge of the topics, read the entire chapter. Table 15-1 lists the major headings in this chapter and their corresponding "Do I Know This Already?" quiz questions. You can find the answers in Appendix A, "Answers to the 'Do I Know This Already?' Quizzes."

Table 15-1 "Do I Know This Already?" Section-to-Question Mapping

Foundation Topics Section	Questions
Intrusion Prevention System Essentials	1, 2
Best Practices for Intrusion Policy Deployment	3
Configuring a Network Analysis Policy	4
Configuring an Intrusion Policy	5
Policy Deployment	6
Verification	7

CAUTION   The goal of self-assessment is to gauge your mastery of the topics in this chapter. If you do not know the answer to a question or are only partially sure of the answer, you should mark that question as wrong for purposes of the self-assessment. Giving yourself credit for an answer you correctly guess skews your self-assessment results and might provide you with a false sense of security.

1. Which of the following policy configurations can influence the behavior of the intrusion prevention functionality of a threat defense?

    a. Network analysis policy

    b. Intrusion policy

    c. Access control policy

    d. All of these answers are correct.

2. Which of the following numbering schemes is correct for a Snort rule?

   a. A standard text rule uses GID 1.

   b. A preprocessor rule can use any GID except 1–3.

   c. A local rule uses SID 1,000,000 or higher.

   d. All of these answers are correct.

3. Which of the following base policies is recommended by Cisco?

   a. Connectivity over Security

   b. Balanced Security and Connectivity

   c. Security over Connectivity

   d. Maximum Detection

4. Which of the following policies can play a critical role in normalizing SCADA networking traffic?

   a. Network Analysis Policy

   b. Intrusion Policy

   c. Access Control Policy

   d. File & Malware Policy

5. Which of the following options is mandatory if you want to drop an intrusion attempt or block a packet that may constitute a potential cyber attack?

   a. The interface set must be in inline, routed, or transparent mode.

   b. The inspection mode must be set to prevention mode.

   c. The rule action must be configured to block packets.

   d. All of these answers are correct.

6. What can an intrusion policy be applied to?

   a. The network traffic before an access control rule is determined for it.

   b. The filtered network traffic after matching an access control rule.

   c. The network traffic that does not match any access control rule.

   d. All of these answers are correct.

7. If you set the inspection mode to detection mode but the intrusion rule action is set to block packets, what would happen in Secure Firewall deployed in inline mode?

   a. The matching traffic will be dropped due to the intrusion rule action.

   b. The matching traffic will flow without interruption, but the intrusion event would be marked visually as *would have dropped*.

   c. The Detection inspection mode works only with the passive interface mode. Therefore, it has no impact on an inline deployment.

   d. All of these answers are correct.

Foundation Topics

Intrusion Prevention System Essentials

To simplify and accelerate the initial configuration of the intrusion prevention system, Secure Firewall comes with many built-in intrusion policies. You can select one of them in a few clicks for matching traffic (through an access control rule) and for unmatching traffic (through a default action), as shown in Figure 15-1. If your organization's cybersecurity strategy warrants more granular inspection services, you can customize the default settings in a built-in policy. However, a customization can involve several policy components. For example,

- **Network analysis policy:** This policy works in conjunction with inspectors (in Snort 3) and preprocessors (in Snort 2) to normalize traffic.

- **Intrusion policy:** This policy employs the Snort rules and variables to perform deep packet inspection.

- **Access control policy:** This policy allows you to filter specific network traffic and applies the network analysis and intrusion policies to it.

The following sections describe all the components that are essential to an overarching inspection policy.

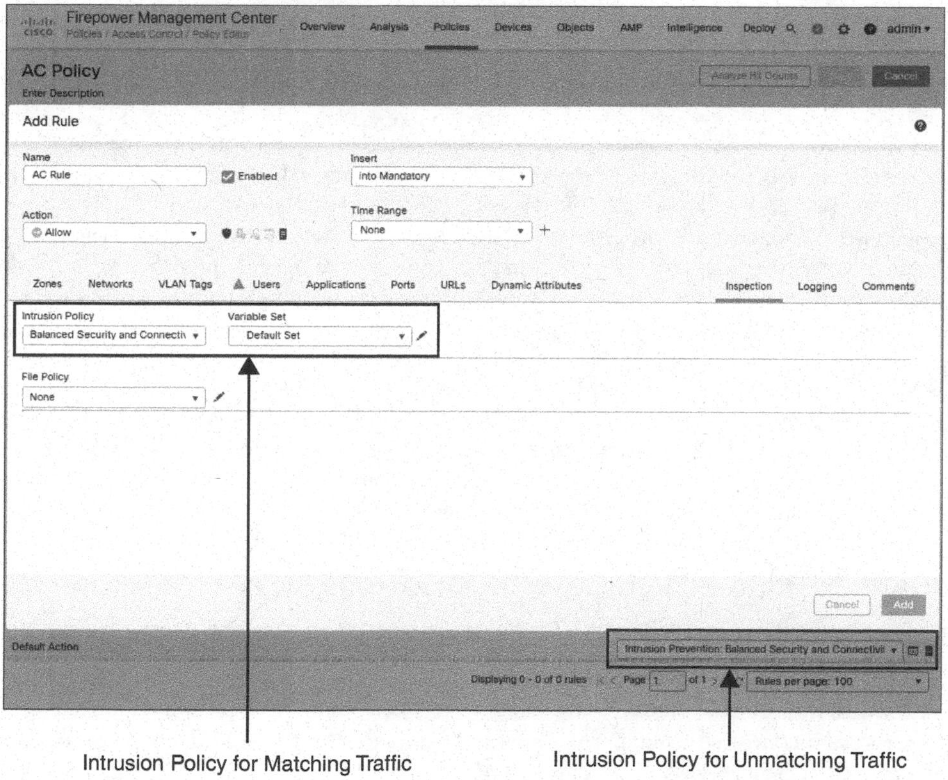

Intrusion Policy for Matching Traffic   Intrusion Policy for Unmatching Traffic

Figure 15-1 *Simple Options to Select the Built-in Intrusion Policy*

Network Analysis Policy

Before performing deep packet inspection, the Snort engine decodes a packet and stream-lines its header and payload into a standard format that a Snort rule can analyze easily. The component that performs this normalization is called a *preprocessor* (in Snort 2) or an *inspector* (in Snort 3). Snort has many protocol-specific preprocessors or inspectors. They can identify anomalies within the stream of packets, detect evasion techniques, and drop packets when there is an inconsistency, such as an invalid checksum or unusual ports. The settings of Snort 2 preprocessors are not in one-to-one mapping with Snort 3 inspectors. Also, their implementations on open-source Snort and proprietary Cisco Secure Firewall are not the same. The management center GUI offers a user-friendly network analysis policy editor to enable, disable, and fine-tune the settings of preprocessors or inspectors.

Figure 15-2 shows the basic architecture of the open-source Snort. Here, all the preprocessor plug-ins operate at the same level—after decoding a packet and before the Snort rule inspection.

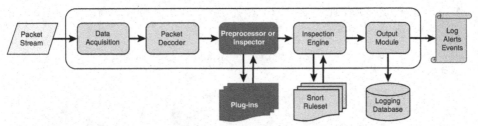

Figure 15-2 *Open-Source Snort Implementing Preprocessor Plug-ins*

Figure 15-3 illustrates the multiphase implementation of preprocessors or inspectors on a threat defense. The Snort engine uses them to decode and normalize traffic in multiple phases as the packets go through advanced security checks. If a preprocessor or an inspector is manually disabled but Snort requires its service to support an active intrusion rule, the threat defense overrides the manual setting and engages that relevant preprocessor or inspector to ensure maximum efficacy. However, the settings remain visually disabled on the management center GUI.

Intrusion Policy

An intrusion policy allows you to enable, disable, or set a rule state for matching traffic. After decoding and normalizing a packet, the threat defense uses the intrusion ruleset to perform deep packet inspection. An intrusion rule is written based on Snort rule syntax and contains the signature of a specific vulnerability. Therefore, both terms *intrusion rule* and *Snort rule* are interchangeable in this chapter. Secure Firewall supports Snort rules from various sources, including the following:

- **Standard text rules:** The Cisco Talos threat intelligence group writes these rules in cleartext format. The Snort detection engine uses them to analyze packets.

- **Shared object (SO) rules:** Cisco Talos writes SO rules in the C programming language and compiles them. SO rules are used for a variety of reasons, including proprietary agreements between Cisco and third-party vendors.

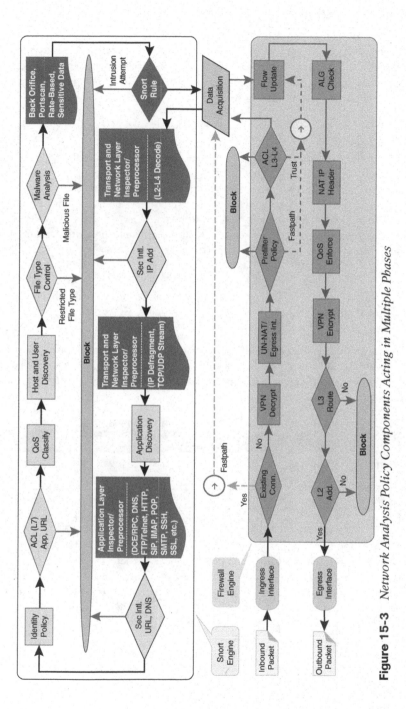

Figure 15-3 *Network Analysis Policy Components Acting in Multiple Phases*

■ **Preprocessor rules:** The Snort development team creates these rules, which you can use to control alerts that come from the preprocessors.

■ **Local rules:** The management center enables you to create custom Snort rules either by using the built-in rule editor in the GUI or by importing rules written in a plaintext file. After the custom Snort rules are found, the management center categorizes them as *local rules*. Similarly, if you obtain Snort rules from a third party, the system considers them to be local rules as well.

> **NOTE**   Although Secure Firewall supports third-party rules or locally created rules, always consider using the Cisco-provided intrusion rules over any local rules that protect against the same vulnerability. Cisco-provided rules are developed by Talos—a group of dedicated world-class researchers who are primarily responsible for writing and updating Snort rules. An ill-structured Snort rule can negatively impact the threat defense's performance. To craft a highly effective custom Snort rule, you need to be an expert of Snort rule syntax, which is beyond the scope of this chapter. To learn more about custom rule writing, read the documentation on open-source Snort at www.snort.org.

Figure 15-4 shows the possible verdicts of packet analysis on a threat defense. An intrusion policy is one of the last phases of the inspection process. However, any bypassed or trusted traffic is not subject to Snort rule inspection.

Snort uses a unique generator ID (GID) and Snort rule ID (SID) to identify a rule. Depending on who creates a rule, the numbering schemes of GIDs and SIDs are different. Table 15-2 provides the identification numbers that you can use to distinguish one type of Snort rule from another.

Table 15-2   Types of Snort Rules and Their Identification Numbers

Type of Rule	Identification Number
Standard text rule	GID is 1. SID is lower than 1,000,000.
Shared object rule	GID is 3.
Preprocessor rule	GID can be anything other than 1–3.
Local rule	SID is 1,000,000 or higher.

Snort IPS technology goes through continual development and maintenance processes. It ensures the best-in-class protection and performance. The latest version of Snort is 3, which is popular for its multithreaded inspection capability. Snort 3 delivers higher performance and efficiency. This book is primarily written based on Secure Firewall software version 7.0, which supports both Snort 2 and Snort 3. For your comprehensive understanding, both Snort versions are discussed in the configuration examples of this chapter.

15

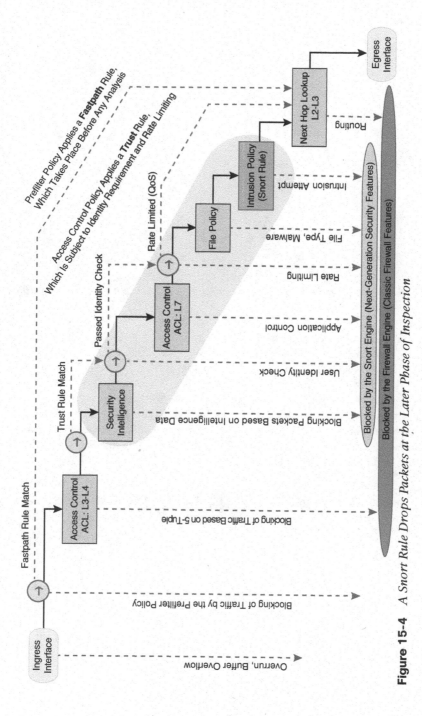

Figure 15-4 *A Snort Rule Drops Packets at the Later Phase of Inspection*

Figure 15-5 shows a newly created network analysis policy (top image) and an intrusion policy (bottom image). You can choose either Snort 2 or Snort 3 to modify the settings in the policies.

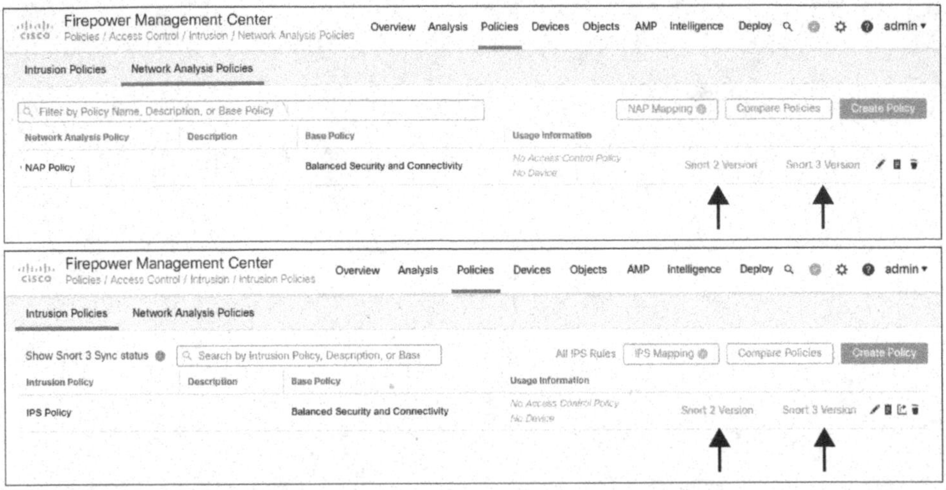

Figure 15-5 *Both Snort Versions Are Supported on the Network Analysis and Intrusion Policies*

You can use the management center GUI to find additional information about a Snort rule. You can go to **Objects > Intrusion Rules**, and select the desired Snort version to view the rule, as shown in Figure 15-6. The figure exhibits the retrieval of the Telnet-specific rule 1:718 in the Snort 3 rule viewer. This rule can block a Telnet connection attempt when a user enters incorrect login credentials. You can also view a rule in the Snort 2 rule viewer, and even edit the rule options to create your own version. Figure 15-7 shows the retrieval of rule 1:718 in the rule editor. Note that any customization of a Cisco-provided rule turns the rule into a local rule. As indicated in Table 15-2, Secure Firewall automatically assigns an SID of 1,000,000 or higher to a local rule.

NOTE   Throughout this chapter, Snort rule 1:718 or SID:718 is used as an example to explain various scenarios. You can replace it with any standard Snort rule for your lab exercise.

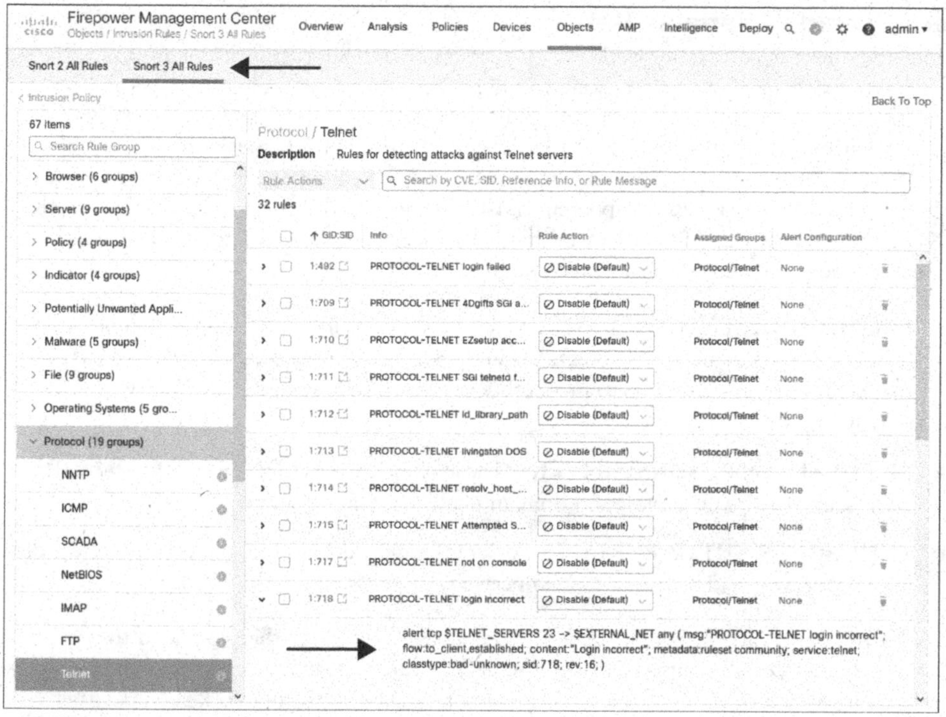

Figure 15-6 *Viewing the Detail of a Snort Rule*

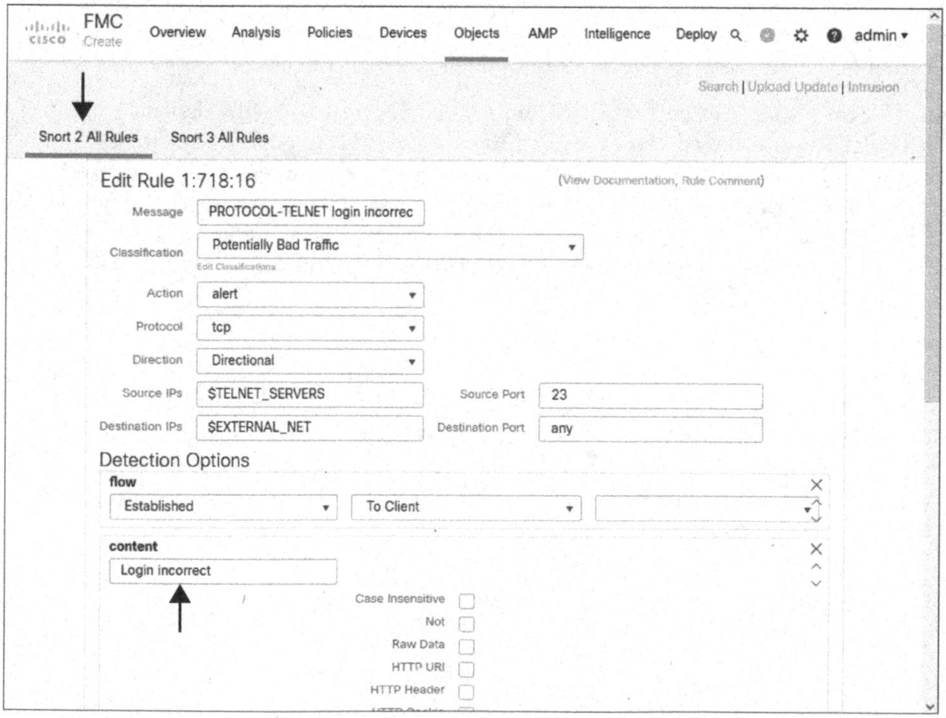

Figure 15-7 *Editing a Cisco-Provided Snort Rule*

System-Provided Variable Sets

Besides the direct use of static IP address or port number, a Snort rule also supports variables to represent the source and destination IP addresses and port numbers. This empowers you to deploy Snort rules in any network without modifying the original rule constraints; you simply need to adjust the values of the variable according to the new network environment. By default, Secure Firewall comes with many default variables. The purposes of the **system-provided variables** are apparent in their names. For instance, names ending with $*_NET, $*_SERVERS, and $*_PORTS define network addresses, IP addresses, and port numbers, respectively. Let's look at some examples:

- **$HOME_NET, $EXTERNAL_NET:** $HOME_NET includes the internal network resources that you need to protect. $EXTERNAL_NET specifies the external network that you are not responsible to protect—outside of your organization's networking jurisdiction.

- **$HTTP_SERVERS, $DNS_SERVERS:** These names are used to define the static IP addresses of the web servers and domain name servers, respectively.

- **$FTP_PORTS, $HTTP_PORTS:** These names are used to define the port numbers of the FTP servers and web servers, respectively.

The $HOME_NET variable is used to define the internal networks that you need to protect with your threat defense. Out of the box, the default values of many server-specific variables are set to *any* or *$HOME_NET*. However, in an organization, the network servers either don't occupy all the available IP addresses or a server doesn't utilize all the possible ports. You must replace the default values with actual server IP addresses and port numbers to increase efficacy and reduce false positive alerts. Specifying the addresses and ports minimizes the number of times a Snort rule gets evaluated by the inspection engine. Thus, customization of default variables can improve overall system performance.

Figure 15-8 shows some examples of system-provided Snort variables. By default, HOME_NET is set to any, and HTTP_SERVERS is set to HOME_NET. It renders the HTTP_SERVERS variable to include all IP addresses. However, in a real-world organization, it is impractical to run web servers on all possible IP addresses. So, you must specify both HOME_NET and HTTP_SERVERS based on your own network environment. Likewise, Oracle applications don't run on any possible ports. Therefore, the ORACLE_PORTS variable needs to be defined precisely as well.

This chapter uses Snort rule 1:718 to demonstrate the operation of an intrusion policy. As illustrated in Figure 15-9, Snort rule 1:718 analyzes traffic from the $TELNET_SERVERS variable to detect a potential brute-force attack. You must define both variables—$HOME_NET and $TELNET_SERVERS—to trigger the SID:718 properly. If you do not change the default value of the $TELNET_SERVERS variable, Snort may analyze packets from additional IP addresses—along with your real Telnet server—to find the "Login incorrect" content within the payloads.

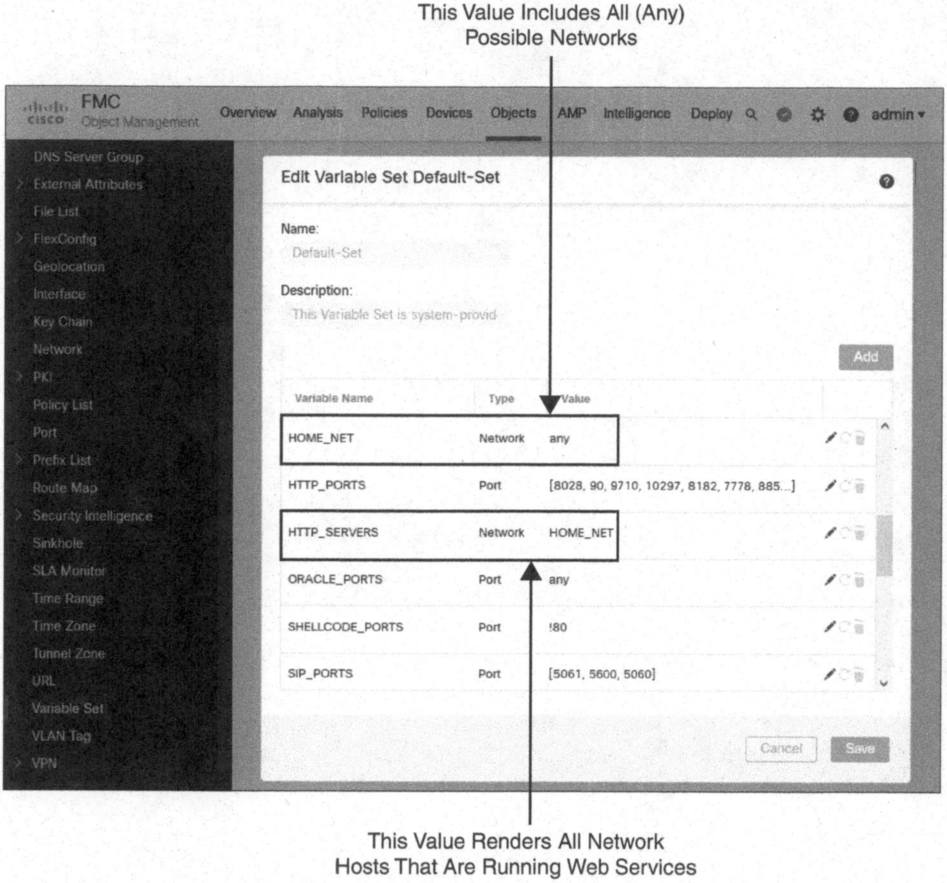

This Value Includes All (Any)
Possible Networks

This Value Renders All Network
Hosts That Are Running Web Services

Figure 15-8 *Default Values of the Snort Variables Set (Requires Customization)*

System-Provided Base Policies

To help you with initial deployment, Secure Firewall software comes with several precon-figured network analysis and intrusion policies. You can deploy one of them directly, or use one as a baseline for your custom intrusion policy:

- **Balanced Security and Connectivity:** This base policy is the best starting point to create your own intrusion policy that can address the critical vulnerabilities while maintaining system performance.

- **Connectivity over Security:** This policy prioritizes connection speed by reducing the detection of older or less critical vulnerabilities.

- **Security over Connectivity:** This policy prioritizes network security over connectivity by enabling a greater number of rules and setting more rules to drop offending traffic over the other default policies.

- **Maximum Detection:** Security has supreme priority over business continuity. Due to the deeper inspection of packets with this policy, end users may experience latency, and a threat defense may drop some legitimate traffic.

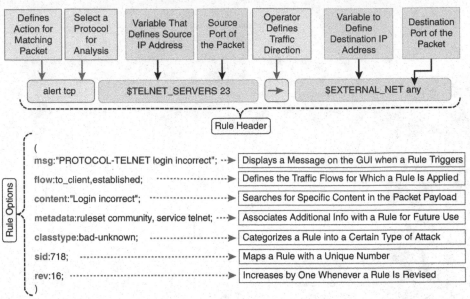

Figure 15-9 *Anatomy of Snort Rule 1:718 (Where GID:1 and SID:718)*

Figure 15-10 shows the system-provided base policies that you can find in Secure Firewall out of the box. Each management center comes with four network analysis policies and five intrusion policies. The No Rules Active base policy allows you to create an empty intrusion policy with all the intrusion rules disabled. This policy can be used as a tool to investigate any technical issues with the Snort engine.

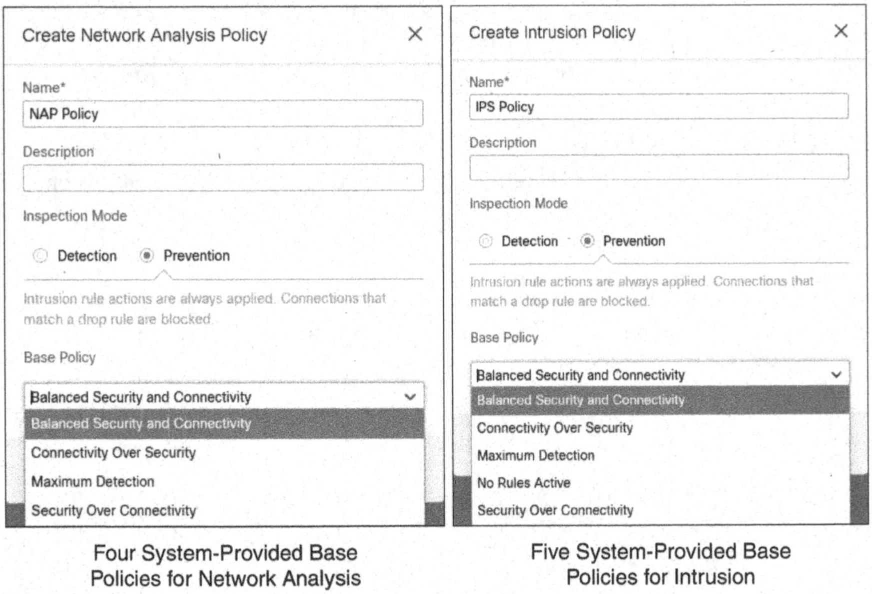

Four System-Provided Base
Policies for Network Analysis

Five System-Provided Base
Policies for Intrusion

Figure 15-10 *System-Provided Built-in Base Policies*

The number of rules enabled by default in a system-provided policy varies. Cisco uses the Common Vulnerability Scoring System (CVSS) score to determine whether a rule should be enabled in a system-provided policy. See Table 15-3 to understand the eligibility criteria for including a Snort rule in a system-provided policy.

Table 15-3   CVSS Scores of the System-Provided Policies

Intrusion Policy	CVSS Score	Age of Vulnerability
Connectivity over Security	10	Current year plus two prior years
Balanced Security and Connectivity	9 or higher	Current year plus two prior years
Security over Connectivity	8 or higher	Current year plus three prior years
Maximum Detection	7.5 or higher	All the years since 2005

Figure 15-11 shows the correlation among the system-provided intrusion policies, their detection coverages, and processing overheads. The higher the threat coverage, the higher the utilization of the threat defense resources.

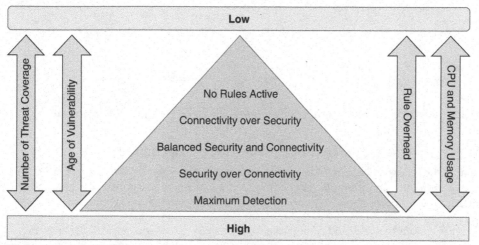

Figure 15-11   *Differences Between the System-Provided Policies, Coverages, and Processing Overheads*

Cisco releases rule updates periodically. You can configure the management center to download the latest ruleset automatically from the cloud and install it through a scheduled task. You can also manually download a rule update file and upload it to the management center for installation. Each rule update comes with a unique ruleset. Although the total number of available rules on a specific rule update package is unpredictable, the proportions of enabled to disabled rules in different base policies are almost identical. In general, the Maximum Detection policy and Security over Connectivity policy have more intrusion rules enabled than the Connectivity over Security policy and **Balanced Security and Connectivity policy**.

Figure 15-12 shows the number of rules in various categories on a newly deployed Secure Firewall running software version 7.0. The images are taken from the intrusion policy editor based on Snort 3.

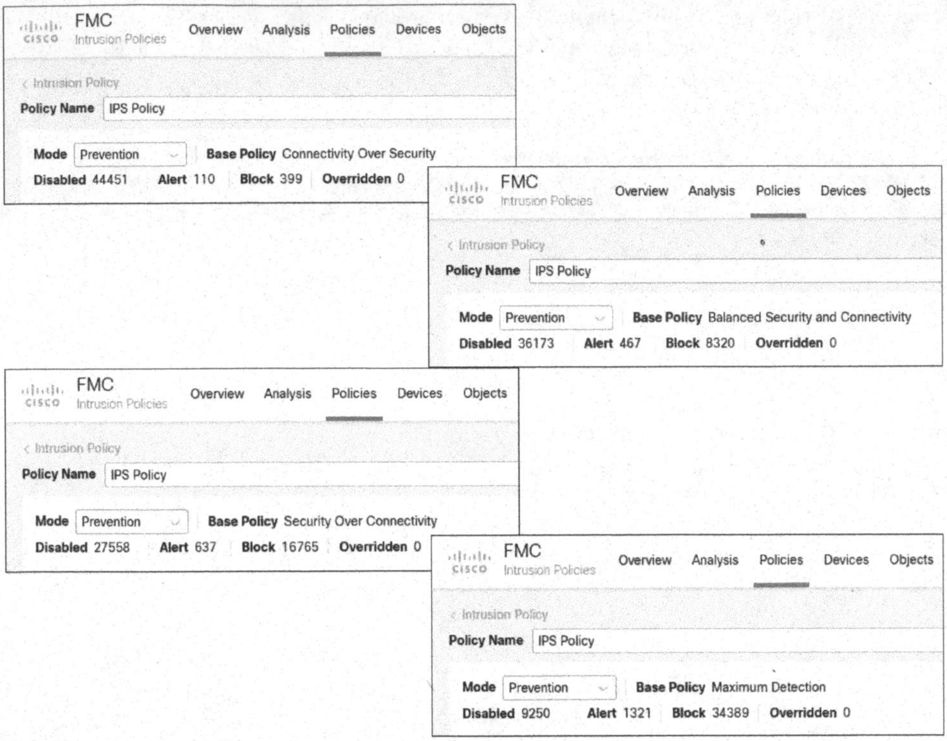

Figure 15-12 *Determining the Number of Rules on a Base Policy and Their Status*

Best Practices for Intrusion Policy Deployment

Consider the following best practices when you deploy Secure Firewall to protect your network from intrusion attempts. They can help you to achieve an optimal experience. The configuration details of these items are described in later sections of this chapter.

■ If you want to match and filter packets based on 5-tuple—source port, destination port, source address, destination address, and protocol—you should consider using an access control rule or prefilter rule, but not an intrusion rule. The purpose of a Snort-based intrusion rule is to perform advanced deep packet inspection.

■ Select the Balanced Security and Connectivity policy as the base policy when you create a new network analysis policy and intrusion policy. The ruleset in this policy provides greater security coverage against the latest threats while ensuring optimized performance. This base policy is also recommended by Cisco.

Figure 15-13 shows the selection of Balanced Security and Connectivity as the base policy for both the network analysis policy (left) and intrusion policy (right).

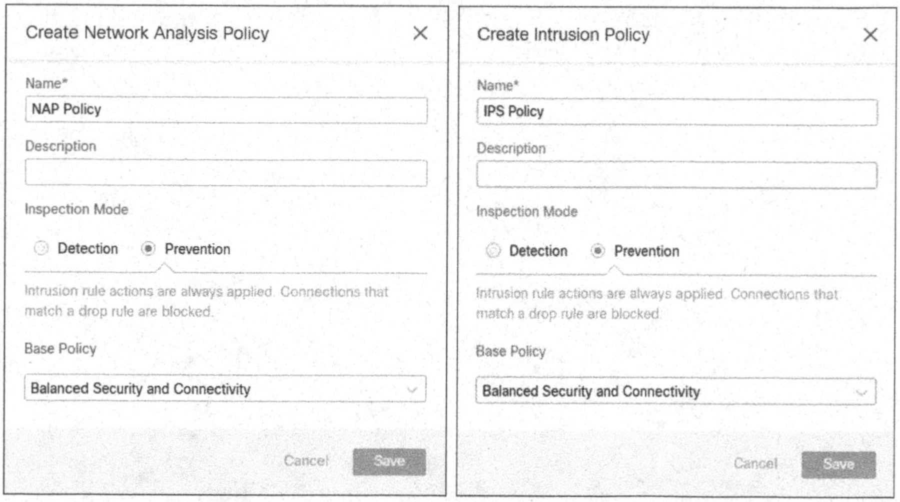

Create Network Analysis Policy ✕

Name*
NAP Policy

Description

Inspection Mode

○ Detection   ⦿ Prevention

Intrusion rule actions are always applied. Connections that match a drop rule are blocked.

Base Policy

Balanced Security and Connectivity ⌄

Cancel   Save

Create Intrusion Policy ✕

Name*
IPS Policy

Description

Inspection Mode

○ Detection   ⦿ Prevention

Intrusion rule actions are always applied. Connections that match a drop rule are blocked.

Base Policy

Balanced Security and Connectivity ⌄

Cancel   Save

Figure 15-13 *Separate Policy Creation Windows for the Network Analysis and Intrusion Policies*

- Use the intrusion rule recommendations feature within the intrusion policy. It utilizes the network discovery data, correlates that data with any associated vulnerabilities that are recorded in the Vulnerability Database (VDB), and recommends Snort rules that are developed to address those vulnerabilities. The steps to enable rule recommendations are described in detail in the "Incorporating Intrusion Rule Recommendations" section later in this chapter.

Furthermore, you can automate the rule recommendation generation and policy deployment processes using the task scheduling feature of the management center. It ensures periodic enablement of intrusion rules based on the recently discovered applications and hosts in your network.

Figure 15-14 shows the task scheduling feature on the management center. You can schedule recurring or one-time tasks to generate rule recommendations, deploy policies, and perform many more jobs.

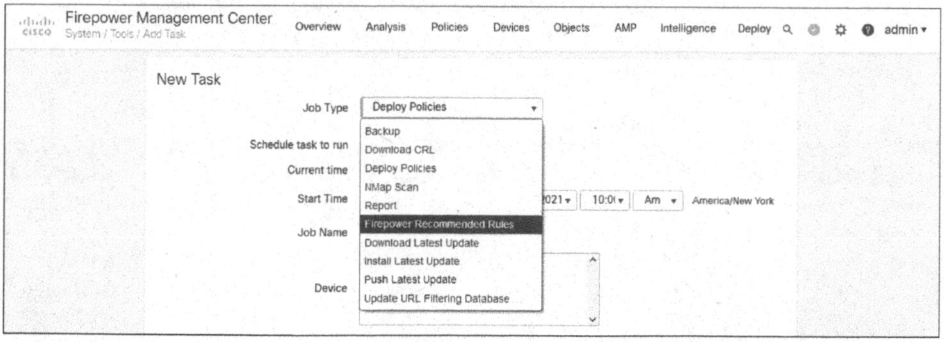

Figure 15-14 *Task Scheduling Functionality for Intrusion Rule Recommendations*

■ Enhance detection by selecting both advanced options, Adaptive Profiles and Enable Profile Update. These options allow a Secure Firewall to leverage service metadata and intelligently apply enabled intrusion rules to relevant traffic.

Figure 15-15 shows the detection enhancement settings in an access control policy where you can configure the Adaptive Profiles and Enable Profile Update settings. To implement an intrusion policy based on Snort 3, you must select both Enable and Enable Profile Updates options, as shown in this figure.

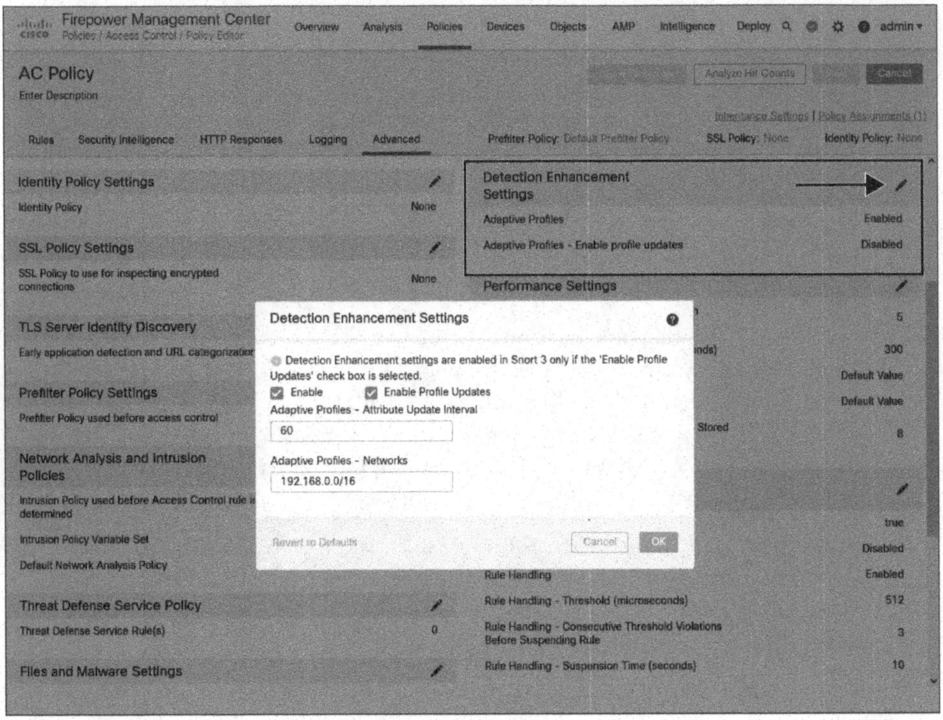

Figure 15-15 *Adaptive Profile Configurations*

Table 15-4 shows the differences between the intrusion rule recommendations and enable profile update features. Although both features work together to enable traffic-specific intrusion rules, there are some differences between them.

Table 15-4 Intrusion Rule Recommendations Versus Enable Profile Update

Intrusion Rule Recommendations	Enable Profile Update
Recommends enabling and disabling intrusion rules, based on the discovered applications and hosts.	Compares rule metadata with the applications and operating systems of a host and determines whether the threat defense should apply a certain rule to certain traffic from that host.
Can enable a disabled rule if the rule relates to a host and application in the network.	Does not change the state of a disabled rule. Works only on the enabled rules in an intrusion policy.
Configured within an intrusion policy.	Configured within an access control policy.

> **TIP**   Enable both features—enable profile update and intrusion rule recommendations—at
> the same time. Doing so allows a threat defense to enable or disable the intrusion rules that
> are related to the hosts, applications, and services running on a network and then apply the
> enabled rules to relevant traffic from those hosts.

Some of the best practices are applicable to a particular deployment mode and depend on
your traffic handling policy. For example:

- If you want to prevent cyber attacks by blocking intrusion attempts, you need to
deploy the threat defense as a bump in the wire (BITW). The BITW deployment
requires an inline interface pair. You include the ingress and egress interfaces of an
inline interface pair and then assign the interface pair to an inline set. To learn more
about inline mode, see Chapter 6, "IPS-Only Deployment in Inline Mode."

- If your goal is to deploy a threat defense for detection-only purposes—because you
do not want to block intrusion attempts in real time—consider deploying the threat
defense in inline tap mode instead of in passive mode. Doing so enables you to switch
to inline mode faster, without the need for a cabling change. This is critical in case of
an emergency. To learn more, read Chapter 7, "Deployment in Detection-Only Mode."

- If you choose to deploy your threat defense in passive mode, make sure the Adaptive
Profiles option is enabled in the advanced settings section of the access control policy.
This option enables a threat defense to adapt intrusion rules dynamically based on the
metadata of the service, client application, and host traffic.

- When a threat defense prompts you to select a firewall mode (during initialization
after a reimage), choose routed mode. Although transparent mode can block intrusion
attempts, you could accomplish the same goal—transparency or a bump in the wire—
by using inline mode, which has less configuration overhead. Using the threat defense
CLI, you can switch between routed mode and transparent mode. To learn more about
routed mode, read Chapter 4, "Firewall Deployment in Routed Mode."

Configuring a Network Analysis Policy

Let's begin the configurations. Here are the steps to create a new network analysis policy
from scratch:

Step 1.   Navigate to **Policies > Access Control > Intrusion**, and then select the
Network Analysis Policies tab.

Step 2.   Click the **Create Policy** button. The Create Network Analysis Policy configuration window appears (see Figure 15-16).

Step 3.   Select **Prevention** as the inspection mode.

Step 4.   Select **Balanced Security and Connectivity** as the base policy.

Step 5.   Click **Save**. After the policy is created, you then return to the Network Analysis
Policies tab.

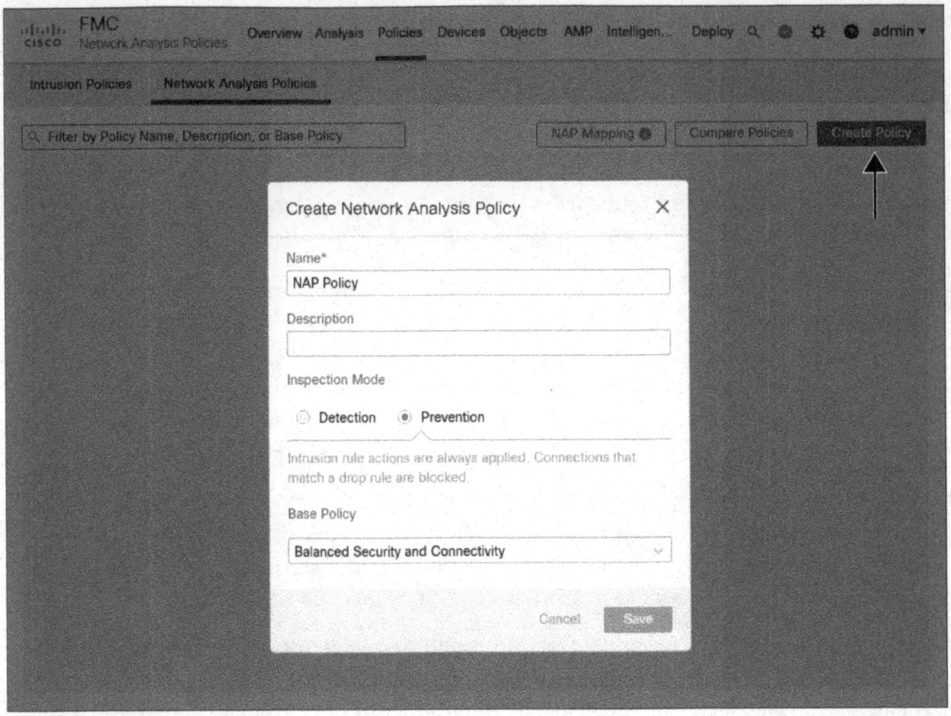

Figure 15-16 *Network Analysis Policy Configuration*

Secure Firewall enables you to customize the default settings of a network analysis policy. This flexibility enables you to implement any special requirements of your organization's cybersecurity policy. If you need to modify the default settings of the network analysis policy, read on to learn the process; otherwise, skip to the "Configuring an Intrusion Policy" section.

CAUTION A network analysis policy is an advanced feature. Misconfiguration of this policy can impact the traffic flow and system performance. Cisco recommends that only expert users should modify its settings when necessary.

On software version 7.0 or higher, you can choose either Snort 2 or Snort 3, as shown in Figure 15-17, to modify a network analysis policy. You do not need to customize the same policy using both Snort versions. However, this section demonstrates both policy editors for your comprehensive understanding.

Key Topic

There are plenty of options to customize in a network analysis policy. For training purposes, this section shows you how to enable the inspectors (in Snort 3) or preprocessors (in Snort 2) for protocols that are used in a supervisory control and data acquisition (SCADA) network. Some examples of SCADA networking protocols are Modbus, DNP3, CIP, and S7Commplus. Because these protocols are exclusively designed for industrial control system architecture, they are disabled by default.

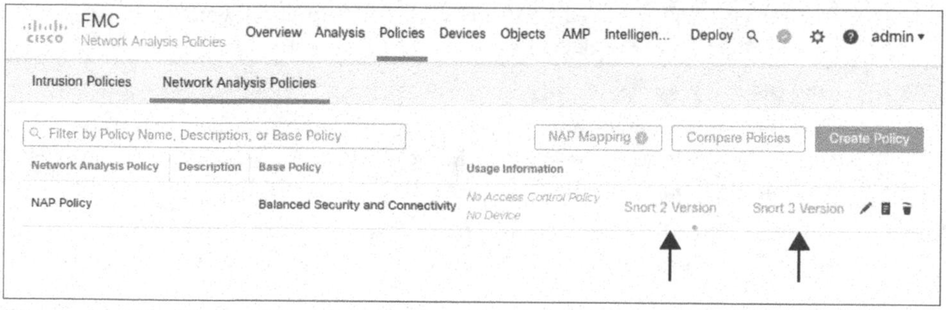

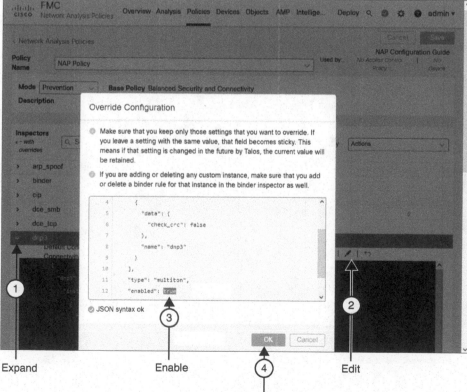

Figure 15-17   *Network Analysis Policy Can Be Customized with Both Snort 2 and Snort 3*

To enable them, select the desired Snort version for your network analysis policy. A warning message appears to remind you about the negative impact of any misconfigurations. Click Yes to continue.

If you selected Snort 3 Version, perform the following tasks in the network analysis policy editor (illustrated in Figure 15-18):

Step 1.   Find **dnp3** from the list of inspectors. Expand it to view the current settings.

Figure 15-18   *Network Analysis Policy Editor (Based on Snort 3)*

Step 2. Click the pencil icon to edit. The Override Configuration window opens. Here, you can customize the default settings of the inspector.

Step 3. Find the line with "enabled": and change its value from **false** to **true**.

Step 4. Click **OK** to save the custom settings. The GUI returns to the list of inspectors. Here, you can continue to enable other relevant SCADA inspectors, such as Modbus, CIP, and S7Commplus.

Step 5. Finally, click the **Save** button to save the changes, and then select **Network Analysis Policy** to return to the Network Analysis Policies tab (see Figure 15-19).

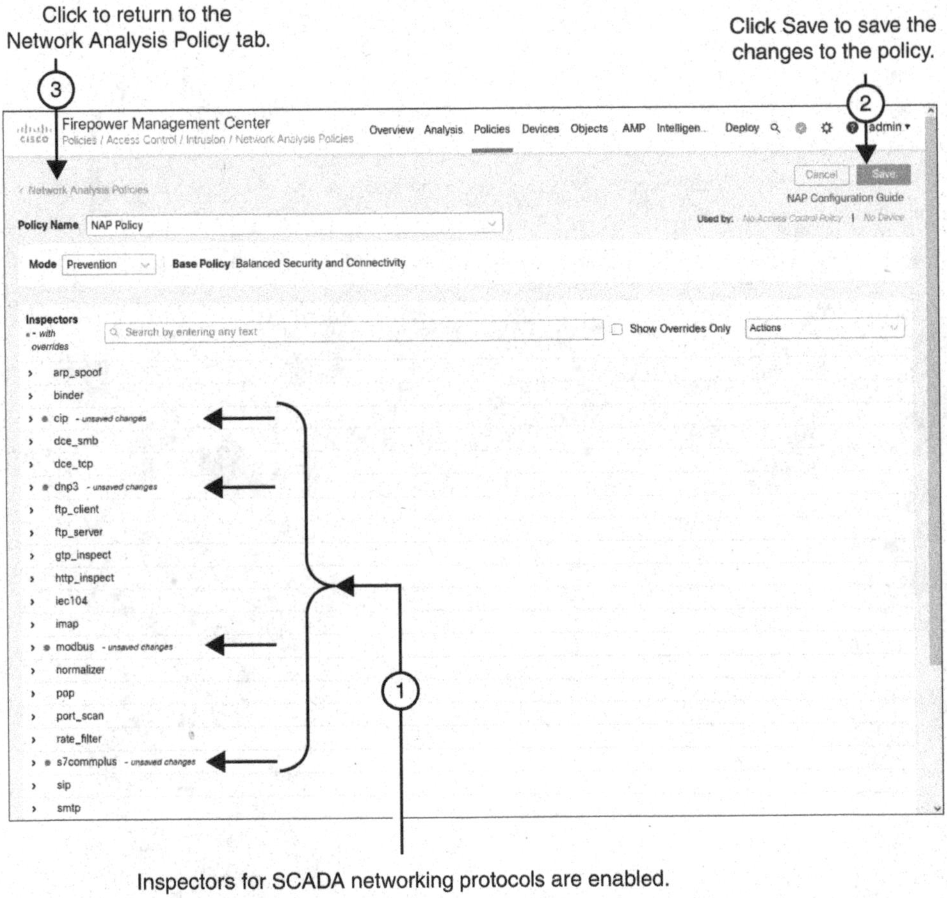

Figure 15-19 *Saving the Changes on a Network Analysis Policy Editor (Based on Snort 3)*

If you selected Snort 2 Version, perform the following tasks in the network analysis policy editor (see Figure 15-20):

Step 1. On the left panel, select **Settings**. On the Settings page, scroll down to find the SCADA Preprocessors section.

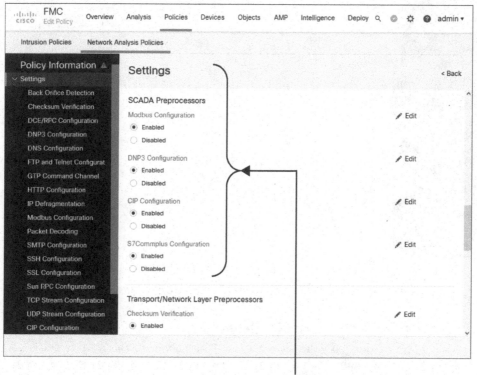

Preprocessors for SCADA Networking
Protocols Are Enabled

Figure 15-20 *Network Analysis Policy Editor (Based on Snort 2)*

Step 2. From the list of SCADA preprocessors, select **Enabled** for the protocols that are relevant to your network.

Step 3. After the desired preprocessors are selected, go to the Policy Information page from the left panel. Select the **Commit Changes** button to save the changes to the policy (see Figure 15-21) and to return to the Network Analysis Policies tab.

At this point, customizations are saved to the network analysis policy; however, they are not associated and applied to a threat defense. Before you do that, let's configure an intrusion policy in the next section.

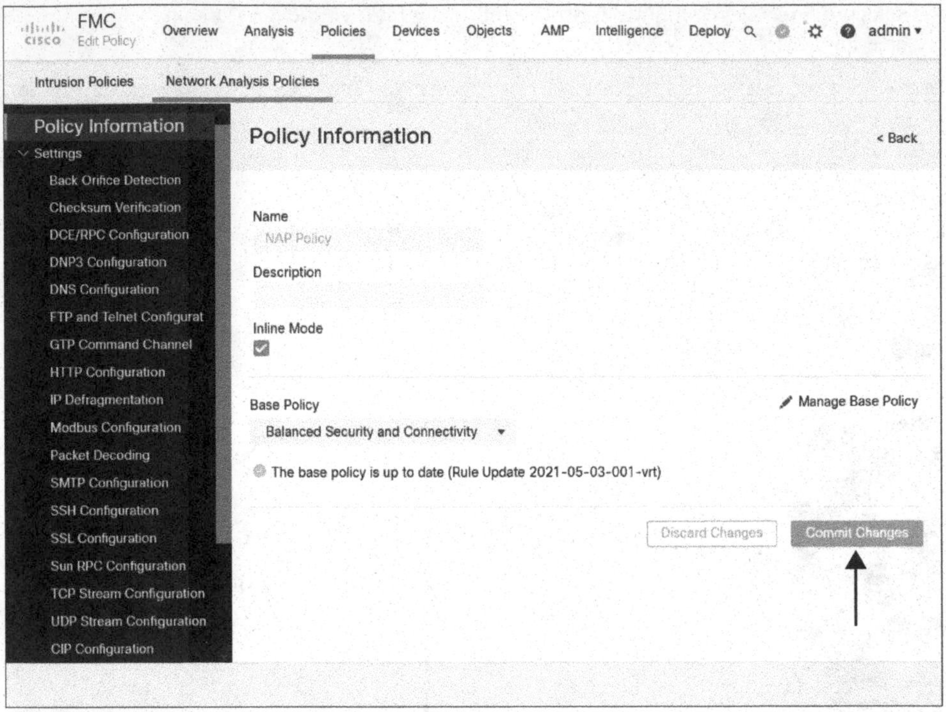

Figure 15-21 *Saving the Changes on a Network Analysis Policy (Based on Snort 2)*

Configuring an Intrusion Policy

Intrusion policy configuration is the key part of an IPS deployment. This is where you select an intrusion ruleset and define the rule actions. You can start with one of the system-provided base policies and build your own ruleset on top of it. An intrusion policy pairs with the variable sets that define the network environment. Variable sets are critical to the efficacy and performance. Speaking of performance, you can also take advantage of the system-generated intrusion rule recommendations feature to improve system performance. You learn all these key elements of the IPS functionality in the following sections.

Creating a Policy with a Default Ruleset

To create an intrusion policy, follow these steps:

Step 1. Navigate to **Policies > Access Control > Intrusion**, and select the **Intrusion Policies** tab. The intrusion policy configuration page appears.

Step 2. Click the **Create Policy** button. The Create Intrusion Policy window appears (see Figure 15-22).

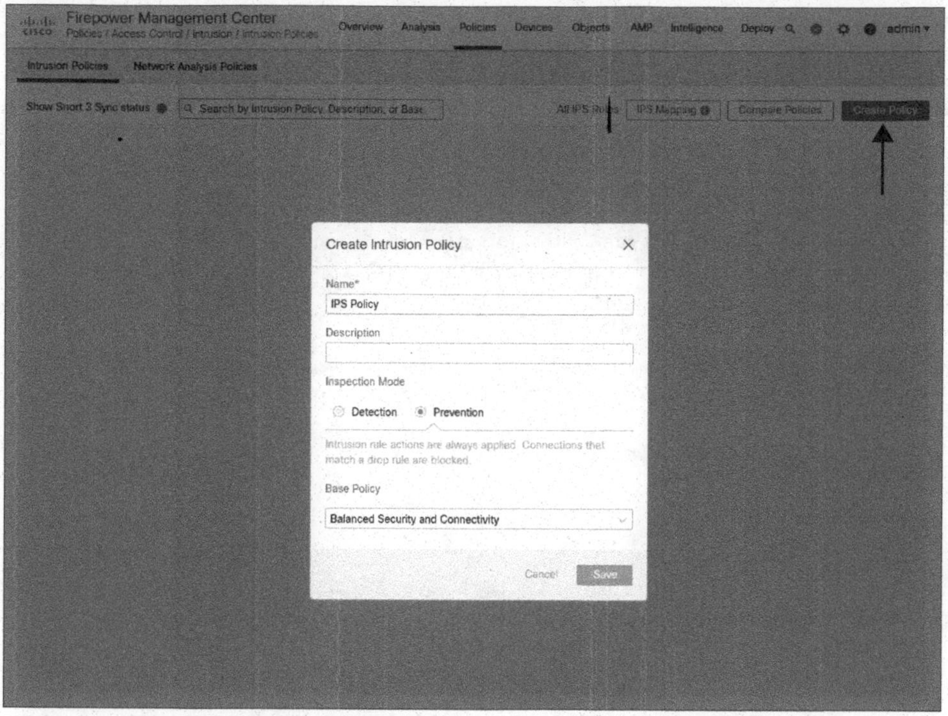

Figure 15-22 *Configuration Window to Create an Intrusion Policy*

Step 3. Name the policy.

Step 4. Select the **Prevention** inspection mode. Selecting this option can drop packets in inline, routed, or transparent mode. Enabling this option, however, does not affect the traffic flow if you configure the threat defense interfaces in inline tap or passive mode.

Step 5. Select **Balanced Security and Connectivity** as the base policy. This policy provides the best system performance without compromising the detection of the latest and critical vulnerabilities.

Step 6. Click the **Save** button to create an intrusion policy using the default settings. When this policy is created, you return to the Intrusion Policies tab.

Incorporating Intrusion Rule Recommendations

The intrusion rule recommendations feature is disabled, by default. However, you should leverage this feature to optimize the ruleset in your intrusion policy. It enables your Secure Firewall to analyze your network discovery data, correlates them with any associated vulnerabilities found in the Vulnerability Database, and then recommends intrusion rules that are relevant only to your network environment. The data is gathered as a result of the deployed network discovery policy, which enables Secure Firewall to identify the operating systems, services, and applications running in a network environment (Chapter 9, "Network Discovery Policy," describes this policy in detail).

CAUTION Generate and use intrusion rule recommendations *after* the majority of the hosts in your network are discovered. If you apply recommendations prematurely, Secure Firewall may recommend disabling many intrusion rules, which can result in diminishing protections against critical vulnerabilities.

To generate and use intrusion rule recommendations, edit the intrusion policy where you want to enable this feature. You can edit an intrusion policy using either Snort 2 or Snort 3 versions. Click your desired Snort version (see Figure 15-23). Depending on the Snort version you select, the intrusion policy editor looks different.

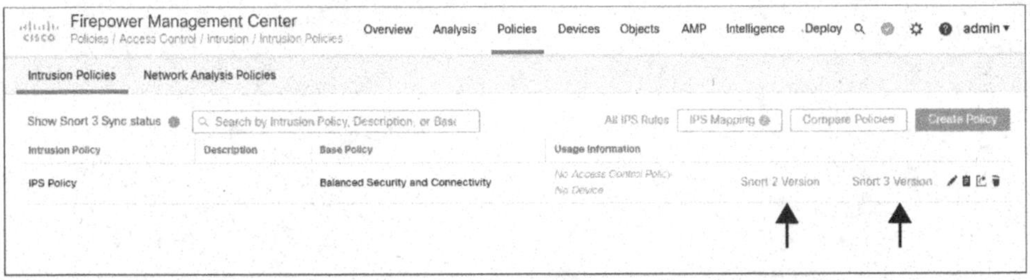

Figure 15-23 *Available Snort Versions to Edit an Intrusion Policy*

If you selected Snort 3 Version, perform the following tasks in the intrusion policy editor:

Step 1.   On the intrusion policy editor page, select the **Recommendations** button on the left panel. The Rule Recommendations window appears (see Figure 15-24).

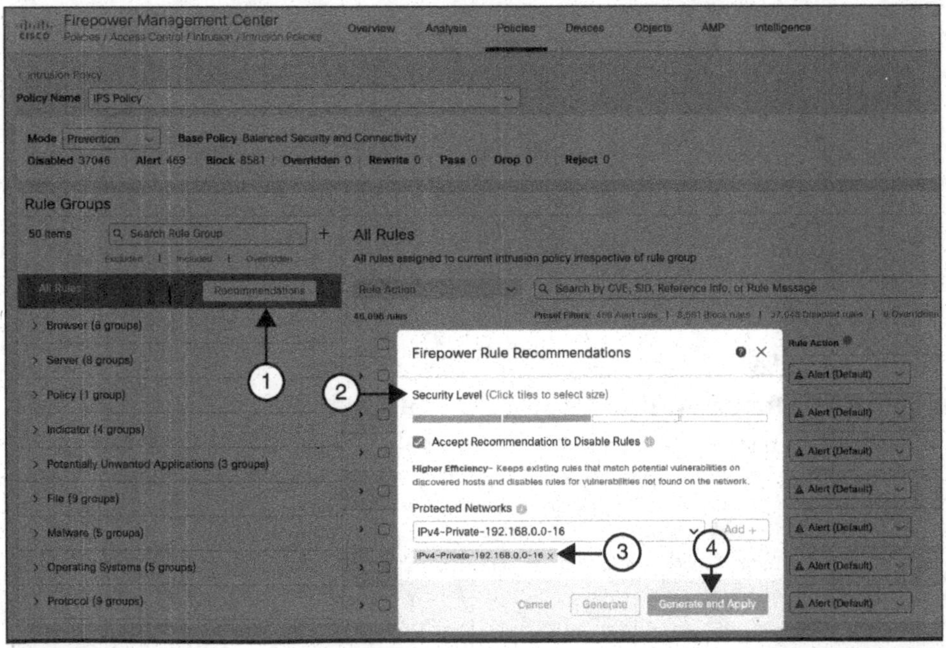

Figure 15-24 *Rule Recommendations Setup—Based on the Snort 3 Intrusion Policy Editor*

NOTE   Although this book primarily uses Secure Firewall software version 7.0 in its screenshots, only Figure 15-24 uses version 7.1 to capture the screenshot. We made this exception because the rule recommendations feature on the Snort 3 version of the intrusion policy is introduced in software version 7.1. To understand the difference, you can compare Figure 15-24 (captured using version 7.1) with Figure 15-26 (captured using version 7.0), and notice that the Recommendations button is missing in Figure 15-26. On software version 7.0, you can still use the rule recommendation feature using the Snort 2 version of the intrusion policy editor, as shown in Figure 15-25.

Step 2.   Select the desired **Security Level** and the **Protected Networks.** The number of recommended rules can substantially differ based on your selections for these two options. A higher security level and broader protected networks generate more recommendations.

Step 3.   Finally, select the **Generate and Apply** button to incorporate the rule recommendations into your intrusion policy.

If you selected Snort 2 Version, perform the following tasks in the intrusion policy editor:

Step 1.   On the intrusion policy editor page, select **Firepower Recommendations** on the left panel. The Firepower Recommended Rules Configuration page appears (see Figure 15-25).

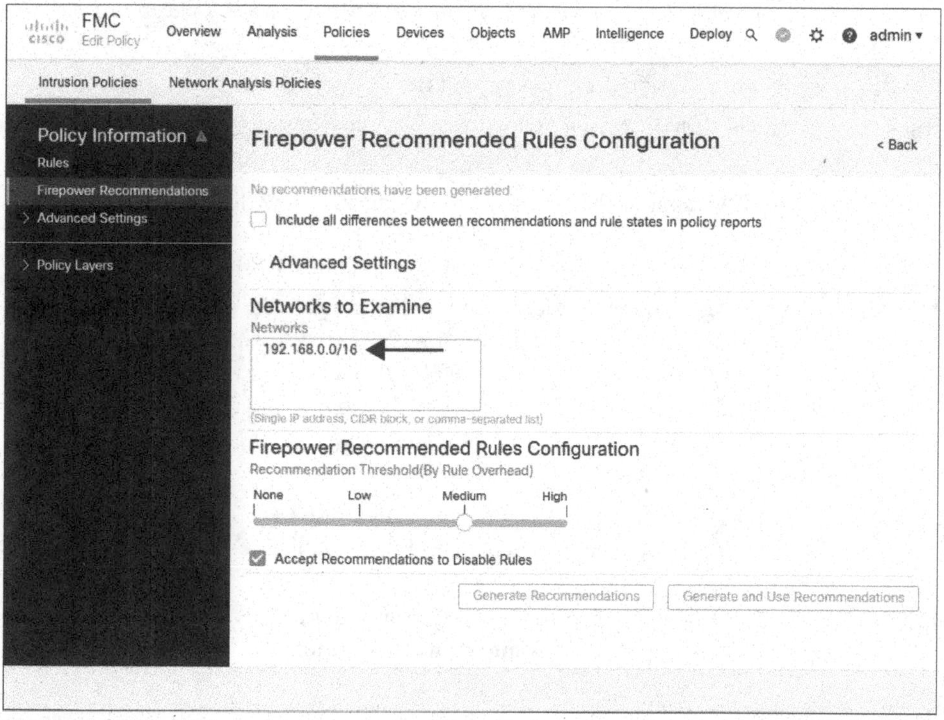

Figure 15-25   *Rule Recommendations Setup—Based on the Snort 2 Intrusion Policy Editor*

Step 2. In the Networks to Examine field, enter the internal networks that you want to protect with the intrusion policy. Optionally, you can set Recommendation Threshold (by Rule Overhead) to **Medium** so that the intrusion rules with higher processing overhead are not included in the recommended ruleset. Note that the number of recommended rules can substantially differ based on your selections for these two options.

Step 3. Click the **Generate and Use Recommendations** button to generate rule recommendations and incorporate them into the intrusion policy. If the recommendations were generated before, you would notice different types of buttons, such as Update Recommendations and Do Not Use Recommendations.

Step 4. Finally, go to the Policy Information page and make sure to save the changes by clicking the **Commit Changes** button.

Enabling or Disabling an Intrusion Rule

Secure Firewall is equipped with thousands of intrusion rules, but not all of them are enabled at the same time. You learned about it in the "System-Provided Base Policies" section. To enable or disable an additional Snort rule in an intrusion policy, edit the policy with your desired Snort version, and follow the steps shown here. For demonstration purposes, this exercise shows how to enable Snort rule 1:718 (SID:718) to drop packets.

If you selected Snort 3 Version of the intrusion policy editor, follow these steps:

Step 1. Enter the Snort rule ID (such as SID:718) to retrieve the desired rule directly from the database, as shown in Figure 15-26. Alternatively, you can use the left panel to find a rule from its relevant rule groups.

Step 2. Use the **Rule Action** drop-down to set the desired action.

Step 3. Finally, click the **Intrusion Policy** to save the changes to the policy.

If you selected Snort 2 Version of the intrusion policy editor, follow these steps:

Step 1. Select **Rules** in the left panel. This displays a glimpse of the available rules.

Step 2. Rules are organized in a variety of ways. You can use the category panel to find your desired rule, as shown in Figure 15-27. Alternatively, if you know the Snort rule ID, you can enter it directly in the Filter field.

Step 3. When you find the desired rule, select its check box and set the Rule State to **Drop and Generate Events**. It enables a Snort rule to block matching packets and to trigger an alert.

Figure 15-27 illustrates the steps to find a Telnet-specific rule using the Snort 2 version of the intrusion policy editor and then enable the rule to drop and generate events.

Step 4. Go to the Policy Information page. Make sure to save any changes to the intrusion policy by clicking the **Commit Changes** button.

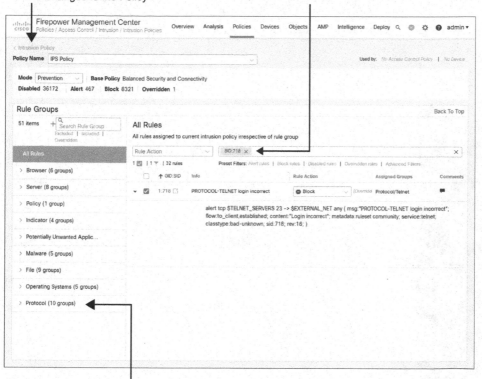

Click **Intrusion Policy** to Save
the Changes to the Policy

Option 1: Enter the Snort Rule ID

Option 2: Expand the Relevant Rule Groups to Find the Rule

Figure 15-26   *Enabling a Snort Rule on the Snort 3 Version of the Intrusion Policy Editor*

Setting Up a Variable Set

One of the important steps to enable intrusion prevention functionality is to associate the intrusion policy with a variable set that precisely reflects your network environment. Because Secure Firewall does not force an administrator to customize the values of the default variables, this essential step is often overlooked. At a minimum, you must define the $HOME_NET variable to include the network that you wish to protect with your intrusion policy.

Generally speaking, if a threat defense is deployed to inspect the northbound and southbound traffic, you may assume $EXTERNAL_NET=!$HOME_NET for that environment. However, if you deploy your threat defense to inspect eastbound and westbound traffic, you should define the variables precisely. If the default value of any server-specific variables are set to any or $HOME_NET, you must replace them with the original network addresses. Doing so makes a Snort rule more effective and reduces the probability of false positive alerts. Thus, a proper variable setting can improve overall system performance.

To add a new variable set and modify the default values, follow these steps:

Step 1. Navigate to **Objects > Object Management**.

Step 2. Select **Variable Set** from the menu on the left. The list of available variable sets appears.

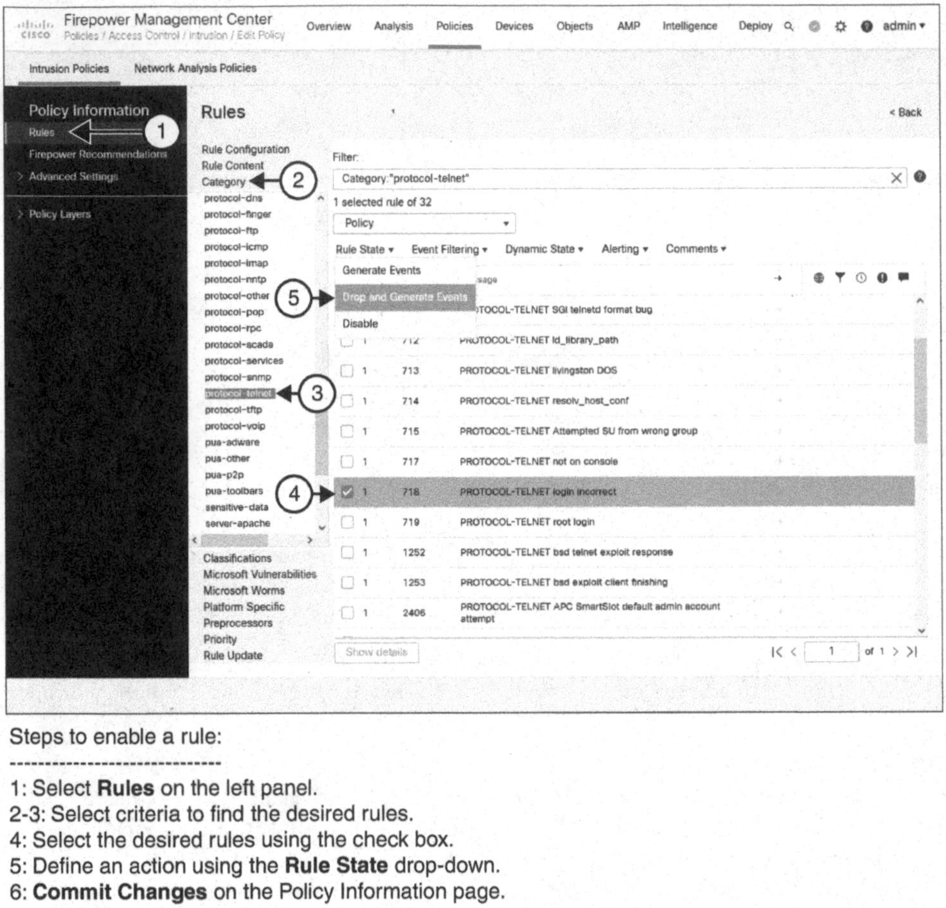

Steps to enable a rule:

1: Select **Rules** on the left panel.
2-3: Select criteria to find the desired rules.
4: Select the desired rules using the check box.
5: Define an action using the **Rule State** drop-down.
6: **Commit Changes** on the Policy Information page.

Figure 15-27 *Enabling a Snort Rule on the Snort 2 Version of the Intrusion Policy Editor*

Step 3. Here, you can edit an existing variable set or choose to create a new one. To create a new variable set, click the **Add Variable Set** button. The New Variable Set configuration window appears.

Step 4. Find the default variables that need to be updated. Use the pencil icon to modify their default values with predefined network objects. The management center also allows you to create a new network object on the fly. When the variables are customized, they are listed under the Customized Variables category, as shown in Figure 15-28.

Step 5. When the variable values are updated based on your own network environment, save the configurations.

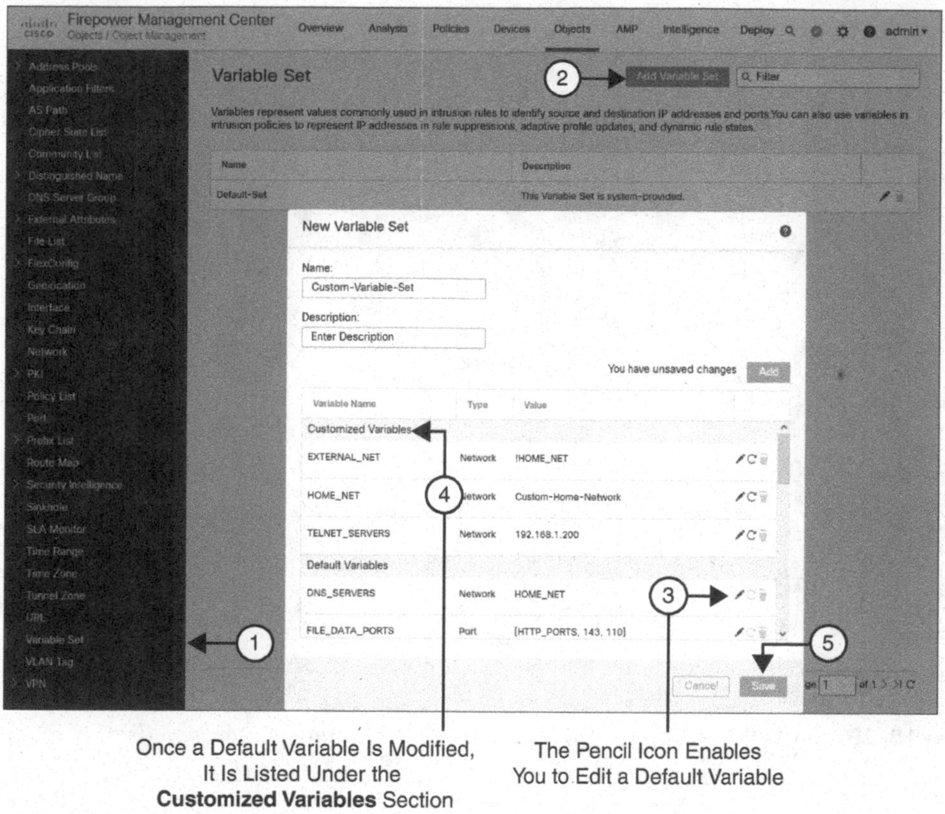

Figure 15-28 *Creating a Custom Variable Set*

Policy Deployment

So far, you have configured various parts of an intrusion detection and prevention system. They do not begin acting on live traffic until and unless you bring together all the policy components and deploy them on the threat defense. An access control policy acts as the central place for invoking all other security settings and policies, such as network analysis policies and intrusion policies. Let's work on an access control policy now.

Step 1.   Navigate to **Policies > Access Control > Access Control**. The available access control policies appear. You can modify one of the existing policies or click **New Policy** to create a new one.

Step 2.   When the access control policy editor opens, go to the Advanced tab. Modify the **Network Analysis and Intrusion Policies** section (see Figure 15-29). Here, you can select an intrusion policy that can process network traffic before an access control rule is determined for the traffic. You can also select a network analysis policy and a variable set to use by the intrusion policy.

Step 3.   For any traffic that does not match any access control rule, you can select a system-provided or custom intrusion policy as the default action, as shown in Figure 15-30.

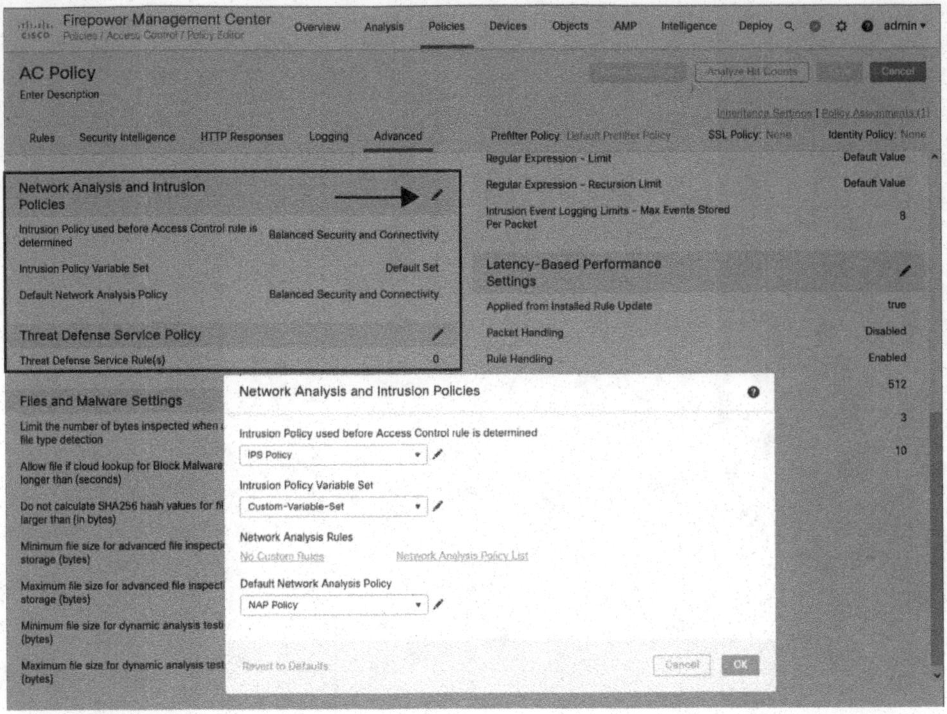

Figure 15-29 *Invoking Policies Before an Access Control Rule Is Determined*

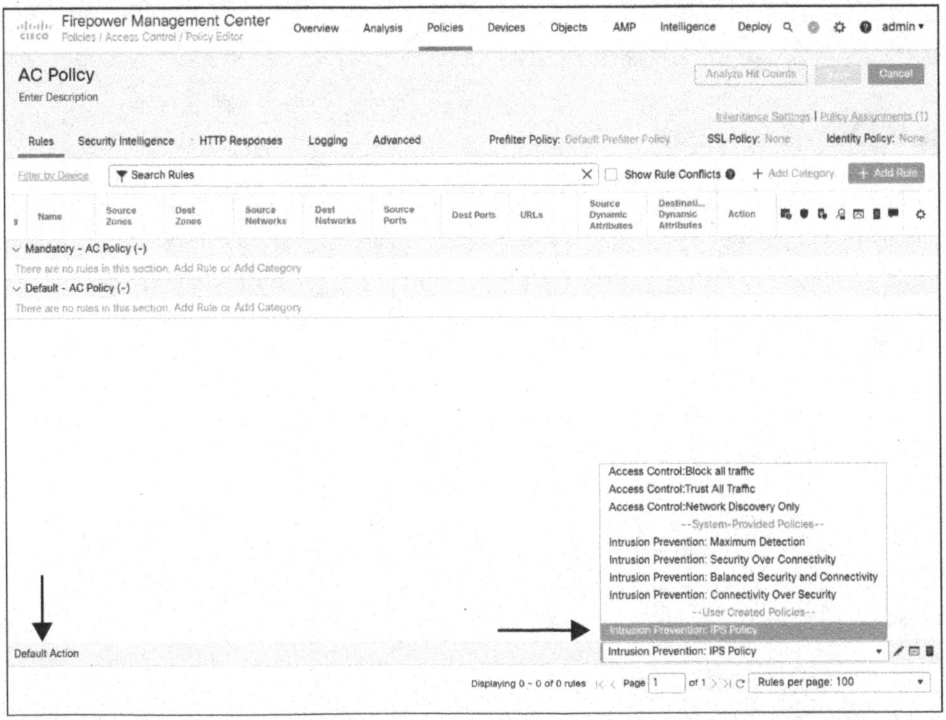

Figure 15-30 *Default Intrusion Policy for Traffic That Does Not Match Any Access Control Rules*

Step 4.   You can also set an inspection policy per access control rule. When you are adding or editing an access control rule, go to the **Inspection** tab and use the drop-down to select an intrusion policy and variable set for the matching traffic. Figure 15-31 shows the selection of an intrusion policy and a variable set within an access control rule. When a packet matches the condition of this access control rule, it is subject to the intrusion inspection based on this intrusion policy and variable set.

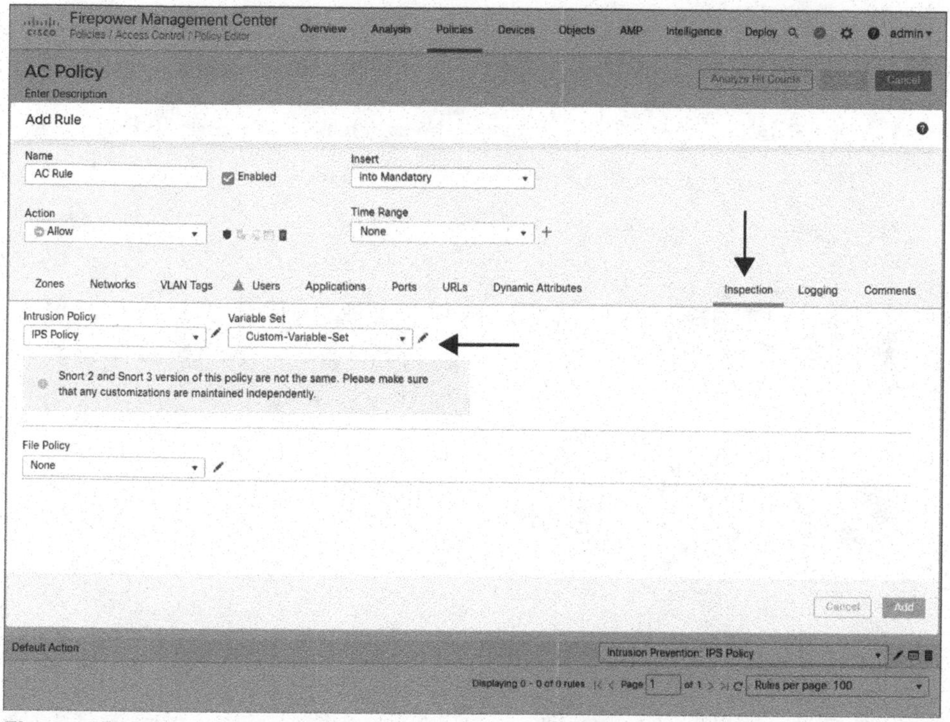

Figure 15-31   *Intrusion Policy for Traffic That Matches an Access Control Rule*

Step 5.   After you invoke all the desired policies in your access control policy, click the **Save** button to store the configurations locally.

Step 6.   Finally, go to **Deploy > Deployment** to deploy the policy to your threat defense.

Verification

To verify whether an intrusion policy is active, you can run traffic to and from hosts on either side of the threat defense. However, if the traffic does not carry a signature of any vulnerability, the threat defense does not trigger an intrusion alert for it. To verify the action of an intrusion policy, this chapter uses the simple Snort rule 1:718. Here is the rule syntax:

```
alert tcp $TELNET_SERVERS 23 -> $EXTERNAL_NET any (msg:"PROTOCOL-
TELNET login incorrect"; flow:to_client,established; content:"Login
incorrect"; metadata:ruleset community, service telnet;
classtype:bad-unknown; sid:718; rev:16; )
```

According to the syntax of this rule, when a Telnet server does not approve an authentication request (typically due to the user supplying incorrect login credentials) and responds to the client with a Login incorrect message (contained in the payload of the packet), the threat defense triggers the rule to prevent any potential brute-force attacks. Assuming the variable set is customized precisely, this rule analyzes Telnet traffic (port 23) destined to the $EXTERNAL_NET network. It should not evaluate any Telnet traffic destined to the $HOME_NET network.

Figure 15-32 shows the topology that is used in the lab exercises in this chapter. If you attempt to connect to your Telnet server from an external network host and enter valid login credentials, you will be able to access the server as usual. However, if you enter incorrect credentials, the server sends the Login incorrect message. Any subsequent connection attempts on that Telnet session are blocked by the threat defense; more specifically, they are blocked by Snort rule 1:718.

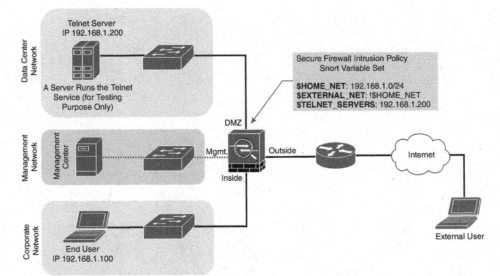

Figure 15-32 *Lab Topology Used in This Chapter*

Example 15-1 shows the messages on the CLI when you attempt to connect to a Telnet server running on a Linux-based system. Note the Login incorrect message when the login attempt is unsuccessful.

Example 15-1 *Telnet Server Connection Attempts*

```
! When a login attempt is unsuccessful

end-user@Linux:~$ telnet 192.168.1.200
Trying 192.168.1.200... Open
Connected to 192.168.1.200.

learner login: student
Password: <incorrect_password_is_entered>
```

```
Login incorrect
learner login:


| When a login attempt is successful

end-user@Linux:~$ telnet 192.168.1.200
Trying 192.168.1.200... Open
Connected to 192.168.1.200.


learner login: student
Password: ********

Welcome to Ubuntu 18.04.5 LTS (GNU/Linux 4.15.0-122-generic x86_64)
student@Server:~$
```

15

TIP   Some Telnet servers may return a different failure message, such as Login Failed. To detect this string, a different Snort rule, 1:492, is available.

Key Topic

Depending on the settings for rule action, interface mode, and inspection mode, the threat defense can act differently on the same Snort rule. The management center also indicates it with different types of events. For example, if the interface mode is set to inline mode, the inspection mode is set to Prevention, and the rule action is set to block packets, a threat defense drops any matching packets. However, if the inspection mode is set to Detection, or if the interface mode is set to inline tap or passive mode, the management center shows a "would have dropped" event.

When a connection is blocked by an intrusion rule, you can find the corresponding events on both the Connection Events page and Intrusion Events page. The Connection Events page distinguishes an intrusion attempt by displaying the Reason field of the associated connection event. You can view it by navigating to **Analysis > Connections > Events** (see Figure 15-33).

To find the intrusion events only, you can navigate to **Analysis > Intrusions > Events**. Figure 15-34 illustrates different types of intrusion events triggered by the same Snort rule 1:718.

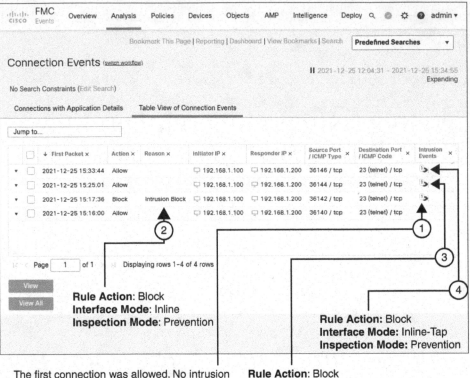

Figure 15-33   *Connection Events for Traffic Matching an Intrusion Rule*

The management center supports the download of a packet that triggered an intrusion event. The downloaded packet can be used for offline analysis on third-party software. By navigating to **Analysis > Intrusions > Events,** you can select the events that you want to download and click the Download Packets button to download them (see Figure 15-34). The packets are saved in .pcap file format, which is supported by most packet analyzer tools. Figure 15-35 displays packet data in the Wireshark packet analyzer tool. This packet is captured when you enter an incorrect credential to connect to a Telnet server. Snort rule 1:718 can detect the payload of this packet.

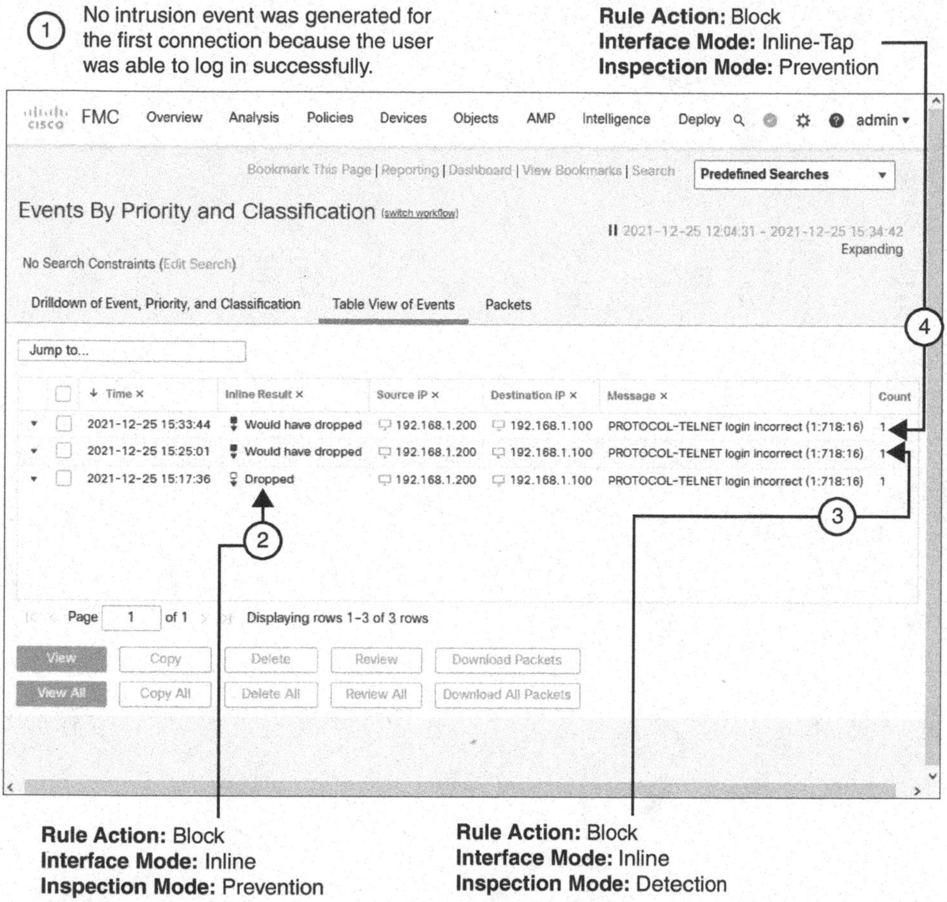

① No intrusion event was generated for the first connection because the user was able to log in successfully.

Rule Action: Block
Interface Mode: Inline-Tap
Inspection Mode: Prevention

Rule Action: Block
Interface Mode: Inline
Inspection Mode: Prevention

Rule Action: Block
Interface Mode: Inline
Inspection Mode: Detection

Figure 15-34 *Snort Rule 1:718 Generating Intrusion Events in Different Settings*

The Intrusion Events dashboard is also a great place to view a summary of all the intrusion activities by your threat defense. As you can see in Figure 15-36, you can use the built-in widgets and add custom widgets to monitor various critical data points of your intrusion detection and prevention system.

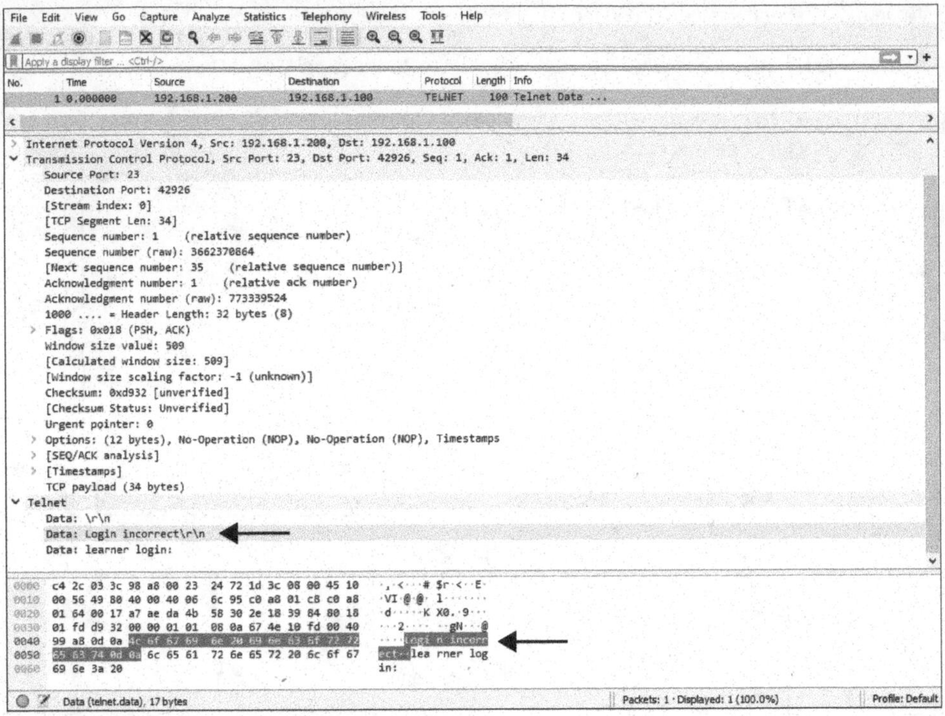

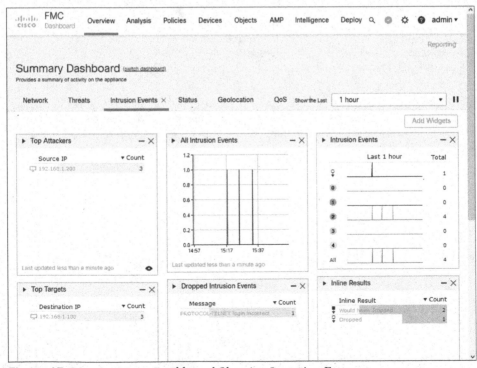

Figure 15-35   *Packet Analyzer Showing Detail Information About an Event and a Packet*

Figure 15-36   *Summary Dashboard Showing Intrusion Events*

Summary

This chapter describes one of the most important and widely used features of the Secure Firewall: the Snort-based intrusion prevention system. In this chapter, you learn how to configure a threat defense as a dedicated IPS, how to optimize an intrusion policy by incorporating system-generated intrusion rule recommendations, how to apply various policies in an access control policy, and how to drill down into intrusion events for advanced analysis.

Exam Preparation Tasks

As mentioned in the section "How to Use This Book" in the Introduction, you have a couple of choices for exam preparation: the exercises here, Chapter 22, "Final Preparation," and the exam simulation questions in the Pearson Test Prep practice test software.

Review All Key Topics

15

Review the most important topics in this chapter, noted with the Key Topic icon in the outer margin of the page. Table 15-5 lists a reference of these key topics and the page numbers on which each is found.

Key Topic

Table 15-5   Key Topics for Chapter 15

Key Topic Element	Description	Page
List	Types of Snort rules	346
Paragraph	Snort versions	348
Paragraph	Snort variables	352
List	Base policy	353
Paragraph	SCADA networking protocol	360
Paragraph	Rule recommendation	365
Paragraph	Would have dropped event	375

Complete Tables and Lists from Memory

Print a copy of Appendix C, "Memory Tables" (found on the companion website), or at least the section for this chapter, and complete the tables and lists from memory. Appendix D, "Memory Tables Answer Key," also on the companion website, includes completed tables and lists to check your work.

Define Key Terms

Define the following key terms from this chapter, and check your answers in the Glossary:

Balanced Security and Connectivity policy, system-provided variable, shared object (SO) rules, preprocessor rules, local rules

## CHAPTER 16

Malware and File Policy

This chapter provides an overview of the following topics:

File Policy Essentials: This section describes two major features of a file policy: detecting file types and analyzing malicious files.

Best Practices for File Policy Configuration: This section provides some tips to configure and deploy a file policy on Secure Firewall.

Fulfilling Prerequisites: This section explains various requirements for enabling and updating the malware detection capability on Secure Firewall.

Configuring a File Policy: This section walks you through the steps to create a file policy and to deploy the policy to your threat defense.

Verification: In this section, you learn how to analyze file events and malware events using the Secure Firewall GUI and CLI.

The objectives of this chapter are to learn about

- Architecture of Cisco Secure Firewall's malware defense technology (also known as advanced malware protection or AMP)

- Implementing malware defense on Secure Firewall

- Configuration of the malware and file policy

- Verification of malware and file policy operation

- Analysis of file events using event viewer and dashboard

As a security professional, you might not want your users to download and open random files from the Internet. Although you allow your users to visit most websites, you might want to block their attempts to download malicious files from the sites they visit or to upload internal files to external websites. Unsafe downloads can spread viruses, malware, exploit kits, and other dangers on your network, and they can make the entire network vulnerable to various types of attacks. Likewise, to comply with your organization's policies, you might not want your users to upload any particular types of files to the Internet from your corporate network. Secure Firewall enables you to block the download and upload of files based on file type (.png, .pdf, .exe, and others) and file disposition (malware).

"Do I Know This Already?" Quiz

The "Do I Know This Already?" quiz enables you to assess whether you should read this entire chapter thoroughly or jump to the "Exam Preparation Tasks" section. If you are in doubt about your answers to these questions or your own assessment of your knowledge of the topics, read the entire chapter. Table 16-1 lists the major headings in this chapter and their corresponding "Do I Know This Already?" quiz questions. You can find the answers in Appendix A, "Answers to the 'Do I Know This Already?' Quizzes."

Table 16-1 Do I Know This Already?" Section-to-Question Mapping

Foundation Topics Section	Questions
File Policy Essentials	1
Best Practices for File Policy Configuration	2
Fulfilling Prerequisites	3
Configuring a File Policy	4
Verification	5

CAUTION The goal of self-assessment is to gauge your mastery of the topics in this chapter. If you do not know the answer to a question or are only partially sure of the answer, you should mark that question as wrong for purposes of the self-assessment. Giving yourself credit for an answer you correctly guess skews your self-assessment results and might provide you with a false sense of security.

1. Which type of analysis requires an external connection from a management center?
   a. Local
   b. Dynamic
   c. High-fidelity
   d. All of these answers are correct.

2. Which of the following is recommended when enabling a file policy?
   a. Use the Reset Connection option on a file rule to block a file.
   b. Avoid storing clean files using a file rule.
   c. Keep the captured file size lower for optimal performance.
   d. All of these answers are correct.

3. Which of the following does not require a malware license?
   a. Sending a file to the cloud for dynamic analysis
   b. Enabling a local analysis engine
   c. Performing a cloud lookup without blocking a file
   d. Blocking a file transfer based on its file format

4. Which of the following statements is incorrect in a file policy operation?
   a. A threat defense can interrupt traffic flow if a cloud lookup fails or takes a long time.
   b. A file policy uses the adaptive profile feature.
   c. The management center sends a query to the cloud to detect the file type.
   d. The management center connects to the cloud to obtain new signatures for malware.

5. Which of the following is not a valid malware disposition?

    a. Malware

    b. Clean

    c. Unknown

    d. Virus

Foundation Topics

File Policy Essentials

To monitor and control network-based file transfers, Secure Firewall offers a standalone policy known as a *file policy*. A file policy enables you to detect any file type, such as media files (.mp3, .mpeg) and executable files (.exe, .rpm). In addition, a threat defense can analyze a file for potential malware when the file traverses a network. By design, a threat defense can detect and block files based on their type before it performs lookups for malware.

Figure 16-1 shows the architectural diagram of the Secure Firewall engines. The figure highlights both components of a file policy—file type control and malware analysis—which are described in the following sections.

File Type Detection

Secure Firewall uses the *file magic numbers* to identify the file format. The file magic numbers are a sequence of unique hex characters that are encoded in file headers. When a file traverses a network, a threat defense can match the file magic numbers from the stream of packets to determine the file format. For example, for a Microsoft executable (MSEXE) file, the file magic number is 4D 5A, and it is located at the beginning of the file. To find this number, Snort uses the following rule on the threat defense:

```
file type:MSEXE; id:21; category:Executables,Dynamic Analysis
Capable,Local Malware Analysis Capable; msg:"Windows/DOS
executable file "; rev:1; content: | 4D 5A|; offset:0;
```

Figure 16-2 demonstrates the magic number on a TCP packet. This packet is captured when a client downloads an executable file from a website. After completing the TCP three-way handshake, the server sends this information to the client.

Malware Analysis

To protect a network from the latest malware, Cisco Secure Firewall is empowered with the malware defense technology (also known as advanced malware protection or AMP). This technology enables a threat defense to analyze a file for potential malware and viruses while the file traverses a network. To expedite the analysis process and to conserve resources, the threat defense can perform both local and dynamic analysis. Let's take a look at the technologies behind them.

Figure 16-3 illustrates the purposes of any interactions between Secure Firewall and the Cisco clouds.

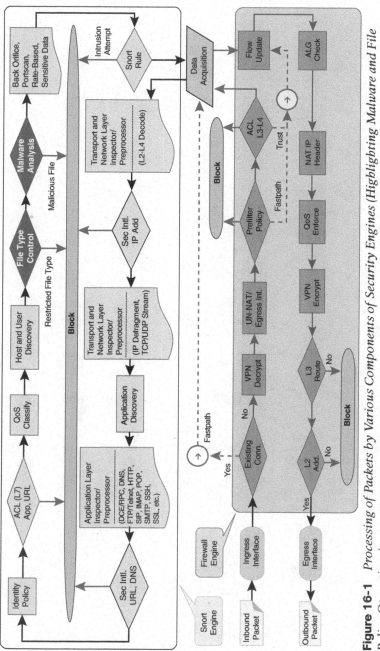

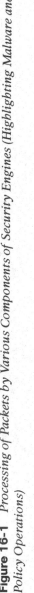

Figure 16-1 *Processing of Packets by Various Components of Security Engines (Highlighting Malware and File Policy Operations)*

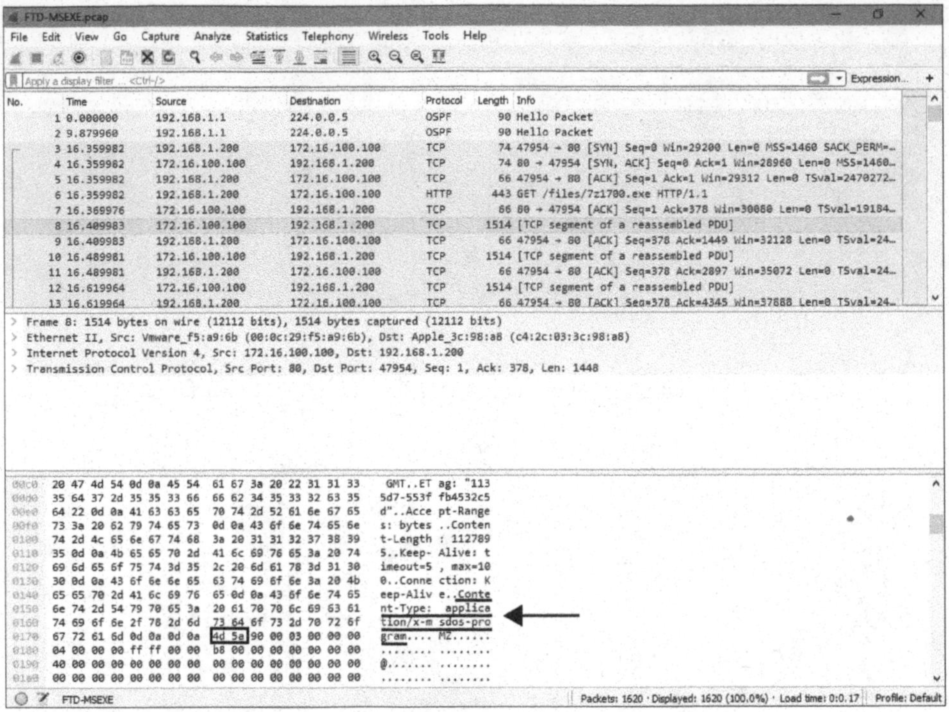

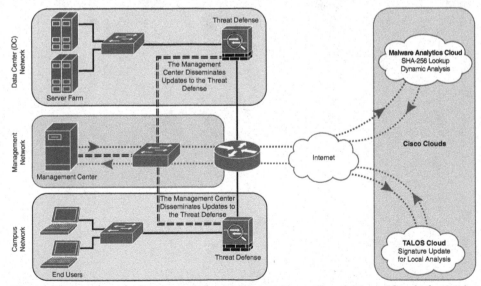

Figure 16-2 *Retrieving the Magic Number from the Stream of Packets*

Figure 16-3 *Communications Between Secure Firewall and Cisco Clouds for Malware Analysis*

The threat defense calculates the SHA-256 hash value (Secure Hash Algorithm with 256 bits) of a file and uses the value to determine a file's **disposition** (malware, clean, unknown, unavailable). The management center caches previous cloud lookups and begins the process of disposition checking by performing a lookup in its local cache before it sends a new query to the malware analytics cloud (also known as AMP cloud). It provides a faster lookup result and improves overall performance. Depending on the action you select in a file policy, Secure Firewall can perform additional advanced analysis in the following order:

- **Spero analysis:** The Spero analysis engine examines MSEXE files only. It analyzes the structural metadata and header of an MSEXE file and submits them in the form of a Spero signature to the malware analytics cloud. You can configure a file policy to perform Spero analysis locally without submitting any information to the malware analytics cloud.

- **Local analysis:** The local analysis engine enables a threat defense to inspect files locally. It uses rules provided by the Cisco Talos threat intelligence group to detect the most common types of malware. Since the analysis is performed locally in the system without sending the query to the malware analytics cloud, the local analysis engine can help save time and resources.

  A threat defense uses two types of rulesets for local analysis: high-fidelity rules and pre-classification rules. The management center downloads high-fidelity malware signatures from Talos and disseminates the rulesets to its managed threat defense devices. The threat defense matches the patterns and analyzes files for known malware. It also uses the file pre-classification filters to optimize resource utilization.

- **Dynamic analysis:** The dynamic analysis feature submits a captured file to the Cisco malware analytics sandbox for dynamic analysis. Sandboxing can be performed either in the cloud or by way of an on-premises appliance on the local network. Upon analysis, the sandbox returns a threat score, which is a scoring system for determining whether a file should be considered malicious. The file policy allows you to adjust the threshold level of the dynamic analysis threat score. Thus, you can define when a threat defense should treat a file as potential malware.

  Dynamic analysis provides an option called *capacity handling* that allows Secure Firewall to store a file temporarily if the system fails to submit the file to a sandbox environment. Some of the potential reasons for such a failure include communication issues between Secure Firewall and the sandbox (cloud or on-premises) or exceeding the daily file submission limit.

Figure 16-4 shows an architectural workflow of the malware analysis techniques on Secure Firewall.

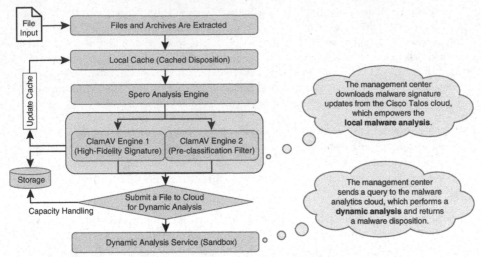

Figure 16-4 *Architecture of the Malware Defense Technology*

Best Practices for File Policy Configuration

You should consider the following best practices when you configure a file policy:

- When you want to block a file by using a file policy, use the Reset Connection option. It enables the application sessions to close before the connection times out by itself.

- You can use a threat defense to capture and store files that are detected by the threat defense. Avoid storing clean files because they can quickly fill up the storage. Store the files only when an offline forensic analysis is needed. If your incident response team wants to download a captured file from Secure Firewall to a local computer for advanced forensic analysis, take an extra precaution before the download. When a file is blocked and captured by a threat defense for its malicious activities, it indicates that the file might be infected with malware. To store a higher volume of files, Cisco offers a malware storage pack as an add-on.

- You can limit the size of files to capture. Keeping the file size limit lower is critical for optimal performance. The file size limit can be set in the access control policy advanced settings page. File size limits can impact the following activities:

  - Sending files to the cloud for dynamic analysis

  - Storing files locally

  - Calculating the SHA-256 hash value of files

- In case of any communication issues between Secure Firewall and the Cisco cloud, the threat defense can hold the transfer of a file for a short period of time when the file matches a rule with the Block Malware action. Although this holding period is configurable, Cisco recommends that you use the default value of two seconds to mitigate latency due to long file disposition lookups.

Figure 16-5 displays the advanced settings of an access control policy where you can define the file holding period and file size limits.

Figure 16-5 displays FMC Policy Editor interface showing:

AC Policy — Enter Description

Tabs: Rules | Security Intelligence | HTTP Responses | Logging | Advanced | Prefilter Policy: Default Prefilter Policy | SSL Policy: None | Identity ...

| Intrusion Policy Variable Set | Default Set |
| Default Network Analysis Policy | Balanced Security and Connectivity |

Threat Defense Service Policy

| Threat Defense Service Rule(s) | 0 |

Files and Malware Settings

Limit the number of bytes inspected when doing file type detection	1460
Allow file if cloud lookup for Block Malware takes longer than (seconds)	2
Do not calculate SHA256 hash values for files larger than (in bytes)	10485760
Minimum file size for advanced file inspection and storage (bytes)	6144
Maximum file size for advanced file inspection and storage (bytes)	1048576
Minimum file size for dynamic analysis testing (bytes)	6144

Latency-Based Performance Settings

Applied from Installed Rule Update	true
Packet Handling	Disabled
Rule Handling	Enabled
Rule Handling – Threshold (microseconds)	512
Rule Handling – Consecutive Threshold Violations Before Suspending Rule	3
Rule Handling – Suspension Time (seconds)	10

File Size Limits   File Holding Period

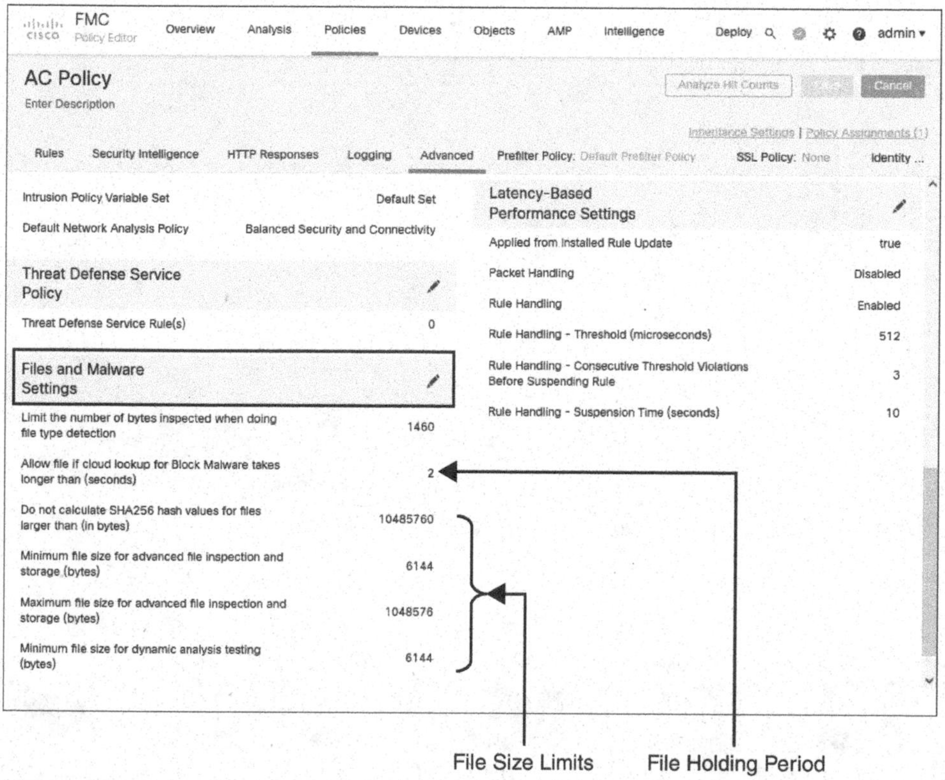

Figure 16-5 *Configuration of the File Holding Period and File Size Limits*

Fulfilling Prerequisites

The following items are necessary for a successful file policy deployment:

- Make sure to install the appropriate licenses. With the installation of a threat license, a threat defense can control the transfer of files based on their types. In other words, if you are currently using the security intelligence and intrusion prevention features on your threat defense, you can control the file transfer based on file type without installing any additional licenses. However, to perform a malware analysis, the threat defense requires a malware license.

    Figure 16-6 shows the actions and features you can enable by using the threat and malware licenses.

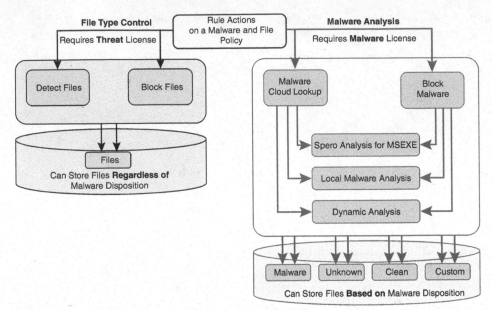

Figure 16-6 *Actions on a File Rule and Their Necessary Licenses*

Table 16-2 summarizes the differences between the capabilities of a threat license and a malware license.

Table 16-2 Differences Between a Threat License and a Malware License

When Only a Threat License Is Applied...	When a Malware License Is Also Applied...
A threat defense can block a file based on its file type.	A threat defense can block a file based on its malware disposition.
A threat defense utilizes the file's magic numbers to determine the file type.	A threat defense matches malware signatures to perform local malware analysis.
A threat defense does not require a connection to the cloud for file type detection.	A threat defense needs to connect to the cloud for various purposes—for example, to update the signature of the latest malware, to send a file to the cloud to perform dynamic file analysis, and to perform an SHA-256 lookup.
You can apply only two rule actions: Detect Files and Block Files.	You can apply any rule actions available, including Malware Cloud Lookup and Block Malware.

In short, to control the transfer of files based on file type, you need only a threat license. To perform malware analysis, you need a malware license in addition to the threat license.

■ A file policy uses the adaptive profiles feature. Make sure the feature is enabled in the advanced settings of the access control policy (see Figure 16-7).

■ Make sure the Enable Automatic Local Malware Detection Updates option is checked (see Figure 16-8). It enables the management center to communicate with the Talos cloud every 30 minutes for updates. When a new ruleset is available, the management center downloads it to enrich the local malware analysis engine.

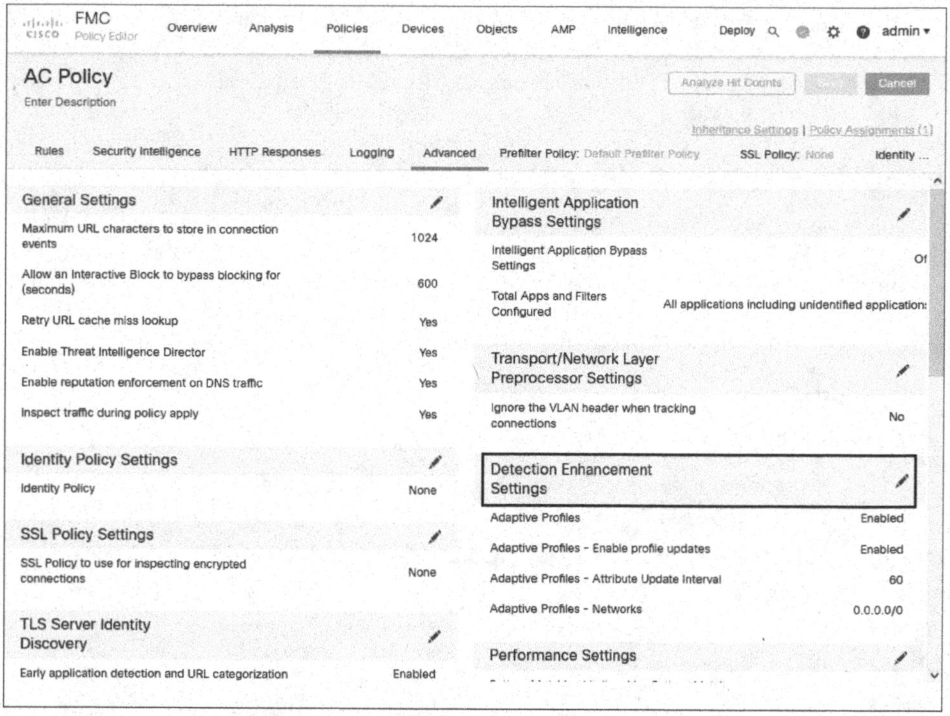

Figure 16-7 *Option to Enable Adaptive Profile Updates*

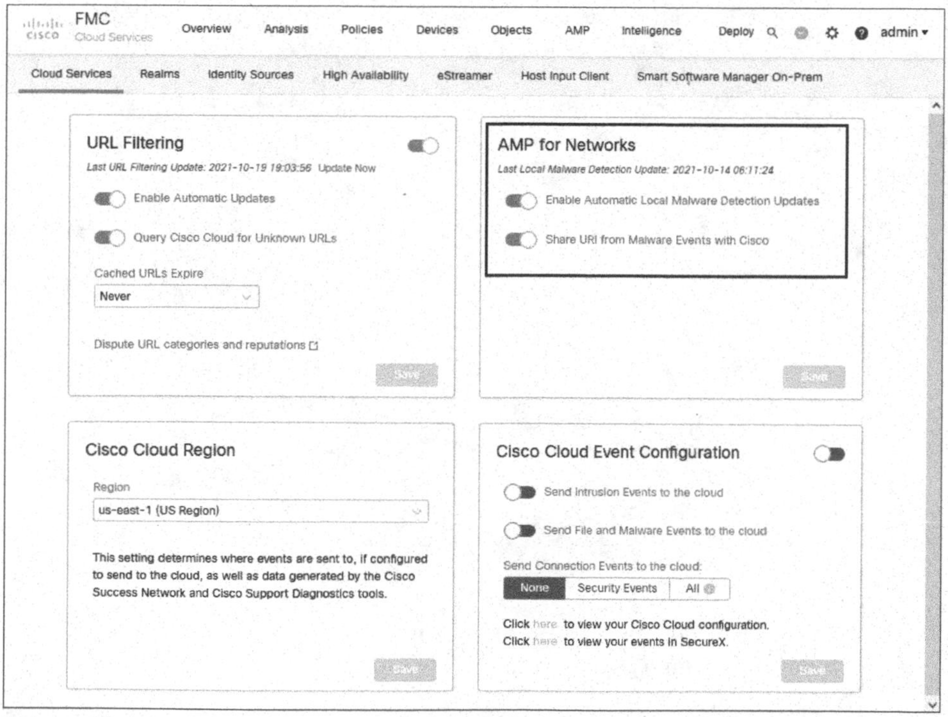

Figure 16-8 *Option to Enable the Automatic Local Malware Detection Updates*

■ A file policy leverages application detection functionality to determine whether an application is capable of transmitting a file. Make sure your network discovery policy is deployed and configured to discover applications. To learn about application detection and control, read Chapter 9, "Network Discovery Policy."

Configuring a File Policy

Deploying a file policy is a multistep process. First, you need to create a file policy and add file rules to it. A file rule allows you to select the file type category, application protocol, direction of transfer, and action. However, you cannot add any source or destination details in a file rule. To assign source and destination IP addresses, create an access control rule in your access control policy and invoke the file policy within the access control rule.

Creating a File Policy

To create a file policy, follow these steps:

Step 1. Navigate to **Policies > Access Control > Malware & File**. The Malware & File Policy page appears.

Step 2. Click the **New File Policy** button, and the New File Policy window appears (see Figure 16-9).

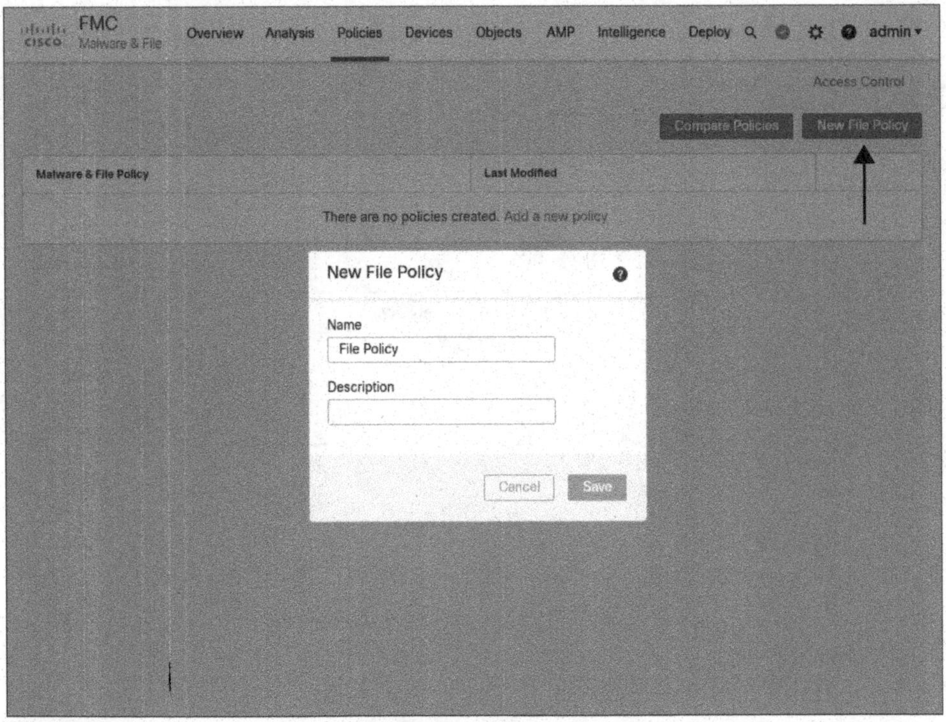

Figure 16-9 *Creating a New File Policy*

Step 3. Name the policy and click the **Save** button. The file policy editor appears.

Step 4. Click the **Add Rule** button. The file rule editor appears.

Step 5. Select **Any** from the Application Protocol drop-down to detect files over multiple application protocols.

Step 6. Make a selection from the Direction of Transfer drop-down. Depending on the underlying application protocol for a file transfer, the direction can be limited. For example, the HTTP, FTP, and NetBIOS-ssn (SMB) protocols can be monitored for file transfers in any direction—upload or download. However, SMTP (upload only) and POP3/IMAP (download) support only unidirectional file transfers.

Figure 16-10 explains the reasons for unidirectional transfer with the SMTP, POP3, and IMAP protocols. Whereas SMTP is used for outbound transfers, POP3/IMAP is used to download incoming emails and any attachments.

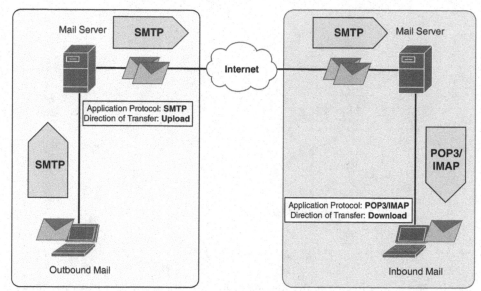

Figure 16-10 *Directions of Protocols Associated with Inbound and Outbound Emails*

Step 7. Select the file type categories you want to process and click **Add** to add them to the rule. You can also search for specific file types directly in the search field.

Step 8. Select an action from the Action drop-down. You will find four options in the drop-down:

- **Detect Files:** This action detects a file transfer and logs it as a file event without interrupting the transfer.

- **Block Files:** This action blocks files—based on the file types selected in the rule.

- When blocking a file, optionally you can select the Reset Connection option. It allows the blocked application session to close before the connection times out by itself, which may take several minutes depending on the application.

■ Figure 16-11 displays a file rule that blocks the transfer of any system and executable files without analyzing them for malware. According to the configuration, when a file matches this rule, a threat defense sends reset packets to terminate any associated connection.

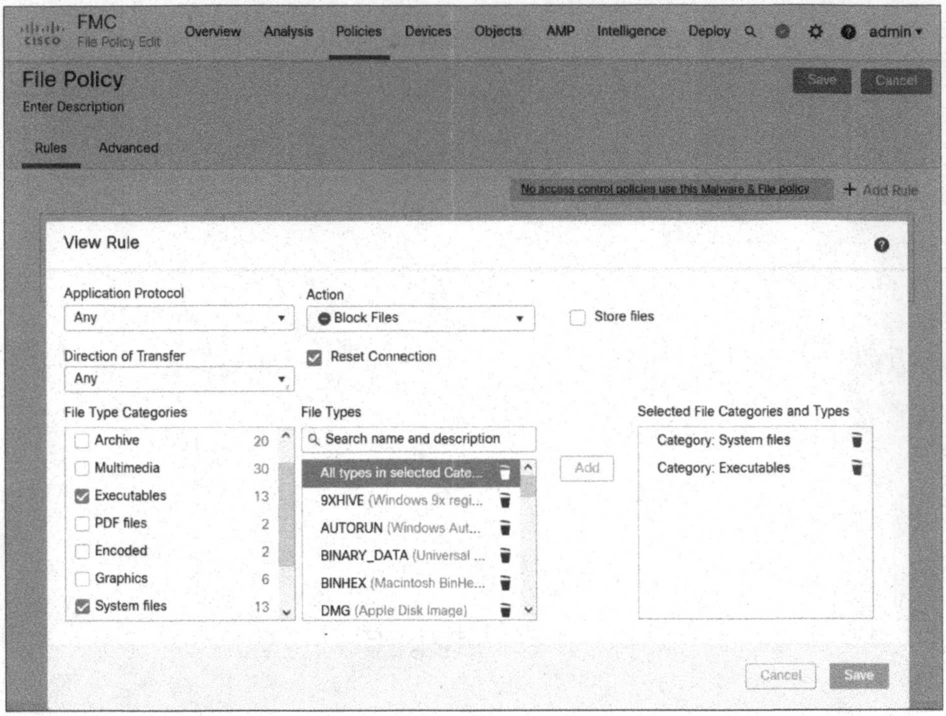

Figure 16-11 *A File Rule with the Block Files Action*

■ Figure 16-12 displays a file rule that can detect the transfer of Office documents, archive, and PDF files. This rule is not set to analyze any files for malware; however, when there is a match, it lets the threat defense store the detected files in its local storage.

■ **Malware Cloud Lookup:** This action enables a threat defense to perform malware analysis locally and remotely. The threat defense allows an uninterrupted file transfer regardless of the file's disposition.

■ **Block Malware:** This action is similar to the Malware Cloud Lookup action, but it enables the threat defense to block files that return a disposition of malware.

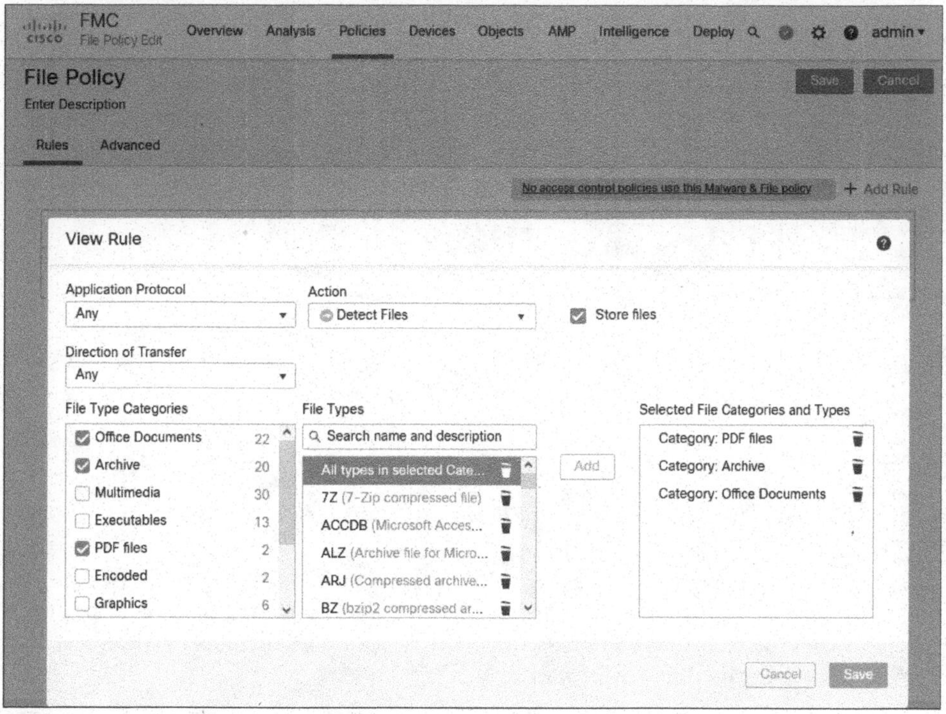

Figure 16-12 *Detection-Only File Rule*

In a nutshell, the first two options—Detect Files and Block Files—allow you to control files based on their types. The last two options—Malware Cloud Lookup and Block Malware—enable you to control files based on file disposition, and the use of these options requires the malware license.

A file policy does not evaluate file rules based on its position; rather, it uses the order of actions. The order of actions is Block Files, Block Malware, Malware Cloud Lookup, and Detect Files. When performing advanced analysis, a threat defense can engage Spero analysis, local malware analysis, and dynamic analysis. You can enable these detection features by selecting the check box for each in the rule editor.

Step 9. After you add rules with the desired conditions and options, click the **Save** button in the Add Rule window. The browser returns to the Malware and File Policy editor page.

Figure 16-13 shows the creation of two file rules. The first rule blocks system and executable files with connection reset enabled. The second rule can detect only archive file types, Office documents, and PDF files. Files that match this rule are also stored.

The New Malware & File Policy is
Not Used by Any Access Control Policy Yet

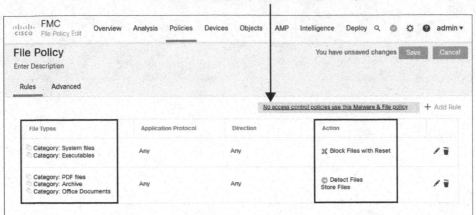

Figure 16-13 *Two File Rules for Different File Types Applying Different Actions*

The previous two file rules are able to detect and block files solely based on their file types. Those files may or may not contain malware. However, if you want to detect and block those files only when the files contain malware, you can select the **Block Malware** action.

Figure 16-14 shows an alternative—but intelligent—way to block files. This particular rule (which requires a malware license) enables a threat defense to block the transfer of a file and to store it locally if the file is infected with malware. When blocking the file transfer, the threat defense sends reset packets to terminate any associated connection. This rule does not allow a threat defense to store a file if the file appears to be clean. This prevents storage from getting full of clean or benign files.

Step 10. Optionally, on the Advanced tab, you can enable additional features for advanced analysis and inspection. Figure 16-15 shows the advanced settings of the file policy. For example, here you can adjust the threshold level of the dynamic analysis threat score for blocking files based on threat score, enable inspection of archive file types, define the depth of inspection for nested archive files, and so on.

Step 11. Click the **Save** button on the policy editor to save the changes on the file policy.

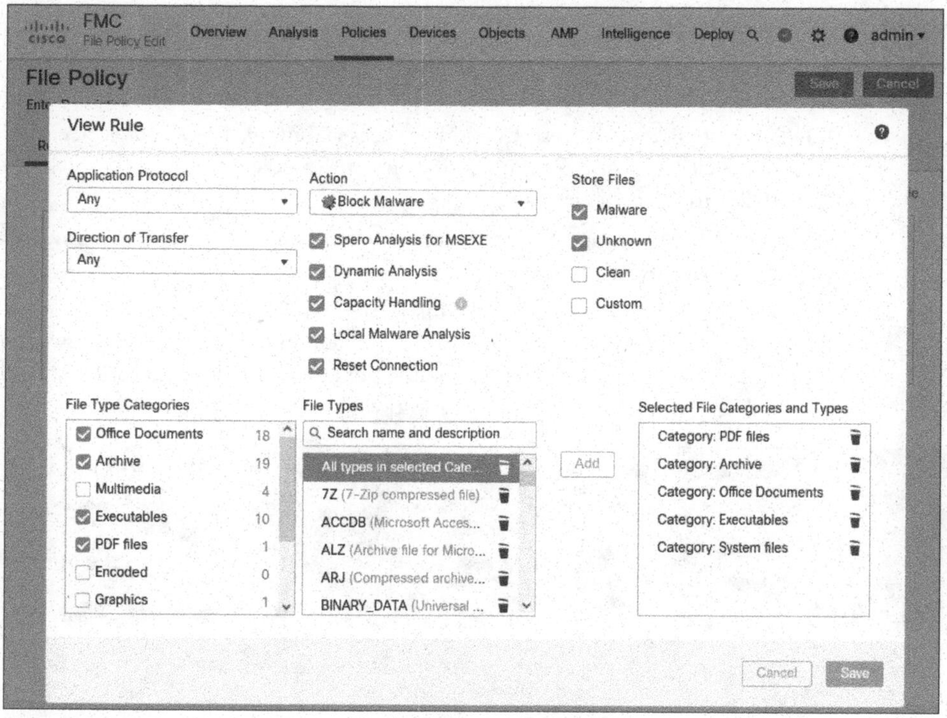

Figure 16-14 *A File Rule with a Block Malware Action*

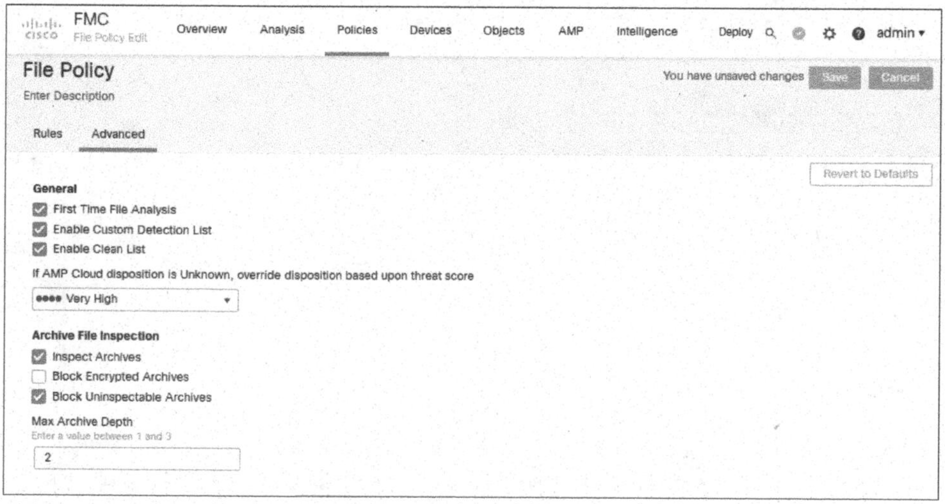

Figure 16-15 *Advanced Settings of a File Policy*

Deploying a File Policy

To apply a file policy on a threat defense, you need to create an access control rule and invoke the file policy into it. Here are the detailed steps:

Step 1. Navigate to **Policies > Access Control > Access Control**. The available access control policies appear. You can modify one of the existing policies or click **New Policy** to create a new one.

Step 2. On the policy editor page, you can edit an existing rule or create a new rule by clicking the **Add Rule** button.

Step 3. On the rule editor window, go to the Inspection tab. You will notice dropdowns for Intrusion Policy, Variable Set, and File Policy. Figure 16-16 shows the drop-downs on the Inspection tab. The file policy you configured earlier should be listed here, under the File Policy drop-down.

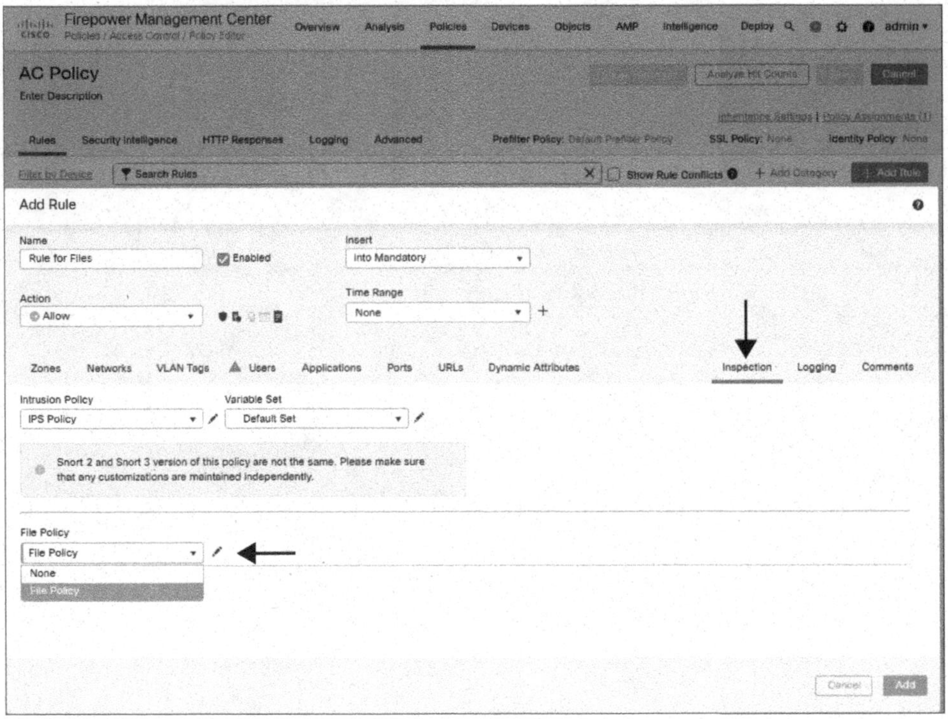

Figure 16-16 *Selecting a File Policy for an Access Control Rule*

Step 4. Choose a policy from the File Policy drop-down. Doing so automatically enables logging for the file event. You can verify it by viewing the settings on the Logging tab (see Figure 16-17). Additionally, to view the connection event that is associated with a file transfer, you can manually enable **Log at End of Connection**.

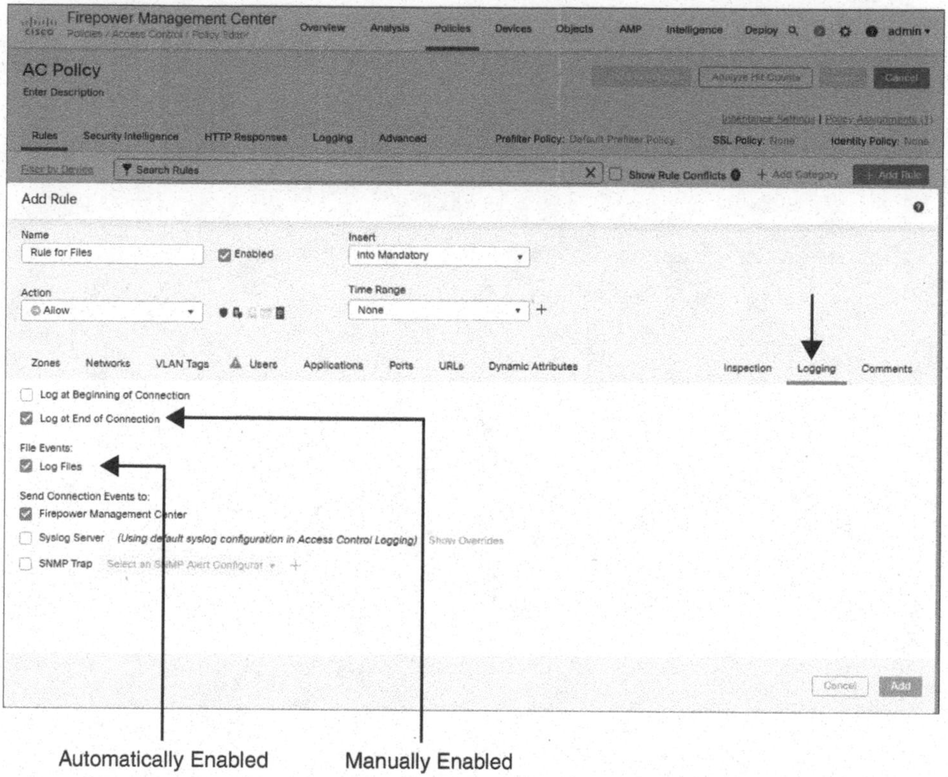

Automatically Enabled   Manually Enabled

Figure 16-17   *Options to Enable Logging for File Events and Connection Events*

Step 5.   Click the **Add** button to save the changes. You return to the access control policy editor page. If you are editing an existing access control rule, you can click the **Save** button instead.

Step 6.   In the access control policy editor page, select a default action. Note that you cannot select a file policy as the default action of an access control policy (see Figure 16-18). You can invoke a file policy only within an individual access control rule.

Step 7.   Finally, click **Save** to save the changes, and go to **Deploy > Deployment** to deploy the configuration to your threat defense.

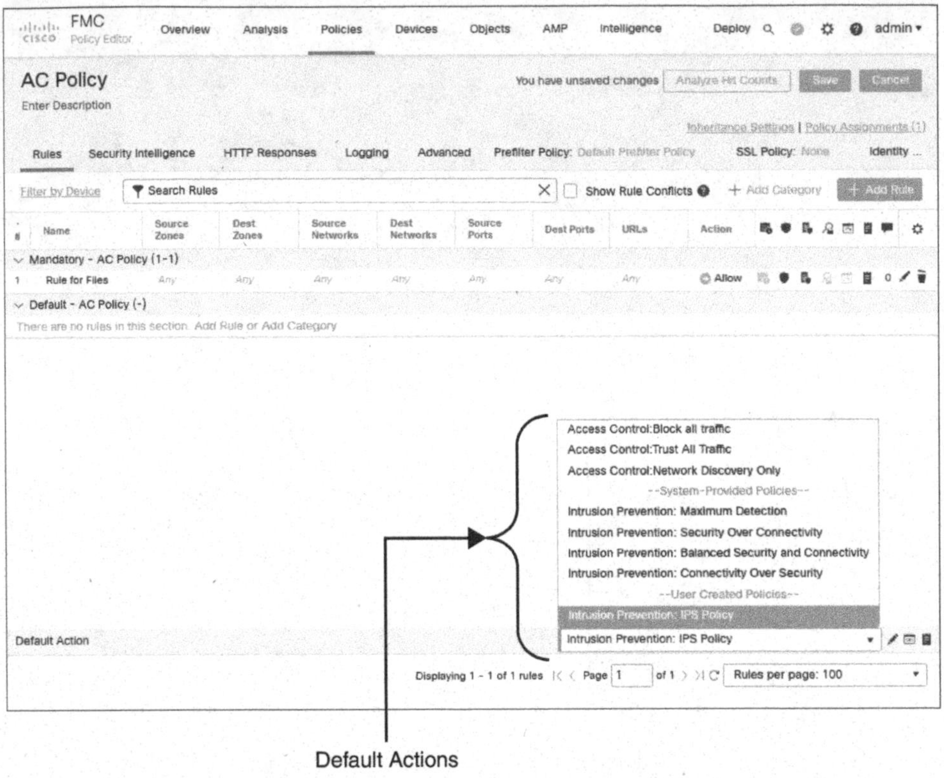

Figure 16-18 *Independent File Policy Is Not an Option for Default Action*

Verification

A file policy primarily generates two types of events: file events and malware events. A threat defense generates a *file event* when it detects or blocks a certain type of file without a malware lookup. The threat defense generates a *malware event* when it performs an analysis for malware or blocks a file due to malware disposition. There is also another type of event, called a retrospective malware event. Cisco updates its malware analytics cloud regularly as it discovers additional information about a file. If a file was thought to be clean initially but later was found harmful, or vice versa, the malware analytics cloud updates its disposition accordingly. If a Secure Firewall previously sent a query to the malware analytics cloud for a file, but the disposition for that file has changed since then, the cloud can retrospectively notify the Secure Firewall about the new disposition. In such case, management center generates a retrospective malware event.

The following sections of this chapter demonstrate the operation of both file type detection and malware analysis. In this scenario, a client downloads files with two different formats: the Microsoft executable (MSEXE) file format and Portable Document Format (PDF). As a security engineer, you need to verify whether a file policy is operational and whether the transfer of files complies with the active file policy.

Figure 16-19 shows the topology that is used in the configuration examples in this chapter. To demonstrate various scenarios, the end user downloads different files from a server, and the threat defense in the LAN acts on them, per the file policy.

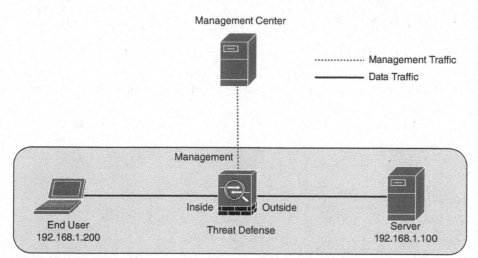

Figure 16-19   *Topology Used in the Lab Exercises in This Chapter*

Analyzing File Events

Using a web browser on your client computer, you can attempt to download two files—7z1900.exe and userguide.pdf—from a web server. If the threat defense is running a file policy configured as previously described, it should block the download of the 7z1900.exe file and simply detect the download of userguide.pdf file.

Figure 16-20 shows the currently enabled rules in the file policy. The first rule detects and blocks files in four categories, and the second rule only detects files in four different categories. The page also confirms that the file policy is Used by 1 Access Control Policy.

| cisco FMC File Policy Edit | Overview | Analysis | Policies | Devices | Objects | AMP | Intelligence | Deploy | admin ▼ |

File Policy
Enter Description

Rules   Advanced

Used by 1 access control policy   + Add Rule

File Types	Application Protocol	Direction	Action		
Category: System files Category: Executables	Any	Any	✗ Block Files with Reset	✎	🗑
Category: PDF files Category: Archive Category: Office Documents	Any	Any	⊙ Detect Files Store Files	✎	🗑

The New Malware and File Policy
Is Used by an Access Control Policy

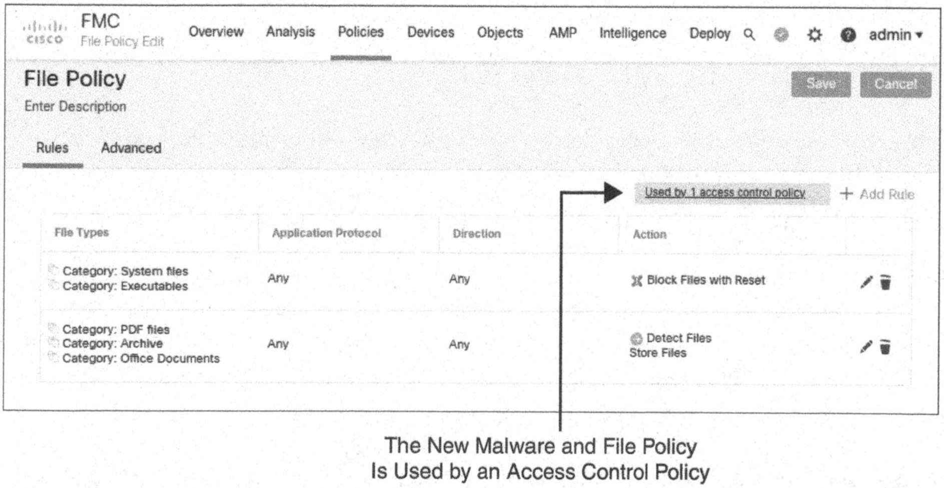

Figure 16-20   *Overview of the Active Rules Used in This Exercise*

Navigate to **Files > File Events** to view the file events. By default, the management center shows the File Summary page. However, to find useful contextual information about file events, you should also check the Table View of File Events page.

Figure 16-21 confirms the blocking and detection of an MSEXE file and a PDF file. Because the Block Files action does not perform malware analysis, the Disposition column is blank.

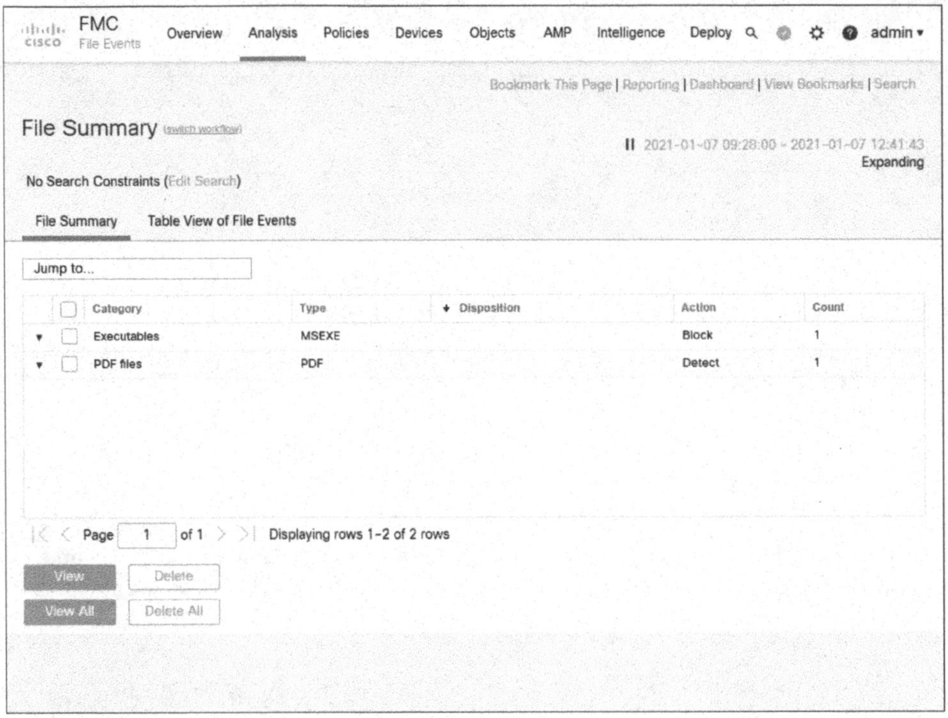

Figure 16-21   *Summary View of File Events*

Figure 16-22 shows detailed information about the detected and blocked files and their associated source and destination hosts. The SHA256 and Threat Score columns are blank because the threat defense does not perform any kind of malware analysis but takes an action based on file type only.

Figure 16-23 shows the data from file events visually in various widgets. To find this dashboard, go to **Overview > Dashboards > Files Dashboard**. The widgets in the Files Dashboard display various file event data. In this example, the File Dispositions widget shows no data because the currently deployed file rules do not check for any malware.

If you do not see a file event that you expected to see, you can use the CLI to debug the action of a file rule and verify the operation of the file policy. If you run the **system support firewall-engine-debug** command while you attempt to transfer a file, you see detailed logs associated with file inspection and analysis.

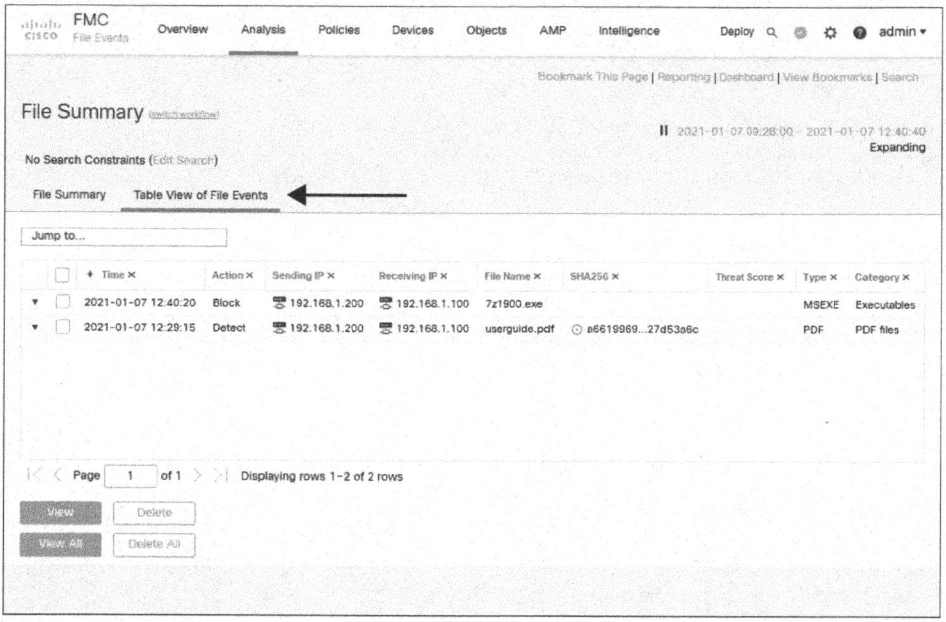

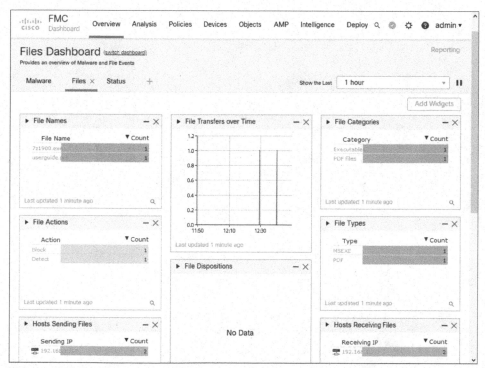

Figure 16-22   *The Table View of File Events Provides Additional Data*

Figure 16-23   *The Files Dashboard Provides an Insight on File Transfer Activities*

Example 16-1 shows the detailed debugging messages that appear when a client computer attempts to download the executable file 7z1900.exe and the threat defense blocks it due to the action configured in the Block Files rule.

Example 16-1 *Blocking a Microsoft Executable (MSEXE) File*

```
! First, run the debug command and specify necessary parameters.


> system support firewall-engine-debug

Please specify an IP protocol: tcp
Please specify a client IP address: 192.168.1.100
Please specify a client port:
Please specify a server IP address:
Please specify a server port:
Monitoring firewall engine debug messages

192.168.1.100-46592 > 192.168.1.200-80 6 AS 4-4 I 0 new firewall session
192.168.1.100-46592 > 192.168.1.200-80 6 AS 4-4 I 0 using HW or preset rule order 2,
'Rule for Files', action Allow and prefilter rule 0
192.168.1.100-46592 > 192.168.1.200-80 6 AS 4-4 I 0 HitCount data sent for rule id:
268461056,
192.168.1.100-46592 > 192.168.1.200-80 6 AS 4-4 I 0 allow action
192.168.1.100-46592 > 192.168.1.200-80 6 AS 4-4 I 0 IP SI: HTTP HOST
"http://192.168.1.200/files/7z1900.exe" has embedded IP
192.168.1.100-46592 > 192.168.1.200-80 6 AS 4-4 I 0 File policy verdict is Type,
Malware, and Capture
192.168.1.100-46592 > 192.168.1.200-80 6 AS 4-4 I 0 File type verdict Reject,
fileAction Block, flags 0x00003500, and type action Reject for type 21 of instance 0
192.168.1.100-46592 > 192.168.1.200-80 6 AS 4-4 I 0 File type event for file named
7z1900.exe with disposition Type and action Block
192.168.1.100-46592 > 192.168.1.200-80 6 AS 4-4 I 0 deleting firewall session flags
= 0x14001, fwFlags = 0x1100
192.168.1.100-46592 > 192.168.1.200-80 6 AS 4-4 I 0 Logging EOF as part of session
delete with rule_id = 268461056 ruleAction = 4 ruleReason = 16
.

<Output omitted for brevity>
.

^C
Caught interrupt signal
Exiting.

>
```

Example 16-2 shows the debugging messages that appear when a client computer downloads the file userguide.pdf. The threat defense generates a log, but it does not block the PDF file because the rule action is Detect Files.

Example 16-2 *Detecting a Portable Document Format (PDF) File*

```
> system support firewall-engine-debug

Please specify an IP protocol: tcp
Please specify a client IP address: 192.168.1.100
Please specify a client port:
Please specify a server IP address:
Please specify a server port:
Monitoring firewall engine debug messages

192.168.1.100-46590 > 192.168.1.200-80 6 AS 4-4 I 0 new firewall session

192.168.1.100-46590 > 192.168.1.200-80 6 AS 4-4 I 0 using HW or preset rule order 2,
'Rule for Files', action Allow and prefilter rule 0

192.168.1.100-46590 > 192.168.1.200-80 6 AS 4-4 I 0 HitCount data sent for rule id:
268461056,

192.168.1.100-46590 > 192.168.1.200-80 6 AS 4-4 I 0 allow action

192.168.1.100-46590 > 192.168.1.200-80 6 AS 4-4 I 0 IP SI: HTTP HOST
"http://192.168.1.200/files/userguide.pdf" has embedded IP

192.168.1.100-46590 > 192.168.1.200-80 6 AS 4-4 I 0 File policy verdict is Type,
Malware, and Capture

192.168.1.100-46590 > 192.168.1.200-80 6 AS 4-4 I 0 File type verdict Unknown,
fileAction Log, flags 0x00201100, and type action Log for type 286 of instance 0

192.168.1.100-46590 > 192.168.1.200-80 6 AS 4-4 I 0 File type storage finished
within signature using verdict Log

192.168.1.100-46590 > 192.168.1.200-80 6 AS 4-4 I 0 File signature reserved file
data of a6619969f016b6be5b9a1a3fc014005f7cdc47784edc26f2ee5a06f627d53a6c with flags
0x00201100 and status Initialized

192.168.1.100-46590 > 192.168.1.200-80 6 AS 4-4 I 0 File signature verdict Log and
flags 0x00201100 for a6619969f016b6be5b9a1a3fc014005f7cdc47784edc26f2ee5a06f627d53a6c
of instance 0

192.168.1.100-46590 > 192.168.1.200-80 6 AS 4-4 I 0 File event for a6619969f016b-
6be5b9a1a3fc014005f7cdc47784edc26f2ee5a06f627d53a6c, size 657777 queued to DM status
Sent, action Store, type 9, disp Type, spero Type, storage pending, score 0

192.168.1.100-46590 > 192.168.1.200-80 6 AS 4-4 I 0 File type event for
a6619969f016b6be5b9a1a3fc014005f7cdc47784edc26f2ee5a06f627d53a6c named userguide.pdf
with disposition Type and action Log

192.168.1.100-46590 > 192.168.1.200-80 6 AS 4-4 I 0 Archive childs been processed No

192.168.1.100-46590 > 192.168.1.200-80 6 AS 4-4 I 0 IP SI: HTTP HOST
"http://192.168.1.200/favicon.ico" has embedded IP

192.168.1.100-46590 > 192.168.1.200-80 6 AS 4-4 I 0 File policy verdict is Type,
Malware, and Capture

192.168.1.100-46590 > 192.168.1.200-80 6 AS 4-4 I 0 IP SI: HTTP HOST
"http://192.168.1.200/files/userguide.pdf" has embedded IP

192.168.1.100-46590 > 192.168.1.200-80 6 AS 4-4 I 0 File policy verdict is Type,
Malware, and Capture

192.168.1.1' repeated 1 times, suppressed by syslog-ng on ThreatDefense
```

16

```
192.168.1.100-46590 > 192.168.1.200-80 6 AS 4-4 I 0 deleting firewall session flags =
0x14001, fwFlags = 0x1100

192.168.1.100-46590 > 192.168.1.200-80 6 AS 4-4 I 0 Logging EOF as part of session
delete with rule_id = 268461056 ruleAction = 2 ruleReason = 8

.

<Output omitted for brevity>

.

^c

Caught interrupt signal

Exiting.

>
```

Analyzing Malware Events

When you attempt to download the same MSEXE file 7z1900.exe as you did previously, you will notice different behavior on the threat defense because it applies a different rule action—Block Malware instead of Block Files. You analyze the following scenarios in this section:

■ The management center is unable to communicate with the cloud.

■ The management center performs a cloud lookup.

■ The threat defense blocks malware.

Figure 16-24 shows a file rule that can block the transfer of any system files, PDF files, executables, and archive and Office documents if the files contain malware. When a file is identified as malicious, this rule allows a threat defense to store the file in local storage and to send reset packets to terminate any associated connection. To conserve disk space, files with a clean disposition are not stored.

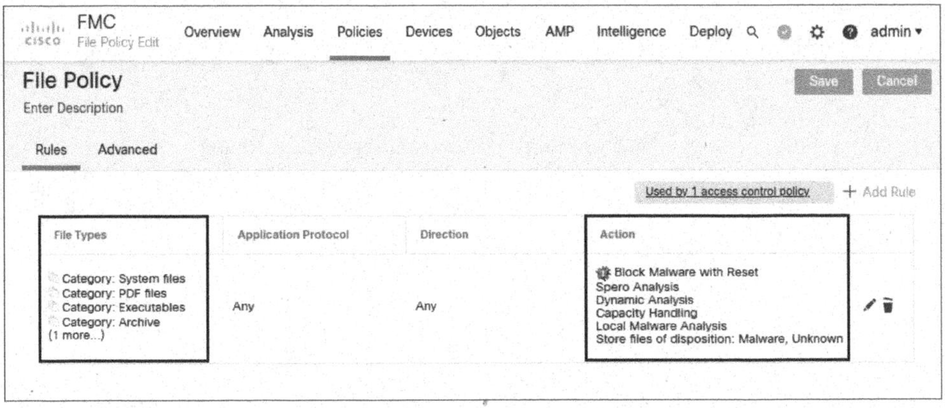

Figure 16-24 *Overview of the Active Rule Used in This Exercise*

The Management Center Is Unable to Communicate with the Cloud

After deploying the file policy with the Block Malware rule action, you can attempt to download the same MSEXE file 7z1900.exe as you did previously. In this instance, the threat defense calculates the file's SHA-256 hash and attempts to perform a cloud lookup for the hash value.

Figure 16-25 shows a file event (table view) for downloading the same 7z1900.exe file. Because the file policy enables malware analysis, the threat defense calculates the SHA-256 hash value. However, the cloud lookup process times out.

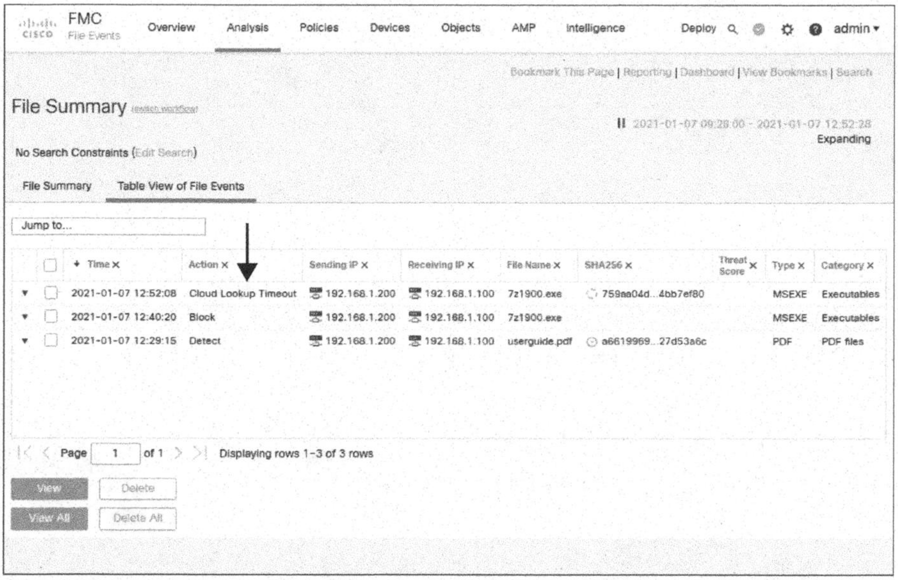

Figure 16-25   *Malware Analysis Verdict—Cloud Lookup Timeout*

Figure 16-26 shows the summary view of the file events. Due to the cloud lookup timeout, the malware disposition is listed as *Unavailable*.

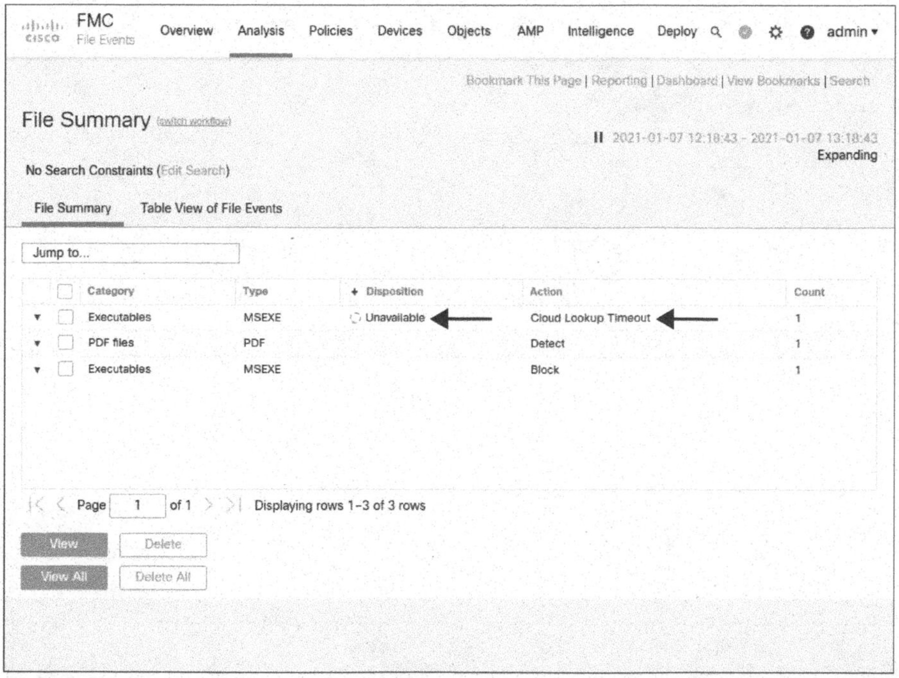

Figure 16-26   *The Malware Disposition Is Unavailable Due to a Cloud Lookup Timeout*

Example 16-3 demonstrates that the threat defense is able to calculate the SHA-256 checksum locally. However, when it sends the calculated hash value for a lookup, the query times out (due to a communication failure to the Cisco cloud). This leads the management center to display the disposition as Unavailable.

Example 16-3 *The Management Center Calculates the SHA-256 Hash Value but Is Unable to Complete a Lookup*

```
> system support firewall-engine-debug


Please specify an IP protocol: tcp
Please specify a client IP address: 192.168.1.100
Please specify a client port:
Please specify a server IP address:
Please specify a server port:
Monitoring firewall engine debug messages

192.168.1.100-46598 > 192.168.1.200-80 6 AS 4-4 I 0 new firewall session

192.168.1.100-46598 > 192.168.1.200-80 6 AS 4-4 I 0 using HW or preset rule order 2,
'Rule for Files', action Allow and prefilter rule 0

192.168.1.100-46598 > 192.168.1.200-80 6 AS 4-4 I 0 HitCount data sent for rule id:
268461056,

192.168.1.100-46598 > 192.168.1.200-80 6 AS 4-4 I 0 allow action

192.168.1.100-46598 > 192.168.1.200-80 6 AS 4-4 I 0 IP SI: HTTP HOST
"http://192.168.1.200/files/7z1900.exe" has embedded IP

192.168.1.100-46598 > 192.168.1.200-80 6 AS 4-4 I 0 File policy verdict is Type,
Malware, and Capture

192.168.1.100-46598 > 192.168.1.200-80 6 AS 4-4 I 0 File type verdict Unknown,
fileAction Malware Lookup, flags 0x01B9DA00, and type action Stop for type 21 of
instance 0

192.168.1.100-46598 > 192.168.1.200-80 6 AS 4-4 I 0 File signature verdict Unknown
and flags 0x01B9DA00 for partial file of instance 0

192.168.1.100-46598 > 192.168.1.200-80 6 AS 4-4 I 0 File signature 759aa04d5b03e-
beee13ba01df554e8c962ca339c74f56627c8bed6984bb7ef80 ShmDBLookupFile returned 0

192.168.1.100-46598 > 192.168.1.200-80 6 AS 4-4 I 0 File signature cache query returned
Cache Miss for 759aa04d5b03ebeee13ba01df554e8c962ca339c74f56627c8bed6984bb7ef80 with
disposition Cache Miss, spero Cache Miss, severity 0, and transmit Not Sent

192.168.1.100-46598 > 192.168.1.200-80 6 AS 4-4 I 0 File signature reserved file
data of 759aa04d5b03ebeee13ba01df554e8c962ca339c74f56627c8bed6984bb7ef80 with flags
0x01B9DA00 and status Exceeded Max Filesize

192.168.1.100-46598 > 192.168.1.200-80 6 AS 4-4 I 0 File signature verdict Pending
and flags 0x01B9DA00 for 759aa04d5b03ebeee13ba01df554e8c962ca339c74f56627c8bed6984b-
b7ef80 of instance 0

.

<Output omitted for brevity>

.

Caught interrupt signal
Exiting.

>
```

To find the root cause of a lookup failure, you can analyze the syslog messages on the management center. To view the messages, you can use Linux commands, such as **less**, **cat**, or **tail**, as needed. Note that the timestamps of messages use coordinated universal time (UTC).

> **TIP**   Cloud Lookup Timeout in the Action column indicates that the management center is unable to connect to the cloud. When you see this, check whether the management interface of the management center is connected to the Internet. If the Internet connectivity is operational, make sure the management center can resolve a DNS query.

Example 16-4 shows various states of the management center cloud communication. The syslog messages are automatically generated and stored by the Secure Firewall software. To view them in real time, you can use the **tail** command with the **-f** parameter.

Example 16-4   *Analyzing Syslog Messages for Management Center Communications to the Cloud*

```
admin@FMC:~$ sudo tail -f /var/log/messages
Password:
.

<Output is omitted for brevity>
.

! If management center is connected to the internet, but fails to resolve a DNS
query, the following error message appears in the Syslog.

[timestamp] FMC stunnel: LOG3[3953:140160119551744]: Error resolving 'cloud-sa.amp.
sourcefire.com': Neither nodename nor servname known (EAI_NONAME)

.


! After you fix any communication issues, management center should be able to con-
nect to the cloud. The following Syslog messages confirm a successful connection.
.

[timestamp] FMC SF-IMS[25954]: [26657] SFDataCorrelator:FireAMPCloudLookup [INFO]
cloud server is cloud-sa.amp.sourcefire.com
[timestamp] FMC SF-IMS[25954]: [26657] SFDataCorrelator:imcloudpool [INFO] connect
to cloud using stunnel
.


! Once the management center is connected to the cloud, it begins the registra-
tion process. The following messages confirm successful registrations to the Cisco
Clouds.
.

[timestamp] FMC SF-IMS[25954]: [26657] SFDataCorrelator:FireAMPCloudLookup [INFO]
Successfully registered with fireamp cloud
[timestamp] FMC SF-IMS[25954]: [25954] SFDataCorrelator:FileExtract [INFO] Success-
fully registered with sandbox cloud
.
```

16

```
! Upon successful registration, management center is able to perform cloud lookup
and obtains updates. The following messages confirm a successful check for malware
database update.
.
[timestamp] FMC SF-IMS[25275]: [25275] CloudAgent:CloudAgent [INFO] ClamUpd, time to
check for updates
.
[timestamp] FMC SF-IMS[25275]: [25298] CloudAgent:CloudAgent [INFO] Nothing to do,
database is up to date
.
```

Figure 16-27 shows the DNS setting on the management interface of a management center. To find this page, go to **System > Configuration** and select Management Interfaces. Make sure the management center can communicate with the configured DNS server and resolve a domain name using this DNS server.

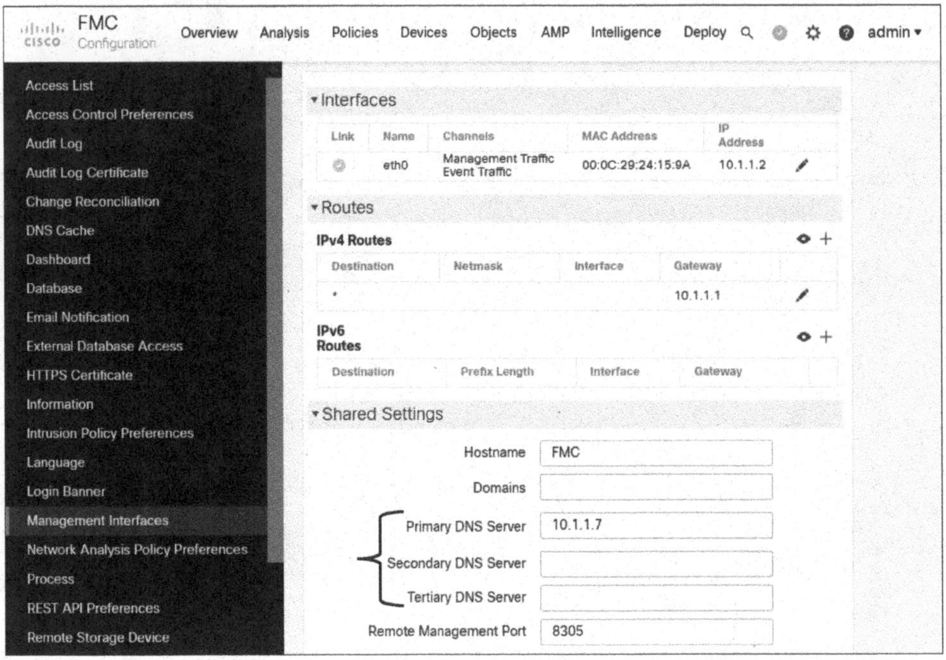

Figure 16-27 *DNS Settings on a Management Center*

The Management Center Performs a Cloud Lookup

If the management center is able to resolve a DNS query, it should be able to connect and register with the Cisco cloud as well. Registration with the cloud allows the management center to perform cloud lookups for malware disposition. This section assumes that you have fixed any connectivity or DNS issues you experienced in the previous section. Here you will download the MSEXE file 7z1900.exe once again. You should notice a different type of event this time.

Figure 16-28 shows two different actions on file events for downloading the same file. Because the management center can communicate with the Cisco clouds, the threat defense returns Malware Cloud Lookup instead of Cloud Lookup Timeout.

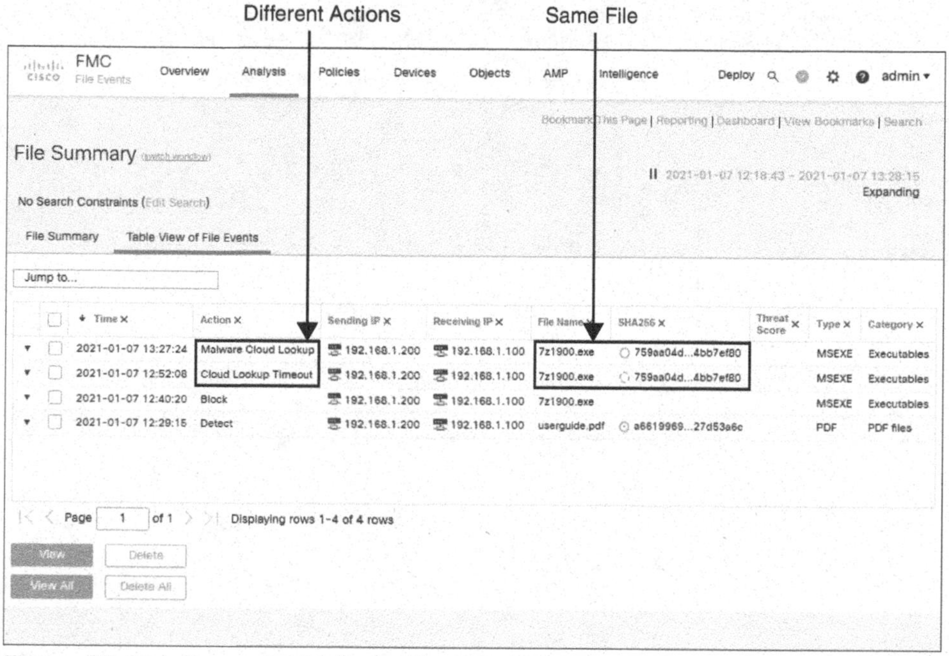

Figure 16-28 *Successful Malware Cloud Lookup*

You can go to the File Events page to find the dispositions of any detected files. The Cisco cloud can return one of the following dispositions for a query:

- **Malware:** If Cisco determines that a file is malware
- **Clean:** If Cisco finds no malicious pattern on a file
- **Unknown:** If Cisco has not assigned a disposition (malware or clean) to a file

Figure 16-29 compares two types of dispositions—unknown and unavailable—for the 7z1900.exe file. Unknown confirms a successful cloud communication with no cloud-assigned category, whereas Unavailable indicates an issue with cloud communication.

The Threat Defense Blocks Malware

This section shows how to analyze the operations and actions of Secure Firewall on malware. To emulate a malicious file, this chapter leverages an antimalware test file available at the European Institute for Computer Antivirus Research (EICAR) website, the **EICAR test file**. Cisco does not develop or maintain this test file; however, you can download the latest copy from eicar.org. Alternatively, you can create a test file on your own using a text editor. It consists of the following characters:

X5O!P%@AP[4\PZX54(P^)7CC)7}$EICAR-STANDARD-ANTIVIRUS-TEST-FILE!$H+H*

Figure 16-30 shows the creation of suspicious.exe, an antimalware test file. The example uses Notepad—a text editor for Microsoft Windows—to create the file. The file simply contains the test string. After you copy the string, save the file in the Windows executable (.exe) format.

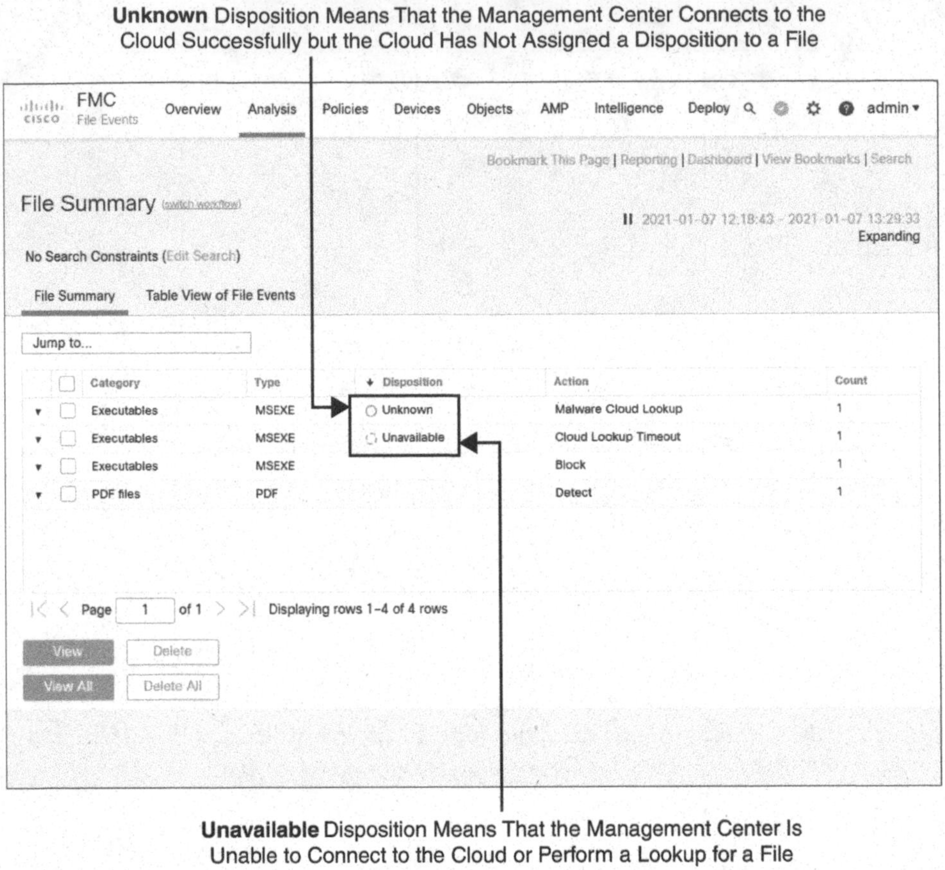

Unknown Disposition Means That the Management Center Connects to the
Cloud Successfully but the Cloud Has Not Assigned a Disposition to a File

Unavailable Disposition Means That the Management Center Is
Unable to Connect to the Cloud or Perform a Lookup for a File

Figure 16-29 *Malware Disposition—Unknown Versus Unavailable*

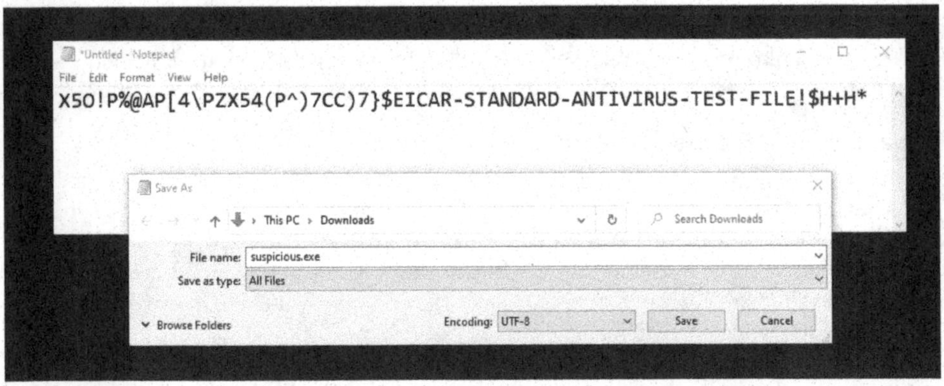

Figure 16-30 *Creating an Antimalware Test File Using a Text Editor*

To perform an experiment, at first, store the antimalware test file (suspicious.exe) on a web server in your lab network. Then attempt to download the test file to a client computer by using a web browser. The threat defense should block the attempt.

Figure 16-31 demonstrates that the threat defense blocks the client's multiple attempts to download the suspicious.exe file. The cloud lookup returns a very high threat score for this antimalware test file because the cloud detects the test string within the file and considers it malware.

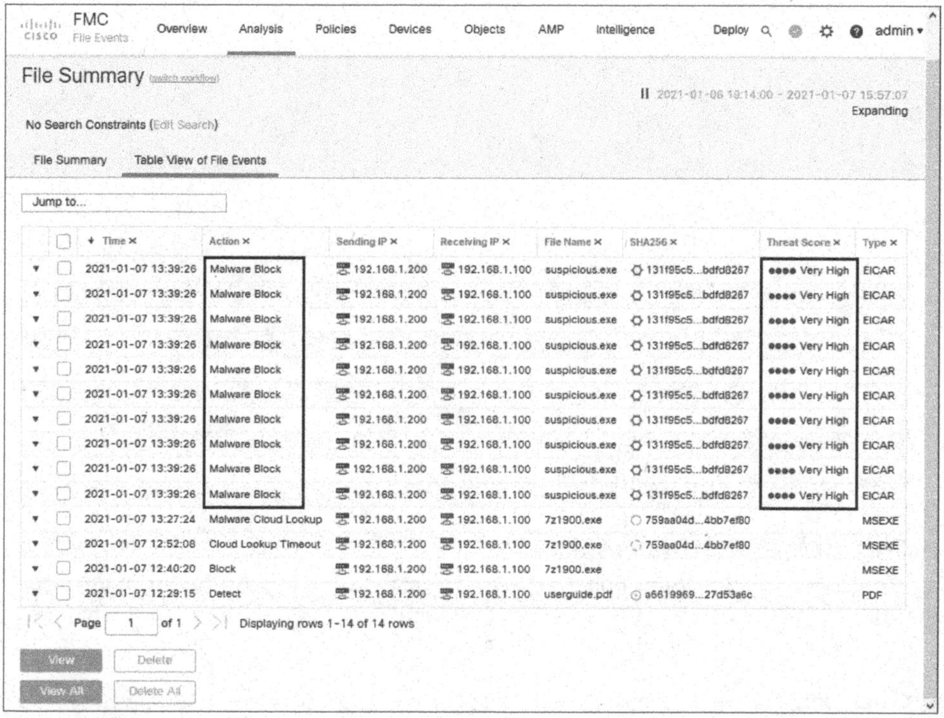

Figure 16-31 *The Threat Defense Blocking a File with a Very High Threat Score*

Likewise, if you navigate to the Files Dashboard, the File Disposition widget should show data (see Figure 16-32). There was no data displayed in this widget previously (refer to Figure 16-23).

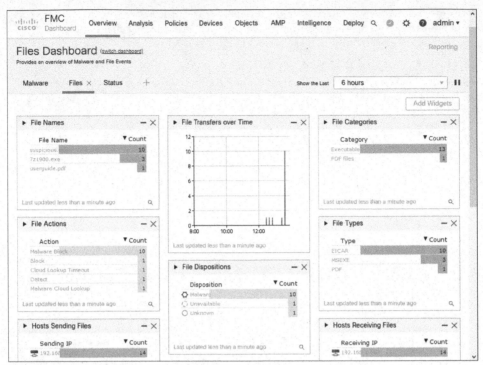

Figure 16-32   *The File Disposition Widget Shows Data*

Overriding a Malware Disposition

If you disagree with a file disposition—whether it is analyzed locally by the threat defense or dynamically by the cloud—the management center allows you to override this outcome by using a file list. There are two types of file lists:

- **Clean list:** If a threat defense blocks a file because the Cisco malware analytics cloud identifies the file as a malware, you could manually allow the file by adding it to the clean list. This lets the file go through as if it were a clean file even though the cloud has it marked as malicious.

- **Custom detection list:** If the local or dynamic analysis engine identifies a file as clean or unknown and the threat defense allows the file to transfer, you could change this behavior by adding the file to the custom detection list. By doing so, future detections of the file will result in a block regardless of the disposition reported by the local or dynamic analysis engines.

In short, the clean list allows you to allow a file, whereas you can block a file by adding it to the custom detection list. To deploy a new file list, the threat defense must be running a file policy with the following rule conditions:

- The rule matches the same file type as your selected file format for a file list. For example, if you want to add an executable file to the clean or custom detection list, a rule in the file policy must match the file type configured in the rule.

- The action of the rule is set to one of the malware analysis rules, such as malware cloud lookup or block malware.

When these conditions are fulfilled, you can add a file to a file list in two ways: by using the right-click context menu or by using a file list object. The context menu enables you to add a file on the fly.

Figure 16-33 shows the addition of the 7z1900.exe file to the clean list through the context menu.

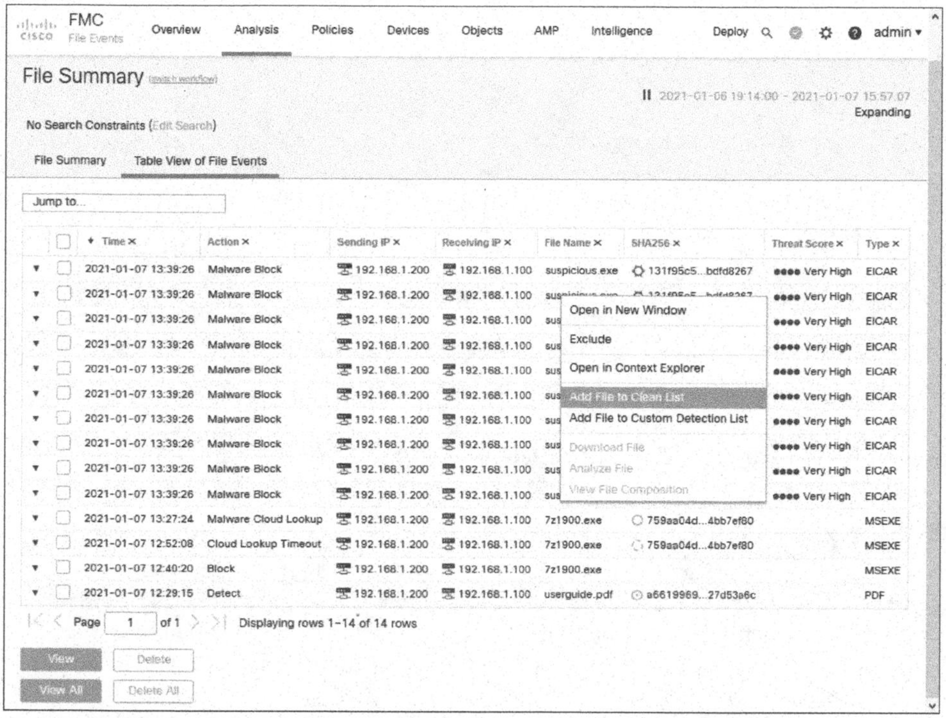

Figure 16-33 *Adding a File to the Clean List by Using the Context Menu*

After you add your desired file to the clean list, you can attempt to redownload the file that was blocked previously. The client should be able to download the file this time.

Network Trajectory

The management center allows you to track and visualize the path of a file by using the network file trajectory feature. This feature can save you analysis time when you want to determine the spread of a suspicious file. You can look up a particular file by entering its SHA-256 hash value after navigating to **Files > Network Trajectory**.

Figure 16-34 shows the network file trajectory for the 7z1900.exe file. Throughout the exercises on this chapter, the file has gone through various disposition states that you can see on this page.

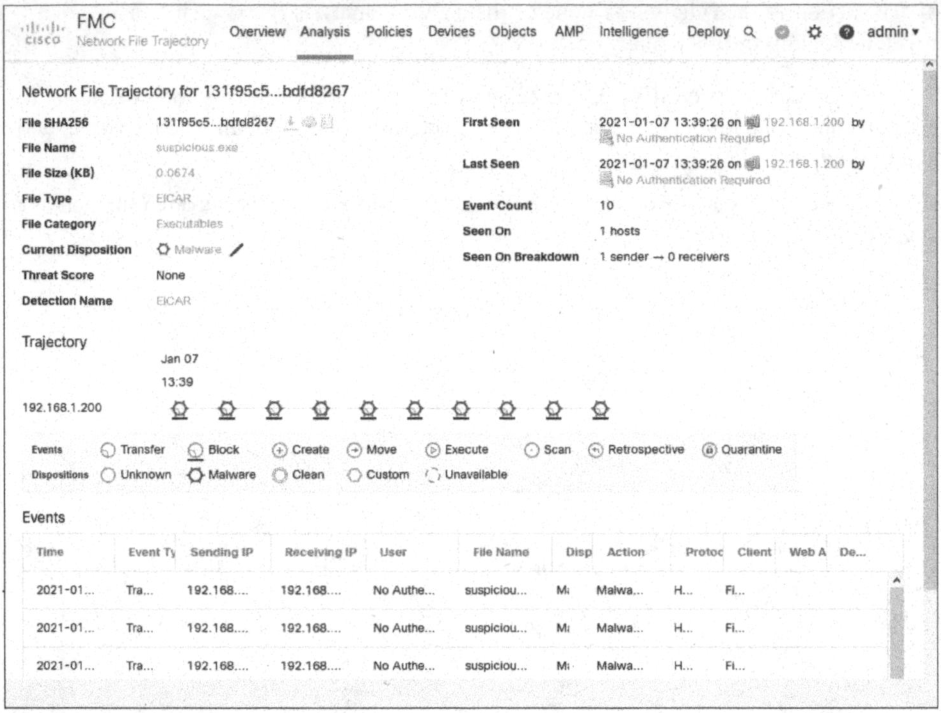

Figure 16-34 *Network File Trajectory Page*

Summary

Cisco integrates the malware defense technology with Secure Firewall. This chapter explains how they work together to help you detect and block the spread of infected files across your network. This chapter also shows the configurations and operations of a file policy on Secure Firewall. It also explains various logs and debug messages that are useful to determine any issues with cloud lookup and file disposition.

Exam Preparation Tasks

As mentioned in the section "How to Use This Book" in the Introduction, you have a couple of choices for exam preparation: the exercises here, Chapter 22, "Final Preparation," and the exam simulation questions in the Pearson Test Prep practice test software.

Review All Key Topics

Review the most important topics in this chapter, noted with the Key Topic icon in the outer margin of the page. Table 16-3 lists a reference of these key topics and the page numbers on which each is found.

Key Topic

Table 16-3   Key Topics for Chapter 16

Key Topic Element	Description	Page
Bullet list	Malware analysis engines	385
Bullet list and Table 16-2	Licensing requirements	387
Step list	File rule actions	391

Complete Tables and Lists from Memory

Print a copy of Appendix C, "Memory Tables" (found on the companion website), or at least the section for this chapter, and complete the tables and lists from memory. Appendix D, "Memory Tables Answer Key," also on the companion website, includes completed tables and lists to check your work.

Define Key Terms

Define the following key terms from this chapter, and check your answers in the Glossary:

disposition, Spero analysis, local analysis, dynamic analysis, clean list, EICAR test file

16

CHAPTER 17

Network Address Translation (NAT)

This chapter provides an overview of the following topics:

NAT Essentials: This section describes the Network Address Translation (NAT) operations and elaborates on different techniques to implement NAT on Secure Firewall.

Best Practices for NAT Deployment: This section discusses some of the best practices to enable NAT on Secure Firewall while delivering optimal performance.

Fulfilling Prerequisites: This section highlights the threat defense interface requirements to enable NAT.

Configuring NAT: This section walks you through the steps to configure NAT in various use cases and validate configurations using the CLI.

The objectives of this chapter are to learn about

- Network Address Translation (NAT) and Port Address Translation (PAT) technologies

- Implementation of various NAT techniques on Secure Firewall

- Verification and troubleshooting of address translation operation

- Introduction to platform settings

Any external user, whether an attacker or a legitimate Internet user, should have no visibility into your internal network. You can hide the internal addresses of your network by masquerading them into public addresses. However, assigning a dedicated public address to each of the internal hosts is not a feasible option. You can solve this challenge by enabling the Network Address Translation (NAT) functionality on a threat defense. This chapter demonstrates how to configure NAT and how NAT can masquerade an internal IP address as a public IP address.

NOTE In this chapter, the terms *translating* and *masquerading* refer to the same operation and are interchangeable. In other words, *translating* an address and *masquerading* an address refer to the same technology—NAT.

"Do I Know This Already?" Quiz

The "Do I Know This Already?" quiz enables you to assess whether you should read this entire chapter thoroughly or jump to the "Exam Preparation Tasks" section. If you are in doubt about your answers to these questions or your own assessment of your knowledge of the topics, read the entire chapter. Table 17-1 lists the major headings in this chapter and their corresponding "Do I Know This Already?" quiz questions. You can find the answers in Appendix A, "Answers to the 'Do I Know This Already?' Quizzes."

Table 17-1 "Do I Know This Already?" Section-to-Question Mapping

Foundation Topics Section	Questions
NAT Essentials	1
Best Practices for NAT Deployment	2
Fulfilling Prerequisites	3
Configuring NAT	4

CAUTION The goal of self-assessment is to gauge your mastery of the topics in this chapter. If you do not know the answer to a question or are only partially sure of the answer, you should mark that question as wrong for purposes of the self-assessment. Giving yourself credit for an answer you correctly guess skews your self-assessment results and might provide you with a false sense of security.

1. Which NAT section has the highest priority during rule evaluation?
   a. NAT Rules Before
   b. Auto NAT Rules
   c. NAT Rules After
   d. All of them have the same priority.

2. After you deploy a new NAT policy, if a connection still uses a rule from the prior version of the NAT policy, how could you ensure that the threat defense will use the new policy?
   a. Deploy the NAT policy one more time.
   b. Make the NAT rule more specific.
   c. Clear the current translation table.
   d. All of these answers are correct.

3. Which deployment mode supports NAT?
   a. Firewall mode
   b. Inline mode
   c. Inline-tap mode
   d. All of these answers are correct.

4. Which command enables you to determine whether a connection matches a NAT rule and how many times it has matched?

   a. show nat

   b. show nat detail

   c. show xlate detail

   d. show conn detail

Foundation Topics

NAT Essentials

NAT enables a threat defense to translate an internal IP address into an address from a different subnet. The NAT process is transparent to both internal and external hosts. When NAT is in action, an internal host is unaware that its original IP address is being translated or masqueraded to a public address, while the external host assumes that the public address is the actual address of the internal host.

Figure 17-1 shows that the NAT operations of a threat defense take place on the firewall engine.

Another advantage of NAT is the ability to route private traffic to the Internet. An organization's internal hosts use private IP addresses for internal communication, as defined in RFC 1918 (see Table 17-2). Private IP addresses are not routable to the Internet unless you map or translate them into public addresses. In fact, this "limitation" of private address space enables different organizations to reuse the same addresses in their internal networks and to maintain them regardless of any changes in their public IP address. Thus, it conserves the use of public IP addresses. The Internet Assigned Numbers Authority (IANA) reserves additional nonroutable IP addresses that you can use in a test network and in documentation. They are described in RFC 5737 (see Table 17-3).

Table 17-2 Private IP Addressing in Classes A, B, and C, as Defined in RFC 1918

Class	Range of IP Addresses	Number of Hosts
Class A	10.0.0.0–10.255.255.255	$2^{24} - 2 = 16,777,214$
Class B	172.16.0.0–172.31.255.255	$2^{20} - 2 = 1,048,574$
Class C	192.168.0.0–192.168.255.255	$2^{16} - 2 = 65,534$

Table 17-3 IP Addresses Reserved for Testing and Documentation, as Defined in RFC 5737

Address Block	Range of IP Addresses	Number of Hosts
192.0.2.0/24	192.0.2.0–192.0.2.255	$2^8 - 2 = 254$
198.51.100.0/24	198.51.100.0–198.51.100.255	$2^8 - 2 = 254$
203.0.113.0/24	203.0.113.0–203.0.113.255	$2^8 - 2 = 254$

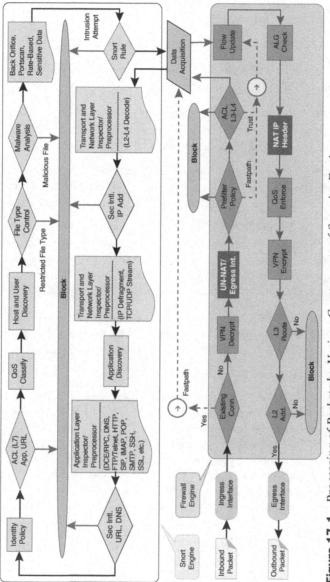
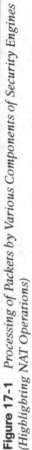

Figure 17-1 *Processing of Packets by Various Components of Security Engines (Highlighting NAT Operations)*

17

NAT Techniques

NAT enables you to masquerade IP addresses in various scenarios, such as one-to-one, one-to-many, many-to-one, many-to-many, few-to-many, and many-to-few. However, before you enable NAT, you need to answer the following questions:

- How does a threat defense select a masqueraded or translated address? Is it predefined statically or allocated dynamically?

- How many external or public addresses are available for selection? One or more?

Your answers to these questions can help you determine the types of translations to enable. You can categorize NAT mainly into three types:

- **Static NAT:** A threat defense permanently maps the original IP address with a translated IP address. Because the mapping is permanent, either the internal or an external host is able to initiate a connection.

- **Dynamic NAT:** Instead of a permanent mapping, a threat defense selects an IP address from a predefined address pool and translates an original internal address into the selected IP address. The selection of an address is on a first-come, first-served basis.

- **Port Address Translation (PAT):** If a dynamic address pool has fewer external addresses than there are internal hosts, it is impossible for all the internal hosts to connect to external networks at the same time. To address this issue, a threat defense can translate both the IP address and port number of a connection (as opposed to just the IP address) and can multiplex over 65,000 connections over a single IP address.

    RFC documents describe this feature as Network Address and Port Translation (NAPT), but due to the nature of its operation, this feature is also known as *Port Address Translation (PAT)*, *NAT overload*, and *IP masquerading*.

Figure 17-2 shows the major differences between NAT and PAT.

A threat defense can use the IP address of the egress interface for PAT operation. This means that when any internal host connects to a resource over the Internet, the source IP address of the connection appears as the egress interface of the threat defense instead of as the original internal host address. However, if the number of concurrent connections exceeds its limit, any additional hosts are unable to connect to the external network. To address this issue, you can combine the PAT functionality with a dynamic address pool. This allows a threat defense to select a new IP address from the pool when the first selection from the pool is no longer available for multiplexing a new connection.

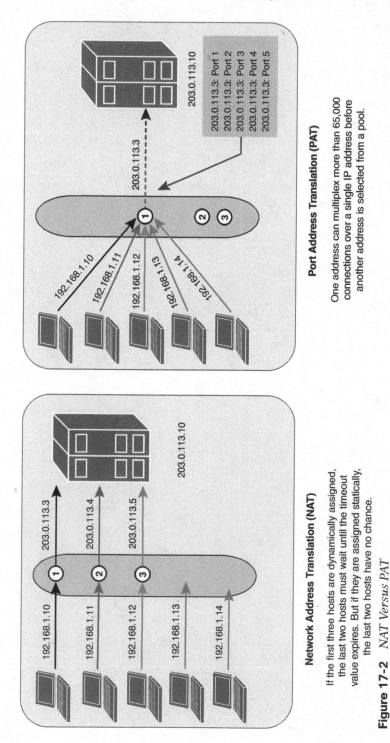

Port Address Translation (PAT)

One address can multiplex more than 65,000 connections over a single IP address before another address is selected from a pool.

Network Address Translation (NAT)

If the first three hosts are dynamically assigned, the last two hosts must wait until the timeout value expires. But if they are assigned statically, the last two hosts have no chance.

Figure 17-2 *NAT Versus PAT*

NAT Rule Types

A threat defense offers two options to configure a NAT rule condition:

- **Auto NAT:** An Auto NAT rule can translate one address—either a source or destination address—in a single rule. This means that to translate both source and destination addresses, two separate Auto NAT rules are necessary.

- **Manual NAT:** A Manual NAT rule allows the translation of both source and destination addresses within the same rule. A Manual NAT rule may be necessary when you want to make an exception for translation.

Figure 17-3 compares the available translation options in the NAT rule editor. An Auto NAT Rule supports the translation of one address per rule, while a Manual NAT Rule allows you to translate both source and destination addresses in a single rule.

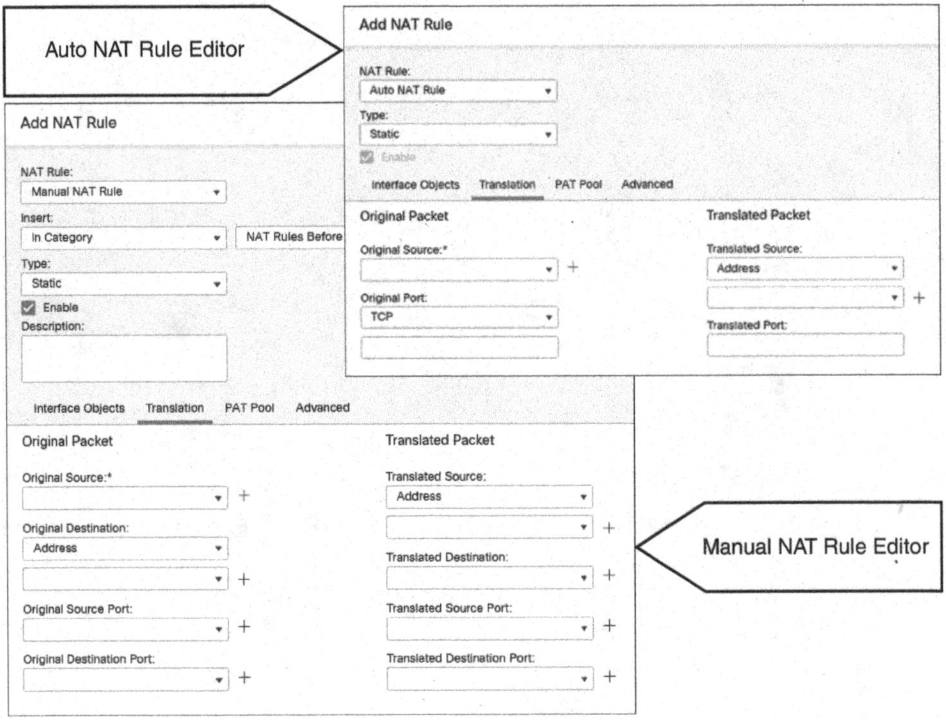

Figure 17-3 *Auto NAT Versus Manual NAT—Comparison of Rule Editor Windows*

A NAT policy editor categorizes NAT rules into three groups: NAT Rules Before, Auto NAT Rules, and NAT Rules After. In the CLI, you can view the rules under Section 1, Section 2, and Section 3, respectively. During evaluation, the threat defense begins with the rules under Section 1. Until there is a match, the threat defense continues evaluating the rules in the next sections.

Any rules under the NAT Rules Before and NAT Rules After sections are part of manual NAT policies. Their names and priorities are relative to the Auto NAT Rules, which allow you to translate one type of address at a time. To translate destination addresses, a separate Auto NAT rule is necessary.

Figure 17-4 describes the priority of each section in a NAT policy. In this chapter, you learn how to configure Auto NAT rules with both static and dynamic types.

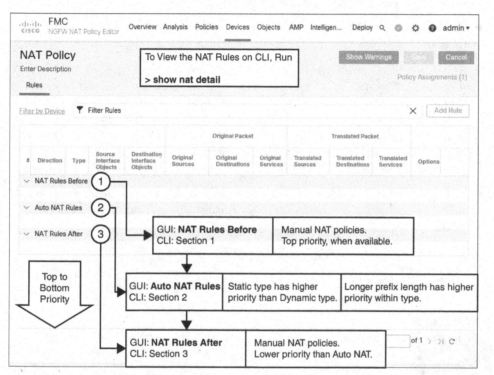

Figure 17-4   *Priorities of Rules in a NAT Policy*

Best Practices for NAT Deployment

Consider the following best practices when you plan to enable NAT on a threat defense:

- Configuring an Auto NAT rule is simpler than configuring a Manual NAT rule. Cisco recommends that you choose an Auto NAT rule because you can easily implement most of the common NAT scenarios with it. A Manual NAT rule may be necessary when you want to make an exception for translation.

- If you modify an existing NAT rule or redeploy a new NAT policy, you may find that the new policy is not in action until the timer for any existing connections expires. To have a threat defense act on the latest NAT policy immediately, you can clear the current translations by running the **clear xlate** command on the threat defense.

- The larger the translation table, the higher the processing overhead. If the number of translated connections grows excessively, it can affect the CPU and memory utilization of a threat defense.

- To improve performance, prefer static NAT to dynamic NAT or PAT.

- Review the addresses on dynamic and static NAT rules carefully before you apply them. Avoid creating rules with overlapping IP addresses.

- Ensure that any applications running on a network terminate connections gracefully to prevent a threat defense from handling stale connections.

- Make sure the global idle timeout durations for Translation Slot (xlate), Connection (Conn), and Xlate-PAT are set for optimal performance. You can adjust the timeout values for your threat defense by navigating to **Devices > Platform Settings** in your management center. The Platform Settings page allows you to manage a wide range of administrative settings to harden your threat defense. The settings are device specific, but they can be shared among multiple threat defense devices through a platform settings policy.

Figure 17-5 shows the global idle timeouts. If you are unsure about the timeout duration, use the default settings. Do not enter them arbitrarily because doing so can introduce unplanned connectivity issues.

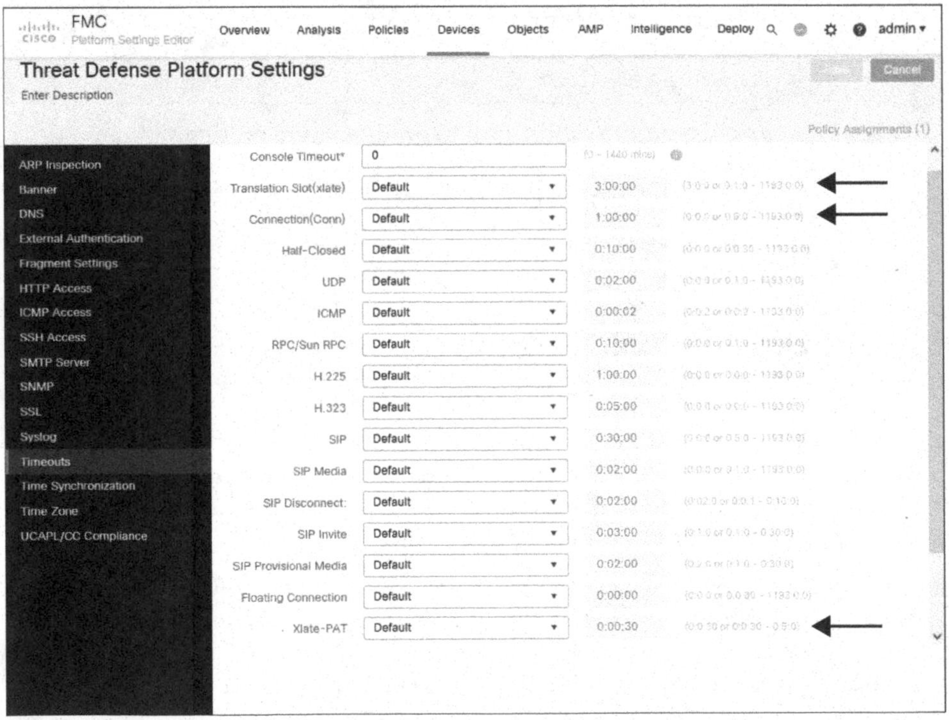

Figure 17-5 *Platform Settings Page Showing Global Timeouts*

Fulfilling Prerequisites

Before you add a NAT rule, ensure that you understand and fulfill the following items:

- Any associated interfaces that participate in a NAT configuration have to be in a regular firewall mode—routed or transparent. A threat defense does not support NAT on IPS-only interface types, such as inline, inline-tap, and passive. Figure 17-6 shows the available modes of a threat defense physical interface. Select None to enable the regular router interface mode, which supports NAT. Chapter 4, "Firewall Deployment in Routed Mode," and Chapter 5, "Firewall Deployment in Transparent Mode," describe the firewall deployment modes in detail.

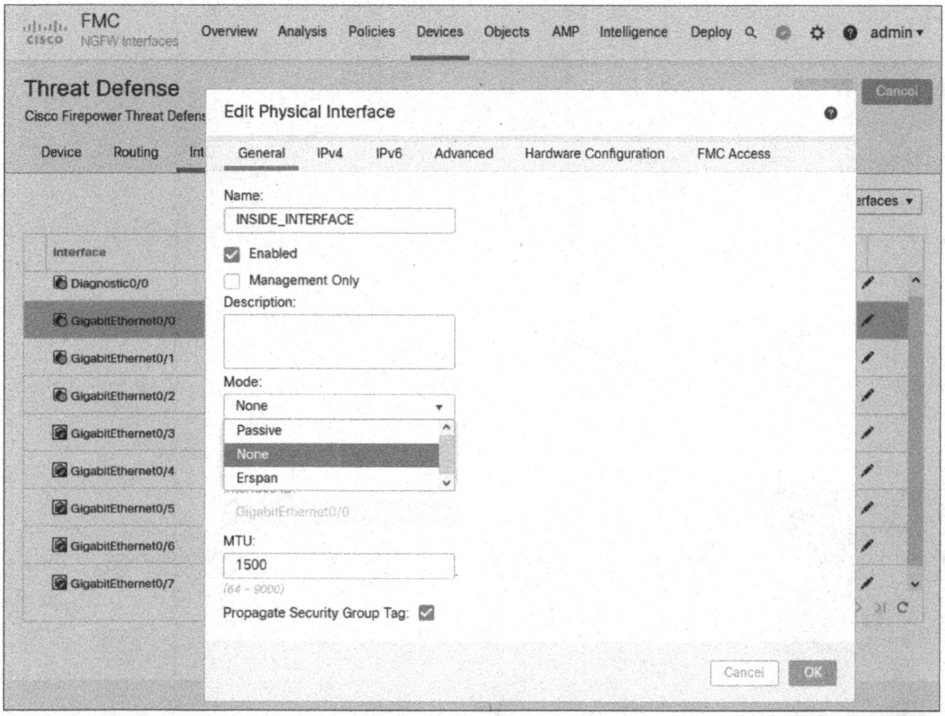

Figure 17-6 *Using the None Option to Turn an Interface into a Regular Firewall Interface*

- If you used a threat defense in an IPS-only mode, make sure all the associated interfaces where you want to enable NAT are now configured with IP address and security zones. Figure 17-7 shows the allocation of IP addresses and security zones in a threat defense. The lab topology in this chapter uses three routed interfaces on a threat defense—GigabitEthernet0/0, GigabitEthernet0/1, and GigabitEthernet0/2.

- Before you begin the process of adding a NAT rule, define any network objects that may be invoked within a NAT rule. To add a network object, go to **Objects > Object Management** and select the **Add Network** menu. Figure 17-8 shows the network objects that are used in the configuration examples in this chapter. You can add any additional objects needed for your own deployment.

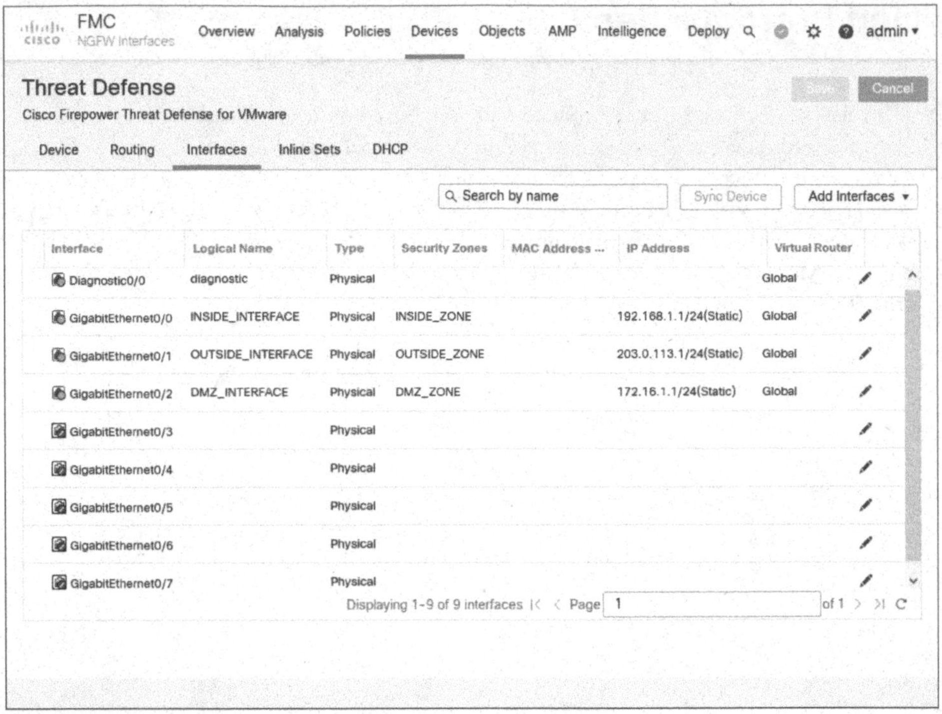

Figure 17-7 *Allocating IP Addresses and Security Zones on Threat Defense Routed Interfaces*

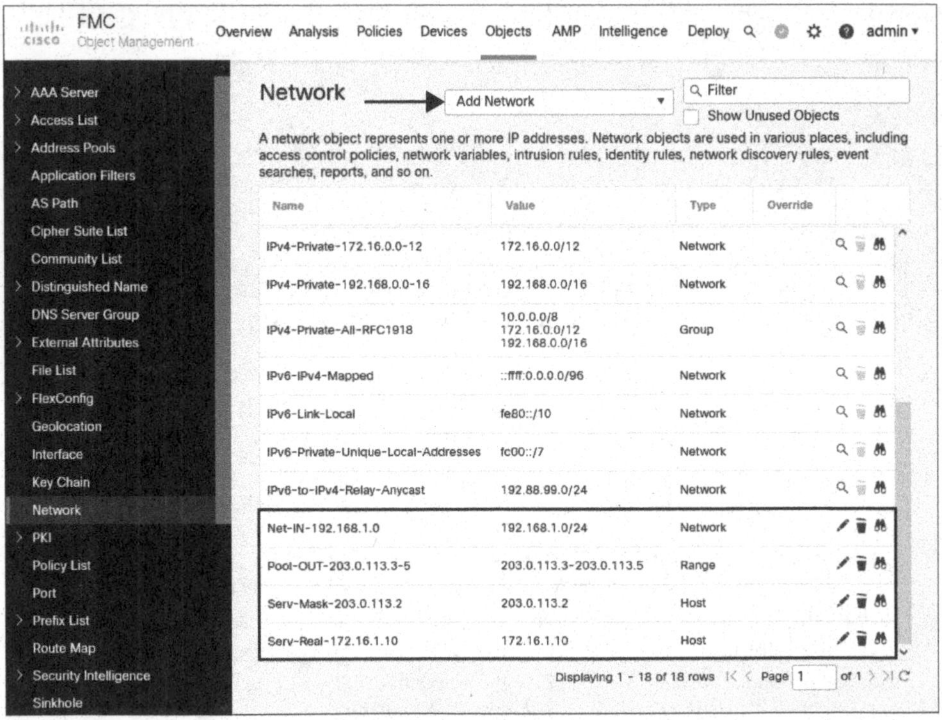

Figure 17-8 *Network Object Configuration Page*

Configuring NAT

A threat defense enables you to accomplish translation in various ways. You can select any type (static versus dynamic) with any combination of NAT rule (Auto versus Manual). However, Cisco recommends that you use Auto NAT rule because it is easier to configure and simpler to troubleshoot. In the following sections, you learn how to configure Auto NAT to masquerade IP addresses in the following real-world deployment scenarios:

- *Masquerading a source address* when an internal host initiates a connection to an external server

- Allowing an external host to connect to an internal host when an external host uses a *masqueraded destination address*

Masquerading a Source Address (Source NAT for Outbound Connection)

When an internal host initiates a connection to the Internet, a threat defense can translate the internal IP address to a public IP address. In other words, the threat defense can masquerade the source addresses of outbound connections. This section describes various methods to select a public IP address for an outbound connection.

> **NOTE**   This section assumes that you have already configured any necessary objects described in the "Fulfilling Prerequisites" section earlier in this chapter.

17

Figure 17-9 shows a scenario where an internal host connects to an external host through a threat defense. When an end user initiates a connection using the original source IP address, the threat defense translates (masquerades) the original source IP address into an address that is predefined in an address pool.

Configuring a Dynamic NAT Rule

The management center offers two types of NAT policies: the Firepower NAT Policy and Threat Defense NAT Policy. The former is used to enable NAT on classic hardware models, such as the 7000 and 8000 Series. To enable NAT on a threat defense, you need to deploy the Threat Defense NAT Policy to it. To do so, follow these steps:

Step 1.   Navigate to **Devices > NAT**. The NAT Policy window appears.

Step 2.   To create a new NAT policy for a threat defense, select **Threat Defense NAT Policy** (see Figure 17-10).

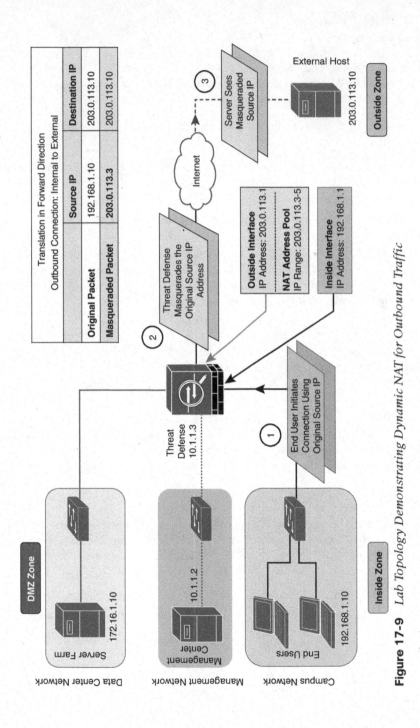

Figure 17-9 *Lab Topology Demonstrating Dynamic NAT for Outbound Traffic*

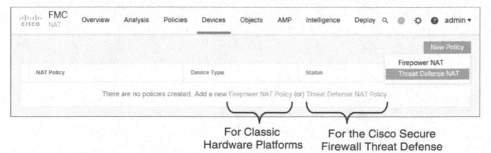

Figure 17-10   *NAT Policy Configuration Options for Different Hardware Models*

Step 3.   When the New Policy window appears, name your policy and add your threat defense from the list of available devices to the policy (see Figure 17-11). Click the **Save** button. The NAT policy editor page appears.

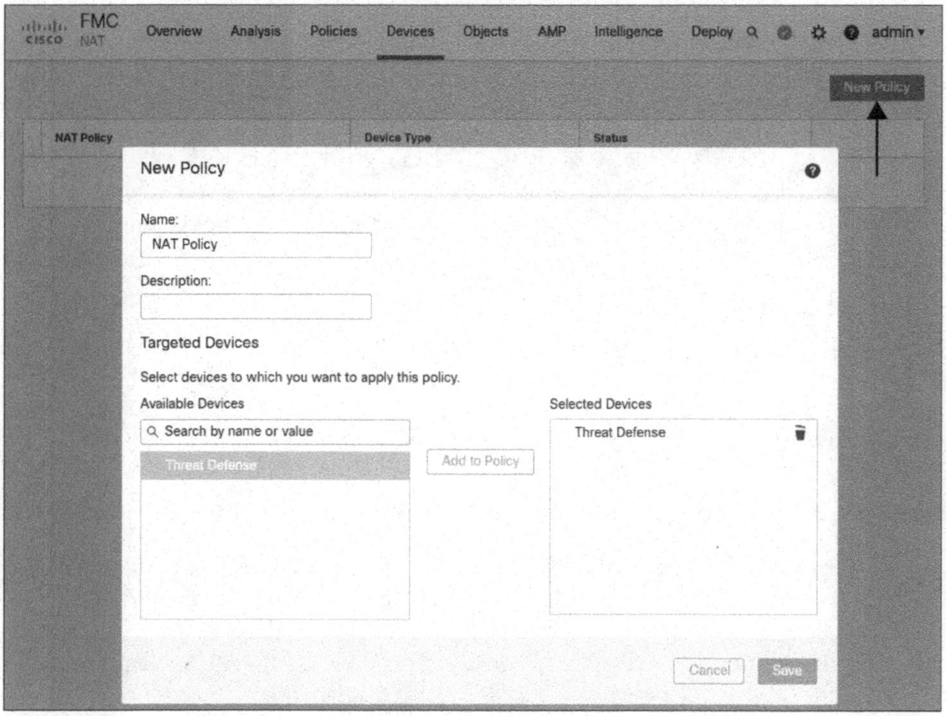

Figure 17-11   *Assigning a NAT Policy to a Threat Defense*

Step 4.   On the policy editor page, click the **Add Rule** button to create a NAT rule. The Add NAT Rule window appears.

Step 5.   From the NAT Rule drop-down, select **Auto NAT Rule**, and from the Type drop-down, select **Dynamic**. Depending on your selections in both of these drop-downs, you will find different configurable options on the Translation tab. For instance, for an Auto NAT Rule with Dynamic type, you need to configure the Original Source and Translated Source.

Step 6. Use the Original Source drop-down to define the source IP addresses of the packets that you want to masquerade. You can select a network object that you defined in the "Fulfilling Prerequisites" section earlier in this chapter. If you did not create an object earlier, you can create one on the fly by clicking the green plus icon next to a drop-down.

Step 7. Define a translated address—the address that appears as the source address of a translated packet. You need to select one of the following translation methods on the Translation or PAT Pool tab, depending on the type of NAT (static or dynamic) you want to configure.

- **Destination Interface IP:** This method allows a threat defense to use the same IP address as the egress interface of the threat defense.

- **Address:** This method enables a threat defense to select an address from a predefined address pool.

Table 17-4 shows a matrix of various Auto NAT rule selections. In this section, you implement dynamic NAT with an address pool.

Table 17-4 Auto NAT Rule—Major Configurable Options

Type	Translation Tab (Translated Source)	Translation Tab (Port Translation)	PAT Pool Tab
Static	Destination Interface IP	Configurable	Not Configurable
Static	Address	Configurable	Not Configurable
Dynamic	Destination Interface IP	Not Configurable	Not Configurable
Dynamic	Address	Not Configurable	Unselected
Dynamic	Address	Not Configurable	Enabled with Address
Dynamic	Address	Not Configurable	Enabled with Destination Interface IP

Figure 17-12 shows the configuration of original and translated addresses in a dynamic Auto NAT rule. If a custom PAT pool is chosen on the PAT Pool tab, also select **Flat Port Range** and **Include Reserve Ports** to enable a threat defense to use the complete range of port numbers, 1 to 65535, even though the same source port number is unavailable for mapping.

Figure 17-13 shows another option to configure address translation. In this case, because the IP address of the destination interface is used as the translated source, a custom PAT pool is unnecessary; hence, it is disabled.

Step 8. At this point, you can click the **OK** button, save the configurations, and deploy the policy on the threat defense. Alternatively, you can continue enhancing the NAT rule with additional rule constraints. For example, on the Interface Objects tab (see Figure 17-14), you can select the ingress and egress interfaces for the traffic that you want to translate. The Available Interface Objects field shows the associated security zones that you assigned by going to **Devices > Devices Management**.

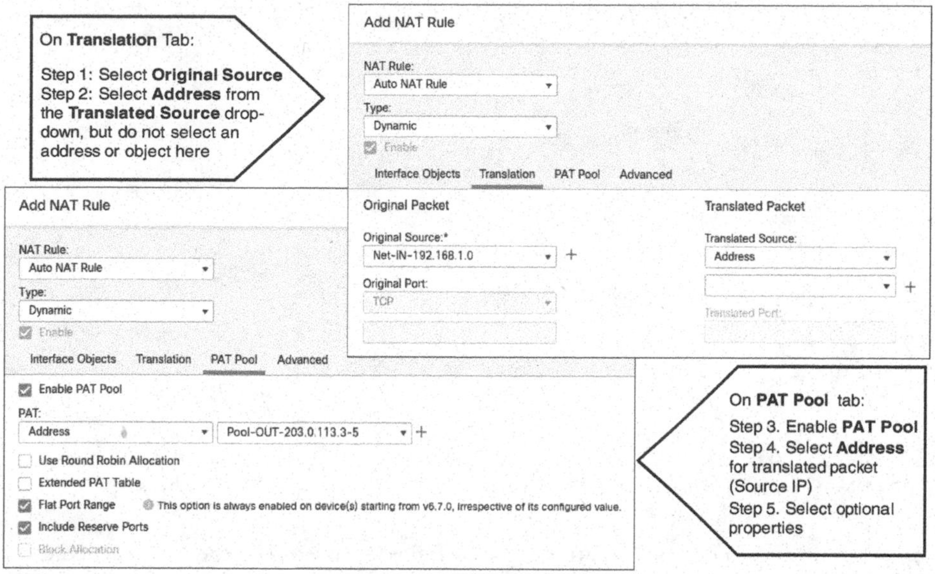

On **Translation** Tab:

Step 1: Select **Original Source**
Step 2: Select **Address** from
the **Translated Source** drop-
down, but do not select an
address or object here

Add NAT Rule

NAT Rule:
Auto NAT Rule

Type:
Dynamic

☑ Enable

Interface Objects   Translation   PAT Pool   Advanced

Original Packet

Original Source:*
Net-IN-192.168.1.0   +

Original Port:
TCP

Translated Packet

Translated Source:
Address

+

Translated Port:

Add NAT Rule

NAT Rule:
Auto NAT Rule

Type:
Dynamic

☑ Enable

Interface Objects   Translation   PAT Pool   Advanced

☑ Enable PAT Pool

PAT:
Address | Pool-OUT-203.0.113.3-5   ▾   +

☐ Use Round Robin Allocation

☐ Extended PAT Table

☑ Flat Port Range   ⓘ This option is always enabled on device(s) starting from v6.7.0, irrespective of its configured value.

☑ Include Reserve Ports

☐ Block Allocation

On **PAT Pool** tab:

Step 3. Enable **PAT Pool**
Step 4. Select **Address**
for translated packet
(Source IP)

Step 5. Select optional
properties

Figure 17-12   *Defining a Dynamic Auto NAT Rule Using the Custom PAT Pool*

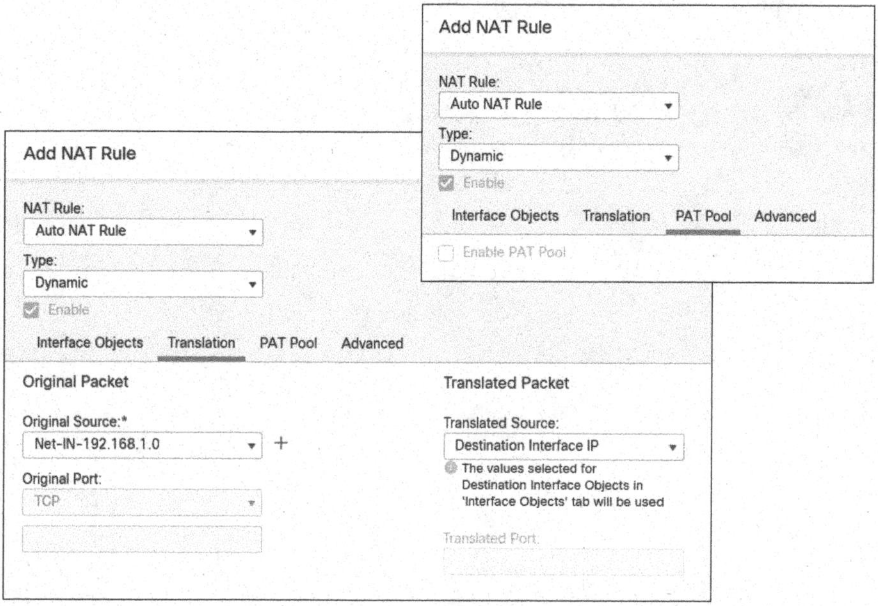

17

Add NAT Rule

NAT Rule:
Auto NAT Rule

Type:
Dynamic

☑ Enable

Interface Objects   Translation   PAT Pool   Advanced

☐ Enable PAT Pool

Add NAT Rule

NAT Rule:
Auto NAT Rule

Type:
Dynamic

☑ Enable

Interface Objects   Translation   PAT Pool   Advanced

Original Packet

Original Source:*
Net-IN-192.168.1.0   +

Original Port:
TCP

Translated Packet

Translated Source:
Destination Interface IP   ▾

ⓘ The values selected for
Destination Interface Objects in
'Interface Objects' tab will be used

Translated Port:

Figure 17-13   *Defining a Dynamic Auto NAT Rule Using Destination Interface Address*

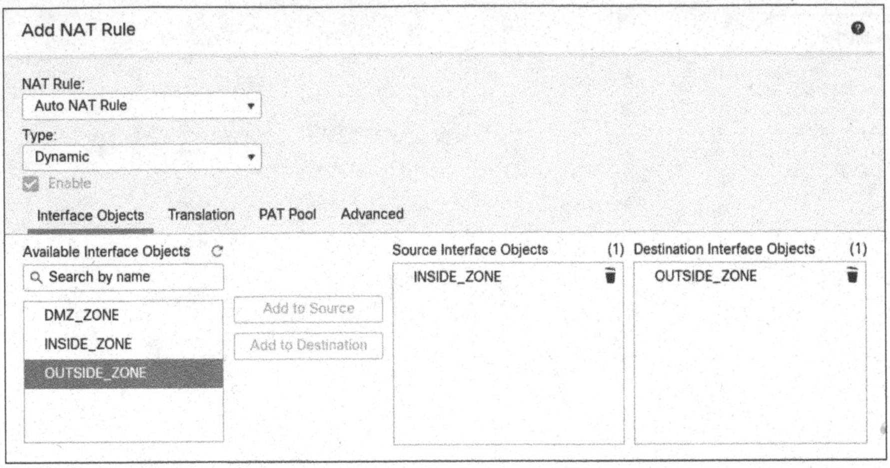

Figure 17-14 *Selecting Source and Destination Interface Objects to Match Traffic*

Step 9. When you complete all the steps, click the **OK** button on the NAT rule editor window to create the NAT rule. The browser returns to the NAT policy editor, where you can see the NAT rule you have just created. To activate the policy, first click **Save** to save the policy, and then navigate to **Deployment > Deploy** to deploy the policy on your threat defense.

Figure 17-15 shows a dynamic Auto NAT rule that translates the source IP addresses of any hosts from the INSIDE_ZONE to the OUTSIDE_ZONE. The translated packet uses an address from the address pool, Pool-OUT-203.0.113.3-5, as its source IP address.

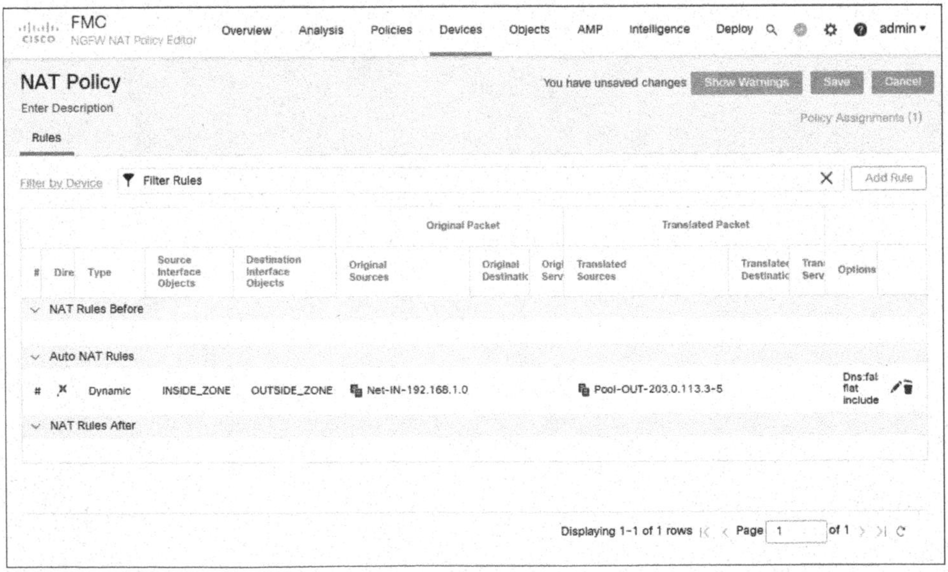

Figure 17-15 *Defining a Dynamic NAT Rule to Translate Outbound Connections*

In the following sections, you learn how to verify the configuration on the CLI and how to determine whether a threat defense is translating addresses as expected.

Verifying the Configuration

After you deploy a NAT policy, you can run the **show running-config nat** command in the CLI to view the latest NAT configurations and to confirm whether the desired policy is active.

Example 17-1 exhibits the running configurations of NAT and the definitions of any associated objects that are invoked in a NAT rule.

Example 17-1 *Defining a NAT Rule and Any Associated Objects*

```
! To view the NAT configurations:

> show running-config nat
!
object network Net-IN-192.168.1.0
 nat (INSIDE_INTERFACE,OUTSIDE_INTERFACE) dynamic pat-pool Pool-OUT-203.0.113.3-5
flat include-reserve
>


! To determine the scope of an object:

> show running-config object
object network Net-IN-192.168.1.0
 subnet 192.168.1.0 255.255.255.0
object network Pool-OUT-203.0.113.3-5
 range 203.0.113.3 203.0.113.5
>
```

You can also run the **show nat detail** command to display more detailed information about a NAT policy, such as the priority of a rule (Auto NAT versus Manual NAT) or the type of a rule (static versus dynamic). The output of this command also displays the number of matching connections in both forward and reverse directions, through the translate_hits and untranslate_hits counters, respectively.

Example 17-2 shows an Auto NAT rule (dynamic PAT) for translating traffic from the 192.168.1.0/24 network to the address pool 203.0.113.3 to 203.0.113.5. The zero hit count indicates that the rule has not matched any connections.

Example 17-2 *Output of the* show nat detail *Command*

```
> show nat detail
Auto NAT Policies (Section 2)
1 (INSIDE_INTERFACE) to (OUTSIDE_INTERFACE) source dynamic Net-IN-192.168.1.0 pat-
pool Pool-OUT-203.0.113.3-5 flat include-reserve
    translate_hits = 0, untranslate_hits = 0
    Source - Origin: 192.168.1.0/24, Translated (PAT): 203.0.113.3-203.0.113.5
>
```

17

Examples 17-1 and 17-2 display the source (INSIDE_INTERFACE) and destination (OUT-SIDE_INTERFACE) defined in a NAT rule. However, the output in these examples does not show the status, IP address, or name of an interface. You can find them by running other commands, such as **show nameif** and **show interfaces ip brief**.

Example 17-3 shows how to map the physical interfaces with their logical names. It also shows how to verify the IP address and status of an interface.

Example 17-3 *Viewing Various Parameters of Threat Defense Interfaces*

```
! To view the mapping of physical interfaces with their logical names:


> show nameif
Interface              Name                   Security
GigabitEthernet0/0     INSIDE_INTERFACE          0
GigabitEthernet0/1     OUTSIDE_INTERFACE         0
GigabitEthernet0/2     DMZ_INTERFACE             0
Management0/0          diagnostic                0
>


! To view the status and IP addresses of the threat defense interfaces:


> show interface ip brief
Interface              IP-Address     OK? Method Status                 Protocol
GigabitEthernet0/0     192.168.1.1    YES manual up                         up
GigabitEthernet0/1     203.0.113.1    YES manual up                         up
GigabitEthernet0/2     172.16.1.1     YES manual up                         up
GigabitEthernet0/3     unassigned     YES unset  administratively down up
GigabitEthernet0/4     unassigned     YES unset  administratively down up
GigabitEthernet0/5     unassigned     YES unset  administratively down up
GigabitEthernet0/6     unassigned     YES unset  administratively down up
GigabitEthernet0/7     unassigned     YES unset  administratively down up
Internal-Control0/0    127.0.1.1      YES unset  up                         up
Internal-Control0/1    unassigned     YES unset  up                         up
Internal-Data0/0       unassigned     YES unset  up                         up
Internal-Data0/0       unassigned     YES unset  up                         up
Internal-Data0/1       169.254.1.1    YES unset  up                         up
Internal-Data0/2       unassigned     YES unset  up                         up
Management0/0          unassigned     YES unset  up                         up
>
```

Verifying the Operation: Inside to Outside

This section describes how to verify the NAT operation on a threat defense. To demonstrate the translation process, this example uses SSH traffic.

Let's initiate a connection from an internal host 192.168.1.10 to an external SSH server 203.0.113.10. If NAT is operational on the threat defense, the external SSH server sees 203.0.113.3 as the source IP address of the internal host instead of its original source IP address, 192.168.1.10.

Example 17-4 shows an SSH connection between the internal client and the external server. The connection table shows the original IP address (192.168.1.10) of the internal server with a translation (**xlate**) ID. However, you can determine the masqueraded or translated address (203.0.113.3) from the translation table.

Example 17-4   *Connection and Translation Tables*

```
> show conn detail
1 in use, 3 most used
Inspect Snort:
        preserve-connection: 1 enabled, 0 in effect, 2 most enabled, 0 most in
effect
Flags: A - awaiting responder ACK to SYN, a - awaiting initiator ACK to SYN,
       b - TCP state-bypass or nailed,
       C - CTIQBE media, c - cluster centralized,
       D - DNS, d - dump, E - outside back connection, e - semi-distributed,
       F - initiator FIN, f - responder FIN,
       G - group, g - MGCP, H - H.323, h - H.225.0, I - initiator data,
       i - incomplete, J - GTP, j - GTP data, K - GTP t3-response
       k - Skinny media, L - decap tunnel, M - SMTP data, m - SIP media
       N - inspected by Snort (1 - preserve-connection enabled, 2 - preserve-
connection in effect)
       n - GUP, O - responder data, o - offloaded,
       P - inside back connection, p - passenger flow
       q - SQL*Net data, R - initiator acknowledged FIN,
       R - UDP SUNRPC, r - responder acknowledged FIN,
       T - SIP, t - SIP transient, U - up,
       V - VPN orphan, v - M3UA W - WAAS,
       w - secondary domain backup,
       X - inspected by service module,
       x - per session, Y - director stub flow, y - backup stub flow,
       Z - Scansafe redirection, z - forwarding stub flow


TCP OUTSIDE_INTERFACE: 203.0.113.10/80 INSIDE_INTERFACE: 192.168.1.10/47958,
    flags Ux N1, qos-rule-id 268462080, idle 8s, uptime 8s, timeout 1h0m, bytes 0,
xlate id 0x2b7716a7a780
  Initiator: 192.168.1.10, Responder: 203.0.113.10
  Connection lookup keyid: 2158727

>
```

17

```
> show xlate detail

1 in use, 2 most used

Flags: D - DNS, e - extended, I - identity, i - dynamic, r - portmap,
        s - static, T - twice, N - net-to-net

TCP PAT from INSIDE_INTERFACE:192.168.1.10/47958 to OUTSIDE_INTER-
FACE:203.0.113.3/47958 flags ri idle 0:00:04 timeout 0:00:30 refcnt 1 xlate id
0x2b7716a7a780

>
```

By looking at the output of the **show nat detail** command, you can determine whether the traffic matches a particular NAT rule and how many times a rule finds a match.

Example 17-5 confirms that the Auto NAT rule found one matching connection when a host sent traffic from INSIDE_INTERFACE to OUTSIDE_INTERFACE.

Example 17-5 *Matching One Connection in the Forward Direction*

```
> show nat detail

Auto NAT Policies (Section 2)
1 (INSIDE_INTERFACE) to (OUTSIDE_INTERFACE) source dynamic Net-IN-192.168.1.0 pat-
pool Pool-OUT-203.0.113.3-5 flat include-reserve
    translate_hits = 1, untranslate_hits = 0
    Source - Origin: 192.168.1.0/24, Translated (PAT): 203.0.113.3-203.0.113.5

>
```

To analyze the NAT operation further, you can capture traffic in real time as a threat defense translates the original addresses. Chapter 8, "Capturing Traffic for Advanced Analysis," describes the steps to capture traffic using the management center GUI. As an alternative, you can also capture traffic directly using the threat defense CLI. The examples in this chapter demonstrate how to use the CLI tools to capture and examine live traffic.

Example 17-6 demonstrates the capture of any SSH traffic on the inside interface. Later, you will analyze the translation of these packets.

Example 17-6 *Capturing SSH Traffic on the Threat Defense Inside Interface*

```
! Begin the capture of SSH traffic on inside interface.


> capture ssh_traffic_inside trace interface INSIDE_INTERFACE match tcp any any
eq 22



! Verify if the threat defense is running a capture for SSH traffic.


> show capture
capture ssh_traffic_inside type raw-data trace interface INSIDE_INTERFACE [Capturing
- 0 bytes]
    match tcp any any eq ssh

>
```

At this stage, you can initiate an SSH connection from the internal host to the external SSH server. The threat defense should capture the traffic on the inside interface. You can view the packets in the CLI.

Example 17-7 shows the first few captured packets for an SSH connection. Later, it analyzes the first packet to demonstrate the detailed operation of an address translation.

Example 17-7 *Analyzing Captured Packets*

```
! To view all of the captured packets (press Ctrl+C to exit from a long show):
> show capture ssh_traffic_inside

81 packets captured

   1: 02:59:47.220310   192.168.1.10.41934 > 203.0.113.10.22:
S 1482617093:1482617093(0) win 29200 <mss 1460,sackOK,timestamp 15243390
0,nop,wscale 7>
   2: 02:59:47.221149   203.0.113.10.22 > 192.168.1.10.41934:
S 1409789153:1409789153(0) ack 1482617094 win 28960 <mss 1380,sackOK,timestamp
17762742 15243390,nop,wscale 7>
   3: 02:59:47.221256   192.168.1.10.41934 > 203.0.113.10.22: . ack 1409789154
win 229 <nop,nop,timestamp 15243390 17762742>
   4: 02:59:47.221729   192.168.1.10.41934 > 203.0.113.10.22:
P 1482617094:1482617135(41) ack 1409789154 win 229 <nop,nop,timestamp 15243391
17762742>
   5: 02:59:47.222186   203.0.113.10.22 > 192.168.1.10.41934: . ack 1482617135
win 227 <nop,nop,timestamp 17762742 15243391>
.
.
<Output is omitted for brevity>



! To analyze the first captured packet:

> show capture ssh_traffic_inside packet-number 1 trace

81 packets captured

   1: 02:59:47.220310 192.168.1.10.41934 > 203.0.113.10.22:
S 1482617093:1482617093(0) win 29200 <mss 1460,sackOK,timestamp 15243390
0,nop,wscale 7>
Phase: 1
Type: CAPTURE
Subtype:
Result: ALLOW
Config:
```

17

```
Additional Information:
MAC Access list

Phase: 2
Type: ACCESS-LIST
Subtype:
Result: ALLOW
Config:
Implicit Rule
Additional Information:
MAC Access list

Phase: 3
Type: ROUTE-LOOKUP
Subtype: Resolve Egress Interface
Result: ALLOW
Config:
Additional Information:
found next-hop 203.0.113.10 using egress ifc OUTSIDE_INTERFACE

Phase: 4
Type: ACCESS-LIST
Subtype: log
Result: ALLOW
Config:
access-group CSM_FW_ACL_ global
access-list CSM_FW_ACL_ advanced permit ip any any rule-id 268435457
access-list CSM_FW_ACL_ remark rule-id 268435457: ACCESS POLICY: AC Policy
- Mandatory/1
access-list CSM_FW_ACL_ remark rule-id 268435457: L7 RULE: Traffic Selection
Additional Information:
 This packet will be sent to snort for additional processing where a verdict will be
reached

Phase: 5
Type: CONN-SETTINGS
Subtype:
Result: ALLOW
Config:
class-map class-default
 match any
policy-map global_policy
 class class-default
 set connection advanced-options UM_STATIC_TCP_MAP
```

```
service-policy global_policy global
Additional Information:


Phase: 6
Type: NAT
Subtype:
Result: ALLOW
Config:
object network Net-IN-192.168.1.0
 nat (INSIDE_INTERFACE,OUTSIDE_INTERFACE) dynamic pat-pool Pool-OUT-203.0.113.3-5
flat include-reserve
Additional Information:
Dynamic translate 192.168.1.10/41934 to 203.0.113.3/41934


Phase: 7
Type: NAT
Subtype: per-session
Result: ALLOW
Config:
Additional Information:


Phase: 8
Type: IP-OPTIONS
Subtype:
Result: ALLOW
Config:
Additional Information:


Phase: 9
Type: NAT
Subtype: per-session
Result: ALLOW
Config:
Additional Information:


Phase: 10
Type: IP-OPTIONS
Subtype:
Result: ALLOW
Config:
Additional Information:


Phase: 11
Type: FLOW-CREATION
```

```
Subtype:
Result: ALLOW
Config:
Additional Information:
New flow created with id 442, packet dispatched to next module


Phase: 12
Type: EXTERNAL-INSPECT
Subtype:
Result: ALLOW
Config:
Additional Information:
Application: 'SNORT Inspect'


Phase: 13
Type: SNORT
Subtype:
Result: ALLOW
Config:
Additional Information:
Snort Verdict: (pass-packet) allow this packet


Phase: 14
Type: ROUTE-LOOKUP
Subtype: Resolve Egress Interface
Result: ALLOW
Config:
Additional Information:
found next-hop 203.0.113.10 using egress ifc OUTSIDE_INTERFACE


Phase: 15
Type: ADJACENCY-LOOKUP
Subtype: next-hop and adjacency
Result: ALLOW
Config:
Additional Information:
adjacency Active
next-hop mac address 0023.2472.1d3c hits 139985869104448


Phase: 16
Type: CAPTURE
Subtype:
Result: ALLOW
Config:
```

```
Additional Information:
MAC Access list

Result:
input-interface: OUTSIDE_INTERFACE
input-status: up
input-line-status: up
output-interface: OUTSIDE_INTERFACE
output-status: up
output-line-status: up
Action: allow



1 packet shown
>
```

Verifying the Operation: Outside to Inside

The NAT rule you created earlier evaluates the forward traffic—the traffic that originates from INSIDE_INTERFACE and is destined for OUTSIDE_INTERFACE. However, any traffic in the reverse direction does not match this rule. You can verify this by capturing SSH traffic on OUTSIDE_INTERFACE and by analyzing the trace data.

Example 17-8 shows how to enable the **capture** tool on the outside interface.

Example 17-8   *Capturing SSH Traffic on the Threat Defense OUTSIDE_INTERFACE*

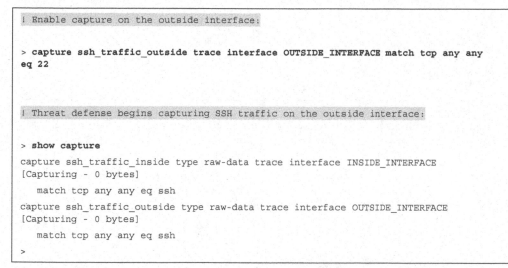

```
! Enable capture on the outside interface:

> capture ssh_traffic_outside trace interface OUTSIDE_INTERFACE match tcp any any
eq 22


! Threat defense begins capturing SSH traffic on the outside interface:

> show capture
capture ssh_traffic_inside type raw-data trace interface INSIDE_INTERFACE
[Capturing - 0 bytes]
    match tcp any any eq ssh
capture ssh_traffic_outside type raw-data trace interface OUTSIDE_INTERFACE
[Capturing - 0 bytes]
    match tcp any any eq ssh
>
```

Now if you attempt to connect from an external host to an internal host, regardless of the destination IP address you choose—either original or masqueraded—the connection attempt fails.

Example 17-9 shows the failed connection attempts from the external host 203.0.113.10 to the same internal host—through the masqueraded IP address 203.0.113.3 and the original IP address 192.168.1.10.22.

Example 17-9 *Captured Traffic on the Threat Defense OUTSIDE_INTERFACE Shows Only SYN (S) Packets*

```
> show capture ssh_traffic_outside

8 packets captured

  1: 03:56:51.100290 203.0.113.10.48400 > 203.0.113.3.22: S 3636330443:3636330443(0)
win 29200 <mss 1460,sackOK,timestamp 18618684 0,nop,wscale 7>
  2: 03:56:52.097269 203.0.113.10.48400 > 203.0.113.3.22: S 3636330443:3636330443(0)
win 29200 <mss 1460,sackOK,timestamp 18618934 0,nop,wscale 7>
  3: 03:56:54.101343 203.0.113.10.48400 > 203.0.113.3.22: S 3636330443:3636330443(0)
win 29200 <mss 1460,sackOK,timestamp 18619435 0,nop,wscale 7>
  4: 03:56:58.105478 203.0.113.10.48400 > 203.0.113.3.22: S 3636330443:3636330443(0)
win 29200 <mss 1460,sackOK,timestamp 18620436 0,nop,wscale 7>



  5: 03:57:22.069759 203.0.113.10.53048 > 192.168.1.10.22:
S 1744936567:1744936567(0) win 29200 <mss 1460,sackOK,timestamp 18626426 0,nop,
wscale 7>
  6: 03:57:23.066250 203.0.113.10.53048 > 192.168.1.10.22:
S 1744936567:1744936567(0) win 29200 <mss 1460,sackOK,timestamp 18626676 0,nop,
wscale 7>
  7: 03:57:25.070369 203.0.113.10.53048 > 192.168.1.10.22:
S 1744936567:1744936567(0) win 29200 <mss 1460,sackOK,timestamp 18627177 0,nop,
wscale 7>
  8: 03:57:29.082469 203.0.113.10.53048 > 192.168.1.10.22:
S 1744936567:1744936567(0) win 29200 <mss 1460,sackOK,timestamp 18628180 0,nop,
wscale 7>
8 packets shown
>
```

Example 17-10 analyzes the trace data of the first captured packet, where the external host tries to connect to the internal host using its masqueraded IP address, 203.0.113.3.

Example 17-10 *Trying to Connect to the Masqueraded IP Address of an Internal Host*

```
> show capture ssh_traffic_outside packet-number 1 trace

8 packets captured

  1: 03:56:51.100290 203.0.113.10.48400 > 203.0.113.3.22: S 3636330443:3636330443(0)
win 29200 <mss 1460,sackOK,timestamp 18618684 0,nop,wscale 7>
Phase: 1
```

```
Type: CAPTURE
Subtype:
Result: ALLOW
Config:
Additional Information:
MAC Access list

Phase: 2
Type: ACCESS-LIST
Subtype:
Result: ALLOW
Config:
Implicit Rule
Additional Information:
MAC Access list

Phase: 3
Type: ROUTE-LOOKUP
Subtype: Resolve Egress Interface
Result: ALLOW
Config:
Additional Information:
found next-hop 203.0.113.3 using egress ifc OUTSIDE_INTERFACE

Result:
input-interface: OUTSIDE_INTERFACE
input-status: up
input-line-status: up
output-interface: OUTSIDE_INTERFACE
output-status: up
output-line-status: up
Action: drop
Drop-reason: (nat-no-xlate-to-pat-pool) Connection to PAT address without pre-exist-
ing xlate


1 packet shown
>
```

Example 17-11 analyzes the trace data of the fifth captured packet where the external host tries to connect to the internal host by using its original IP address, 192.168.1.10.

Example 17-11 *Trying to Connect to the Original IP Address of an Internal Host*

```
> show capture ssh_traffic_outside packet-number 5 trace

8 packets captured

  5: 03:57:22.069759 203.0.113.10.53048 > 192.168.1.10.22: S 1744936567:
1744936567(0) win 29200 <mss 1460,sackOK,timestamp 18626426 0,nop,wscale 7>
Phase: 1
Type: CAPTURE
Subtype:
Result: ALLOW
Config:
Additional Information:
MAC Access list


Phase: 2
Type: ACCESS-LIST
Subtype:
Result: ALLOW
Config:
Implicit Rule
Additional Information:
MAC Access list


Phase: 3
Type: ROUTE-LOOKUP
Subtype: Resolve Egress Interface
Result: ALLOW
Config:
Additional Information:
found next-hop 192.168.1.10 using egress ifc INSIDE_INTERFACE


Phase: 4
Type: ACCESS-LIST
Subtype: log
Result: ALLOW
Config:
access-group CSM_FW_ACL_ global
access-list CSM_FW_ACL_ advanced permit ip any any rule-id 268435457
access-list CSM_FW_ACL_ remark rule-id 268435457: ACCESS POLICY: AC Policy
- Mandatory/1
access-list CSM_FW_ACL_ remark rule-id 268435457: L7 RULE: Traffic Selection
Additional Information:
```

This packet will be sent to snort for additional processing where a verdict will be reached

```
Phase: 5
Type: CONN-SETTINGS
Subtype:
Result: ALLOW
Config:
class-map class-default
 match any
policy-map global_policy
 class class-default
 set connection advanced-options UM_STATIC_TCP_MAP
service-policy global_policy global
Additional Information:

Phase: 6
Type: NAT
Subtype: per-session
Result: ALLOW
Config:
Additional Information:

Phase: 7
Type: IP-OPTIONS
Subtype:
Result: ALLOW
Config:
Additional Information:

Phase: 8
Type: NAT
Subtype: rpf-check
Result: DROP
Config:
object network Net-IN-192.168.1.0
 nat (INSIDE_INTERFACE,OUTSIDE_INTERFACE) dynamic pat-pool Pool-OUT-203.0.113.3-5
flat include-reserve
Additional Information:

Result:
input-interface: OUTSIDE_INTERFACE
input-status: up
input-line-status: up
output-interface: INSIDE_INTERFACE
```

```
output-status: up
output-line-status: up
Action: drop
Drop-reason: (acl-drop) Flow is denied by configured rule


1 packet shown
>
```

Connecting to a Masqueraded Destination (Destination NAT for Inbound Connection)

When external hosts access any services of your company, they should access through the public IP address of your organization. Any internal addressing scheme must be invisible to the external users. In this section, you learn how to connect to an internal host by using a masqueraded public IP address.

Figure 17-16 illustrates a scenario where an external host connects to an internal DMZ server of a company. When an external host initiates a connection to a masqueraded public address, the threat defense translates the address into an internal original address.

Configuring a Static NAT Rule

Because in the previous section you created an Auto NAT rule with a dynamic type and analyzed its detailed operation, this section does not duplicate the same procedures for creating a NAT policy from scratch. You can just add a new NAT rule as illustrated in Figure 17-16 and then redeploy the NAT policy. If the policy deployment is successful, the threat defense should let an external host connect to an internal DMZ server using a masqueraded public IP address. Because the threat defense in this case translates a public destination address to an internal address, this translation is known as destination NAT.

Figure 17-17 illustrates a static NAT rule that enables an outside host to connect to a DMZ server (internal IP address 172.16.1.10) via the SSH service (internal port 22) without knowing the internal addressing scheme. The outside host can access the DMZ server only if the outside host uses the masqueraded IP address 203.0.113.2 and port 2200 as its destination.

Figure 17-18 shows two rules in a NAT policy; the static Auto NAT rule (bottom) has just been created to translate inbound connections. The dynamic NAT rule (top) was added earlier to translate outbound connections.

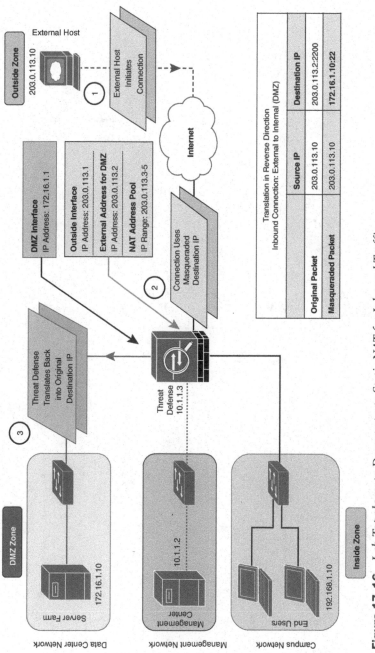

Figure 17-16 *Lab Topology to Demonstrate Static NAT for Inbound Traffic*

17

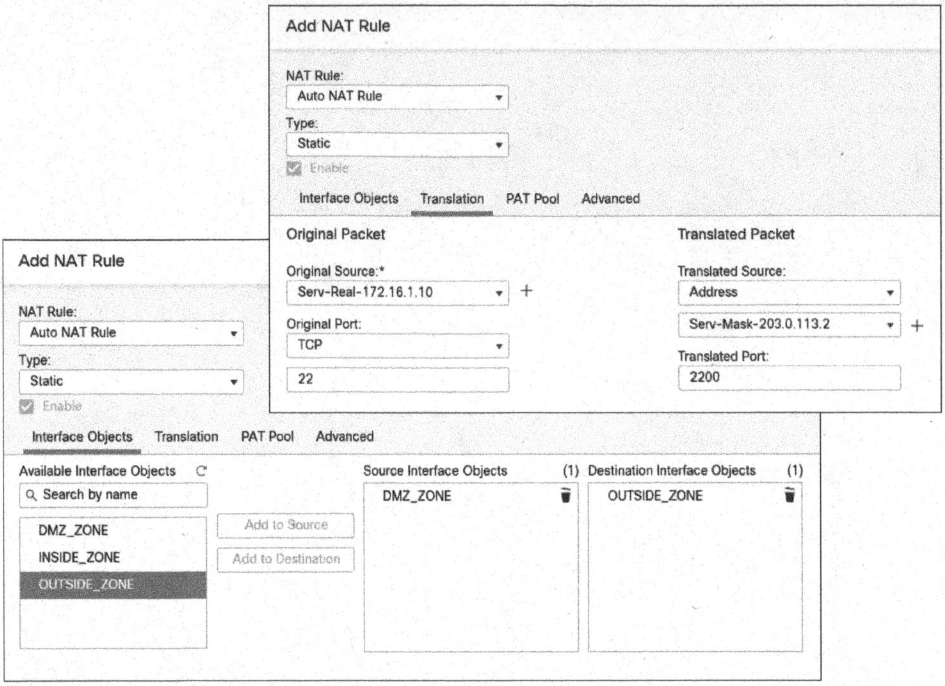

Figure 17-17 *Defining a Static Auto NAT Rule for Inbound Connections*

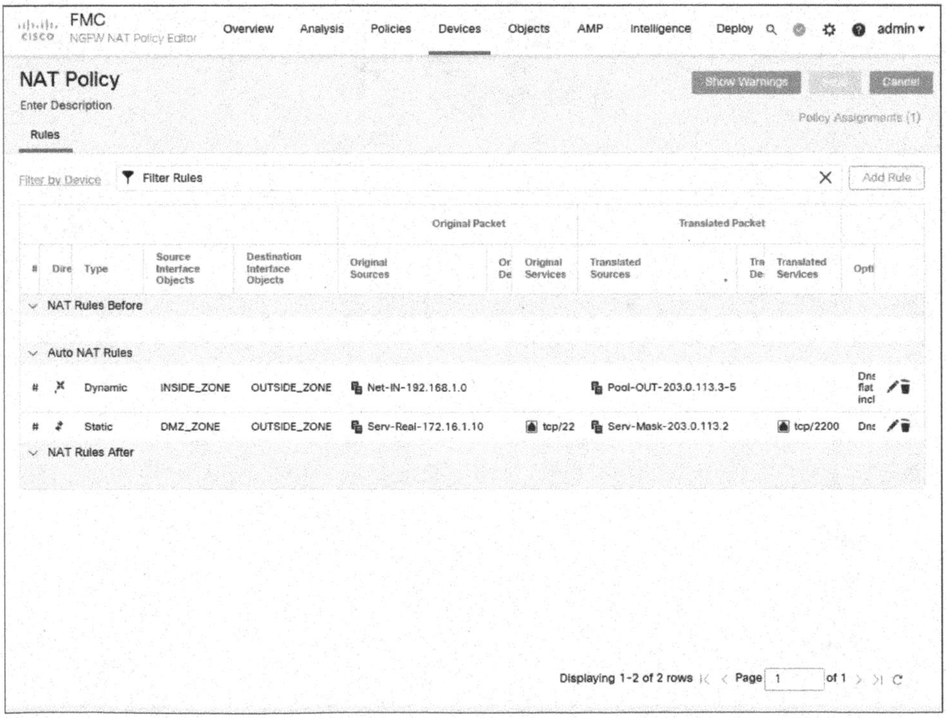

Figure 17-18 *Dynamic NAT and Static NAT Rules for Outbound and Inbound Traffic*

After you add a new NAT rule, you must click the **Save** button to save the policy. Finally, navigate to **Deploy > Deployment** to deploy the new NAT policy to your threat defense.

Verifying the Operation: Outside to DMZ

This section demonstrates the operation of a static Auto NAT rule on a threat defense. As in the previous exercise, this one also uses the SSH service to generate traffic. However, unlike in the previous exercise, the SSH connection is initiated by an external host.

Before you begin, you should clear the NAT counters and any existing translations so that you will be able to notice any new changes quickly:

```
> clear nat counters
```

```
> clear xlate
```

Now you can try to access the internal DMZ server from an external host. Using an SSH client, connect to port 2200 of the translated (masqueraded) IP address 203.0.113.2. You are connected to the internal DMZ server, although the original IP address of the server is 172.16.1.10, and the server listens to port 22 for SSH connections. This happens due to the static NAT on the threat defense.

Example 17-12 shows confirmation that the inbound SSH traffic matches the first rule on the Auto NAT policy. The untranslate_hits counter confirms the matching of one connection in the reverse direction.

Example 17-12 *Matching a Connection in the Reverse Direction*

```
> show nat detail

Auto NAT Policies (Section 2)
1 (DMZ_INTERFACE) to (OUTSIDE_INTERFACE) source static Serv-Real-172.16.1.10
Serv-Mask-203.0.113.2 service tcp ssh 2200
    translate_hits = 0, untranslate_hits = 1
    Source - Origin: 172.16.1.10/32, Translated: 203.0.113.2/32
    Service - Protocol: tcp Real: ssh Mapped: 2200
2 (INSIDE_INTERFACE) to (OUTSIDE_INTERFACE) source dynamic Net-IN-192.168.1.0
pat-pool Pool-OUT-203.0.113.3-5 flat include-reserve
    translate_hits = 0, untranslate_hits = 0
    Source - Origin: 192.168.1.0/24, Translated (PAT): 203.0.113.3-203.0.113.5
>
```

Example 17-13 shows the status of the current translations. The flag confirms a static port translation between an external host and an internal DMZ server.

Example 17-13 *Real-Time Translation Status*

```
> show xlate detail
1 in use, 2 most used
Flags: D - DNS, e - extended, I - identity, i - dynamic, r - portmap,
       s - static, T - twice, N - net-to-net
```

```
TCP PAT from DMZ_INTERFACE:172.16.1.10 22-22 to OUTSIDE_INTERFACE:203.0.113.2
2200-2200
        flags sr idle 0:00:54 timeout 0:00:00 refcnt 1 xlate id 0x7f516987ee00
>
```

To better understand the NAT operation, you can capture SSH traffic on an outside interface (on the translated port) and analyze it (see Example 17-14).

Example 17-14 *Capturing SSH Traffic on an Outside Interface (on a Translated Port)*

```
! Enable capture on outside interface:

> capture ssh_traffic_outside_masked trace interface OUTSIDE_INTERFACE match tcp any
any eq 2200


! Verify that the capture is running:

> show capture
capture ssh_traffic_inside type raw-data trace interface INSIDE_INTERFACE
[Capturing - 0 bytes]
 match tcp any any eq ssh
capture ssh_traffic_outside type raw-data trace interface OUTSIDE_INTERFACE
[Capturing - 0 bytes]
 match tcp any any eq ssh
capture ssh_traffic_outside_masked type raw-data trace interface OUTSIDE_INTERFACE
[Capturing - 0 bytes]
 match tcp any any eq 2200

>


! Now, initiate an SSH connection from the external host to the internal DMZ server.
Use the masqueraded IP address and port number. It generates the following traffic.


> show capture ssh_traffic_outside_masked

59 packets captured

  1: 05:21:23.785436 203.0.113.10.41760 > 203.0.113.2.2200: S
2089153959:2089153959(0) win 29200 <mss 1460,sackOK,timestamp 19887065 0,nop,
wscale 7>
  2: 05:21:23.786168 203.0.113.2.2200 > 203.0.113.10.41760: S 29917599:29917599(0)
ack 2089153960 win 28960 <mss 1380,sackOK,timestamp 19892875 19887065,nop,wscale 7>
  3: 05:21:23.786336 203.0.113.10.41760 > 203.0.113.2.2200: . ack 29917600 win 229
<nop,nop,timestamp 19887065 19892875>
  4: 05:21:23.786855 203.0.113.10.41760 > 203.0.113.2.2200:
```

```
P 2089153960:2089154001(41) ack 29917600 win 229 <nop,nop,timestamp 19887066
19892875>

  5: 05:21:23.787312 203.0.113.2.2200 > 203.0.113.10.41760: . ack 2089154001 win 227
<nop,nop,timestamp 19892876 19887066>

 .

 .

<Output is omitted for brevity>
```

Example 17-15 shows how to analyze the tracing data of a captured packet. The threat defense translates and allows the packet as you are connecting through IP address 203.0.113.2 and port 2200.

Example 17-15 *Analyzing a Translated Packet (Where the Packet Matches a Rule)*

```
> show capture ssh_traffic_outside_masked packet-number 1 trace

59 packets captured

  1: 05:21:23.785436 203.0.113.10.41760 > 203.0.113.2.2200:
S 2089153959:2089153959(0) win 29200 <mss 1460,sackOK,timestamp 19887065 0,nop,
wscale 7>
Phase: 1
Type: CAPTURE
Subtype:
Result: ALLOW
Config:
Additional Information:
MAC Access list


Phase: 2
Type: ACCESS-LIST
Subtype:
Result: ALLOW
Config:
Implicit Rule
Additional Information:
MAC Access list


Phase: 3
Type: UN-NAT
Subtype: static
Result: ALLOW
Config:
object network Serv-Real-172.16.1.10
 nat (DMZ_INTERFACE,OUTSIDE_INTERFACE) static Serv-Mask-203.0.113.2 service tcp ssh
2200
```

17

```
Additional Information:
NAT divert to egress interface DMZ_INTERFACE
Untranslate 203.0.113.2/2200 to 172.16.1.10/22


Phase: 4
Type: ACCESS-LIST
Subtype: log
Result: ALLOW
Config:
access-group CSM_FW_ACL_ global
access-list CSM_FW_ACL_ advanced permit ip any any rule-id 268435457
access-list CSM_FW_ACL_ remark rule-id 268435457: ACCESS POLICY: AC Policy
- Mandatory/1
access-list CSM_FW_ACL_ remark rule-id 268435457: L7 RULE: Traffic Selection
Additional Information:
 This packet will be sent to snort for additional processing where a verdict will be
reached


Phase: 5
Type: CONN-SETTINGS
Subtype:
Result: ALLOW
Config:
class-map class-default
 match any
policy-map global_policy
 class class-default
 set connection advanced-options UM_STATIC_TCP_MAP
service-policy global_policy global
Additional Information:


Phase: 6
Type: NAT
Subtype: per-session
Result: ALLOW
Config:
Additional Information:


Phase: 7
Type: IP-OPTIONS
Subtype:
Result: ALLOW
Config:
Additional Information:
```

```
Phase: 8
Type: NAT
Subtype: rpf-check
Result: ALLOW
Config:
object network Serv-Real-172.16.1.10
 nat (DMZ_INTERFACE,OUTSIDE_INTERFACE) static Serv-Mask-203.0.113.2 service tcp
ssh 2200
Additional Information:

Phase: 9
Type: NAT
Subtype: per-session
Result: ALLOW
Config:
Additional Information:

Phase: 10
Type: IP-OPTIONS
Subtype:
Result: ALLOW
Config:
Additional Information:

Phase: 11
Type: FLOW-CREATION
Subtype:
Result: ALLOW
Config:
Additional Information:
New flow created with id 505, packet dispatched to next module

Phase: 12
Type: EXTERNAL-INSPECT
Subtype:
Result: ALLOW
Config:
Additional Information:
Application: 'SNORT Inspect'

Phase: 13
Type: SNORT
Subtype:
Result: ALLOW
```

```
Config:
Additional Information:
Snort Verdict: (pass-packet) allow this packet

Phase: 14
Type: ROUTE-LOOKUP
Subtype: Resolve Egress Interface
Result: ALLOW
Config:
Additional Information:
found next-hop 172.16.1.10 using egress ifc DMZ_INTERFACE

Phase: 15
Type: ADJACENCY-LOOKUP
Subtype: next-hop and adjacency
Result: ALLOW
Config:
Additional Information:
adjacency Active
next-hop mac address a4ba.db9f.9460 hits 5205

Result:
input-interface: OUTSIDE_INTERFACE
input-status: up
input-line-status: up
output-interface: DMZ_INTERFACE
output-status: up
output-line-status: up
Action: allow


1 packet shown
>
```

Instead of using the translated address, if you attempt to connect using the original IP address, the connection attempt should fail. To verify it, you can use the command shown in Example 17-16, which analyzes the tracing data of a captured packet. The threat defense captures the packet when an external host attempts to connect to the internal DMZ server using its original IP address, but the attempt fails.

Example 17-16 *Analyzing a Packet (Where the Packet Does Not Match a Rule)*

```
> show capture ssh_traffic_outside packet-number 1 trace

6 packets captured

  1: 05:19:16.438255 203.0.113.10.48556 > 172.16.1.10.22: S 1315278899:1315278899(0)
win 29200 <mss 1460,sackOK,timestamp 19855229 0, nop,wscale 7>
Phase: 1
Type: CAPTURE
Subtype:
Result: ALLOW
Config:
Additional Information:
MAC Access list


Phase: 2
Type: ACCESS-LIST
Subtype:
Result: ALLOW
Config:
Implicit Rule
Additional Information:
MAC Access list


Phase: 3
Type: ROUTE-LOOKUP
Subtype: Resolve Egress Interface
Result: ALLOW
Config:
Additional Information:
found next-hop 172.16.1.10 using egress ifc DMZ_INTERFACE


Phase: 4
Type: ACCESS-LIST
Subtype: log
Result: ALLOW
Config:
access-group CSM_FW_ACL_ global
access-list CSM_FW_ACL_ advanced permit ip any any rule-id 268435457
access-list CSM_FW_ACL_ remark rule-id 268435457: ACCESS POLICY: AC Policy
- Mandatory/1
access-list CSM_FW_ACL_ remark rule-id 268435457: L7 RULE: Traffic Selection
Additional Information:
```

17

```
  This packet will be sent to snort for additional processing where a verdict will be
reached

Phase: 5
Type: CONN-SETTINGS
Subtype:
Result: ALLOW
Config:
class-map class-default
 match any
policy-map global_policy
 class class-default
 set connection advanced-options UM_STATIC_TCP_MAP
service-policy global_policy global
Additional Information:

Phase: 6
Type: NAT
Subtype: per-session
Result: ALLOW
Config:
Additional Information:

Phase: 7
Type: IP-OPTIONS
Subtype:
Result: ALLOW
Config:
Additional Information:

Phase: 8
Type: NAT
Subtype: rpf-check
Result: DROP
Config:
object network Serv-Real-172.16.1.10
 nat (DMZ_INTERFACE,OUTSIDE_INTERFACE) static Serv-Mask-203.0.113.2 service tcp ssh
2200
Additional Information:

Result:
input-interface: OUTSIDE_INTERFACE
input-status: up
input-line-status: up
```

```
output-interface: DMZ_INTERFACE
output-status: up
output-line-status: up
Action: drop
Drop-reason: (acl-drop) Flow is denied by configured rule


1 packet shown
>
```

Summary

This chapter describes various types of NAT on a threat defense. It shows the steps to configure a NAT rule and demonstrates how a threat defense can leverage NAT technology to masquerade internal IP addresses in a real-world scenario.

Exam Preparation Tasks

As mentioned in the section "How to Use This Book" in the Introduction, you have a couple of choices for exam preparation: the exercises here, Chapter 22, "Final Preparation," and the exam simulation questions in the Pearson Test Prep practice test software.

Review All Key Topics

Review the most important topics in this chapter, noted with the Key Topic icon in the outer margin of the page. Table 17-5 lists a reference of these key topics and the page numbers on which each is found.

Table 17-5   Key Topics for Chapter 17

Key Topic Element	Description	Page
Paragraph	Private IP addresses	418
List	Static NAT vs. dynamic NAT	420
List	Port Address Translation (PAT)	420
List	Auto NAT vs. manual NAT	422
Paragraph	NAT policy editor	422
List	Platform settings	424

Complete Tables and Lists from Memory

Print a copy of Appendix C, "Memory Tables" (found on the companion website), or at least the section for this chapter, and complete the tables and lists from memory. Appendix D, "Memory Tables Answer Key," also on the companion website, includes completed tables and lists to check your work.

Define Key Terms

Define the following key terms from this chapter, and check your answers in the Glossary:

static NAT, dynamic NAT, Port Address Translation (PAT), Auto NAT, Manual NAT

CHAPTER 18

Traffic Decryption Policy

This chapter provides an overview of the following topics:

Traffic Decryption Essentials: This section describes different techniques to decrypt traffic using Secure Firewall. It summarizes the evolution of encryption protocols and explains the TLS handshakes.

Best Practices for Traffic Decryption: This section shares the best practices for positioning the decryption rules in an SSL policy.

Configuring a Decryption Policy: This section demonstrates the steps to configure an SSL policy to decrypt network traffic and then enable a next-generation security policy to analyze the decrypted traffic further.

Verification: In this section, you learn how to use the management center event viewer and dashboard to realize the benefits of decrypting traffic.

The objectives of this chapter are to learn about

- SSL and TLS protocols

- Traffic decryption techniques

- Implementation of an SSL policy on Secure Firewall

- Public Key Infrastructure (PKI) certificate-based objects

- Verification of traffic decryption operation on threat defense

The majority of Internet traffic is now encrypted. While legitimate users are using encryption technologies to secure communication, bad actors are also taking advantage of them. Malicious activities are now increasingly obfuscated using modern encryption protocols. Because of this exploitation, malware and ransomware can remain invisible when they traverse over an encrypted tunnel. Cisco Secure Firewall can decrypt the encrypted traffic, inspect the decrypted traffic further for intrusion detection and malware analysis, enforce any next-generation security policies, and then finally re-encrypt the traffic like a man-in-the-middle. This chapter describes the steps to implement a traffic decryption policy on Secure Firewall and demonstrates the benefit of decrypting traffic.

"Do I Know This Already?" Quiz

The "Do I Know This Already?" quiz enables you to assess whether you should read this entire chapter thoroughly or jump to the "Exam Preparation Tasks" section. If you are in doubt about your answers to these questions or your own assessment of your knowledge of the topics, read the entire chapter. Table 18-1 lists the major headings in this chapter and their corresponding "Do I Know This Already?" quiz questions. You can find the answers in Appendix A, "Answers to the 'Do I Know This Already?' Quizzes."

Table 18-1 "Do I Know This Already?" Section-to-Question Mapping

Foundation Topics Section	Questions
Traffic Decryption Essentials	1
Best Practices for Traffic Decryption	2
Configuring a Decryption Policy	3, 4
Verification	5

CAUTION The goal of self-assessment is to gauge your mastery of the topics in this chapter. If you do not know the answer to a question or are only partially sure of the answer, you should mark that question as wrong for purposes of the self-assessment. Giving yourself credit for an answer you correctly guess skews your self-assessment results and might provide you with a false sense of security.

1. An administrator configured an SSL policy and then deployed the policy on a threat defense system right away however, the new configuration does not take any actions on encrypted traffic. Which of the following reasons could be applicable?

a. The default action of the access control policy is set to Network Discovery Only.

b. A file policy was not created and deployed on the threat defense.

c. An SSL policy is not invoked in the access control policy.

d. The SSL decryption license is not applied on the threat defense.

2. Which of the following statements is true?

a. Decryption of encrypted traffic can impact overall throughput.

b. SSL rules that require the least amount of information to determine the outcome should be placed at the top in order.

c. When positioning the SSL rules, place the Block and Do Not Decrypt actions before the rules that have Decrypt Known Key and Decrypt Resign actions.

d. All of these answers are correct.

3. To prevent an end user from downloading an executable file from https://example.com, which of the following actions is required?

a. Add an SSL rule for the matching traffic with the Decrypt - Resign action.

b. Add an access control rule for matching traffic with the Allow action.

c. Add a file rule to block the executable file type.

d. All of these answers are correct.

4. Which of the following options is the supported way to block the SSLv2 protocol?

a. In an access control rule, add a rule condition to block port 443 (under the Ports tab).

b. In an access control rule, add a rule condition to block an HTTPS application (under the Applications tab).

c. In an SSL policy, choose the Block action for an SSLv2 session (under the Undecryptable Action tab).

d. In an SSL rule, add a rule condition to block the SSLv2 protocol (under the Version tab).

5. Which of the following views in the GUI display the SSL status and action?

    a. The connection events page at Analysis > Connections > Events

    b. The file events page at Analysis > Files > File Events

    c. The Connection summary dashboard

    d. All of these answers are correct.

Foundation Topics

Traffic Decryption Essentials

Secrecy and privacy are of vital importance for communication. Prior to the electronic communication era, a person was appointed as a messenger. Sometimes, a pigeon was used for its homing instinct. However, neither a person nor a pigeon was able to ensure the confidentiality of a message. The longer the distance they had to travel, the more vulnerable the messengers and their messages were. Furthermore, to decode any messages, the recipient had to know the sender's secret key and encoding technique. Sending secrets along with the messages was not a wise decision. Thus, *cryptanalysis* began to evolve hundreds of years ago. Cryptanalysis is a domain in which the methods of decrypting any encrypted messages are studied. Al-Kindi (Born: 801 AD, Iraq) is known as the father of cryptanalysis.

Figure 18-1 shows the design of a simple algorithm to encipher any plaintexts. Here, each letter in the English alphabet is shifted by 3. It means, in ciphertext, the letter *A* represents the letter *D* (A+3).

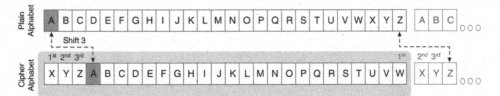

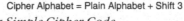

Cipher Alphabet = Plain Alphabet + Shift 3

Figure 18-1 *Designing a Simple Cipher Code*

Figure 18-2 displays two different approaches to encipher the word *CRYPTOGRAPHY*. It uses the **cipher** alphabet shown in Figure 18-1. Modern cryptographic algorithms are so complicated that they require computers with higher computational power for encryption and decryption operations (see Figure 18-3). The new generation of Cisco Secure Firewall comes with dedicated processors for cryptographic operations.

Overview of SSL and TLS Protocols

The Secure Socket Layer (SSL) protocol was originally developed by Taher Elgamal (Born: 1955 AD, Egypt) when he was working at Netscape Communications. Since its first draft, the SSL protocol has gone through many revisions and improvements to ensure protection against any new vulnerabilities. When SSL protocol version 3 was revised to address a vulnerability with a man-in-the-middle attack (known as the POODLE attack), the new edition of the protocol was renamed the Transport Layer Security (TLS).

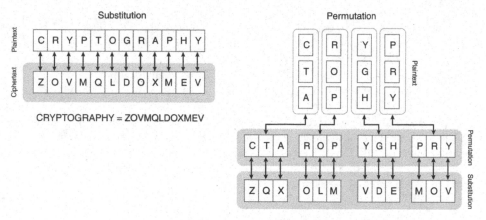

CRYPTOGRAPHY = ZOVMQLDOXMEV

CRYPTOGRAPHY = ZQXOLMVDEMOV

Figure 18-2   *Concept of Encryption and Decryption Using a Simple Cipher*

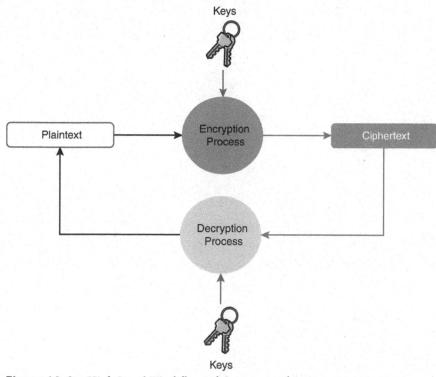

Figure 18-3   *High-Level Workflow of Cryptographic Operations*

NOTE Although the SSL protocol is deprecated, many people still use the pioneering term *SSL* to refer to its successor, the TLS protocol. For example, on the Secure Firewall GUI, you add an "SSL Rule" in an "SSL Policy" to decrypt traffic that can be encrypted by either SSL or TLS protocol. Here, both protocols—SSL and TLS—are used interchangeably.

The TLS protocol has also gone through several revisions since its first release. TLS 1.2 has been a widely deployed cryptographic protocol. Ten years after its release, the Internet Engineering Task Force (IETF) defined its successor—TLS 1.3—in RFC 8446 in 2018. Figure 18-4 shows the evolution of SSL and TLS protocol versions, their release dates, and references to the standardized documents.

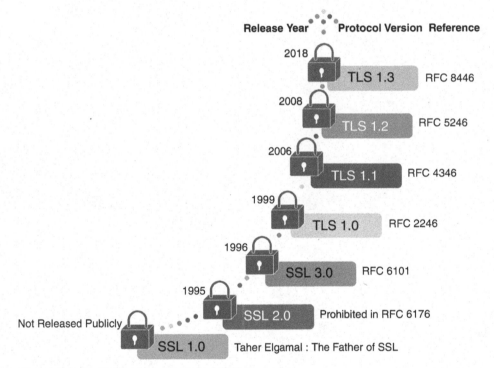

Figure 18-4 *Evolution of SSL and TLS Protocols*

 Secure Firewall uses the protocol handshake to determine the exact protocol version used in an encrypted session. After the TCP three-way handshake (SYN, SYN-ACK, ACK) is complete, the TLS handshake begins with a Hello message from the client, followed by another Hello message from the server, as a response. During the TLS handshake, the client and server negotiate the security parameters they can support and exchange encryption keys to establish a secure TLS connection. Depending on the TLS version, the client/server handshake may differ (see Figure 18-5 and Figure 18-6). TLS 1.2 requires two round trips to complete its handshake. However, TLS 1.3 allows a client and server to complete the handshake in just in one round trip. This reduces latency introduced by the encryption process, as illustrated in Figure 18-7. TLS 1.3 also deprecates obsolete ciphers and algorithms that are known for potential security vulnerabilities, such as RC4, DES, and MD5. The list of supported cipher suites in TLS 1.3 is much shorter than the list for TLS 1.2.

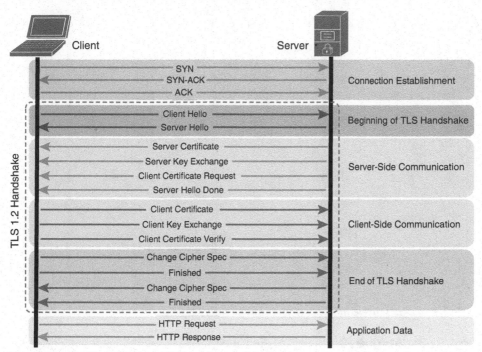

Figure 18-5 *Detail View of TLS 1.2 Handshakes*

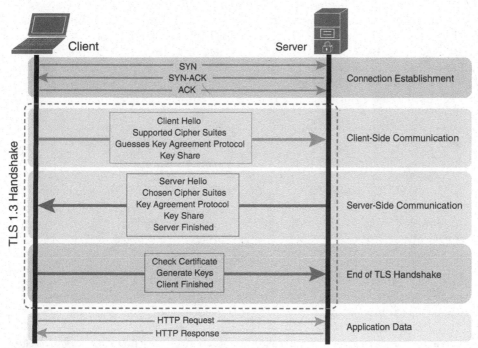

Figure 18-6 *Detail View of TLS 1.3 Handshakes*

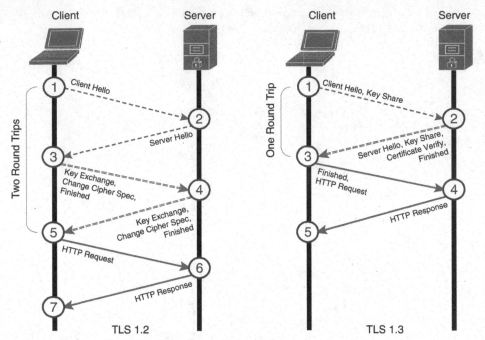

Figure 18-7   *Round Trips Comparison by TLS 1.2 and TLS 1.3*

Decryption Techniques on Secure Firewall

The full suite of access control rule capabilities can be performed only on nonencrypted traffic. To decrypt, inspect, and block encrypted traffic, you need to configure an SSL policy and select the SSL policy from within your access control policy. When an SSL policy is associated with an access control policy, Secure Firewall uses that SSL policy to act on any encrypted traffic before the traffic can be evaluated by the access control policy rules. Depending on the direction of traffic, Secure Firewall offers two techniques to decrypt traffic (see Figure 18-8): decryption by resigning (for outgoing traffic) and decryption using known key (for incoming traffic).

■ **Decryption by resigning (for outgoing traffic):** This technique is used to decrypt *outgoing* traffic from an internal end user—when the user attempts to connect to an external web server located outside your organization. It enables Secure Firewall to intercept outgoing encrypted traffic much like a proxy or man-in-the-middle. It completes the SSL handshake on behalf of the client that initiated the connection and is then able to decrypt the traffic for evaluation by the access control policy and perform further inspection if further inspection is configured in the rule that allows the traffic. If the traffic passes inspection, it re-encrypts the traffic and sends it off to its destination.

Using this method, a threat defense builds a TLS tunnel with the internal end user using a preconfigured trusted **certificate** issued by an internal certificate authority (CA). On the other side, a separate TLS tunnel is established simultaneously between the threat defense and the destination website. From the end user's perspective, the connection is transparent and the user is not aware that an intermediate device, Secure Firewall, between the user and the destination has intervened.

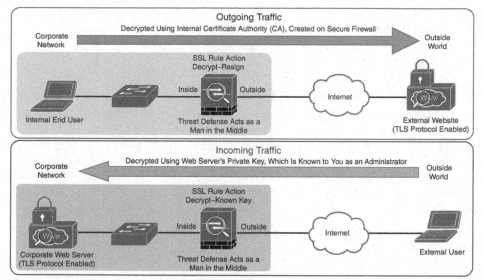

Figure 18-8 *Decryption Techniques Are Influenced by Traffic Direction*

- **Decryption by known key (for incoming traffic):** This technique is used to decrypt *incoming* traffic—in other words, traffic from external sources destined for servers that belong to you located behind Secure Firewall. Because you or your organization owns the server, you can gain access to the server's private key, if needed. In other words, the server's private key is known to you.

  To implement this method, you upload the server's private key to the management center. After the SSL policy deployment, the threat defense can use this private key to decrypt and re-encrypt any incoming traffic. This way, you can protect your internal web server from an external attack.

> **NOTE**   Secure Firewall software version 7.1 introduces the Encrypted Visibility Engine, which can passively identify client software information and threats within encrypted traffic. It uses the machine learning technology based on TLS fingerprinting. Secure Firewall obtains the latest fingerprints through the Vulnerability Database (VDB) package update. In the advanced settings section of an access control policy, you can find many modern techniques to handle encrypted traffic.

Best Practices for Traffic Decryption

Enabling traffic decryption functionality introduces additional CPU overhead, which can impact the overall throughput of the system. Therefore, you should consider the following best practices when you configure an SSL policy:

- SSL rules are evaluated in top-to-bottom order. Place the SSL rules with Block and Do Not Decrypt actions before the rules that have Decrypt Known Key and Decrypt Resign actions.

18

■ When you add SSL policy rules, place the rules with specific conditions before the rules with broader conditions. In general, rules that require the least amount of information to determine the outcome should be placed closer to the top of the SSL policy rule base.

Configuring a Decryption Policy

In the following sections, you learn how to configure an SSL policy to decrypt network traffic, and then enable a next-generation security policy, such as a file policy, to analyze the decrypted traffic further. You begin the process by creating public key infrastructure (PKI) objects. Next, you configure an SSL policy using the PKI objects. To demonstrate the benefits of traffic decryption, you can also create or reuse a file policy. Alternatively, an intrusion policy could be used to show deep packet inspection. Finally, you must associate your SSL policy with the access control policy that you intend to deploy to your threat defense.

Figure 18-9 summarizes the steps to implement traffic decryption functionality on Secure Firewall.

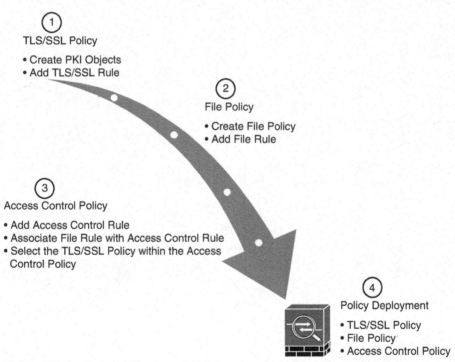

Figure 18-9 *Steps to Implement Decryption with Next-Generation Security*

PKI Objects

In an SSL policy, you use a combination of PKI objects and standard objects to establish the matching criteria for SSL rules. PKI objects can represent your internal public key infrastructure components. Before you create an SSL policy, add the following types of PKI objects by navigating to **Objects > Object Management**.

Internal CAs Object

The internal certificate authority object represents the certificates from internal CAs that you control. When you invoke this object in an SSL policy rule and select the Decrypt - Resign action, Secure Firewall uses the internal CA certificate object to re-sign the server certificate that is passed to the client from the external server the client wants to communicate with. It enables Secure Firewall to decrypt matching outgoing traffic and re-encrypt traffic that passes inspection to its destination.

To configure a self-signed Internal CAs object, use the following steps:

Step 1. Go to **Objects > Object Management.**

Step 2. On the left panel, select **PKI > Internal CAs,** as shown in Figure 18-10.

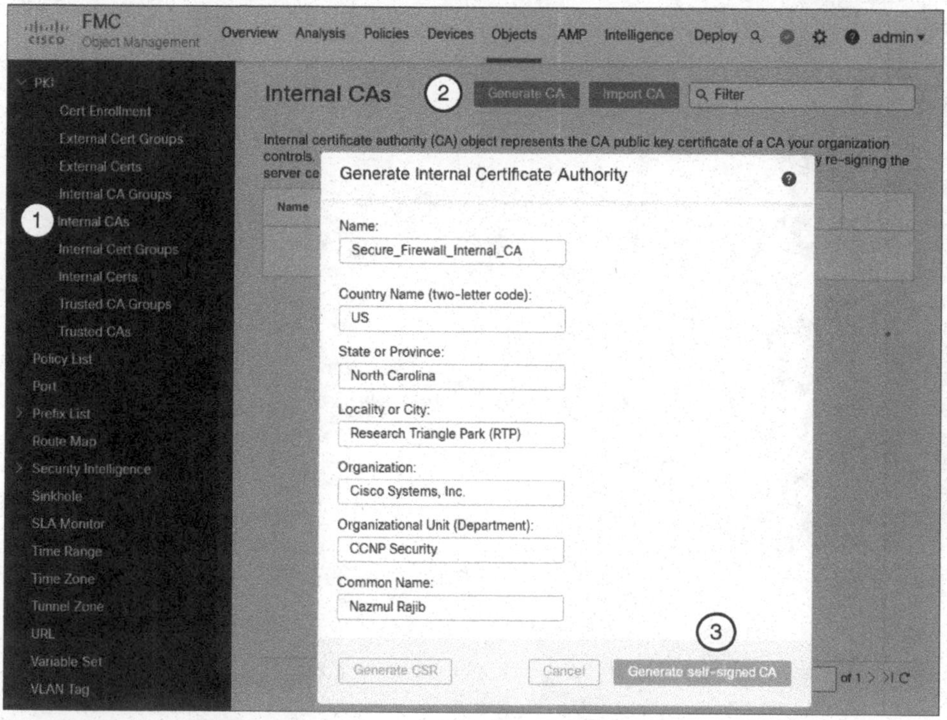

Figure 18-10 *Generation of Internal Certificate Authority*

Step 3. Click the **Generate CA** button.

Step 4. Complete the form with necessary information.

Step 5. Click the **Generate Self-Signed CA** button.

Internal Certs Object

The internal certificate object represents the certificates of servers that your organization administers. To configure an internal certificate object, you upload the server certificate and private key. When you invoke this object in an SSL rule and select the Decrypt - Known Key action, Secure Firewall uses the uploaded private key to decrypt any matching incoming traffic.

To configure an Internal Certs object, use the following steps:

Step 1.   Go to **Objects > Object Management**.

Step 2.   On the left panel, select **PKI > Internal Certs**, as shown in Figure 18-11.

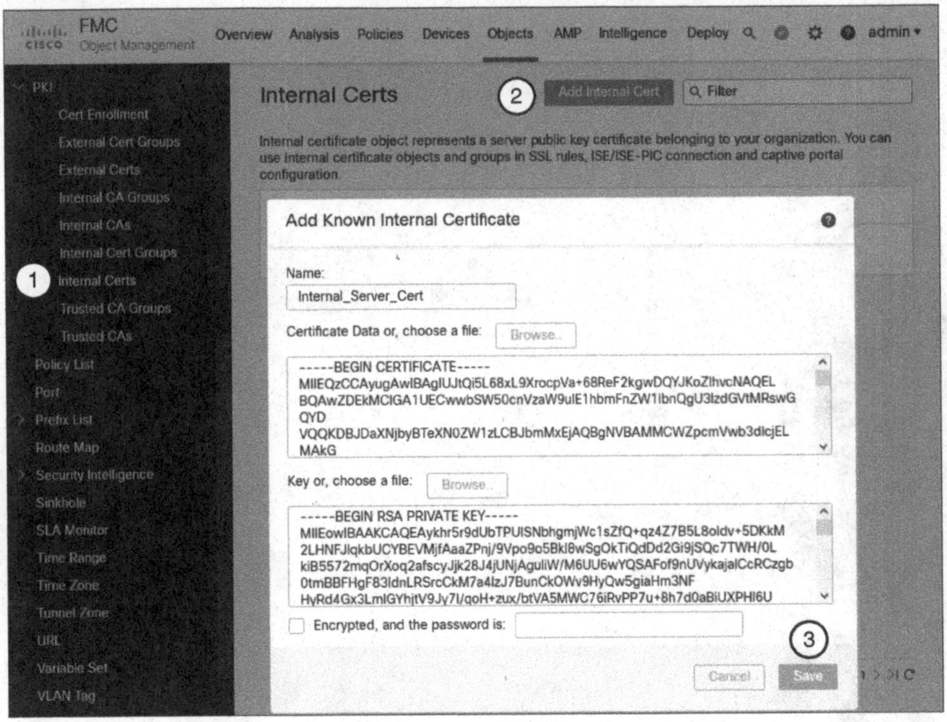

Figure 18-11   *Addition of a Known Internal Certificate*

Step 3.   Click the **Add Internal Cert** button.

Step 4.   Click the **Browse** buttons to upload the certificate and key files of your internal web server.

Step 5.   Click the **Save** button.

SSL Policy

After you create the necessary PKI objects, you can create an SSL policy by using the following steps:

Step 1.   On the management center, navigate to **Policies > Access Control > SSL**. The SSL policy configuration page appears.

Step 2.   To create a new policy, click the **New Policy** button. The New SSL Policy configuration window appears (see Figure 18-12).

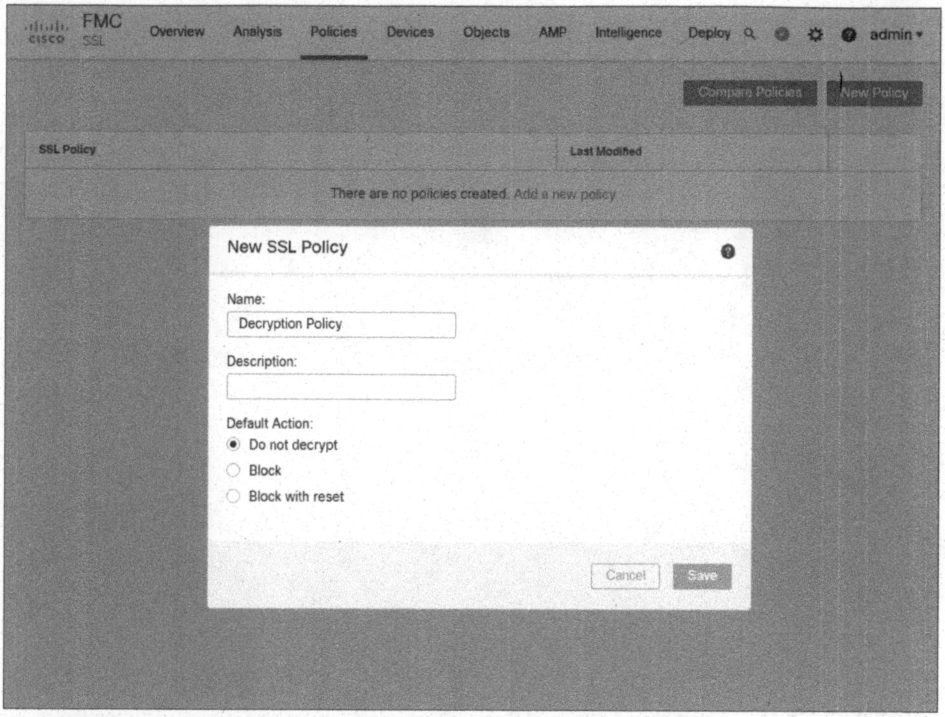

Figure 18-12 *New SSL Policy Configuration Window*

Step 3.   Give a name to the policy and select **Do Not Decrypt** as the default action. The option you select for the default action is used to handle the traffic that does not match any SSL rules. Click the **Save** button to save the policy. The new policy opens in the SSL policy editor.

Step 4.   In the policy editor page, click the **Add Rule** button. This opens the Add Rule configuration window. On this window, you define your SSL rule matching conditions and rule action.

Step 5.   Name the SSL rule, define the direction of the encrypted traffic, and select an action and PKI object based on the traffic direction. For example:

■ Select the action **Decrypt - Resign** for the outgoing traffic, which will flow from inside to the outside zone. Then select an Internal CA object (see Figure 18-13).

■ Select the **Decrypt - Known Key** action to handle incoming traffic, which will flow from the outside zone to the internal zones. Then select an Internal Cert object (see Figure 18-14).

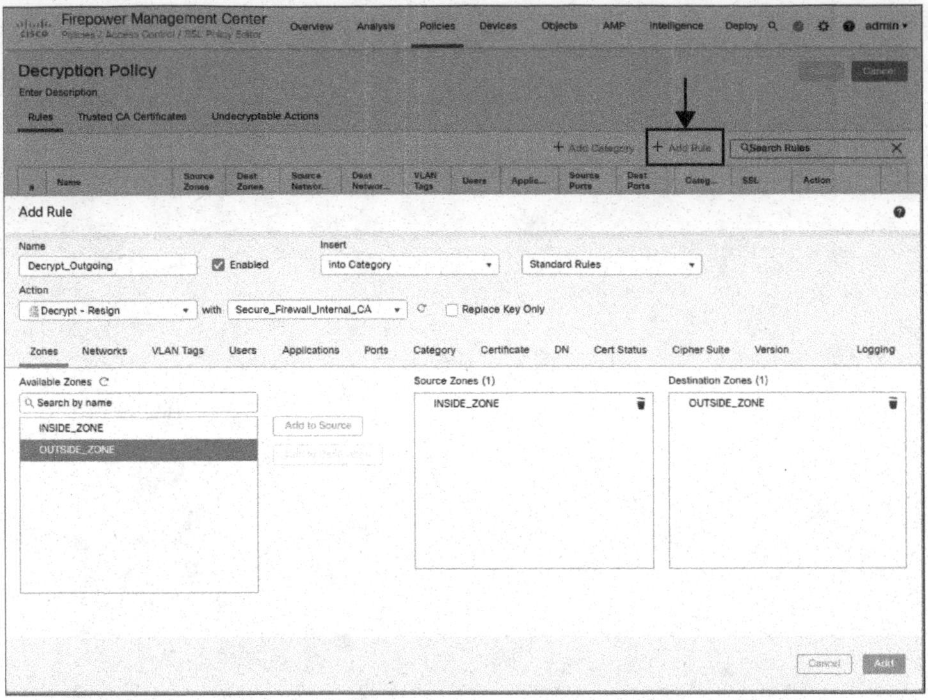

Figure 18-13 *SSL Rule with the Decrypt - Resign Action Matching Outbound Traffic*

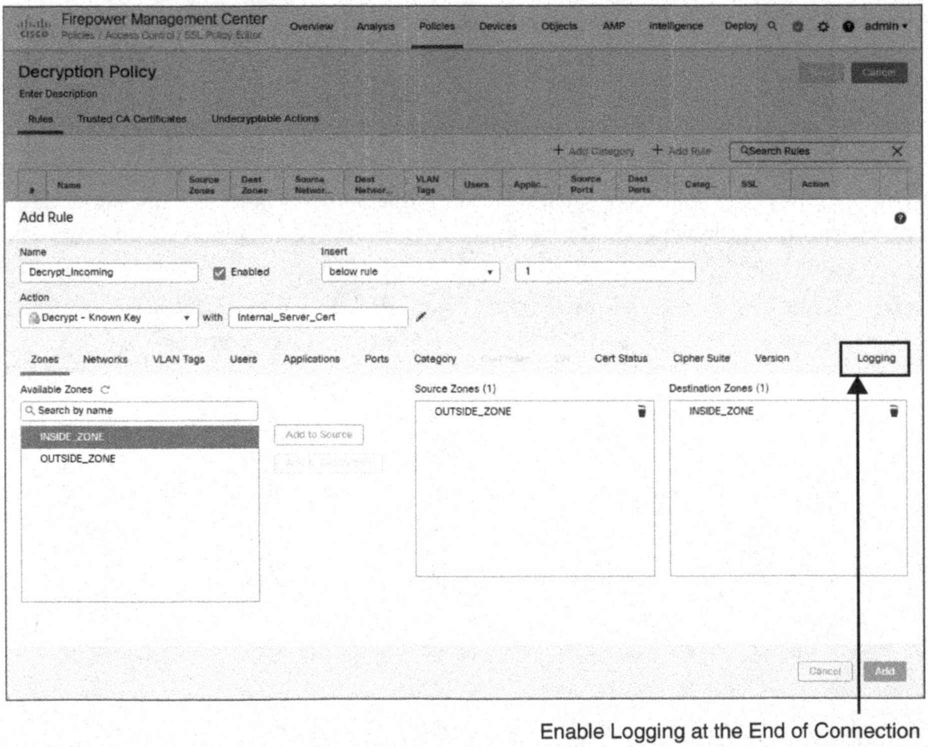

Enable Logging at the End of Connection

Figure 18-14 *SSL Rule with the Decrypt - Known Key Action Matching Inbound Traffic*

Step 6. Optionally, for all SSL rules, enable logging for matching encrypted traffic. In the Add Rule window, go to the **Logging** tab and select **Log at the End of Connection** to enable logging for matching encrypted connections. After you complete the logging configuration, click the **Add** button to create the SSL rule. The GUI returns to the SSL policy editor page.

Step 7. Similarly, you can enable logging for any traffic that can match the default action. On the policy editor page, click the logging icon next to the drop-down for default action, as shown in Figure 18-15.

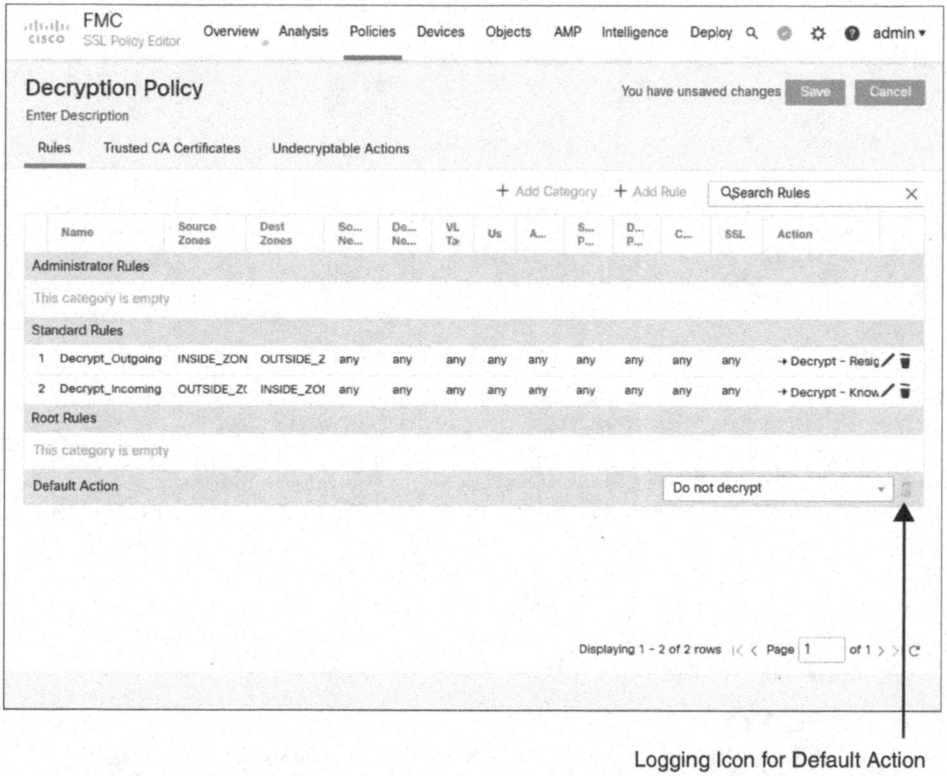

Logging Icon for Default Action

Figure 18-15 *Configuration of SSL Rules to Match Traffic from Both Directions*

Step 8. Finally, define how Secure Firewall will handle the undecryptable traffic. Navigate to the Undecryptable Actions tab and modify the selections using the drop-down as desired. For example, if you do want to deny any SSLv2 traffic, you can select **Block** action from the drop-down, as shown in Figure 18-16. After the desired changes are made, save the configurations.

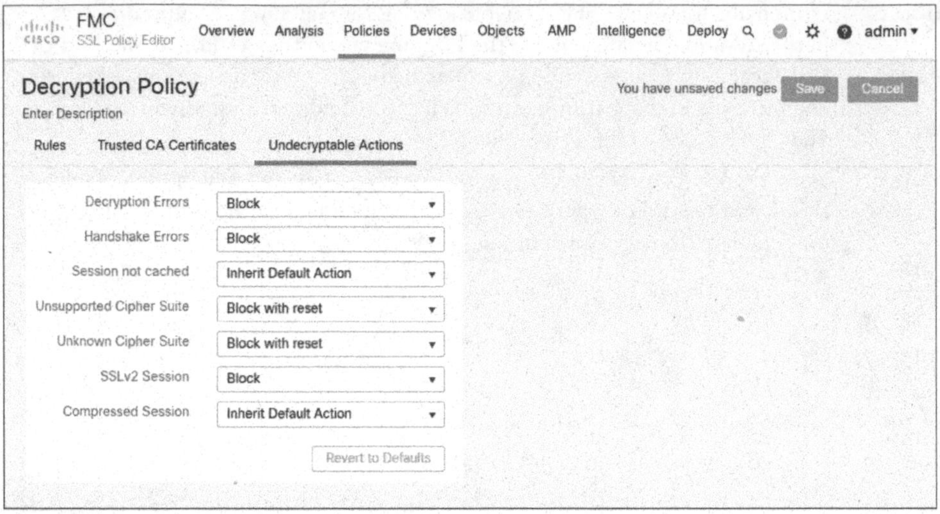

Figure 18-16   *Actions for Undecryptable Traffic*

File Policy

Creating a file policy is not a requirement for traffic decryption; however, it allows you to experience the benefits of decryption. For example, if a file policy is deployed to block executable (EXE) files, but there is no SSL policy deployed on Secure Firewall, you can still transfer over protocols that support file transfers. In this case, the file policy is rendered ineffective because encryption prevents the access control policy rules from being able to evaluate the traffic. However, when an SSL policy is enabled to decrypt traffic and a file policy is also deployed to block file downloads, Secure Firewall can precisely block the transfer of files. The "Verification" section later in this chapter demonstrates this operation in detail, but for now, just configure a simple file policy to block the executable files, as shown in Figure 18-17. This figure shows the file rule condition only; however, the step-by-step instructions on File Policy configuration are described in Chapter 16, "Malware and File Policy."

Access Control Policy

After you configure an SSL policy and a file policy, you must invoke them in the access control policy you intend to use. You can modify an existing access control policy by navigating to **Policies > Access Control** or create a new one if existing policies do not meet your needs. After you enter the access control policy editor, complete the following steps to invoke the file policy and SSL policy:

Step 1.   Click the **Add Rule** button to create an access control rule to match the source and destination of the encrypted sessions. Alternatively, you can modify an existing access control rule that matches the encrypted traffic.

Step 2.   On the rule configuration window, select the **Allow** action and define all the matching conditions for the rule.

Step 3.   On the Inspection tab, select the **File Policy** you created in the previous section (see Figure 18-18). This is the place to map a file policy with the matching traffic.

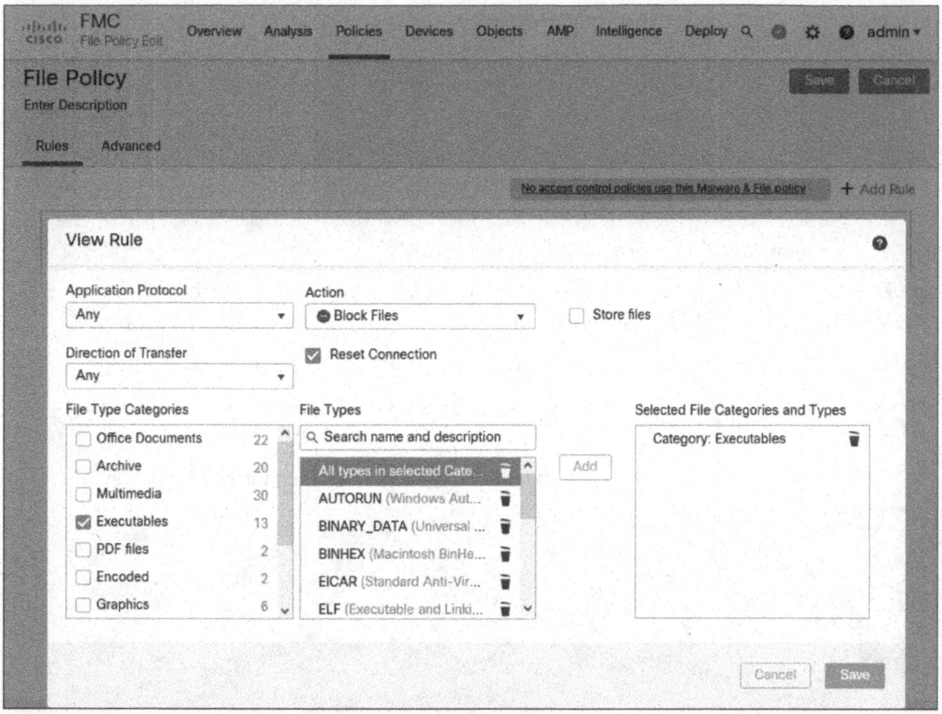

Figure 18-17 *File Rule to Block the Transfer of Any Executable Files*

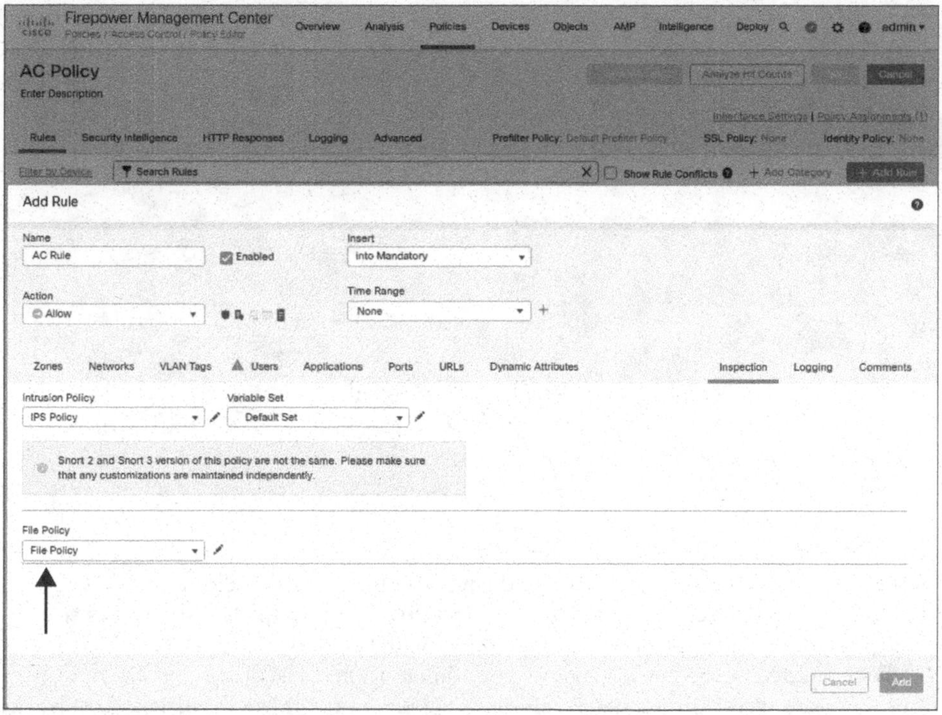

Figure 18-18 *Mapping a File Policy with Matching Traffic*

Step 4. On the Logging tab, enable **Log at the End of Connection**. This option allows you to see connection events when the rule matches traffic.

Step 5. Click the **Add** button on the rule configuration window. The GUI returns to the access control policy editor page.

Step 6. On the access control policy editor, you will find a link to the currently selected SSL policy. If this is a new configuration, the link is SSL Policy: None. Click the **None** link. This opens a pop-up window that displays a list of the available SSL policies, as shown in Figure 18-19.

Step 7. Use the drop-down to select the SSL policy you created earlier. After it is selected, click the **OK** button to return to the policy editor page.

Step 8. Click **Save** on the access control policy editor page to save the configurations.

Step 9. Navigate to **Deploy > Deployment**. Deploy the policies to your threat defense.

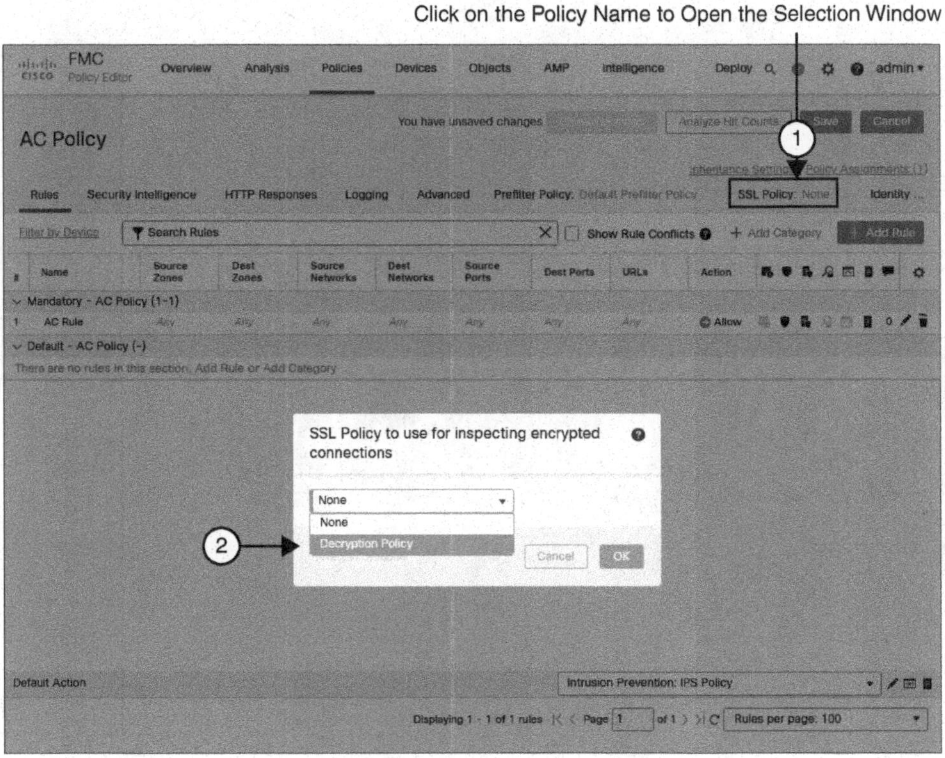

Figure 18-19 *Invoking an SSL Policy into an Access Control Policy*

Verification

It's time to test your configurations and see the magic—how a threat defense analyzes encrypted traffic and blocks a file despite its transfer over an encrypted session. This section assumes that your lab environment has a web server with the TLS protocol enabled. The web server is located at the outside zone of your threat defense installation, as shown in Figure 18-20. The site displays a file directory, where one of the files is of the executable file type (.exe extension).

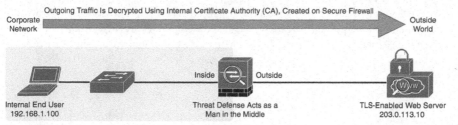

Figure 18-20 *Lab Environment Used in This Chapter to Demonstrate Traffic Decryption*

Perform the following tasks:

1. First, log in to the internal end-user computer (IP: 192.168.1.100) and open a browser.

2. Using the browser, access an external website (IP: 203.0.113.10). Because the TLS protocol is enabled on the website, you should enter **https://203.0.113.10** in the URL bar.

3. Attempt to download the EXE file from the site. (The file was uploaded previously as a part of the lab preparation.)

The file download attempt should be unsuccessful due to the file policy you deployed earlier (refer to Figure 18-17). To give you a better understanding, Figure 18-21 shows the capture of an HTTPS session where an end user's attempt to download an executable file from an external website is blocked by an intermediate threat defense. The capture shows the beginning of the TCP three-way handshake, followed by the TLS handshake, and finally, a reset packet that terminated the encrypted session.

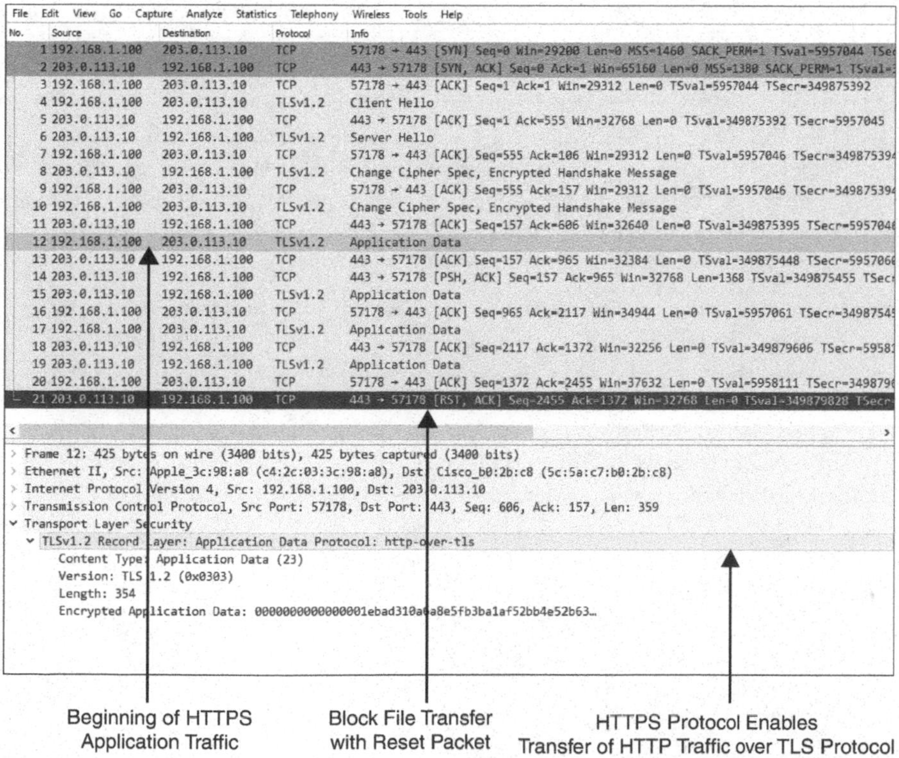

```
File  Edit  View  Go  Capture  Analyze  Statistics  Telephony  Wireless  Tools  Help
No.    Source          Destination      Protocol   Info
    1 192.168.1.100   203.0.113.10     TCP        57178 → 443 [SYN] Seq=0 Win=29200 Len=0 MSS=1460 SACK_PERM=1 TSval=5957044 TSec
    2 203.0.113.10    192.168.1.100    TCP        443 → 57178 [SYN, ACK] Seq=0 Ack=1 Win=65160 Len=0 MSS=1380 SACK_PERM=1 TSval=3
    3 192.168.1.100   203.0.113.10     TCP        57178 → 443 [ACK] Seq=1 Ack=1 Win=29312 Len=0 TSval=5957044 TSecr=349875392
    4 192.168.1.100   203.0.113.10     TLSv1.2    Client Hello
    5 203.0.113.10    192.168.1.100    TCP        443 → 57178 [ACK] Seq=1 Ack=555 Win=32768 Len=0 TSval=349875392 TSecr=5957045
    6 203.0.113.10    192.168.1.100    TLSv1.2    Server Hello
    7 192.168.1.100   203.0.113.10     TCP        57178 → 443 [ACK] Seq=555 Ack=106 Win=29312 Len=0 TSval=5957046 TSecr=349875394
    8 203.0.113.10    192.168.1.100    TLSv1.2    Change Cipher Spec, Encrypted Handshake Message
    9 192.168.1.100   203.0.113.10     TCP        57178 → 443 [ACK] Seq=555 Ack=157 Win=29312 Len=0 TSval=5957046 TSecr=349875394
   10 192.168.1.100   203.0.113.10     TLSv1.2    Change Cipher Spec, Encrypted Handshake Message
   11 203.0.113.10    192.168.1.100    TCP        443 → 57178 [ACK] Seq=157 Ack=606 Win=32640 Len=0 TSval=349875395 TSecr=5957046
   12 192.168.1.100   203.0.113.10     TLSv1.2    Application Data
   13 203.0.113.10    192.168.1.100    TCP        443 → 57178 [ACK] Seq=157 Ack=965 Win=32384 Len=0 TSval=349875448 TSecr=5957066
   14 203.0.113.10    192.168.1.100    TCP        443 → 57178 [PSH, ACK] Seq=157 Ack=965 Win=32768 Len=1368 TSval=349875455 TSecr
   15 203.0.113.10    192.168.1.100    TLSv1.2    Application Data
   16 192.168.1.100   203.0.113.10     TCP        57178 → 443 [ACK] Seq=965 Ack=2117 Win=34944 Len=0 TSval=5957061 TSecr=34987545
   17 192.168.1.100   203.0.113.10     TLSv1.2    Application Data
   18 203.0.113.10    192.168.1.100    TCP        443 → 57178 [ACK] Seq=2117 Ack=1372 Win=32256 Len=0 TSval=349879606 TSecr=59581
   19 203.0.113.10    192.168.1.100    TLSv1.2    Application Data
   20 192.168.1.100   203.0.113.10     TCP        57178 → 443 [ACK] Seq=1372 Ack=2455 Win=37632 Len=0 TSval=5958111 TSecr=3498796
   21 203.0.113.10    192.168.1.100    TCP        443 → 57178 [RST, ACK] Seq=2455 Ack=1372 Win=32768 Len=0 TSval=349879828 TSecr

> Frame 12: 425 bytes on wire (3400 bits), 425 bytes captured (3400 bits)
> Ethernet II, Src: Apple_3c:98:a8 (c4:2c:03:3c:98:a8), Dst: Cisco_b0:2b:c8 (5c:5a:c7:b0:2b:c8)
> Internet Protocol Version 4, Src: 192.168.1.100, Dst: 203.0.113.10
> Transmission Control Protocol, Src Port: 57178, Dst Port: 443, Seq: 606, Ack: 157, Len: 359
∨ Transport Layer Security
   ∨ TLSv1.2 Record Layer: Application Data Protocol: http-over-tls
        Content Type: Application Data (23)
        Version: TLS 1.2 (0x0303)
        Length: 354
        Encrypted Application Data: 0000000000000001ebad310a0a8e5fb3ba1af52bb4e52b63...
```

Beginning of HTTPS Application Traffic   Block File Transfer with Reset Packet   HTTPS Protocol Enables Transfer of HTTP Traffic over TLS Protocol

Figure 18-21 *Capture of an Encrypted Session Shows the Blocking of a File Transfer*

For blocking a file, a connection event should be triggered. The event should also indicate that the connection is decrypted. Navigate to **Analysis > Connections > Events** to view the connection events (see Figure 18-22). Similarly, if you go to the Connection Summary dashboard, you can view various decryption-related statistics in widgets (see Figure 18-23).

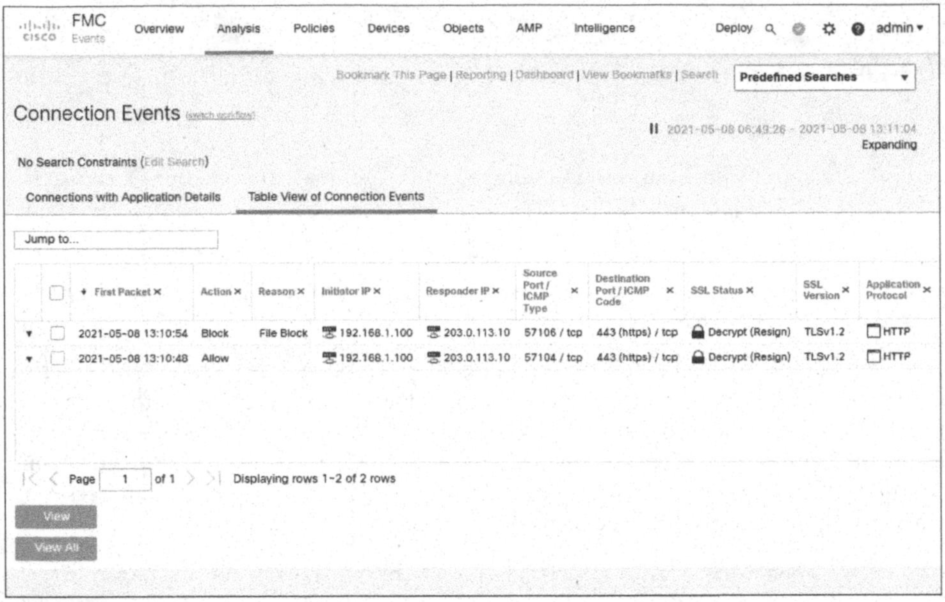

Figure 18-22 *Connection Events Show the Blocking of a File Transfer Through a TLS Session*

To understand the benefit of the SSL policy, let's perform another test: remove the association of the SSL policy from the access control policy. You can do it by entering the access control policy editor and changing the SSL policy selection from Decryption Policy to None (the navigation and option are displayed in Figure 18-19). After you change the selection, save the access control policy and redeploy it to the threat defense.

Now, attempt to access the same external website (IP: 203.0.113.10) once again from your browser. Enter **https://203.0.113.10** in the URL bar. Attempt to download the EXE file from the site. This time, the file should be downloaded successfully. On the **Analysis > Connections > Events** page, you will notice that the connection events are no longer decrypted. Hence, the file transfer was not blocked per the file policy (see Figure 18-24). The application protocol is now considered HTTPS (HTTP over TLS). Notably, the destination port number 443 remains unchanged in both tests—with and without decryption.

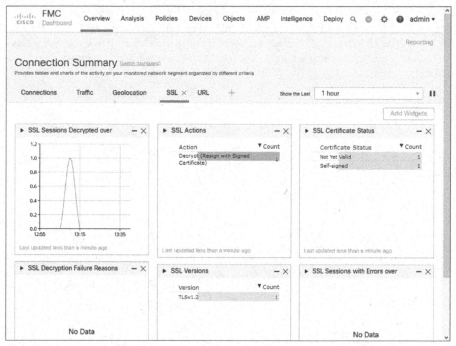

Figure 18-23 *Dashboard Widgets Show the Blocking of a File Transfer Through a TLS Session*

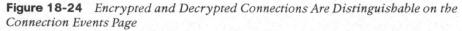

Figure 18-24 *Encrypted and Decrypted Connections Are Distinguishable on the Connection Events Page*

For additional clarification, if you go to **Analysis > Files > File Events** to view the file events, you will notice that the file was blocked only during the first test (see Figure 18-25). The event was logged when the SSL policy was deployed on the threat defense. However, no file event was triggered during the second test because the file policy was ineffective without traffic decryption.

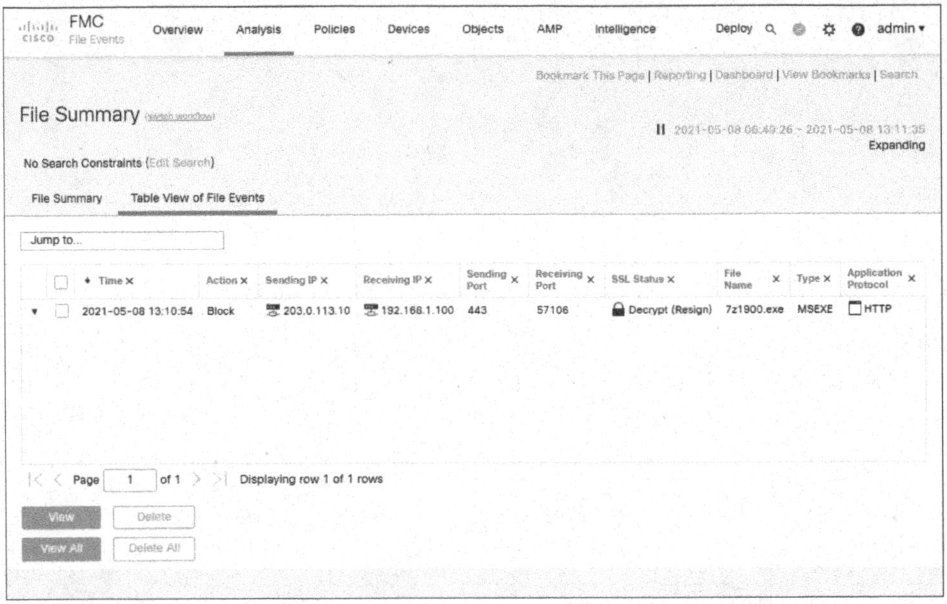

Figure 18-25 *The File Event Confirms the Blocking of an Executable File*

Summary

This chapter provides an overview of the SSL and TLS protocols, and explains the methods that Secure Firewall uses to decrypt the encrypted traffic. Finally, the chapter shows how to implement an SSL policy and enable a file policy to demonstrate the decryption functionality in a lab exercise.

Exam Preparation Tasks

As mentioned in the section "How to Use This Book" in the Introduction, you have a couple of choices for exam preparation: the exercises here, Chapter 22, "Final Preparation," and the exam simulation questions in the Pearson Test Prep practice test software.

Review All Key Topics

Review the most important topics in this chapter, noted with the Key Topic icon in the outer margin of the page. Table 18-2 lists a reference of these key topics and the page numbers on which each is found.

Table 18-2   Key Topics for Chapter 18

Key Topic Element	Description	Page
Paragraph	TLS handshake	464

Complete Tables and Lists from Memory

There are no Memory Tables or Lists for this chapter.

Define Key Terms

Define the following key terms from this chapter, and check your answers in the Glossary:

cipher, certificate, decryption by resigning, decryption by known key

18

## CHAPTER 19

Virtual Private Network (VPN)

This chapter provides an overview of the following topics:

> **VPN Essentials:** This section discusses two predominant VPN architectures: site-to-site VPN and remote access VPN.
>
> **IPsec Essentials:** This section describes various protocols and algorithms that are used in different stages of VPN connections and operations.
>
> **Site-to-Site VPN Deployment:** This section demonstrates the steps to deploy site-to-site VPN on Secure Firewall. It also shows various command-line tools that you can use to verify the VPN configurations.
>
> **Remote Access VPN Deployment:** This section details the phases of remote access VPN configurations, and presents key commands that you can run to determine the VPN status.

The objectives of this chapter are to learn about

- Virtual Private Network (VPN) technologies and protocols
- Implementation of site-to-site VPN topology
- Implementation of remote access VPN topology
- Verification and troubleshooting of VPN configurations

A virtual private network (VPN) allows you to transfer data securely over the insecure public Internet while maintaining anonymity and privacy of the sender and receiver. When you use a VPN tunnel to connect your computer (source host) with a remote system (destination host), both the source and destination hosts communicate with each other as if they are part of the same local network. Any random users on the Internet can see the tunneled traffic, but they are unable to determine the actual payload or the original IP addresses of the source and destination hosts. Because modern VPN technologies can ensure confidentiality, integrity, and availability (CIA), many companies are now confidently adapting hybrid work models. This chapter explains the complex operations of different VPN technologies on Secure Firewall.

"Do I Know This Already?" Quiz

The "Do I Know This Already?" quiz enables you to assess whether you should read this entire chapter thoroughly or jump to the "Exam Preparation Tasks" section. If you are in doubt about your answers to these questions or your own assessment of your knowledge of the topics, read the entire chapter. Table 19-1 lists the major headings in this chapter and their corresponding "Do I Know This Already?" quiz questions. You can find the answers in Appendix A, "Answers to the 'Do I Know This Already?' Quizzes."

Table 19-1 "Do I Know This Already?" Section-to-Question Mapping

Foundation Topics Section	Questions
VPN Essentials	1
IPsec Essentials	2, 3, 4, 5
Site-to-Site VPN Deployment	6
Remote Access VPN Deployment	7

CAUTION The goal of self-assessment is to gauge your mastery of the topics in this chapter. If you do not know the answer to a question or are only partially sure of the answer, you should mark that question as wrong for purposes of the self-assessment. Giving yourself credit for an answer you correctly guess skews your self-assessment results and might provide you with a false sense of security.

1. Which site-to-site VPN network topology is supported by Cisco Secure Firewall?

    a. Point-to-Point

    b. Hub and Spoke

    c. Full Mesh

    d. All of these answers are correct.

2. Which protocol is not part of the IPsec framework?

    a. Authentication Header (AH)

    b. Generic Routing Encapsulation (GRE)

    c. Internet Key Exchange (IKE)

    d. Encapsulating Security Payload (ESP)

3. Which of the following protocols is used for encryption?

    a. AES

    b. ECDH

    c. DH

    d. SHA

4. Which of the following protocols is used for data integrity?

   a. AES

   b. ECDH

   c. SHA

   d. DH

5. Which of the following protocols is used to exchange secret keys?

   a. IKE

   b. ISAKMP

   c. ECDH

   d. All of these answers are correct.

6. For site-to-site VPN deployment on Secure Firewall, which of the following is true?

   a. When you are registering a management center with Cisco Smart Software Licensing, the export-controlled functionality must be allowed for stronger encryption algorithms.

   b. Secure Firewall supports the configuration of a site-to-site virtual private network using both IKEv1 and IKEv2 protocols.

   c. If an interface of the threat defense is configured with NAT and VPN, you need to exempt the internal traffic from being translated.

   d. All of these answers are correct.

7. For a remote access VPN deployment of Secure Firewall, which of the following is false?

   a. Secure Firewall supports the SSL protocol only to establish a secure connection with remote users.

   b. The Simple Certificate Enrollment Protocol (SCEP) allows a threat defense to act as a CA server for a remote user.

   c. When connecting to a remote access VPN, the remote user connects to the organization's authentication server directly for credential validation.

   d. All of these answers are correct.

Foundation Topics

VPN Essentials

VPN technology leverages a variety of protocols and algorithms to provide information security services. In VPN architectures, confidentiality is maintained by encrypting the packet, integrity is guaranteed by validating the hash function, and availability to authorized users is confirmed by matching the secret keys. Figure 19-1 shows three main components of information security—confidentiality, integrity, and availability, which is known as the CIA triad.

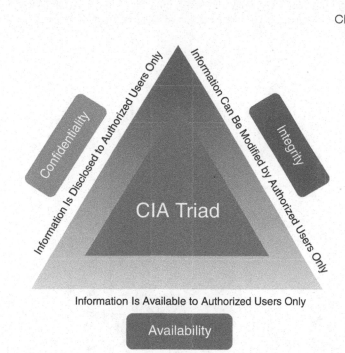

Figure 19-1 *CIA Triad Information Security Model*

You can enable VPN services on many modern networking platforms, such as a router, a firewall, and even on the public cloud. When it is enabled, the platform builds a secure tunnel over the Internet, encapsulates the packets from your private network, and sends them through that secure tunnel. Likewise, on the other end of the secure tunnel, another VPN-enabled device receives the packets, decapsulates them, and sends them to a destination endpoint that is located at another private network. Regardless of the platform you deploy, the VPN architectures are mainly two types:

- **Site-to-Site VPN** (S2S VPN)

- **Remote Access VPN** (RAVPN)

Figure 19-2 shows the processing of packets through the VPN components of Secure Firewall.

Site-to-Site VPN

In a site-to-site virtual private network, the VPN gateways located in geographically separated networks connect each other via a secure tunnel over the Internet. This connection makes all the hosts in participating sites a part of the same virtual network. This network enables the hosts to connect to each other through a secure tunnel built by their respective gateways. You can configure a threat defense to act as a VPN gateway. Secure Firewall can support three types of site-to-site VPN topologies:

- **Point-to-Point:** Two VPN gateways are connected via a secure tunnel.

- **Hub and Spoke:** A VPN gateway (hub) connects to multiple VPN gateways (spoke nodes) via independent secure tunnels.

- **Full Mesh:** VPN gateways in a group connect to each other via multiple secure tunnels.

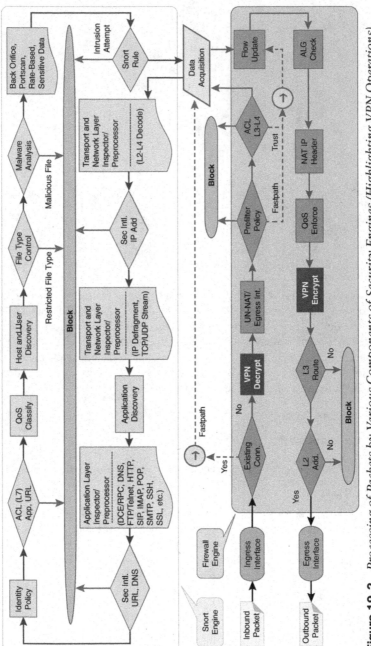

Figure 19-2 *Processing of Packets by Various Components of Security Engines (Highlighting VPN Operations)*

Figure 19-3 shows a high-level design of a site-to-site virtual private network with point-to-point topology.

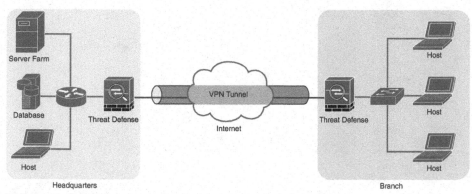

Figure 19-3   *Site-to-Site VPN: Point-to-Point Topology*

Figure 19-4 shows a high-level design of a site-to-site virtual private network with hub-and-spoke topology.

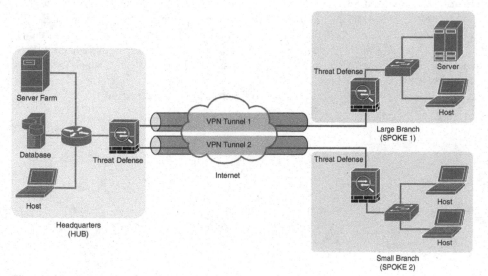

Figure 19-4   *Site-to-Site VPN: Hub-and-Spoke Topology*

Figure 19-5 shows a high-level design of a site-to-site virtual private network with full mesh topology.

19

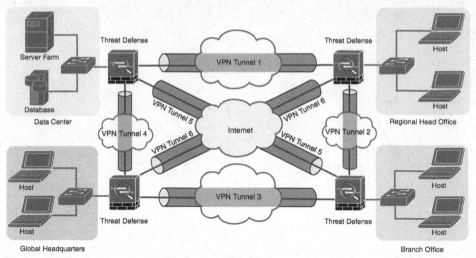

Figure 19-5 *Site-to-Site VPN: Full Mesh Topology*

Remote Access VPN

Key Topic

In a remote access virtual private network, an endpoint device located in a remote network can connect to an organization's internal network over the Internet via a secure channel. The endpoint device uses Cisco AnyConnect Secure Mobility Client to establish a secure tunnel with a threat defense, which is deployed in an organization network as a remote access VPN headend. The AnyConnect client supports Windows, Mac, Linux, Apple iOS, and Android operating systems. Therefore, you can use your laptop, smartphone, or tablet as an endpoint device to connect to your organization's network remotely via a secure tunnel.

Figure 19-6 shows a high-level design of a remote access virtual private network.

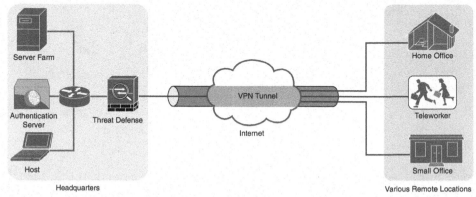

Figure 19-6 *Remote Access VPN Topology*

NOTE In this chapter, the terms *VPN gateway*, *VPN headend*, *VPN peer*, and *VPN device* refer to the Cisco Secure Firewall Threat Defense with VPN services enabled.

IPsec Essentials

Internet Protocol Security (IPsec) is not a single networking protocol. It encompasses a group of protocols and algorithms that work together to establish a secure connection over the public Internet. The Internet Engineering Task Force (IETF) defines the standards for implementing IPsec using three distinct protocols: Authentication Header (AH), Encapsulating Security Payload (ESP), and **Internet Key Exchange (IKE)**. Figure 19-7 displays the major components that are used to establish an IPsec tunnel, and Table 19-2 delineates their security functions.

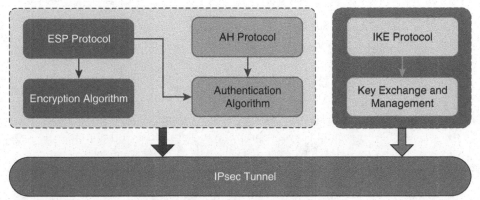

Figure 19-7   *Major Protocols Used to Build an IPsec Tunnel*

Table 19-2   Three Major Security Protocols of the IPsec Framework

Protocol Name	Functions	Protocol/Port Number	References
Authentication Header (AH)	Integrity, authentication, anti-replay	IP Protocol 51	RFC 4302
Encapsulating Security Payloads (ESP)	Confidentiality, integrity, authentication, anti-replay	IP Protocol 50	RFC 4303
Internet Key Exchange (IKE)	Key exchange	UDP 500	RFC 7296

As the technologies are evolving fast, and modern computers are coming up with higher computational power, attackers are able to break the older algorithms. Therefore, it is critical to consider the stronger algorithms when implementing an IPsec tunnel. Cisco regularly reviews the vulnerabilities and weaknesses of protocols, and it stops supporting the less secure ciphers and algorithms in Secure Firewall. For example, from Version 6.7 or higher, Secure Firewall does not support the 3DES, AES-GMAC, AES-GMAC-192, and AES-GMAC-256 encryption algorithms. The only exception in supporting weaker encryption algorithms is DES. Secure Firewall allows you to enable the DES algorithm in Evaluation Mode or in a deployment without export-controlled licenses. Table 19-3 provides some examples of cryptographic algorithms to strengthen the security of a tunnel.

Table 19-3   Cryptographic Algorithms and Their Strengths

Purpose	Cryptographic Algorithm	Reference	Key Strength
Encryption	Advanced Encryption Standard (AES)	FIPS 197	AES256
	Data Encryption Standard (DES)	FIPS 46-3	3DES (Triple DES)
Integrity	Secure Hash Algorithm (SHA)	FIPS 180-4	SHA-2 with 512-bit digest
	Message-Digest Algorithm	RFC 1321	MD5
Key Exchange	Diffie-Hellman (DH) Key Agreement Algorithm	RFC 3526	DH Group 14 (2048-bit modulus)
	Elliptic-Curve Diffie-Hellman (ECDH)	RFC 5903	DH Group 21 (521-bit random elliptic curve)

CAUTION   The stronger the algorithm you implement, the higher the CPU utilization would be on a threat defense. Therefore, when selecting a threat defense model for your network, you must carefully consider your throughput requirements and compare the maximum limits with the specifications provided in the product datasheet (published at cisco.com).

Mode of Operation

An IPsec tunnel between two VPN gateways can operate in two modes:

■ **Transport mode:** In this mode, only the payload is encrypted or authenticated. The original IP header remains unmodified and unencrypted.

■ **Tunnel mode:** In this mode, the entire packet (IP header and payload) is encrypted, authenticated, and then encapsulated into a new IP packet, which uses a new IP header.

You can configure the VPN peers with the AH or ESP protocol individually (such as only the AH protocol or only the ESP protocol), or in combination with both AH and ESP protocols at the same time. For example, Figure 19-8 shows the insertion of authentication header in both transparent mode and tunnel mode. In transport mode, an authentication header is inserted after the original IP header of a packet and before the next layer protocol (such as TCP, UDP, or ICMP). In tunnel mode, the original IP header is encapsulated by a new IP header and an authentication header. Similarly, Figure 19-9 shows the insertion of the ESP header in both modes, and Figure 19-10 shows the insertion of both AH and ESP headers together at the same time.

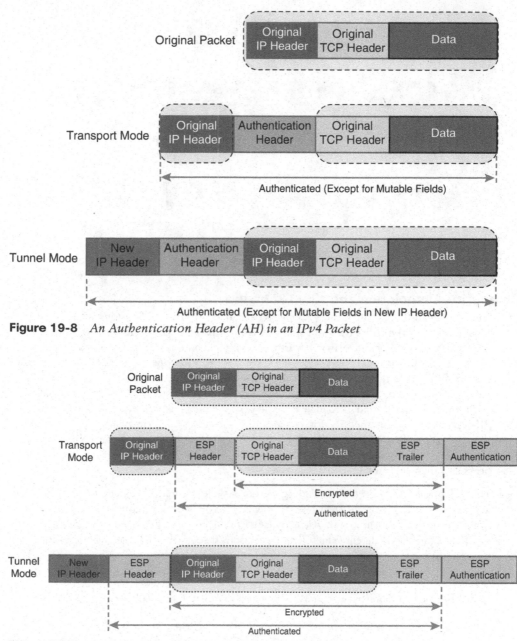

Figure 19-8 *An Authentication Header (AH) in an IPv4 Packet*

Figure 19-9 *An Encapsulating Security Payload (ESP) Header in an IPv4 Packet*

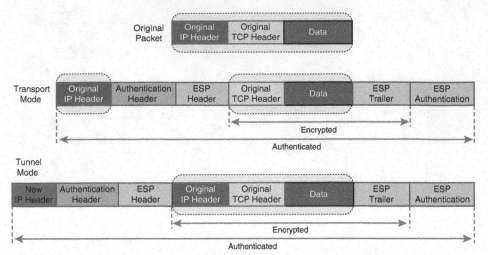

Figure 19-10 *Encapsulation of AH and ESP Headers Simultaneously*

Security Association and Key Exchange

Key Topic

To establish an IPsec tunnel, the VPN peers exchange a proposal of various security protocols and algorithms that they can support. This proposal is known as a *transform set*. Depending on your organization's security policy, you can combine the desired security attributes in the proposal. After negotiating a proposal, VPN peers establish a security association (SA) between them. Establishment of a security association indicates that the VPN peers have agreed on the security attributes that they will use to protect user data. To build a security association and exchange secret keys, VPN peers use the Internet Key Exchange (IKE) protocol and Internet Security Association and Key Management Protocol (ISAKMP) framework. Figure 19-11 shows an example of proposing various security attributes in the transform set. This packet is captured during an IKE protocol negotiation between two VPN peers and then analyzed in a packet analyzer.

The IKE protocol has been enhanced significantly since its first implementation, IKEv1. The new version of IKE—called IKEv2—introduces stronger security features and offers additional reliability, resiliency, and efficiency (see RFC 7296 for detail). The operations of IKEv1 and IKEv2 are also different. The following sections discuss the steps of IKE operations in both versions.

IKEv1

The IKEv1 negotiations between two VPN peers complete in two phases:

- **IKEv1 Phase 1:** In this phase, both VPN peers authenticate each other and establish a security association to perform an IKE operation. Phase 1 allows the peers to communicate securely in phase 2.

  IKE phase 1 can operate in two modes: main mode and aggressive mode. The main mode exchanges six messages to complete its operation, whereas the aggressive mode can complete its operation in three messages. Although the aggressive mode is faster, the main mode is more secure.

■ **IKEv1 Phase 2:** In this phase, both VPN peers use the secure communication channel that was established in phase 1 to negotiate security associations for IPsec operation. IKE phase 2 operates only in one mode, known as quick mode.

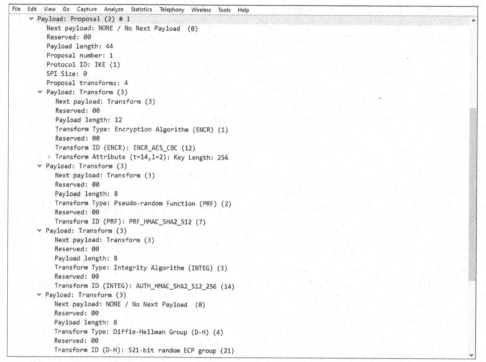

```
File  Edit  View  Go  Capture  Analyze  Statistics  Telephony  Wireless  Tools  Help
  ∨ Payload: Proposal (2) # 1
      Next payload: NONE / No Next Payload  (0)
      Reserved: 00
      Payload length: 44
      Proposal number: 1
      Protocol ID: IKE (1)
      SPI Size: 0
      Proposal transforms: 4
  ∨ Payload: Transform (3)
      Next payload: Transform (3)
      Reserved: 00
      Payload length: 12
      Transform Type: Encryption Algorithm (ENCR) (1)
      Reserved: 00
      Transform ID (ENCR): ENCR_AES_CBC (12)
    > Transform Attribute (t=14,l=2): Key Length: 256
  ∨ Payload: Transform (3)
      Next payload: Transform (3)
      Reserved: 00
      Payload length: 8
      Transform Type: Pseudo-random Function (PRF) (2)
      Reserved: 00
      Transform ID (PRF): PRF_HMAC_SHA2_512 (7)
  ∨ Payload: Transform (3)
      Next payload: Transform (3)
      Reserved: 00
      Payload length: 8
      Transform Type: Integrity Algorithm (INTEG) (3)
      Reserved: 00
      Transform ID (INTEG): AUTH_HMAC_SHA2_512_256 (14)
  ∨ Payload: Transform (3)
      Next payload: NONE / No Next Payload  (0)
      Reserved: 00
      Payload length: 8
      Transform Type: Diffie-Hellman Group (D-H) (4)
      Reserved: 00
      Transform ID (D-H): 521-bit random ECP group (21)
```

Figure 19-11 *Proposal of Security Protocols and Algorithms in a Real Packet*

Figure 19-12 shows various phases to establish and terminate an IPsec tunnel.

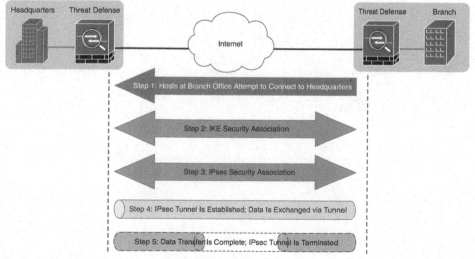

Figure 19-12 *IPsec Tunnel Creation and Termination*

IKEv2

In IKEv2, the VPN peers usually exchange four messages in a request-response manner. The names of those messages and their primary functions follow:

- **IKE_SA_INIT:** This is the first pair of messages where the VPN peers negotiate cryptographic algorithms, exchange random numbers (known as cryptographic nonces), and perform a key exchange. Using the security attributes negotiated at this stage, VPN peers protect the following messages cryptographically.

- **IKE_AUTH:** This is the second pair of messages that authenticate the previous messages, exchange identities and certificates, and establish the first Child SA.

- **CREATE_CHILD_SA:** The exchange of this message creates new Child SAs and rekeys both IKE SAs and Child SAs. Any of the participating VPN peers can initiate this message.

- **INFORMATIONAL:** VPN peers can exchange this message to notify each other of events related to IKE operation. The INFORMATIONAL messages are secured with the same security attributes that are negotiated during the exchange of initial messages.

TIP The exchanges of IKEv2 messages are not categorized in various phases like IKEv1. However, for ease of understanding, you can interpret the exchanges of IKE_SA_INIT and IKE_AUTH by analogy with the IKEv1 Phase 1 and the exchange of CREATE_CHILD_SA with IKEv1 Phase 2.

Figure 19-13 shows the format of an IKEv2 header. To understand its practical usage, you can compare the fields in this figure with Figure 19-14, which shows various components of ISAKMP in a live packet capture. The exchange of this packet, IKE_SA_INIT, is the first step to establish an IPsec tunnel using IKEv2 negotiation.

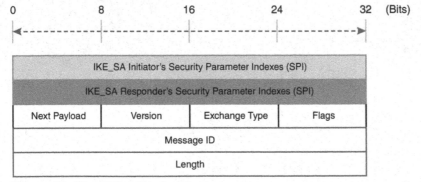

Figure 19-13 *IKEv2 Header Format*

```
File  Edit  View  Go  Capture  Analyze  Statistics  Telephony  Wireless  Tools  Help
No.      Time        Source          Destination       Protocol   Length  Info
       1 0.000000   203.0.113.1     203.0.113.2       ISAKMP     492 IKE_SA_INIT MID=00 Initiator Request
<

> Frame 1: 492 bytes on wire (3936 bits), 492 bytes captured (3936 bits)
> Ethernet II, Src: Cisco_b0:2b:c9 (5c:5a:c7:b0:2b:c9), Dst: Cisco_a1:4f:c9 (5c:5a:c7:a1:4f:c9)
> Internet Protocol Version 4, Src: 203.0.113.1, Dst: 203.0.113.2
> User Datagram Protocol, Src Port: 500, Dst Port: 500
v Internet Security Association and Key Management Protocol
     Initiator SPI: 129dfd8e2e2367f5
     Responder SPI: 0000000000000000
     Next payload: Security Association (33)
  >  Version: 2.0                                                    ─────▶ IKEv2 Header
     Exchange type: IKE_SA_INIT (34)
  >  Flags: 0x08 (Initiator, No higher version, Request)
     Message ID: 0x00000000
     Length: 450
  > Payload: Security Association (33)
  > Payload: Key Exchange (34)
  > Payload: Nonce (40)
  > Payload: Vendor ID (43) : Cisco Delete Reason Supported
  > Payload: Vendor ID (43) : Cisco Copyright
  > Payload: Notify (41) - NAT_DETECTION_SOURCE_IP
  > Payload: Notify (41) - NAT_DETECTION_DESTINATION_IP
  > Payload: Notify (41) - IKEV2_FRAGMENTATION_SUPPORTED
  > Payload: Vendor ID (43) : Cisco Fragmentation
```

Figure 19-14 *Analysis of IKEv2 Header in a Live Packet*

Authentication

Key Topic

During the IKE negotiation process, the VPN peers can authenticate each other by using preshared keys. Preshared keys are simple to configure and feasible to deploy in a smaller network. However, they are not scalable in a large VPN deployment. For scalability, you can use digital certificates. The VPN peers can obtain digital certificates from the certificate authority (CA) of a public key infrastructure (PKI) system. A CA is responsible for signing and issuing digital certificates, which are used to validate the identity of the VPN peers. In the real world, you do not want a threat defense to serve as a certificate authority; instead, you enroll the participating threat defense devices with a certificate authority server. Upon a successful certificate enrollment, the threat defense devices—the VPN peers—exchange their identity certificates to validate each other.

Figure 19-15 shows the communications between a certificate authority and the threat defense in a PKI.

Additionally, the IKEv2 protocol includes support of the Extensible Authentication Protocol (EAP) authentication framework to authenticate the IKE SAs. The authentication methods in EAP-IKEv2 protocol are based on asymmetric key pairs, passwords, and symmetric keys.

19

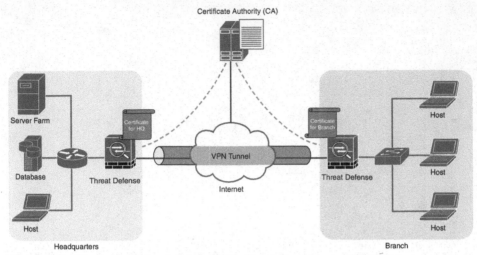

Figure 19-15 *Secure Firewall in a Public Key Infrastructure (PKI)*

Site-to-Site VPN Deployment

The following sections describe how to implement the site-to-site VPN using Secure Firewall.

Prerequisites

Before you begin the core configuration of the site-to-site VPN, fulfill the following prerequisites:

- When registering your management center with Cisco Smart Software Licensing, you must allow the export-controlled functionality, as shown in Figure 19-16. It allows you to enable strong cryptographic features on your Cisco Secure Firewall. If the export-controlled functionality is not allowed, you can use only the Data Encryption Standard (DES) algorithm to encrypt data. Likewise, if you run Secure Firewall in evaluation mode, DES is the only encryption algorithm you can implement.

- In a site-to-site VPN network, two or more threat defense devices are connected to each other over the public Internet (see the examples of various VPN topologies in Figure 19-3, Figure 19-4, and Figure 19-5). This chapter uses the point-to-point network topology, illustrated in Figure 19-17, to demonstrate the configuration and operation of a site-to-site VPN. To emulate the headquarters and branch sites, additional threat defense devices are registered to the management center (see Figure 19-18). The device registration process is described step by step in Chapter 3, "Licensing and Registration."

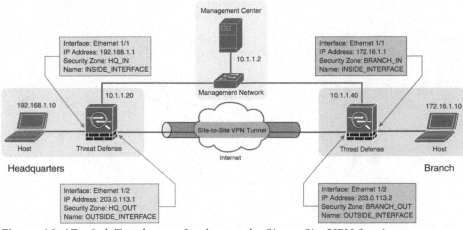

Figure 19-16 *Allowing Export-Controlled Functionality*

Figure 19-17 *Lab Topology to Implement the Site-to-Site VPN Services*

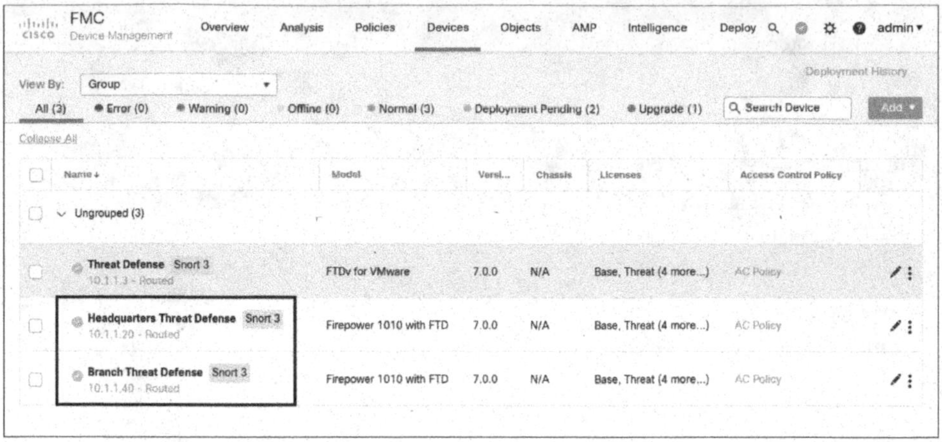

Figure 19-18 *Registration of Multiple Threat Defense Devices with the Management Center*

- After the threat defense devices are registered, configure the interfaces of both devices to match the settings on the topology diagram in Figure 19-17. Figure 19-19 shows the configurations of both threat defense devices located at headquarters and branch sites.

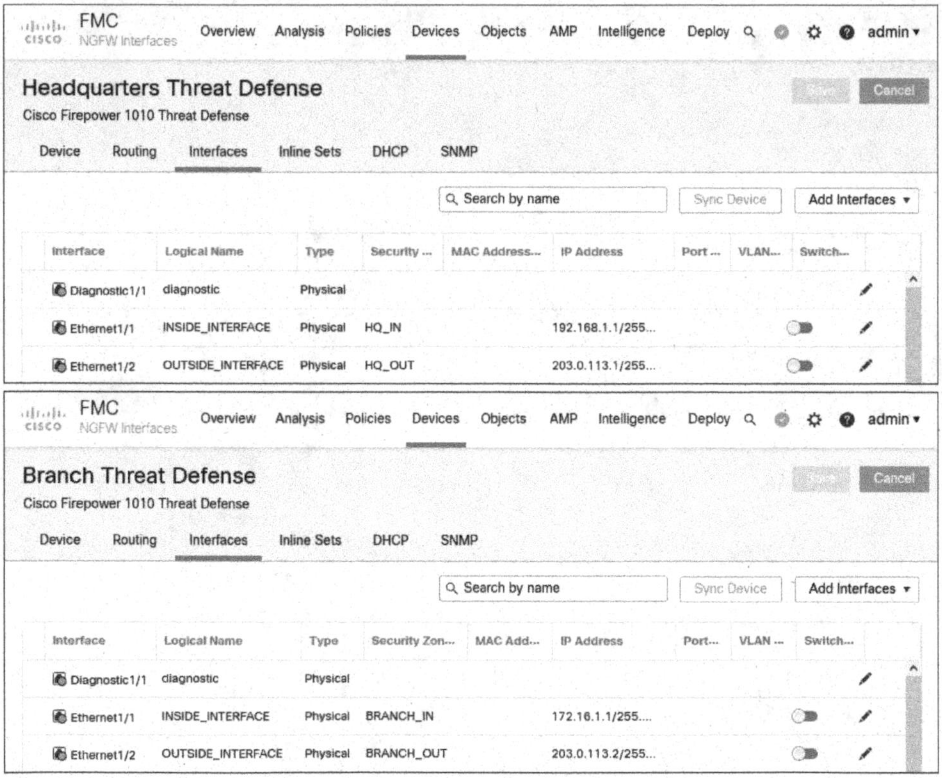

Figure 19-19 *Interface Configurations of a Threat Defense*

■ Create network objects for the headquarters and branch networks. You can create them by navigating to **Objects > Object Management** before you configure the VPN topology. Alternatively, you can add the objects on the fly when you are on the VPN configuration wizard. Figure 19-20 shows two custom network objects to represent the local-area networks (LANs) of headquarters and branch sites.

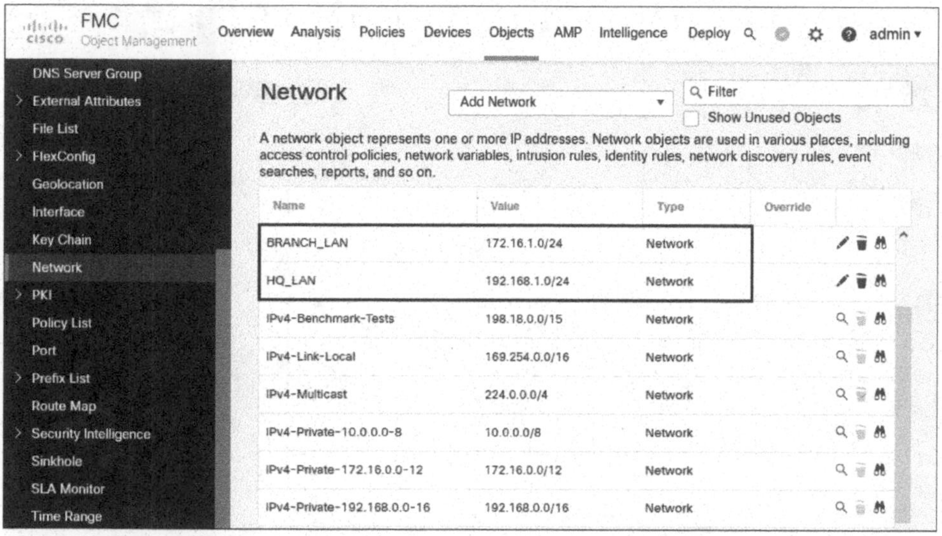

Figure 19-20   *Network Objects for Headquarters and Branch Networks*

Configurations

When the prerequisites are fulfilled, use the following steps to configure a site-to-site VPN on Secure Firewall:

Step 1.   On your management center, navigate to **Devices > VPN > Site To Site**. The site-to-site VPN configuration page appears.

Step 2.   From the Add VPN drop-down, select **Firepower Threat Defense Device**. The Create New VPN Topology configuration window appears.

Step 3.   On the Create New VPN Topology window, name the VPN topology, select a network topology type, and choose the desired IKE version.

Figure 19-21 shows navigation to the site-to-site VPN topology configuration page. For this site-to-site VPN configuration, a policy-based point-to-point network topology has been chosen with IKE version 2.

19

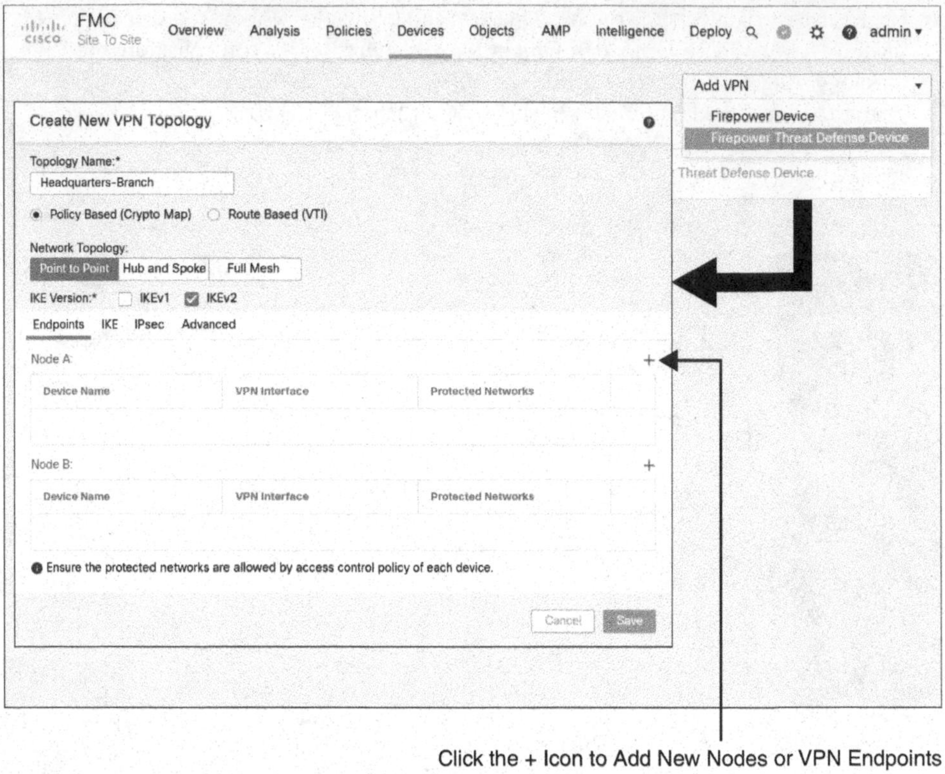

Click the + Icon to Add New Nodes or VPN Endpoints

Figure 19-21   *Site-to-Site VPN Topology Configuration*

Step 4.   On the Endpoints tab, click the **+** icon to add the details of the Node A side of the configuration—the threat defense at headquarters site. The Add Endpoint configuration window appears.

Step 5.   On the Add Endpoint window, select the threat defense and its interface. The interface IP address should auto-populate.

Step 6.   Click the **+** icon on the Add Endpoint window to add the networks whose traffic will be protected through the VPN tunnel. If a desired network object is not predefined on the **Objects > Object Management** page, you can create it now on the fly.

Step 7.   Click **OK** to return to the Create New VPN Topology window. Node A (the headquarters site) is configured at this stage.

Step 8.   Repeat Steps 4 to 7 to add Node B (the branch site). Figure 19-22 shows the configurations of Node A and Node B.

Step 9.   After both nodes are added (see Figure 19-23), click the **Save** button to save the VPN topology.

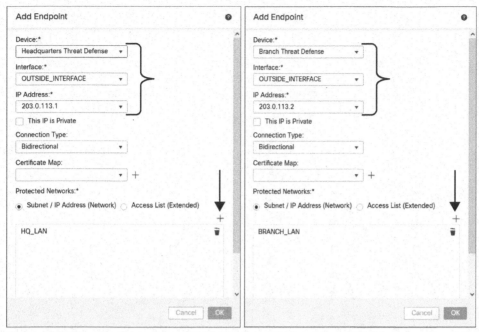

Figure 19-22   *Configuration of Endpoints in a Point-to-Point Topology*

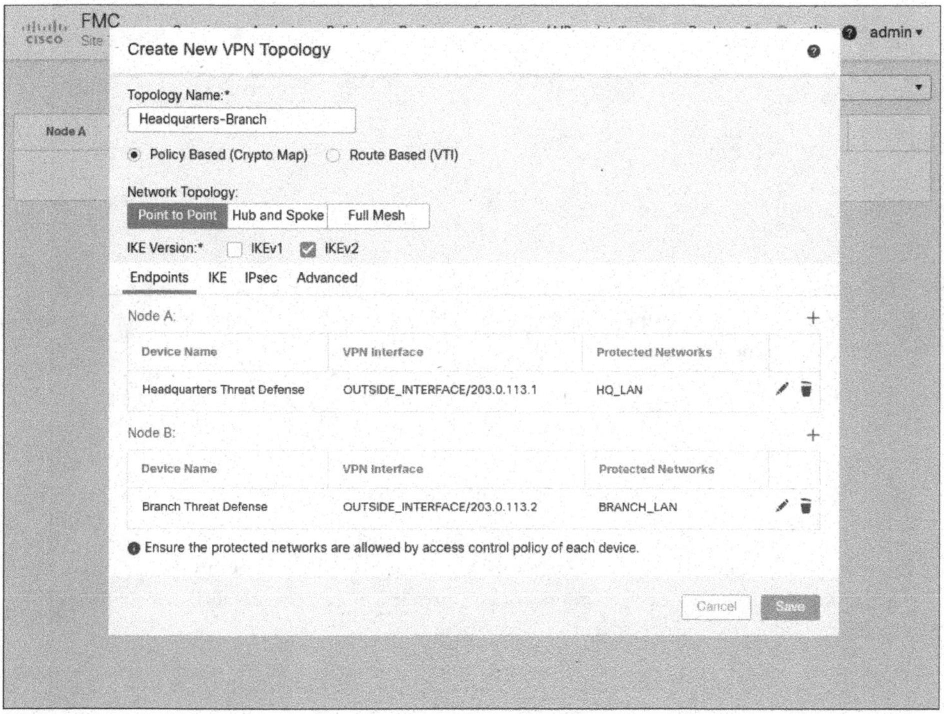

Figure 19-23   *Creation of a New VPN Topology with Two Nodes*

Step 10. If you deploy the configurations at this stage, both threat defense devices should be able to establish a site-to-site VPN tunnel between them. However, if you want to strengthen the VPN tunnel security, there are numerous options to configure in this Create New VPN Topology window. For instance, under the IKE tab, you can create your own IKEv2 policy with stronger security attributes and select it for your site-to-site VPN tunnel (see Figure 19-24).

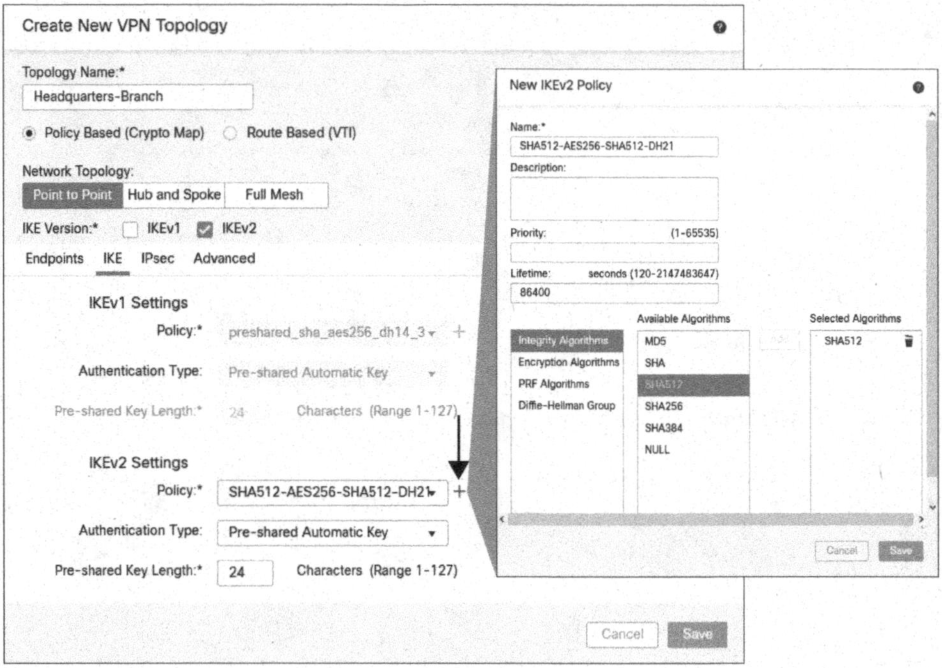

Figure 19-24 *Creation of a New IKEv2 Policy*

If you configure any additional options for your VPN topology, don't forget to save the configurations. Deploy the configuration changes on both threat defense devices by navigating to **Deploy > Deployment**.

When the deployment is successful, you are ready to test the communication between the headquarters and branch sites through the VPN tunnel. From one of the hosts in the headquarters, attempt to connect to a host in the branch site. If the hosts are able to communicate, that's great. You can move to the Configuration Verification section to analyze the IPsec tunnel statistics.

If the hosts between the headquarters and branch sites are unable to communicate through the VPN tunnel, analyze the connection events and review any existing settings that may be blocking the traffic. The following sections help you to solve this issue.

Access Control Policy

If end-user traffic is blocked by the access control policy, you can allow the traffic in two ways:

- **Option 1:** You can add access control rules explicitly to match and allow traffic between both LANs (headquarters and branch), as shown in Figure 19-25. In this case, if the access control policy is set to block all traffic by default, the end-user traffic between both sites is still allowed by the access control rules. If you assign an intrusion policy for each access control rule, the matching traffic is also subject to deep packet intrusion inspection.

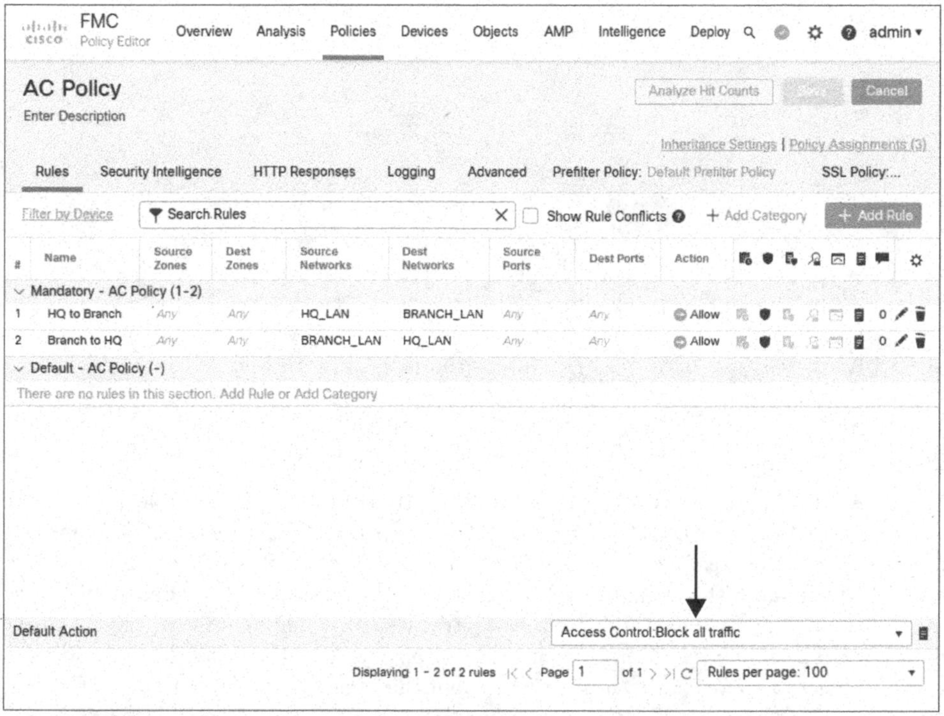

Figure 19-25 *Allowing End-User Traffic Specifically Between Two Sites*

- **Option 2:** If no access control rule is added to match the LAN traffic, the default action of the access control policy can permit the traffic. Figure 19-26 shows the selection of an intrusion policy as the default action. Allowing traffic without any sort of inspection would introduce security risks.

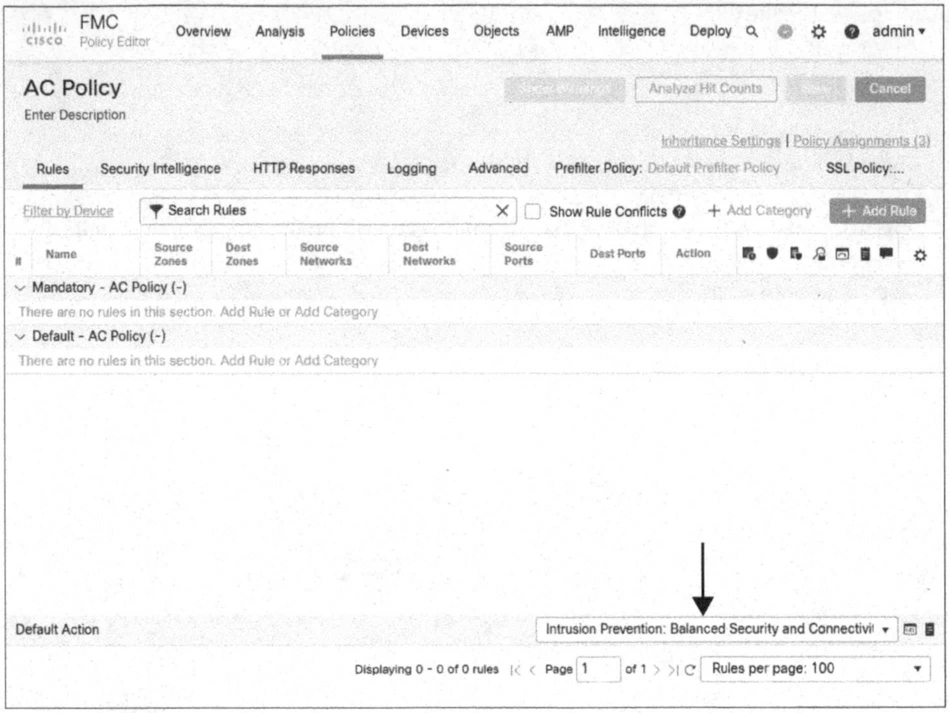

Figure 19-26 *Allowing All Traffic After Intrusion Inspection*

NAT Policy

Network Address Translation is discussed in the aptly titled Chapter 17, "Network Address Translation (NAT)." NAT is used to translate private IP addresses into routable, public addresses. In a real-world scenario, if an interface of the threat defense is configured to perform address translation as well as to establish a site-to-site VPN tunnel, you need to exempt the internal traffic from being translated by adding an identity NAT rule. This is known as a NAT exemption. In an identity NAT rule, the original source address and the translated source address are usually kept the same. The same is true for the destination address: the original destination address and the translated destination remain the same.

For example, Figure 19-27 shows a dynamic NAT rule that translates all the internal IP addresses into the outside interface address. Because the outside interface is also configured to establish a site-to-site VPN tunnel, an identity NAT rule is configured to exclude the internal traffic from being translated, as shown in Figure 19-28.

Figure 19-29 and Figure 19-30 show two different identity NAT rules in two separate NAT policies that can be deployed in headquarters and branch threat defense devices.

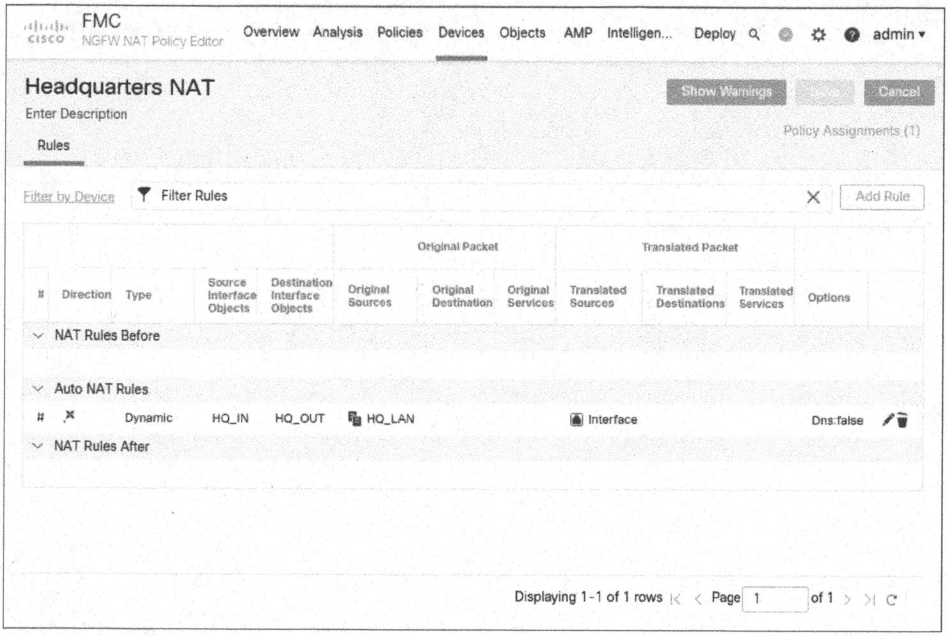

Figure 19-27   *NAT Rule to Translate Internal Addresses to Destination Interface IP Addresses*

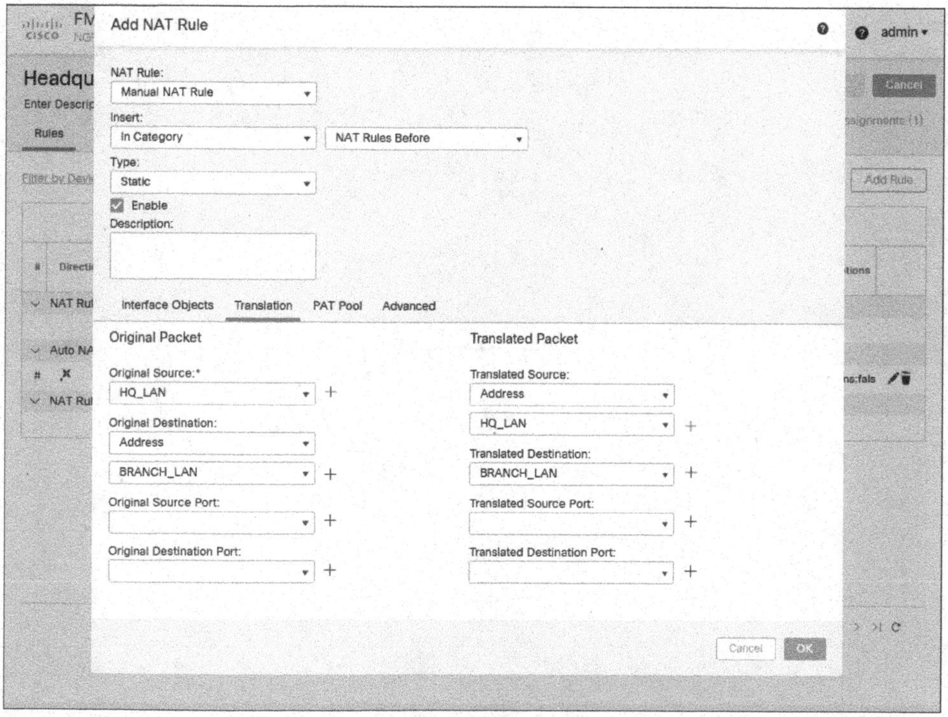

Figure 19-28   *Identity NAT Rule Configuration*

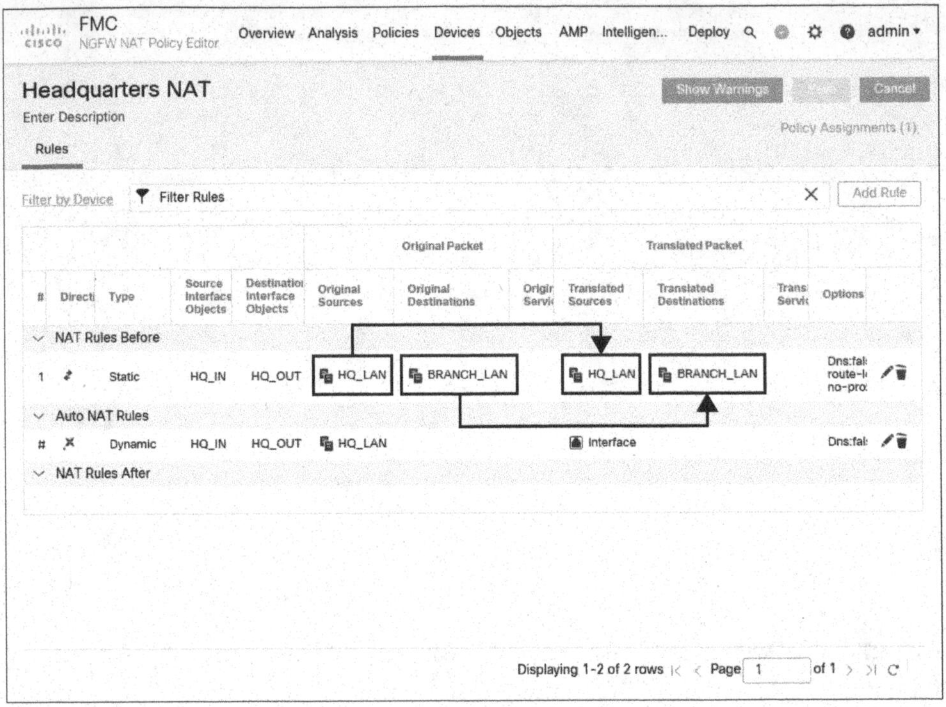

Figure 19-29 *NAT Policy for Headquarters to Perform a NAT Exemption*

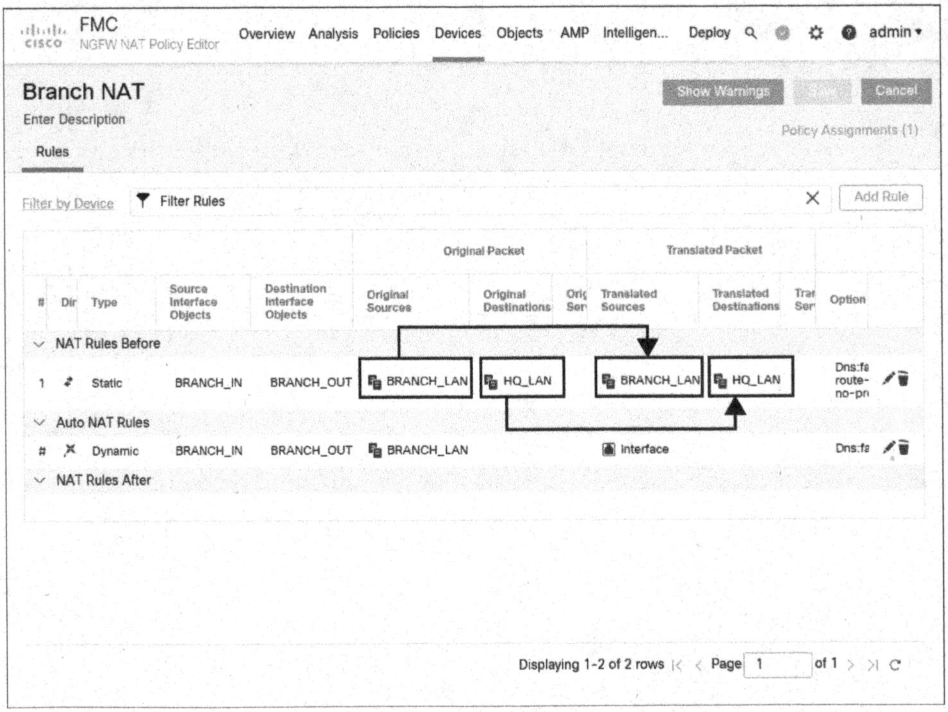

Figure 19-30 *NAT Policy for a Branch Site to Perform a NAT Exemption*

Verification

This section assumes that end users between the headquarters and branch sites can communicate successfully over the IPsec tunnel. To verify the operations of an IPsec tunnel, you can use one of the hosts in the headquarters to connect to a host in the branch office. Sending a simple ICMP ping request, as shown in Example 19-1, would establish a connection over the IPsec VPN tunnel.

Example 19-1   *Successful Ping Test Through an IPsec VPN Tunnel*

```
user@Headquarters:~$ ping 172.16.1.10
PING 172.16.1.10 (172.16.1.10) 56(84) bytes of data.
64 bytes from 172.16.1.10: icmp_seq=2 ttl=64 time=2.34 ms
64 bytes from 172.16.1.10: icmp_seq=3 ttl=64 time=2.15 ms
64 bytes from 172.16.1.10: icmp_seq=4 ttl=64 time=2.30 ms
64 bytes from 172.16.1.10: icmp_seq=5 ttl=64 time=2.08 ms
^C
--- 172.16.1.10 ping statistics ---
5 packets transmitted, 4 received, 20% packet loss, time 4023ms
rtt min/avg/max/mdev = 2.087/2.221/2.342/0.110 ms
user@Headquarters:~$
```

When the policy deployment is successful, you can use the CLI of the threat defense to review the configurations. As you know, you can run the **show running-config** command to view the running configuration. Adding the **crypto** parameter with the command displays the VPN configurations only, as shown in Example 19-2.

Example 19-2   *IPsec Site-to-Site VPN Configurations on a Threat Defense*

```
> show running-config crypto

crypto ipsec ikev2 ipsec-proposal CSM_IP_1
 protocol esp encryption aes-gcm-256 aes-gcm-192 aes-gcm
 protocol esp integrity null
crypto ipsec security-association pmtu-aging infinite
crypto map CSM_Outside_Interface_map 1 match address CSM_IPSEC_ACL_1
crypto map CSM_Outside_Interface_map 1 set peer 203.0.113.2
crypto map CSM_Outside_Interface_map 1 set ikev2 ipsec-proposal CSM_IP_1
crypto map CSM_Outside_Interface_map 1 set reverse-route
crypto map CSM_Outside_Interface_map interface OUTSIDE_INTERFACE
crypto ca trustpool policy
crypto ikev2 policy 1
 encryption aes-256
```

19

```
  integrity sha512
  group 21
  prf sha512
  lifetime seconds 86400
crypto ikev2 enable OUTSIDE_INTERFACE
crypto ikev1 am-disable
>
```

Figure 19-31 shows the exchange of two pairs of packets for IKEv2 negotiation followed by the four pairs of packets for the ping test. The packets for ICMP requests and responses are encapsulated by the ESP header.

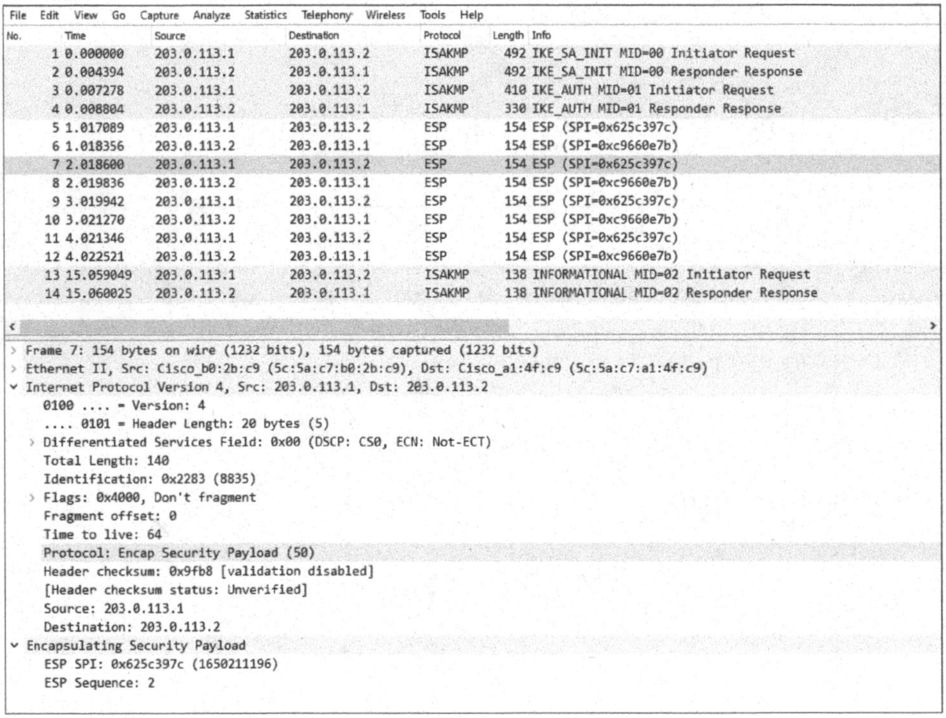

Figure 19-31 *ICMP Packets Through an IPsec VPN Tunnel*

To find detailed statistics about the VPN sessions in a threat defense, run the **show vpn-sessiondb detail** command. To view details of IKEv2 and IPsec attributes used in the VPN sessions, add the **l2l** (alpha lowercase *L*, numeric 2, and a second alpha lowercase *L*) parameters with the command, as shown in Example 19-3.

Example 19-3 *Displaying VPN Session Details*

```
! To display VPN session statistics:

> show vpn-sessiondb detail


----------------------------------------------------------------------
VPN Session Summary
----------------------------------------------------------------------

                    Active : Cumulative : Peak Concur : Inactive
                 ---------------------------------------------------
Site-to-Site VPN    :    1 :          1 :           1
  IKEv2 IPsec       :    1 :          1 :           1
----------------------------------------------------------------------
Total Active and Inactive:  1            Total Cumulative :     1
Device Total VPN Capacity: 75
Device Load            : 1%
----------------------------------------------------------------------


----------------------------------------------------------------------
Tunnels Summary
----------------------------------------------------------------------

                    Active : Cumulative : Peak Concurrent
                 ---------------------------------------------------
IKEv2               :    1 :          1 :           1
IPsec               :    1 :          1 :           1
----------------------------------------------------------------------
Totals              :    2 :          2
----------------------------------------------------------------------


>

! To display LAN-to-LAN VPN session information:

> show vpn-sessiondb detail 121

Session Type: LAN-to-LAN Detailed

Connection   : 203.0.113.2
Index        : 1                   IP Addr      : 203.0.113.2
Protocol     : IKEv2 IPsec
Encryption   : IKEv2: (1)AES256  IPsec: (1)AES-GCM-256
Hashing      : IKEv2: (1)SHA512  IPsec: (1)none
Bytes Tx     : 3780                Bytes Rx     : 3780
```

19

```
Login Time     : 22:02:36 UTC Sat Mar 27 2021
Duration       : 0h:04m:11s
Tunnel Zone    : 0

IKEv2 Tunnels: 1
IPsec Tunnels: 1

IKEv2:
  Tunnel ID    : 1.1
  UDP Src Port : 500              UDP Dst Port : 500
  Rem Auth Mode: preSharedKeys
  Loc Auth Mode: preSharedKeys
  Encryption   : AES256           Hashing      : SHA512
  Rekey Int (T): 86400 Seconds    Rekey Left(T): 86148 Seconds
  PRF          : SHA512           D/H Group    : 21
  Filter Name  :

IPsec:
  Tunnel ID    : 1.2
  Local Addr   : 192.168.1.0/255.255.255.0/0/0
  Remote Addr  : 172.16.1.0/255.255.255.0/0/0
  Encryption   : AES-GCM-256      Hashing      : none
  Encapsulation: Tunnel
  Rekey Int (T): 28800 Seconds    Rekey Left(T): 28548 Seconds
  Rekey Int (D): 4608000 K-Bytes  Rekey Left(D): 4607997 K-Bytes
  Idle Time Out: 30 Minutes       Idle TO Left : 26 Minutes
  Bytes Tx     : 3780             Bytes Rx     : 3780
  Pkts Tx      : 45               Pkts Rx      : 45

>
```

After an IPsec tunnel is established successfully, you can view the detailed statistics of the security associations from the CLI. Run the **show crypto ikev2 sa detail** command (see Example 19-4) for IKEv2 security associations and the **show crypto ipsec sa detail** command for IPsec security associations (see Example 19-5).

Example 19-4 *IKEv2 Security Association Detail*

```
> show crypto ikev2 sa detail

IKEv2 SAs:

Session-id:1, Status:UP-ACTIVE, IKE count:1, CHILD count:1
```

```
Tunnel-id    Local              Remote             Status     Role
 19066247    203.0.113.1/500    203.0.113.2/500    READY      INITIATOR
      Encr: AES-CBC, keysize: 256, Hash: SHA512, DH Grp:21, Auth sign: PSK, Auth
verify: PSK
      Life/Active Time: 86400/216 sec
      Session-id: 1
      Status Description: Negotiation done
      Local spi: 1BBE8980EB3784BB       Remote spi: 91154FB2E3E310F0
      Local id: 203.0.113.1
      Remote id: 203.0.113.2
      Local req mess id: 18            Remote req mess id: 0
      Local next mess id: 18          Remote next mess id: 0
      Local req queued: 18            Remote req queued: 0
      Local window: 1                 Remote window: 1
      DPD configured for 10 seconds, retry 2
      NAT-T is not detected
      IKEv2 Fragmentation Configured MTU: 576 bytes, Overhead: 28 bytes, Effective
MTU: 548 bytes
Parent SA Extended Status:
      Delete in progress: FALSE
      Marked for delete: FALSE
Child sa: local selector  192.168.1.0/0 - 192.168.1.255/65535
          remote selector 172.16.1.0/0 - 172.16.1.255/65535
          ESP spi in/out: 0xe62a8d7b/0xbc4877fd
          AH spi in/out: 0x0/0x0
          CPI in/out: 0x0/0x0
          Encr: AES-GCM, keysize: 256, esp_hmac: N/A
          ah_hmac: None, comp: IPCOMP_NONE, mode tunnel
>
```

Example 19-5 *IPsec Security Association Detail*

```
> show crypto ipsec sa detail

interface: OUTSIDE_INTERFACE
    Crypto map tag: CSM_Outside_Interface_map, seq num: 1, local addr: 203.0.113.1

      access-list CSM_IPSEC_ACL_1 extended permit ip 192.168.1.0 255.255.2S55.0
172.16.1.0 255.255.255.0
      local ident (addr/mask/prot/port): (192.168.1.0/255.255.255.0/0/0)
      remote ident (addr/mask/prot/port): (172.16.1.0/255.255.255.0/0/0)
      current_peer: 203.0.113.2

      #pkts encaps: 45, #pkts encrypt: 45, #pkts digest: 45
      #pkts decaps: 45, #pkts decrypt: 45, #pkts verify: 45
```

19

```
#pkts compressed: 0, #pkts decompressed: 0
#pkts not compressed: 45, #pkts comp failed: 0, #pkts decomp failed: 0
#pre-frag successes: 0, #pre-frag failures: 0, #fragments created: 0
#PMTUs sent: 0, #PMTUs rcvd: 0, #decapsulated frgs needing reassembly: 0
#TFC rcvd: 0, #TFC sent: 0
#Valid ICMP Errors rcvd: 0, #Invalid ICMP Errors rcvd: 0
#pkts no sa (send): 0, #pkts invalid sa (rcv): 0
#pkts encaps failed (send): 0, #pkts decaps failed (rcv): 0
#pkts invalid prot (rcv): 0, #pkts verify failed: 0
#pkts invalid identity (rcv): 0, #pkts invalid len (rcv): 1396264912
#pkts invalid pad (rcv): 0,
#pkts invalid ip version (send): 0, #pkts invalid ip version (rcv): 0
#pkts invalid len (send): 0, #pkts invalid len (rcv): 0
#pkts invalid ctx (send): 0, #pkts invalid ctx (rcv): 0
#pkts invalid ifc (send): 0, #pkts invalid ifc (rcv): 0
#pkts failed (send): 0, #pkts failed (rcv): 0
#pkts replay rollover (send): 0, #pkts replay rollover (rcv): 0
#pkts replay failed (rcv): 0
#pkts min mtu frag failed (send): 0, #pkts bad frag offset (rcv): 0
#pkts internal err (send): 0, #pkts internal err (rcv): 0

local crypto endpt.: 203.0.113.1/500, remote crypto endpt.: 203.0.113.2/500
path mtu 1500, ipsec overhead 55(36), media mtu 1500
PMTU time remaining (sec): 0, DF policy: copy-df
ICMP error validation: disabled, TFC packets: disabled
current outbound spi: BC4877FD
current inbound spi : E62A8D7B

inbound esp sas:
  spi: 0xE62A8D7B (3861548411)
     SA State: active
     transform: esp-aes-gcm-256 esp-null-hmac no compression
     in use settings ={L2L, Tunnel, IKEv2, }
     slot: 0, conn_id: 1, crypto-map: CSM_Outside_Interface_map
     sa timing: remaining key lifetime (kB/sec): (4101116/28719)
     IV size: 8 bytes
     replay detection support: Y
     Anti replay bitmap:
      0x00003FFF 0xFFFFFFFF
outbound esp sas:
  spi: 0xBC4877FD (3158865917)
     SA State: active
     transform: esp-aes-gcm-256 esp-null-hmac no compression
     in use settings ={L2L, Tunnel, IKEv2, }
```

```
        slot: 0, conn_id: 1, crypto-map: CSM_Outside_Interface_map
        sa timing: remaining key lifetime (kB/sec): (4055036/28719)
        IV size: 8 bytes
        replay detection support: Y
        Anti replay bitmap:
         0x00000000 0x00000001

>
```

If the NAT exemption is enabled on a VPN gateway to exclude the translation of internal IP addresses, you can confirm the deployment of an identity NAT rule by looking into the output of the **show running-config nat** command (see Example 19-6). Additionally, the **show xlate detail** command confirms the exemption from address translation performed by an identity rule.

Example 19-6 *Implementation of a NAT Exemption*

```
> show running-config nat
nat (INSIDE_INTERFACE,OUTSIDE_INTERFACE) source static HQ_LAN HQ_LAN destination
static Branch_LAN Branch_LAN no-proxy-arp route-lookup
!
object network HQ_LAN
 nat (INSIDE_INTERFACE,OUTSIDE_INTERFACE) dynamic interface
>


> show xlate detail
2 in use, 2 most used
Flags: D - DNS, e - extended, I - identity, i - dynamic, r - portmap,
       s - static, T - twice, N - net-to-net
NAT from INSIDE_INTERFACE:192.168.1.0/24 to OUTSIDE_INTERFACE:192.168.1.0/24
    flags sIT idle 0:00:00 timeout 0:00:00 refcnt 0 xlate id 0x2b8047a7a3c0
NAT from OUTSIDE_INTERFACE:172.16.1.0/24 to INSIDE_INTERFACE:172.16.1.0/24
    flags sIT idle 0:00:00 timeout 0:00:00 refcnt 0 xlate id 0x2b8047a7a1c0

>
```

Remote Access VPN Deployment

The following sections describe how to implement the remote access VPN using Secure Firewall.

Prerequisites

Before you begin configuring the remote access VPN services, fulfill the following prerequisites:

Key Topic

■ Register a threat defense, which will provide remote access VPN services in the head-quarters, with a management center. Configure the ingress and egress interfaces of the threat defense in routed mode with the necessary IP addresses. If the interfaces of the Headquarters Threat Defense are configured as a part of the site-to-site VPN lab exercises (as shown in Figure 19-19), you can reuse them now. Note that, unlike the site-to-site VPN lab exercises, the remote access VPN lab requires only one threat defense, which will act as a headend (see Figure 19-32).

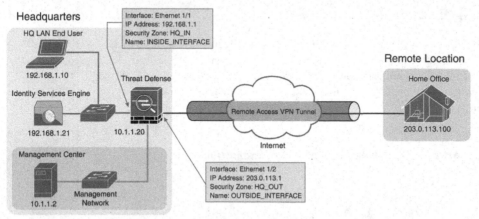

Figure 19-32 *Lab Topology to Implement the Remote Access VPN Services*

■ When registering your management center with Cisco Smart Software Licensing, you must allow the export-controlled functionality, as shown in Figure 19-16. It allows you to enable strong cryptographic features on your Cisco Secure Firewall. If the export-controlled functionality is not allowed, you can use only the Data Encryption Standard (DES) algorithm to encrypt data. Likewise, if you run Secure Firewall in Evaluation Mode, DES is the only encryption algorithm you can implement.

■ Acquire and enable one of the AnyConnect features licenses for your threat defense. There are three tiers of AnyConnect licenses: AnyConnect Plus, AnyConnect Apex, and AnyConnect VPN Only. The AnyConnect Plus license offers the basic remote-access VPN services, whereas the AnyConnect Apex license allows you to enable many advanced features in addition to the basic features provided by the AnyConnect Plus license.

If you choose between AnyConnect Plus and AnyConnect Apex license tiers, you must consider the total number of unique users who may be using remote access VPN services at any time. In contrast, the AnyConnect VPN Only license allows any number of unique users to connect to a threat defense. However, in this case, the total number of simultaneous connections processed by a specific threat defense at any time is limited by the AnyConnect VPN Only license.

Key Topic

TIP   The performance of remote access VPN services depends on the threat defense model and the AnyConnect license you choose. In other words, when designing a remote access VPN service for your organization, you must carefully estimate the maximum bandwidth requirements of your organization as well as the maximum number of simultaneous remote user sessions that will be processed by a headend threat defense. Therefore, read the Secure Firewall datasheet and orderability guide to select an appropriate device model and AnyConnect license tier.

■ Enable the AnyConnect licenses on the threat defense using the management center. To enable the license, go to **Devices > Device Management**, and edit the device settings of the threat defense where you want to configure the remote access VPN. On the Device tab, as shown in Figure 19-33, you can enable your desired license types.

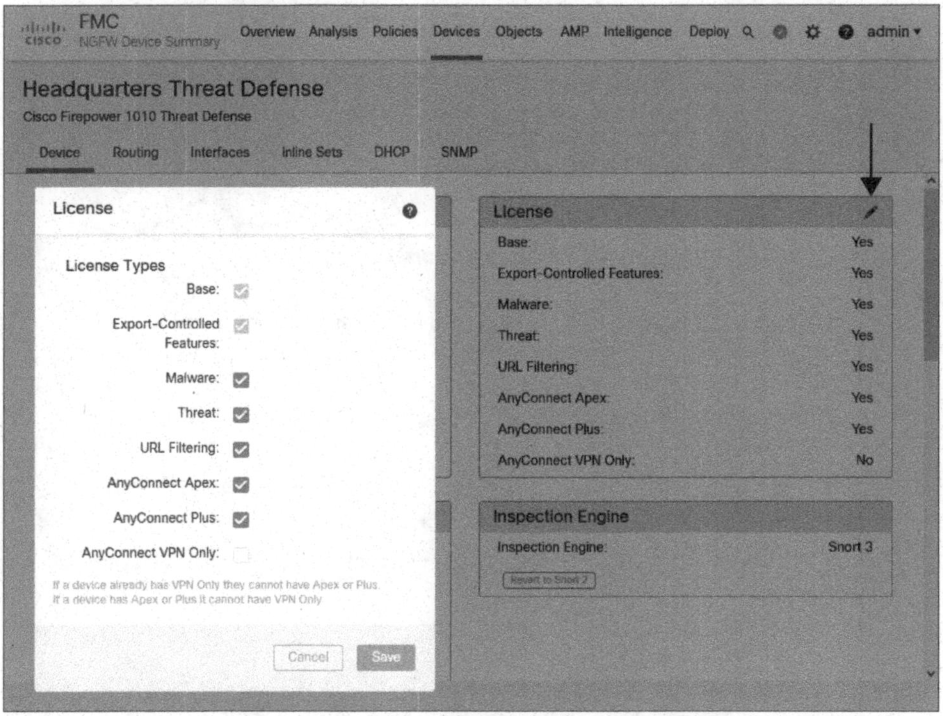

Figure 19-33   *Enabling the AnyConnect License on Secure Firewall*

■ Secure Firewall Version 7.x or higher supports local user authentication. You can use its local user database to authenticate users for remote access VPN connections. Although setting up a few local users may be a faster way to demonstrate the remote-access VPN operations, a large organization requires a dedicated AAA server to manage thousands of users. In a real-world scenario, you enable local authentication as a fallback mechanism. You can add a new realm for local users by going to **System > Integration > Realms** (see Figure 19-34).

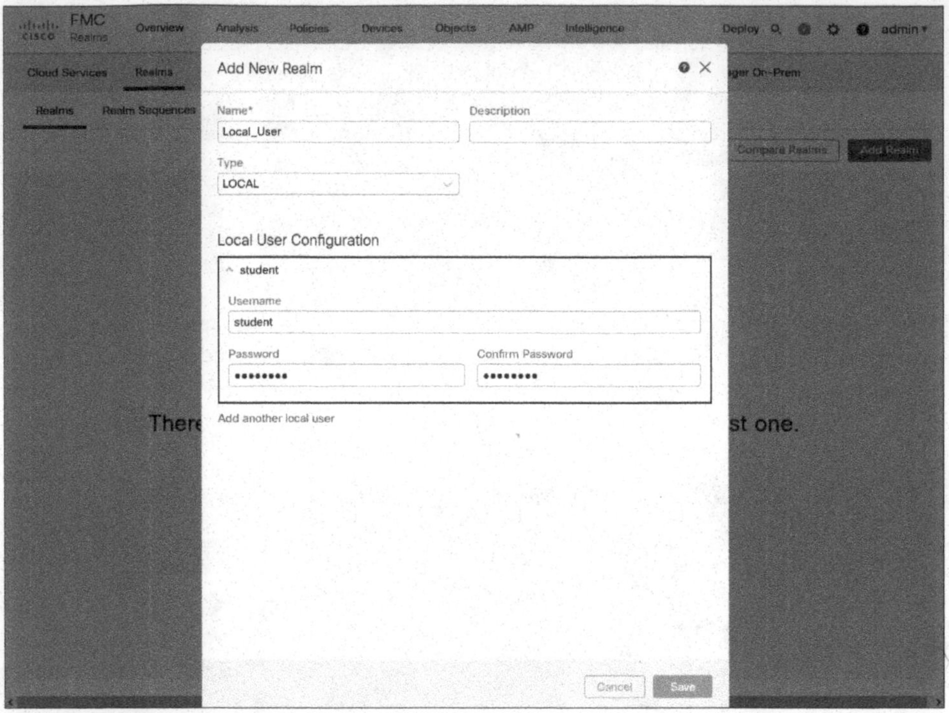

Figure 19-34 *Local User Configuration on the Management Center*

If your Secure Firewall runs an earlier software version, a separate AAA server is necessary to authenticate the remote access VPN users. The lab exercises in this chapter use the Cisco Identity Service Engine (ISE) as the primary AAA server and the local user database as a fallback. For your lab testing, you can choose to use both or any one of the authentication methods. Describing an ISE server is beyond the scope of this book, but you can find details in the ISE configuration guide, published at cisco.com.

Figure 19-35 shows the workflow for validating a remote user credential by an AAA server through a VPN gateway.

Configuration

Implementation of remote access VPN services on Secure Firewall is not a straightforward process. Before you begin the core part of the remote access VPN configuration, you need to define several components in various types of objects. When the necessary objects are configured, you invoke them into the Remote Access VPN Policy Wizard to configure the remote access VPN. The following sections walk you through all the necessary configurations.

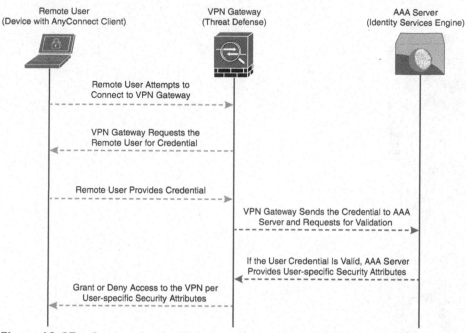

Figure 19-35   *Communication Between a Remote User, VPN Gateway, and AAA Server*

AnyConnect File

The AnyConnect Secure Mobility Client software empowers a remote user to connect to the internal network of an organization from any geographic location. It supports both SSL and IPsec IKEv2 protocols to establish a secure connection. The AnyConnect client supports various operating systems, such as Windows, Mac OS, and Linux. You can download the software package for your desired operating system from the Cisco Software Download Center. After you download the files, you need to upload them to the management center. Follow these steps to upload:

Step 1.   Navigate to **Objects > Object Management** on your management center.

Step 2.   Select **VPN > AnyConnect File** from the left panel.

Step 3.   Click the **Add AnyConnect File** button to upload the client software package files.

Figure 19-36 shows the upload of three different AnyConnect client software package files for Linux, Mac OS, and Windows operating systems.

19

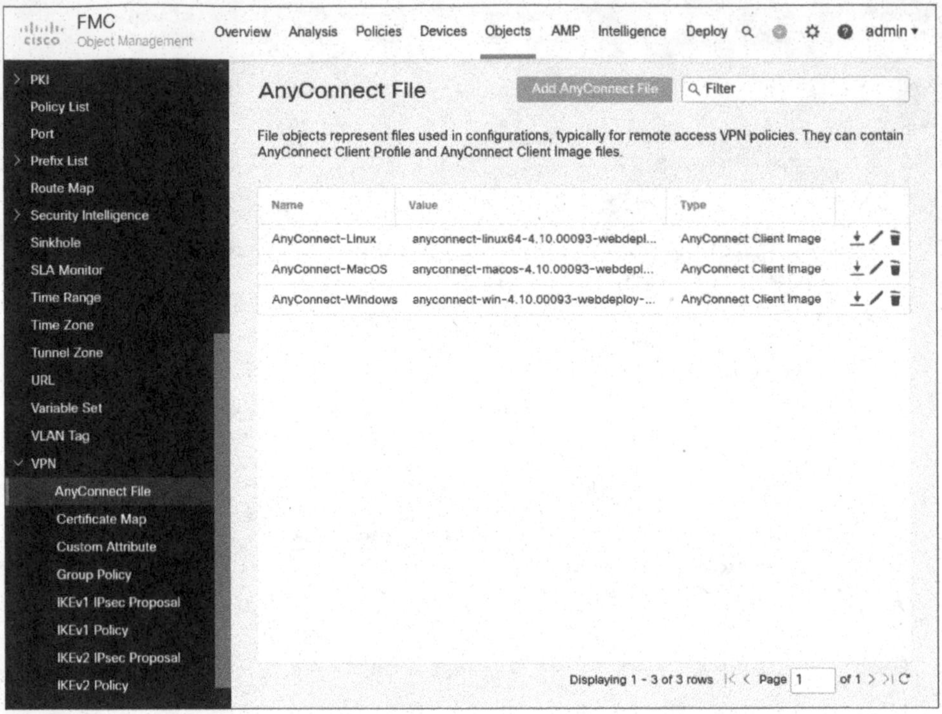

Figure 19-36　*Uploading the AnyConnect Files to the Management Center*

RADIUS Server Group

Using the **AAA Server > RADIUS Server Group** object, you can add a single server or a group of servers that can be used to authenticate many remote access VPN users. The lab exercises in this chapter use an ISE server for AAA services. (Optionally, a local user is also added as a fallback, as shown in Figure 19-34.)

Figure 19-37 shows the creation of a RADIUS Server Group object, named Identity_Services_Engine, to describe the connection parameters of an authentication server. In the Key and Confirm Key fields, enter the shared secret key that is also used in the ISE server. This key is used to encrypt data between the threat defense and the ISE server.

Certificate Enrollment

You can use the Cert Enrollment object to enter information about the certification authority (CA) server in your public key infrastructure (PKI). This information is necessary to create a certificate signing request (CSR) and to obtain an identity certificate. Secure Firewall offers four ways to select an enrollment type:

- **PKCS12 File:** Import a Public Key Cryptography Standard (PKCS) file into Secure Firewall. A PKCS12 file is a single encrypted file that can contain information about the server certificate, any intermediate certificates, and the private key.

- **SCEP:** Use the Simple Certificate Enrollment Protocol (SCEP) to establish a direct connection between a threat defense and a CA server, and allow the threat defense to obtain an identity certificate directly from the CA.

■ **Manual:** Copy the certificate information that you obtain from a CA server and paste it manually on Secure Firewall.

■ **Self-signed:** Allow the threat defense to act as a CA server using its self-signed root certificate.

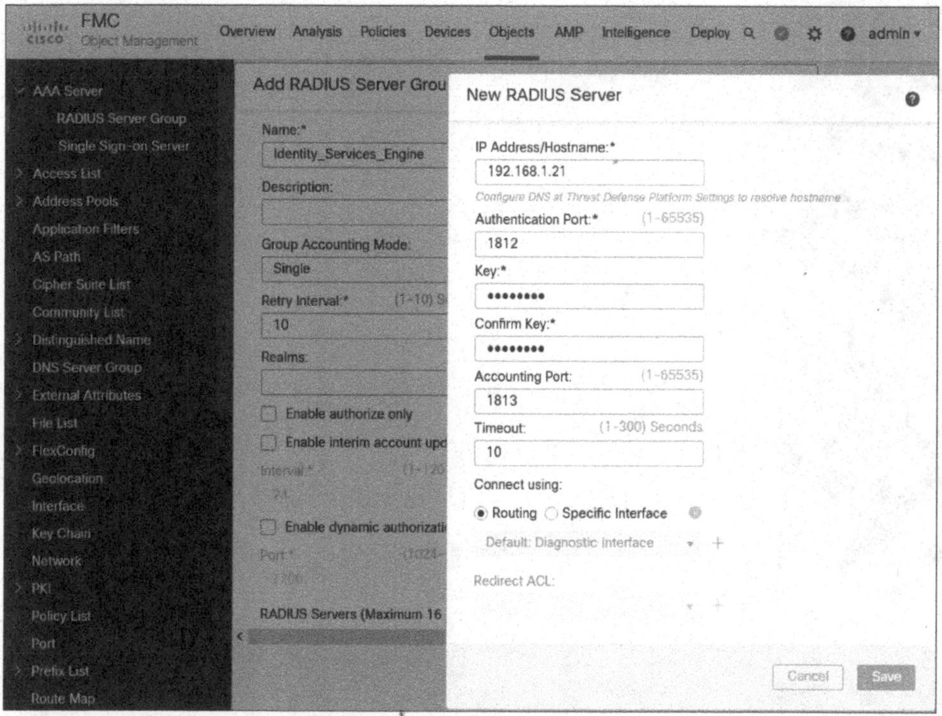

Figure 19-37 *Object to Define the User Authentication Server*

Because describing the configuration and deployment of an external CA server is beyond the scope of this book, this chapter uses the self-signed certificate to demonstrate the configuration of remote access VPN services on a threat defense. Use the following steps to add a self-signed certificate to a threat defense:

Step 1. Go to **Objects > Object Management**.

Step 2. Select **PKI > Cert Enrollment** on the left panel.

Step 3. Click the **Add Cert Enrollment** button. It opens the Add Cert Enrollment configuration window.

Step 4. On the CA Information tab, select **Self Signed Certificate** from the Enrollment Type drop-down.

Step 5. When you select the self-signed certificate enrollment type, you also need to provide a Common Name (CN). This field is located on the Certificate Parameters tab, as shown in Figure 19-38.

Step 6. Click the **Save** button to save the Cert Enrollment object.

Step 7. After adding the object, go to **Devices > Certificates** to add the certificate to your Secure Firewall (see Figure 19-39). After the certificate is added successfully, you can view the identity certificate by clicking the **ID** button (see Figure 19-40).

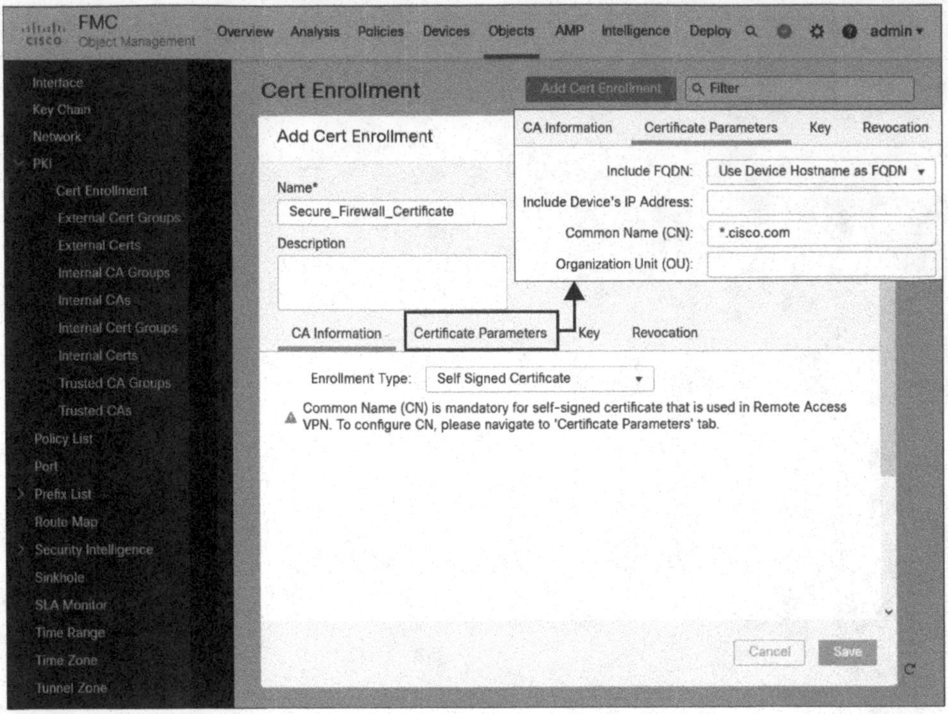

Figure 19-38 *Creating a Certificate Enrollment Object*

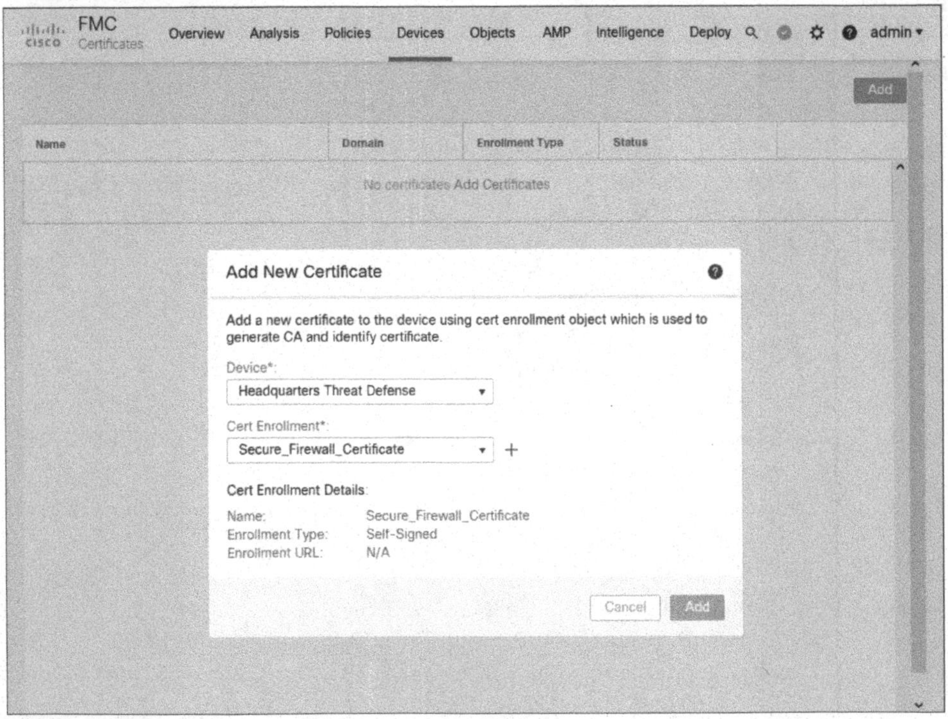

Figure 19-39 *Adding a Certificate to the Threat Defense*

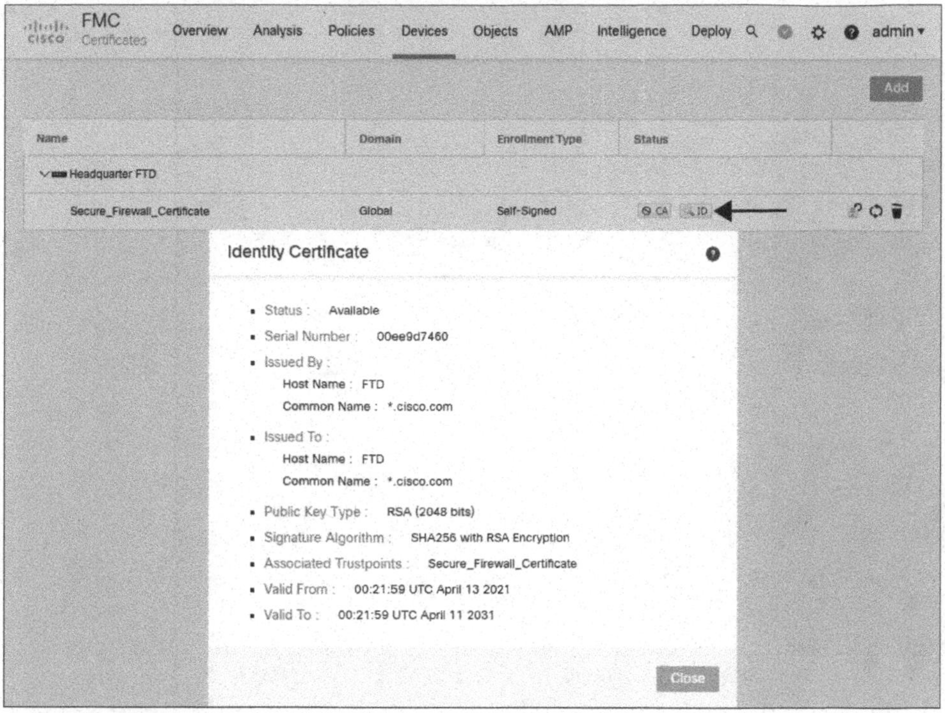

Figure 19-40   *Viewing the Detail of an Identity Certificate*

Network and IP Address Pool

To represent the IP addresses of both local-area network users and the remote access users, you can add the following types of objects after navigating to **Objects > Object Management:**

- **Network:** A network object can be added to represent the local-area network at headquarters. If you created network objects for the site-to-site VPN lab exercises in the previous section, you could reuse them here.

- **Address pools:** An address pool object contains the pre-allocated IP addresses for remote users. An IP address from this pool is assigned to a remote user when the user connects to the organization's internal network over the Internet using the remote-access VPN tunnel.

Figure 19-41 shows the addition of two objects. The top part of the figure shows the HQ_LAN network object, which defines the local-area network of the headquarters. Likewise, the bottom part of the figure shows the RAVPN_IP_Pool object, which defines an IPv4 address pool for remote users.

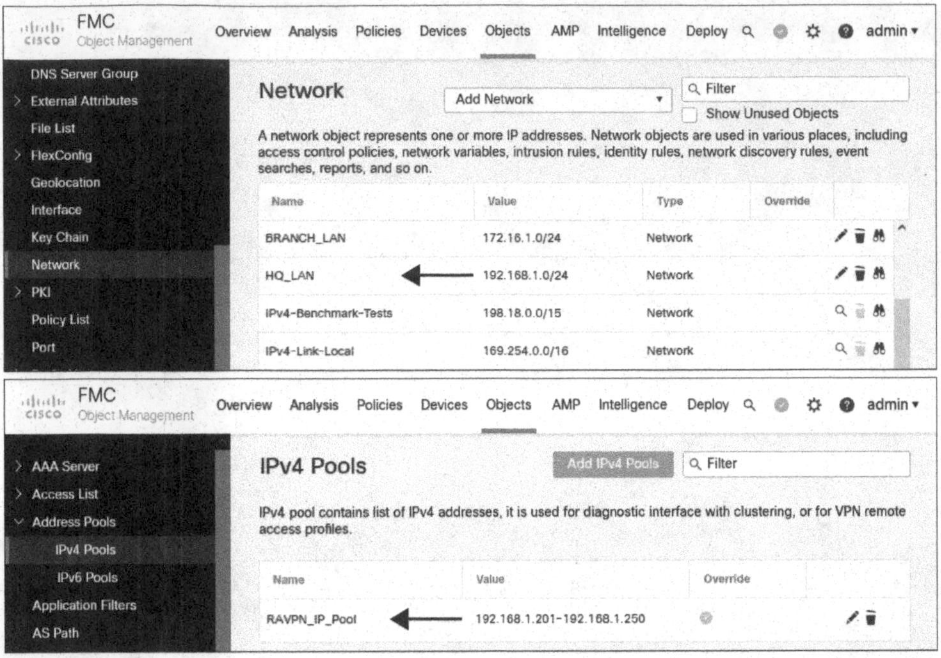

Figure 19-41 *Objects to Represent the LAN and Remote Users' Network Addresses*

Remote Access VPN Policy

Now is the time to put all the parts together. In the following steps, you use a wizard to configure a remote access VPN policy:

Step 1. Navigate to **Devices > VPN > Remote Access**.

Step 2. Click the **Add** button to create a new remote access VPN policy. The Remote Access VPN Policy Wizard opens. The policy wizard takes you through the necessary configuration steps, one by one.

Step 3. At first, configure the Policy Assignment, as shown in Figure 19-42.

    a. Name this remote access VPN policy.

    b. Select the protocols for the VPN tunnel. You can select either SSL or IPsec IKEv2, or both.

    c. Add the threat defense where this policy will be deployed.

Step 4. Next, configure the Connection Profile.

    a. Choose an Authentication Method for the remotely connected users. This lab exercise uses AAA Only (see Figure 19-43).

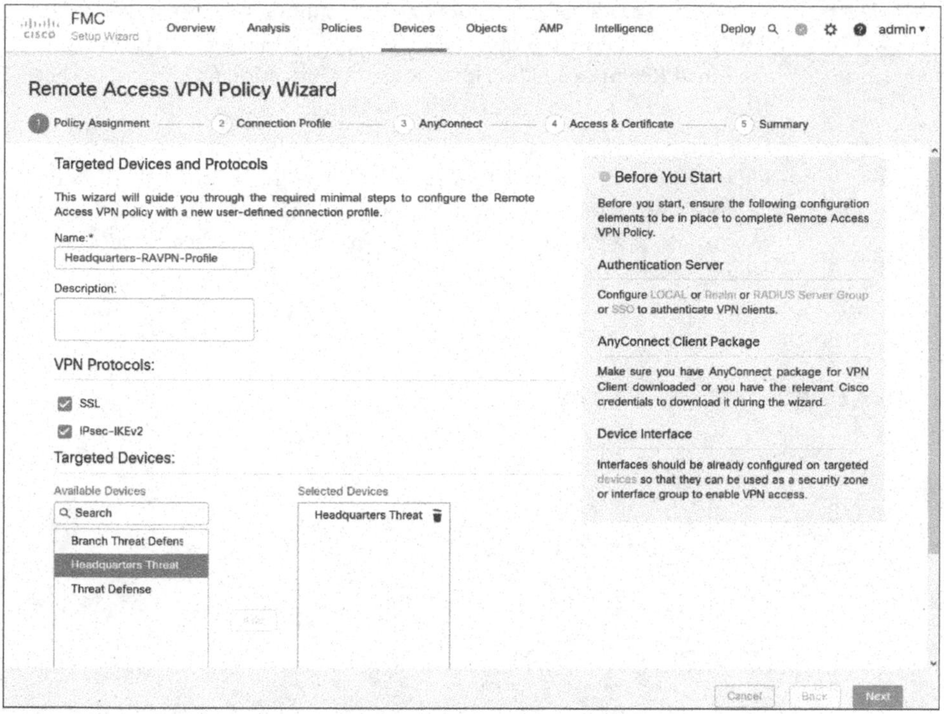

Figure 19-42   *Remote Access VPN Policy Assignment Configuration*

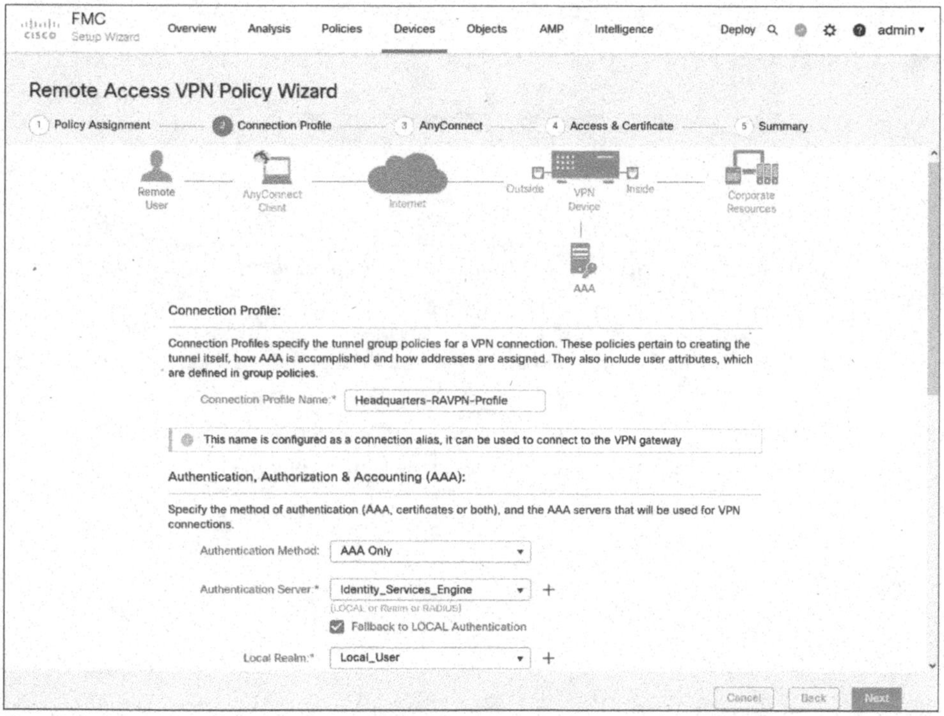

Figure 19-43   *Connection Profile Page (Top Part)—Authentication Method Selection*

b. For authentication, authorization, and accounting services, select the **RADIUS Server Group** object that you created earlier. Optionally, select the **Local Realm** as a fallback to local authentication (described in the "Prerequisites" section; refer to Figure 19-34).

c. Define a method to assign IP addresses to remote users. As shown in Figure 19-44, the threat defense will assign addresses from the RAVPN_IP_Pool when remote users connect to the organization's network via the remote access VPN tunnel. You created this object earlier (refer to Figure 19-41).

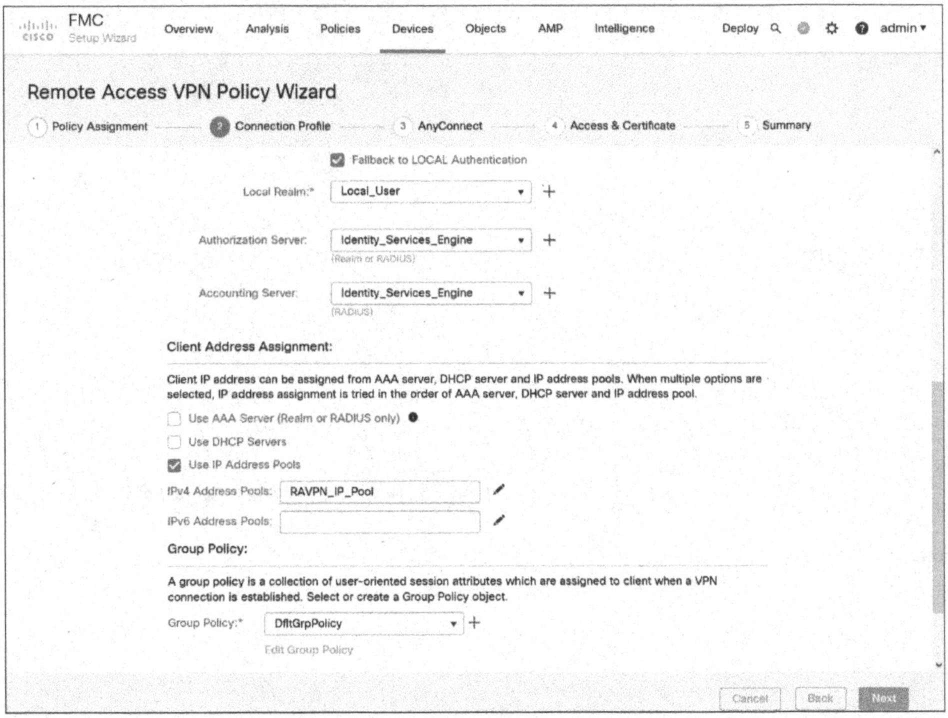

Figure 19-44 *Connection Profile Page (Bottom Part)—Client Address and Group Policy Assignment*

d. For Group Policy, you can create and select a new policy. For this chapter, select **DfltGrpPolicy**, which is the default group policy.

Step 5. In the next section, select one or more AnyConnect client images that you uploaded to the management center earlier (see Figure 19-45).

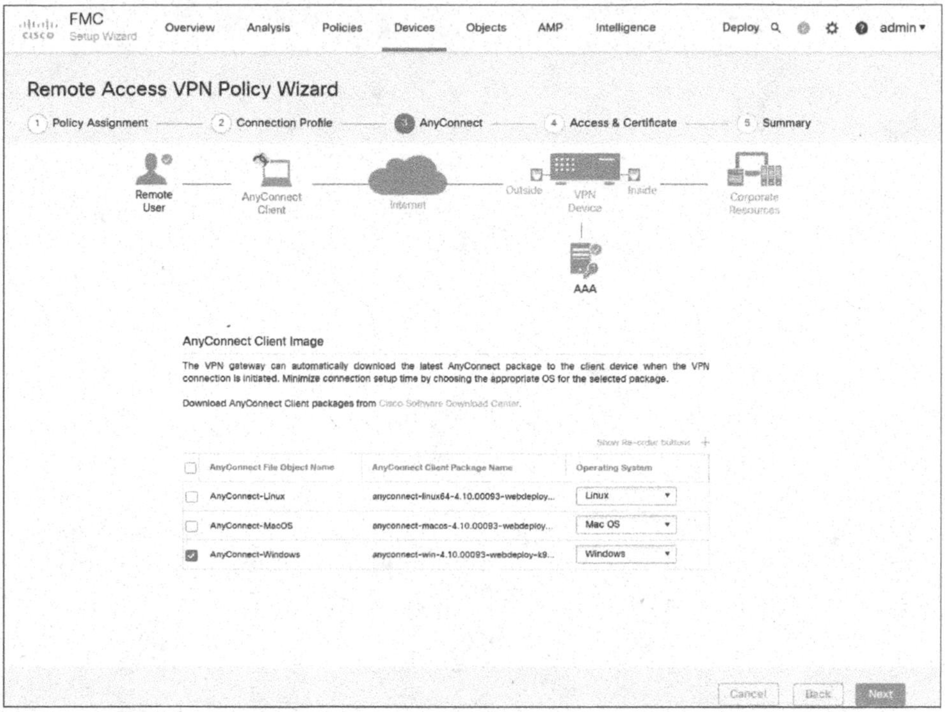

Figure 19-45 *AnyConnect Client Image Selection in a Policy*

Step 6. Finally, in the Access & Certificate section, choose the desired options from the drop-down, as displayed in Figure 19-46.

    a. Select the security zone, HQ_OUT, which is associated with the outside interface of the threat defense. In the remote access VPN lab topology, the remote users use the outside interface to connect to the organization network.

    b. Select **Secure_Firewall_Certificate**, which you installed on the threat defense earlier. This certificate is used to authenticate the VPN headend.

Step 7. The Summary section shows all the options you configured so far (see Figure 19-47). Click **Finish** if everything looks good.

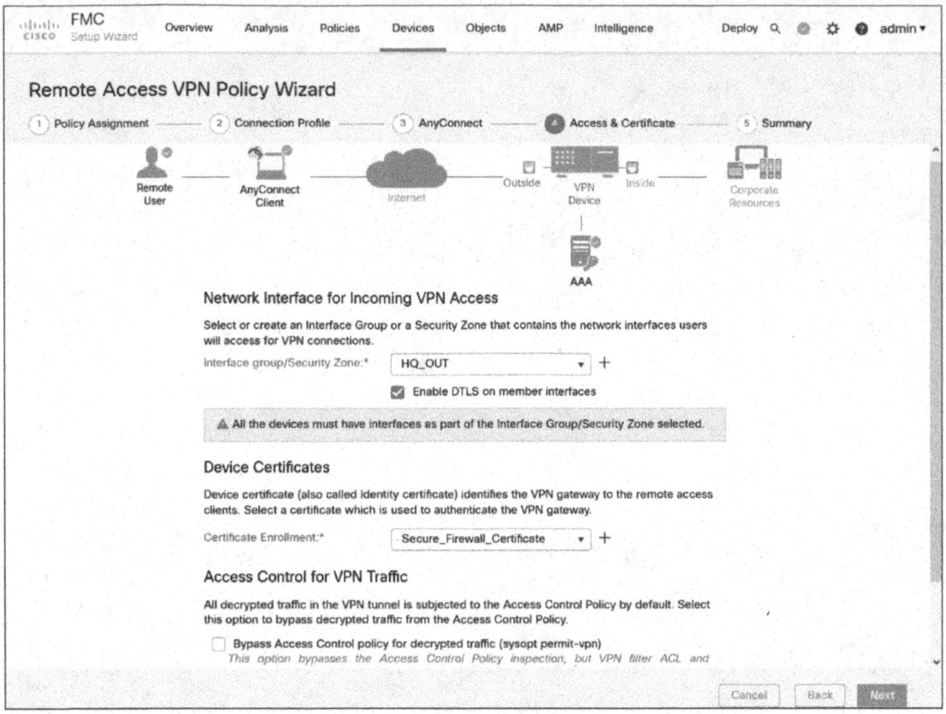

Figure 19-46   *Configurations for Incoming VPN Access*

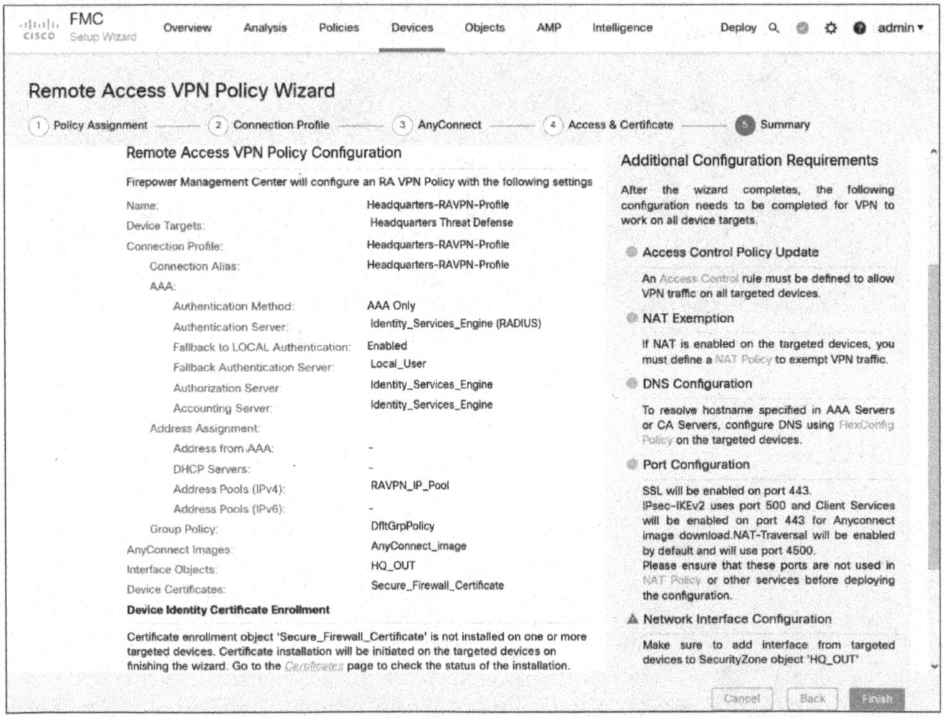

Figure 19-47   *Summary of Remote Access VPN Policy Configurations*

Step 8.   Navigate to the **Deploy > Deployment** page to deploy the remote access VPN policy to your threat defense.

Verification

When the remote access VPN policy is deployed on the threat defense, you can test the successful operation by using a browser in the remote host, as shown in the following steps:

Step 1.   Log in to the remote host machine and open a browser.

Step 2.   On the URL bar of the browser, enter the IP address of the threat defense's outside interface. If the browser can connect to the threat defense successfully, it should prompt with a security warning because a browser does not trust a self-signed certificate, by default (see Figure 19-48).

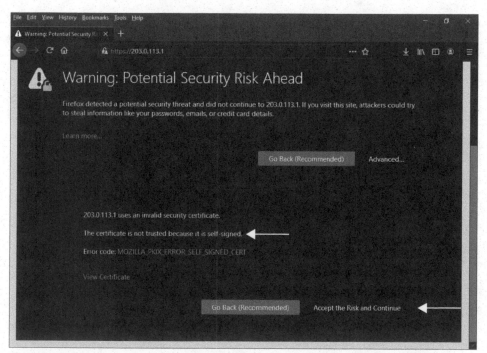

Figure 19-48   *Security Warning on the Browser Due to Self-Signed Certificate*

19

TIP   If the browser is unable to connect to the threat defense's outside interface, check whether any existing settings on the threat defense, such as an access control policy or NAT policy, are blocking the connection. The "Verification" section under "Site-to-Site VPN Policy Deployment" describes the process.

Step 3.   Because you used your Secure Firewall to generate this certificate earlier, you can accept the risk and continue this exercise in your lab environment.

Step 4.   After you accept the risk, the login prompt appears (see Figure 19-49). Enter the username and password. The AAA server deployed in this lab environment validates this user credential. (The communication workflow between a remote user and AAA server is illustrated in Figure 19-35.)

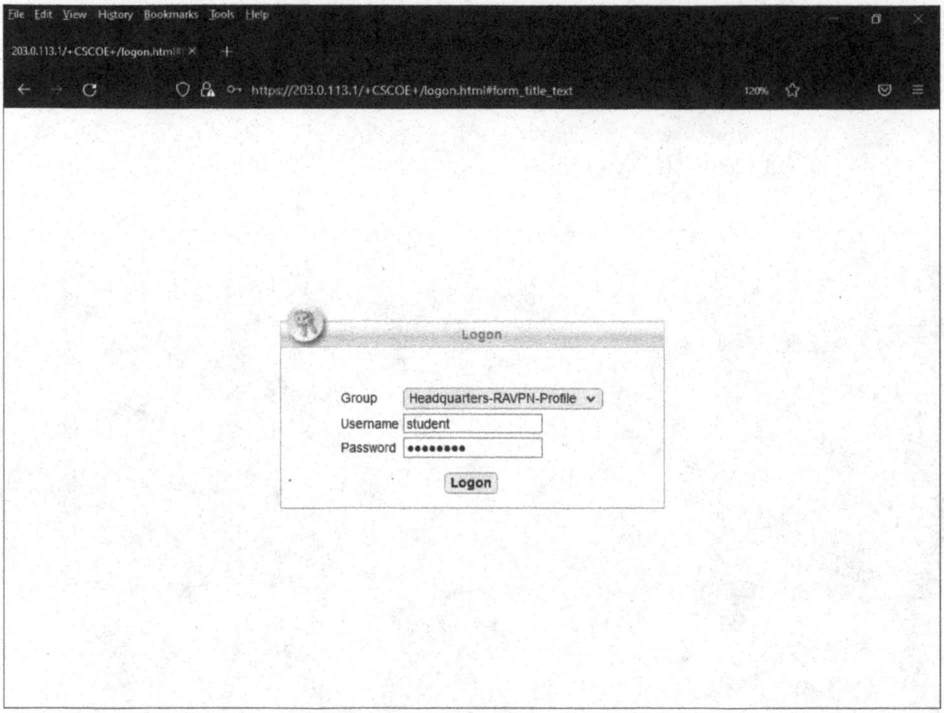

Figure 19-49   *Connection Attempt to the Corporate Network Shows a Login Prompt*

Step 5.   Click the **Logon** button. The browser prompts you to download and install the AnyConnect Secure Mobility Client (see Figure 19-50). Download the software and install it on your computer.

Step 6.   When the installation is complete, open the AnyConnect client software and perform the following tasks on the client:

    a.   Enter the IP address of the threat defense outside interface on the client software.

    b.   Click the **Connect** button. A login window appears (see Figure 19-51).

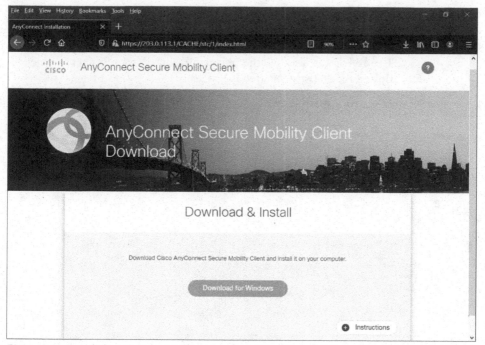

Figure 19-50 *The Ability to Download and Install AnyClient Client Software Is Offered*

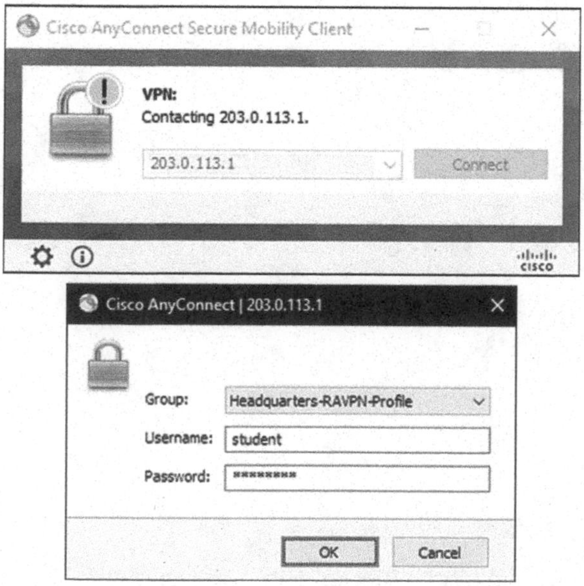

Figure 19-51 *AnyConnect Client Login Prompt*

c.   Enter the username and password (the same credential that you entered in Step 4).

d.   Click **OK** to log in. The AnyConnect client establishes a VPN session.

Step 7.   You can verify the remote access connection status in various ways:

   a.   As a remote user, you can open the AnyConnect client software to view the VPN connection status on the Message History tab (see Figure 19-52). You can also find the assigned IP address for this remote connection on the Statistics tab (see Figure 19-53).

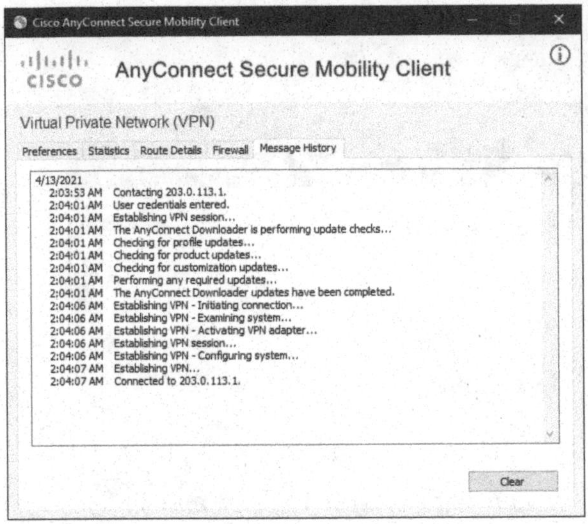

Figure 19-52   *The AnyConnect Client Establishes a VPN Connection*

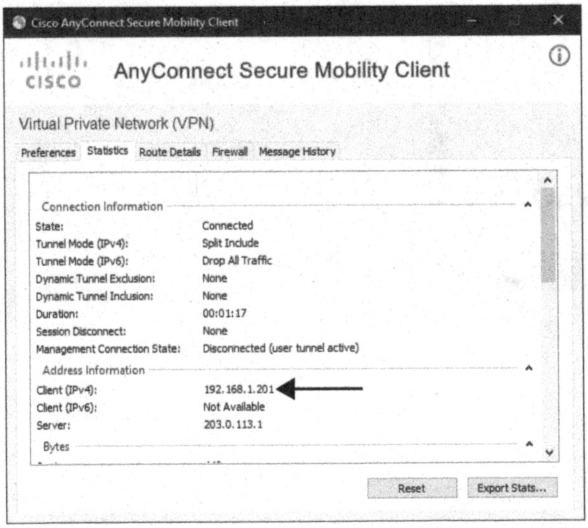

Figure 19-53   *A Remote User Obtains an IP Address from the Threat Defense IPv4 Address Pool*

b. As a firewall administrator, you can log in to the management center and navigate to the Access Controlled User Statistics dashboard. The VPN tab displays various statistics about the active session in different widgets (see Figure 19-54).

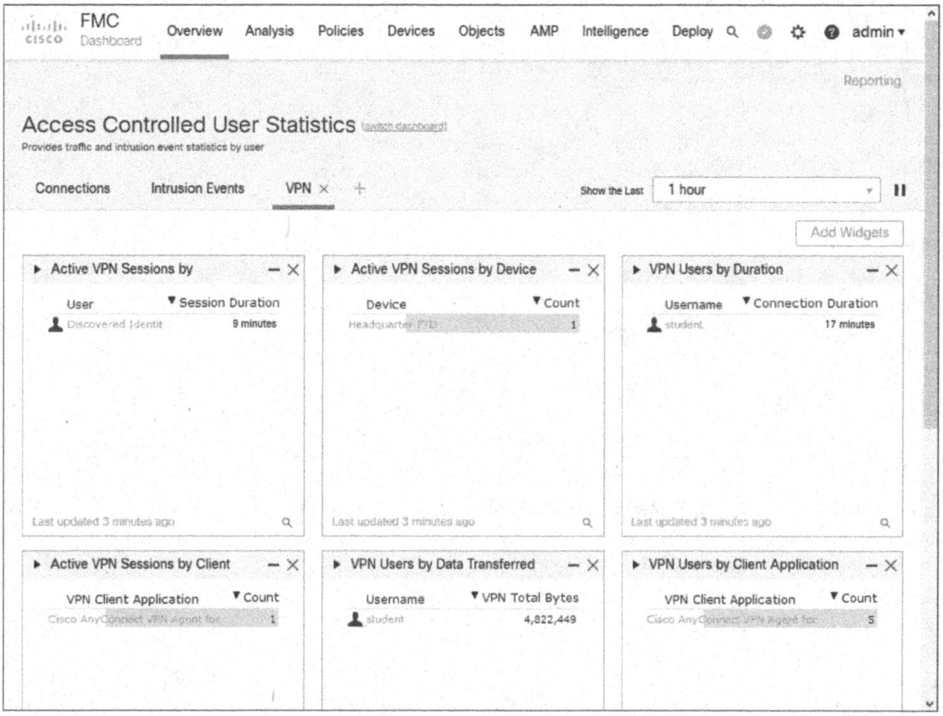

Figure 19-54   *The Management Center Dashboard Shows VPN User Sessions*

Example 19-7, Example 19-8, and Example 19-9 provide commands that you can run on the threat defense CLI to view the remote access VPN sessions. The command outputs in these examples represent a single user connection in this lab exercise.

Example 19-7   *Viewing the VPN Session Database*

```
> show vpn-sessiondb detail
------------------------------------------------------------------
VPN Session Summary
------------------------------------------------------------------

                   Active : Cumulative : Peak Concur : Inactive
                   ------------------------------------------------
AnyConnect Client  :     1 :          1 :           1 :        0
  SSL/TLS/DTLS     :     1 :          1 :           1 :        0
                   ------------------------------------------------
```

```
Total Active and Inactive    :     1      Total Cumulative :     1
Device Total VPN Capacity    :     75
Device Load                  :     1%
----------------------------------------------------------------


----------------------------------------------------------------
Tunnels Summary
----------------------------------------------------------------

                       Active : Cumulative : Peak Concurrent
                  ----------------------------------------------

AnyConnect-Parent  :     1 :          1 :              1
SSL-Tunnel         :     1 :          1 :              1
DTLS-Tunnel        :     1 :          1 :              1

----------------------------------------------------------------

Totals             :     3 :          3
----------------------------------------------------------------


>
```

Example 19-8   *Viewing the AnyConnect Client Details*

```
> show vpn-sessiondb anyconnect

Session Type: AnyConnect


Username     : student              Index       : 10
Assigned IP  : 192.168.1.201        Public IP   : 203.0.113.100
Protocol     : AnyConnect-Parent SSL-Tunnel DTLS-Tunnel
License      : AnyConnect Premium
Encryption   : AnyConnect-Parent: (1)none  SSL-Tunnel: (1)AES-GCM-256
DTLS-Tunnel: (1)AES-GCM-256
Hashing      : AnyConnect-Parent: (1)none  SSL-Tunnel: (1)SHA384  DTLS-Tunnel: (1)
SHA384
Bytes Tx     : 15844                Bytes Rx    : 104
Group Policy : DfltGrpPolicy
Tunnel Group : Headquarters-RAVPN-Profile
Login Time   : 02:14:06 UTC Tue Apr 13 2021
Duration     : 0h:01m:13s
Inactivity   : 0h:00m:00s
VLAN Mapping : N/A                  VLAN        : none
Audt Sess ID : 000000000000a0006074fe6e
Security Grp : none                 Tunnel Zone : 0


>
```

Example 19-9 *Viewing the Detail Session*

```
> show vpn-sessiondb detail anyconnect

Session Type: AnyConnect Detailed

Username    : student              Index       : 10
Assigned IP : 192.168.1.201        Public IP   : 203.0.113.100
Protocol    : AnyConnect-Parent SSL-Tunnel DTLS-Tunnel
License     : AnyConnect Premium
Encryption  : AnyConnect-Parent: (1)none  SSL-Tunnel: (1)AES-GCM-256  DTLS-Tunnel:
(1)AES-GCM-256
Hashing     : AnyConnect-Parent: (1)none  SSL-Tunnel: (1)SHA384  DTLS-Tunnel: (1)
SHA384
Bytes Tx    : 15844                Bytes Rx    : 104
Pkts Tx     : 12                   Pkts Rx     : 2
Pkts Tx Drop : 0                   Pkts Rx Drop : 0
Group Policy : DfltGrpPolicy
Tunnel Group : Headquarters-RAVPN-Profile
Login Time  : 02:14:06 UTC Tue Apr 13 2021
Duration    : 0h:04m:06s
Inactivity  : 0h:00m:00s
VLAN Mapping : N/A                 VLAN        : none
Audt Sess ID : 000000000000a0006074fe6e
Security Grp : none                Tunnel Zone : 0

AnyConnect-Parent Tunnels: 1
SSL-Tunnel Tunnels: 1
DTLS-Tunnel Tunnels: 1

AnyConnect-Parent:
  Tunnel ID   : 10.1
  Public IP   : 203.0.113.100
  Encryption  : none                Hashing     : none
  TCP Src Port : 55911              TCP Dst Port : 443
  Auth Mode   : userPassword
  Idle Time Out: 30 Minutes         Idle TO Left : 25 Minutes
  Client OS   : win
  Client OS Ver: 10.0.19042
  Client Type : AnyConnect
  Client Ver  : Cisco AnyConnect VPN Agent for Windows 4.10.00093
  Bytes Tx    : 7922                Bytes Rx     : 0
  Pkts Tx     : 6                   Pkts Rx      : 0
  Pkts Tx Drop : 0                  Pkts Rx Drop : 0
```

19

```
SSL-Tunnel:
  Tunnel ID    : 10.2
  Assigned IP  : 192.168.1.201        Public IP    : 203.0.113.100
  Encryption   : AES-GCM-256          Hashing      : SHA384
  Ciphersuite  : ECDHE-RSA-AES256-GCM-SHA384
  Encapsulation: TLSv1.2              TCP Src Port : 55920
  TCP Dst Port : 443                  Auth Mode    : userPassword
  Idle Time Out: 30 Minutes           Idle TO Left : 26 Minutes
  Client OS    : Windows
  Client Type  : SSL VPN Client
  Client Ver   : Cisco AnyConnect VPN Agent for Windows 4.10.00093
  Bytes Tx     : 7922                 Bytes Rx     : 104
  Pkts Tx      : 6                    Pkts Rx      : 2
  Pkts Tx Drop : 0                    Pkts Rx Drop : 0

DTLS-Tunnel:
  Tunnel ID    : 10.3
  Assigned IP  : 192.168.1.201        Public IP    : 203.0.113.100
  Encryption   : AES-GCM-256          Hashing      : SHA384
  Ciphersuite  : ECDHE-ECDSA-AES256-GCM-SHA384
  Encapsulation: DTLSv1.2             UDP Src Port : 64814
  UDP Dst Port : 443                  Auth Mode    : userPassword
  Idle Time Out: 30 Minutes           Idle TO Left : 26 Minutes
  Client OS    : Windows
  Client Type  : DTLS VPN Client
  Client Ver   : Cisco AnyConnect VPN Agent for Windows 4.10.00093
  Bytes Tx     : 0                    Bytes Rx     : 0
  Pkts Tx      : 0                    Pkts Rx      : 0
  Pkts Tx Drop : 0                    Pkts Rx Drop : 0

>
```

Summary

This chapter describes the wide variety of security protocols and techniques that are used in a virtual private network. After discussing the VPN fundamentals, this chapter demonstrates the steps to configure a site-to-site VPN. It then describes the processes to connect a remote user to a corporate network using remote access VPN functionality. Throughout the chapter, you use many command-line tools to verify the VPN configurations and operations on Secure Firewall.

Exam Preparation Tasks

As mentioned in the section "How to Use This Book" in the Introduction, you have a couple of choices for exam preparation: the exercises here, Chapter 22, "Final Preparation," and the exam simulation questions in the Pearson Test Prep practice test software.

Review All Key Topics

Review the most important topics in this chapter, noted with the Key Topics icon in the outer margin of the page. Table 19-4 lists a reference of these key topics and the page numbers on which each is found.

Key Topic

Table 19-4   Key Topics for Chapter 19

Key Topic Element	Description	Page
Paragraph	What is site-to-site VPN?	485
Paragraph	What is remote access VPN?	488
Paragraph	Protocols of the IPsec framework	489
Paragraph	Purpose of IKE and ISAKMP protocols	492
Paragraph	Role of a digital certificate in VPN	495
List	VPN license requirements	496
Paragraph	NAT exemption	504
List	AnyConnect license types	514
Tip	Remote access VPN performance	515
List	Certificate enrollment types	518

Complete Tables and Lists from Memory

Print a copy of Appendix C, "Memory Tables" (found on the companion website), or at least the section for this chapter, and complete the tables and lists from memory. Appendix D, "Memory Tables Answer Key," also on the companion website, includes completed tables and lists to check your work.

Define Key Terms

Define the following key terms from this chapter, and check your answers in the Glossary:

site-to-site VPN, remote access VPN, Internet Protocol Security (IPsec), Internet Key Exchange (IKE)

19

## CHAPTER 20

Quality of Service (QoS)

This chapter provides an overview of the following topics:

Quality of Service Essentials: This section describes various QoS techniques and explains the QoS operation on a threat defense from an architectural standpoint.

Best Practices for Enabling QoS: This section suggests the best practice to position a threat defense with a QoS policy.

Fulfilling Prerequisites: This section highlights various modes of threat defense and discusses the required mode for QoS implementation.

Configuring QoS Policy: This section demonstrates the steps to configure a QoS policy using a management center and to deploy it to a threat defense.

Verification: This section provides useful tips to analyze QoS configuration and operation using the CLI.

The objectives of this chapter are to learn about

- Quality of service (QoS) operation on Secure Firewall
- Implementation of QoS on threat defense
- Verification of QoS configurations on threat defense

Cisco Secure Firewall can limit the rate of network traffic after the traffic is allowed or trusted by an access control rule. However, it does not regulate the rate of any particular traffic when a prefilter policy applies the Fastpath action on them. Limiting the rate of traffic is a way to manage the bandwidth of a network and to ensure quality of service (QoS) for business-critical applications. This chapter discusses the steps to configure a QoS policy on Secure Firewall, deploy the policy from the management center to a threat defense, and verify the QoS operations on the threat defense.

"Do I Know This Already?" Quiz

The "Do I Know This Already?" quiz enables you to assess whether you should read this entire chapter thoroughly or jump to the "Exam Preparation Tasks" section. If you are in doubt about your answers to these questions or your own assessment of your knowledge of the topics, read the entire chapter. Table 20-1 lists the major headings in this chapter and their corresponding "Do I Know This Already?" quiz questions. You can find the answers in Appendix A, "Answers to the 'Do I Know This Already?' Quizzes."

Table 20-1 "Do I Know This Already?" Section-to-Question Mapping

Foundation Topics Section	Questions
Quality of Service Essentials	1, 2
Best Practices for Enabling QoS	3
Fulfilling Prerequisites	4
Configuring QoS Policy	5
Verification	6

1. Which of the following statements is correct?

    a. The Snort engine not only evaluates but also enforces a QoS rule.

    b. The Snort engine rate-limits traffic as soon as it receives it.

    c. The firewall engine enforces the actual rate limit.

    d. All of these answers are correct.

2. Which step is necessary to view any QoS-related events?

    a. In a QoS policy, enable logging at the beginning of a connection.

    b. In a QoS policy, enable logging at the end of a connection.

    c. In an access control policy, enable logging for a QoS rule.

    d. In an access control policy, enable logging at the end of a connection.

3. How many rules can be added in a QoS policy?

    a. 8

    b. 16

    c. 24

    d. 32

4. To enable a QoS policy on an interface, a threat defense should be deployed in which mode?

    a. Routed mode

    b. Inline mode

    c. Passive mode

    d. Switched mode

5. To limit the download rate to 5 MB/sec, which value should you enter in a QoS rule?

    a. 4

    b. 5

    c. 40

    d. 50

6. Which of the following commands confirms whether traffic is rate-limited by the threat defense?

    a. **show service-policy police**

    b. **show conn detail**

    c. **show asp drop**

    d. All of these answers are correct.

Foundation Topics

Quality of Service Essentials

There are multiple ways to enable quality of service (QoS) in a network. A threat defense implements the **traffic policing** mechanism to limit the rate of traffic. With this method, the threat defense drops excessive traffic when the traffic rate reaches a predefined limit. As of this writing, the threat defense does not support **traffic shaping**, where excessive traffic is queued in a buffer—rather than being dropped—for later transmission.

Figure 20-1 illustrates the crests and troughs of the traffic pattern when a threat defense rate-limits traffic using the policing method.

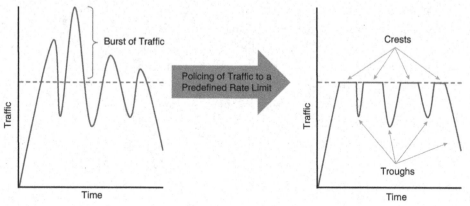

Figure 20-1 *Traffic Policing Method Dropping Excessive Traffic*

Figure 20-2 shows a typical graph illustrating traffic that is rate-limited by the shaping mechanism.

You can activate only one QoS policy on a threat defense at any given time. However, you can add multiple QoS rules within a single QoS policy. Each QoS rule must be associated with a source interface and a destination interface, where both of them have to be routed interfaces. You can set separate upload and download speed limits for the traffic that matches the conditions of a QoS rule. Furthermore, you can define the QoS rule conditions based on advanced networking characteristics, such as network address, port number, application, URL, and user identity.

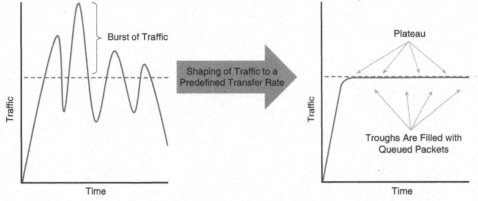

Figure 20-2   *Traffic Shaping Queues Excessive Traffic for Later Transmission*

The Snort engine evaluates a QoS rule and classifies traffic. When a packet matches with a QoS rule, the Snort engine sends the ID of the matching rule to the firewall engine. The firewall engine limits the rate of individual flows based on the download and upload speed limits defined on the QoS rule. You must enable logging at the end of a connection to view QoS-related information.

Figure 20-3 shows the workflow of QoS implementation on Secure Firewall. You use the management center to configure and apply a QoS policy and view any QoS events. The threat defense ensures that the traffic conforms to the QoS rule. Figure 20-4 highlights the operations of a QoS policy in a threat defense architecture.

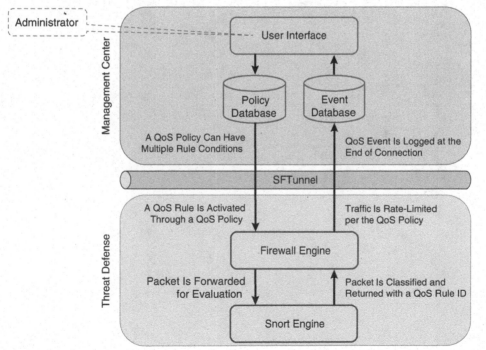

Figure 20-3   *QoS Implementation on the Secure Firewall*

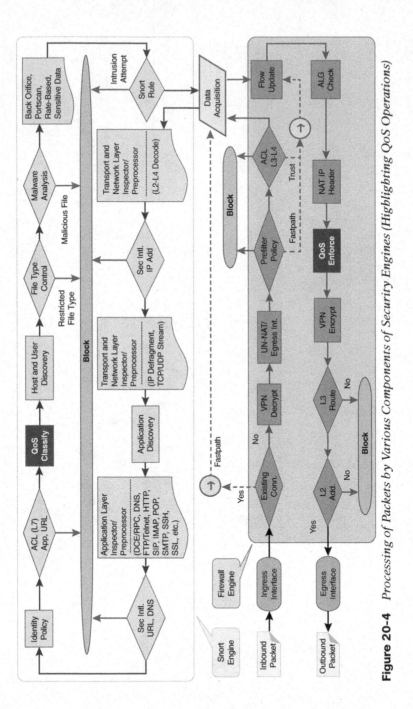

Figure 20-4 *Processing of Packets by Various Components of Security Engines (Highlighting QoS Operations)*

Best Practices for Enabling QoS

As of this writing, Secure Firewall supports up to 32 QoS rules within a single QoS policy. You can add different rule conditions for different network segments that are connected to different threat defense interfaces. However, when you want to implement a QoS policy, you should position the threat defense as close to the source as possible to ensure that the traffic does not consume the network and system resources more than it should.

Figure 20-5 shows a typical network where the threat defense enables different QoS rules through the same QoS policy. Traffic is originated from different source networks and rate-limited by different QoS rules.

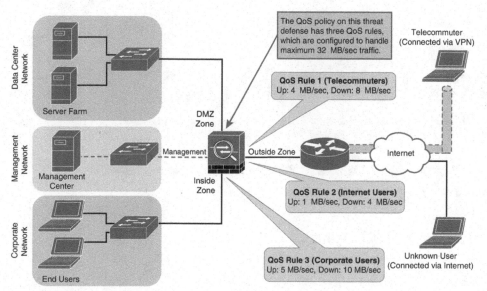

Figure 20-5   *Different QoS Rules Can Be Applied to Different Types of Users*

Fulfilling Prerequisites

Each interface participating in a QoS policy must be in routed mode and associated with an interface object. You cannot apply a QoS policy to an interface that is in inline mode, passive mode, or switched mode. (Read Chapter 4, "Firewall Deployment in Routed Mode," to learn about routed mode.)

Figure 20-6 shows the configuration of the threat defense interface. Both of the participating interfaces are in routed mode (assigned with IP addresses) and associated with security zones (interface objects).

20

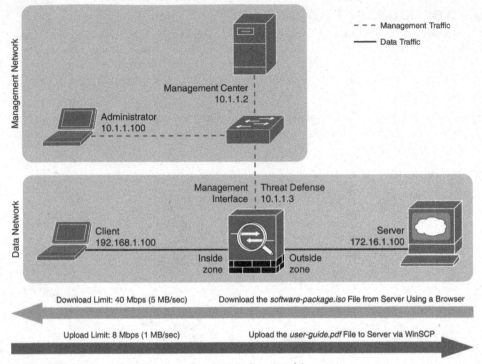

Figure 20-6 *Interface Settings for QoS Policy Enablement*

Configuring QoS Policy

Follow these steps to create a QoS policy and add a rule within it:

Step 1. Navigate to **Devices > QoS**. Secure Firewall does not come with a default QoS policy, so click the **New Policy** button to create one (see Figure 20-7). The New Policy window appears.

QoS Policy	Status	Last Modified
There are no policies created. Add a new policy		

Figure 20-7 *Home Page for the QoS Policy*

Step 2. Name the new policy and add a target device to which you want to apply this policy. Click **Save** to save the changes. The QoS policy editor page appears.

Step 3. Select a device for the new QoS policy you want to create and click **Add to Policy** (see Figure 20-8). Then click **Save**.

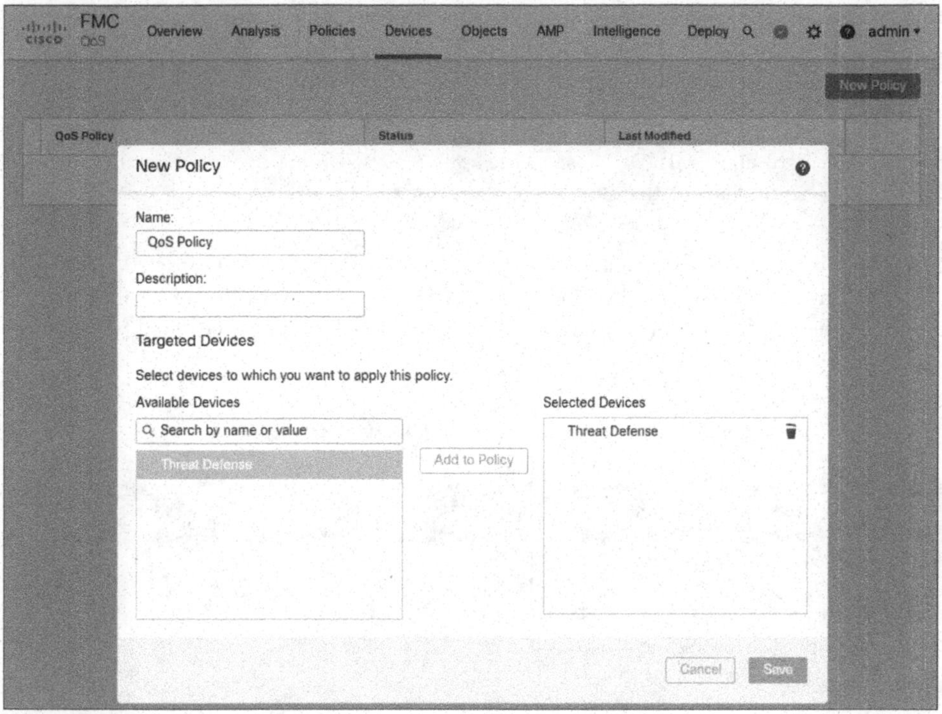

Figure 20-8 *Assigning a QoS Policy to a Threat Defense*

Step 4.   On the QoS policy editor page, notice that there is a link to the Policy Assignments option that you can use to associate a new managed device with this policy. Click the **Add Rule** button (see Figure 20-9). The Add Rule window appears, and in it you can define a rule condition.

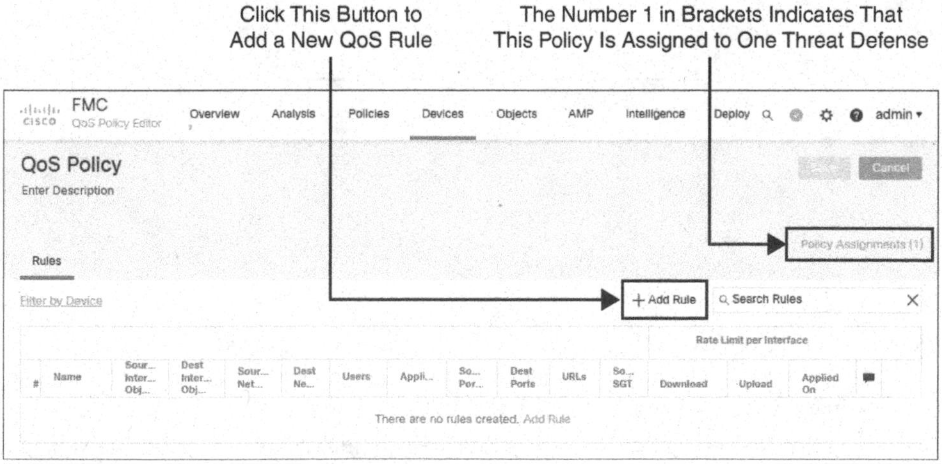

Figure 20-9 *The QoS Policy Editor Page*

Step 5. Name the new QoS rule. Using the Apply QoS On drop-down, define where you want to rate-limit traffic. In addition, on the Interface Objects tab, add a source and destination interface to the rule condition.

> **TIP** You should rate-limit traffic as close to the source as possible to ensure that the traffic rate does not go beyond an entitled limit throughout the network.

Figure 20-10 shows a new QoS rule, named QoS Rule, that is applied on Interfaces in Source Interface Objects. This rule limits traffic rates only when the traffic originates from the Inside_Zone interface and is destined for the Outside_Zone.

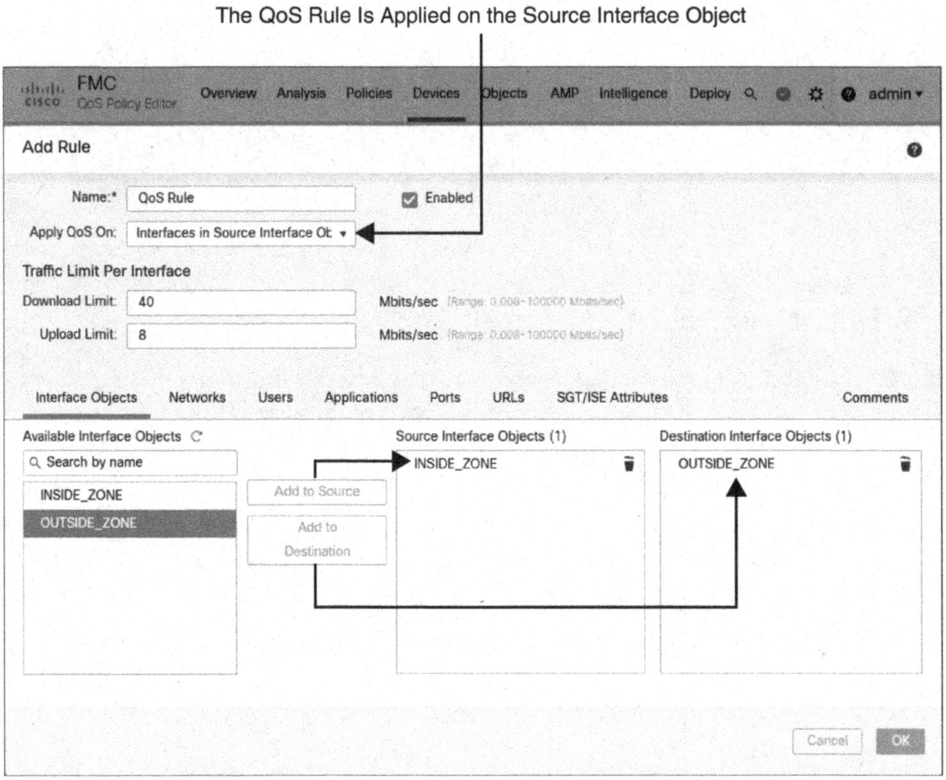

The QoS Rule Is Applied on the Source Interface Object

Figure 20-10 *Selecting Interface Objects in a Rule*

Key Topic

Step 6. Enter a desired traffic limit for the interface. You can provide upload and download limits separately. If you do not enter a value, the threat defense enables the maximum throughput for that physical interface.

Table 20-2 provides a conversion chart for commonly used traffic rates. When you enter a traffic limit, the threat defense considers the value as megabits per second (Mbps), not megabytes per second (MB/sec). The highlighted rows of this table are used in the configuration example in this chapter.

Table 20-2   Megabits per Second to Megabytes per Second Conversion Table

Megabits per Second (Mbps)	Megabytes per Second (MB/sec)
1 Mbps	0.125 MB/sec
4 Mbps	0.5 MB/sec
8 Mbps	1 MB/sec
10 Mbps	1.25 MB/sec
16 Mbps	2 MB/sec
40 Mbps	5 MB/sec
80 Mbps	10 MB/sec
100 Mbps	12.5 MB/sec

NOTE   A threat defense supports the rate limit of 0.008 to 100,000 Mbps per interface. If you want to allocate *below* 0.008 Mbps to any hosts, it implies that those hosts are not important to you. You may just want to consider blocking them by using an access rule or a prefilter rule.

Figure 20-11 shows the traffic limits for download and upload flows, 40 Mbps and 8 Mbps, respectively.

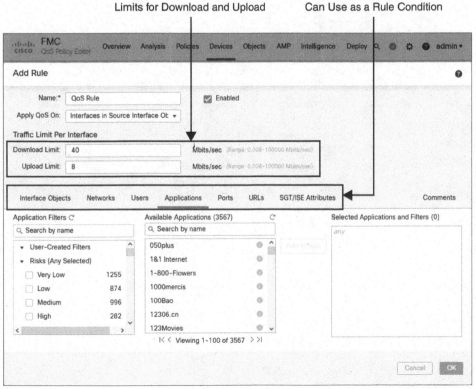

Figure 20-11   *Traffic Limit for a QoS Rule*

Step 7. Optionally, add a precise rate-limiting condition based on any additional networking characteristics, such as network address, port number, application, URL, and user identity.

Step 8. After you outline a rule condition, click the **OK** button to create the QoS rule. The browser returns to the QoS policy editor page. Click the **Save** button to preserve the QoS rules you have created.

Figure 20-12 shows the custom QoS rule you just created.

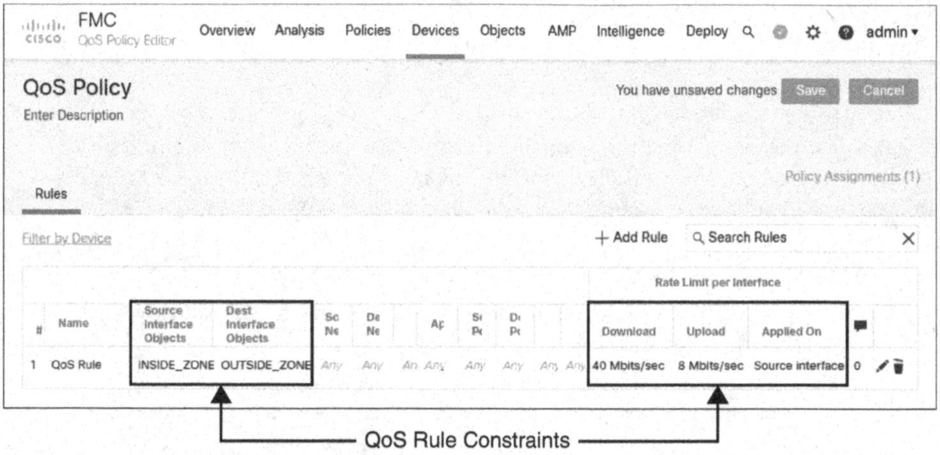

Figure 20-12 *Viewing Available QoS Rules on the QoS Policy Editor Page*

At this point, you can go to **Deploy > Deployment** to activate a QoS rule, but by default, the threat defense does not generate any log when it triggers a QoS rule. A QoS policy does not offer an option for logging. If you want to view QoS-related statistics for any specific connection, you must identify the associated access rule that triggers the QoS rule and enable logging at the end of that connection. To accomplish that, you have to edit the access control policy and redeploy the revised policy.

Figure 20-13 shows the option to enable logging for traffic matching the default action. Because this exercise does not use any custom access rules, you can enable logging for the default action to generate QoS data when a connection hits the default action.

Verification

After you successfully deploy a QoS policy, you can verify the deployment status from the threat defense CLI. Example 20-1 shows confirmation of the QoS policy configurations and the interface where the policy is deployed.

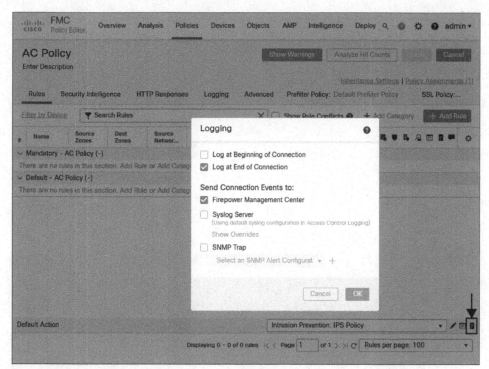

Figure 20-13 *Enabling Logging for the Default Action of an Access Control Policy*

Example 20-1 *Policy Map Showing the Active QoS Policy on an Interface*

```
! To view the rate-limiting settings:

> show running-config policy-map
!
policy-map type inspect dns preset_dns_map
 parameters
  message-length maximum client auto
  message-length maximum 512
  no tcp-inspection
policy-map type inspect ip-options UM_STATIC_IP_OPTIONS_MAP
 parameters
  eool action allow
  nop action allow
  router-alert action allow
policy-map global_policy
 class inspection_default
  inspect dns preset_dns_map
```

20

```
  inspect ftp
  inspect h323 h225
  inspect h323 ras
  inspect rsh
  inspect rtsp
  inspect sqlnet
  inspect skinny
  inspect sunrpc
  inspect xdmcp
  inspect sip
  inspect netbios
  inspect tftp
  inspect icmp
  inspect icmp error
  inspect snmp
  inspect ip-options UM_STATIC_IP_OPTIONS_MAP
 class class_snmp
  inspect snmp
 class class-default
  set connection advanced-options UM_STATIC_TCP_MAP
policy-map policy_map_INSIDE_INTERFACE
 match flow-rule qos 268462080
  police input 8000000 250000
  police output 40000000 1250000
!
>


! To determine where a policy is applied:

> show running-config service-policy
service-policy global_policy global
service-policy policy_map_INSIDE_INTERFACE interface INSIDE_INTERFACE
>
```

Now, you can verify the impact of the QoS policy you have deployed. First, download a file from the server to a client system. Then upload a file from the client PC to the server. You should notice two different traffic rates.

Figure 20-14 shows a simple lab topology that you can use to limit and verify the download and upload speeds through a threat defense.

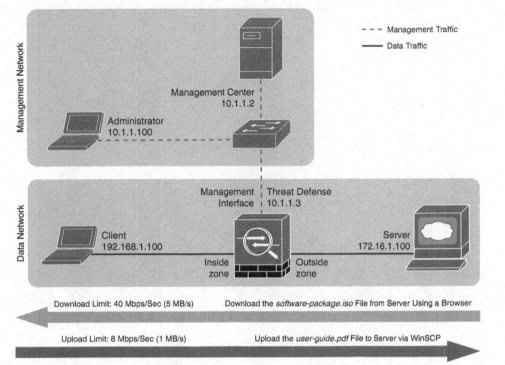

Figure 20-14 *Lab Topology to Test the Rate-Limiting of Traffic Through a Threat Defense*

Figure 20-15 shows the download of a software image file. The threat defense enforces the download rate up to 5 MB/sec, per the QoS policy.

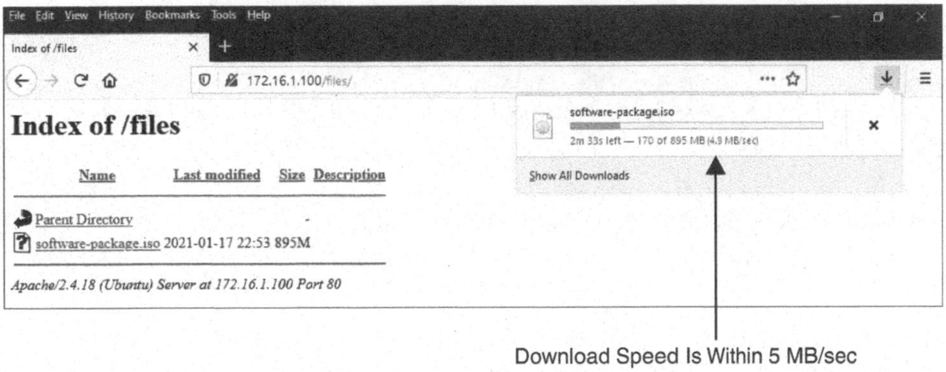

Figure 20-15 *Compliance of the Download Rate (Defined in the QoS Policy)*

Figure 20-16 shows the upload of a PDF file. The threat defense regulates the upload rate below 1 MB/sec, per the QoS policy.

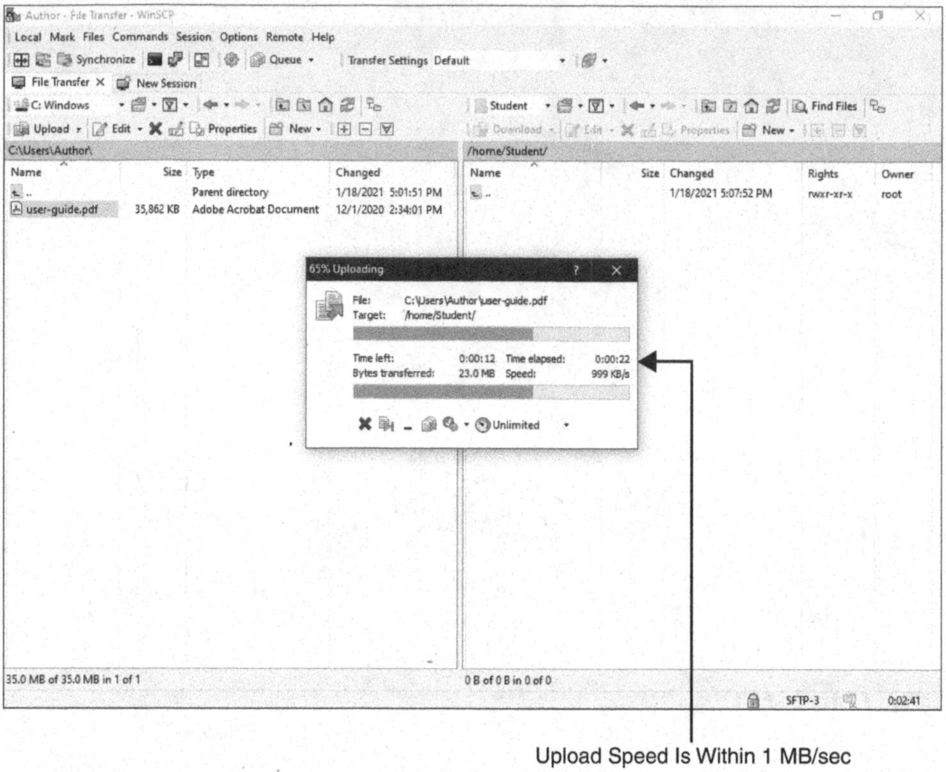

Upload Speed Is Within 1 MB/sec

Figure 20-16 *Compliance of the Upload Rate (Defined in the QoS Policy)*

Both of these transfers—download of the ISO and upload of the PDF—are initiated by a host that is located at the inside zone. Therefore, the traffic matches the QoS rule, and the threat defense regulates the traffic rate. However, if the connection is initiated by an outside system, it does not match the QoS rule condition. Hence, the QoS policy does not limit the traffic rate; the source and destination hosts should be able to utilize the full capacity of the threat defense interface bandwidth.

Analyzing QoS Events and Statistics

If you have enabled logging for the connections that also match your QoS rule conditions, you can view the QoS-related statistics in the Connection Events page. Here are the steps to view them:

Step 1.   Navigate to **Analysis > Connections > Events**.

Step 2.   Select **Connection Events** as the table view.

Step 3.   Expand the Search Constraints arrow on the left.

Step 4.   Select the necessary QoS-related data points.

Figure 20-17 shows two connection events. The bottom connection is originated by an inside client, which matched the conditions in the QoS Rule, and the traffic rate is limited accordingly. However, the connection at the top is not rate-limited because it is initiated by a host located at the outside zone.

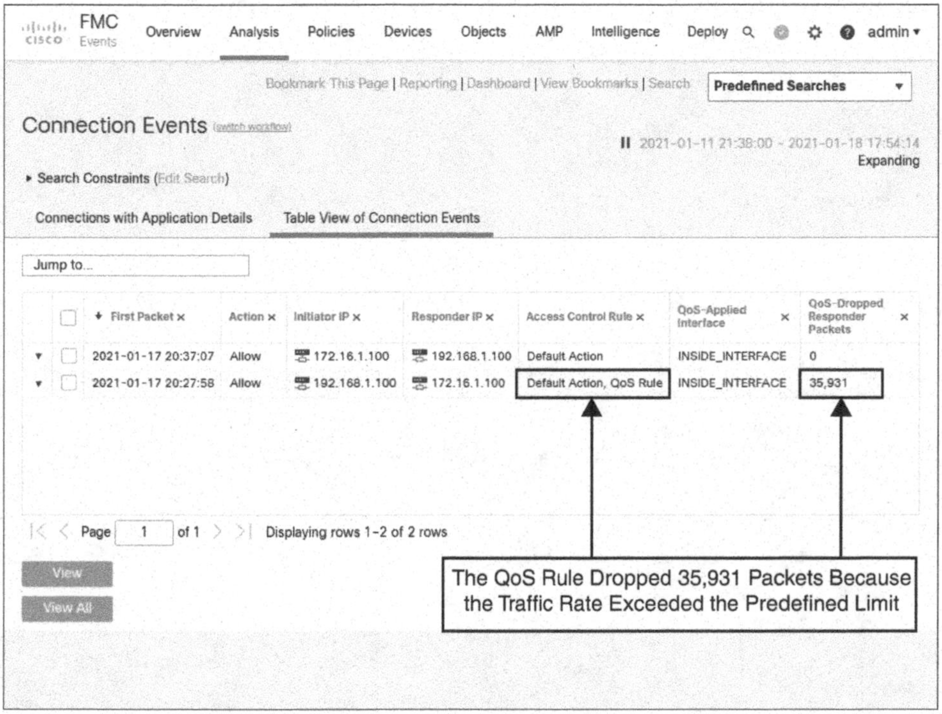

Figure 20-17 *Connection Events Showing Associated QoS Rules*

Example 20-2 demonstrates the actions of a QoS policy on a threat defense. This example provides two commands that you can use to determine any drop due to a QoS rule during a file transfer.

Example 20-2 *Statistics of Dropped Packets Due to a QoS Policy*

```
! Record on the service policy statistics

> show service-policy police
Interface INSIDE_INTERFACE:
  Service-policy: policy_map_INSIDE_INTERFACE
    Flow-rule QoS id: 268462080
      Input police Interface INSIDE_INTERFACE:
        cir 8000000 bps, bc 250000 bytes
        conformed 309884 packets, 233417067 bytes; actions:  transmit
        exceeded 10459 packets, 14979835 bytes; actions:  drop
        conformed 454552 bps, exceed 29168 bps
      Output police Interface INSIDE_INTERFACE:
        cir 40000000 bps, bc 1250000 bytes
```

```
         conformed 499249 packets, 673878828 bytes; actions:  transmit
        exceeded 58971 packets, 84562922 bytes; actions:  drop
         conformed 1312296 bps, exceed 164672 bps
>


! Statistics of the Accelerated Security Path (ASP) counts

> show asp drop

Frame drop:
  No route to host (no-route)                            2049
  Reverse-path verify failed (rpf-violated)              137
  Flow is denied by configured rule (acl-drop)           1946
  First TCP packet not SYN (tcp-not-syn)                 53
  TCP failed 3 way handshake (tcp-3whs-failed)           30
  Output QoS rate exceeded (rate-exceeded)               69430
  Slowpath security checks failed (sp-security-failed)   173
  FP L2 rule drop (l2_acl)                               705
  Interface is down (interface-down)                     5

Last clearing: Never
Flow drop:
Last clearing: Never
>
```

Example 20-3 reveals the connections that are rate-limited by a QoS rule. The flags associated with a connection confirm whether the traffic is going through a deep packet inspection process. To determine the meaning of each flag, you can use the **detail** keyword. For example, the flag **N** confirms that the Snort engine is inspecting the connection.

Example 20-3 *Identifying the Status of a Rate-Limited Connection*

```
> show conn detail
1 in use, 6 most used
Inspect Snort:
        preserve-connection: 1 enabled, 0 in effect, 6 most enabled, 0 most in
effect
Flags: A - awaiting responder ACK to SYN, a - awaiting initiator ACK to SYN,
       b - TCP state-bypass or nailed,
       C - CTIQBE media, c - cluster centralized,
       D - DNS, d - dump, E - outside back connection, e - semi-distributed,
       F - initiator FIN, f - responder FIN,
       G - group, g - MGCP, H - H.323, h - H.225.0, I - initiator data,
```

```
        i - incomplete, J - GTP, j - GTP data, K - GTP t3-response

        k - Skinny media, L - decap tunnel, M - SMTP data, m - SIP media

        N - inspected by Snort (1 - preserve-connection enabled, 2 - preserve-
connection in effect)

        n - GUP, O - responder data, o - offloaded,

        P - inside back connection, p - passenger flow

        q - SQL*Net data, R - initiator acknowledged FIN,

        R - UDP SUNRPC, r - responder acknowledged FIN,

        T - SIP, t - SIP transient, U - up,

        V - VPN orphan, v - M3UA W - WAAS,

        w - secondary domain backup,

        X - inspected by service module,

        x - per session, Y - director stub flow, y - backup stub flow,

        Z - Scansafe redirection, z - forwarding stub flow


TCP OUTSIDE_INTERFACE: 172.16.1.100/80 INSIDE_INTERFACE: 192.168.1.100/63860,
    flags UIO N1, qos-rule-id 268462080, idle 0s, uptime 50s, timeout 1h0m, bytes
283367890
  Initiator: 192.168.1.100, Responder: 172.16.1.100
  Connection lookup keyid: 4524219


>
```

Example 20-4 shows the real-time debug messages generated by the firewall and Snort engines, due to the match of a QoS rule (ID: 268442624).

Example 20-4   *Debugging the QoS Rule–Related Events in Real Time*

```
! Debug messages in the firewall engine:


> system support firewall-engine-debug


Please specify an IP protocol: tcp
Please specify a client IP address:
Please specify a client port:
Please specify a server IP address:
Please specify a server port:


Monitoring firewall engine debug messages


! Output is truncated for brevity

    .
    .
    .
192.168.1.100-63883 > 172.16.1.100-80 6 AS 1-1 I 0 Starting QoS with minimum 0, id 0
and SrcZone first with zones 1 -> 2, geo 0 -> 0, vlan 0, source sgt type: 0, source
sgt tag: 0, ISE sgt id: 0, dest sgt type: 0, ISE dest sgt tag: 0, svc 0, payload 0,
client 0, misc 0, user 9999997, icmpType 0, icmpCode 0
```

20

```
192.168.1.100-63883 > 172.16.1.100-80 6 AS 1-1 I 0 match rule order 1, id 268462080
action Rate Limit
192.168.1.100-63883 > 172.16.1.100-80 6 AS 1-1 I 0 QoS policy match status (match
found), match action (Rate Limit), QoS rule id (268462080)

^c
Caught interrupt signal
Exiting.


>
```

The statistics in these examples were captured when a client PC was downloading a large ISO file from the server using a web browser. You could perform a similar analysis on uploaded traffic. Before you begin uploading a file from the client PC to the server, you can run the following commands to reset the counters.

```
> clear service-policy interface INSIDE_INTERFACE
```

```
> clear asp drop
```

Summary

This chapter explains the steps to configure a QoS policy on a threat defense. It also provides an overview to the common rate-limiting mechanisms and how a threat defense implements QoS. Finally, this chapter provides the command-line tools you can use to verify the configuration and operation of QoS policies in the threat defense.

Exam Preparation Tasks

As mentioned in the section "How to Use This Book" in the Introduction, you have a couple of choices for exam preparation: the exercises here, Chapter 22, "Final Preparation," and the exam simulation questions in the Pearson Test Prep practice test software.

Review All Key Topics

Review the most important topics in this chapter, noted with the Key Topic icon in the outer margin of the page. Table 20-3 lists a reference of these key topics and the page numbers on which each is found.

Key Topic

Table 20-3   Key Topics for Chapter 20

Key Topic Element	Description	Page
Step list	Understanding throughput calculation	544

Complete Tables and Lists from Memory

Print a copy of Appendix C, "Memory Tables" (found on the companion website), or at least the section for this chapter, and complete the tables and lists from memory. Appendix D, "Memory Tables Answer Key," also on the companion website, includes completed tables and lists to check your work.

Define Key Terms

Define the following key terms from this chapter, and check your answers in the Glossary:

traffic policing, traffic shaping

20

## CHAPTER 21

System Logging (Syslog)

This chapter provides an overview of the following topics:

Secure Firewall Logging Essentials: This section describes the syslog implementation over UDP and TCP, and different components of the syslog messages, such as security levels and facilities.

Best Practices for Logging: This section provides tips to optimize Secure Firewall performance when syslog is enabled in a large-scale deployment.

Prerequisites: This section discusses the key requirements to connect a syslog server to Secure Firewall successfully.

Sending Syslog from Threat Defense: This section demonstrates how to use the platform settings to add a syslog server and send logs from a threat defense.

Sending Syslog from Management Center: This section explains the steps to send messages to a syslog server directly from a management center. It also describes the techniques to correlate different types of events and sends alerts to a syslog server only when a certain condition is fulfilled.

Troubleshooting Logs: This section explains the process to generate troubleshooting files that include all the configuration and log files from Secure Firewall.

The objectives of this chapter are to learn about

- Syslog messages, security levels, and facilities

- Configuration of syslog services on Secure Firewall

- Configuration of correlation policy

- Configuration of alerts for security and system events

- Generation and collection of troubleshooting logs using GUI

Logging helps you to understand the behavior of a computer system. You can use logging for real-time alerting as well as for auditing purposes. The Internet Engineering Task Force (IETF) standardizes **system logging (syslog)** in RFC 5424. Secure Firewall supports sending syslog messages to third-party syslog servers and security information and event management (SIEM) tools. It enables you to monitor, audit, and debug the operations of Secure Firewall. Syslog can be a great troubleshooting tool in your toolbox. This chapter describes the procedures to enable logging on both the management center and a threat defense.

"Do I Know This Already?" Quiz

The "Do I Know This Already?" quiz enables you to assess whether you should read this entire chapter thoroughly or jump to the "Exam Preparation Tasks" section. If you are in doubt about your answers to these questions or your own assessment of your knowledge of the topics, read the entire chapter. Table 21-1 lists the major headings in this chapter and their corresponding "Do I Know This Already?" quiz questions. You can find the answers in Appendix A, "Answers to the 'Do I Know This Already?' Quizzes."

Table 21-1 "Do I Know This Already?" Section-to-Question Mapping

Foundation Topics Section	Questions
Secure Firewall Logging Essentials	1
Best Practices for Logging	2
Prerequisites	3
Sending Syslog from Threat Defense	4
Sending Syslog from Management Center	5
Troubleshooting Logs	6

CAUTION The goal of self-assessment is to gauge your mastery of the topics in this chapter. If you do not know the answer to a question or are only partially sure of the answer, you should mark that question as wrong for purposes of the self-assessment. Giving yourself credit for an answer you correctly guess skews your self-assessment results and might provide you with a false sense of security.

1. Which of the following keywords does not represent a severity level?
   a. ALERT
   b. AUDIT
   c. DEBUG
   d. INFO

2. Which of the following statements is false?
   a. Secure Firewall can rate-limit syslog messages based on severity levels.
   b. Secure Firewall can send syslog messages for connection events.
   c. Syslog over UDP can introduce extra overhead in a large deployment.
   d. If the TCP syslog server goes down, user traffic cannot continue through Secure Firewall.

3. What is the standard port number of the syslog protocol?
   a. UDP 514
   b. TCP 1470
   c. Both UDP 514 and TCP 1470
   d. None of these answers are correct.

4. Which of the following options can be configured in the Platform Settings policy?

   a. Adding a custom banner

   b. Setting up time synchronization

   c. Sending syslog messages

   d. All of these answers are correct.

5. Which of the following event types can be used as a constraint in a correlation rule?

   a. Discovery events

   b. Intrusion and file events

   c. Connection events

   d. All of these answers are correct.

6. What is included in the Secure Firewall troubleshooting file package?

   a. Command output

   b. Database search queries

   c. Syslogs of running processes

   d. All of these answers are correct.

Foundation Topics

Secure Firewall Logging Essentials

Secure Firewall can generate syslog alerts for various security events, such as intrusion policies, file and malware policies, discovery policies, and access control policies. It can also send syslog alerts to provide the health status of its various hardware and software components. You can configure a management center to generate and send syslog messages directly to a syslog server. Alternatively, a threat defense device can also send the syslog messages directly to one or more syslog servers. Depending on your use case, which is described later in this chapter, you should select one originator for logging. Configuring both devices—management center and threat defense—for the same syslog messages can be resource intensive.

Secure Firewall can send syslog messages over TCP as well as UDP. When you choose a transport layer protocol, carefully consider its merits and demerits. For example, if TCP is chosen to send syslog messages, Secure Firewall opens multiple connections to the syslog server to ensure that syslog messages are not lost during transmission. In a large deployment, when a syslog server is configured to collect logs from many originators, the volume of TCP connections can be very high; it can introduce excessive overhead to the syslog server. In this case, syslog over UDP may be a more beneficial solution. Keep in mind that UDP may be a low-overhead protocol, but the syslog messages over UDP can be lost due to congestion or any sporadic networking issues. To learn more about the syslog protocol and its implementation over different protocols, you can read the RFC documents listed on Table 21-2.

Table 21-2   RFC Documents Describing Syslog Implementations

RFC	Description
RFC 5424	The Syslog Protocol
RFC 5426	Transmission of Syslog Messages over UDP
RFC 6587	Transmission of Syslog Messages over TCP
RFC 5425	Transport Layer Security (TLS) Transport Mapping for Syslog

Key Topic

Syslog messages can be generated by many processes and subsystems of a computer system, such as the authentication subsystem, networking subsystem, or mail subsystem. Each syslog message is associated with a **severity level**. As the name implies, a severity level indicates the significance of a message. It enables a system administrator to decide whether and when an action should be taken to address the issue described in a syslog message. The IETF uses the term **facility** to refer to various subsystems. RFC 5424 describes various severity levels and facilities that can be used by a syslog server. You can find them in Table 21-3 and Table 21-4, respectively.

Table 21-3   Syslog Messages Severity Levels

Severity Level (0–7)	Messages That Describe...
EMERG	An emergency condition where the system is unusable
ALERT	A condition where an action must be taken immediately to fix the issue
CRIT	A critical condition that indicates a failure in the primary system
ERR	An error condition
WARNING	A warning condition
NOTICE	A condition that does not indicate an error but may require special attention
INFO	An informational message
DEBUG	Debug-level information to help the developers of an application or system

Table 21-4   Syslog Messages Facilities

Facility Level (0–23)	Messages That Are Associated With...
KERN	Kernel
USER	User-level process
MAIL	Mail system
DAEMON	System daemon
AUTH	Security/authentication subsystem
SYSLOG	System logging daemon (syslogd)
LPR	Line printer subsystem
NEWS	Network news subsystem

Facility Level (0–23)	Messages That Are Associated With...
UUCP	Unix-to-Unix copy subsystem
CRON	Clock/scheduling daemon
	(Used by Syslog server running on a Linux OS)
AUTHPRIV	Security/authentication system
FTP	FTP daemon
NTP	NTP subsystem
AUDIT	Audit subsystem (Security log audit)
ALERT	Alerting subsystem (Console)
CLOCK	Clock/scheduling daemon
	(Used by Syslog server running on Windows OS)
LOCAL0–LOCAL7	Locally defined facilities

Best Practices for Logging

Consider the following issues when configuring Secure Firewall to send alerts to a syslog server:

- If your syslog server uses TCP, enable the Allow User Traffic to Pass When TCP Syslog Server Is Down option. It enables the traffic flow to continue in case of any issues with the syslog server (shown later in Figure 21-9).

- To prevent a syslog server from crashing, you can enable rate limiting for certain types of syslog messages (shown later in Figure 21-11).

- Syslog over TCP can introduce overhead in a large deployment. In this scenario, syslog over UDP can improve performance.

- Do not associate a syslog server with an access control rule that has the potential to match a higher volume of traffic because it can send a lot of connection events for matching traffic.

Prerequisites

To learn and test the syslog configuration, you can utilize the same lab that you built in previous chapters. You can simply install the syslog service to your administrator computer. Figure 21-1 shows the lab topology used in the exercises of this chapter. Besides adding a syslog server, ensure the following items:

- Make sure your management center and threat defense can reach the syslog server. While the management center uses its management interface for external communication, you can configure a threat defense device to use either its management interface or its named data interface to communicate with the syslog server (see Figure 21-2).

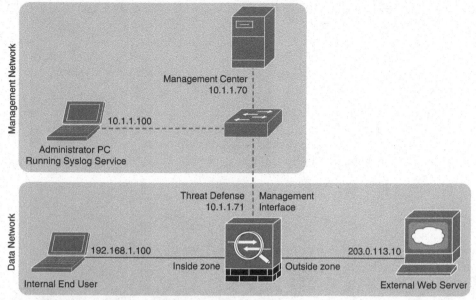

Figure 21-1 *Lab Topology Used in This Chapter*

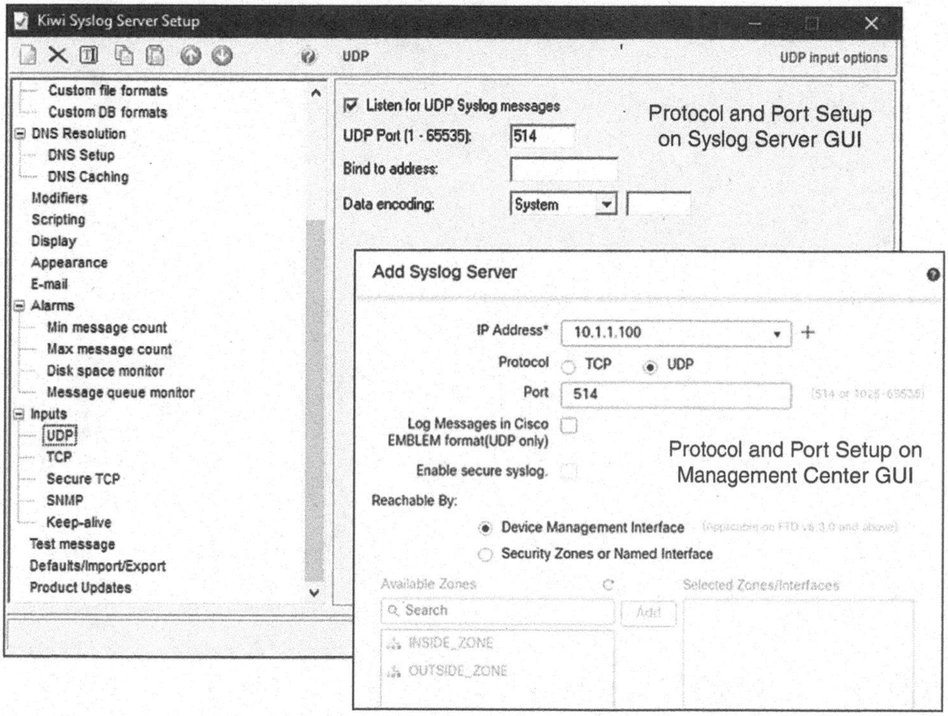

Figure 21-2 *The Protocol and Port Number Need to Match on the Client and Server*

■ The syslog server should be configured to accept incoming syslog messages. The protocol and port number must match on both the client and server sides—Secure Firewall and the syslog server. Figure 21-2 shows that Secure Firewall is configured to send syslog messages over UDP port 514, and the syslog server also listens for syslog messages over UDP port 514. For the TCP protocol, syslog uses port 1470, by default.

■ Add any necessary rules in the security policies that will trigger syslog alerts in your lab environment. For example, in the following sections, you will enable Secure Firewall to send syslog messages for file events and intrusion events. The file rule (shown in Figure 21-3) and the intrusion rule (shown in Figure 21-4) can do that job.

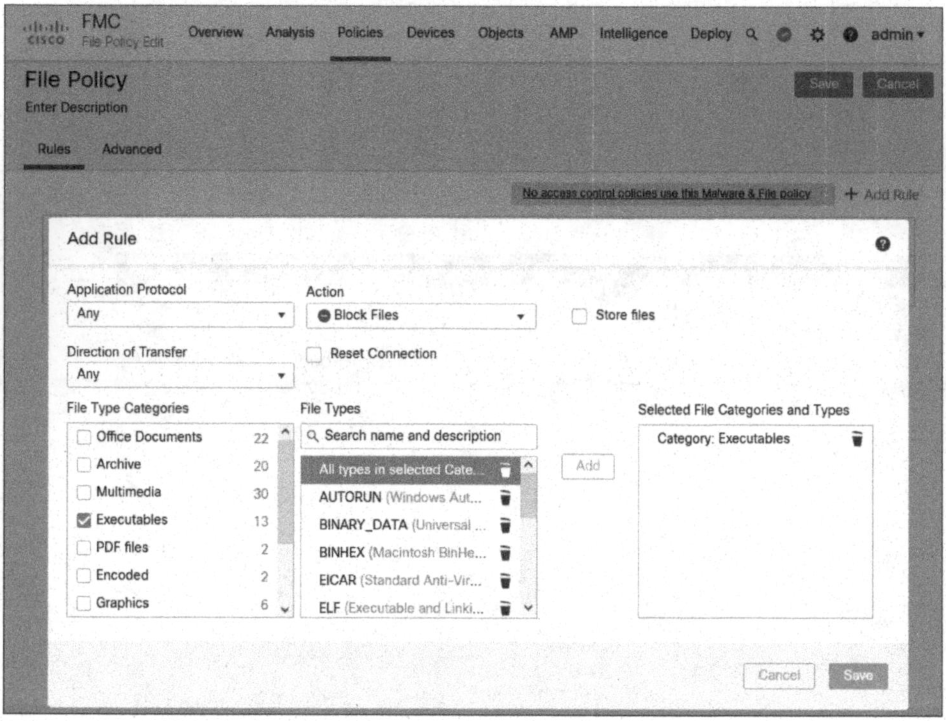

Figure 21-3 *File Rule to Block Executable (MSEXE) Files*

■ Add an access control rule to match the traffic between the internal end user and external web server. Associate the intrusion policy and file policy with the access control rule, as shown in Figure 21-5.

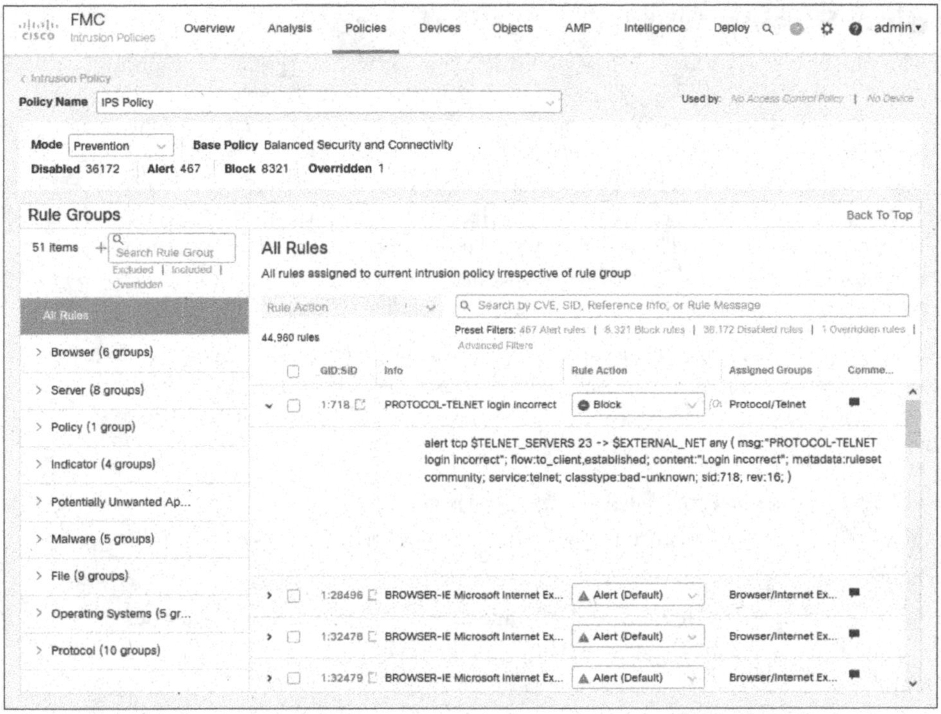

Figure 21-4   *Intrusion Rule to Block Incorrect Login Attempts over Telnet*

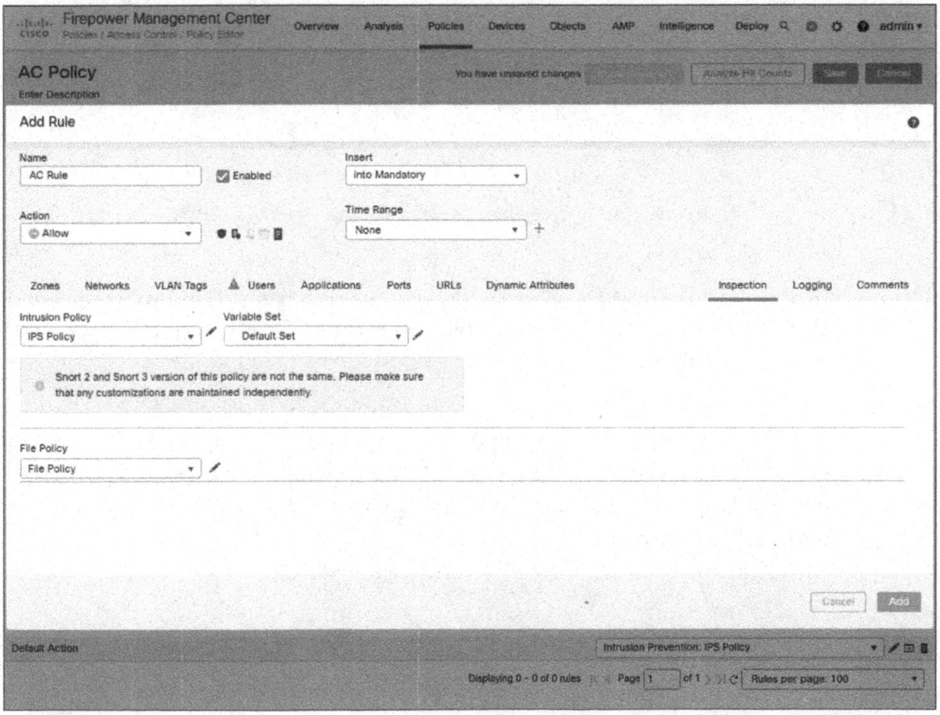

Figure 21-5   *Association of Intrusion and File Policies with an Access Control Rule*

Sending Syslog from Threat Defense

By using the platform settings policy, you can deploy different logging configurations to different threat defense devices. The platform settings policy allows you to configure many device-specific options in one place and then deploy them to one or more threat defense devices as needed. For example, you can add a custom banner to appear during a threat defense login; allow the hosts that can communicate with a threat defense over SSH, HTTPS, and ICMP protocols; define how the threat defense device will synchronize time with its management center or an NTP server; provide health monitoring status over the Simple Network Management Protocol (SNMP); send security events and system messages to an external syslog server in addition to other configurations and settings.

The platform settings configuration page presents many granular settings for syslog. The following configuration example uses minimal steps to enable syslog. To learn about every option in the platform settings, read the official user guide available at cisco.com.

Add a Syslog Server on Platform Settings

To add a syslog server on Secure Firewall using the platform settings policy, follow these steps:

Step 1. Navigate to **Devices > Platform Settings**. Click the **New Policy** button and select **Threat Defense Settings**, as shown in Figure 21-6.

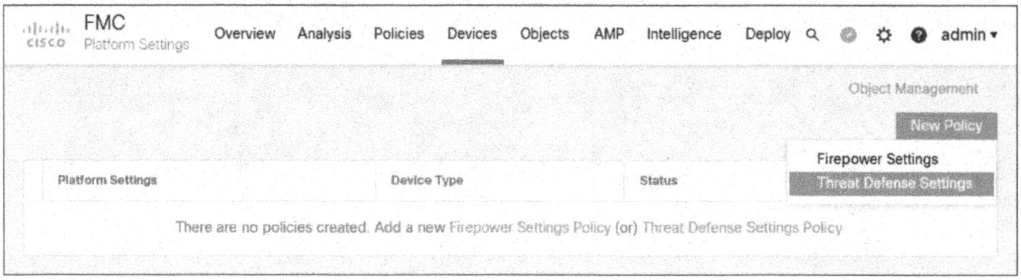

Figure 21-6 *Navigating to the Platform Settings Page for a Threat Defense*

Step 2. On the New Policy window, name the policy, add your threat defense to it, and click the **Save** button to save the policy (see Figure 21-7). The platform settings configuration page appears.

Step 3. On the left panel of the platform settings configuration page, click **Syslog**. The syslog configuration page appears.

Step 4. Under the Logging Setup tab, select **Enable Logging**, as shown in Figure 21-8. You can leave the remaining options on this tab unchecked because they are optional for this lab exercise.

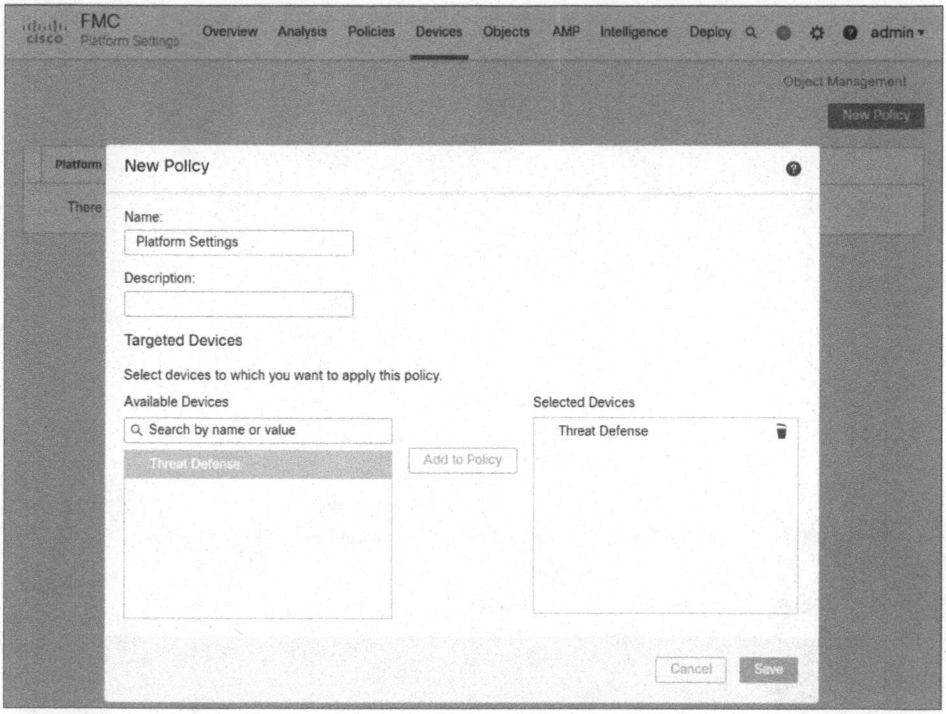

Figure 21-7 *Creating a New Policy for Threat Defense Platform Settings*

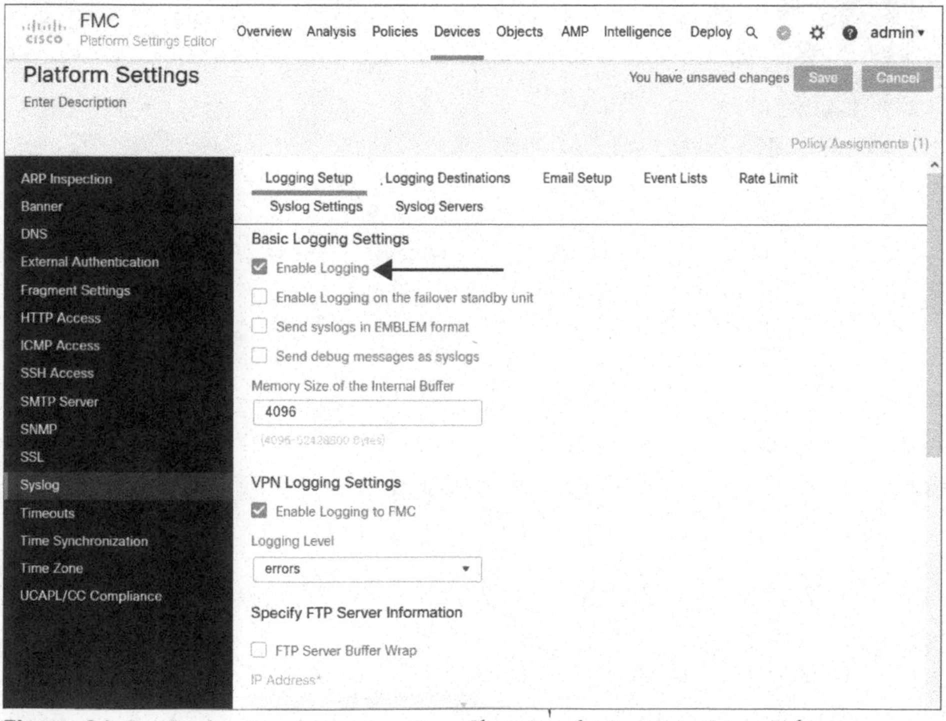

Figure 21-8 *Syslog Configuration Page Showing the Logging Setup Tab*

Step 5. Navigate to the Syslog Servers tab and click **Add.** It opens the Add Syslog Server window. Enter the syslog server IP address, transport protocol, and port number. Because the syslog server in this lab environment is deployed in the management network, select the **Device Management Interface** for its reachability. Click **OK.** Now the tab should look like the one shown in Figure 21-9.

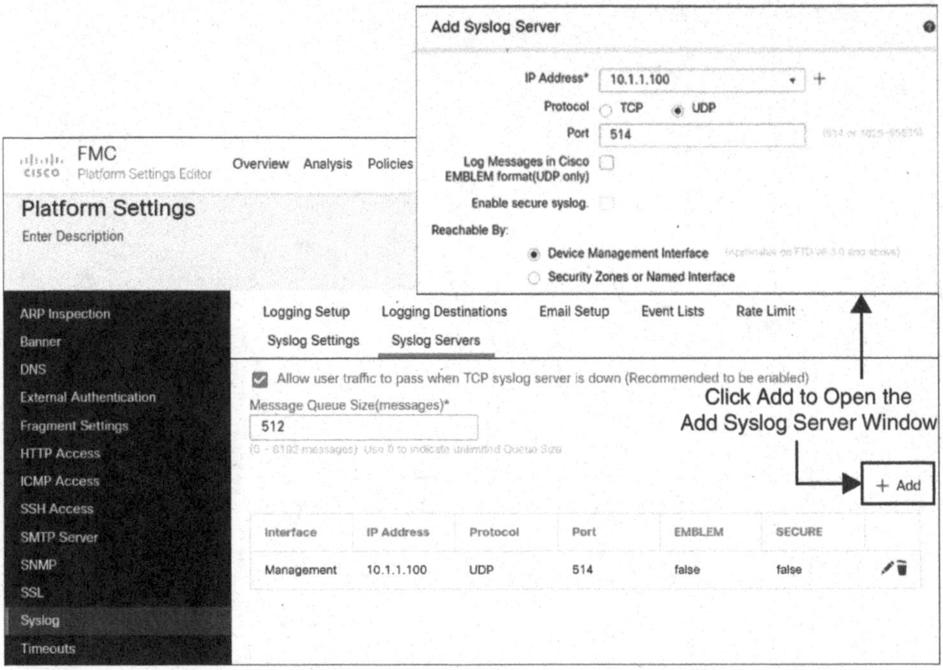

Figure 21-9 *Syslog Configuration Page Showing the Syslog Servers Tab*

Step 6. At this stage, you could save the platform settings configurations and move to the next section. However, if you would like to enhance the syslog messaging, you can enable additional options. For example, you can insert a timestamp and an originator device ID into the syslog messages (see Figure 21-10). Likewise, you can enable various fine-tuning features, such as rate limiting of syslog messages based on syslog ID or their severity levels, to improve Secure Firewall performance (see Figure 21-11).

Step 7. After you finish enabling any optional settings, click **Save** to save the configurations to the platform settings policy.

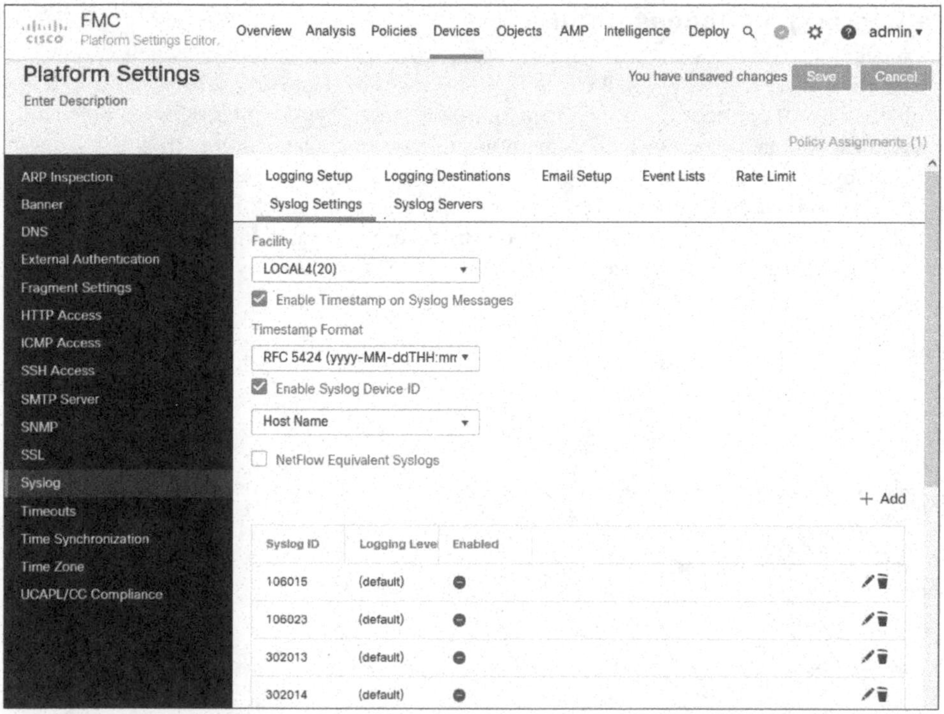

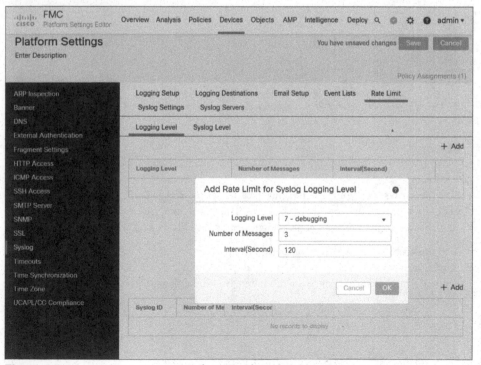

Figure 21-10 *Enabling a Timestamp and a Device ID for Syslog Messages*

Figure 21-11 *Rate Limiting of Debug-Level Syslog Messages*

Enable Logging on Access Control Policy

In the preceding section, you added a syslog server in the platform settings policy. Next, you need to instruct Secure Firewall to send log messages to the syslog server configured in the policy. You can configure an access control policy to send syslog messages for intrusion events and file and malware events. This method of producing syslog events from the access control policy is global and simple to configure. After you open the desired access control policy in the policy editor, go to the Logging tab and select the check boxes as shown in Figure 21-12. Make sure to save the changes on the access control policy. Finally, deploy the policy to your threat defense device by navigating to **Deploy > Deployment**.

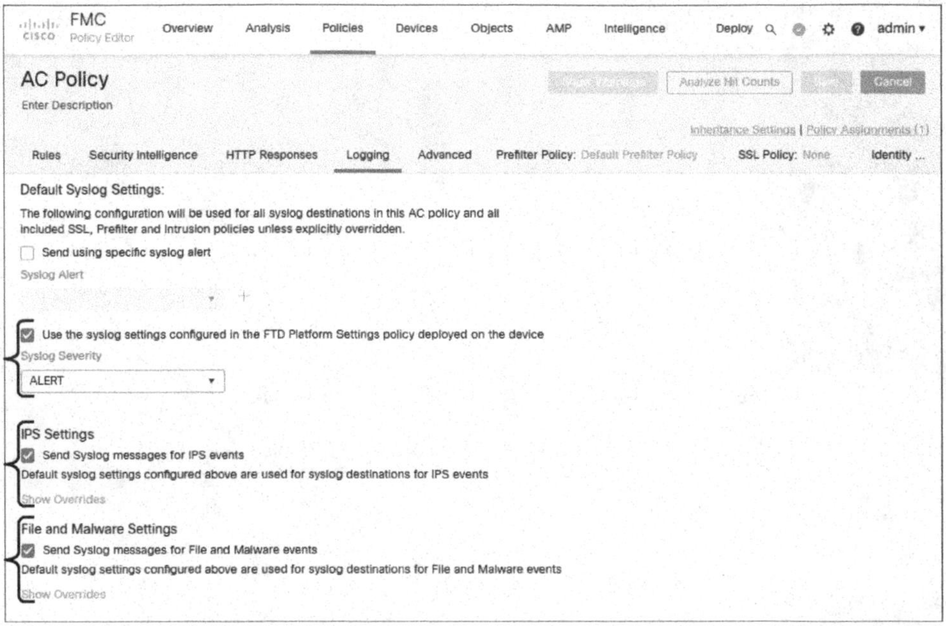

Figure 21-12　*Enable Logging Globally for Intrusion and File Events*

Verification

After the policy has been successfully deployed, you can perform the following tests:

- Use the browser of your internal end-user computer and attempt to download an executable (.exe) file from the web server. The threat defense device should block the download attempt, and the management center should display a file event.

- Use the CLI of the end-user computer to connect to the web server over the Telnet protocol. If you enter incorrect credentials, the threat defense device should block the login attempt, and the management center should display an intrusion event.

For both blocked attempts, the threat defense device should also send syslog messages to the syslog server (Figure 21-13 shows an example). Note that both messages are originated from the threat defense device (Syslog device ID/hostname: ThreatDefense, Originator IP address 10.1.1.71).

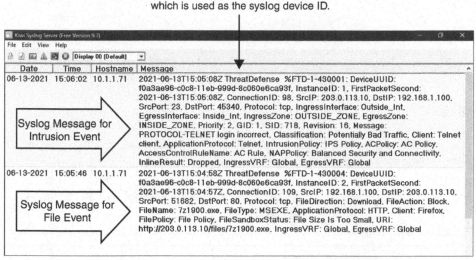

ThreatDefense is the hostname of the threat defense device, which is used as the syslog device ID.

Figure 21-13 *Syslog Server Showing Messages for Intrusion and File Events*

Sending Syslog from Management Center

The previous sections described how to use the platform settings policy to enable a threat defense device to send messages directly to a syslog server. In the following sections, you learn how to enable a management center to send log messages directly to a syslog server. If a threat defense device detects and blocks malicious file transfers or intrusion attempts, sending syslog messages directly from the threat defense would be the optimal choice. However, if you want to receive syslog messages for the events that need to be processed and correlated by the management center, you should configure the management center to send syslog alerts directly.

Create Syslog Alerts

The following steps show how to generate syslog events from the management center:

Step 1. On the management center, go to **Policies > Actions > Alerts**. The Alerts page appears.

Step 2. On the Alerts tab, click the **Create Alert** drop-down menu and select **Create Syslog Alert** (see Figure 21-14). The Edit Syslog Alert Configuration window opens.

21

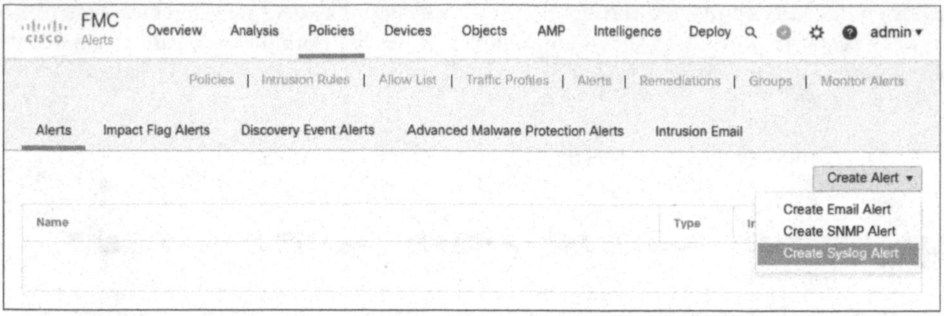

Figure 21-14   *Navigating to the Syslog Alerts Creation Menu*

Step 3.   In the configuration window, name the configuration and enter the relevant information of the syslog server you wish to use. Secure Firewall uses the IP address and port number you enter in this window to communicate with the syslog server.

Step 4.   Choose a facility and severity levels as described in Table 21-3 and Table 21-4. Optionally, provide a unique tag to distinguish any messages from the management center to the syslog server. Figure 21-15 shows an example of syslog alert configuration.

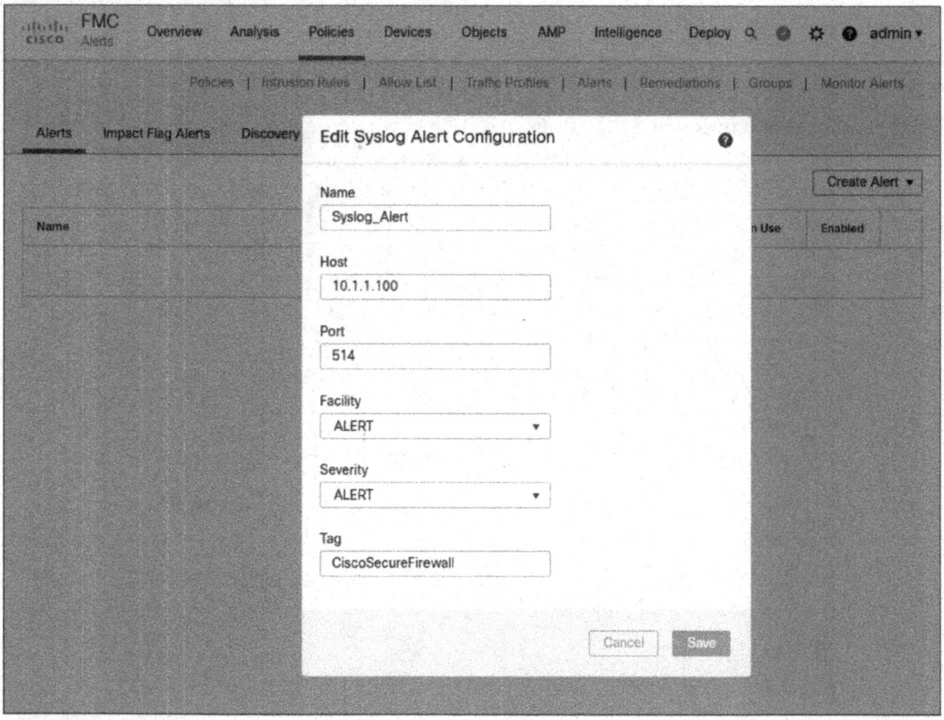

Figure 21-15   *Syslog Alert Configuration Example*

Step 5.   Click **Save** to save the configuration. The GUI returns to the Alerts tab. Make sure the newly created alerting system is enabled.

Step 6.   At this stage, you can choose the types of events for which you want to receive alerts on the syslog server. For example, you can enable the syslog notification for all event types under the Impact Flag Alerts and Discovery Event Alerts tabs, as shown in Figure 21-16 and Figure 21-17. Note that, to trigger these alerts, the management center requires an active Network Discovery policy (Network Discovery is described in detail in Chapter 9, "Network Discovery Policy").

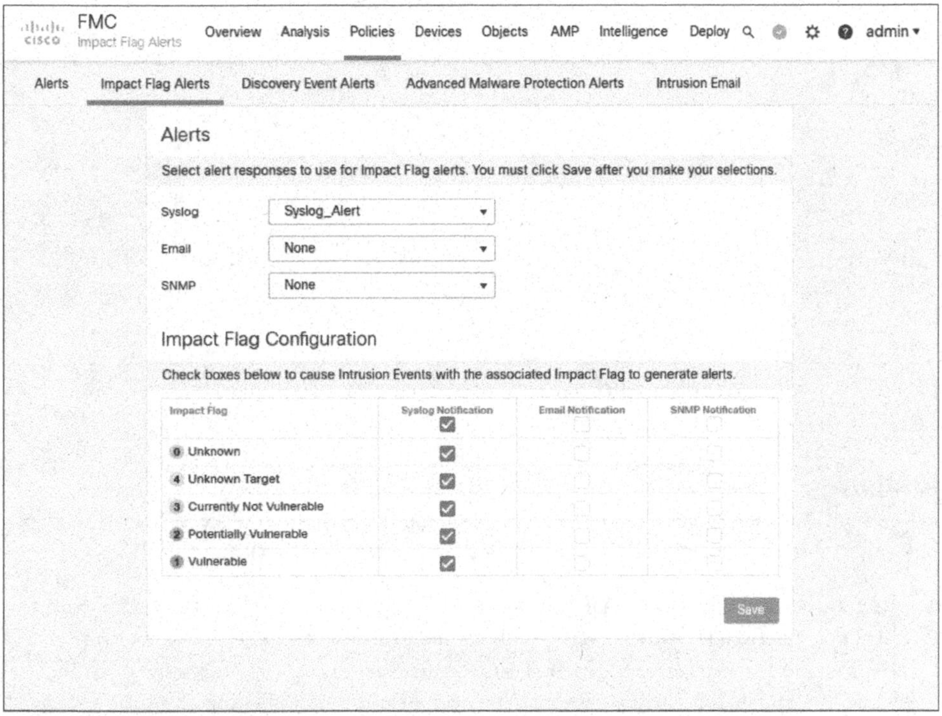

Figure 21-16   *Enabling Syslog Notifications for Impact Flag Alerts*

Step 7.   Make sure to use the **Save** button to save any configuration changes.

21

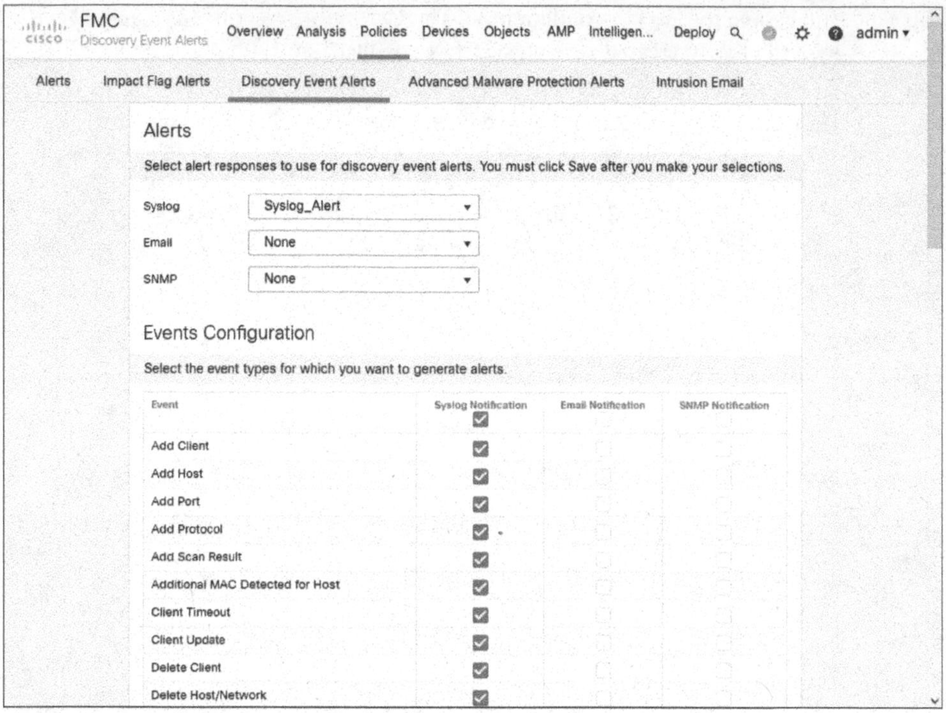

Figure 21-17 *Enabling Syslog Notifications for Discovery Event Alerts*

Verification

After the configuration is saved, perform the following tests. Although the verification steps are the same as before, the syslog server shows different results this time.

■ Use the browser of your internal end-user computer and attempt to download an executable (.exe) file from the web server. The threat defense device should block the download attempt, and the management center should produce a file event. At the same time, the syslog server should display messages from both Secure Firewall components. In Figure 21-18, as the threat defense (IP: 10.1.1.71, Device ID: ThreatDefense) sends a message for the file event, the management center (IP: 10.1.1.70, Device ID: CiscoSecureFirewall) sends several syslog messages for different types of discovery events.

■ As a second test, use the CLI of the end-user computer to connect to the web server over Telnet. If you enter incorrect credentials, Secure Firewall blocks further login attempts, and the management center should produce an intrusion event. At the same time, the syslog server should display messages from both Secure Firewall components. In Figure 21-19, as the threat defense (IP: 10.1.1.71, Device ID: ThreatDefense) sends a message for the intrusion event, the management center (IP: 10.1.1.70, Device ID: CiscoSecureFirewall) sends several syslog messages for the discovery of a new host, protocol, and operating system. Finally, the management center performs impact correlation to determine the impact flag to associate with the event (potentially vulnerable), and sends a syslog message for it as well.

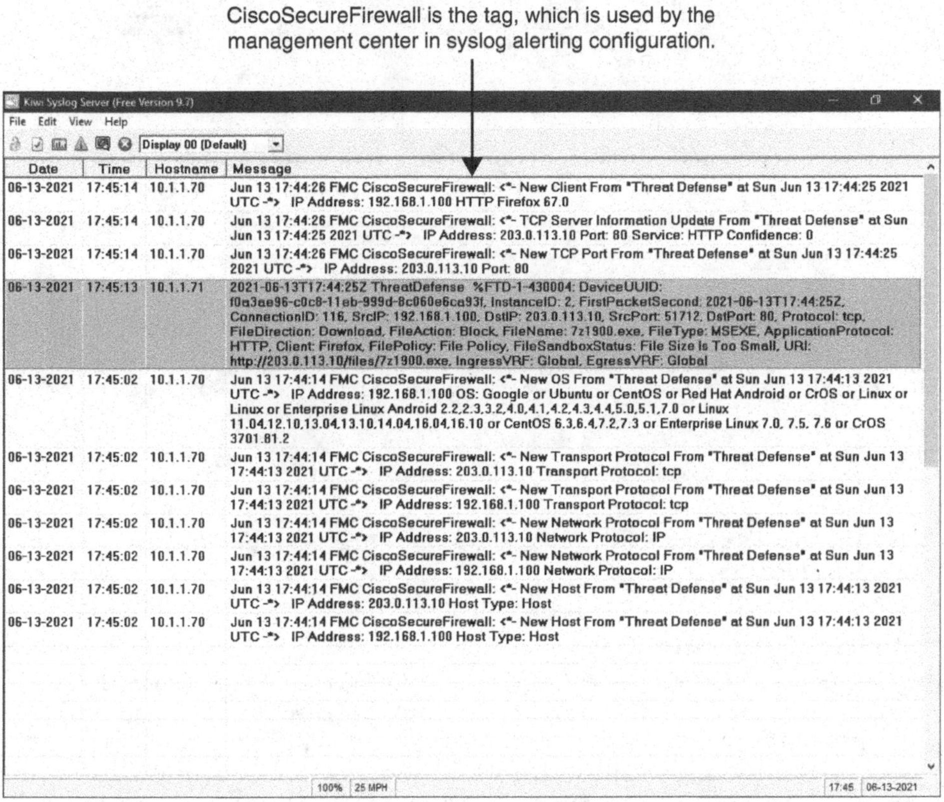

CiscoSecureFirewall is the tag, which is used by the management center in syslog alerting configuration.

Figure 21-18 *Syslog Server Showing Messages for a File Event and Associated Discovery Events*

21

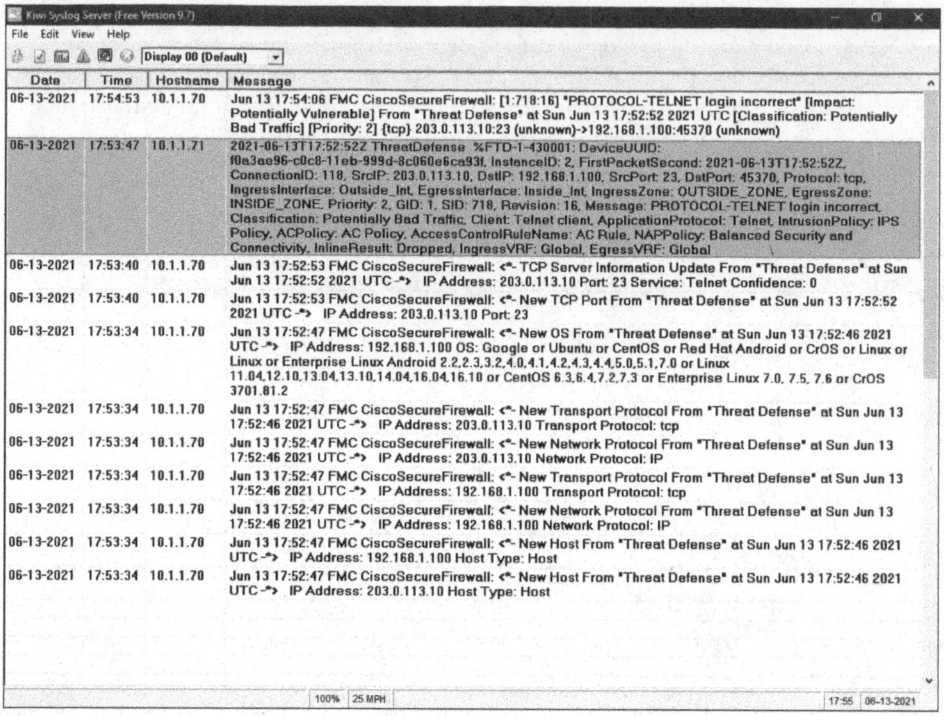

Figure 21-19 *Syslog Server Showing Messages for an Intrusion Event, Discovery Events, and the Associated Impact*

Correlate Events to Send Syslog Alerts

The previous section showed syslog alerts between two hosts in a lab environment. In the real world, when thousands of an organization's users access network resources, they can trigger a substantially higher volume of syslog messages. In this case, if you want to receive syslog messages only for an event that is generated during a very specific circumstance, you can leverage the functionality of the correlation policy to produce syslog events under the specific set of conditions you are interested in logging.

As the name suggests, a correlation policy enables the management center to correlate various datapoints and events that are received from threat defense devices. You can create correlation rules based on discovery events, intrusion events, file events, connection events, and a variety of other conditions. The management center can use correlation rule constraints to match an event generated under very specific circumstances. As a response to the rule match, you can instruct the management center to send alerts to a syslog server in your correlation policy configuration.

The following steps demonstrate how to create a correlation rule to match a specific malware event and then send a syslog alert as a response to a violation of that rule:

Step 1.   Navigate to **Policies > Correlation**. Select the **Rule Management** tab. The rule management page appears (see Figure 21-20).

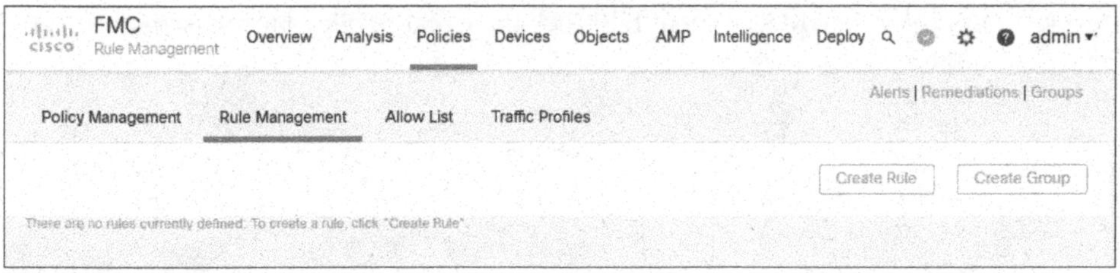

Figure 21-20 *The Rule Management Tab Provides an Option to Create a New Correlation Rule*

Step 2. Click the **Create Rule** button. The correlation rule editor page appears.

Step 3. Under the Rule Information tab, name the rule. Then, under the Select the Type of Event for This Rule section, you can use the drop-down to develop rule conditions. Use the **Add Condition** and **Add Complex Condition** buttons to define the rule logic, as necessary. When you are done, click the **Save** button to save the rule.

Figure 21-21 displays a correlation rule that detects the download of malicious files on two specific hosts. In a real-world scenario, they might be two important hosts: the chief executive officer (CEO) and chief financial officer (CFO) of a company.

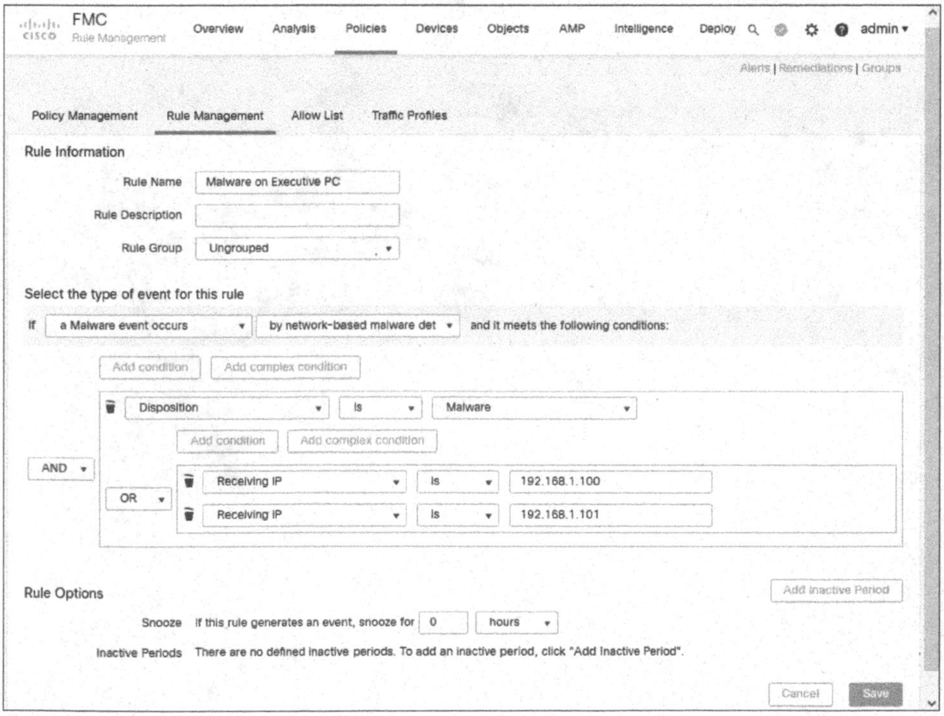

Figure 21-21 *A Correlation Rule*

Step 4. On the Policy Management tab, click the **Create Policy** button (see Figure 21-22).

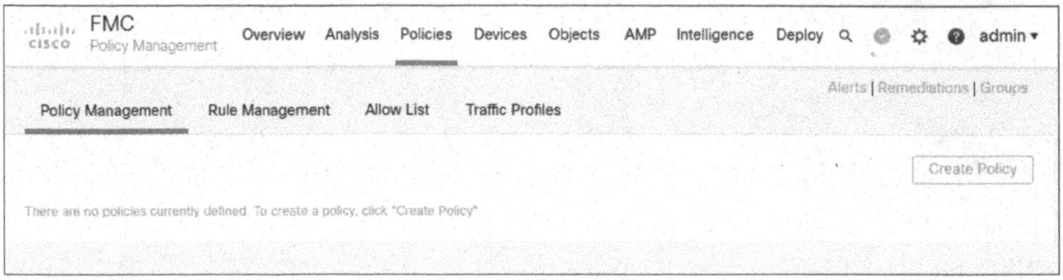

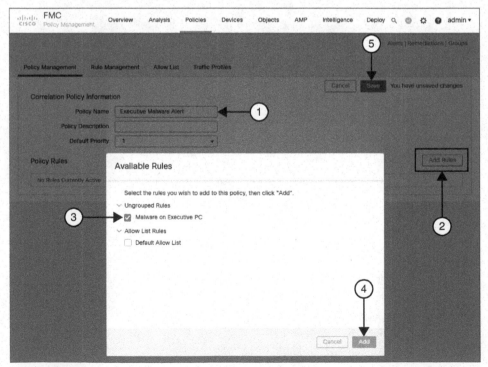

Figure 21-22 *The Policy Management Tab Provides an Option to Create a New Correlation Policy*

Step 5. Give a name to the correlation policy. Click the **Add Rules** button. It shows the available correlation rules in a window.

Step 6. On the Available Rule window, select the correlation rule you have just created and click the **Add** button (see Figure 21-23). The GUI returns to the Policy Management page. The correlation policy that you just created appears.

Step 7. Select the callout icon next to the policy name. When the response selection window appears, move the preconfigured syslog alert response to the **Assigned Responses** section, as shown in Figure 21-24.

Figure 21-23 *List of Available Correlation Rules*

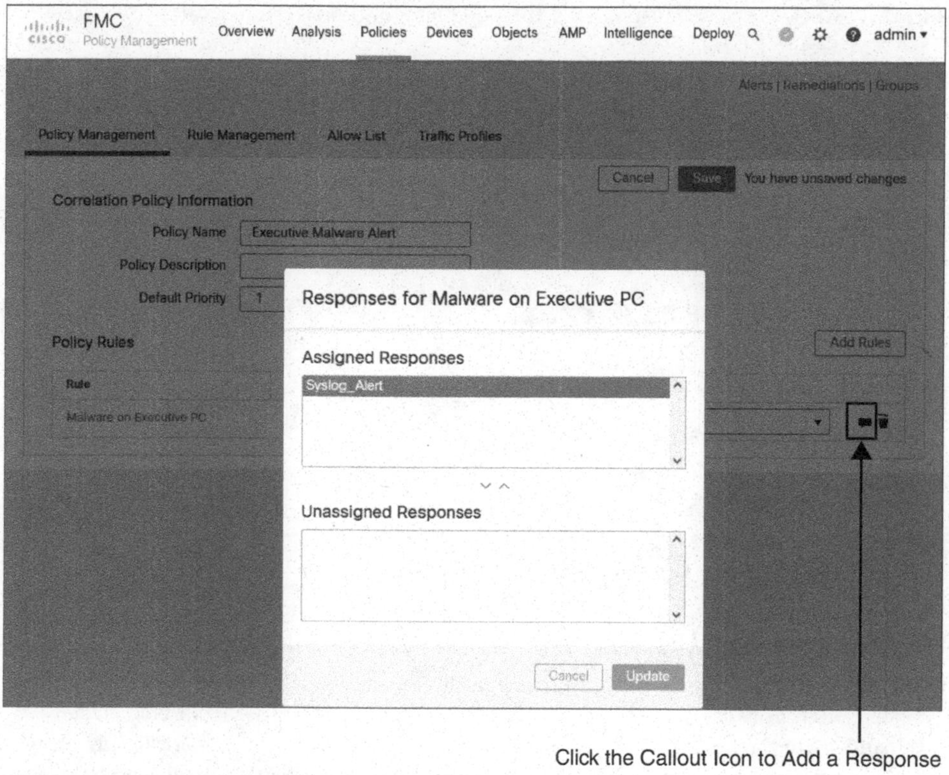

Click the Callout Icon to Add a Response

Figure 21-24 *List of Available Responses*

Step 8. Click the **Update** button. The GUI returns to the policy management window and displays the mapping of a correlation rule with a response, as shown in Figure 21-25.

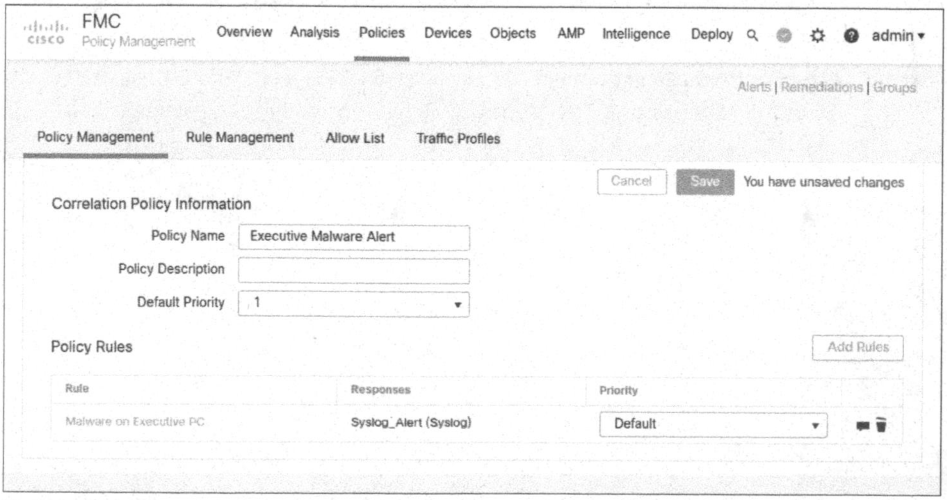

Figure 21-25 *The Correlation Policy Shows the Mapping Between a Correlation Rule and a Response*

Step 9.   Click the **Save** button. After the policy is saved, make sure to activate it (see Figure 21-26).

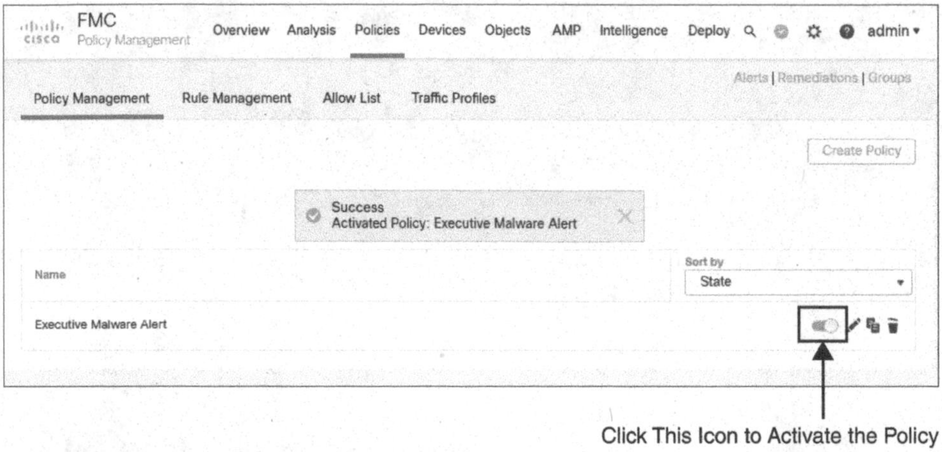

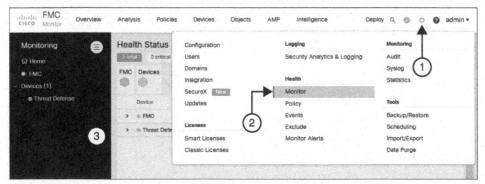

Figure 21-26   *Activating a Correlation Policy*

Troubleshooting Logs

In case of any technical issues with Secure Firewall, you can contact the Cisco technical assistance center. You may be requested to obtain troubleshooting files from your Secure Firewall and share the files with Cisco for advanced analysis. The troubleshooting files contain log messages of various processes, copies of configuration files, results of database queries, various command outputs, and so on. The files are critical to determine the root cause of any technical issues with Secure Firewall.

You can use the management center GUI to generate troubleshooting files from any threat defense devices as well as the management center. Following are steps to generate and download the files:

Step 1.   On your management center GUI, open the **System** menu and navigate to **Health > Monitor** (see Figure 21-27). The health monitoring page appears.

Figure 21-27   *Navigating to the Health Monitoring Page*

Step 2. On the left panel, you will find the management center and all the threat defense devices that are part of your Secure Firewall deployment. Select the device from which you want to generate the troubleshooting file.

Step 3. When the device-specific health status is displayed, select **General Trouble-shooting Files.** The Troubleshooting Options window appears. Include all data, as shown in Figure 21-28.

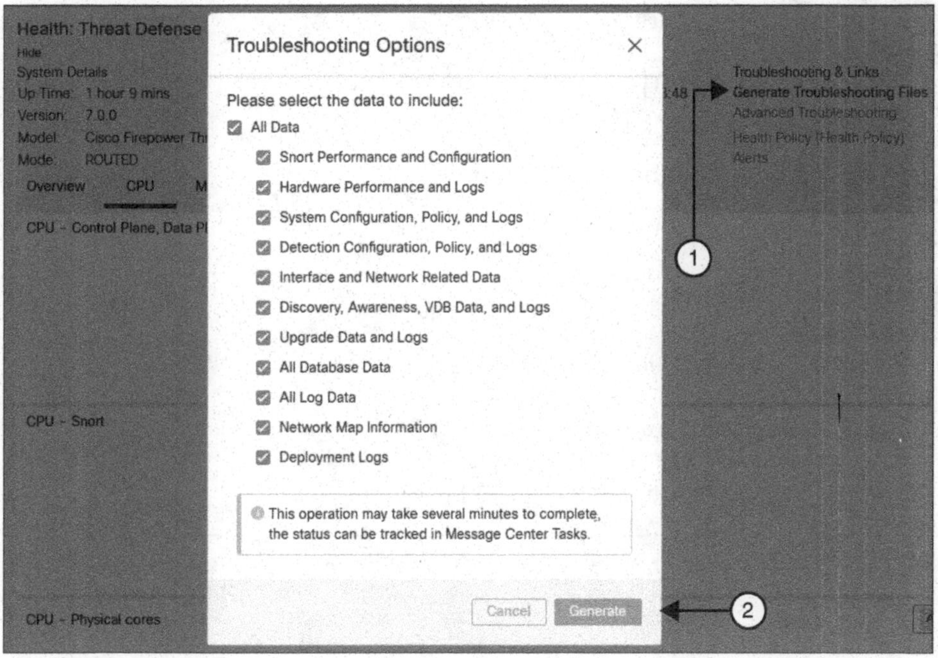

Figure 21-28 *Selecting Troubleshooting Logs*

Step 4. Click the **Generate** button to begin the troubleshooting file-generation process. After the file is generated, you can download it using the task status window (see Figure 21-29).

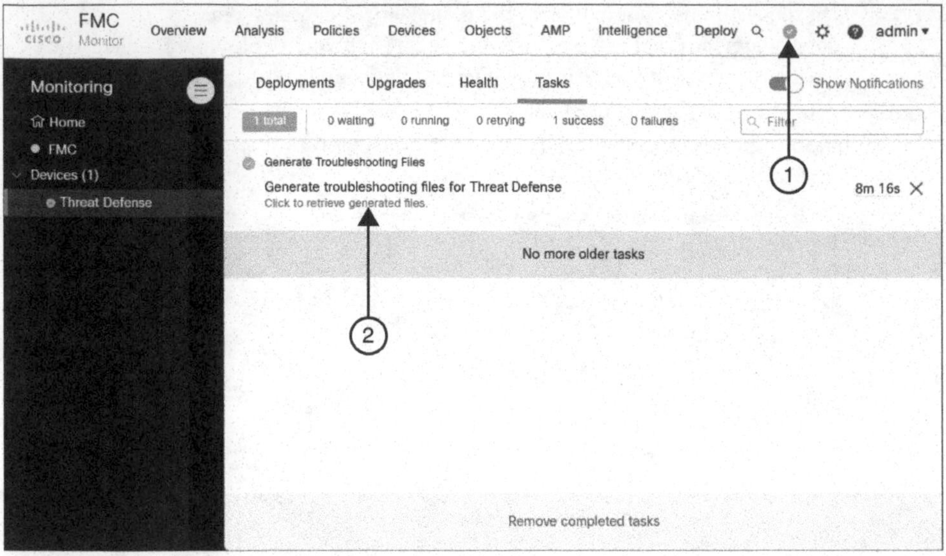

Figure 21-29   *Link to Download Troubleshooting Files*

If you simply want to view the syslog messages of the management center on the fly without generating the comprehensive troubleshooting files, you can click the System menu and navigate to **Monitoring > Syslog**, as shown in Figure 21-30.

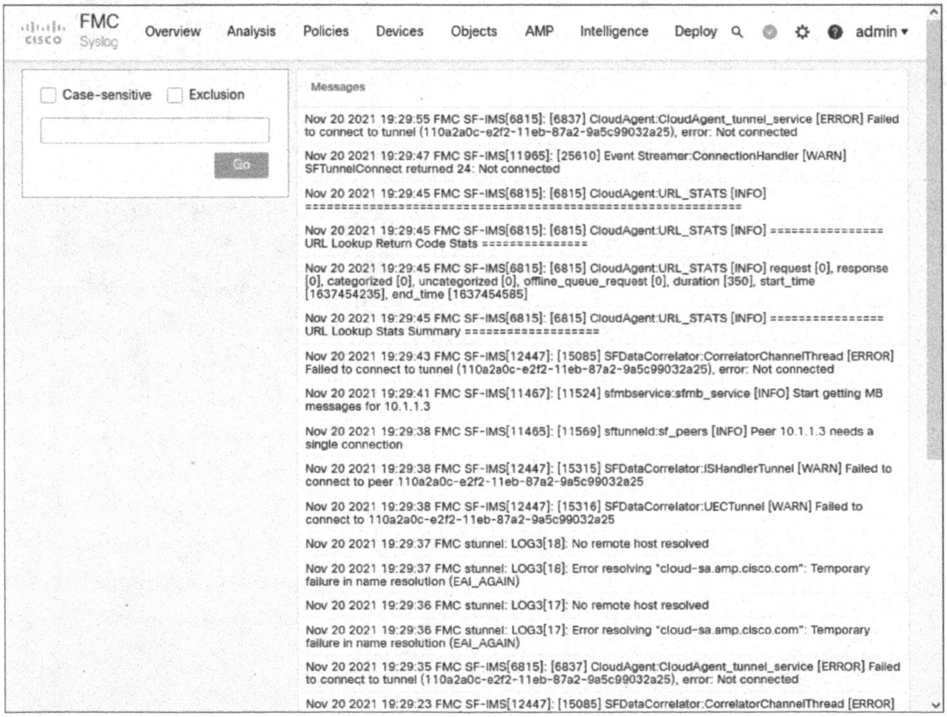

Figure 21-30   *Retrieving Syslog Messages on the Management Center GUI*

Summary

This chapter demonstrates the generation of different types of security events and the ability to send corresponding syslog messages to an external syslog server. It delineates the procedures for sending syslog messages from the management center and threat defense devices using two different options: platform settings policy and alert responses. Finally, it describes the steps to create a correlation policy to issue syslog alerts in response to correlation policy rule violations.

Exam Preparation Tasks

As mentioned in the section "How to Use This Book" in the Introduction, you have a couple of choices for exam preparation: the exercises here, Chapter 22, "Final Preparation," and the exam simulation questions in the Pearson Test Prep practice test software.

Review All Key Topics

Review the most important topics in this chapter, noted with the Key Topic icon in the outer margin of the page. Table 21-5 lists a reference of these key topics and the page numbers on which each is found.

Key Topic

Table 21-5   Key Topics for Chapter 21

Key Topic Element	Description	Page
Paragraph	Choosing TCP or UDP for Syslog	558
Paragraph	Security level and facility	559
List	Syslog ports	562
Paragraph	Understanding correlation policy	574

Complete Tables and Lists from Memory

Print a copy of Appendix C, "Memory Tables" (found on the companion website), or at least the section for this chapter, and complete the tables and lists from memory. Appendix D, "Memory Tables Answer Key," also on the companion website, includes completed tables and lists to check your work.

Define Key Terms

Define the following key terms from this chapter, and check your answers in the Glossary:

system logging (syslog), facility, severity level

21

## CHAPTER 22

Final Preparation

Congratulations! You have got through all the chapters in this book. Now it's time to get ready for the exam. This chapter helps you to get over the finish line.

In the first 7 chapters of this book, you learned about the deployment of Cisco Secure Firewall and Intrusion Prevention System (IPS) in various modes. The next 14 chapters elaborated on the implementation of security policies and the techniques to verify the policy operations. All chapters provide essential knowledge, recommend best practices, suggest a simple lab design, and describe the configuration steps. Practicing the lab exercises that are demonstrated in this book and validating the Secure Firewall operations in a lab environment are key to passing the exam.

Although the exam topics are described thoroughly in the preceding chapters, as an exam candidate, you should be familiar with the latest developments and implementations of the outlined features. The contents in this book are static, but the exam outlines are dynamic. Cisco reserves the right to update the exam outline anytime. Besides, Cisco Secure Firewall and IPS go through a continuous development cycle. The GUI navigation and appearance may be slightly different in different software versions. To learn about the new features and options, read the version-specific official product documentations, which are available at the official Cisco website. After you finish this book, the next best resource to check is cisco.com. Cisco often publishes e-learning resources on the CCNP Security certification curriculum, which could be a great supplement to an official certification guide.

Getting Ready for the Exam

Now that you have finished this book, you can register for the exam and take the test. However, if you first spend some time thinking about your exam-day expectations, learning about the user interface of a real Cisco exam, and knowing about your testing center, you will be better prepared to take the exam, particularly if this is your first Cisco exam. You are very close to the finish line, so now it's time put forth one last effort.

Tools for Final Review

Here, we suggest some tools and resources that you can consider for your final exam preparation. Certainly, you can develop your own plan or use this list partially or as is. You may consider the following items in your plan:

- **Progress Tracker:** Each chapter provides a short list of learning objectives. All objectives are also listed together in a table that you can find in the Introduction to this book. Use that table as your preparation checklist, and ensure that you have studied all the topics.

- **Study Notes:** While you were reading the book, you likely took notes or highlighted the lines that are important to you. Review them now to boost your confidence.

- **Key Topics:** Use the Key Topics tables to review the important topics in each chapter. If you find any knowledge gaps, take some time to consider these topics further.

- **"Do I Know This Already?" (DIKTA) Quizzes:** Take the "Do I Know This Already?" (DIKTA) quizzes for each chapter and review the answers.

- **Pearson Test Prep Practice Test Engine:** Use the Pearson Test Prep practice test engine to practice. This bank of unique exam-realistic questions is available only with this book.

Exam Day

Here are some additional tips to ensure that you are ready for this rewarding exam:

- **Get some rest:** Most students report success after getting plenty of rest the night before the exam. All-night cram sessions are not always helpful.

- **Bring your valuables:** Bring all your valuables but prepare to lock them up. The testing center does not allow you to take your phone, smart watch, wallet, and other such items into the exam room. You will be provided a secure place to store them while taking the exam.

- **Plan your travel time:** Give yourself extra time to find the center and get checked in. Be sure to arrive early.

- **Budget your time for exam questions:** Do the math to find the average time to answer each question. If the average does not sound like enough time, realize that many questions are straightforward and require only 15 to 30 seconds to answer. Being able to answer some questions quickly builds time for other questions as you take your exam.

- **Watch the clock:** Check in on the time remaining periodically as you are taking the exam. You might even find that you can slow down dramatically as you have built up a nice block of extra time.

Practice Tests

The following sections discuss the available tools to practice model tests and quizzes, and how to access them.

Pearson Cert Practice Test Engine and Questions on the Website

Register this book to get access to the Pearson IT Certification test engine (software that displays and grades a set of exam-realistic, multiple-choice questions). Using the Pearson Test Prep practice test engine, you can either study by going through the questions in Study Mode or take a simulated (timed) exam.

The Pearson Test Prep practice test software comes with two full practice exams. These practice tests are available to you either online or as an offline Windows application. To access the practice exams that were developed with this book, please see the instructions in the card inserted in the sleeve in the back of the book. This card includes a unique access code that enables you to activate your exams in the Pearson Test Prep software.

Accessing the Pearson Test Prep Software Online

The online version of this software can be used on any device with a browser and connectivity to the Internet, including desktop machines, tablets, and smartphones. To start using your practice exams online, simply follow these steps:

Step 1.   Go to http://www.PearsonTestPrep.com.

Step 2.   Select **Pearson IT Certification** as your product group.

Step 3.   Enter the email/password for your account. If you don't have an account on PearsonITCertification.com or CiscoPress.com, you will need to establish one by going to PearsonITCertification.com/join.

Step 4.   On the My Products tab, click the **Activate New Product** button.

Step 5.   Enter the access code printed on the insert card in the back of your book to activate your product. The product will then be listed in your My Products page.

Step 6.   Click the **Exams** button to launch the exam settings screen and start your exam.

Accessing the Pearson Test Prep Software Offline

If you wish to study offline, you can download and install the Windows version of the Pearson Test Prep software. There is a download link for this software on the book's companion website, or you can just enter this link in your browser:

http://www.pearsonitcertification.com/content/downloads/pcpt/engine.zip

To access the book's companion website and software, simply follow these steps:

Step 1.   Register your book by going to PearsonITCertification.com/register and entering the ISBN: **9780136589709**.

Step 2.   Respond to the challenge questions.

Step 3.   Go to your account page and select the **Registered Products** tab.

Step 4.   Click the **Access Bonus Content** link under the product listing.

Step 5.   Click the **Install Pearson Test Prep Desktop Version** link under the Practice Exams section of the page to download the software.

Step 6.   After the software finishes downloading, unzip all the files on your computer.

Step 7.   Double-click the application file to start the installation and follow the on-screen instructions to complete the registration.

Step 8.   When the installation is complete, launch the application and select the **Activate Exam** button on the My Products tab.

Step 9.   Click the **Activate a Product** button in the Activate Product Wizard.

Step 10.   Enter the unique access code found on the card in the sleeve in the back of your book and click the **Activate** button.

Step 11.   Click **Next** and then the **Finish** button to download the exam data to your application.

Step 12. You can now start using the practice exams by selecting the product and clicking the **Open Exam** button to open the exam settings screen.

Note that the offline and online versions will synch together, so saved exams and grade results recorded on one version will be available to you on the other as well.

Customizing Your Exams

When you are in the exam settings screen, you can choose to take exams in one of three modes:

- Study Mode
- Practice Exam Mode
- Flash Card Mode

Study Mode enables you to fully customize your exams and review answers as you are taking the exam. This is typically the mode you would use first to assess your knowledge and identify information gaps. Practice Exam Mode locks certain customization options, as it is presenting a realistic exam experience. Use this mode when you are preparing to test your exam readiness. Flash Card Mode strips out the answers and presents you with only the question stem. This mode is great for late-stage preparation when you really want to challenge yourself to provide answers without the benefit of seeing multiple-choice options. This mode will not provide the detailed score reports that the other two modes will, so you should not use it if you are trying to identify knowledge gaps.

In addition to these three modes, you will be able to select the source of your questions. You can choose to take exams that cover all the chapters, or you can narrow your selection to just a single chapter or the chapters that make up specific parts in the book. All chapters are selected by default. If you want to narrow your focus to individual chapters, simply deselect all the chapters and then select only those on which you wish to focus in the Objectives area.

You can also select the exam banks on which to focus. Each exam bank comes complete with a full exam of questions that cover topics in every chapter. The two exams printed in the book are available to you as well as two additional exams of unique questions. You can have the test engine serve up exams from all four banks or from just one individual bank by selecting the desired banks in the exam bank area.

There are several other customizations you can make to your exam from the exam settings screen, such as the time of the exam, the number of questions served up, whether to randomize questions and answers, whether to show the number of correct answers for multiple-answer questions, or whether to serve up only specific types of questions. You can also create custom test banks by selecting only questions that you have marked or questions on which you have added notes.

Updating Your Exams

If you are using the online version of the Pearson Test Prep software, you should always have access to the latest version of the software as well as the exam data. If you are using the Windows desktop version, every time you launch the software, it will check to see if there

22

are any updates to your exam data and automatically download any changes that were made since the last time you used the software. This requires that you are connected to the Internet at the time you launch the software.

Sometimes, due to many factors, the exam data may not fully download when you activate your exam. If you find that figures or exhibits are missing, you may need to manually update your exams.

To update a particular exam that you have already activated and downloaded, simply select the Tools tab and select the Update Products button. Again, this is only an issue with the Windows desktop application.

If you wish to check for updates to the Pearson Test Prep exam engine software, Windows desktop version, simply select the Tools tab and select the Update Application button. This will ensure you are running the latest version of the software engine.

Premium Edition

In addition to the free practice exam provided on the website, you can purchase additional exams with expanded functionality directly from Pearson IT Certification. The Premium Edition of this title contains an additional two full practice exams and an eBook (in both PDF and ePub format). In addition, the Premium Edition title also has remediation for each question to the specific part of the eBook that relates to that question.

Because you have purchased the print version of this title, you can purchase the Premium Edition at a deep discount. A coupon code in the book sleeve contains a one-time-use code and instructions for where you can purchase the Premium Edition.

To view the premium edition product page, go to www.informit.com/title/9780136733799.

Chapter-Ending Review Tools

At the end of each chapter, you will find several features in the "Exam Preparation Tasks" section. You might have already worked through these in each chapter. It can also be useful to use these tools again as you make your final preparations for the exam.

Summary

The tools and suggestions in this chapter have been designed with one goal in mind: to help you develop the skills required to pass the CCNP Security exam, concentrating on Cisco Secure Firewall and IPS (formerly Cisco Firepower). This book has been developed from the beginning to not just tell you the facts but to also help you learn how to apply the facts in the real world. No matter what your experience level leading up to when you take the exams, it is our hope that the broad range of preparation tools and the contents in this book will help you to become an expert on Cisco Secure Firewall and IPS.

We hope you do well on the exam. We encourage you to celebrate when you pass. Share your success story in your blog posts. Congratulations on achieving a major milestone in your career.

Answers to the "Do I Know This Already?" Questions

Chapter 1

1. C. Next-generation firewall. An NGFW is designed to provide application visibility and control, as well as to perform deep packet inspection at layers 3–7 to prevent a network from intrusion attempts.

2. D. All of these answers are correct. You have three options to manage a threat defense, depending on how you want to manage it—remotely using management center, locally via device manager, or from cloud-based Cisco Defense Orchestrator.

3. C. Secure Firewall Device Manager. Device Manager allows you to manage a single threat defense locally without registering it to any remote management platform.

4. C. XLTR. The Extra Long-Term Release (XLTR) offers the longest lifecycle and is chosen for government certification.

5. B. SRU/LSP. The rule update package for Snort 2 is known as Cisco Secure Rule Update (SRU). In Snort 3, this rule update package is called the Lightweight Security Package (LSP).

6. C. VDB. VDB is a database that stores vulnerability information and fingerprints of various applications, services, and operating systems (OSs).

7. A. Clustering. With clustering, you can simply add extra threat defense devices to your existing deployment and group them into a single logical cluster to support additional throughput.

8. D. All of these answers are correct. Multi-instance capability enables you to isolate many critical firewall elements, such as firewall policy management, software maintenance tasks, any failure and troubleshooting, and data traffic processing.

Chapter 2

1. D. You can deploy Secure Firewall Version 7.0 on VMware ESXi Version 6.5 or later. Other virtualization platforms, such as VMware Workstation, VMware Player, VMware Fusion, VMware vCloud Director, and VirtualBox, are not supported by Secure Firewall Version 7.0.

2. C. The recommended amount of memory for a management center virtual appliance to manage up to 25 threat defense devices is 32 GB.

3. B. The Virtual Machine Disk (.vmdk) file is a compressed virtual disk that stores the Secure Firewall software.

4. C. The throughput of a VMXNET3 adapter is 10 Gbps, whereas the legacy default adapter E1000 supports up to 1 Gbps.

5. D. A threat defense virtual appliance requires four interfaces—one interface for management communication and three interfaces for traffic inspection.

6. D. Promiscuous mode must be enabled in all the data interfaces of a threat defense virtual appliance.

7. D. SSH access to the management center and threat defense is enabled by default.

8. B. Only protocols such as HTTPS and SSH that support encrypted communication are used in Secure Firewall for management communication.

Chapter 3

1. D. Secure Firewall can connect to the Cisco SSM to obtain a license directly over the Internet and via an on-premises server. When Internet connectivity is restricted, you can also manually copy and paste the information between Secure Firewall and the Cisco license server.

2. A. To enable intrusion prevention functionality, you must apply a valid threat license to your Secure Firewall.

3. C. In the smart licensing model, you can enable the next-generation security features free of cost for 90 days.

4. B. By enabling the Smart License Monitor module in the health policy, you can receive health alerts if there is any communication issue between your management center and the Cisco Smart Licensing Cloud, or if the license is expired or out of compliance.

5. D. During device registration, you must select and deploy an access control policy to the threat defense. This is part of the registration process.

6. C. You can run the **show managers** command on a threat defense to determine its current manager.

Chapter 4

1. C. You cannot change the firewall mode until you unregister the desired threat defense from the management center.

2. C. Changing the firewall mode wipes out any existing configurations on a threat defense.

3. B. The **configure firewall routed** command is used to configure a threat defense from transparent to routed mode.

4. A. A threat defense data interface can be configured with a static IP address, as well as a dynamically assigned IP address.

5. C. The **debug icmp trace** command is used to debug and analyze ping requests.

6. D. All of these commands—**show interface ip brief**, **show interface** *interface_ID*, **show running-config interface**—are useful when you want to investigate an issue with an interface.

Chapter 5

1. D. All of these answers are correct.

2. D. Changing a firewall to transparent deployment mode erases any existing configuration.

3. C. Issuing the **configure firewall transparent** command in the threat defense CLI.

4. C. The BVI's IP address is used as the source IP address for packets that originate from a threat defense.

5. C. The Access Control: Block All Traffic policy is equivalent to the **deny tcp any any** access control rule.

6. A. The **show access-list** command displays the access control rule entries.

7. D. All of these answers are correct. IRB enables switching between interfaces and subinterfaces. It also supports routing between bridge groups and between a bridge group and a routed interface.

Chapter 6

1. A. You can enable Network Address Translation (NAT) in the transparent mode; however, a threat defense does not support NAT in the inline mode.

2. D. All of these answers are correct. Enabling portfast on the switch ports where inline interfaces are connected allows those switch ports to transition to the forwarding state immediately and reduces hardware bypass time. Also, enabling the fail open features for the inline interface set allows a threat defense to continue moving traffic through it without any interruption in case of an inspection failure. Finally, allowing the inline set to propagate its link state reduces the routing convergence time when one of the interfaces in an inline set goes down.

3. D. The Propagate Link State feature is not enabled by default on an inline set.

4. D. All of these answers are correct. Both interface pairs should be included in the same inline set to ensure the recognition of asynchronous traffic. Also, the fail open feature allows a threat defense to continue its traffic flow through the device by bypassing the detection. Finally, Propagate Link State reduces the routing convergence time when one of the interfaces in an inline set goes down.

5. B. The **show inline-set** command displays the advanced settings of an inline interface set.

Chapter 7

1. C. In inline tap mode and in passive mode, if you apply an access control rule or intrusion rule with a block or drop action, a threat defense does not actually block the original traffic. It only generates an event and lets the original traffic go through the threat defense.

2. B. A network TAP is dedicated hardware that is designed to replicate and transfer traffic. A SPAN port, in contrast, drops packets if the utilization of a SPAN link exceeds its capacity.

Appendix A: Answers to the "Do I Know This Already?" Questions 591

A

3. D. All of these answers are correct. Passive mode can work with just one interface, whereas an inline set requires at least two interfaces. An inline interface does not require that port mirroring features, such as a TAP or SPAN port, be available. Transition between detection-only mode and prevention mode is faster and easier in inline tap mode.

4. C. You can easily transition to the inline mode without touching any physical cables.

5. C. If the ultimate plan is to deploy a threat defense in detection-only mode permanently, choose passive mode over inline tap mode to eliminate any chance of traffic interruption due to an accidental outage of the threat defense. Furthermore, depending on the traffic, the inline tap mode configurations can impact the threat defense performance more than the passive mode configurations.

6. B. The **show inline-set** command can confirm whether an interface is set to inline tap mode.

7. B. If an interface on a threat defense is configured in passive mode, the **show interface** *<interface_name>* command shows IPS Interface-Mode: Passive in its output.

8. D. A threat defense operates in detection-only mode when the interface is set to inline tap or passive mode, regardless of the inspection mode selected in the intrusion policy. When configured in inline interface mode, a threat defense can also inspect traffic in a non-blocking mode (alert only) if you select detection inspection mode in the intrusion policy.

Chapter 8

1. D. All of these answers are correct. A threat defense analyzes packets with the help of the Snort engine as well as the ASA and Lina engines.

2. D. All of these answers are correct. Capturing traffic can increase the CPU utilization of a threat defense. A threat defense is designed to capture traffic only for troubleshooting purposes, and you can use the management center GUI to capture traffic from the threat defense interfaces.

3. C. It stops a threat defense from capturing traffic when the buffer is full.

4. D. All of these answers are correct. You can store captured packets into a file directly using the management center. You can store the traces of captured packets into a cleartext format. Packets that are seen live by the threat defense interfaces can be viewed offline.

Chapter 9

1. D. All of these answers are correct. Internal detectors are always on; they are built in the software. Secure Firewall software comes with a set of application detectors, by default. The management center leverages OpenAppID to create custom detectors.

2. C. The Vulnerability Database contains fingerprints.

3. D. All of these answers are correct. A network discovery policy allows Secure Firewall to discover hosts, users, and applications.

4. D. For precise detection of the latest applications, you must keep the Vulnerability Database (VDB) version up to date.

5. C. One of the best practices for a network discovery policy configuration is to exclude the IP addresses of any NAT and load-balancing devices from the list of monitored networks.

6. A. If you want to discover certain subnets or ports, do not use an access control rule or a prefilter rule to trust connections from those subnets or ports because the trusted connections are not subject to deep inspection or discovery; hence, they do not contain detailed information during discovery.

7. C. This statement is false because Secure Firewall allows you to create objects for network addresses, port numbers, interfaces, VLAN tags, URLs, time ranges, and for many more variable components.

8. B. If some operating systems appear as pending, the reason is that the threat defense is currently analyzing the collected data or waiting on further information to reach a conclusion.

Chapter 10

1. A. On the access control's policy editor page, you can select a default action for unmatched traffic.

2. D. All these answers are correct. These choices could improve system performance. You should place the precisely defined rules before a broader rule. To filter traffic solely based on 5-tuple, you should consider using prefilter rules instead of access control rules. Finally, the rules with a block action should be placed at the top of the access control ruleset for faster processing.

3. C. The Show Rule Conflict option in the access control policy editor allows you to identify duplicate and overlapping rules (also known as shadowed rules).

4. D. You select a default action for the entire access control policy, not for every access control rule.

5. C. The **system support firewall-engine-debug** command enables you to debug the operation of the access control policy on a threat defense.

Chapter 11

1. D. All of these answers are correct. The rule options provided in A, B, and C can bypass security inspection.

2. D. All of these answers are correct. The differences provided in A, B, and C are applicable.

3. D. All of these answers are correct. The choices provided in A, B, and C are the best practices for rule creation.

4. B. Enabling logging in a prefilter rule is not a mandatory step to deploy a prefilter policy.

Appendix A: Answers to the "Do I Know This Already?" Questions   593

A

5. C. An access control rule with Trust action supports granular filters based on Security Intelligence data, application fingerprints, URL filtering, user identities, and so on.

6. A. You can use the **show access-list** command to view the list of prefilter rules as well as access control rules that are active on a threat defense.

7. D. All of these answers are correct. Secure Firewall supports various encapsulation protocols, such as Generic Routing Encapsulation (GRE), IP-in-IP, IPv6-in-IP, and Teredo encapsulation protocols.

Chapter 12

1. B. Security Intelligence is one of the earliest lines of defense in the Snort engine.

2. C. The Add IP to Block List option in the context menu enables you to block an address without redeploying an access control policy.

3. D. All of these answers are correct. These options—feed, list, and context menu—can be used to block IP addresses.

4. A. If your goal is to block traffic based on 5-tuple—source port, destination port, source IP, destination IP, and protocol—you should consider deploying a prefilter rule instead of engaging Security Intelligence as the primary method for blocking traffic. It ensures optimal system performance.

5. B. On a newly installed management center, the list of intelligence-based objects may not be available for selection. To populate them in the list of available objects and use them as a rule constraint, you need to update the Cisco intelligence feed from the Cisco cloud, which requires Internet connectivity.

6. C. The **egrep** *ip_address* *.blf* command displays an exact IP address and confirms that the address is included in the current Block List file.

7. C. Any address that you block by selecting the Add IP to Block List option is included in the Global Block List category. So, if you want to unblock the address again, go to **Object Management > Security Intelligence** and remove the address from the Global Block List.

8. C. You can create a text file to include custom IP addresses in bulk and input the file directly into a management center.

9. A. After obtaining the indicators from various sources, the management center publishes the observables to its managed threat defense. In a TID deployment, managed devices are known as elements.

Chapter 13

1. D. The monitor action allows a packet to go through a threat defense; however, it can log the packet transfer as an event.

2. B. A sinkhole is configured to respond with a spoofed DNS server address.

3. C. A threat defense does not download the intelligence feed; the management center downloads the feed and deploys it to its managed threat defense devices.

4. D. All of these answers are correct. These options can help expedite the enforcement of a new DNS policy.

5. A. A threat license is required.

6. D. All of these answers are correct. They are true for a DNS policy.

7. B. The DNS policy-related configurations are stored at /var/sf/sidns_download.

Chapter 14

1. C. Both the management center and threat defense can collectively resolve URLs on the Internet.

2. D. All of these answers are correct.

3. D. A threat license is a prerequisite to enable URL Filtering. In addition, a URL Filtering license is necessary to deploy an access control rule with any URL-based conditions.

4. D. All of these answers are correct. These options can be considered the best practices. Enabling a health module for URL Filtering can confirm the successful downloading and deployment of URL datasets. Enabling automatic updates for URL Filtering ensures that Secure Firewall's URL database is up to date. Avoiding a smaller cache for URLs can make sure that the system is not always staying busy with frequent queries to the Cisco Cloud.

5. D. All of these answers are correct.

Chapter 15

1. D. All of these answers are correct. A network analysis policy works in conjunction with preprocessor rules to normalize traffic. An intrusion policy employs the Snort rules to perform deep packet inspection. However, an access control policy has to invoke both the desired network analysis policy and intrusion policy for matching access control rules.

2. D. All of these answers are correct. Depending on the purpose and type of rule, Snort uses a different numbering scheme to distinguish the rules. For example, standard text rules use GID 1. Preprocessor rules use any GID except 1–3. Local rules use SID 1,000,000 or higher.

3. B. Cisco Talos recommends the Balanced Security and Connectivity policy for the best system performance without compromising the detection of the latest critical vulnerabilities.

4. A. The Snort engine uses the settings on a network analysis policy to decode and normalize traffic as the packets go through advanced security checks.

5. D. All of these answers are correct. The interface set, inspection mode, and rule action must be configured properly to block an intrusion attempt.

6. D. All of these answers are correct. Secure Firewall can ensure deep packet inspection whether the packets match any access control rules or not.

7. B. The matching traffic will flow without interruption, but the intrusion event would be marked visually as *would have dropped*.

Chapter 16

1. B. The dynamic analysis feature submits a captured file to the malware analytics sandbox for dynamic analysis. A sandbox environment can be available in the cloud or on-premises. Upon analysis, the sandbox returns a threat score—a scoring system for considering a file as potential malware.

2. D. All of these answers are correct. These options are recommended.

3. D. To block a file transfer solely based on its file format, a threat license is sufficient.

4. C. The management center does not need to send a query to the cloud to detect a file type.

5. D. Virus is not a valid type of malware disposition. The valid dispositions for any detected files are shown on the File Events page.

Chapter 17

1. A. NAT Rules Before. A NAT policy editor categorizes NAT rules into three groups: NAT Rules Before, Auto NAT Rules, and NAT Rules After. In the CLI, you can find the rules under Section 1, Section 2, and Section 3, respectively. During evaluation, the threat defense begins with the rules under Section 1, which is basically NAT Rules Before in the GUI.

2. C. Clearing the current translation table ensures that the threat defense will use the new policy.

3. A. Firewall mode supports NAT. Any associated interfaces that participate in a NAT configuration have to be in a regular firewall mode—routed or transparent. A threat defense does not support NAT on IPS-only interface types, such as inline, inline-tap, and passive.

4. B. The **show nat detail** command enables you to determine whether a connection matches a NAT rule and how many times it has matched.

Chapter 18

1. C. An SSL policy is not invoked in the access control policy.

2. D. All of these answers are correct.

3. D. All of these answers are correct.

4. C. In an SSL policy, choose the Block action for an SSLv2 session (under the Undecryptable Action tab).

5. D. All of the views in the GUI display the SSL status and action.

Chapter 19

1. D. All of these answers are correct. Secure Firewall supports all three network topologies—Point-to-Point, Hub and Spoke, and Full Mesh—in a VPN configuration.

2. B. Generic Routing Encapsulation (GRE). AH, ESP, and IKE are the three major protocols in an IPsec framework.

3. A. AES. The Advanced Encryption Standard (AES) is a data encryption protocol that is standardized in FIPS 197.

4. C. SHA. The Secure Hash Algorithm (SHA) is used for data integrity and is standardized in FIPS 180-4.

5. D. All of these answers are correct. IKE, ISAKMP, and ECDH—all these protocols are used for key exchange.

6. D. All of these answers are correct. When you are registering a management center with Cisco Smart Software Licensing, the export-controlled functionality must be allowed to enable modern encryption algorithms. Secure Firewall supports the configuration of a site-to-site virtual private network using both IKEv1 and IKEv2 protocols. If an interface of the threat defense is configured with NAT and VPN, you need to exempt the internal traffic from being translated using an identity NAT rule. This process is called NAT exemption.

7. D. All of these answers are correct. Secure Firewall supports both SSL and IKEv2 protocols in remote access VPN configuration. SCEP protocol allows Secure Firewall to obtain a certificate directly from the certificate authority. When remote users connect to a threat defense for VPN access, the threat defense communicates to an authentication server for credential validation.

Chapter 20

1. C. The Snort engine evaluates a QoS rule and classifies traffic. When a packet matches with a QoS rule, the Snort engine sends the ID of the matching rule to the firewall engine. Later, the firewall engine limits the rate of individual flows based on the download and upload speed limits defined on a QoS rule.

2. D. In an access control policy, enable logging at the end of a connection.

3. D. Secure Firewall supports up to 32 QoS rules within a single QoS policy.

4. A. Each interface participating in a QoS policy must be in routed mode. You cannot apply a QoS policy to an interface that is in inline mode, passive mode, or switched mode.

5. C. 40 Mbps = 5 MB/sec.

6. D. All of these answers are correct. These commands can provide information about the traffic rate limit and quality of service policy.

Chapter 21

1. B. The AUDIT keyword is used as a facility level to represent the audit subsystem.

2. C. Syslog over TCP can introduce extra overhead in a large deployment.

3. C. Syslog messages can be sent over both UDP and TCP. The default ports are UDP 514 and TCP 1470.

4. D. All of these answers are correct. Using platform settings, you can add a custom banner to appear during threat defense login; allow the hosts that can communicate with the threat defense over SSH, HTTPS, and ICMP protocols; define how the threat defense will synchronize time with its management center or an NTP

server; provide health monitoring status over Simple Network Management Protocol (SNMP); send security events and system messages to an external syslog server; and many more.

5. D. All of these answers are correct. You can create a correlation rule based on discovery events, intrusion events, file events, connection events, and many other constraints.

6. D. All of these answers are correct. The troubleshooting file package contains log messages of various system processes, copies of configuration files, results of database queries, various command outputs, and so on.

CCNP Security Cisco Secure Firewall and Intrusion Prevention System Official Cert Guide Updates

Over time, reader feedback allows Pearson to gauge which topics give our readers the most problems when taking the exams. To assist readers with those topics, the author creates new materials clarifying and expanding on those troublesome exam topics. As mentioned in the Introduction, the additional contents about the exam are contained in a PDF on this book's companion website, at www.ciscopress.com/title/9780136589709.

This appendix is intended to provide you with updated information if Cisco modifies the exam upon which this book is based. When Cisco releases an entirely new exam, the changes are usually too extensive to provide in a simple update appendix. In those cases, you might need to consult the new edition of the book for the updated content. This appendix attempts to fill the void that occurs with any print book. In particular, this appendix does the following:

- Mentions technical items that might not have been mentioned elsewhere in the book

- Covers new topics if Cisco adds anything new to the exam over time

- Provides a way to get up-to-date information and references about an exam topic

Always Get the Latest at the Book's Product Page

You are reading the version of this appendix that was available when your book was printed. However, given that the main purpose of this appendix is to be a living, changing document, it is important that you look for the latest version online at the book's companion website. To do so, follow these steps:

Step 1. Browse to www.ciscopress.com/title/9780136589709.

Step 2. Click the **Updates** tab.

Step 3. If there is a new Appendix B document on the page, download the latest Appendix B document.

NOTE The downloaded document has a version number. Comparing the version of the print Appendix B (Version 1.0) with the latest online version of this appendix, you should do the following:

- **Same version:** Ignore the PDF that you downloaded from the companion website.

- **Website has a later version:** Ignore this Appendix B in your book and read only the latest version that you downloaded from the companion website.

Technical Content

The current Version 1.0 of this appendix does not contain additional technical coverage.

Analyze Hit Counts   An option to determine whether there are any access control rules that do not match any traffic.

Auto NAT   A type of NAT rule that allows the translation of one address—either source or destination address—in a single rule. This means that to translate both source and destination addresses, two separate Auto NAT rules are necessary.

Balanced Security and Connectivity policy   A policy recommended by Cisco Talos for the best system performance without compromising the detection of the latest critical vulnerabilities.

base license   A license that enables you to update the system and perform basic switching, routing, and NAT functionality. However, you cannot enable any advanced next-generation security features with it.

bridge group   A unique Layer 2 environment in transparent firewall mode. Each bridge group comes with a Bridge Virtual Interface (BVI). Although you can create multiple bridge groups on a single threat defense in transparent mode, the hosts within different bridge groups cannot communicate with each other without a router.

certificate   An electronic document that is used to ensure the identity of a network resource in the public key infrastructure (PKI). The client and server use the certificate information during the TLS handshake to establish an encrypted session. A certificate is issued by a certificate authority (CA). In a lab environment, a certificate can be self-signed as well.

cipher   A method of encoding regular plaintext into a substitute format that should be understandable by its authorized recipients only.

Cisco Defense Orchestrator (CDO)   A cloud-based management platform that enables you to configure and manage policies simultaneously for different Cisco security platforms, such as Secure Firewall threat defense, Adaptive Security Appliances (ASA), and Meraki MX.

Cisco Smart Software Manager (SSM)   An application that allows you to administer the licenses and subscription entitlements for the Cisco products in your organization. It is available in both a cloud version (hosted at cisco.com) and an on-premises version (for your virtual environment).

clean list   A list in which files are not blocked by a threat defense due to their malware disposition. You could manually allow such files by adding them to the clean list. This lets the files go through the threat defense moving forward.

clustering   A technique that offers higher performance, scalability, and resiliency at the same time. With clustering, you can simply add extra threat defense devices to your existing deployment and group them into a single logical cluster to support additional throughput.

connection event   A log that is generated and sent to the management center when a connection is established between a source and destination through a threat defense.

Context Menu   A menu on the management center GUI, providing shortcuts to various features that are pertinent to a particular type of event. To open the context menu, go to an event view page and simply right-click or left-click on the event (depending on the mouse settings on computer).

decryption by known key   A decryption technique that is used to decrypt incoming traffic from an external user—when the user attempts to connect to an internal web server located inside of your organization. This technique assumes that you own the internal web server, and therefore you have the private key of your web server. In other words, the server's private key is known to you.

decryption by resigning   A decryption technique that is used to decrypt outgoing traffic from an internal end user—when the user attempts to connect to an external web server located outside of your organization. It enables a threat defense to intercept outgoing encrypted traffic like a man-in-the-middle and then decrypt it for further evaluation against an access control policy.

default action   An action that defines how the traffic that does not match any access control rule conditions is handled by a threat defense.

DHCP   Dynamic Host Configuration Protocol; a network protocol that can be used to dynamically assign IP addresses to connected hosts.

disposition   The state of a file determining whether it is malware, clean, or unknown. A threat defense calculates the SHA-256 hash value (Secure Hash Algorithm with 256 bits) of a file and uses the value to determine a disposition. The management center performs a lookup on the cached disposition before it sends a new query to the malware analytics cloud.

DNS Policy   A policy on Cisco Secure Firewall that is based on the Security Intelligence feature, which allows the detection and control of connections to a susceptible DNS query.

dynamic analysis   A type of analysis in which a captured file is submitted to the Cisco malware analytics sandbox. A sandbox environment can be available in the cloud or on-premises.

dynamic NAT   The selection of an IP address from a predefined address pool and translation of an original internal address into the selected IP address. The selection of an address from the address pool is on a first-come, first-served basis.

EICAR test file   An antimalware test file that emulates a malicious file; it is available at the European Institute for Computer Antivirus Research (EICAR) website. Cisco does not develop or maintain this test file; however, you can download the latest copy from eicar.org.

ERSPAN   A technology that transports mirrored traffic over a Layer 3 network by encapsulating it using the Generic Routing Encapsulation (GRE) tunneling protocol.

export-controlled license   A license that utilizes strong encryption technologies. It is subject to the approval of Cisco and permission from the local government.

facility   The many processes and subsystems of a computer system, such as the authentication subsystem, networking subsystem, and mail subsystem, in which syslog messages can be generated. The Internet Engineering Task Force (IETF) uses the term *facility* to refer to these subsystems.

fastpath rule   A prefilter rule or tunnel rule with Fastpath action. It can enable a threat defense to bypass traffic before a packet even reaches the firewall engine and Snort engine.

feature license   A license that is necessary to enable security features. It is not hardware specific. A feature license entitles you to enable a particular security feature on a managed threat defense device.

feed   A Cisco-provided list of harmful IP addresses, domains, and URLs. The Cisco threat intelligence research team consistently analyzes suspicious Internet activities, identifies potentially malicious addresses (IP, domain, and URL), categorizes them based on their contents and behavior on the Internet, and packages them in a file for download. You can configure a management center to download that file directly from the Cisco cloud, and incorporate the feedback automatically into the access control policy.

Geolocation Database (GeoDB)   A database that stores the geographical information of an IP address; for example, country name or flag.

hardware bypass   A fault-tolerance feature that ensures continuity of traffic flow between an inline interface pair in case of any unplanned failure. The feature is very helpful if your threat defense experiences any software reboot, hardware crash, or even a power outage. The support of this feature depends on your threat defense model and its network module.

high availability   A deployment architecture that ensures business continuity during an unplanned outage. In a high availability deployment, one device operates actively while the other device stays in standby. A standby device does not actively process traffic or security events.

inline mode   An interface mode that logically establishes connections between two data interfaces and enables the device to act like a bump on the wire for the connected network hosts. Inline interfaces on an interface pair are network agnostic. They can send and receive any traffic, as long as the policies permit. No IP addresses need to be configured on any of the member interfaces of an inline pair.

inline set   A logical group of one or more interface pairs. In inline mode, the ingress and egress interfaces are bundled into an interface pair. Each pair must be associated with an inline set.

integrated routing and bridging (IRB)   A technique that enables a threat defense to support Layer 2 bridging and Layer 3 routing simultaneously.

Internet Key Exchange (IKE)   A type of protocol that VPN peers use to build a security association and exchange secret keys.

Internet Protocol Security (IPsec)   A group of protocols and algorithms that work together to establish a secure connection over the public Internet; it is not a single networking protocol. The Internet Engineering Task Force (IETF) defines the standards for implementing IPsec using three distinct protocols: Authentication Header (AH), Encapsulating Security Payload (ESP), and Internet Key Exchange (IKE).

Lightweight Security Package (LSP)   The rule update package for Snort 3.

list   A custom method to input addresses in bulk for blocking. You can list the addresses in a text file and upload the file manually to the management center through a web browser.

Local Analysis   A malware analysis engine that enables a threat defense to inspect files locally. It uses rules provided by Cisco Talos to detect the most common types of malware.

local rules   Snort rules that you create and import into the management center. If you obtain a Snort rule from a community-based Internet forum, the system considers it a local rule as well.

manifest (.mf) file   A clear-text file that stores the SHA1 digests of the OVF and VMDK files in a package.

Manual NAT   A type of NAT rule that allows the translation of both source and destination addresses within the same rule. A Manual NAT rule may be necessary when you want to make an exception for translation.

multi-instance   A technology that enables the creation and operation of multiple application instances on the same chassis, but with a small subset of the total hardware resources. It enables the isolation of many critical elements of an application.

NXDOMAIN   A nonexistent domain name. The NXDOMAIN message indicates that the requested domain name does not exist. The browser cannot resolve the IP address for a domain. Consequently, a user fails to access the website.

Open Virtual Format (.ovf) file   An XML file used to store references of virtual machine elements.

OpenAppID   An open-source application detection module. Secure Firewall uses application detectors to identify the network applications running on a monitored network. Behind the scenes, it leverages OpenAppID.

packet analyzer   A tool used to capture traffic and to analyze it on demand.

PCAP file   A file that stores packet data captured from the IP communication channel.

Permanent License Reservation (PLR)   The ability to reserve licenses from your smart account in a more restricted network where Internet connectivity to management network is prohibited. In the PLR licensing model, the management center can operate without any connection to the Cisco SSM cloud application. You can manually copy and paste licensing information between the management center and cisco.com to check the licenses in and out.

Port Address Translation (PAT)   A translation technique by which both the IP address and port number of a connection (as opposed to just the IP address) can be translated and multiplexed over 65,000 connections over a single IP address. If a dynamic address pool has fewer external addresses than the number of internal hosts, it is impossible for all the internal hosts to connect to external networks at the same time. PAT can address this limitation.

prefilter rule   A rule that allows you to filter traffic based on basic networking constraints, such as IP address, port number, VLAN tag, and interface.

preprocessor rules   Rules created by the Snort development team. The Snort engine uses them to decode packets with various protocols.

promiscuous mode   An operating mode that allows a virtual network interface to see any packet in a network segment—even packets that are not aimed at that interface.

Propagate Link State   A feature that automatically brings down the remaining interface if one interface in an inline pair goes down. When one of the links of a pair goes down, the other link could stay up to receive traffic. However, this feature makes a threat defense not transfer traffic through an interface that has no link. This feature improves routing convergence time by not trying to send traffic through a failed link.

remote access VPN   A type of virtual private network in which an endpoint device located in a remote network can connect to an organization's internal network over the Internet via a secure channel.

routed mode   The operating mode that enables a Secure Firewall threat defense to function as the next Layer 3 hop in a network. Each interface you enable with routed mode represents a separate Layer 3 network; hence, each interface is configured with separate subnet.

Secure Firewall Device Manager (FDM)   A device manager that enables you to manage a single threat defense locally without registering it to any remote management platform.

Secure Firewall Management Center (FMC)   The management center that enables you to manage multiple threat defenses from a centralized location.

Secure Rule Update (SRU)   The rule update package for Snort 2.

Security Intelligence   An early line of defense that enables you to block a suspicious address automatically using reputation-based intelligence.

severity level   A keyword that indicates the significance of a syslog message. Each syslog message is associated with a severity level. It enables a system administrator to decide whether and when an action should be taken to address the issue described in a syslog message.

shadowed rules   Access control rules that use a broader overlapping subnet.

shared object (SO) rules   Rules written in the C programming language by Talos and compiled for Snort use. The content of an SO rule is made irretrievable for various reasons, such as proprietary agreements between Cisco and third-party vendors.

Show Rule Conflict   An option to determine any duplicate or overlapping rules (also known as shadowed rules) in an access control policy.

sinkhole   An option that enables a threat defense to respond to a DNS query with a false IP address. The browser on the client machine does not realize that an intermediate security device—the threat defense in this example—acts as a spoof DNS server, and it responds to its query with a false IP address.

site-to-site VPN   A type of virtual private network in which the VPN gateways located in geographically separated networks can connect each other via a secure tunnel over the Internet. It makes all the hosts in the configured sites appear as a part of the same virtual network.

Spero analysis   A type of analysis in which the engine examines the MSEXE files only.

static NAT   The permanent mapping of an original IP address with a translated IP address. Because the mapping is permanent, either the internal or an external host is able to initiate a connection.

switch port   A port that forwards traffic at Layer 2. There are two types of switch ports: access and trunk. Access ports forward untagged traffic to only one VLAN, whereas trunk ports forward traffic to multiple VLANs.

Switched Port Analyzer (SPAN)   A switch port that is enabled with the port mirroring feature.

system logging (syslog)   A short form of the term *system logging*. It produces system-level events to inform you of how the various components of the operating system and its processes are performing. You can use logging for real-time alerting as well as for auditing purposes. The Internet Engineering Task Force (IETF) standardized syslog in RFC 5424.

system-provided variable   A variable used to represent source and destination information in a Snort rule. Variables can empower you to enable a rule in any network environment without modifying the original Snort rule.

TAP   A dedicated hardware that is designed to replicate and transfer traffic.

thick provision   An option to provision virtual disk space at the time of the virtual disk creation.

thin provision   An option to provision virtual disk space on demand. The size of a virtual disk grows whenever there is a need, up to the maximum allocated limit.

traffic policing   A method that drops excessive traffic when the traffic rate reaches a predefined limit.

traffic shaping   A method that queues excessive traffic in a buffer—rather than dropping it—for later transmission.

transparent mode   The mode in which a threat defense allows you to control your network traffic like a firewall, while the threat defense stays invisible to the hosts in your network.

trust rule   An access control rule with Trust action. It can match and trust traffic based on applications, URLs, users, and so on. Unlike a prefilter rule, an access control rule uses the innermost header of a packet to filter traffic.

tunnel rule   A rule that filters tunnel traffic that is encapsulated by an additional IP header—for example, GRE, IP-in-IP, and IPv6-in-IP.

uncategorized URLs   URLs are marked as Uncategorized by a management center if the cloud lookup times out, or if the query to the Cisco Cloud Services is disabled due to privacy concerns. You can configure a management center to send queries to the Cisco Cloud Services if its local database lookup does not return a result—a predefined category for the requested URL.

URL database   The database where URL reputation information is stored. Cisco Cloud publishes two types of URL datasets—20 million URLs and 1 million URLs. Secure Firewall downloads them depending on the size of its available memory. After the initial download of a database, the management center receives updates from the cloud periodically, as long as the automatic update is enabled. The periodic updates are incremental and smaller.

URL reputation   Different levels of reputation used by the management center to indicate the trustworthiness of websites. The Secure Firewall URL database uses a Web Reputation Index (WRI), which is calculated dynamically based on data points from various sources, such as age and history of the site, reputation and location of the hosting IP address, subject and context of the content, and so on.

Virtual Machine Disk (.vmdk) file   A compressed virtual machine disk file for a virtual appliance.

VMXNET3   An advanced network adapter designed to minimize network processing overhead in a virtual environment. The difference between an E1000 and a VMXNET3 adapter is in throughput. The throughput of a VMXNET3 adapter is 10 Gbps, whereas an E1000 adapter supports up to 1 Gbps.

Vulnerability Database (VDB)   A database that contains the fingerprints of various applications, operating systems, services, and client software. It also keeps a record of known vulnerabilities.

Index

Numerics

5–tuple, 5

A

access control lists, verifying, 115–118

access control policy, 194. *See also* prefilter policy

best practices, 199–200

configuring, 200–201

enable logging on, 568

establishing trust, 237–240

fulfilling prerequisites, 201

invoking a prefilter policy, 235–236

invoking file and SSL policy, 474–476

options, 196–197

prefilter policy, Fastpath, 227

reusable objects, 181–183

rule editor, 198–199

rules, creating, 202–207

selecting a default action, 108–111

on site-to-site VPN, 503–504

verifying

debug messages, 210–211

bit counts, 208–210

trace data analysis, 213–222

access control rule, 176

adding to a routing protocol, 111–115

creating, 202–207

actions

DNS policy, 292–293

domain not found, 291

drop, 288–291

sinkhole, 291–292

prefilter policy, 227

bypassing deep packet inspection, 227–229

Fastpath action, 227

Trust, 228

alerts, syslog

correlating events to send, 574–578

creating, 569–571

verifying, 572–574

Al-Kindi, 462

AMP (advanced malware protection), 382–386

application detectors, 175–176, 186–187

ARP (Address Resolution Protocol), 104

authentication, IPsec, 495

automatic IP addressing, routed mode configuration, 80–82

AVC (application visibility and control), 172, 176

B

base policy, 353–356

best practices

for access control policy, 199–200

for blocking DNS queries, 295–296

for detection-only mode, 143–145

for device registration, 61

for file policy, 386–387

for inline mode, 125–126

for intrusion policy, 356–359

for logging, 560

for NAT deployment, 423–424

for network discovery, 178–179

for prefilter policy, 230

for QoS, 541

for routed mode, 73

for Security Intelligence, 256

for traffic decryption, 467–468

for transparent mode, 93–94

for URL filtering, 317–322

for virtual environment, 30–31

block actions, 122–123, 143

block list, Security Intelligence

    adding an address, 267–268

    manual blocking, 270–272

    removing an address, 268–269

blocking

  DNS queries, 285–289, 295–296

  URLs, 323–324

branding

  Cisco Secure architecture, 13

  Cisco Secure Firewall management platforms, 11

  Firepower, 11

bump in the wire, 125

BVI (bridge virtual interface), 92, 118, 125

C

CA (certificate authority), 495

cabling, threat defense, 142–143

capturing traffic, 156, 162–165

  best practices, 160

  packet drop analysis, 158

  packet tracer tool, 169–170

  using Cisco Secure Firewall, 162–165

  verification, 165–169

cat command, 303–304

CIA (confidentiality, integrity, and availability) triad, 484–485

Cisco Secure Firewall, 8. *See also* IPS (intrusion prevention systems); network discovery; policy; threat defense

  access control policy

    configuring, 200–201

    creating rules, 202–207

    debug messages, 210–211

    establishing trust, 237–240

    fulfilling prerequisites, 201

    hit counts, 208–210

    invoking a prefilter policy, 235–236

    trace data analysis, 213–222

  blocking a DNS query, 285–289

  capturing traffic, 162–165

  clustering, 18–19

  DNS policy

    adding a rule, 298–301

    configuring, 297–298

    invoking, 301

    verifying, 302–307

encapsulated traffic inspection, 242–245

Encrypted Visibility Engine, 467

Evaluation Mode, 56–59

export-controlled license, 55–56

feature license, 54–55

GeoDB (Geolocation Database), 16

hardware architecture, 16–17

high availability, 20–21

HLD (high-level design), 8

logging, 556, 558. *See also* logging

    adding a syslog server on platform settings, 564–566

    best practices, 560

    creating syslog alerts, 569–571

    prerequisites, 560–563

    RFC documents describing, 559

    syslog message facilities, 559–560

    syslog message severity levels, 559

    troubleshooting, 578–580

    verifying, 568–569

LTR (Long-Term Release), 13

management communication over the Internet, 65–67

management solutions, 8–10

    branding, 11

    CDO (Cisco Defense Orchestrator), 9

    FDM (Secure Firewall Device Manager), 8–9

    FMC (Secure Firewall Management Center), 9

network discovery, 180–181

    application detectors, 175–176

    best practices, 178–179

    fulfilling prerequisites, 179–180

    host discovery analysis, 186–188

    operations, 176–177

    policy configuration, 183–186

    policy verification, 186

    reusable objects, 181–183

    undiscovered new hosts, 188–191

Network Trajectory, 413–414

policy editor, 196

prefilter policy, 224

    actions, 227

    best practices, 230

    bypassing deep packet inspection, 227–229

    enabling bypass through a, 230

fulfilling prerequisites, 230–231

rules, 226–227, 230–235

product evolution and lifecycle, 11–14

resiliency, 21–22

rule editor, 198–199

scalability, 18, 19–20

Security Intelligence, 248, 251–253

    adding an address to the block list, 267–268

    automatic blocking using Cisco intelligence feed, 259–260

    best practices, 256

    blocking suspicious addresses, 254–255, 262–263

    context menu, 254–255

    fulfilling prerequisites, 256–259

    manual blocking using custom list, 270–272

    Monitor-only mode, 272–274

    overriding Cisco intelligence feed outcome, 265–267

    removing an address from the block list, 268–269

software

    architecture, 14–16

    release cycle, 13

sources of intelligence, 293

    comparing, 294

    feed, 293

    list, 293

STR (Short-Term Release), 13

system-provided base policies, 353–356

system-provided variable sets, 352–354

TID (Threat Intelligence Director), 274–275

    adding sources, 277–278

    enabling, 276–277

    importing indicators, 278–280

URL filtering, 310, 312

    allowing a specific URL, 329–331

    analyzing the default category override, 331–335

    best practices, 317–322

    blocking URLs, 323–324

    Cloud Services and, 314–315, 318

    debugging a connection to an uncategorized URL, 339–340

    enabling, 322

    fulfilling prerequisites, 315–317

    handling uncategorized URLs, 335–338

    health module, 317–318

    investigating uncategorized URLs, 338

    resolving URLs, 315–316

    updates, 319

    verifying, 325–331

    web reputation levels, 312–314

validation

    of licensing, 59–61

    of registration, 67–68

VDB (Vulnerability Database), 15–16

on a virtual platform, 26–27

    best practices, 30–31

    configuration, 31–32

    hosting environment settings, 27

    management center specifications, 28

    software package selection, 28–29

    system initialization and validation, 41–45

    threat defense specifications, 28

    virtual machine creation, 35–40

    virtual network for data traffic, 33–34

    virtual network for management traffic, 32–33

    virtual resource allocation, 28

classic license, 48, 50–51

Cloud Services, URL filtering and, 314–315, 318

clustering

    Cisco Secure Firewall, 18–19

    inter-chassis, 18

    intra-chassis, 18

    multi-instance, 20

commands

    configure firewall routed, 75

    configure firewall transparent, 95

    configure manager add, 62

    debug, 82–84, 106–107

    debug dhcpd packet, 88

    debug icmp trace, 107

    egrep, 305

    firewall-engine-debug, 326–329, 332–335

    head, 304–305

    Linux

        cat, 303–304

        telnet, 374–375

    nslookup, 306–307

    ping, 507

    show access-list, 115–118, 240–241

    show arp, 107, 108

show asp drop, 552

show capture ssh_traffic_inside, 437–441

show conn detail, 435–436, 552–553

show dhcp binding, 87

show firewall, 75, 96

show inline-set, 134

show interface, 85–86

show interface ip brief, 85, 104, 133, 434

show ip, 85

show managers, 67, 74, 94–95

show nameif, 434

show nat detail, 433–434, 436, 449

show running-config, 73, 93

show running-config crypto, 507–508

show running-config interface, 86–87, 103

show running-config nat, 433, 513

show running-config policy-map, 547–548

show service-policy police, 551–552

show vpn-sessiondb anyconnect, 532–534

show vpn-sessiondb detail, 509–510, 531–532

show xlate detail, 449–450

telnet, 374–375

configure firewall routed command, 75

configure firewall transparent command, 95

configure manager add command, 62

configuring

    access control policy, 200–201

    file policy, 390

    inline mode, 126–127

        event analysis in IPS-only mode, 135–136

        fulfilling prerequisites, 126–127

        inline set configuration, 129–131

        interface setup, 127–130

        verification, 132–134

    inline tap mode, 145–147

    NAT (Network Address Translation). *See* NAT (Network Address Translation)

    network analysis policy, 359–361

    network discovery policy, 183–186

    packet capture, 162–165

    passive interface mode, 149–151

        SPAN ports, 151–152

        verification, 152–153

    prefilter policy, rules, 230–235

    QoS policy, 542–547

    threat defense, firewall mode, 73–74

    transparent mode, interfaces, 96–102

VPN (virtual private network)

    remote access, 516–522

    site-to-site, 499–502

connectivity, verifying, 104–108

control unit, 18

creating

    file policy, 390–394, 474–475

    inline set, 127–130

    intrusion policy, 364–365

    network discovery policy, 183–186

    rules, 202–207

    SSL policy, 470–474

    syslog alerts, 569–571

cryptanalysis, 462–463

cryptography, 462, 490. *See also* **decryption**

CVSS (Common Vulnerability Scoring System), 354–355

D

data unit, 18

debug command, 82–84, 106–107

debug dhcpd packet command, 88

debug icmp trace command, 107

decryption, 463, 466–467. *See also* SSL (Secure Socket Layer)

    best practices, 467–468

    by known key, 467

    policy

        configuring, 468–476

        verifying, 476–480

    by resigning, 466–467

detection-only mode, 141

    best practices, 143–145

    event analysis, 153–154

    inline tap mode, 145

        configuring, 145–147

        verifying configuration, 147–149

    passive interface mode, 149

        configuring, 149–151

        SPAN port, configuring on a switch, 151–152

    passive monitoring technology, 141–143

direct cloud access architecture, 52

DNS (Domain Name System), 284–285

    blocking, 285–289, 295–296

    policy

adding a rule, 298–301

configuring, 297–298

fulfilling prerequisites, 296–297

invoking, 301

verifying, 302–307

rule actions, 287–288, 292–293

domain not found, 291

drop, 288–291

sinkhole, 291–292

Docker, multi-instance, 19–20

domain not found action, 291

drop action, 288–291

dynamic NAT, 420

E

editing, intrusion policy, 364–368

egrep command, 305

Elgamal, T., 462

encapsulated traffic inspection, 242–245

Encrypted Visibility Engine, 467

encryption, 463

ERSPAN (encapsulated remote switched port analyzer) port, 141–142

EtherChannel, 21–22

evaluation license, 56–59

events

analyzing, 153–154

file policy, 398, 399–404

malware, 404

management center performs a cloud lookup, 408–410

management center unable to communicate with the cloud, 404–408

threat defense blocks malware, 409–412

QoS (quality of service), 550–551

export-controlled license, 55–56

F

Fastpath action, 227

FDM (Secure Firewall Device Manager), 8–9

feature license, 54–55

file policy, 382–383

best practices, 386–387

configuring, 390

creating, 390–394, 474–475

deployment, 396–397

events, 398

analyzing, 399–402

blocking a Microsoft executable file, 402

detecting a PDF file, 403–404

file type detection, 382–384

fulfilling prerequisites, 387–390

invoking, 474–476

malware analysis, 382–386

dynamic analysis, 385–386

local analysis, 385

verifying, 398–399

final preparation, 582

accessing the Pearson test prep software, 584–585

chapter-ending review tools, 586

customizing your exams, 585

exam day, 583

getting ready for the exam, 582

practice tests, 583

premium edition, 586

tools for final review, 582–583

updating your exams, 585–586

Firepower, branding, 11

firewall. *See also* Cisco Secure Firewall; NGFW (next-generation firewall)

host-based, 4

network-based, 5

next-generation, 6–8

stateful, 6

stateless, 5

firewall-engine-debug command, 326–329, 332–335

G-H

GRE (Generic Routing Encapsulation), encapsulated traffic inspection, 242–245

hardware architecture, Cisco Secure Firewall, 16–17

hardware bypass, 22

head command, 304–305

health module, URL filtering, 317–318

high availability, Cisco Secure Firewall, 20–21

hit counts, 208–210

host discovery, 186–188

host-based firewall, 4

I

IDS (intrusion detection systems), 123, 342–343
IKEv1, 492–493
importing, TID indicators, 278–280
initialization
    firewall mode configuration, 73–74
    management center virtual appliance, 29–42
    threat defense virtual appliance, 43–44
inline mode, 120, 126–127, 142
    best practices, 125–126
    event analysis in IPS-only mode, 135–136
    fulfilling prerequisites, 126–127
    inline set configuration, 129–131
    interface setup, 127–130
    versus passive mode, 123–124
    versus transparent mode, 124–125
    verifying, 132–134
inline tap mode, 145
    configuring, 145–147
    verifying configuration, 147–149
inter-chassis clustering, 18
interface modes, 142–143
intra-chassis clustering, 18
intrusion policy, 345, 346–351. See also IPS
    (intrusion prevention systems)
    base, 353–356
    best practices, 356–359
    creating, 364–365
    CVSS (Common Vulnerability Scoring System),
        354–355
    deployment, 371–373
    enabling/disabling rules, 368
    setting up a variable set, 369–370
    verifying, 373–378
invoking, DNS policy, 301
IP addressing. See also NAT (Network Address
    Translation)
    addresses reserved for testing and documentation,
        418
    BVI (bridge virtual interface), 92
    NAT (Network Address Translation), 416. See also
        NAT (Network Address Translation)
        best practices, 423–424
        configuring, 427
        connecting to a masqueraded destination,
            446–447

fulfilling prerequisites, 425–426
private IP addressing, 418
rules, 422–423
techniques, 420
    remote access VPN, 521–522
    static, routed mode configuration, 76–79
IPS (intrusion prevention systems), 4, 123, 342–343,
    345
    intrusion policy, 346–351
        creating, 364–365
        deployment, 371–373
        enabling/disabling rules, 368
        incorporating rule recommendations,
            364–368
        setting up a variable set, 369–370
        verifying, 373–378
    network analysis policy, 346–347
        configuring, 359–361
        Snort and, 361–363
    Snort
        rules, 346–351
        system-provided variable sets, 352–354
    system-provided base policies, 353–356
IPsec, 489. See also remote access VPN; site-to-site
    VPN
    authentication, 495
    cryptographic algorithms, 490
    mode of operation, 490–492
    security association and key exchange, 492
        IKEv1, 492–493
        IKEv2, 494–495
    security protocols, 489
    transform set, 492
    verifying, 507, 513
        displaying session details, 509–510
        security association, 510–513
        site-to-site VPN configurations on a threat
            defense, 507–508
        successful ping test through a tunnel, 507
IRB (integrated routing and bridging), 118

J-K-L

Layer 2 networks, configuring transparent mode
    in, 96
Layer 3 networks, deploying a threat defense
    between, 108–109

license(s)

classic, 48

comparison of smart and classic, 50–51

evaluation, 56–59

export-controlled, 55–56

feature, 54–55

malware, 388–389

PLR (Permanent License Reservation), 53–54

SLR (Specific License Reservation), 54

smart, 48

direct cloud access, 52

offline access, 53–54

on-premises server access, 52–53

SSM (Cisco Smart Software Manager), 51

subscription options, 55

threat, 388–389

URL Filtering, 315–317

validation of, 59–61

Linux

cat command, 303–304

telnet command, 374–375

logging, 556, 558

adding a syslog server on platform settings, 564–566

best practices, 560

enable on access control policy, 568

prerequisites, 560–563

RFC documents describing, 559

sending syslog

from management center, 569

from threat defense, 564

syslog alerts

correlating events to send, 574–578

creating, 569–571

verifying, 572–574

syslog message

facilities, 559–560

severity levels, 559

troubleshooting, 578–580

verifying, 568–569

M

malware

analysis, 382–385

dynamic, 385–386

license, 388–389

local, 385

events, 404

management center performs a cloud lookup, 408–410

management center unable to communicate with the cloud, 404–408

threat defense blocks malware, 409–412

Network Trajectory feature, 413–414

overriding a file disposition, 412–413

management center

adding to a threat defense, 62

registration, 63–65

management solutions

CDO (Cisco Defense Orchestrator), 9

Cisco Secure Firewall, 8–10

FMC (Secure Firewall Management Center), 9

Monitor-only mode, Security Intelligence, 272–274

multi-instance, 19–20

N

NAT (Network Address Translation), 416, 418

addresses reserved for testing and documentation, 418

best practices, 423–424

configuring, 427

connecting to a masqueraded destination, 446–447

analyzing a packet, 455–457

analyzing a translated packet, 451–454

capturing SSH traffic on an outside interface, 450–451

configuring a static NAT rule, 446–449

matching a connection in the reverse direction, 449

real-time translation status, 449–450

verifying outside to DMZ operation, 449–457

fulfilling prerequisites, 425–426

masquerading a source address, 427–428

configuring a dynamic NAT rule, 427–433

verifying inside to outside operation, 434–441

verifying outside to inside operation, 441–446

verifying the configuration, 433–434

private IP addressing, 418

rules, 422–423

dynamic, 427–433

static, 446–449

on site-to-site VPN, 504–506

techniques, 420

network analysis policy, 346–347

base, 353–356

configuring, 359–361

Snort and, 361–363

network discovery, 174, 180–181

application detectors, 175–176, 186–187

best practices, 178–179

fulfilling prerequisites, 179–180

host discovery analysis, 186–188

operations, 176–177

policy configuration, 183–186

reusable objects, 181–183

undiscovered new hosts, 188–191

Network Trajectory, 413–414

network-based firewall, 5

NGFW (next-generation firewall), 6–8. *See also* Cisco Secure Firewall

Cisco Secure Firewall, 8

high availability, 20–21

HLD (high-level design), 8

management solutions, 8–10

nslookup command, 306–307

O

offline access architecture, 53–54

OSI (Open Systems Interconnection) model, 5

overriding Cisco intelligence feed outcome, 265–267

P

packet capture, 158

best practices, 160

versus packet tracer tool, 169–170

using Cisco Secure Firewall, 162–165

verification, 165–169

passive interface mode, 149

configuring, 149–151

SPAN port, configuring on a switch, 151–152

verifying, 152–153

passive mode, versus inline mode, 123–124

passive monitoring technology, detection-only mode, 141–143

PAT (Port Address Translation), 420

phishing, Security Intelligence and, 263

ping command, 507

PKI objects

Internal CAs object, 469

Internal Certs object, 469–470

PLR (Permanent License Reservation), 53–54

policing, 538

policy

access control, 194

creating rules, 202–207

debug messages, 210–211

enable logging on, 568

establishing trust, 237–240

hit counts, 208–210

invoking file and SSL policy, 474–476

options, 196–197

policy editor, 198–199

reusable objects, 181–183

rule editor, 198–199

selecting a default action, 108–111

on site-to-site VPN, 503–504

trace data analysis, 213–222

base, 353–356

CVSS (Common Vulnerability Scoring System), 354–355

decryption

configuring, 468–476

verifying, 476–480

DNS (Domain Name System), 282

actions allowing DNS queries, 292–293

adding a rule, 298–301

configuring, 297–298

domain not found action, 291

drop action, 288–291

fulfilling prerequisites, 296–297

invoking, 301

sinkhole action, 291–292

verifying, 302–307

file, 382–383

best practices, 386–387

configuring, 390

creating, 390–394, 474–475

deployment, 396–397

file type detection, 382–384

fulfilling prerequisites, 387–390

invoking, 474–476

malware analysis, 382–386

verifying, 398–399

intrusion, 345, 346–351

base, 353–356

best practices, 356–359

creating, 364–365

CVSS (Common Vulnerability Scoring System), 354–355

deployment, 371–373

editing, 364–368

enabling/disabling rules, 368

setting up a variable set, 369–370

verifying, 373–378

network analysis, 346–347

configuring, 359–361

Snort and, 361–363

network discovery, creating, 183–186

prefilter, 224

actions, 227

best practices, 230

bypassing deep packet inspection, 227–229

enabling bypass through a, 230

fulfilling prerequisites, 230–231

invoking into an access control policy, 235–236

rules, 226–227, 230–235

verifying, 240–242

QoS (quality of service), 538–539

configuring, 542–547

verifying, 546–550

remote access VPN, 522–527

SSL, 468

creating, 470–474

Internal CAs object, 469

Internal Certs object, 469–470

invoking, 474–476

PKI objects, 468

policy editor, 196

prefilter policy, 224

actions, 227

best practices, 230

bypassing deep packet inspection, 227–229

enabling bypass through a, 230

fulfilling prerequisites, 230–231

invoking into an access control policy, 235–236

rules, 226–227, 230–235

verifying, 240–242

on-premises server architecture, 52–53

promiscuous mode, 141

Q

QoS (quality of service), 536, 539–540

best practices, 541

debugging, 553–554

events, 550–551

fulfilling prerequisites, 541–542

identifying the status of a rate-limited connection, 552–553

policing, 538

policy, 538–539

configuring, 542–547

verifying, 546–550

statistics, 551–552

traffic shaping, 539

R

registration

adding a management center to a threat defense, 62

configurations on management center, 63–65

management communication over the Internet, 65–67

threat defense device, 61

validation of, 67–68

remote access VPN, 488, 513

configuring, 516

AnyConnect file, 517–518

certificate enrollment, 518–521

network and IP address pool, 521–522

RADIUS server group, 518

policy, 522–527

prerequisites, 513–517

verifying, 527–534

reputation levels, URL, 312–314

resiliency, Cisco Secure Firewall, 21–22

reusable objects, 181–183

routed mode, 70, 72

automatic IP addressing, 80–82

best practices, 73

enabling, 75

fulfilling prerequisites, 73–74

static IP addressing, 76–79

validation of interface configuration, 82

    debug command, 82–84

    debug dhcpd packet command, 88

    show dhcp binding command, 87

    show interface command, 85–86

    show interface ip brief command, 85

    show ip command, 85

    show running-config interface command, 86–87

routing protocols, adding an access control rule, 111–115

rule editor, 198–199

rules

adding to a DNS policy, 298–301

creating, 202–207

CVSS (Common Vulnerability Scoring System), 354–355

intrusion policy

    editing, 365–368

    enabling/disabling, 368

NAT (Network Address Translation), 422–423

    dynamic, 427–433

    static, 446–449

prefilter policy, 226–227, 230–235

Snort, 346–351, 352–354

URL filtering, 325–331

S

scalability, Cisco Secure Firewall, 18

clustering, 18–19

multi-instance, 19–20

Security Intelligence, 248, 251–253, 264–265

adding an address to the block list, 267–268

automatic blocking using Cisco intelligence feed, 259–260

best practices, 256

blocking suspicious addresses, 254–255, 262–263

context menu, 254–255

fulfilling prerequisites, 256–259

manual blocking using custom list, 270–272

Monitor-only mode, 272–274

overriding Cisco intelligence feed outcome, 265–267

removing an address from the block list, 268–269

show access-list command, 115–118, 240–241

show arp command, 107, 108

show asp drop command, 552

show capture ssh_traffic_inside command, 437–441

show conn detail command, 435–436, 552–553

show dhcp binding command, 87

show firewall command, 75, 96

show inline-set command, 134

show interface command, 85–86

show interface ip brief command, 85, 104, 133, 434

show ip command, 85

show managers command, 67, 74, 94–95

show nameif command, 434

show nat detail command, 433–434, 436, 449

show running-config command, 73, 93

show running-config crypto command, 507–508

show running-config interface command, 86–87, 103

show running-config nat command, 433, 513

show running-config policy-map command, 547–548

show service-policy police command, 551–552

show vpn-sessiondb anyconnect command, 532–534

show vpn-sessiondb detail command, 509–510, 531–532

show xlate detail command, 449–450

sinkhole action, 291–292

site-to-site VPN, 485–488, 496

access control policy, 503–504

configuring, 499–502

NAT policy, 504–506

prerequisites, 496–499

SLR (Specific License Reservation), 54

Smart Agent, 52

smart license, 48

comparison of SLR and PLR models, 54

comparison with classic license, 50–51

direct cloud access, 52

offline access, 53–54

on-premises server access, 52–53

Snort, 158, 346. *See also* **IPS (intrusion prevention systems)**

intrusion policy, editing, 364–368

network analysis policy options, 361–363

rules, 346–351

    syntax, 373–374

    system-provided variable sets, 352–354

software architecture, Cisco Secure Firewall, 14–16

Sourcefire, 11

sources of intelligence

    comparing, 294

    feed, 293

    list, 293

SPAN (switched port analyzer) port, 141–142, 151–152

SSH traffic

    capturing on an outside interface, 450–451

    trace data analysis, 218–222

SSL (Secure Socket Layer), 462–464

    policy, 468

        creating, 470–474

        Internal CAs object, 469

        Internal Certs object, 469–470

        invoking, 474–476

        PKI objects, 468

SSM (Cisco Smart Software Manager), 51

stateful firewall, 6

stateless firewall, 5

static IP addressing, routed mode configuration, 76–79

static NAT, 420, 446–449

statistics, QoS (quality of service), 551–552

subscription options, Cisco Secure Firewall, 55

syntax, Snort rule 1:718, 373–374

syslog, 558

    adding a server on platform settings, 564–566

    alerts

        correlating events to send, 574–578

        creating, 569–571

        verifying, 572–574

    best practices, 560

    enable on access control policy, 568

    message facilities, 559–560

    message severity levels, 559

    prerequisites, 560–563

    RFC documents describing, 559

    sending from management center, 569

    sending from threat defense, 564

    troubleshooting, 578–580

    verifying, 568–569

T

TAP, 142

TCP (Transmission Control Protocol), 5

telnet command, 374–375

Telnet traffic, trace data analysis, 214–215

threat defense. *See also* network discovery

    access control policy, selecting a default action, 108–111

    adding a management center, 62

    block actions, 122–123, 143

    cabling, 142–143

    Cloud Services and, 315

    deploying between Layer 3 networks, 108–109

    detection-only mode, 141

        best practices, 143–145

        event analysis, 153–154

        passive monitoring technology, 141–143

    device registration, 61

    inline mode, 120, 126–127, 142

        best practices, 125–126

        event analysis in IPS-only mode, 135–136

        fulfilling prerequisites, 126–127

        inline set configuration, 129–131

        interface setup, 127–130

        versus passive mode, 123–124

        versus transparent mode, 124–125

        verifying, 132–134

    inline tap mode, 145

        configuring, 145–147

        verifying configuration, 147–149

    interface modes, 142–143

    management communication over the Internet, 65–67

    network discovery, 174, 180–181

        application detectors, 175–176

        best practices, 178–179

        fulfilling prerequisites, 179–180

        host discovery analysis, 186–188

        operations, 176–177

        policy configuration, 183–186

        policy verification, 186

        reusable objects, 181–183

        undiscovered new hosts, 188–191

    packet capture, 160

    packet drops, 158

passive interface mode, 149

    configuring, 149–151

    SPAN port, configuring on a switch, 151–152

    verifying, 152–153

passive mode, 123–124

promiscuous mode, 141

QoS (quality of service), 536

    best practices, 541

    policing, 538

    traffic shaping, 539

routed mode, 70, 72

    best practices, 73

    configuring interfaces with automatic IP addressing, 80–82

    configuring interfaces with static IP addresses, 76–79

    enabling, 75

    fulfilling prerequisites, 73–74

    validation of interface configuration, 82–88

sending syslog from, 564

transparent mode, 70, 92–93

    configuring in a Layer 2 network, 96

    enabling, 95–96

    fulfilling prerequisites, 94–95

    interface configuration, 96–102

    verifying basic connectivity and operations, 104–108

    verifying the interface status, 103–104

unregistering, 74

URL filtering

    best practices, 317–322

    resolving URLs, 315–316

    web reputation levels, 312–314

threat license, 388–389

TID (Threat Intelligence Director), 274–275

    adding sources, 277–278

    enabling, 276–277

    importing indicators, 278–280

TLS (Transport Layer Security), 462–464. *See also* **decryption**

    client/server handshake, 464–466

    evolution of, 464

tools

    capture, 441–446

    for final review, 582–583

Network Trajectory, 413–414

packet tracer, 169–170

trace data analysis

    of live SSH traffic, 218–222

    of live Telnet traffic, 214–215

    of live web traffic, 215–218

traffic shaping, 539

transform set, 492

transparent mode, 70, 92–93

    best practices, 93–94

    configuring in a Layer 2 network, 96

    enabling, 95–96

    fulfilling prerequisites, 94–95

    versus inline mode, 124–125

    interface

        configuring, 96–102

        verifying status of, 103–104

    verifying basic connectivity and operations, 104–108

troubleshooting, logging, 578–580

Trust action, 228, 237–240

tunneling protocol, encapsulated traffic inspection, 242–245. *See also* **IPsec; VPN (virtual private network)**

U

undiscovered hosts, data analysis, 188–191

unregistering, threat defense, 74

URL filtering, 310, 312

    allowing a specific URL, 329–331

    analyzing the default category override, 331–335

    best practices, 317–322

    blocking URLs, 323–324

    Cloud Services and, 314–315, 318

    debugging a connection to an uncategorized URL, 339–340

    enabling, 322

    fulfilling prerequisites, 315–317

    handling uncategorized URLs, 335–338

    health module, 317–318

    investigating uncategorized URLs, 338

    resolving URLs, 315–316

    updates, 319

    verifying, 325–331

    web reputation levels, 312–314

V

validating
  interface configuration
    debug command, 82–84
    debug dhcpd packet command, 88
    show dhcp binding command, 87
    show interface command, 85–86
    show interface ip brief command, 85
    show ip command, 85
    show running-config interface command, 86–87
  registration, 67–68
variable set, associating with an intrusion policy, 369–370
verifying
  access control lists, 115–118
  access control policy
    debug messages, 210–211
    hit counts, 208–210
    trace data analysis, 213–222
  Cisco intelligence feed, 262
    files containing intelligence-based IP addresses, 262–263
    inclusion of specific IP addresses, 264
    IP addresses susceptible to phishing, 263
  DNS policy, 303–304
    files containing the DNS addresses and policy configurations, 302–303
    identifying the DNS intelligence category for domains, 305
    resolving domain names, 306–307
    viewing the list of domains in a category, 304–305
  file policy, 398–399
  inline mode, 132–134
  inline tap mode, 147–149
  intrusion policy, 373–378
  IPsec, 507, 513
    displaying session details, 509–510
    security association, 510–513
    site-to-site VPN configurations on a threat defense, 507–508
    successful ping test through a tunnel, 507
  NAT configuration, 433–434
    inside to outside, 434–441
    outside to inside, 441–446
  network discovery policy, 186
  packet capture, 165–169
  passive interface mode, 152–153
  prefilter policy, 240–242
  QoS policy, 546–550
  remote access VPN, 527–534
  syslog, 568–569
  syslog alerts, 572–574
  transparent mode
    basic connectivity and operations, 104–108
    interface status, 103–104
  URL filtering, 325–331
virtual environment, Cisco Secure Firewall deployment, 26–27
  best practices, 30–31
  configuration, 31–32
  hosting environment settings, 27
  management center specifications, 28
  software package selection, 28–29
  system initialization and validation, 41–45
  threat defense specifications, 28
  virtual machine creation, 35–40
  virtual network for data traffic, 33–34
  virtual network for management traffic, 32–33
  virtual resource allocation, 28
VPN (virtual private network), 482
  architectures, 485
  CIA (confidentiality, integrity, and availability) triad, 484–485
  IPsec, 489
    cryptographic algorithms, 490
    IKEv1, 492–493
    IKEv2, 494–495
    mode of operation, 490–492
    security association and key exchange, 492
    security protocols, 489
    transform set, 492
    verifying, 507–513
  remote access, 488, 513
    AnyConnect file, 517–518
    certificate enrollment, 518–521
    configuring, 516
    network and IP address pool, 521–522
    policy, 522–527

prerequisites, 513–517

RADIUS server group, 518

verifying, 527–534

site-to-site, 485–488, 496

access control policy, 503–504

configuring, 499–502

NAT policy, 504–506

prerequisites, 496–499

VT (Virtualization Technology), enabling, 27

W-X-Y-Z

web traffic, trace data analysis, 215–218

websites, 174

REGISTER YOUR PRODUCT at CiscoPress.com/register
Access Additional Benefits and SAVE 35% on Your Next Purchase

- Download available product updates.
- Access bonus material when applicable.
- Receive exclusive offers on new editions and related products.
  (Just check the box to hear from us when setting up your account.)
- Get a coupon for 35% for your next purchase, valid for 30 days.
  Your code will be available in your Cisco Press cart. (You will also find
  it in the Manage Codes section of your account page.)

Registration benefits vary by product. Benefits will be listed on your account page under Registered Products.

CiscoPress.com – Learning Solutions for Self-Paced Study, Enterprise, and the Classroom
Cisco Press is the Cisco Systems authorized book publisher of Cisco networking technology, Cisco certification self-study, and Cisco Networking Academy Program materials.

At **CiscoPress.com** you can
- Shop our books, eBooks, software, and video training.
- Take advantage of our special offers and promotions (ciscopress.com/promotions).
- Sign up for special offers and content newsletters (ciscopress.com/newsletters).
- Read free articles, exam profiles, and blogs by information technology experts.
- Access thousands of free chapters and video lessons.

Connect with Cisco Press – Visit CiscoPress.com/community
Learn about Cisco Press community events and programs.

Cisco Press